PARENT
TRAINING

Foundations of Research and Practice

Edited by
RICHARD F. DANGEL/RICHARD A. POLSTER
The University of Texas at Arlington

Foreword by Nathan H. Azrin

THE GUILFORD PRESS
New York/London

To our parents, who never even heard of parent training.

© 1984 The Guilford Press
A Division of Guilford Publications, Inc.
200 Park Avenue South, New York, N.Y. 10003
All rights reserved

Printed in the United States of America

Second printing, August 1986

LIBRARY OF CONGRESS CATALOGING IN PUBLICATION DATA

Main entry under title:

Parent training.

Bibliography: p.
Includes indexes.
1. Parenting—Study and teaching—Addresses, essays, lectures.   I. Dangel, Richard F.   II. Polster, Richard A.
[DNLM: 1. Child rearing.   2. Behavior therapy.   3. Parent-Child relations.   4. Parents. WS 105.5.C3 P227]
HQ755.8.P376 1984   649′.1′07   82-15508
ISBN 0-89862-627-7

CONTRIBUTORS

Donald M. Baer, PhD, Department of Human Development and Family Life, University of Kansas, Lawrence, Kansas

Harriet H. Barrish, PhD, Department of Continuing Education, Shawnee Mission Medical Center, and private practice, Shawnee Mission, Kansas

I. Jay Barrish, PhD, Department of Continuing Education, Shawnee Mission Medical Center, and private practice, Shawnee Mission, Kansas

Martha E. Bernal, PhD, Department of Psychology, University of Denver, Denver, Colorado

Sidney W. Bijou, PhD, Department of Psychology and Special Education, The University of Arizona, Tuscon, Arizona

Elaine A. Blechman, PhD, Department of Psychology, Wesleyan University, Middletown, Connecticut

Curtis J. Braukmann, PhD, Department of Human Development and Family Life and Bureau of Child Research, University of Kansas, Lawrence, Kansas

Karen S. Budd, PhD, Meyer Children's Rehabilitation Institute, University of Nebraska Medical Center, Omaha, Nebraska

Robert L. Burgess, PhD, College of Human Development, The Pennsylvania State University, University Park, Pennsylvania

Michael F. Cataldo, PhD, John F. Kennedy Institute and Johns Hopkins University School of Medicine, Baltimore, Maryland

Edward R. Christophersen, PhD, Department of Pediatrics, University of Kansas Medical Center, Kansas City, Kansas

Miki R. Christophersen, BSN, Department of Continuing Education, Shawnee Mission Medical Center, Shawnee Mission, Kansas

Richard F. Dangel, PhD, Graduate School of Social Work, The University of Texas at Arlington, Arlington, Texas

Jean E. Dumas, MS, Child Study Centre, University of Ottawa, Ottawa, Ontario, Canada

Glen Dunlap, PhD, Social Process Research Institute, University of California at Santa Barbara, Santa Barbara, California

Lynne H. Embry, PhD, Bureau of Child Research, University of Kansas, Lawrence, Kansas

Pamela L. Fabry, MA, Meyer Children's Rehabilitation Institute, University of Nebraska Medical Center, Omaha, Nebraska

Rex Forehand, PhD, Department of Psychology, University of Georgia, Athens, Georgia

Israel Goldiamond, PhD, Departments of Psychiatry and Behavioral Sciences (Biopsychology), Committee on Human Nutrition and Nutritional Biology, University of Chicago, Chicago, Illinois

MARILYN C. HALL, EdD, Responsive Management, Inc., Shawnee Mission, Kansas, and Bureau of Child Research, University of Kansas, Lawrence, Kansas

BILL L. HOPKINS, PhD, Department of Human Development and Family Life, University of Kansas, Lawrence, Kansas

JEAN JOHNSON, BA, Speech and Hearing Department, University of California at Santa Barbara, Santa Barbara, California

KATHRYN KIRIGIN RAMP, PhD, Department of Human Development and Family Life and Bureau of Child Research, University of Kansas, Lawrence, Kansas

ROBERT L. KOEGEL, PhD, Speech and Hearing Department, University of California at Santa Barbara, Santa Barbara, California

CRAIG R. LOFTIN, BS, Portage Project, Portage, Wisconsin

JOHN R. LUTZKER, PhD, Behavior Analysis and Therapy Program, Rehabilitation Institute, Southern Illinois University at Carbondale, Carbondale, Illinois

ROBERT J. MCMAHON, PhD, Department of Psychology, University of British Columbia, Vancouver, British Columbia, Canada

ROBERT E. O'NEILL, MA, Speech and Hearing Department, University of California at Santa Barbara, Santa Barbara, California

ELSIE M. PINKSTON, PhD, School of Social Service Administration, University of Chicago, Chicago, Illinois

RICHARD A. POLSTER, PhD, Graduate School of Social Work, The University of Texas at Arlington, Arlington, Texas

RHONDA A. RICHARDSON, MA, College of Human Development, The Pennsylvania State University, University Park, Pennsylvania

LAURA SCHREIBMAN, PhD, Department of Psychology, Claremont McKenna College, Claremont, California

DAVID E. SHEARER, PhD, Exceptional Children's Center, Utah State University, Logan, Utah

DRENDA M. TIGNER, MA, Department of Human Development and Family Life and Bureau of Child Research, University of Kansas, Lawrence, Kansas

ROBERT G. WAHLER, PhD, Psychology Department, University of Tennessee, Knoxville, Tennessee

MONTROSE M. WOLF, PhD, Department of Human Development and Family Life and Bureau of Child Research, University of Kansas, Lawrence, Kansas

ACKNOWLEDGMENTS

Several individuals made substantial contributions to the development of this book. We would like to extend our appreciation to our graduate students Sam Quattrochi, Sue Ann Pike, Gene Ross, Helen Smith, Sandra Penn, and Dawson Moorer, and to Cindi Jarvis, Dawson's disco partner. A special note of thanks is due Judith Sears, who held the project together, and Jodie Collins, who organized the first National Conference on Parent Training. Paul Glasser, Dean of the Graduate School of Social Work at The University of Texas at Arlington, has been more supportive of our work than anyone could be expected to be.

The book would not exist if our contributors had not carved huge chunks of time from their tightly packed schedules to prepare chapters. The Administration for Children, Youth, and Families, particularly Dr. Ray Rackley, provided moral and financial support.

Richard Dangel would like to thank Bill Hopkins, his tutor for several years, whose technological contributions are reflected in Chapter 8, and Rod Conard and Art Willans, who helped Bill develop the APPLE teacher training program, the predecessor to WINNING! He also thanks his wife, Bonnie, for everything. Finally, he expresses his amazement that Richard Polster has put up with him for so long.

Richard Polster would like to thank Mary Ann Lynch for her interest during his work on this project. He also would like to thank Elsie Pinkston for introducing him to parent training and for her continued encouragement. Last, but certainly not least, he thanks Richard Dangel, who makes tedious tasks enjoyable.

FOREWORD

This book is impressive as a compilation of the procedures, theories, and research basis of the behavioral approach to teaching parenting. The editors have managed to put together in this volume contributions by the knowledgeable innovators in this rapidly expanding field, with the result that in-depth coverage is obtained of the procedural details, in addition to conceptual explication of this subject matter. No single author could have provided this information as well as have the contributors to this book.

The title of this book, at first glance, seems somewhat overstated in that it purports to encompass various approaches to parent training, rather than the purely behavioral approach. But the wealth of procedural detail, extent of application, and experimental basis in evaluation presented in the several chapters gives credibility to the implicit conviction that the behavioral approach is dominant and needs no comparative treatment to justify its existence as the treatment choice.

The broad conceptual basis of behavioral parenting is well described by Bijou, one of its originators, as well as by Burgess and Richardson, who relate the approach to sociological theory. Hopkins explains how the approach relates to basic behavioral methodology; Bernal relates the approach to the multiple concerns and diversity of opinion concerning parenting practices; and Goldiamond describes an insightful framework of attribution of causality, which enables us to appreciate the findings in this area in the larger context of psychological treatment.

Applications of the approach to specific programs include programs for autistic children, described by Koegel and his colleagues; programs for child-abusing and lower-socioeconomic-status families, described by Lutzker; programs for physically impaired children, described by Cataldo; programs for pediatric settings, described by the Christophersens and the Barrishes; programs for social service agencies, described by Pinkston and by Embry; programs for preschoolers, described by Shearer and Loftin; programs for large-scale groups, described by Hall; programs for group homes, described by Braukmann and his colleagues; and so on. Each subpopulation and delivery system entail procedural and conceptual variations, which have been described in great detail. In almost every case, the program descriptions are accompanied by rigorous experimental evaluations that demonstrate the substantial effectiveness of the parenting program.

Especially exciting is the extent to which several investigators have discovered in their own research how parent–child practices are related to other factors impinging on the family. Wahler and Dumas; McMahon and Forehand; Lutzker; and Goldiamond present evidence from their respective vantage points of the role that stress, alternative reinforcers, social context, and other relevant parent influences play in parenting practices. These findings suggest that such problems as depression, anxiety, and alcoholism will eventually be integrated in a common set of principles of behavior, of which parenting behavior will be one component.

The series of studies performed by Forehand and his colleagues is especially informative in answering such questions as "Will generalization occur?"; "How long do the benefits last?"; "Can instructional manuals be used for effective teaching?" Their results and those of others have established the effectiveness of the detailed parent training programs and go further to isolate the role of specific components, as well as to determine the boundaries of effectiveness. These boundaries are found to extend quite widely; they show, surprisingly, that instructional manuals are very effective and, not surprisingly, that teaching the parents general reinforcement principles is also beneficial.

What emerges from the contributions, separately and collectively, is that behavioral parent training has matured into a distinct subject matter of demonstrated effectiveness, with a distinctive methodology, increasingly widespread application, and its own theoretical formulation.

This book stands as a reference source for all those who desire practical application to specific subpopulations of troubled children and their parents.

NATHAN H. AZRIN

CONTENTS

PART II: PROGRAMS AND APPLICATIONS

PART III: ISSUES AND DIRECTIONS

BEHAVIORAL PARENT TRAINING
Where It Came from and Where It's At

Richard A. Polster
Richard F. Dangel
The University of Texas at Arlington

EMPLOYMENT OPPORTUNITIES

> One couple to procreate and raise a child. No experience necessary. Applicants must be available 24 hours per day, 7 days per week, and must provide food, shelter, clothing, and supervision. No training provided. No salary; applicants pay $140,000 over the next 18 years. Accidental applications accepted. Single people may apply but should be prepared for twice the work.

3,500,000 people successfully applied for this job in 1979 (U.S. Department of Commerce Bureau of the Census, 1980).

PARENTS' PLACE IN SOCIETY — BETWEEN A ROCK AND A HARD PLACE

In a recent comic strip, a little girl asked if she could see her mother's parenting license. The mother answered that a license was not required to be a mother. The child replied, "Gee, that's scary." The little girl may have a point. It is not that parents should be licensed, but that no quality controls exist to govern who become parents or how parents perform their jobs. This may be particularly disconcerting if one considers that it is parents who, through their influence on the kind of adults their children become, play a primary role in determining the future of the culture. While this may be cause for concern, parents' on-the-job performance is rarely scrutinized—yet the human race has survived, for the most part pretty well. Traditionally, child-rearing practices were passed down from experienced parent to new mother, and were based on individual intelligence, experience, intuition, and luck.

Consider this analogy. Would someone commission a carpenter to build kitchen cabinets if he or she were quite intelligent but could make only these claims to woodworking proficiency: "My parents were carpenters, I really love wood, and I have used cabinets myself"? A cabinet built by this carpenter may fall off the wall at first use. Initially, it may seem odd to draw an analogy between parents and carpenters, but another comparison strengthens the relationship. Both are held responsible for their end products, children and cabinets. If the cabinets fell off the wall, the client would call the carpenter to correct his work. In the same vein, when children cause problems, parents are called.

When Dennis "the Menace" Mitchell tramples the flower bed, Mr. Wilson calls Mrs. Mitchell. Mr. Wilson expects Mrs. Mitchell to do something to Dennis so he will not trample the flowers again. The next week Dennis's teacher calls Mrs. Mitchell because Dennis stuck Margaret's pigtails in the inkwell. The teacher expects Mrs. Mitchell to do something to Dennis so he does not cause mischief again in school. These examples reflect society's expectations for parents to be responsible for their children's behavior—expectations apparent even in the law.

Legal codes of several states hold parents liable for their children's behavior. In California, parents are liable for up to $2000 for their children's vandalism, and for up to $30,000 for damage to property, injury, or death as a result of their minor (under 15) children's shooting a firearm (*West's Annotated Civil Codes*, 1973). In Montana, parents are liable up to $2500 for damage caused by their minor (under 18) children (*Laws and Resolutions of the State of Montana*, 1977).

Since parents do not receive formalized training before having children, how can they know what to do when their children misbehave? Where can parents learn how to prevent their children's misbehavior? How do parents know the long-term effects of their management techniques? If parents have received a variety of recommendations from different sources (e.g., professionals, their own parents, neighbors, television or other media, college courses), how do they know which are correct? If parents try a recommended procedure and it does not work, what should they do next? With so many questions, and the likelihood of being held responsible for not having the right answers, it is a wonder that humans persist in becoming parents.

PARENTS GET MANY CHILD-REARING SUGGESTIONS

A look at the past shows that parenting has long been a popular concern. Beekman (1977), in an extensive review of child care information, found 2000-year-old child-rearing suggestions. When the printing press was introduced in the 1400s, parenting information was among the first topics published. Some of the older manuscripts included archaic suggestions—for example, wrapping infants tightly with cloth to insure development of straight bones, submerging babies in freezing rivers to build strength and resistance to illness, and using opium to quiet cranky infants and help children fall asleep at bedtime. The amazing number (over 800) of manuals and pamphlets Beekman found demonstrates the lavish attention parenting has received.

A quick perusal of the 100 or so child care books available today at most bookstores shows that authors currently discuss many of the same issues addressed hundreds of years ago: how to put a cranky child to bed, what to do about a child's temper tantrums, how to help a baby stay healthy, and how to handle a child's noncompliance. Unfortunately, even though so many sources of child care recommendations are available to parents, no dependable way has been offered for parents to determine whether or not the suggestions are correct or applicable to their children.

Authors often base their ideas on personal experience, untested assumptions, and social convention. For example, liberal and conservative social conditions have influenced the emphasis placed on discipline. The more conservative the social climate, the more common the recommendations for punishment as a child management technique. Beekman illustrated this correspondence through a reference to Spock's child care manuals (1946, 1957). After World War II, in response to Nazism and Fascism, the social climate in the United States was liberal. At that time Spock (1946) referred to physical punishment as something only a "grim minority of parents will use." A decade later, under conservative social conditions, a new edition of Spock's child care manual (1957) stated that physical punishment might help clear the air between parents and children and might be better than a long period of disapproval.

We recently reviewed authors' recommendations for parents' use of physical punishment and found that many opinions changed within short periods of time (Dangel, Polster, & Ross, 1982). From 1964 to 1967, 67% of the authors recommended using physical punishment; from 1968 to 1971, 72%; from 1972 to 1975, 52%; and from 1976 to 1979, 87%. While causal relationships between recommendations to use particular child management techniques and social conditions may be difficult to demonstrate, it may be that these dramatic changes reflect authors' responses to general societal changes in attitudes about child rearing.

CHILD REARING TODAY:
TOUGHER THAN EVER

On top of the concerns addressed in most child-rearing books, parents face new problems. Industrialization, urbanization, and economic hard times have drastically changed family structure and life styles. These changes include the disintegration of the extended family, and an increase in parents who work outside the home and in single-parent households. Risley, Clark, and Cataldo (1976) point out that a few generations ago, when people lived together in extended families, new mothers had access to others who had child-rearing experience and could share parenting tasks. Now, people live apart from their extended families, and it is common for new mothers to live in neighborhoods with other new mothers. Most have little parenting experience and no one available to help with child care responsibilities.

Another contemporary social situation, difficult economic conditions, forces parents to work outside the home. In 1950, only 20% of the mothers with children under 18 years of age were employed; in 1978 this percentage reached over 50% (Ruopp, Travers, Glantz, & Coelen, 1979). When parents work away from home, they have less time for child care and household responsibilities, and thus fewer opportunities to influence their children. Employed parents must frequently rely on some form of day care for their children. In 1978, almost 52% of the families, which included more than 5 million children, had a work-related need for some form of day care for at least 30 hours per week (Ruopp et al., 1979). When children are in day care, other adults assume child-rearing tasks and may influence some of the behaviors children develop. Unfortunately, some of these influences may compete with the objectives parents set for their children. This creates additional problems for working parents: Not only do they have less time to influence their children, but they may have to spend some of their time competing with the effects of others.

Single parenting, an increasing social phenomenon, can exacerbate the difficulties of child-rearing. In 1970, 85% of all dependent children (under 18) lived in two-parent families. By 1978, this percentage had decreased markedly to 78% (U.S. Department of Commerce Bureau of the Census, 1979). Blechman (1982), in her review of research on the effects of children being raised by one parent, points out that 90% of single parents are women, that many of these women must work, and that women typically have lower incomes than men. Blechman also found that in addition to decreased finances, single parents often experience extreme losses of social status when a spouse leaves or dies. These conditions intensify the rigors of shouldering all the household responsibilities and child-rearing tasks without a spouse to share the load.

Loss of extended family supports, worsening of economic conditions, and an increase in single-parent households combine to make parenting tougher than ever. Perhaps it is not surprising that in a recent survey, Ann Landers (1976) found that 70% of the responding parents would not take the job of parent again if given the choice.

The difficulties of contemporary child rearing can be seen in recent statistics showing that approximately 550,000 children were reported abused and neglected, with an estimated half million more cases unreported (Helfer & Kempe, 1976). While most parents do not go to these extremes, the strain of contemporary parenting may manifest itself in other ways. Juvenile crime statistics show that the number of delinquency cases brought before the courts has nearly tripled since 1960, and in 1979, almost 25% of all serious crimes (e.g., rape, robbery, assault) were committed by juveniles (U.S. Department of Commerce Bureau of the Census, 1980). In 1977, nationwide vandalism of public schools cost an estimated $600,000,000, triple the cost of vandalism in 1971 ("Vandalism in the Schools," 1979).

Statistics on child abuse and juvenile crime dramatize the difficulties of parenting in contemporary society. Generally, parents have fewer social supports and more responsibilities. In spite of these social changes, society persists in its expectation that parents have the primary influence over their children's behavior.

HOW MUCH INFLUENCE DO PARENTS REALLY HAVE?

Horowitz (1976) points out that how much influence parents have over their children will not be known until many empirical questions about child rearing and child development have been answered. Fundamental questions include the following: What in a child's environment affects the child's development? How much of the effects are parents responsible for? How much impact does the physical environment have? How much of the child's repertoire is actually shapable? These issues are part of a basic quest to identify manipulable variables that influence the kinds of individuals children become. Martin (1972), in his comprehensive literature review, found that investigators have identified at least seven broad categories of parent behaviors that influence child development. These behaviors include enforcing rules consistently, discussing rules with children, using reinforcement for appropriate behavior more often than punishment for inappropriate behavior, accepting and nurturing, assigning responsibility, and modeling the behaviors the parents expect their children to perform. However, a fundamental question remains: Are there specific, correct ways parents should perform these behaviors so they have optimal effects on their children? Researchers have been trying to answer this question.

AN EMPIRICAL APPROACH
TO CHILD REARING

In the early 1900s, some parenting specialists adopted scientific methods to study child rearing. Noyes (1913), as cited in Beekman (1977), employed rigorous observational procedures for 2 years, and published a detailed description of the methods she used to keep her baby healthy. In 1919, McCandless started the Iowa Child Welfare Research Station to study child development and to train people in parenting (Horowitz, 1976). From 1919 to 1925, Gesell observed and measured children's motor performance and physical growth as the children matured. As a result of this work, he established a summary of performance norms for child development. In the 1920s and 1930s, Gesell incorporated his research in guidebooks for parents (Gesell, 1928, 1934).

Scientific methods helped parenting specialists identify potentially relevant variables in child rearing, but evidence of cause-and-effect relationships between specific parent and child behaviors was lacking. Researchers' use of science was not sufficient to answer many parental concerns, and through the 1920s parents still received conflicting information. As had been the case for centuries, most authors of child care manuals continued to support one of two basic positions on child rearing: that parents were completely responsible for the types of people their children became, or that parents were only supporters of the individuals their children were destined to become.

BEHAVIORAL PARENT TRAINING

Currently, there are many well-known child care books that address various parenting concerns. For examples of some of these, see Dodson (1970), Dreikurs and Grey (1970), Ginott (1969), T. Gordon (1975), and Spock (1977). One method of addressing parenting concerns that has received a great deal of attention is behavioral parent training. Because extensive reviews of this approach already exist (see Berkowitz & Graziano, 1972; S. B. Gordon & Davidson, 1981; Johnson & Katz, 1973; and O'Dell, 1974), we do not examine the literature here.

Behavioral parent trainers began developing their methods in the 1950s and early 1960s when applied behavior analysts (Baer, Wolf, & Risley, 1968), sometimes known as behavior modifiers, were moving their research from restricted settings, such as state hospitals, to natural environments, such as schools and homes. The first formal account of behavioral parent training was published by Williams in 1959.

Behavioral parent training involves systematically teaching parents to implement specific child management techniques. The effects of the training procedures are assessed through data collected on parent and child behaviors. Since the 1960s, behavioral parent trainers have tested a variety of training techniques with an assortment of child behaviors and parent–child relationship problems. Research has been conducted in homes, clinics, public places, schools, and other natural settings. The results of some of these studies have found their way into the popular child care market. Procedural manuals are available on toilet training (Azrin & Foxx, 1976), bedwetting (Azrin & Besalel, 1981), shopping in public places (Greene, Clark, & Risley, 1977), and general child rearing (Becker, 1971; Patterson, 1973; Patterson & Gullion, 1973).

THE FOCUS OF THIS BOOK

For the first time, pioneers and innovators in behavioral parent training have been brought together in one book. These influential researchers and practitioners have conducted parent training projects in universities, research centers, social service agencies, hospitals, low-income housing projects, schools, and homes. Their projects have affected the lives of thousands of parents and children. The authors provide detailed explanations, critical analyses, and practical recommendations concerning the procedures, outcomes, and issues in parent training.

This book is organized into three parts: "Goals and Objectives," "Programs and Applications," and "Issues and Directions."

Part I: Goals and Objectives

In this part, the authors address a fundamental issue in behavioral parent training: the potential benefits, for parents and children, of participation in a parent training program. The authors discuss factors that practitioners, researchers, and administrators should consider when determining the design, purpose, and desired outcomes for parent training programs.

In Chapter 1, Bijou discusses the differences between traditional and behavioral approaches to parent training. He also presents a general overview of the strengths and weaknesses of some of the parent training research, and makes recommendations for improving the technology and expanding the applicability of the procedures.

In Chapter 2, Hopkins describes procedures for developing data-based parent training programs. He emphasizes that a commitment to measurement, as part of original project design, provides accessible data during program development and implementation. Hopkins explains that these data can be used to assess whether program objectives are met.

Blechman, in Chapter 3, operationally defines parent and child "competence," and reviews her research on the effects of familial competence on success in parent training. She also discusses two important questions: Which parents are most likely to benefit from parent training, and what constitutes a satisfactory outcome in parent training? Blechman disputes the notion that every parent can benefit from parent training and discusses the need for broad-based family interventions that might help families increase their accomplishments in parent training.

Part II: Programs and Applications

The authors in this part present comprehensive descriptions of their parent training work. They explain the unique aspects of their particular projects and discuss topics that are relevant across projects. The chapters include descriptions of program development and content, participant characteristics, staff and parent training procedures, dissemination efforts, and future plans. The authors also delineate evaluation methods, present data, and analyze program effectiveness.

Hall, in Chapter 4, charts the development of the widely disseminated Responsive Parenting Program. Originally designed for parents of children with special education needs (e.g., autistic, hearing-impaired, and mentally retarded children), it is now used by parents of all types of children and for a broad range of problems. More than 3000 parents have been taught, in groups, to develop, implement, and evaluate intervention procedures for their children's behavior. Unique to this program, Responsive Parenting trains program veterans, parents, to be parent trainers themselves. The majority of participants have made important changes and have been highly satisfied with the program's effectiveness.

Shearer and Loftin, in Chapter 5, describe the Portage Project, a program for parents of handicapped preschoolers. Begun in rural Wisconsin, it has been disseminated throughout the United States and several foreign countries. One important component of the Portage Project is a home teacher, who helps parents in their homes to develop objectives and implement interventions. Research has demonstrated qualitative improvement in parent–child relationships and substantial increases in children's IQ scores.

In Chapter 6, Christophersen, Barrish, Barrish, and Christophersen explain their educational program designed for parents of infants and toddlers. Parents meet in groups, where instructors give lectures and handouts on child development and child management, demonstrate how to use time-out procedures, and show films on health and safety. Instructors also teach parents how to communicate with a pediatrician, administer medication according to prescription, and perform appropriate child feeding and hygiene tasks. In the last two years, 150 families have completed this economical program; all have given it very high ratings.

Braukman, Kirigin Ramp, Tigner, and Wolf, in Chapter 7, identify the empirical foundation of the program design and goals of Achievement Place, a community-based model of group homes for delinquents. The authors detail the training program individuals complete to become teaching-parents. All 170 Achievement Place homes use the same systematic procedures to train teaching-parents. New teaching-parents are taught by professional staff and former and current teaching-parents through lectures, modeling, written exercises, and feedback during rehearsals in training and performance on the job. The Achievement Place model has been highly successful: Consumers are satisfied, and delinquent behavior is reduced during treatment.

We ourselves, in Chapter 8, describe WINNING!, a systematic, empirical approach to parent training. We used a Parents' Advisory Council to help develop a packaged training program for parents from diverse ethnic and socioeconomic backgrounds, whose 3- to 12-year-old children have a variety of behavior problems. WINNING! incorporates videotape skill lessons in a self-paced, cost-effective program that can be conducted by paraprofessionals. Over 2000 parents in 16 states have participated in WINNING!. They showed substantial changes in child management skills and parent–child interactions, and rated their satisfaction with the program highly.

In Chapter 9, Pinkston discusses her parent education program for home and school behavior problems. She used structured interviews and standardized teaching methods to develop individualized programs across both settings. Pinkston coordinated program responsibilities between parents and teachers to support improved child behaviors at home and at school. The 100 parents who completed this program consistently gave it high ratings.

Burgess and Richardson, in Chapter 10, present an overview of child maltreatment. They describe the environmental factors, skill deficits, and interpersonal coercion associated with abuse, and they review recent intervention projects. The authors stress the importance of programs that emphasize prevention and the amelioration of environmental conditions that appear to foster child abuse.

Lutzker, in Chapter 11, describes Project 12-Ways, an ecobehavioral program for abusive and neglectful parents. Project 12-Ways uses a multifaceted approach to ameliorate a number of problems related to child abuse. Over 300 parents, most of whom are agency-referred, have participated in individualized programs, such as parent training (which replicates Forehand's program), job-hunting skills training, money management, and stress-reduction assertiveness training. Outcome data indicate that most participants attain their treatment goals and suggest that child abuse decreases in geographical areas served by Project 12-Ways.

In Chapter 12, McMahon and Forehand review their efforts to evaluate the generality of parent training program effects. The authors examine generalization across settings, siblings, behavior, and time with over 100 mother–child pairs. They also assess the effects of adjunct programs: written instructions, self-control training, lessons in social learning principles, and multimodal family therapy.

In Chapter 13, Cataldo discusses unique problems of parent training with parents of handicapped and ill children. He explains that even parents with good parenting skills may not know how to apply them with children who have multiple problems. Cataldo relies on experience with over 3000 cases to delineate important considerations for work with this population. He uses case studies to illustrate how training parents in generalized compliance procedures can improve a broad range of child behavior and can enhance generalization of child management skills to other child behaviors. Cataldo also discusses the occurrence of symptom substitution, presents examples, and recommends procedures to avoid this problem.

In Chapter 14, Koegel, Schreibman, Johnson, O'Neill, and Dunlap explain difficulties parents can have in managing autistic children. The authors delineate their work and elaborate specific concerns that are critical for parent training with this population. They describe a six-step parent training program, which includes systematic teaching and feedback in the home and clinic. The authors examine side effects of parent training and compare various outcome measures across two groups of parents: One group participated in parent training, while the other received clinic treatment.

In Chapter 15, Wahler and Dumas analyze the difficulties of multiply coerced parents in maintaining parent training effects. The authors review their research and use case examples to explain how coercive environmental situations, poverty, and social isolation can profoundly affect parents' continued use of systematic child management procedures. Wahler and Dumas are currently working on two program adjuncts, accurate attending and mand review, that may enhance training effects with insular populations.

Budd and Fabry, in Chapter 16, explain that economical, systematic behavioral assessment procedures have not been available to practitioners who conduct parent training within the time and financial constraints of clinic settings. They describe the development of an efficient, economical assessment procedure that can be used by practitioners and researchers. The authors delineate five structured assessment situations in which parents demonstrate child management skills before and after parent training. Budd and Fabry use several case examples to demonstrate that parent trainers easily learn to implement the assessment procedures.

In Chapter 17, Embry discusses variables that can interfere with parents' success in parent training. She proposes a systematic method, the taxonomic key, to match client characteristics with specific intervention strategies, thereby developing a comprehensive plan and improving parents' chances for positive outcomes. Embry details her 3-year-old parent training program and describes factors that have affected the performance of 45 families.

Part III: Issues and Directions

In this part, the authors cover consumer issues, ethical considerations, and future directions—topics that affect parent training participants, practitioners, and researchers.

Bernal, in Chapter 18, reviews her work comparing the outcomes of behavioral parent training, client-centered parent counseling, and an 8-week waiting-list control group. She also discusses client behaviors that may predict dropout and suggests interventions to curb it. To address consumer issues, Bernal answers several questions parents may have about parent training, such as these: For what child problems is parent training useful? What happens in parent training? How will I know if it is effective? These answers can help parents become informed consumers.

In Chapter 19, Goldiamond presents a fresh approach to ethics in parent training. He addresses both parent trainers and ethicists in his explanation of linear and nonlinear behavior analysis. Goldiamond uses case studies to illustrate these two approaches to treatment planning. He then details the rationale for conducting nonlinear analyses, and discusses the pitfalls of using only linear procedures. The author addresses ethical concerns through a payoff matrix, which can demonstrate the relative costs and benefits of client participation in selected interventions.

Baer, in Chapter 20, discusses future directions for parent training. He reviews the accomplishments of parent training and concludes that many important milestones have been achieved. Baer cautions researchers against allowing marker-variable relationships to become the goal of research, rather than discriminative stimuli for different research. He stresses the importance of adhering to rigorous scientific practices, sharing information with colleagues, assessing the social validity of interventions, and analyzing behaviors within the social context.

References

Azrin, N. H., & Besalel, V. A. *A parent's guide to bedwetting control: A step-by-step method.* New York: Pocket Books, 1981.

Azrin, N. H., & Foxx, R. M. *Toilet training in less than a day.* New York: Pocket Books, 1976.

Baer, D. M., Wolf, M. M., & Risley, T. R. Some current dimensions of applied behavior analysis. *Journal of Applied Behavior Analysis*, 1968, *1*, 91–97.

Becker, W. C. *Parents are teachers: A child management program.* Champaign, Ill.: Research Press, 1971.

Beekman, D. *The mechanical baby: A popular history of the theory and practice of child raising.* Westport, Conn.: Lawrence Hill, 1977.

Berkowitz, B. P., & Graziano, A. M. Training parents as behavior therapists: A review. *Behaviour Research and Therapy*, 1972, *10*, 297–317.

Blechman, E. A. Are children with one parent at psychological risk?: A methodological review. *Journal of Marriage and the Family*, 1982, *44*, 179–195.

Dangel, R. F., Polster, R. A., & Ross, G. *What parents and professionals think about physical punishment.* Manuscript submitted for publication, 1982.

Dodson, F. *How to parent.* New York: Signet, 1970.

Dreikurs, R., & Grey, L. *A parents' guide to child discipline.* New York: Hawthorn Books, 1970.

Gesell, A. *Infancy and human growth.* New York: Macmillan, 1928.

Gesell, A. *The atlas of infant behavior.* New Haven: Yale University Press, 1934.

Ginott, H. G. *Between parent and child.* New York: Avon, 1969.

Gordon, S. B., & Davidson, N. Behavioral parent training. In A. S. Gurman & D. P. Kniskern (Eds.), *Handbook of family therapy.* New York: Brunner/Mazel, 1981.

Gordon, T. *Parent effectiveness training: The tested new way to raise responsible children.* New York: Plume Books, 1975.

Greene, B. F., Clark, H. B., & Risley, T. R. *Shopping with children: Advice for parents.* San Rafael, Calif.: Academic Therapy Publications, 1977.

Helfer, R. E., & Kempe, C. H. *Child abuse and neglect: The family and the community.* Cambridge, Mass.: Ballinger, 1976.

Horowitz, F. D. Directions for parenting. In E. J. Mash, L. A. Hamerlynck, & L. C. Handy (Eds.), *Behavior modification and families.* New York: Brunner/Mazel, 1976.

Johnson, C. A., & Katz, R. C. Using parents as change agents for their children: A review. *Journal of Child Psychology and Psychiatry and Allied Disciplines,* 1973, *14,* 181–200.

Landers, A. Ann Landers. *Dallas Times-Herald,* January 23, 1976, p. 20.

Laws and Resolutions of the State of Montana (Section 40-6-237, Montana Legislative Council). Bozeman: Color World of Montana, 1977.

Martin, B. Parent–child relations. In T. Thompson & W. S. Dockens (Eds.), *Application of behavior modification.* New York: Academic Press, 1972.

O'Dell, S. Training parents in behavior modification: A review. *Psychological Bulletin,* 1974, *81,* 418–433.

Patterson, G. R. *Families: Applications of social learning to family life.* Champaign, Ill.: Research Press, 1973.

Patterson, G. R., & Gullion, M. E. *Living with children: New methods for parents and teachers.* Champaign, Ill.: Research Press, 1973.

Risley, T. R., Clark, H. B., & Cataldo, M. F. Behavioral technology for the normal middle-class family. In E. J. Mash, L. A. Hamerlynck, & L. C. Handy (Eds.), *Behavior modification and families.* New York: Brunner/Mazel, 1976.

Ruopp, R., Travers, J., Glantz, F., & Coelen, C. *Children at the center: Summary findings and their implications.* Cambridge, Mass.: Abt Books, 1979.

Spock, B. *Common sense book of baby and child care* (1st ed.). Toronto: Collins, 1946.

Spock, B. *Common sense book of baby and child care* (2nd ed.). New York: Duell, Sloan & Pearce, 1957.

Spock, B. *Baby and child care* (3rd ed.). New York: Wallaby, 1977.

U.S. Department of Commerce Bureau of the Census. *Current Population Reports* (Series P.20, No. 338). Washington, D.C.: U.S. Government Printing Office, 1979.

U.S. Department of Commerce Bureau of the Census. *Statistical Abstracts of the United States.* Washington, D.C.: U.S. Government Printing Office, 1980.

Vandalism in the schools. *U.S. News and World Report,* January 29, 1979, p. 55.

West's Annotated Civil Codes (Sections 1714.1 & 1714.3, Official California Civil Code Classification). St. Paul, Minn.: West Publications, 1973.

Williams, C. D. The elimination of tantrum behaviors by extinction procedures. *Journal of Abnormal and Social Psychology,* 1959, *59,* 269–270.

GOALS AND OBJECTIVES

PARENT TRAINING
Actualizing the Critical Conditions of Early Childhood Development

Sidney W. Bijou
The University of Arizona

INTRODUCTION

Parent training, in the broadest sense of the term, has had a long history, probably beginning with the extended family. In all likelihood, initially it consisted of advice, verbal formulas ("Give him plenty of love"), and admonitions from friends, relatives, and authority figures. With the advent of mass communication and the decline of the extended family, parent training expanded to include numerous indirect methods: first, how-to-do-it books, pamphlets, and newspaper articles, and then radio, television, and multimedia packages such as audiocassettes and film strips with accompanying workbooks. And now in the offing are videocassettes and videodiscs to show and tell parents "how to do it."

Proliferation of the so-called helping professions—those dedicated to health, education, and welfare—has served to increase the ranks of trainers and advice givers to include nursery-, elementary-, and high-school teachers; early childhood educators; social workers; clinical, child, and developmental psychologists; child psychiatrists; counselors; and home economists. All engage in some form of face-to-face parent training in educational groups, individual consultations, or tutorials in learning or home settings, and all distribute their wares on radio, television, or wherever there is an available audience. Further inflating the ranks are paraprofessionals, parents, journalists, and self-styled therapists.

Obviously, all parent training approaches have high interest value for parents, as evidenced by their unquestioning purchase of recommended publications, their faithfulness in listening to and watching programs on child care, and their attendance at parent education meetings. Just how much actual

15

benefit is derived is impossible to determine, since no reliable data exist to show that these parental activities have resulted in positive changes in the parents or children. Undoubtedly, some parents do benefit, either because they become less concerned about a problem ("It's only natural that siblings fight and bicker, particularly during adolescence"), or because they have already been questioning the efficacy of their child-rearing practices and have been contemplating changes when the advice offered by an "authority" prompts them to take action.

It is fairly safe to say, however, that many parents probably derive little or no benefit from typical parent training programs. For one thing, the goals of such training are usually so general that either they do not apply specifically to the problem a parent is coping with, or the parent cannot judge whether or not the goals have been achieved. Furthermore, although the techniques advocated are generally purported to be applications of a developmental theory, they are usually not. In fact, they are usually only vaguely based on one or several principles extracted from the works of Freud, Rogers, Dreikurs, Gesell, Maslow, Skinner, and others. So the resulting prescriptions turn out to be generalized statements that vacillate with the fads and fashions in child-rearing practices and are often rigid and contradictory as well.

There is also the question of motivation. These parent trainers assume that through insight, understanding, and allegedly new modes of communication, parents will be able and willing to put into effect a recommended child-rearing program and to carry it out to completion. Even though most parents are sincerely eager to do so, the kind of motivation that might be generated through insight and understanding is too weak and too unfocused to bring about and sustain significant behavior changes in the parents themselves, and hence in their children.

Fortunately, there exists a contrasting, relatively recent approach to parent training known as "behavior modification." Although behavior modification is made up of two major theoretical subdivisions—behavior therapy and applied behavior analysis—this discussion focuses on applied behavior analysis (Baer, Wolf, & Risley, 1968) and considers only direct, face-to-face approaches. The indirect approaches—for example, how-to-do-it books—require separate and quite different consideration.

One of the assumptions of applied behavior analysis is that a child's behavior, whether normal, deviant, or retarded, is related to his or her past interactions with people, places, and things, and to his or her current environmental circumstances. The most important of these is the behavior of significant people: father, mother, siblings, close relatives, and friends. Consequently, when the objective is to change the behavior of a child—that is, to help him or her make a new kind of adjustment to different situations—then the behavior of these significant people must also be changed. Another assumption is that changes in functional relationships between stimuli and responses can be identified only if the stimulating conditions and the behaviors of those involved are defined in observable terms. For this reason, objective definitions and recording systems are essential and integral parts of this approach. This is one of the striking differences between the usual parent training approaches and those of applied behavior analysis.

The strategy behind applied behavior analysis consists of training parents in the use of behavioral techniques (hereafter referred to as "parent training proper") and supervising implementation of the training with the child in the home, rather than in a clinical or educational setting. Parent training proper includes four basic procedures: (1) setting attainable goals in objectively defined terms, in light of the child's competence and the programmed material available; (2) helping the child attain the objectives by means of behaviorally based teaching techniques; (3) monitoring progress by systematic record-keeping methods, and modifying the teaching techniques on the basis of what the records show; and (4) modifying the conditions as necessary so as to maintain and generalize the desirable changes that have been acquired (Bijou, 1977, 1981a; Schiefelbusch & Hoyt, 1978).

A review of the parent behavior training endeavor, an assessment of accomplishments, and a summary of some future challenges follow.

RESEARCH

Early Studies

Two particular studies mark the beginning of the application of learning principles to parent training. Both were concerned with the effectiveness of parent intervention for changing a child's aversive behavior, and both were conducted in the home, using a single-subject design. In the first study, Williams (1959) demonstrated that the tyrant-like tantrum behavior of a 21-month-old boy could be eliminated by the operant extinction procedure. The child, who had been seriously ill for much of his first 18 months, finally became normally healthy, yet continued to demand the same kind of attention he had received previously. Particularly upsetting to the parents was his insistence that one of them or his aunt stay with him until he fell asleep at night or at naptime. When they refused, he had violent, uncompromising tantrums.

Treatment to eliminate this behavior consisted of putting him to bed at his usual bedtime, closing the bedroom door, and not responding to his screams and rages. After 10 sessions, the child no longer even whimpered and actually smiled when he was left alone after being put to bed. But when his aunt inadvertently responded to an emotional outbreak on one occasion, the tantrum behavior reoccurred, making a second round of extinction necessary. By the ninth going-to-bed occasion, the tantrums had ceased completely, and no further tantrums were reported during the next 2 years. Nor were there any unfortunate side effects: The child appeared to be friendly, expressive, and outgoing.

The second study, by Hawkins, Peterson, Schweid, and Bijou (1966), was far more exacting and complicated in research design, in the training of the parent, and in the way in which data were collected. The aim was to establish whether a mother with limited training could reduce the tantrums and aggressive, disobedient behavior of her 4-year-old son. After collecting baseline data on the child's behavior in the home, the experimenters taught the mother, through a system of cues from them, how to consequate desirable and undesirable instances of behavior. Under this regime, carried out in two or three sessions per week, the child's undesirable behaviors decreased markedly after only six sessions, and the desirable behaviors increased correspondingly. At that point, for experimental reasons, a reversal procedure was introduced during which the undesirable behaviors were reinforced and the desirable behaviors were ignored, much as the mother had been doing before the experiment began. Soon the undesirable behaviors reappeared. It became evident that there was a functional relationship between the changes in behavior and the mother's management of contingencies. Resumption of the treatment procedure reestablished the desirable behaviors in six sessions. Twenty-four days after the termination of treatment, a 3-day check of the boy in his home showed that the changed behavior he had acquired was being well maintained.

It is interesting to note the sequence of events that led Hawkins *et al.* to study the possibility of training a mother to treat her child's problem behavior at home. In the late 1950s, young children with problems were often referred for treatment to the Child Development Clinic of the University of Washington. There they were diagnosed and treated in the usual manner of that period: A staff member administered psychological tests and then initiated and conducted play therapy sessions modeled after Axline's adaptation of Carl Rogers's client-centered theory (Axline, 1947). The therapist kept the parents apprised of the child's progress and described some of the techniques being used, suggesting that they try them at home. But because of its general ineffectiveness, this approach was abandoned in the early 1960s and was replaced by new techniques based on learning principles. Staff members and students unschooled in the new approach were trained through courses and work supervision that consisted mainly of prompting techniques, including the use of a "bug-in-the-ear" through which only the trainee could hear instructions from the supervisor.

To facilitate discussions during consultations, the parents were asked to observe the sessions either in the therapy room or through a one-way screen. Before long, it became apparent that demonstrations and postsession discussions were not having sufficient effect on the parent–child relationship, so the clinical procedure was altered: The parent (usually the mother) was placed in the role of therapist, and the staff member served as supervisor. Training consisted of orienting the parent to the specific objective of the therapy and teaching her the techniques for achieving this objective through the application of reinforcement principles. Skills in consequating desirable and undesirable behavior were shaped primarily through the use of light signals as prompts. When the mother became proficient in managing the contingencies, the light signals were used to reinforce her appropriate consequations. This procedure has been described in detail by Wahler, Winkel, Peterson, and Morrison (1965) in a study involving three mother–child dyads. The next step toward helping parents help themselves in dealing with their children's problem behavior was to see whether similar procedures could also be used in the home. It was this unknown that Hawkins *et al.* (1966) undertook to investigate.

Studies since the Mid-1960s

The pioneering efforts of the mid-1960s were followed by a steadily increasing number of studies, some with single-subject and some with group research designs (Graziano, 1977; O'Dell, 1974). While certain investigators concerned themselves with specifying the techniques that enhanced the acquisition, maintenance, and generalization of a subject's behavior changes (e.g., Wahler, Berland, & Coe, 1977), others aimed to evaluate the effectiveness of such intervention for treating various kinds of developmental and behavioral problems. Among the latter were studies on modifying negativistic, noncompliant, oppositional, and aggressive behavior in children, as well as a substantial number of studies on autistic behavior, delinquency, speech defects, problems related to somatic illness, and incorrigibility in the home.

Parent educational training procedures took different directions. In some investigations, parents were trained on a one-to-one basis; in others, on a group basis; and in still others, with a combination of both. The phases of parent training proper were also mixed. In some instances, individual or group training preceded parent implementation, a procedure evolving primarily from research in clinical settings; in other instances, training was given in conjunction with implementation, a practice followed mostly in educational programs, such as the Portage Project (Shearer & Shearer, 1976).

Interestingly, only a few investigations were directed toward evaluating effectiveness of procedures and variations in training techniques that are necessary for parents of different educational and socioeconomic status.

EVALUATION

Evaluating the progress of parent behavior training during the past 15 years or so is complicated. One must determine not only whether the research studies have met investigative standards, but also whether the entire enterprise is socially acceptable and economically feasible. Both aspects are considered in the assessment that follows.

Strengths

It is encouraging to note that reviews of the literature indicate a distinct and steady improvement in both quantity and quality of research. Although O'Dell (1974) found few positive things to say about this type of research, he conceded that the field had considerable potential. Graziano's review (1977), only 3 years later, was far more enthusiastic: "Seriously utilizing parents as cooperative change agents and training them in therapeutic skills may be the single most important development in the child therapy area" (p. 257).

More recent research reports note that investigators are more conscientious about their research designs, are supplying more details about their training procedures, and are describing parent and child behaviors more precisely. Furthermore, leading researchers in the field are focusing more on basic processes, including the conditions that promote rapid acquisition of new behavior (e.g., Wahler, Leske, & Rogers, 1979) and its maintenance and generalization (Forehand, Sturgis, McMahon, Aguar, Green, Wells, & Breiner, 1979; Koegel, Glahn, & Nieminen, 1978; Miller & Sloane, 1976).

Parent behavior training currently ranks high among the achievements of behavior modification, along with child therapy, behavior therapy of neurotic behavior in young adults, the Achievement Place model of treating delinquent youths (which includes training their parents), and the special education of handicapped children. Everything considered, parent training has as much validity as do other acceptable clinical and remedial practices. It is a feasible and effective way of dealing with children's behavior problems. It is relatively easy to train parents from a wide range of educational and social backgrounds in the essential behavioral techniques; the procedures are well within prevailing moral, ethical, and legal standards; and parents, as clients and consumers, are generally satisfied and pleased with the results (e.g., Smith, Kushlick, & Glossop, 1977).

Whether these training programs are cost-effective is, at present, difficult to determine for two reasons: (1) The behavioral approach is still in its formative stages, and (2) the standards for financial comparison vary widely. A solution to the first problem must come from the field itself. With the significant advances in and stabilization of procedures and products that can be expected in the next 10 to 15 years of research, determination of the cost of these training programs will be relatively simple. Nevertheless, assessing the costs of comparable programs will remain a problem, because estimates will continue to vary from clear-cut to none at all. An example of an unequivocal standard of comparison is the cost of educating a preschool-age handicapped child in a classroom. Here, the fixed and expendable operating costs determined by specialists are readily compiled. A fluctuating comparative standard, on the other hand, is the cost of providing therapy or a rehabilitation program for a child in a community agency, where the type of facility and the salary ranges of the various professional, paraprofessional, and clerical staffs depend a great deal on the location and economic status of the community. Yet another example—that of no standard at all—is the projected cost in a community in which there are no existing agencies or child care facilities, as in the Third World countries, where establishment of any facility for handling problem children is almost out of the question, considering the myriad problems of mere survival.

Weaknesses

The weaknesses of parent behavior training, many of which are also found in other types of applied investigations, center on details of the research. One glaring deficiency is that of research design. Illustrative is the report by Johnson and Katz (1973), which pointed out that 64% of the studies reviewed contained treatment procedures so poorly described that it was impossible to fathom exactly which functional relationships were being investigated. The prevalence of errors in research strategy reflects not only on the training and standards of the researchers, but on journal reviewers as well. A problem related to the confounding of experimental variables is the interpretation of findings from single-subject design studies on the basis of logic appropriate for group design research. Many investigators appear not to understand that individual-subject research yields data that may or may not demonstrate relationships among functionally defined stimulus and response variables, whereas group design procedures produce information for testing hypotheses about differences in trait or individual populations (Herson & Barlow, 1976; Sidman, 1960; Yates, 1976).

Casual and unclear descriptions of experimental procedures, too, are prevalent in the literature. Again, Johnson and Katz (1973) noted that 65% of the reviewed reports provided only meager descriptions or no descriptions at all of experimental procedures in general, and 33% furnished insufficient information on the reliability of parent and child behavior changes. Whether these shortcomings are the result of vague and poorly thought-out procedures, or whether they reveal an inability to write in precise and descriptive language is beside the point. In either case, as with faulty experimental designs, the net result is that replication of studies that may indeed have inherent merit is impossible.

Also encountered are studies that are, in a sense, incomplete: They fail to describe the conditions that maintain and generalize the newly acquired behaviors. While it is true that all studies need not be concerned with all three phases of behavior change—acquisition, maintenance, and generalization—and that they may rightly concentrate on any one aspect of parent training, investigators who claim that their procedures are effective for changing behavior are obligated to specify the conditions under which such changes are maintained and generalized.

FUTURE CHALLENGES

The first challenge facing workers in this field, and the one deserving highest priority, is to improve the quality of parent training through systematic research and theory construction. The second is to combine parent training with educational techniques for the purpose of large-scale prevention of sociocultural retardation and behavior disorders.

Improving Techniques

It should be apparent from the previous discussion that all three aspects of parent training research need improvement in (1) the parent implementation aspect of training, (2) the procedures for parent training proper, and (3) the procedures for maintaining and generalizing changes in behavior.

Parent Implementation

Little more can be said about research on parent implementation of the training received, other than to reiterate the importance of complying with established research designs and experimental procedures and the necessity for exploring variations (e.g., Herbert & Baer, 1972).

Parent Training Proper

A glossing over of the description of parent training proper—a tendency in many investigations concerned with a comparative analysis of remedial or therapeutic approaches—should be replaced with a specific account of the training procedure, similar to that usually devoted to the other components of the experimental procedures. Also included in the description should be measures of the parents' proficiencies at the end of training. Training parents, even in a carefully conceived program, is no guarantee that each will emerge with the same level of proficiency. In order to report that each parent in a study was comparably trained to implement an educational or therapeutic program, data should be available to show that each indeed demonstrated comparable mastery. This requirement may pose a problem for research on models in which parent training occurs during the initial stages of implementation—for example, the Portage Project (Shearer & Shearer, 1976). Nevertheless, it should be possible to set up criteria for proficiency and to find measures that indicate the degree of attainment.

As has been noted previously, investigators have become keenly aware that changes in a child's behavior brought about in the home are of limited value unless they can be maintained and generalized to other situations and circumstances. They are, therefore, directing much of their research in that direction (e.g., Braukmann, Kirigin, & Wolf, 1981). The problem of generalizing acquired behavior to new situations poses more of a challenge than does maintenance, because it most often requires changes in the behavior of other persons outside of the home, such as teachers, community workers, and the like.

Behavior Theory

Few will contend that current behavior theory is sufficiently comprehensive for effective application to any and all practical problems. Improvement in behavior theory will evolve through the efforts of critics of psychological theory (philosophers of science) and basic and applied experimental psychologists. Applied researchers working on parent training problems can contribute to theory revision and construction by devoting more time and effort to investigating the conditions that bring about behavior changes in children, rather than concentrating further on response contingencies. Among these other areas are analyses of (1) the role of precurrent interactions, such as attending and perceiving (stimulus control or discrimination); (2) the relationships among setting factors and changes in the functional properties of stimuli and responses; and (3) language-referential behavior. Findings in these areas will lead to revisions and improvements in behavior theory and will extend the range of conditions that can be managed by a parent to effect change in a child's behavior.

Application to Broad-Scale Programs

In a large majority of physically normal children who are considered retarded, the retardation comes about through socioculturally disadvantageous conditions. When substandard social and economic conditions constitute the environment of children, they serve to restrict and limit opportunities for them to grow, develop, and learn. More specifically, the families and teachers of these children do not or cannot provide them with the physical and social experiences generally available to middle-class children; do not or cannot reinforce acquisition of academic skills, knowledge, and effective work habits, such as concentrating on academic tasks and working independently; do not or cannot stimulate and encourage conventional forms of language development; and do not or cannot generate motivation for academic achievement and excellence (Bijou, 1981b).

Preventing this kind of retardation, usually mild or moderate, can most constructively be achieved through a comprehensive program beginning in the very first year of a child's life and continuing until the end of the fourth grade. An intervention strategy of this sort could consist of an integration of parent training, compensatory preschool, and a special elementary-school program. Parent training would be designed to assist parents to promote early development of their child's language, social skills, and cognitive skills (e.g., Shearer & Shearer, 1976). The preschool would afford opportunities to learn the skills and knowledge required for success in the first grade (e.g., Bijou, 1972, 1977), and the special elementary-school program would help in the mastery of language and academic skills so that the children could apply them to practical situations with little or no assistance (e.g., Becker & Carnine, 1981). Parent training, in a specially adapted form, would be pivotal to the entire program.

The same approach could be used as the basis for preventing problem behaviors. Here, more emphasis would be placed on development and maintenance of social, ethical, and moral behavior (e.g., Gelfand & Hartmann, 1977).

Other Implications

Parent training could well become the method of choice in the education and training of retarded persons in foreign countries. The Portage Project model, for example, has been used as a basis for intervention programs in retardation in England (Smith *et al.*, 1977) and Wales (Revill & Blunden, 1979), and research from those countries has shown that the procedures are highly effective and well received by the clients. Other adaptations are being tried in several South American and Asian countries, where the parent training format is attractive to those who work with families (e.g., Jesien, Aliaga, & Llanos, 1979). The limited funds available to these workers for the education and training of the retarded can be spent most profitably on training parents and child care personnel to work with retarded children in the home or in some kind of community facility. It is therefore easy to understand the widespread interest in adopting and adapting American-developed parent training programs and techniques to the needs of other countries worldwide.

References

Axline, V. M. *Play therapy*. Boston: Houghton Mifflin, 1947.

Baer, D. M., Wolf, M. M., & Risley, T. R. Some current dimensions of applied behavior analysis. *Journal of Applied Behavior Analysis*, 1968, *1*, 91–97.

Becker, W. C., & Carnine, D. W. Direct instruction: A behavioral theory model for comprehensive educational intervention with the disadvantaged. In S. W. Bijou & R. Ruiz (Eds.), *Behavior modification: Contributions to education*. Hillsdale, N.J.: Erlbaum, 1981.

Bijou, S. W. These kids have problems and our job is to do something about them. In J. B. Jordon & L. S. Robbins (Eds.), *Let's try doing something else kind of thing.* Arlington, Va.: Council for Exceptional Children, 1972.

Bijou, S. W. Practical implication of an interactional model of child development. *Exceptional Children*, 1977, *44*, 6–14.

Bijou, S. W. Essential steps in the education and training of retarded children. In S. W. Bijou & G. Becerra (Eds.), *Modificación de conducta: Aplicaciones sociales.* Mexico City: Trillas, 1981. (a)

Bijou, S. W. The prevention of retarded development in disadvantaged children. In M. Begab, H. C. Haywood, & H. L. Gerber (Eds.), *Psychosocial influences in retarded performance* (Vol. 1, *Issues and theories in development*). Baltimore: University Park Press, 1981. (b)

Braukmann, C. J., Kirigin, K. A., & Wolf, M. M. Behavioral treatment of juvenile delinquency. In S. W. Bijou & R. Ruiz (Eds.), *Behavior modification: Contributions to education.* Hillsdale, N.J.: Erlbaum, 1981.

Forehand, R., Sturgis, E. T., McMahon, R. J., Aguar, D., Green, K., Wells, K. C., & Breiner, J. Parent behavior training to modify child noncompliance. *Behavior Modification*, 1979, *3*, 3–25.

Gelfand, D. M., & Hartmann, D. P. The prevention of childhood behavior disorders. In B. B. Lahey & A. E. Kazdin (Eds.), *Advances in child clinical psychology* (Vol. 1). New York: Plenum Press, 1977.

Graziano, A. M. Parents as behavior therapists. In M. Hersen, R. M. Eisler, & P. M. Miller (Eds.), *Progress in behavior modification* (Vol. 4). New York: Academic Press, 1977.

Hawkins, R. P., Peterson, R. F., Schweid, E., & Bijou, S. W. Behavior therapy in the home: Amelioration of problem parent–child relations with the parent in a therapeutic role. *Journal of Experimental Child Psychology*, 1966, *4*, 99–107.

Herbert, E. W., & Baer, D. M. Training parents as behavior modifiers: Self-recording contingent attention. *Journal of Applied Behavior Analysis*, 1972, *5*, 139–149.

Hersen, M., & Barlow, D. H. *Single case experimental designs.* New York: Pergamon Press, 1976.

Jesien, G., Aliaga, J., & Llanos, M. *Validation of the Portage model in Peru.* Paper presented at the Interamerican Congress of Psychology, Lima, Peru, July 1979.

Johnson, C. A., & Katz, R. C. Using parents as change agents for their children: A review. *Journal of Child Psychology and Psychiatry and Allied Disciplines*, 1973, *14*, 181–200.

Koegel, R. L., Glahn, T. J., & Nieminen, G. S. Generalization of parent training results. *Journal of Applied Behavior Analysis*, 1978, *11*, 95–109.

Miller, S. J., & Sloane, H. N., Jr. The generalization effects of parent training across stimulus settings. *Journal of Applied Behavior Analysis*, 1976, *9*, 355–370.

O'Dell, S. Training parents in behavior modification: A review. *Psychological Bulletin*, 1974, *81*, 418–433.

Revill, S., & Blunden, R. A home training service for preschool developmentally handicapped children. *Behaviour Research and Therapy*, 1979, *17*, 207–214.

Schiefelbusch, R. L., & Hoyt, R. J., Jr. Three years past 1984. In M. C. Reynolds (Ed.), *Futures of education for exceptional children: Emerging structures.* Minneapolis: University of Minnesota Press, 1978.

Shearer, D. E., & Shearer, M. S. The Portage Project: A model for early childhood intervention. In T. D. Tjossem (Ed.), *Intervention strategies for high risk infants and young children.* Baltimore: University Park Press, 1976.

Sidman, M. *Tactics of scientific research.* New York: Basic Books, 1960.

Smith, J., Kushlick, A., & Glossop, C. *The Wessex Portage Project: A home teaching service for families with a preschool mentally handicapped child* (Research Report No. 125). Winchester, England: Health Care Evaluation Research Team, Dawn House, 1977.

Wahler, R. G., Berland, R. M., & Coe, T. D. Generalization processes in child behavior change. In B. B. Lahey & A. E. Kazdin (Eds.), *Advances in child clinical psychology* (Vol. 2). New York: Plenum Press, 1977.

Wahler, R. G., Leske, G., & Rogers, E. S. The insular family: A deviance support system for oppositional children. In L. A. Hamerlynck (Ed.), *Behavioral systems for the developmentally disabled* (Vol. 1, *School and family environments*). New York: Brunner/Mazel, 1979.

Wahler, R. C., Winkel, G. H., Peterson, R. F., & Morrison, D. C. Mothers as behavior therapists for their own children. *Behaviour Research and Therapy*, 1965, *3*, 113-124.

Williams, C. D. The elimination of tantrum behavior by extinction procedures. *Journal of Abnormal and Social Psychology*, 1959, *59*, 269.

Yates, A. R. Research methods in behavior modification: A comparative evaluation. In M. Hersen, R. M. Eisler, & P. M. Miller (Eds.), *Progress in behavior modification* (Vol. 2). New York: Academic Press, 1976.

THE DATA-BASED DEVELOPMENT OF PARENT TRAINING PROGRAMS

Bill L. Hopkins
University of Kansas

Unlike all of the other contributors to this volume, I know nothing about parent training. I have neither trained parents nor conducted parent training research. I have not read the parent training research literature during the last 5 years. I have nothing against parent training work; I simply have been preoccupied with other kinds of problems. Perhaps I write from a perspective that is uncluttered by experience, by obligations to justify my particular parent training program, or, for that matter, by practical considerations.

I have been asked to comment on parent training from the perspective of a person who has done similar kinds of work. I state that perspective here. I have trained teachers, and I have trained safety professionals. They, like parents, try to influence the behaviors of other people. Therefore, I think I understand the fundamental problem of the parent trainer: trying to affect one person's behavior so that it will affect another person's behavior. I have gotten as close to parent training as supervising graduate students who have developed treatment programs for tantrum-throwing, noncompliant, and aggressive children. I think I am familiar with many of the problem behaviors that the parent trainer might try to control. These experiences have given me exposure to the two kinds of technology the parent trainer must have: methods to affect parents' behaviors, and methods parents can use to affect their children's behaviors. I have also worked in human service organizations such as schools, universities, mental health agencies, and community organizations. I think I know the workings of the agencies most parent trainers probably work in.

My intent is to sketch how I would go about developing a parent training program, what research I would conduct, and some of the issues that might be important to my long-range goals. I plan to do this before reading the other chapters in the volume in order to avoid biasing my views more than they are already biased.

My biases are simple and few in number. I am an empiricist. I tend to believe things only after objective evidence is available to indicate that they are true. This objective evidence, in areas of psychology, tends to take the form of objective data and experimentally produced results to allow for statements of causality. I have found claims to be abundant and experimentally derived facts to be precious commodities in psychology. Beyond this bias for science, I have few preferences. My own work has fallen within what might be called applied behavior analysis, or the application of principles of operant conditioning to human behavior, for a number of years. However, that preference is a result of the above-stated preference for the objective and in no way is as fundamental an assumption as the allegiance to empiricism. I hope I follow whichever kind of technology produces desirable objective results, regardless of how well that technology fits with my theoretical positions.

I necessarily express several views about good ways to develop treatment programs. I have few well-developed models to follow in this area, because so few behavioral programs have been developed to their logical limits. Often, it seems, researchers and program developers have preferred either to try to sell or put into practice a relatively untested program, or to develop the very beginnings of programs and spend years testing various aspects and assumptions in these programs. I try here to present an alternative to these two extremes.

This alternative neither tries to sell untested snake oil, nor does it insist on experimental evidence for every possible assumption. Rather, it makes a commitment to a set of goals and tests program assumptions against these goals. However, it does not test hypotheses unless they are reasonably related to the practical goal. I have already stated that I do not have many models to follow in trying to describe this kind of program development. To the best of my knowledge, there have been only two behavioral programs that have followed this approach. One is the Achievement Place programs; the other is the Behavior Analysis Follow Through programs at the University of Kansas. I have enjoyed watching both of these programs develop over several years. Their methods of development have much to recommend them.

SETTING GOALS

The first step in systematic development of a parent training program would be to determine the long-range goals of the effort. Goals are broad, general statements about what a program will accomplish. What will be done? For whom will it be done? Under what time and financial constraints will it be done?

It is useful to recognize early that goals are personal statements. Essentially, each goal is a statement about reinforcers for one or more persons. What do the planners of a program want accomplished? What would be reinforcing for certain parents? What would benefit a certain group of children? It is important to recognize that goals, as statements about reinforcers, are not perfectly reliable. A person may predict that some outcome will be a reinforcer for him or her. Ten years from now, when that outcome is produced, it may be far less reinforcing than the person predicted.

The purposes in setting goals are straightforward. First, the establishment of the goals will eventually lead to means for evaluating the programs being developed. Second, this evaluation will allow the planners to make corrections in their work as they receive information about whether the programs are operating as intended. There is a broad assumption, still largely unproven, that people are much more likely to reach their goals if they know what they are than if the goals are poorly stated or implicit.

The fact that so many different people—program developers, parents, children, taxpayers—have some say about goals means that the results are likely to represent a number of compromises. Professionals are not entirely free to pursue their goals independently of what parents want done. Parents can get only those services that professionals are willing to provide.

The fact that goals are personal means that there is some latitude for different people to arrive at different goals while working on essentially the same problem. Therefore, an observer should expect to see different program personnel trying to achieve different things, and considerable variation in programs aimed at similar populations of parents and children.

To illustrate the process, I will assume that I am developing a parent training program and will carry out, in a hypothetical fashion, the various steps. My very broad goals would be "to make the world a better place through parent training." I would ask myself, as well as a lot of parents and young and old people, what young people might do differently so that the world would be a better place. At this point, I can think of no reason for asking such a question of a specialized set of parents. Therefore, I would try to obtain a random or representative sample of parents.

I have no unique skills for predicting behavior. Therefore, my predictions about the results of such questioning should be treated as rough guesses. Nevertheless, I would expect that the kinds of things that would be most frequently mentioned would be that young people should know, better than is ordinarily the case, such things as how to get along happily with other people, how to work creatively and productively with various resources and opportunities, and how to handle various common crises with equanimity.

I expect much parent training is aimed at quite different behaviors: ensuring that children complete school, minimizing the hassles parents endure during child rearing, and reducing the frequency with which various authorities complain about specific children and adolescents. These are reasonable goals. I only doubt that they are anything close to the dominant concerns of a representative cross-section of our culture. Rather, they are the concerns of strong special-interest groups.

If program developers choose to work with the narrow goals of special-interest groups, they must expect a relatively narrower and more unpredictable base of support for their work.

DERIVING OBJECTIVES

The second step in systematic program development is to translate broad program goals into specific objectives. Goals can be implicit, fuzzy concepts. Objectives are statements that are so concrete and detailed that any two reasonably informed people will agree that particular behavioral events are or are not instances of particular objectives.

Professionals are eventually going to observe and measure whether or not objectives occur, or whether or not objectives are closer to being met. Therefore, the process of specification must be careful and thorough enough to allow for quantified observations. The criterion for objectivity will ultimately rest on the extent of agreement among different people. Presumably, that agreement will depend on the specificity of the objectives.

I am not sure which objectives would result from my goals. I expect that there would be different objectives for children of different ages, and certainly that there would be a lot of guesswork about which behaviors of 5-year-olds are precursors for other wanted behaviors of 12-year-olds. Certainly the list of objectives would be quite long. It is likely that the objectives would include such things as minimizing the numbers of fights and arguments children have at school; setting wide limits for amounts of time children spend with other people or alone; and improving many situational behaviors, such as finding appropriate activities when children are prohibited from engaging in preferred other activities and responding in certain ways to common opportunities.

As this list of objectives is being developed, I would spend a great deal of time talking with parents to insure that the objectives are related to the more general goals and that the objectives completely cover the goals.

DEVELOPING MEASUREMENT SYSTEMS

Adequately specified objectives allow for the direct development of objective measurement. This is true because the test of the adequacy of specification of an objective is that two people are able to agree on the occurrence or nonoccurrence of the events involved in the objective.

However, the fact that such observations can be made does not mean that they can be made simply or inexpensively. Considerations of costs and economics dictate that all measurement be based on samples rather than exhaustive observation. The behavioral events of interest will be observed only part of the time rather than all of the time, and only in some situations rather than in all situations. It is also likely that there will be so many objectives that decisions will be made to measure some but not all of them. Practically, those objectives most likely to be excluded from measurement are those that are most complex or fleeting or that occur in those situations most difficult to observe.

The limits on measurement will leave room for doubting whether particular programs accomplish all of the objectives intended and do so to the extent desired. Nevertheless, incomplete measurement is preferable to no measurement at all. If parent training is like all other fields of human service, some programs will enjoy great short-term popularity that revolves around broadly acceptable goals that have never been translated into objectives. No measurement will be available for these programs and, as a result, there will be no serious evaluation of the extent to which the programs produce the intended goals. These programs, in the absence of measurement, will be closed to validation, improvement, and replication.

The existence of objective measurement systems is a prerequisite to evaluation and to answering questions about the extent to which goals are met. Measurement must be available to allow for improvements. Without measurement, it is impossible to determine whether other people can even carry out a program as its authors intended.

Program authors are likely to talk more about methods than about results. This is useful, because other professionals probably want to learn practical details. However, if a program strikes another professional's fancy, he or she should raise questions about goals, objectives, and results. How could anyone possibly be interested in a set of methods in the absence of information about what those methods produce?

OBJECTIVES DICTATE
NEEDED TECHNOLOGY

Once a measurement system is in place, I would be in a position to begin developing my parent training technology. The technology that is needed is obviously whichever technology will produce the objectives.

In the case of parent training, at least two broad kinds of technology are called for: child development technology and parent training technology. Program planners have to know which parenting methods will produce the wanted child behaviors that are objectives. As these parenting methods are known or developed, the planners will need ways to impart the skills to parents.

As the needed technology is cataloged, it will dictate two courses of action. Parent trainers will obviously want to adopt whichever functional technology is already available, and they will have to develop the needed technology that is not yet available. The search for available technology will lead to the literature. If the parenting literature is like the service literature I know, it will contain many examples of technology that are claimed to produce particular objectives, but these claims will be substantiated by little validating research.

The only productive approach to the shortcomings of the research in the literature is to use what has been reasonably validated and reject what has not been. If the literature provides promising examples of technology that have not yet been validated, professionals should conduct the necessary evaluation research before incorporating the methods into their program.

When parent trainers need particular technology that has not been published, they should conduct development research. In most areas, there appear to be no complex problems in conducting this research. The obligation is to produce technology that will affect certain objectives in certain ways. A measurement system has already been developed to determine the extent to which any procedures affect the objectives. Therefore, validation of new technology is a fairly routine matter.

There will be hundreds of options for which technological methods might be evaluated. Three considerations seem to be important in choosing from among these:

1. What is the probable magnitude of the effects?
2. What are the probable costs of the methods?
3. Are the methods acceptable on moral and ethical grounds?

Some weighting among these considerations is likely to guide researchers toward particular methods and away from other methods.

There are, of course, other ways to select and develop technology. Probably the most common way this is done in psychological services areas is to base decisions on theoretical considerations. Technology is derived from some theory and used without validation; or favored theories are consulted, in the absence of supporting data, in selecting from among technological options. The results, unfortunately, are service approaches that are theoretically attractive but are of little usefulness in producing the desired objectives.

I cannot say which technology is and is not available to my hypothetical effort, because I do not know the parent training literature. Extrapolating from other service areas, I would predict that technology is available to change some more severe behavior problems, such as temper tantrums and bedwetting, while not that much may be known about teaching children to be creative and good at taking advantage of opportunities. Probably a good deal is known about introducing new skills to parents, and little is known about how to get them to use the skills reliably over a long period of time. The first prediction is based on the assumption that, because of social pressures on government funding, more is known about correcting abnormal development than about promoting good development. I predict the second result simply because psychologists and educators consistently seem to assume that training guarantees performance.

WHAT THE DATA SYSTEMS ALLOW

The use of the data systems will insure that the technology included in the parent training program is effective to produce what is intended. If technology is not useful, the data will indicate that so it can be deleted or replaced. The data will indicate shortcomings and errors.

Making corrections and further efforts on the basis of feedback provided by the data will allow for a continuously and gradually improving program. The program will produce known results in given circumstances. Improvements will be obvious and faulty assumptions will be exposed. The eventual result should be reliable and useful parent training programs. There is probably no known alternative approach to program development with this kind of promise.

Acknowledgments

I wish to acknowledge my debts to Montrose Wolf, Lonnie Phillips, Dean Fixsen, Kathi Kirigin Ramp, and Curt Braukmann for their work with the Achievement Place Program, and to Don Bushell and Eugene Ramp for their work with Follow Through.

COMPETENT PARENTS, COMPETENT CHILDREN
Behavioral Objectives of Parent Training

Elaine A. Blechman
Wesleyan University

OVERVIEW OF THE CHAPTER

"Competence" has become a fashionable term in the behavioral science literature and even in the popular press. Since a satisfactory operational definition of the term has yet to be offered, this chapter provides an operational definition of child and adult "competence," describes four combinations of competent and incompetent parents and children, and considers how much each group of families will benefit from behavioral family intervention.

For the past 6 years, my research has included inquiries into improved methods of parent training and basic studies of family interaction. This chapter has provided an opportunity for me to integrate the findings of studies that have, to date, been published in piecemeal fashion. I review the findings of a collaborative study of families successfully engaged in behavioral family intervention; present research on school-based early intervention to illustrate how behavioral family intervention can be modified to suit the needs of incompetent parents; and discuss preliminary findings from research on competent children and their families. Finally, I make recommendations for behavioral family interventions and for alternative interventions with competent and incompetent parents. The framework used to integrate applied and basic research is an operational definition of "competence" and related, low-level assumptions about competent human behavior.

Contemporary discussions of parent training inevitably turn to two questions: "Which parents are most likely to benefit from training?" and "What constitutes a satisfactory outcome of parent training?" In answer to these questions, this chapter disputes the egalitarian assumption that any parent can be successfully trained in effective child-rearing skills; it contends that the purpose of parent training, and of related behavioral family interventions, should be to enhance the competence of parents and children alike.

BEHAVIORAL FAMILY INTERVENTIONS

The term "parent training" is an abbreviation of the phrase "parent contingency management training." It refers to methods of teaching parents to apply principles of behavior analysis to child rearing, with emphasis upon management of reinforcement contingencies. In addition to parent training, there are other behavioral interventions that aim to influence parenting behavior (Blechman, 1981b). These include contingency contracting and family problem-solving training. In parent–child contingency contracting, the details of a contingency management plan are specified in writing and agreed to by all involved parties. Contingency contracting bypasses trial-and-error learning by informing everyone about the occasions for reinforcement; it aims to increase family members' commitment to the contract. Family problem-solving training teaches family members to negotiate and carry out formal contingency contracts, and to achieve informal verbal agreements (Blechman, 1980).

Family problem-solving training aims to prepare family members to solve new problems as they arise, to build an atmosphere of trust, and to acquaint each family member with the others' different perspectives. Contingency contracting and family problem-solving training emphasize stimulus control somewhat more than parent training does. They are more appropriate than is parent training for families with older school-aged and adolescent children, since they involve children as well as parents in training. Both contingency contracting and family problem-solving training aim to convey basic principles of contingency management.

Guided practice and corrective feedback unify these three approaches to behavioral family intervention. The operations to be mastered vary among and within the modes of behavioral family intervention. Operations include making a clear request for desired behavior, reinforcing cooperative behavior with praise, keeping a record of contract compliance, participating in a weekly family conference, and using time out. The family members may receive corrective feedback immediately, if the therapist observes them in the clinic; or they may receive delayed feedback after they provide the therapist with global self-reports and detailed records of events at home.

Guided practice distinguishes behavioral family interventions from approaches that transmit and clarify new skills and attitudes through books, films, and discussion. A better term for the latter approaches is "parent educa-tion," or, if training is directed at other family members, "family life education." Educational programs include workshops in which parents learn principles of contingency management from programmed textbooks (e.g., Patterson & Gullion, 1971). The emphasis on guided practice of new skills also distinguishes behavioral family interventions from systems and strategic family therapies. The latter therapies view family behavior patterns as symbolic epiphenomena less worthy of change than underlying cognitive and affective processes.

In principle, behavioral family interventions train parents and children in new skills; they are not therapies for restoration of functioning lost by the disabled. Unfortunately, this distinction between skill training and therapy is often blurred in practice, perhaps because so little is known about the skills required to build a happy, productive family. Increased knowledge about family competence should enhance the use of behavioral family interventions as methods of skill training, as well as the development of necessary alternatives to child-focused interventions.

A DEFINITION OF "COMPETENCE"

At one time, the terms "normality" and "mental health" described the goals of psychoeducational interventions. "Normality," whether measured by the average statistical response or by cultural convention, has not been a popular treatment goal since the 1950s (Coan, 1974). "Mental health," which can only be detected by the absence of pathology, was rejected as a treatment goal by critics of the medical treatment model (Jahoda, 1958). "Competence" has gained increasing acceptance as the ultimate goal of treatment. The emphasis on "competence," or "self-efficacy" (Bandura, 1977), may be the most enduring product of the community mental health movement.

"Competence" connotes adequate skill at a given pursuit. Since the most elementary human pursuits involve either tasks or interpersonal relationships, a generally competent child or adult performs better than average at both tasks and relationships. In an effort to define "competence" operationally, I might state that competence involves a high level of favorable interpersonal and achievement consequences compared to that of one's peers (Blechman, 1981a). Thus, competence is gauged by the effects of behavior on the environment, not by the topography of behavior (Skinner, 1938).

"Competence" must be distinguished from intrinsic, personal "worth," which is equivalent for all people, regardless of their achievements. Thus the term "incompetence," as used in this chapter, refers to relatively little task and interpersonal success, not to relatively little value as a human being. The definition of "competence" to be offered here is very much a product of the values of Western industrialized society. The importance of this definition is that, for better or worse, people's opinions of themselves and of others are often based on rough indicators of competence. It is a moot point whether competence is also an accurate measure of an individual's contributions to society.

In this definition, "competence" refers to an individual's status as measured at one time, not to an enduring trait or disposition. Assuming an orderly universe, a measure of competence should have predictive validity such that a competent child will become a competent adolescent and adult. There are two components of general competence. The interpersonal component of competence represents self-evaluations and evaluations by others of an individual's role performance. On a classroom choice measure, competent children are frequently nominated by peers and teachers as capable students, talented athletes, and desirable friends. Competent children also tend to nominate themselves for these distinctions. At work, in voluntary community organizations, and in informal meetings of neighbors, competent adults are frequently selected as spokespersons, consulted for advice, and invited to participate in social gatherings. Competent adults are visible in their neighborhoods, well liked, and respected for the contributions they make to the community. Votes for competent children and adults on peer-nomination and community-reputation measures reflect the pleasant interpersonal consequences that competent people generally experience.

The achievement component of competence represents objectively measured outcomes of an individual's performance at school and work, including achievement test scores, occupational ratings, and salary levels. Competent children will score above the median for their grade level on standardized achievement measures. Competent adults will score above the median for their age on measures of education, occupational prestige, and income. These occupational and educational performance scores reflect the pleasant task-related consequences that competent children and adults generally experience.

There appear to be two prerequisites for competence. The first is a repertoire of problem-solving skills, which equip the individual to master rapidly changing social and physical environments. The second prerequisite for competence is "situational freedom," or access to surroundings in which the individual can test problem-solving skills. One of the products of competence is an absence of unexpected crises that inflict intolerable stress. Some of the life crises experienced by the incompetent individual are the direct products of ineffective problem solving; others reflect the lowered situational freedom engendered by incompetence. The objective results of incompetence are acute and chronic crises, disruptions in work and family life, physical illness, and financial instability. The subjective results are low self-esteem, dysphoric mood, and a belief in the uncontrollability of external events. Thus, adults who are generally incompetent are likely to be overrepresented among parents referred by themselves and others for help in rearing their children.

FAMILY COMPETENCE AND BEHAVIORAL FAMILY INTERVENTIONS

Visualize for a moment a distribution of competent to incompetent parents and a second distribution of competent to incompetent children. Four family patterns result: competent parents and children, incompetent parents and children, competent parents of incompetent children, and incompetent parents of competent children. Since unreliable measurement plays a part in this classification system, it helps to focus on the extremes of the distribution (people who score more than two standard deviations above or below the mean). The first group—competent families—has received little attention, even though such families' skills, attitudes, and knowledge provide admirable objectives for behavioral family interventions. The last three groups are potential consumers of behavioral family interventions.

Incompetent adults have received considerable attention, because their lives provide data relevant to arguments about genetic versus environmental contributions to intelligence (Dobzhansky, 1973). Families headed by incompetent parents appear to transmit ineffective problem-solving repertoires from one generation to the next in a pattern of cultural–familial retardation (Zigler, 1966). As long as these families are led by incompetent adults, they might be called incompetent families.

The statement that incompetent families are trapped in a "culture of poverty" (Lewis, 1966) is a sociological comment on the restrictive social environments inhabited by people with deficient problem-solving repertoires. This condition is one I have already referred to as "low situational freedom." Psychiatric hospitals and prisons are extreme examples of environments that restrict future opportunities to develop coping skills and are populated with individuals whose past levels of problem-solving skill have been low. Thus, the inadequate problem-solving repertoires of incompetent families encourage social isolation and deprive younger family members of natural opportunities to learn effective coping habits. Socially isolated families perpetuate themselves but do not flourish in modern urbanized society because they do not make use of technological and cultural advances (Dobzhansky, 1973). It seems reasonable to include among these cultural advances systematic methods of teaching child-rearing skills to parents who lack natural learning opportunities.

Wahler (1980) was the first to point out the relationship between familial isolation and failures in parent training. He described poorly educated, low-income mothers whose insular relationships with outsiders mirrored their coercive relationships with children. For the incompetent parent of a physically or emotionally handicapped child, parent training may be a heroic and impractical effort that requires inordinate time and money and interferes with treatment of the child. Division of scarce resources between parent and child training programs may jeopardize both enterprises. Failures in parent training may also aggravate the child's problems—for example, when unsuccessfully trained parents blame their failures on their children.

Competent parents have, by definition, shown their ability to benefit from experience. Of the three potential groups of consumers of parent training, competent parents of handicapped children seem most likely to benefit from parent training. There is a widespread tendency to blame parents for their children's disabilities. Competent parents of handicapped children suffer from this prejudice more than others. For this reason, they will be encouraged by the behaviorist's reluctance to draw inferences about past events from present behavior, and by the orientation toward the future of skill training programs. Advances in the technology of parent training are most likely to come from experiences with this group of families.

Incompetent parents of competent children have an excess of daily frustrations that interfere with appreciation of their children, as well as few general social skills to ease the child-rearing process. They are likely to be dissatisfied with their children even if (and especially when) their children are competent. Forehand and Wells (1977) have aptly described depressed mothers who request parent training to help them cope with their normal, untroubled children. Thus, the competent children of incompetent parents are at high risk for future life problems (Garmezy, 1974); among those children, however, a few are invulnerable and will survive despite their parents. Because incompetent adults may not respond well to child-focused behavioral family intervention, and because the children of incompetent adults are at risk, interventions must suit the needs of these vulnerable families. Later in this chapter, I describe an intervention that distributes the labor of intervention between home and school and is designed to require only meager parental support.

CHARACTERISTICS OF FAMILIES ENGAGED IN TREATMENT

Does adult competence really affect responsiveness to child-focused interventions? A recent multisite collaboration (Blechman, Budd, Christophersen, Szykula, Wahler, Embry, Kogan, O'Leary, & Riner, 1981) studied the characteristics of families who seek and become engaged in behavioral family intervention. A central question concerned the representation of low-income and one-parent families among those engaged in treatment. The low-income one-parent family has been described repeatedly as hard to keep in parent training (Eyberg & Johnson, 1974). Recipients of parent training have tended to come from the middle class (Hargis & Blechman, 1979). Eight applied research groups, each engaged in the development of methods of behavioral family intervention, cooperated in the execution of the study. Five of the groups participated in both 1978 and 1979. Leaders of these groups completed a questionnaire for a specific number of consecutive clients seen for intake in their clinics (10 in 1978, 20 in 1979). The questionnaire requested the following types of information about each family applying for help: demographics of family members and the family group; descriptions of the types of interventions offered by the clinic to the family; and ratings of the family's subsequent record of treatment attendance.

Over the two years, a total of 181 questionnaires were returned. To illustrate the characteristics of the sample in the second year, 73% of the target children were boys, and 61% were from two-parent families; 79% of the families were white, and 39% had been referred for treatment by a public agency or private practitioner. The mean family income was $11,580. Children's ages ranged from 3.5 to 8.8 years with a mean age of 6 years. The presenting problems most often mentioned by parents were as follows: disturbed parent–child relations (29%), school problems (21%), and antisocial behavior (20%). Validating informal beliefs that the principal difference between sites was type of treatments provided, a stepwise discriminant function analysis found four functions that accounted for 76% of between-locations variance: family communication training, home token economy, marital intervention, and parent support group.

For each family, a composite score was constructed that took into account information about treatment type and treatment disposition, and that indicated whether a client family had become engaged in treatment (i.e., had been offered a specific treatment and accepted the offer). A stepwise discriminant function analysis was executed, with engagement in treatment as the grouping dependent variable. One discriminant function, named "engagement," produced a significant multivariate F ratio. Engaged families tended to receive family communication training, complain of symptomatic child behavior, have mothers and fathers with high occupational prestige ratings, have fathers who worked many hours, and have a high number of natural parents (rather than stepparents). Nonengaged families tended to receive assessment, complain of antisocial child behavior, receive parent–child contracting alone (rather than together with family communication training, as engaged families did), and have many children.

The number of clients engaged in treatment at different locations ranged from 48% to 100%, with a mean of 74%. Because locations also varied in the types of treatment they most often provided, and to a lesser extent in the types of families they most often treated, it would be inappropriate to conclude that one site (or treatment type) was generally more effective than another. The composite engagement score does appear meaningful, since it had the expected relationships with treatment length, treatment completion, and staff ratings of treatment success. Parents' occupational prestige ratings predicted engagement in treatment; this is consistent with evidence that children's life success is best predicted by parent income, occupation, and education (Mosteller & Moynihan, 1972). It is noteworthy that these families were predominantly working-class and lower-middle-class, indicating clearly that parent training was not sought only by an elite group.

Of the two variables initially thought to predict engagement in treatment— number of parents and family income—only the latter (gauged indirectly by parents' occupational prestige ratings) proved to be a useful predictor. Most single parents are women, and the average occupational prestige ratings of women are lower than those of men. Therefore, there is a natural tendency to derive rough estimates of a family's social standing from the number of parents who head the family (Blechman, 1982). For example, families headed by two parents are generally assumed to have higher social standing than are families headed by one parent. Nevertheless, the findings of the collaborative study indicated that only occupational prestige was a useful predictor of engagement in behavioral family treatment.

It seems that competent adults will be most easily engaged in behavioral family intervention. The collaborative study found that the parents who are most likely to receive and persist with some form of behavioral family intervention are adults whose relatively high occupational prestige and family composition indicate effectiveness at pursuits other than child rearing. Since the study sample was predominantly working-class and lower-middle-class, high occupational prestige meant that most of these fathers and mothers were employed at semiskilled or skilled labor. Thus, competent families were not upper-class or wealthy families; however, these competent families were most likely to be engaged in behavioral family intervention. It is conceivable that behavioral family intervention was offered in a more appetizing manner to competent parents, so that they were more likely to accept the offer and remain in treatment. Even so, the bias resulting from the interaction between type of intervention and type of client probably cannot be eliminated without a radical change in the intervention process. For example, behavioral family intervention requires that the parents focus on the child's well-being and the control of impulsive, aggressive, and erratic behavior. Incompetent adults with ineffective work and interpersonal habits may find these demands intolerable, and may not persist in treatment.

ALTERNATIVES TO BEHAVIORAL FAMILY INTERVENTION FOR LESS COMPETENT ADULTS

Child-focused behavioral family interventions demand general competence from adults. For adults with limited competence, other interventions deserve consideration. A strategy has been proposed for matching a client family with an intervention (Blechman, 1981b). The strategy assumes that four conditions are met:

1. Choice of an intervention is guided by easily, inexpensively gathered information.
2. Each of the three child-focused behavioral interventions (parent training, contingency contracting, problem-solving training) is provided with equivalent competence.
3. Once an intervention is selected, reliable, objective data are collected to chart the course of intervention and document its effectiveness.
4. Systematic evidence about the success and failure of the strategy's component rules is used to refine the selection process.

Scrutiny of this assessment strategy reveals that the available array of child-related behavioral family interventions is incomplete. Three interventions might fill gaps in the array. They are parent self-control training, marital problem-solving training, and parent self-sufficiency training.

Parent Self-Control Training

Parent self-control training addresses parents who complain about uncontrolled, aggressive child behavior and who are equally uncontrolled and aggressive themselves. Adults who cannot exercise voluntary control over their own behavior cannot be readily trained in parenting skills. These adults are subject to frequent temper tantrums, and they indulge in verbal and physical abuse of other adults and children. Time out from positive reinforcement, a basic technique in parent training, might be an appropriate remedy for their children. Yet these adults will administer time out with difficulty and in an erratic manner. It is likely that they will add uncalled-for punitive embellishments to the time-out procedure. These poorly controlled parents can be systematically trained to apply time out to themselves. The components of training include the following:

1. Identify instances of one's own explosive behavior from videotapes.
2. Identify antecedents to such behavior on videotape and from memories of recent experiences.
3. Turn off the videotape as soon as critical antecedents are recognized, and engage in systematic, deep relaxation.
4. Record antecedents of poorly controlled behavior at home.
5. Leave the room or change positions in the room when a critical antecedent occurs; then engage in systematic relaxation or an absorbing activity for 5 minutes.

Marital Problem-Solving Training

Marital problem-solving training addresses couples who complain about their children's behavior but are unprepared to cooperate in consistent child-rearing practices. When treatment of a child is necessary, and when marital conflict and inconsistency interfere with treatment, it may be necessary to put one parent in charge of the relationship with the child, or to force consistency and cooperation upon the couple by anticipating each potential disagreement between parents. When complaints about a child merely reflect a couple's dissatisfaction with and mismanagement of family affairs, they might be trained to handle their complaints about each other as solvable problems (Jacobson & Martin, 1976; Vincent, Weiss, & Birchler, 1975; Weiss, 1975), and they might be given repeated experience in cooperatively handling frustrating tasks. A board game has recently been developed to train married couples to resolve problems (including child-related problems) and to behave in a warm and trusting manner during their negotiations (Blechman & Rabin, 1981). There is promising preliminary evidence about this approach from the treatment of normal, unhappy couples in the United States (Rabin, Blechman, & Milton, 1981) and from the treatment of clinically distressed couples in Israel (Rabin, 1981).

Parent Self-Sufficiency Training

Parent self-sufficiency training addresses parents who have problems with child behavior and with maintenance of basic life necessities. Training aims to provide such parents with a problem-solving strategy useful in managing their extrafamilial problems. If successful, training should provide parents with the energy and interest to focus on child behavior problems through any of the three major child-related family interventions. At times, self-sufficiency training may bring about spontaneous improvements in parent–child interaction by altering critical antecedents and consequences. A general problem-solving strategy that parents can apply to a variety of life problems includes these components:

1. Establish priorities.
2. Select one problem.
3. Learn the contingencies, rules, and policies that govern circumstances relevant to that problem.
4. Establish a plan likely to have a good outcome.
5. Put the plan into practice.
6. Gather information about the plan's success over a reasonable time period.
7. Refine the plan if it is moderately successful and continue to use it; return to the planning stage with plans that are clearly unsuccessful.

An Illustration of Self-Sufficiency Training

An illustration of self-sufficiency training as an alternative to child-focused behavioral family intervention is provided by a case study (Blechman & Caple, 1976) of a depressed woman with a history of unsuccessful psychotherapy and drug treatment for depression. The problems of her younger children at school and her older children's difficulties with the police prompted her referral for parent training. In light of the extensiveness and urgency of this woman's life problems, treatment focused on self-sufficiency rather than on parenting. The client's tearful complaints and self-disparagement were gradually channeled into focused discussions of one complaint, with consideration of alternative modes of resolution, and then refinement and implementation of a chosen plan of action. To gauge the impact of intervention, client interaction with unfamiliar adults was sampled before, during, and after treatment. Trained coders rated complaining and problem solving during these 5-minute-long videotaped probes. To document how intervention affected the client's dependency upon prescription drugs, self-reports and dispensary reports of medication usage were monitored.

Mrs. Jones was a 43-year-old, high-school-educated, Catholic woman with six children. Two years before applying for parent training, she was hospitalized briefly for depression and then divorced from her alcoholic husband. In the subsequent 2 years, Mrs. Jones received individual and group therapy from five different nurses and psychiatric residents. Mrs. Jones described herself as unable to manage her finances or her family. Her three young adult sons (two of whom lived with her) included one who abused alcohol, one who was drug-dependent, and one who was AWOL from the Navy. She could not meet the mortgage on her house, and she had no heat, electricity, or telephone. Her medication (200 mg/day of Elavil) provided little help, despite some unpleasant side effects. Mrs. Jones scored 73 on the Cattell Culture Fair Intelligence Test. According to her own report, Mrs. Jones had never lived in a self-sufficient manner during her adult years.

Treatment sessions were spread, at increasingly greater intervals, over 6 months. The first intervention sessions began with a recitation of problems by Mrs. Jones: her own, her children's, and her neighbors'. Each time she raised a problem of her own, the therapist asked her, "What could you do about that?" The trainer changed the subject when Mrs. Jones discussed others' problems or when she denigrated herself. Whenever Mrs. Jones suggested a solution or complimented herself, the trainer showed interest with assent, approval, agreement, or humor. The trainer modeled a problem-solving approach by thinking out loud about issues and presenting alternative solutions from which Mrs. Jones was encouraged to choose. The trainer prompted self-approving statements at the beginning of each session by asking Mrs. Jones what she had done well during the week. Most training sessions ended with the development of a homework assignment, based on a solution that Mrs. Jones had selected: An assignment to contact legal aid included a list of questions to ask the lawyer; an assignment to decide about selling her house included the development of a list of pros and cons. The concepts of assertiveness, self-esteem, and decision making were used by the therapist to label the steps Mrs. Jones was taking. Mrs. Jones read and reread *Your Perfect Right* (Alberti & Emmons, 1974) for encouragement.

During the second intervention phase, an attempt was made to remove the therapist from the problem-solving process. This was done by substituting a programmed game board for the usual discussion. The game board guided Mrs. Jones through steps leading up to selection and evaluation of a solution. Assignments during this phase focused on setting priorities and formulating plans of action in an independent manner. During the third phase of training, the trainer administered three booster training sessions in which Mrs. Jones's active problem solving and self-approval were once again elicited and encouraged.

The results of treatment might be summed up as follows: Problem-solving statements rose from 39% during baseline probes to 59% of Mrs. Jones's comments during third-phase probes. Medication usage dropped from 200 mg/day during baseline to no drugs used during follow-up. There were pretreatment to posttreatment increases in extraversion and reductions in neuroticism on the Eysenck Personality Inventory (Eysenck & Eysenck, 1964), as well as increases in self-sufficiency on the Bernreuter Inventory (Bernreuter, 1933). By the end of treatment, Mrs. Jones had sold her house, paid her outstanding bills, and rented an apartment, which she occupied with her two youngest children, since her older children were now on their own. She bought a car and secured a part-time job. She no longer had complaints about her children's unmanageable behavior. There was evidence of maintenance of positive changes during follow-up. Of course, this case study merely illustrates an alternative to behavioral family intervention; it does not prove the efficacy of self-sufficiency training.

A BEHAVIORAL FAMILY INTERVENTION THAT DISTRIBUTES THE LABOR BETWEEN HOME AND SCHOOL

Parent contingency management training, contingency contracting, and family problem-solving training require considerable parent time, effort, and self-control. Because many parents of high-risk children lack these resources, my colleagues and I decided to modify family problem-solving training by dividing the labor of intervention between home and school. We expected that the resulting intervention would appeal to a broad range of families, including families headed by incompetent adults. Two large-scale studies inquired whether modified family problem-solving training is an effective early intervention for high-risk children and whether family involvement is necessary for successful early intervention (Blechman, Kotanchik, & Taylor, 1981; Blechman, Taylor, & Schrader, 1981). A central question in both studies concerned the willingness of low-income families to participate in and follow through with intervention.

The First Study

The first study (Blechman, Kotanchik, & Taylor, 1981), involved the classes of 13 volunteer teachers of second through fifth grades in 12 public elementary schools in a city of 40,000 with a university clinic. High-risk children were identified at school in the following way: Math and reading classwork were collected daily, scored, and returned to teachers the next day, from the first to the last month of school. The number of correct answers to each assignment was divided by the total number of tasks, and a daily average for all scores was derived. Daily scores were divided by the number of days in the baseline period when the child attended school and was assigned classwork, yielding a baseline mean. A scatter index consisting of the number of daily scores falling at least 12.5% below a child's baseline mean was used to rank children within each class. Inconsistent children were the six children with most baseline math and reading scatter in their class. Stable children were the three children with least scatter in their class. Intermediate children were the remaining children in each class. Three weeks before intervention, inconsistent students were randomly assigned to experimental and control conditions at a ratio of 2 : 1.

The study had a two-way repeated-measures design: condition (experimental, control) × phase (baseline, intervention). The six most inconsistent children in each class were randomly assigned within class, four to the experimental and two to the control condition. A comparison group of stable students included the three in each class with least scatter. Twice as many children were assigned to the experimental as to the control condition, because some families were expected to refuse intervention. During the first week of school, a letter informed parents that if they consented, data concerning their children would be collected throughout the year. Because the classwork of all children was collected throughout the year, the progress of children in the control and stable comparison conditions could be followed without revealing their identities, as could the progress of children whose families declined intervention.

Families who accepted intervention came to the clinic for a 1-hour appointment the week before the note system began. They met a project teacher, learned about intervention, and saw their children's baseline data. They spent up to 15 minutes playing the Solutions board game, which guided them through writing a contingency contract and making decisions about the reward for a "good news" note. The contract target would be the academic subject, math or reading, in which the child was most inconsistent throughout the baseline period; the goal would be performance at or above the child's baseline mean.

After this meeting, the project teacher talked weekly by telephone to parents and children about their contracts. Once the families had written their contracts, teachers began scoring children's work and calculating daily means, using the method employed by project scorers. Each day, project scorers collected all children's classwork, including work by children in the experimental condition already scored by teachers. When children achieved their goals, the teachers were to fill in note forms so that they read, for example, "Good news! John's reading work was 85% correct today." When children did not achieve their goals, no notes were to go home. When teachers assigned no work, notes reading "No work assigned today" were to go home. Teachers were to explain to children how they earned each note by referring to the day's work. Parents were to provide the promised reward when the note came home, but to say nothing when no note came home. Throughout intervention, staff members checked whether teachers sent home notes when merited by the work and whether parents rewarded children as agreed.

The results of the first early-intervention study might be summed up as follows:

1. Dependent measures were reliable, and treatment was carried out as intended. Interscorer reliability for classwork ranged from .36 to 1.00, with a mean of .94. Interrater reliability for coding classroom behavior ranged from .70 to 1.00, with a mean of .91. During intervention, teachers' reliability at giving notes when earned ranged from .13 to 1.00, with a mean of .49. Teachers' reliability at withholding notes when not earned ranged from .05 to 1.00, with a mean of .33. At the end of intervention, teachers guessed which children were in the control condition; only 28% of their guesses were correct. During intervention, the staff teacher spoke weekly to each parent and child in the experimental condition. Judging by these reports, parents regularly provided the agreed-upon rewards.

2. Children with patterns of high classwork scatter differed from classmates who were intermediate and stable workers on several measures of academic performance, interpersonal adequacy, and self-regard. The identification process placed 33 children in the stable comparison group, 105 children in the intermediate group, and 61 children in the inconsistent group. Supporting the assumption that scatter in academic performance is associated with social and behavioral as well as with academic dysfunction, the following significant correlations (Pearson's r, $p < .05$, $n = 199$) between scatter and other measures collected at baseline resulted. High scatter scores in reading were significantly associated with low mean accuracy in reading and math, low teacher ratings of child happiness, low on-task classroom behavior, low self-ratings of "gets along with others" and "likes school," and low sociometric choice, as well as with high math scatter, high probability of being a boy, and high probability of being

nominated by the teacher as an underachiever. An inspection of teacher-constructed ability groupings for math and reading confirmed that scatter detected underachievers rather than low achievers. The inconsistent students came equally from low, average, and high reading groups, and primarily from average math groups. Of the inconsistent students, nine had been legally identified by the school as educationally handicapped and one was deaf; no stable student carried such labels.

One-way analyses of variance (ANOVAs) on baseline scores and significant planned contrasts indicated that each of the three groups (stable, intermediate, inconsistent) differed from the other two on reading scatter, math scatter, reading accuracy, math accuracy, and teacher choice of the child as an underachiever. The inconsistent group looked worst and the stable group looked best on these measures. In addition, the stable group differed significantly from both the intermediate and the identified inconsistent groups on teacher happiness ratings of children, number of children identified by the school as needing special education or as handicapped, children's self-ratings of "happy" and "gets along with others," and sociometric choice. Compared to children in the intermediate and inconsistent groups, children in the stable group were rated happier by teachers, were never identified as needing special education or as handicapped, rated themselves as happier and as getting along better with others, and were more often chosen as best friends by classmates. In sum, there were between-group differences on one of four background variables, four of seven academic variables, and five of eight attitudinal variables.

3. The acceptance rate was 50%, and the follow-through rate was 100%. Of the 61 inconsistent students, 41 were randomly assigned to the experimental and 20 to the control conditions; two of the former were excluded because of teacher disagreement, yielding 39 families invited to participate in intervention. Of the 39, 20 accepted and completed intervention. One-way ANOVAs comparing baseline scores in the experimental (20) and experimental/declined (15) conditions found no significant differences on any of the 19 dependent measures.

4. Intervention had the intended effects on academic performance, along with some unexpected effects on nonacademic domains. It narrowed the gap between inconsistent students and competent students. To test the effects of intervention, 3×2 repeated-measures ANOVAs were used: condition (experimental, experimental/declined, control) $\times$ period (baseline, intervention). Significant interaction and simple main effects indicated that only children in the experimental condition reduced their scatter scores in the target academic subject from baseline to intervention. Children in the experimental condition also made borderline-significant improvements in accuracy in the target academic subject. A borderline-significant interaction suggested that during intervention, as opposed to baseline, children in the experimental condition rated themselves better students; children in the experimental/declined condition did not change their ratings; and children in the control condition rated themselves poorer students.

In light of the significant baseline differences among children in the inconsistent, intermediate, and stable conditions on four academic and five attitudinal measures, one-way ANOVAs were used to determine what differences remained after intervention between children in the experimental and stable groups. During intervention, there no longer were significant differences between the experimental and stable groups on math and reading scatter. The stable group still had significantly higher reading and math accuracy. At the end of intervention, teachers still chose significantly more underachievers from the experimental than from the stable group. There no longer was a significant difference between groups in teachers' ratings of children's happiness. There was a borderline difference between groups on children's self-ratings of happiness; this reversed the baseline difference between groups, since the happiness mean of children in the experimental condition was higher than the mean of children in the stable condition. There no longer were any significant differences between experimental and stable groups on self-ratings of "gets along with others" or on sociogram scores. Thus, only two of four significant baseline differences on classroom variables and one of five significant baseline differences on attitudinal variables distinguished the experimental and stable groups after intervention. The classroom and project teachers independently rated each child's improvement on 0–100 scales. Perfect agreement between these ratings indicated improvement of 50% or more in 15 of the 20 children in the experimental condition.

In sum, competent students whose baseline classwork performance was stable differed on social and emotional as well as academic measures from peers whose classwork was inconsistent. Recruitment of families of inconsistent students to take part in intervention succeeded in engaging 50% of invited families, all of whom followed through. Inconsistent students involved in a collaborative home–school intervention became more consistent in their classwork performance, achieving the primary aim of intervention. Even though these students would have been reinforced if they simply achieved their daily goals, they often did better work than was required. This improved their classwork accuracy and was acknowledged by the children in better ratings of themselves as students. Intervention also narrowed the gap between high-risk and competent children, with no evidence of undesirable side effects. After intervention, only three of nine baseline differences between the experimental and stable groups remained significant.

The findings of the first early-intervention study suggested that a behavioral family intervention can recruit and engage many families in treatment and can benefit early-identified high-risk students without segregating them from their classmates. However, these findings did not establish the necessity of family involvement in intervention. Perhaps the only active intervention ingredient was contingent feedback to children and parents, of the sort provided by the typical home-note system (Atkeson & Forehand, 1979). The second early-intervention study (Blechman, Taylor, & Schrader, 1981) compared the specific and general effects on inconsistent students of family problem-solving training, a home-note system, and no treatment.

The Second Study

The second early-intervention study included the classes of 17 volunteer teachers of second through sixth grades in three public elementary schools. The study had a 3 × 2 repeated-measures design: condition (family problem solving, home note, control) × phase (baseline, intervention). Inconsistent children were identified as in the first study, and the six most inconsistent children in each class were randomly assigned: three to family problem solving, two to home note, and one to control. A comparison group of stable students included the children in each class with the least scatter. Goals for children in the home-note condition were set exactly as in the family problem-solving condition. Families in the home-note condition received a personal letter from the classroom teacher at the beginning of intervention. It might read, for example,

> Dear Mrs. Jones: Starting Monday, November 26, and throughout the school year, I will be sending home a note with your child on days when John does good work in math. When John achieves 80% or better in math, I will send home a "good news" note like the one enclosed. On days when I do not assign written math work, I will send home a "no work assigned today" note so that you will know that John could not have earned a "good news" note that day. I have also enclosed an example of the "no work assigned today" note. On days when I assign math work but your child does not achieve 80% or better, I will not send home a note. It will help John's math work if you congratulate John when he brings home a "good news" note. It will also help if you can reward your child with something special that he likes to do or something that makes him happy. Some rewards might be: half-hour later bedtime, inviting a friend for dinner, 1-hour help with homework, a game of bowling, or extra allowance. If you congratulate John and give a reward when he brings home this note, I am sure it will help John do his best in school.

The family problem-solving intervention was carried out just as it was in the first study.

The results of the second early-intervention study might be summed up this way:

1. Dependent measures were reliable, and intervention was carried out as intended. Interscorer reliability for classwork ranged from .93 to 1.00, with a mean of .98. Interrater reliability for classroom behavior ranged from .76 to 1.00, with a mean of .89. Teachers' total reliability at giving notes when earned and withholding notes when not deserved ranged from .26 to 1.00, with a mean of .80. Judging by parents' and children's reports, parents regularly provided the rewards stipulated by their contracts. A borderline result suggested that teacher reliability for withholding notes was higher in the home-note condition.

Teachers tended to be more lenient and noncontingent in the family problem-solving condition, sometimes sending notes home when not merited by classwork.

2. At baseline, children identified as highly inconsistent in math classwork obtained less favorable scores than their classmates on target and nontarget variables, including teacher ratings of child effort and happiness. They did not differ in frequency of active or passive off-task behavior. Identification placed 100 students in the inconsistent group, 166 in the intermediate group, and 69 in the stable group. The three groups differed significantly from one another, with the inconsistent group scoring in the least favorable direction and the stable group scoring in the most favorable direction on prior identification as needing special education or as handicapped, nomination by the teacher as an underachiever, mean accuracy in math classwork, and math classwork scatter. The inconsistent group differed from the intermediate and consistent groups on Holt math score, teacher happiness rating, and teacher estimation of number of days per week when children did their best work.

3. The acceptance rate for the family problem-solving condition was 64%. Active acceptance was not necessary in the home-note condition. Of the 100 children identified as inconsistent, 13 moved away during baseline, 45 were assigned to the family problem-solving condition, 26 to the home-note condition, and 16 to the control condition. Of the 45 families invited to participate in the family problem-solving condition, 29 accepted, but two subsequently dropped out of the study. Outcome data were analyzed for 27 children in the family problem-solving condition, for 26 in the home-note condition, and for 16 in the control condition. Children whose families accepted family problem solving and those whose families declined were compared on all baseline variables. The only significant difference favored the declined group, in which children more often had two parents, making it unlikely that improvement in the family problem-solving condition was due to differential dropout of disadvantaged children.

4. Compared to no treatment, both family problem-solving and home-note interventions significantly reduced classwork scatter. Preliminary tests revealed no significant difference between the home-note and the family problem-solving conditions in change on classwork scatter. Therefore, the two were combined and compared with the control condition in a $2 \times 3 \times 2$ repeated-measures ANOVA: condition (intervention, control) $\times$ classroom group (1, 2, 3) $\times$ phase (baseline, intervention). A significant condition $\times$ phase interaction effect, and a subsequent test of the simple main effects of phase at each level of condition, indicate a significant reduction in scatter during intervention by the combined intervention condition. Apparently, both interventions achieved their principal aim—to encourage more consistent math performance by erratic students.

5. While children in both the control and home-note conditions became less accurate during intervention, children in the family problem-solving con-

dition maintained their accuracy. The analysis of classwork accuracy scores used a $3 \times 3 \times 2$ repeated-measures covariance analysis: condition (home note, family problem solving, control) $\times$ classroom group (1, 2, 3) $\times$ phase (baseline, intervention). Baseline and intervention classwork scatter scores were the covariates. A significant phase $\times$ condition effect and a subsequent test of the effect of phase at each level of condition indicate a significant reduction in accuracy during intervention by the home-note and control conditions.

6. Children in the family problem-solving condition demonstrated generalization to nonreinforced probes, while children in the home-note condition did not. Children in the famly problem-solving condition were significantly more accurate during probes than during baseline. (Probe days, when no notes could be earned, were scattered throughout intervention.) Analysis of accuracy during three nonreinforced probes used a 2×3 repeated-measures ANOVA: condition (family problem solving, home note) $\times$ trial (baseline mean, intervention mean, probes mean). A condition $\times$ trial effect and subsequent tests of the simple effect of trial at each level of condition indicate that in the family problem-solving condition, a significant trial effect was due to higher accuracy during probes than during baseline.

7. Not only did children receiving intervention of either kind reduce classwork scatter significantly, compared to children in an untreated control condition; but their classwork also became less variable as the classwork of their intermediate and stable peers became more variable. Children in the combined intervention condition did well, despite the increasing difficulty of work assigned. A random subsample of children in the intermediate and stable groups was drawn, providing a comparison group not selected from extremes of the classwork scatter continuum and unlikely to regress toward the mean during intervention; 23% were drawn to provide equal n's. Analysis of the classwork scatter scores of the 53 children who received intervention and the 51 children randomly sampled from the intermediate and stable groups used a 2×2 repeated-measures ANOVA: group (intervention, other classmates) $\times$ phase (baseline, intervention). A significant group main effect resulted, along with a significant group $\times$ phase interaction. Subsequent tests of the simple main effect of phase at each level of group showed a significant reduction in scatter during intervention by the combined intervention group and a significant increase in scatter during intervention by the combined intermediate and stable groups. The net result was that the inconsistent pupils were not significantly more erratic in their math performance during treatment than were the most consistent pupils without treatment.

8. Not only did children in the family problem-solving condition maintain their accuracy while the work of children in the home-note and control conditions dropped in accuracy, but they also maintained their accuracy while the work of children in the intermediate and stable groups dropped in accuracy. A 12% subsample of the combined intermediate and stable groups was drawn. Analysis of classwork accuracy scores used a 2×2 repeated-measures ANOVA:

group (family problem solving, intermediate/stable) × phase (baseline, intervention). A significant group main effect resulted, along with a significant phase × group interaction. Subsequent tests of the simple effects of phase at each level of group indicated a significant drop in accuracy during intervention by the intermediate and stable groups.

9. Although children who received either kind of intervention improved significantly, compared to their own previous academic records and to the current work of their classmates, teachers' opinions about these children's status did not change. Moreover, their performance on a timed math test did not improve. This may have been due to time pressure for which teacher-constructed assignments did not prepare children.

In sum, the second early-intervention study had an even better recruitment record than the first, had the desired treatment and generalization effects, demonstrated the contributions of family involvement to intervention, and showed that inconsistent high-risk children can be encouraged to resemble competent children.

The two early-intervention studies successfully engaged many families of high-risk children. Although single parents have long been considered incompetent, they were no less interested in or responsive to intervention than coupled parents were. Pooling the two early-intervention studies yielded a sample of one- and two-parent families large enough to assess how family type affected participation in and responsiveness to behavioral family intervention (Blechman, 1983). Regardless of family type, intervention significantly improved children's academic performance and classroom behavior. Both one- and two-parent families had high acceptance and low dropout rates. Over the 2 years, there were 115 children identified as inconsistent who were randomly assigned to experimental (79) or control (36) conditions. Of those invited to the experimental condition, 46 accepted and completed intervention (17 one-parent and 29 two-parent families). The rate of acceptance and completion of the intervention was slightly higher for one-parent (68%) than for two-parent (53%) families. After intervention began, two families dropped out, both of whom were two-parent families.

COMPETENT CHILDREN AND THEIR FAMILIES

In 1981 we conducted a series of studies with the objective of learning more about the competence of individual children and the manner in which their families function. The findings reported below result from preliminary analysis of the first study (Blechman, Taylor, & Milton, 1981). Although there has been much discussion of competence in children, few definitions of "competence" have been operationalized and tested for construct validity. This study was

designed to validate a construct of "competence" combining information from two domains: academic achievement and peer nominations. Depending upon their standing relative to the median achievement and peer-nomination scores, children from several elementary schools were grouped in one of four categories, yielding one group of children who excelled in both achievement and the esteem of their classmates, one group of children whose performance was below average on both dimensions, and two groups of children who were strong in one area and weak in another. Independent measures were collected to validate the competence typology. This study was also designed to shed light on the relationship among competence, number of parents, and family size. The latter two characteristics of families have often been taken as rough indicators of family competence.

The study sample was recruited in this way: Teachers in four specific elementary schools were invited to participate because their schools represented all family income levels equally. One month after school began, teachers sent letters to parents of 900 children, inviting participation. The school system had already administered the School College Ability Tests (SCAT), Sequential Tests of Educational Progress (STEP), and Circus Tests of academic aptitude and performance to all children in the schools. During 1½-hour testing sessions, the peer-nomination and validating questionnaires were administered. On the first, children circled any number of classmates' names (including their own) to answer these questions:

> Who would you like to sit next to?
> Who are the best artists?
> Who are the hard workers?
> Who often look happy?
> Who are the best singers and dancers?
> Who are the smart kids?
> Who are the best athletes?
> Who would you like to have for best friends?

Four validating questionnaires were administered to randomly selected subsets of classes: the Children's Locus of Control Scale (Bialer, 1961), the Coopersmith Self-Esteem Scale (Coopersmith, 1967), Hall and Halberstadt's measure of children's sex-typed interests (Hall & Halberstadt, 1980), and Lefkowitz and Tesiny's Inventory of Depression (Lefkowitz & Tesiny, 1980). From among the 43 classroom teachers, volunteers were sought to rate students on dimensions used in the peer-nomination inventory.

In the four elementary schools, 43 of the 49 teachers allowed their classes to be tested. As a result, nine second grades, eight third grades, six fourth grades, ten fifth grades, and ten sixth grades participated. In response to 900 letters to parents requesting children's participation, 71% (641) granted permission, 16% denied it, and 13% did not respond. The proportion of families in each school who agreed to participate ranged from 64% to 74%, with a mean of 71%. Although permission was granted for the participation of 641 children,

75 had no SCAT or STEP scores, yielding 566 children for whom competence scores could be constructed. The sample included 296 girls and 270 boys, ranging in age from 6 to 13 with a mean age of 9 years.

Random assignment within grade levels to subsets of validating questionnaires resulted in the following completion statistics: 22% (125) completed the Locus of Control Questionnaire; 25% (144) completed the Self-Esteem Inventory; and 28% (161) completed the Sex-Typing Questionnaire. Of the 43 classroom teachers, 18 volunteered to rate the children in their classes. They rated 219 children, or 39% of the total sample. The aptitude (SCAT) and performance (STEP) scores were highly correlated ($r = .86$, $p < .001$), and age had a clear and expected effect on these scores. Therefore, the SCAT and STEP scores were transformed to standardized z scores using the means and standard deviations of the child's grade, and the two z scores were combined into a standardized academic performance score. On the standardized academic performance score, girls did significantly better than boys, and children from small families did significantly better than children from large families. Many correlations among peer-nomination items warranted their standardization and combination into a total standardized peer-nomination score. There were no differences by gender, family size, or number of parents on the standardized peer-nomination scores.

The relationship between the standardized academic performance score and the standardized peer-nomination score was positive and significant, but small ($r = .29$, $p < .001$), arguing against a combined competence score. Therefore, the distributions of composite achievement and peer-nomination scores were split at the medians, and each child was placed in one of four groups. The competent group included children who scored above the median on both the achievement and the peer-nomination dimensions. The incompetent group included children who scored below the median on both dimensions. The "bookworm" group and the "social butterfly" group included children who scored above the median on one dimension and below the median on another. As a result, there were 175 children (105 girls, 70 boys) in the competent group, 168 children (86 girls, 82 boys) in the incompetent group, 110 children (60 girls, 50 boys) in the bookworm group, and 113 children (45 girls, 68 boys) in the social butterfly group. The four competence groups did not differ significantly in respect to number of parents heading the family. There were significant differences among groups in family size. Children from larger families were most likely to be in the incompetent group.

Competent and Incompetent Children

If the construct of general competence is valid, then children in the competent group should score in the positive direction on all validating measures, and children in the incompetent group should score in the negative direction on all validating measures. The findings support this hypothesis. The competent group of children scored higher than any other on peer nominations and achievement—higher even than the two groups that scored above the median on one of the two dimensions. The competent group also scored highest of the four groups on teacher nominations, feminine attributes, and internal locus of control. They scored at the mean on self-nominations and social self-esteem. On these two scales, they scored below the social butterfly group. Thus, the children in the competent group were high achievers, were frequently nominated by peers and teachers for excellence, were high in feminine interests, were internal in locus of control, and were average in self-nominations and social self-esteem. The incompetent group scored lowest of the four groups on achievement, peer nominations, femininity, and internality. They scored third lowest on self-nominations and social self-esteem. (Their scores on these measures were higher than those of children in the bookworm group.) In short, the children in the incompetent group scored lowest on all measures except self-nominations and social self-esteem.

Bookworms and Social Butterflies

The children in the bookworm group scored second highest on achievement and third lowest on peer nominations. They scored third lowest on teacher nominations, femininity, and internal locus of control. They scored lowest of all the groups on self-nominations and social self-esteem. In short, children in the bookworm group, despite their relatively high achievement, were rarely nominated for excellence by peers or teachers, were low on feminine attributes and internality, and were exceptionally low on two measures of self-esteem.

The children in the social butterfly group scored second highest on peer nominations and third lowest on achievement. They scored at the mean on teacher nominations, femininity, and locus of control. They scored higher than any other group on self-nominations and social self-esteem. In short, children in the social butterfly group were low achievers who were well liked, self-confident, and average on teacher nominations, femininity, and locus of control.

This study supports the contention that a measure of excellence in achievement and a measure of excellence in social reputation are both required if general competence is to be measured. The achievement and peer-nomination measures provide modestly correlated but not redundant information. Children who scored high on both dimensions excelled more at each dimension than did children who had strengths in only one area. An index that combined scores in the two areas would have obscured important differences between the two intermediate groups. Children who excelled both at achievement and in the eyes of their peers represented a highly competent group, as judged by independent measures administered to subsets of these children. Their frequent endorsement of feminine interests and attitudes indicates an androgynous interest pattern, since this group did not differ from the others on masculinity scores. Feminine interests are positively correlated throughout the sample with high achievement, many peer nominations, and many teacher nominations. The behavior of competent children provides a standard against which the outcome of any child-related intervention might be measured.

The group with the lowest femininity scores of all was the incompetent group. Although the incompetent group functioned poorly in several respects, the self-esteem of this group was higher than the self-esteem of children who were high achievers but rarely nominated by their peers (the bookworms). The academically able but interpersonally inadequate bookworms had the lowest self-esteem of all. Since the self-esteem of the competent group was somewhat lower than that of the social butterflies, it may be that high achievement tends to depress self-esteem, particularly when interpersonal skills are limited. Child-related interventions could gather baseline measures of children's competence in the domains of tasks and relationships relative to peers, and set individual goals that reflect children's strengths and weaknesses. Such an assessment strategy avoids needless child-focused interventions.

Behavior of Competent Children as an External Validator of Treatment Goals and Outcomes

Wolf (1978) reminded behaviorists that clever demonstrations of human behavior change cannot be equated with successful treatment. New behavior must be shown to have "social validity," or subjective value to other people. He suggested that mental health experts rate the appropriateness of samples of new behavior to guide the selection of treatment goals and the evaluation of treatment outcome. The construct of social validity is consistent with growing interest in the effects of behavior on the social ecology (Rogers Warren & Warren, 1977). Evidence accumulates about interventions that strive for local good effects and that unexpectedly produce general bad effects. For example, slum-clearance projects, which strive to improve living conditions for surrounding areas, often deprive people of their homes and export crime and poverty to new regions of the city.

Troubleshooting checks on the social validity of a contemplated behavior change may anticipate negative consequences so that safeguards can be instituted. Suppose that successful parent training increases parents' confidence in their children and that confident parents are often dissatisfied with mediocre teachers who blame poor achievement on children's inadequacies. Suppose, as well, that a few mediocre teachers are asked to rate the behavior of confident parents. These teachers might well show their displeasure with overly confident parents in negative ratings of parent behavior. Thus, when teachers are the source of validating information, confident parent behavior would be judged lacking in social validity. These teacher ratings provide a useful troubleshooting strategy, since they suggest that parent trainers help confident parents become thoughtful advocates for their children.

Social validity, when measured by other people's opinions, is nothing more than social acceptability. This is unfortunate, because an enduring criticism of behavior modification is its perpetuation of the *status quo* (Blechman, 1980). Experts and untroubled peers seem to consult their everyday prejudices as they judge adults and children. When Santrock and Tracy (1978) showed films of child behavior, teachers rated the children healthier if they thought the children had two parents rather than one parent. Although single and coupled parents visited the schools equally often, English schoolteachers judged coupled parents more interested in their children's education (Ferri, 1976). If teachers or other experts are relied on to assess the validity of treatment outcomes, they might judge children with marginal social status as less improved than their more fortunate peers, despite equivalent changes on objective dependent measures. The effects of expectations about sex-role behavior on the judgments of mental health experts and peers are well known. To provide just one example, experts and peers identified comparable noncoercive behaviors as assertive when enacted by men but aggressive when enacted by women (Rich & Schroeder, 1976). If teachers or other experts are relied on to estimate the validity of treatment outcomes, they might regard girls who become more active and boys who become more placid as unimproved, even when these changes in classroom demeanor are accompanied by improved academic performance. Experts are by no means in agreement about the social validity of behavior. This is exemplified by the debate about the work of Rekers and Lovaas (1974), who reported their behavioral treatment of deviant sex-role behaviors in young boys. They argued that the boys' unconventional behaviors predicted later-life adjustment problems (Rekers, Bentler, Rosen, & Lovaas, 1978). Critics who advocated a revised social learning theory (Blechman, 1980) disputed this prediction and recommended androgynous behavior as the appropriate treatment goal (Nordyke, Baer, Etzel, & LeBlanc, 1977).

Despite Skinner's (1938) caveat that the topography of behavior is far less important than the behavior's functional relationships with antecedent, concurrent, and consequent events, experts in human behavior change persist in the assumption that they can identify effective behaviors. An amusing, and discouraging, example of this comes from assertiveness training. Clients who request help because they cannot get a job, advance at work, make a date, or improve a romantic relationship often receive assertiveness training. Countless studies demonstrate the acquisition of assertive behavior repertoires. Yet one hand suffices to count solid evidence that assertive behavior got someone a job, a raise in pay, a date, or a happier marriage (Blechman, 1981a). Assertive behavior may have social or face validity, but for many purposes its predictive validity or effectiveness remains to be demonstrated.

In the design of behavioral family interventions, the primary experts on social validity are parents. Most parents are certain that they know best about good child behavior. It is only reasonable to agree with parents' judgment when their children are healthy, happy at home and school, and maturing at a pace equivalent to that of their peers. When parents request help in raising their children, or when children demonstrate serious behavioral deficiencies, some skepticism about parents' abilities to assess child behavior is in order. The parents' standards for child behavior may differ from the standards held by parents in less troubled families. Most important, troubled parents may give little thought to the effects of child behavior on any one but themselves. Thus an active, curious toddler who gets into cupboards and threatens prized ornaments may be considered hyperactive by a parent who prefers a television-watching, thumb-sucking youngster. The adolescent who asks parents to justify requests may be considered noncompliant when compared to a yea-saying teenager.

In sports, knowledge of effective behaviors is so advanced that experts can look at a batter's swing or a golfer's stroke and predict the outcome with a high degree of accuracy. As a result, sports coaches can train players to reproduce effective behaviors and to achieve desired outcomes. If half the adult male population of the United States spent Monday nights watching children instead of television, the present state of knowledge about effective child behavior would be equally advanced.

There are gaps in our knowledge about the kinds of child and parent behavior most likely to achieve desirable outcomes, and it is risky to rely on the judgment of parents, teachers, and mental health experts. Therefore, behavioral family interventions cannot coach families in set behavior repertoires and merely expect that the families will achieve desirable outcomes—more harmonious interaction; better physical health; better participation in school, work, and play; and more contributions to the community. Planners of interventions can, however, identify competent families who excel in their achievement of desirable task and interpersonal outcomes and whose demographic characteristics make them similar to client families. The *accomplishments* of competent parents and children provide a reasonable standard for evaluating the outcome of interventions. This was the approach used in two studies described earlier (Blechman, Kotanchik, & Taylor, 1981; Blechman, Taylor, & Schrader, 1981). The results were socially as well as statistically significant because family problem-solving training narrowed the gap in *outcomes* achieved by competent and incompetent children. Gurman and Klein (1983) have criticized the matching-to-sample philosophy in any form for its preservation of the *status quo*. Their rejection of matching to sample implies that no contemporary human behavior is worthy of emulation. I disagree and recommend that clinicians and researchers seek out and study exemplars of familial competence.

Task and Relationship Competence as the Goals of Intervention

Although parents may disagree with each other about desirable childhood behaviors, most parents readily agree that they want their children to do well in school and have plenty of friends. Since parents value a balance of task and interpersonal competence, baseline assessment might repeatedly probe a child's standing relative to his or her peers on task and interpersonal accomplishments. When the results show that the child is competent, a family-focused intervention or even a parent-focused intervention is in order. When the results show that the target child and a sibling or two are markedly less competent than peers, an intervention that focuses on the whole family or on only the parents is preferable to treatment aimed at one family scapegoat. When baseline data show that the target child is markedly less competent than peers and siblings, treatment may simply focus on improving relevant accomplishments.

The two studies described earlier (Blechman, Kotanchik, & Taylor, 1981; Blechman, Taylor, & Schrader, 1981) used baseline data from entire classrooms to identify children whose task accomplishments were consistently less adequate than their peers'. Reinforcement contingencies were instituted to reward improved task accomplishments (classwork accuracy at or above the baseline mean). Behaviors that might lead to these accomplishments (e.g., remaining silent and in seat during teacher instruction) were assessed, but were not the targets of intervention. Both studies brought expected improvements in task accomplishments and unplanned improvements in interpersonal accomplishments. Informal observation suggests that the instrumental route to increased task accomplishments varied from one child to the next. To achieve similar results, some children reduced their interaction with peers in the classroom while others increased attentive classroom behavior. Emphasis on outcome forced the children to choose their favorite instrumental behavior.

COMPETENT PARENTS, COMPETENT CHILDREN, AND PARENT TRAINING

In this chapter, I have disputed the egalitarian assumption that any parent can be successfully trained in better child-rearing skills. Competence of adult family heads needs to be considered when an intervention is chosen. I have proposed an operational definition of "competence" and have distinguished competence from human worth. Consideration of the construct of competence reveals that incompetent adults are likely to be overrepresented among clients referred by themselves and others to parent training. Adults who are generally competent may need parent training either because they lack exposure to appropriate child-rearing skills or because their children are handicapped. Incompetent adults with either competent or incompetent children may lack the skills and resources required for child-focused behavioral family intervention. An array of alternatives to behavioral family intervention is available for less competent families. These include parent and self-sufficiency training, parent self-control training, and marital problem-solving training. In addition, behavioral family intervention can be modified to suit the incompetent family. I have described two early-intervention studies that distributed the labor of intervention between home and school, and that successfully engaged many families of high-risk children. Although single parents are often considered to be incompetent, single parents in the early-intervention studies were no less responsive to intervention than coupled parents.

I have contended in this chapter that the purpose of behavioral family intervention should be to enhance the competence of parents and children. In some cases, incompetent adults may not be amenable to child-focused interventions until they have become more self-sufficient and skilled in adult relationships. I have provided preliminary findings from studies of competent children and their families. It seems that the behavior of competent children provides a yardstick for measuring the quality as well as the magnitude of results of behavioral family interventions. Child-related interventions could routinely gather baseline data to determine children's competence, relative to their peers, in task and interpersonal domains. Intervention goals could be set with knowledge of strengths and weaknesses in mind, and needless child-focused interventions could be avoided. When parents apply for help with child-related problems, the parents' cries for help with other life problems often go unheeded. Since the majority of applicants for parent training are women, behavioral family interventions might begin to inquire how much they enhance women's competence (Blechman, 1981a).

Acknowledgments

Preparation of this chapter was partly supported by NIMH Grant 31403 and was facilitated by the cooperation of the Wesleyan University Computing Center.

References

Alberti, R. F., & Emmons, M. L. *Your perfect right*. San Luis Obispo, Calif.: Impact, 1974.

Atkeson, B. M., & Forehand, R. Home-based reinforcement programs designed to modify classroom behavior: A review and methodological evaluation. *Psychological Bulletin*, 1979, *86*, 1298–1308.

Bandura, A. Self-efficacy: Toward a unifying theory of behavioral change. *Psychological Review*, 1977, *84*, 191–215.

Bernreuter, R. G. The measurement of self-sufficiency. *Journal of Abnormal and Social Psychology*, 1933, *26*, 291–300.

Bialer, I. Conceptualization of success and failure in mentally retarded and normal children. *Journal of Personality*, 1961, *29*, 303–320.

Blechman, E. A. Family problem-solving training. *American Journal of Family Therapy*, 1980, *8*, 3–22.

Blechman, E. A. Competence, depression, and behavior modification with women. In M. Hersen (Ed.), *Progress in behavior modification* (Vol. 12). New York: Academic Press, 1981. (a)

Blechman, E. A. Toward comprehensive behavioral family interventions: An algorithm for matching families and interventions. *Behavior Modification*, 1981, *5*, 221–235. (b)

Blechman, E. A. Are children with one parent at psychological risk?: A methodological review. *Journal of Marriage and the Family*, 1982, *44*, 179–195.

Blechman, E. A. *Early intervention with high-risk children from one- and two-parent families.* Unpublished manuscript, Wesleyan University, 1983.

Blechman, E. A., Budd, K. S., Christophersen, E. R., Szykula, S., Wahler, R., Embry, L. H., Kogan, K., O'Leary, K. D., & Riner, L. S. Engagement in behavioral family therapy: A multisite investigation. *Behavior Therapy*, 1981, *12*, 461–472.

Blechman, E. A., & Caple, M. J. *Effects of problem-solving training on a depressed woman's interpersonal behavior and psychotropic drug use: Single-subject case study.* Paper presented at the annual meeting of the Association for Advancement of Behavior Therapy, New York, 1976.

Blechman, E. A., Kotanchik, N. L., & Taylor, C. J. Families and schools together: Early behavioral intervention with high-risk students. *Behavior Therapy*, 1981, *12*, 308–319.

Blechman, E. A., & Rabin, C. *Concepts and methods of explicit marital negotiation with the Marriage Contract Game.* Unpublished manuscript, Wesleyan University, 1981.

Blechman, E. A., Taylor, C. J., & Milton, M. M. *Validity of a construct of childhood task and interpersonal competence.* Paper presented at the annual meeting of the American Psychological Association, Los Angeles, 1981.

Blechman, E. A., Taylor, C. J., & Schrader, S. M. Family problem solving versus home notes as early intervention with high-risk children. *Journal of Consulting and Clinical Psychology*, 1981, *49*, 919–926.

Coan, R. W. *The optimal personality: An empirical and theoretical analysis.* London: Routledge & Kegan Paul, 1974.

Coopersmith, S. *The antecedents of self-esteem.* San Francisco: W. H. Freeman, 1967.

Dobzhansky, T. *Genetic diversity and human equality.* New York: Basic Books, 1973.

Eyberg, S. M., & Johnson, S. M. Multiple assessment of behavior modification with families: Effects of contingency contracting and order of treated problems. *Journal of Consulting and Clinical Psychology*, 1974, *42*, 594–606.

Eysenck, H. J., & Eysenck, S. B. G. An improved short questionnaire for the measurement of extraversion and neuroticism. *Life Sciences*, 1964, *3*, 1103–1109.

Ferri, E. *Growing up in a one-parent family: A long-term study of child development.* Windsor, England: NFER, 1976.

Forehand, R. E., & Wells, K. C. Teachers and parents: Where have all the "good" contingency managers gone? *Behavior Therapy*, 1977, *8*, 1010.

Garmezy, N. The study of competence in children at risk for severe psychopathology. In E. J. Anthony & C. Kupernick (Eds.), *The child in his family: Children at psychiatric risk.* New York: Wiley, 1974.

Gurman, A. S., & Klein, M. H. Marriage and the family: An unconscious male bias in behavioral treatment. In E. A. Blechman (Ed.), *Behavior modification with women.* New York: Guilford Press, 1983.

Hall, J. A., & Halberstadt, A. G. Masculinity and feminity in children: Development of the children's personal attributes questionnaire. *Developmental Psychology*, 1980, *16*, 270–280.

Hargis, K. R., & Blechman, E. A. Social class and training of parents as behavior change agents. *Child Behavior Therapy*, 1979, *1*, 69–74.

Jacobson, N. S., & Martin, B. Behavioral marriage therapy: Current status. *Psychological Bulletin*, 1976, *83*, 540–556.

Jahoda, M. *Current concepts of positive mental health.* New York: Basic Books, 1958.

Lefkowitz, M. M., & Tesiny, E. P. Assessment of childhood depression. *Journal of Consulting and Clinical Psychology*, 1980, *48*, 43–50.

Lewis, O. The culture of poverty. *Scientific American*, 1966, *225*, 19–25.

Mosteller, R., & Moynihan, D. P. (Eds.). *On equality of educational opportunity: Papers deriving from the Harvard University Faculty Seminar on the Coleman Report.* New York: Vantage, 1972.

Nordyke, N. S., Baer, D. M., Etzel, B. C., & LeBlanc, J. Implications of the stereotyping and modification of sex roles. *Journal of Applied Behavior Analysis*, 1977, *10*, 553–557.

Patterson, G. R., & Gullion, M. E. *Living with children: New methods for parents and teachers.* Champaign, Ill.: Research Press, 1971.

Rabin, C. *Treatment of Israeli couples with the Marriage Contract Game.* Unpublished manuscript, University of Tel Aviv, 1981.

Rabin, C., Blechman, E. A., & Milton, M. M. *A multiple-baseline study of the Marriage Contract Game's effects on problem solving and affective behavior.* Paper presented at the annual meeting of the Association for Advancement of Behavior Therapy, Toronto, 1981.

Rekers, G. A., & Lovaas, O. I. Behavioral treatment of deviant sex-role behaviors in a male child. *Journal of Applied Behavior Analysis,* 1974, *7,* 173–190.

Rekers, G. A., Bentler, P. M., Rosen, A. C., & Lovaas, O. I. Child gender disturbances: A clinical rationale for intervention. *Psychotherapy: Theory, Research, and Practice,* 1978, *14,* 2–11.

Rich, A. R., & Schroeder, H. E. Research issues in assertiveness training. *Psychological Bulletin,* 1976, *83,* 1081–1096.

Rogers Warren, A., & Warren, S. F. *Ecological perspectives in behavior analysis.* Baltimore: University Park Press, 1977.

Santrock, J. W., & Tracy, R. L. Effects of children's family structure status on the development of stereotypes by teachers. *Journal of Educational Psychology,* 1978, *70,* 754–757.

Skinner, B. F. *The behavior of organisms.* New York: Appleton, 1938.

Vincent, J. P., Weiss, R. L., & Birchler, G. R. A behavioral analysis of problem solving in distressed and nondistressed married and stranger dyads. *Behavior Therapy,* 1975, *6,* 475–480.

Wahler, R. G. The insular mother: Her problems in parent–child treatment. *Journal of Applied Behavior Analysis,* 1980, *13,* 207–219.

Weiss, R. L. Contracts, cognition and change: A behavioral approach to marital therapy. *The Counseling Psychologist,* 1975, *5,* 15–26.

Wolf, M. M. Social validity: The case for subjective measurement *or* How applied behavior analysis is finding its heart. *Journal of Applied Behavior Analysis,* 1978, *11,* 203–214.

Zigler, E. Mental retardation: Current issues and approaches. In L. W. Hoffman & M. L. Hoffman (Eds.), *Review of child development research* (Vol. 2). New York: Russell Sage Foundation, 1966.

P A R T

II

PROGRAMS AND APPLICATIONS

RESPONSIVE PARENTING
A Large-Scale Training Program
for School Districts, Hospitals,
and Mental Health Centers

Marilyn C. Hall

Responsive Management, Inc., and University of Kansas

INTRODUCTION

The Need for Parent Training

Early studies in the field of parent training identified the need to train parents as behavior managers. Patterson, Littman, and Hinsey (1964) pointed out that the contingencies in a child's social environment are most responsible for the child's behavior, and that retraining the child's parents may be desirable and necessary. Peine (1969) and Patterson, McNeal, Hawkins, and Phelps (1967) suggested that most of the child's behavior is maintained by its effect upon the natural environment, and that it can be effectively modified by changing the consequences supplied by the social agents who live with the child.

Professionals and parents alike have expounded on the increasing need for parenting programs for the improved management of parent–child relationships. Hawkins (1972) and O'Dell (1974) have noted that it appears that only parents and teachers are of sufficient numbers to deal with the problems surfacing today in all aspects of child development. Other experts agree with the solution proposed by Hawkins (1972), suggesting that the number of children with behavioral problems is so large that only a mandatory parent training program initiated and conducted in the public schools can hope to reverse and diminish the trend. One needs only to talk to today's teachers, counselors, or therapists to realize the increasing magnitude of the problem of successful child management by parents.

Training Individual Parents

More recently the question has been not whether to train parents, but how to train them. Numerous studies have indicated that parents can be effective change agents for their children's behavior if taught to use systematic procedures to increase appropriate behaviors and decrease inappropriate ones (e.g., Christophersen, Barnard, Ford, & Wolf, 1976; Hawkins, Peterson, Schweid, & Bijou, 1966; Herbert & Baer, 1972; Nordquist & Wahler, 1973; Zeilberger, Sampen, & Sloane, 1968). However, in most of these early studies, training was done on a one-to-one basis. A professional experimenter supervised observation and recording of data; instructed the parents in specific reinforcement, extinction, or punishment procedures; and carried out behavior analysis procedures to verify the effectiveness of the treatment (R. V. Hall, 1971; R. V. Hall, Axelrod, Tyler, Grief, Jones, & Robertson, 1972; R. V. Hall, Cristler, Cranston, & Tucker, 1970; Patterson & Brodsky, 1966; Williams, 1959; Wolf, Risley, & Mees, 1964). Some parents have been trained in small groups, primarily from a clinical setting (O'Leary, O'Leary, & Becker, 1967; Wagner & Ora, 1970; Wahler, 1969a, 1969b; Wahler, Winkel, Peterson, & Morrison, 1965).

Training Parents in Groups

Although most of the literature reports parent training programs involving from one to five families, large-scale training programs also have been used. As early as 1965, Pumroy reported teaching groups of parents the principles of behavior modification. Walder, Cohen, and Daston (1967), Hirsch and Walder (1969), and Walder, Cohen, Breiter, Daston, Hirsch, and Leibowitz (1967) described programs that taught operant techniques to parents of 19 families. Other programs handling larger groups of parents have also been described in the literature (R. V. Hall, Copeland, & Clark, 1976; Hanf, 1968, 1969; Hanley, 1972; Howard, 1970; O'Leary & Kent, 1974; Patterson, Cobb, & Ray, 1970). A common thread among many of these large-scale training programs was that they were remedial programs, meaning that the training of parents was conducted by a staff of professionals for parents whose children had been referred for some reason.

Another method of training parents suggested by Ora (1970) uses parents (nonprofessionals) to train other parents. Parents who have successfully completed a training program help train other parents in future presentations of that program. In the Regional Intervention Program developed by Ora and his colleagues (Ora, 1970), parents trained other parents, on a one-to-one basis, in behavioral procedures designed to decrease their children's oppositional behaviors.

RESPONSIVE PARENTING:
A LARGE-SCALE PROGRAM

This chapter describes the development, content, and preliminary results of Responsive Parenting, an educational program with both intervention and preventative features. The program is designed to teach parents to observe and measure behavior and to apply social learning theory principles to teaching new behaviors in the home setting. The basic concepts are presented in a large-group setting, followed by small-group interactions in which behavioral situations and rehearsals are used in conjunction with individual home behavior change projects to teach the parents the behavioral skills presented. The *Responsive Parenting Manual* (M. C. Hall, 1981) includes information for parents and for the program directors and group leaders who conduct the sessions. The Manual outlines the organization of the training course and the concepts taught, as well as a description of the program for training parents to function actively as group leaders.

I researched, authored, and developed the Responsive Parenting behavior management program at the University of Kansas, Lawrence, Kansas. The roots of the Responsive Parenting Program were initially implanted when I began developing and using its concepts to meet the special needs of the parents of handicapped children while serving as a special education teacher for emotionally disturbed children in the Shawnee Mission, Kansas, public schools. The experience and expertise I acquired as a teacher and consultant in special education provided the soil for nourishing the early development of Responsive Parenting.

The documentation provided by the numerous studies generated by the program provided further nourishment by indicating that parents could become effective change agents of their children's behavior if guided and instructed. As the dimensions of applied behavior analysis widened and were applied to the Responsive Parenting Program, it truly began to flourish.

The recent updating of the *Responsive Parenting Manual* (M. C. Hall, 1981) provides a guideline to the changes in the Responsive Parenting Program during its development. The program's precepts, originally designed to serve the unique needs of parents of handicapped children, are basic in nature, however, and can be generalized in application to address the needs expressed by all those with the responsibility of adequate child behavior management.

The first preventative Responsive Parenting Program was offered to a group of seven parents 7 years ago in the Shawnee Mission, Kansas, School District. During each of the past few years, several hundred parents have attended Shawnee Mission Responsive Parenting classes. During the past 5 years, Responsive Parenting has been partially supported by a National Institute of Mental Health (NIMH) training grant. Under the auspices of the grant, the Program has been widely disseminated and is currently offered in Kansas, New York, Massachusetts, New Jersey, Illinois, Wisconsin, Missouri, and Mexico through school districts, mental health centers, private clinics, and hospitals.

A unique aspect of the Responsive Parenting Program is that most parents are volunteer subjects. In contrast to many programs, few parents are referred due to some familial disorganization or acute behavioral trauma within the family unit. There are Responsive Parenting Programs presently being carried out with the parents of special children, including second-time juvenile offenders. However, most parents enrolled in the program are concerned with the common misbehaviors encountered in raising children, rather than the more serious disciplinary concerns indicative of a delinquent or quasi-criminal nature. Even so, parents of special education students, who characteristically require additional support and information, have found the program helpful in coping with and educating their deaf, autistic, mentally retarded, learning-disabled, and/or speech/language-impaired youngsters.

Demographic Information

Responsive Parenting has been offered to approximately 3000 parents over the past 8 years in Shawnee Mission, a large middle-class suburb of Kansas City, Kansas, and Kansas City, Missouri. Demographic information obtained during the 1977-1978 school year (M. C. Hall, Grinstead, Collier, & Hall, 1980) typifies the Shawnee Mission Responsive Parenting population.

In the 1977-1978 school year, demographic information was obtained from 274 Responsive Parenting family units (single parents or husband-and-wife pairs) enrolled at nine training sites throughout the Shawnee Mission School District. The median income level of the 194 (71%) families that reported their income level was $25,000-$27,500. Some other characteristics of the parents who participated in Responsive Parenting are presented in Table 4-1.

Format of Training Sessions

The basic purpose of the Responsive Parenting Program is to teach parents how to use applied behavior analysis procedures in managing the behavior of their children. The training format is highly structured; it is divided into eight weekly units, with definite goals, objectives and activities for each unit. Originally this course covered 10 weekly sessions lasting approximately 2 hours each. In the constant monitoring of parent feedback and results of the program, the program format was later altered to eight 2-hour sessions. The 8-week course has proved to be as effective as the longer version.

Table 4-1

Demographic Information on 274 Family Units Enrolled at Nine
Training Sites during the 1977–1978 School Year

Information	Mothers	Fathers	Children[a] Male	Female
Age				
Average	33.9	37.0	8.0	9.0
Range	20–57	23–65	1–19	1–22
n^b	240	213	174	141
Education				
Average	14.4	15.5	—	—
Range	9–20	11–20	—	—
n^b	234	211	—	—

Note. "Family units" included one- and two-parent families. One-parent families accounted for 10.3% of the group. Of the families enrolled, 21% had received other parent training classes.

[a]Children identified by the Parent Evaluation Survey as having behavior of concern to a parent. The average number of children at home was 2.3, with a range of one to six.

[b]Discrepancies in totals are due to the fact that some parents did not respond to every category of the survey.

The Parent Manual: Parents Are Provided a Manual

The *Responsive Parenting Manual* (M. C. Hall, 1981) comes in three sections. The first section is the program director's manual. It spells out the responsibilities of the program director—the person in charge of the overall program. The second section is the group leader's manual. It describes the responsibilities of the group leaders who lead the parents in the small-group activities described below. It outlines the material to be covered in the small-group sessions each week and provides specific instructions for the group leaders to follow. It also provides supplemental materials for the group leader to use with parents of exceptional children and teenagers.

The third section is for the parents. It is divided into eight units. The first unit, covering the material to be learned the first week, is handed out in the first session. One of the several other units is given the parents at each of the weekly sessions that follow. The manual includes a description of the behavioral principles and procedures taught in Responsive Parenting; it also provides definitions of terms, questions, and activities, including behavioral rehearsals to be covered in small-group sessions and weekly assignments to be carried out at home.

The Weekly Sessions

The initial portion of each of the Responsive Parenting sessions is a total-group meeting in which the parent manual is presented, discussed, and demonstrated, and basic concepts are introduced and reviewed. This takes approximately 30 minutes of each session; lecture, demonstration, and discussion formats are used. The number of parent participants attending the large-group meeting generally ranges from 25 to 40, although both larger and smaller groups have been successfully conducted.

Immediately following the large-group presentation, participants gather in smaller groups of 5 to 12 in number. Parents are usually grouped according to the developmental levels of their children (e.g., primary, junior high, high school); by declared interest in a particular age group; or by expressed special needs (i.e., autistic or retarded children, juvenile offenders, etc.). Within the small-group sessions, participants, under the direction of a trained group leader, are given additional information, conduct behavioral role-playing episodes, and individually deal with parental concerns and questions. In the early stages of the development of the Responsive Parenting Program, a quiz on previously covered material was conducted. This was eventually eliminated because parents and staff questioned its usefulness.

Defining the Target Behavior

The central theme of the Responsive Parenting course revolves around a four-step behavioral model:

1. *Define* the behavior of concern.
2. *Measure* the rate, duration, and occurrence of the defined behavior.
3. *Intervene* using natural consequences readily available.
4. *Evaluate* the effectiveness of the treatment procedure.

The first two sessions of the Responsive Parenting course are designed to teach the parents to pinpoint and define behaviors, as well as to acquaint them with the basic techniques of observation and measurement. Parents are taught that the first vital step in managing behavior is developing a precise and accurate definition of the target behavior to be taught, changed, or eliminated. The importance of an accurate description of the behavior using the four Ws— who, what, when, and where—is emphasized, discussed, and demonstrated. Participants learn that a definition of the target behavior includes the following precise information:

1. *Who* exhibits the behavior and *who* will observe it?
2. *What* is the behavior and how will it be measured?

3. *When* will the behavior be observed?
4. *Where* will the behavior be observed?

Participants become acquainted with this fundamental aspect in designing a program to alter the behavior of others constructively by using the technology of behavior analysis.

Measuring the Behavior

Products of behavior, time sampling, event recording or frequency counts, and duration are presented as possible measurement techniques. As soon as possible, each participant selects a behavior of concern, defines it, and obtains a baseline complete with reliability checks. Parents are taught to display their data graphically and are introduced to applied behavior analysis research designs.

Teaching Intervention Strategies

The next three sessions are concerned with the introduction of the basic concepts of systematic reinforcement, including types of reinforcers, token systems, contracts, the effects of schedules, discrimination, generalization, and extinction. The parents are also introduced to concepts and procedures related to giving good instructions, shaping, modeling, and fading. At the same time, they are encouraged to practice the techniques they learn through behavioral rehearsals in the small groups, and in their homes by teaching the new behaviors they have chosen for their home behavior change projects. Encouragement is provided to parents to use the techniques they have learned and to begin applying consequences systematically in order to change the behavior chosen for their project.

In the sixth session, the concepts of punishment, correction, overcorrection, and time out are introduced, discussed, and practiced in behavioral role-playing episodes. The dangers and pitfalls associated with the misuse of punishment are carefully stressed.

The seventh session is used to suggest specific procedures to deal with common problem areas found by many parents. For young children, these might include chores, noncompliance, fighting, toileting, eating habits, shopping, and bedtime. With older children, problem areas might include observing and respecting curfew, running away, smoking, noncompliance, and so forth.

The eighth session stresses ways in which parents can continue to practice and maintain the new skills they have learned. Throughout the course, parents continue to work on their home change projects, frequently carrying out more than one at a time. Climaxing the last session is the sharing with other class members of all projects undertaken by parents. A typical home behavior change project completed by a parent is presented here.

A TYPICAL PARENT BEHAVIOR
CHANGE PROJECT

Subject and Setting

The parent, Mrs. S, was enrolled in the Responsive Parenting Program sponsored by the Shawnee Mission School District. Mrs. S chose her daughter's morning whining/crying behavior as the target of her behavior change project. Eight-year-old Sara reportedly displayed whining/crying behavior in response to clothing prepared for her to wear by her mother, regardless of the choice and combination presented. The project was carried out in the home in the morning on Sundays through Fridays.

Observation and Measurement

Sara's mother recorded the duration of Sara's crying/whining in minutes and fractions thereof, in response to the articles of clothing prepared for her to wear to school or church. Recording was accomplished by timing the number of full minutes of whining/crying behavior as they occurred. At the conclusion of each daily episode, the number of minutes of whining/crying behavior were recorded and plotted on a graph.

On five occasions during the baseline period, the child's father independently recorded the minutes of crying/whining behavior displayed by Sara in response to being told to dress in the clothing prepared by her mother. The percent of agreement in their records was found by dividing the lower number of minutes recorded by the greater number and multiplying by 100. The first two reliability checks indicated less than 100% agreement, with a 2-minute difference in the parents' independent recordings. It was determined that the father was also counting Sara's pouting, sticking her lip out, and sniffling as part of the target behavior. A quick review of the behavioral definition outlined by the mother eliminated this inconsistency. As indicated in Figure 4-1, agreement was always 100% after the behavior definition was reviewed and fully understood by both parents.

Behavior Change Procedures

Baseline

A reversal design was used to analyze the effects of the parents' behavior change procedure on Sara's behavior. Initially, a baseline phase was instituted in which the mother recorded the minutes of whining and crying without attempting to

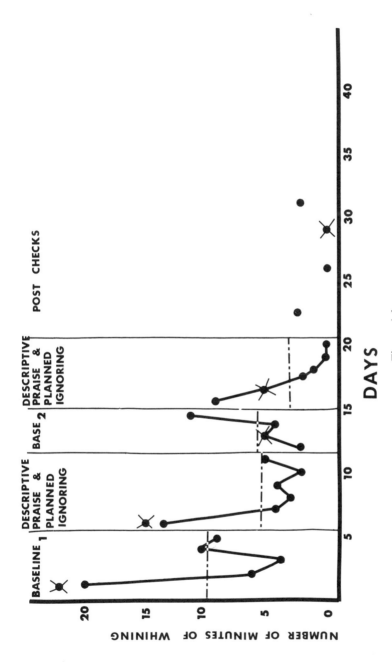

Figure 4-1

Whining behavior of an 8-year-old girl during parent behavior change project.

change her own usual responses of coaxing, yelling, or demanding compliance. Baseline data were recorded for 5 days, ranging from 4 to 20 minutes of whining/crying behavior, with an average of 8.2 minutes for the 5-day period.

Descriptive Praise and Planned Ignoring

After 5 days of baseline, a treatment procedure was instituted in which the mother systematically ignored Sara's uncooperative whining/crying behavior and praised cooperative compliant behavior in connection with the morning dressing task. During this treatment phase, target behavior of whining/crying dropped to a mean of 5 minutes per day for the 6-day period.

Reversal

A 4-day reversal phase was instituted by the parents, who discontinued their praise for cooperation and once again attended to Sara's whining/crying response by coaxing, screaming, and demanding compliance. During the Baseline$_2$ period of 4 days, Sara's crying/whining behavior increased to an average of 5.5 minutes.

Descriptive Praise and Planned Ignoring

Once again, the parents began ignoring uncooperative whining/crying behavior and began praising Sara's cooperative dressing behavior. During this 6-day period, crying/whining behavior ranged from 0 to 9 minutes, with a mean of 2.8. At this time, Sara was also given a choice of two different outfits of clothing chosen by her mother. It was intended that opportunity to choose would be increased to more than two alternatives when the child had learned to make accurate, coordinated choices on her own.

Follow-Up

After the sixth day of reinstatement of treatment, daily recording was discontinued, although the treatment procedure was continued. Follow-up checks were made every 3 days on four occasions after the second treatment phase to determine whether the behavior was being maintained.

Results and Discussion

As is shown in Figure 4-1, during Baseline$_1$ the crying/whining behavior ranged from 4 to 20 minutes in length. During the first week of treatment, there was a slight increase in crying and whining on the first day, then a marked decrease during the remainder of the week. During the 4 days that reversal was instituted, whining/crying behavior began to increase again, slowly at first and then more markedly. When treatment using descriptive praise and planned ignoring was reinstituted, whining/crying behavior soon decreased to a level of 0. Follow-up checks undertaken at 3-day intervals indicated a very low incidence of whining/crying behavior in relation to getting dressed in the mornings. Within a 32-day time span, whining/crying behavior had decreased from a high of as many as 20 minutes to none. The parents also reported improved family relations and a smoother-running household.

A BEHAVIOR CHANGE PROJECT USING A MULTIPLE-BASELINE DESIGN

Another behavior change project in which the parents used a different design and behavior change method is presented here.

Subject and Setting

The parent, Mrs. F, was enrolled in the Responsive Parenting Program sponsored by the University of Kansas and the Shawnee Mission Public Schools at the Indian Creek Site in the spring of 1980. The subject was an 11-year-old male, Geof, whose parents were concerned about his messy personal habits in the bathroom and bedroom areas of his home.

Observation and Measurement

The parents were concerned about teaching Geof to keep the bathroom and the bedroom neat and to make his bed. Their definition of neatness in each of these areas included four items in these different categories, delineated below:

Bathroom
1. Towels hung neatly (vertically and even)
2. Toothpaste and brush put away in appropriate places
3. Reading material stacked neatly
4. Light turned out

Bedroom
1. Dirty clothes placed in hamper
2. Toys and books put away

3. Radio and light off
4. Floor clean of clutter

Bed
1. Sheets smooth
2. Blanket smooth
3. Spread smooth and tucked in
4. Pillow smooth and placed appropriately

Measurement and Treatment

The measurement procedure consisted of direct measurement of permanent products. That is, Geof's mother observed the bathroom, the bedroom, and the bed each weekday morning after Geof left for school and recorded the number of completed task items in each category.

On three occasions throughout this home study, Geof's father independently recorded the number of completed items, and the records were compared. These reliability checks indicated 100% agreement between parents during all three checks.

Behavior Change Procedures

Baseline

A multiple-baseline, across-behaviors design was used to analyze the effects of the behavior change procedure. Prior to any intervention, a baseline record was obtained of all uncompleted items in the three predetermined areas. Throughout this time, Geof's mother continued coaxing, pleading, and reminding Geof in her usual way to get him to improve his sloppy habits.

Contingent Bedtime for Bathroom Neatness

Following baseline, Geof's mother defined for Geof the desired behaviors, as well as the consequences, and a contract was completed. Under the contractual agreement between Mrs. F and Geof, a perfect score resulted in a 15-minute extension of the bedtime hour. Lower scores, dependent on the number of items in each of the three categories that were incomplete, earned an increasingly earlier bedtime. After being given the choice, Geof elected to improved bathroom neatness first. As can be seen in Figure 4-2, Geof had completed an average of only 10% of the tasks in this category for the five days of baseline.

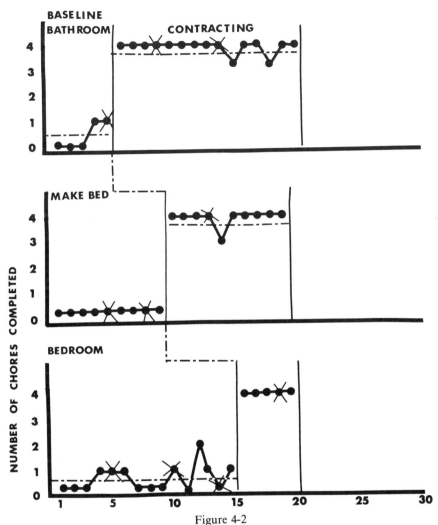

Figure 4-2
Chores completed by an 11-year-old boy during parent behavior change project.

The average increased to 97% within 6 days when the contingencies were applied.

Contingent Bedtime for Bedmaking

Geof then chose to attempt to improve his neatness in bedmaking skills. During the 9 days of baseline phase, his bedmaking score had been 0. Under the contract, within 10 days bedmaking increased to 98%.

Contingent Bedtime for Bedroom Neatness

Geof's final choice was to improve his behavior in the upkeep of his bedroom as defined by the behavioral definition in this behavior change project. Baseline data in this area were recorded for 15 days. As was true in the other two areas, Geof improved his bedroom neatness behavior from the baseline level of 10% to 100% within 5 days of initiating the contract.

Results and Discussion

Within 21 days, this Responsive Parenting participant was able to alter the sloppy personal habits of her child to near-perfect levels and maintain them with the use of natural consequences. The parents were pleased with the results, and, according to their report, the child gained a new sense of self-esteem and accomplishment.

Mrs. F selected contracting because the Responsive Parenting Program suggests that it is an especially good tool to use with preadolescents and teenagers. Contracts seem to help because they list the specific behaviors desired by both parties and tell what consequences will follow. Responsive Parenting contracts have been particularly effective when the youngster is involved in planning the solution and when his or her agreement to complete the contract is obtained.

These successful behavior change projects are typical of those carried out by parents enrolled in Responsive Parenting. Parents are encouraged to use a reversal or multiple-baseline analysis procedure as a learning technique. They report that it is effective in convincing them that what they have done has brought about the behavior change. Currently, the Responsive Parenting staff gives parents the opportunity to practice more than one behavior change procedure formally with more than one behavior during the eight-week course.

PARENTS TRAINING PARENTS

A unique feature of the Responsive Parenting Program is the use of parents and their knowledge, experience, and previous training in the Responsive Parenting Program to train other parents. They serve as the catalyst between the new group of parents enrolled in the program and the informational content of the course. They generate enthusiasm, promote self-confidence, and provide a supportive network for the new enrollees. Through the recommendation of the Responsive Parenting staff members and through additional training and involvement beyond the basic course, parents learn to assist as apprentice group leaders and group leaders. Some parents have even become program directors.

The use of parents to assist in training other parents has some apparent advantages. Using parents as paraprofessional group leaders has helped remove the awe and awkwardness parents frequently exhibit when dealing with a professional staff. The enthusiasm and spirit generated by the interaction among these paraprofessionals and the parents during the course seems to stimulate and encourage the parents to achieve desired behavioral changes. The attitude seems to be, "If they did it and it worked, we can too."

The Apprentice Group Leader

Parents who have completed the Responsive Parenting Program and have successfully carried out at least one behavioral change project as outlined have met one criterion to be considered for appointment as an apprentice group leader. In addition, the parent must demonstrate a working knowledge of the basic principles, concepts, and procedures of behavior management as outlined in the *Responsive Parenting Manual*, the course guideline. Personal qualities, such as good group social skills, resourcefulness, enthusiasm, and organizational skills, are vital considerations in the selection of potential apprentice group leaders. Those selected are recommended jointly by the group leader and the program director, who has also observed the candidates' performances throughout the course.

Those parents who accept the invitation become apprentice group leaders for an entire 8-week course. Apprentice group leaders must be available for a minimum of 3 hours per week to assist the group leader in preparing for and conducting each week's small-group session, for participating in the discussion, and for assisting parents in carrying out their projects. In addition, they are asked to increase their behavioral background through additional related readings (e.g., Azrin, Besalel, Hall, & Hall, 1980; R. V. Hall, 1977) and further discussion. They are also required to complete another behavior change project, using a different behavior analysis design and intervention procedure than in the project they had previously carried out while first taking the course. This requirement is designed to broaden their background and skills for helping other parents. Gradually the apprentice group leader is assigned greater responsibilities. Additional training is accomplished by required attendance at a training workshop, which includes demonstration of role-playing episodes and management techniques for dealing with problem situations that may arise in the sessions. Other training in group leader skills and responsibilities is provided through use of a series of three training tapes (Bureau of Child Research, 1981).

The Group Leader

The group leader has proved to be of critical importance to the realization of the program's objectives. Apprentice group leaders who demonstrate interest and competence by attending regularly, giving clear instructions, providing appropriate feedback to parents, and demonstrating sensitivity to the needs of the group while supporting and helping to produce acceptable behavior change projects may be recommended by the group leader and program director to serve as group leaders. Selection of good group leaders is essential, as course evaluation surveys indicate that parents have consistently rated the group leader and the small-group discussions of the highest importance in the Responsive Parenting course structure. Group leaders were given a rating of 3.83 on a 4-point scale, and small-group discussions were given a rating of 3.76. Thus the group leader is a person of great influence who does a great deal to determine the outcome of the program. The success of the home behavior change projects, as well as the refinement and application of new knowledge and concepts, is dependent upon the group leader's approach and supportive role as the liaison between the parents and the program director.

The main vehicle for training parents to be group leaders is participation in the program. Although they are required to do some outside reading and are encouraged to do even more, the formal training in behavioral approaches is necessarily limited. Therefore, it is important that the program director be available to answer questions that group leaders hesitate to answer independently; to monitor small-group sessions in order to support the group leaders' contributions; and to give feedback on group leaders' comments and answers.

While working closely with the program director and following the guidelines and suggestions provided by the group leader's manual (the second section of the *Responsive Parenting Manual*; see M. C. Hall, 1981), the group leader plans and conducts each week's session with his or her small group of approximately 5 to 12 parents. The group leader guides the parents as they discuss the week's accomplishments or dilemmas, answer questions, review the new concepts and procedures for the week, make plans to try new techniques, practice and review newly acquired skills through behavioral rehearsal, and carry out their home behavior change projects.

Any questions that the group leader is unable to answer are referred to the program director. Group leaders are also responsible for checking attendance and for making phone contact with parents who miss class, are having difficulty, or appear to need additional support. At the conclusion of each session, the group leader gives the parents the next week's unit of the parent manual and collects any response sheets or evaluations that the participants have completed. Prior to each week's meeting with parents, group leaders attend a 30-minute briefing to update general information regarding small-group activities, to discuss problems, and to help the program director plan subsequent sessions. A goal of this preparation is to make each session a viable, dynamic new experience, rather than a boring rehash of material and data.

Since the paraprofessional staff members learn primarily from their group leaders and program directors, it is exceedingly important that the models they observe be good ones. For this reason, it has proved to be better to limit the number of participants and/or to increase the size of groups rather than to settle for inferior group leaders. Poor group leaders will not only provide participants with an inferior program, but will also serve as weak models for subsequent staff members.

The Program Director

In most of the program sites, the program directors are professionals—psychologists, counselors, social workers, teachers, and other related medical-social-educational professionals. There is a need for the program director to have a background of behavioral training and experience in order to be able to provide effective direction of the Responsive Parenting Program. Therefore, although paraprofessionals have served successfully in this position, it is recommended that in most cases program directors have professional training and experience.

Program directors must be able to devote at least 5 hours per week to the program. The director has responsibilities in all phases of the program. He or she is responsible for each of the weekly large-group sessions in which new materials are presented. The program director also helps monitor the small-group activities, answers questions referred by the group leaders, insures the accuracy of the information disseminated, and assists and provides feedback to both group leaders and parent participants. The program director is encouraged to improve his or her behavioral background continually by becoming familiar with the behavioral literature and by attending Responsive Parent training workshops, which are generally offered each spring or summer. The workshops are organized to bring program directors up to date on developments and changes in the Responsive Parenting Program and to provide a forum for answering questions and improving leadership skills.

RESPONSIVE PARENTING TRAINING WORKSHOP

The program director shoulders full responsibility for the accuracy of what is taught in the course, for management of staff, and for all administrative tasks necessary for a smoothly running Responsive Parenting Program. These tasks include helping to arrange for a comfortable environmental setting, making staff assignments, assigning parents to groups, rewarding attendance, and being alert to the special needs of the group. As previously mentioned, the initial large-group session is directed by the program director each week. Close monitoring of the group leaders and apprentice group leaders during the small-group sessions is part of his or her assignment. Making certain that everyone has necessary materials and information is vital for a smooth-running program.

An organizational chart showing the levels of responsibilities of the Responsive Parenting staff is presented in Figure 4-3.

Figure 4-3

Responsive Parenting Program organizational structure and position requirements.

I. The parent being considered as Responsive Parenting staff member will:
   a. Complete the Responsive Parenting course
   b. Complete a home behavior change project
   c. Be recommended by GL as a potential staff member
   d. Demonstrate good social skills
   e. Show enthusiasm for Responsive Parenting Program
II. The apprentice group leader will:
   a. Complete a second home behavior change project
   b. Complete outside reading assignments
   c. Attend all meetings
   d. Help with enrollment
   e. Help with all session activities
   f. Assist group leader
III. The group leader will:
   a. Attend all meetings
   b. Take attendance and help with enrollment
   c. Organize and conduct small-group activities
   d. Help with all session activities
   e. Monitor parents' home behavior change projects
   f. Give feedback to PD
   g. Give feedback to other GLs
   h. Plan with AGL for participation in small groups
   i. Recommend parents to be AGLs
IV. The program director will:
   a. Organize Responsive Parenting Program
   b. Establish meeting place
   c. Make staff assignments
   d. Conduct enrollment and all session activities
   e. Monitor all on-site research
   f. Organize and conduct presentations in large-group session
   g. Prepare agendas for and conduct weekly meetings
   h. Monitor small-group sessions
   i. Give feedback to AGLs and GLs
   j. Recommend parents for AGLs and make recommendations for GLs and PDs

Key: AGL = apprentice group leader; GL = group leader; PD = program director

Certification

Certification procedures for the program director require that a knowledge and complete understanding of the basic principles and procedures of applied behavioral analysis be within his or her level of expertise. This may be fulfilled by the following: (1) passing a concept test based on the *Responsive Parenting Manual*, the *Behavior Management Series* by R. V. Hall (1971), and other readings, and (2) presenting evidence of experience in an academic or applied program that the certifying agent would approve after reviewing the applicant's credentials or following an interview. Other requirements for certification are as follows:

1. Attending the Process Workshop (designed to prepare the program director to organize and manage the administrative aspects of the program, including publicity, keeping records, planning meetings, handling problems, etc.) either at their site or at the Responsive Parenting Institute.
2. Carrying out a Responsive Parenting Program with 6 to 10 parents.
3. Arranging for the Responsive Parenting Institute to send an Institute member to the site to observe a Responsive Parenting class in session, or submitting audiotapes or videotapes of at least two Responsive Parenting class sessions.
4. Generating successful behavior change projects by 60% or more of parents attending a course, submitting copies of the projects including data, and generating parent satisfaction surveys indicating 80% or more positive responses from parents taking the course.
5. Submitting pretraining and posttraining research using the Walker Problem Behavior Identification Checklist (Walker, 1970), Parent Evaluation Survey (PES) (Christophersen *et al.*, 1976), and Behavioral Situations Practice Sheet #3.

When candidates requesting certification have fulfilled the above requirements, certification will be issued.

Other Program Considerations

In a large program such as that at Shawnee Mission, Kansas, monthly meetings of program directors with the district Responsive Parenting coordinator have been an important vehicle for providing further staff training and communication. Frequent visits by the district Responsive Parenting coordinator or other professional staff members have proved to be invaluable as a source of information and reinforcement for the parent staffs at the various sites.

In Shawnee Mission, a Responsive Parenting newsletter was developed and sent to both staff and parents at the various sites. The newsletter presented information and ideas that parents and staff might find helpful. It is recommended that programs with more than one site consider developing a newsletter to enhance communication.

DISCUSSION

The Responsive Parenting Program described here is an attempt to help meet the need for parent training long recognized by behaviorists. The program seeks to provide parents with background knowledge and skills in using applied behavior analysis procedures, in order to help them better understand and manage behavior. It provides them with a basic understanding of social learning theory principles and gives them an opportunity to practice using them with their children. It allows for flexibility in that the parents choose both the behaviors they seek to change and the behavior change procedures they use to modify those behaviors.

The program has been shown to be adaptable for use with both small and large groups of parents in schools, mental health centers, churches, hospitals, and private clinics. Its scope is both remedial and preventative in nature. Although originally designed for use with parents of exceptional children, it has been adapted to provide child-rearing skills for large numbers of parents of "normal" children, from infancy through high school. Thus its emphasis is largely preventative in nature. Nevertheless, its materials are designed and have been used successfully to provide for the needs of parents of special children, including adjudicated second-time juvenile offenders, retarded children and autistic children. Thus, it also serves the needs of parents with common as well as special concerns. Thus far, in addition to the approximately 3000 parents trained in the original program in Shawnee Mission, Kansas, approximately 500 persons have been trained at other sites across the country. This number is rapidly increasing. In addition, 16 paraprofessionals have been certified as program directors and 54 as group leaders.

One parent population this program does not serve in its present form is the low-socioeconomic-level parent with limited reading and verbal skills. The program requires attendance at weekly meetings and high-school-level reading comprehension. These are barriers to those with academic deficits and limited resources for transportation and babysitting. It will therefore require further adaptation and revision if it is to serve such populations. Other models that overcome these problems by serving parents in their homes and that emphasize direct modeling, imitation, and feedback will perhaps be more appropriate for such populations.

An important feature of the Responsive Parenting Program is that it capitalizes on a relatively untouched supply of human resources within the community boundaries. That is, parents assist and train other parents to become better managers in their roles as educators of and models for their children. There are numerous advantages in using parents to assist other parents in acquiring parenting skills. Parents find it easy to respond to other parents as they relate and compare similar problems in management of their offspring. Parents often perceive other parents with less awe and greater realism than they do professionals. As a result, they seem less likely to reject the idea that they can define, measure, and record behavior or learn the procedures presented, since they see first-hand evidence that other parents have done so. Similarly, personal testimonials by parent participants during all phases of the Responsive Parenting Program promote enthusiasm and encourage open discussion and participation.

The most obvious advantage of using parents as staff members relates to cost. In the initial stages of the development of the Responsive Parenting Program, parents chosen to be in leadership roles contributed their time and energy without compensation. Under the sponsorship of the NIMH training grant, parents in the program received compensation. This compensation was in part due to the extra time and effort required for obtaining data for monitoring and evaluating the program. Basic compensation for group leaders was $50 per course, with up to an additional $50 for special research efforts. Program directors received $250 per course, plus additional compensation if they were involved in obtaining more extensive evaluation data and/or developing training materials and workshops.

Each family unit in the Responsive Parenting Program at Shawnee Mission has paid a $20 enrollment fee, which has covered the cost of the manual, coffee, and other materials. Program directors at other sites have generally charged $20 to $25 per family unit if the program has not supported a professional staff. Higher amounts ranging up to $300 per unit have been reported in programs entirely supported by parent fees, as in a clinical setting.

One potential disadvantage of using a largely voluntary paraprofessional staff is that it would seem that there might be problems with attendance and with acceptance of responsibility. Fortunately, this has not proved to be the case. Perhaps the highly organized process, based on performance, by which apprentice group leaders and group leaders are selected is a crucial factor here. As a result, those selected have been generally highly interested, motivated, and responsible staff members. Other factors may be that the group leaders readily perceive that the program depends largely on them and that they receive a great deal of social reinforcement from parents in the small-group sessions. For whatever reasons, there have been very few absences among the staff.

A number of concerns have arisen in trying to evaluate the effectiveness of the Responsive Parenting Program. Several attempts have been made to provide evidence of the program's effectiveness. Perhaps the strongest evidence available comes from the individual behavior change projects carried out by the parents. The project reports turned in by the parents have consistently indicated that changes were brought about in the specific behaviors the parents had selected.

Even so, it has been difficult to assess whether or not the program has resulted in changes in behaviors of parents or children other than those specifically worked with in the behavior change projects. At each training site, two evaluation measures were implemented on a before-and-after basis. These measures were the Walker Problem Behavior Identification Checklist (Walker, 1970) and the PES (Christophersen et al., 1976). These measures indicated significant changes from precourse to postcourse assessments following training, compared to nonsignificant changes in control groups that received no training. Although some attempts were made to get other measures of generalization, they were unsuccessful. However, when outside observers were sent into the homes to make reliability checks on parent observations for their behavior change projects, agreement between the outside observers' and the parents' records was consistently above 90%.

During the early years of development of Responsive Parenting, maintenance meetings and follow-up telephone contacts were implemented. The parents who attended the meetings and who were contacted by telephone consistently reported that the behaviors they had modified in their behavior change projects continued improved. They also reported that they were still using Responsive Parenting procedures in managing behavior in the home, especially systematic attention and approval. However, the maintenance sessions were not well attended; the parents who did attend reported that, although they enjoyed the sessions, they were not functional, since the parents were already maintaining their Responsive Parenting skills. The maintenance sessions were therefore discontinued. On occasion, some parents have re-enrolled in Responsive Parenting in order to improve their skills or get help with a specific problem.

Other evaluation measures implemented on a posttraining basis included measurement of knowledge of social learning theory and Responsive Parenting concepts. These tests over the course content consistently showed that parents scored higher than 85%. At the parents' suggestions, however, these concept tests were discontinued because they were disliked by many and were thought to contribute to the dropout rate in the last sessions.

A consumer satisfaction survey given routinely at the end of the course has indicated a consistently high degree of satisfaction with the program, with scores averaging above 3.5 on a 4-point scale. These surveys have indicated that the group leader, small-group sessions, and the manual are key aspects of the program. There is further evidence that parents who complete the program are satisfied with its results; many, if not most, of those who attend the course are referred by others who have previously taken it. A number of participants have been on waiting lists; for example, one-fifth of 300 participants during spring semester 1979 had been on the waiting list for one semester and had learned of the program from the participants enrolled in the previous semester's course.

Another method of viewing parents' satisfaction with the effectiveness of the Responsive Parenting Program is through the number of parents who have become a part of the training staff. During the 1979–1980 course offering, 18 parents (or 6.6% of those who enrolled) agreed to join the training staff as new apprentice group leaders. Nineteen parents who had been apprentice group leaders continued to participate as group leaders. Thus, 70% of the training staff were parents who had successfully completed the training program.

Another measure for evaluating the Responsive Parenting Program was the attrition rate. During the first years of the program, approximately one out of three families (36%) withdrew their participation in the program by the final session. During 1980, however, this figure was decreased to 25% and finally to 19%. At first glance, these figures may seem high, until one recalls that most parents were self-selected and participating voluntarily, and that their children did not have professionally referred disorders. In the light of these considerations, this attrition rate, especially in the last year, does not seem inordinate.

The pattern of the dropout rate during the first program years indicated that there was a dramatic increase in attrition during the last two sessions. Reasons contributing to this could have been the rather high response cost to parents in filling out the evaluation forms and some parents' reluctance to write up and present their studies in the final session. A decrease in the dropout rate was noted when the course was shortened from the 10-week form to the 8-week form and when the concept exams at each session were discontinued in favor of having parents indicate how they would apply what they had learned in behavioral situations. In spite of the dropout rate even in the early years, it should be remembered that the total number of parents trained is higher than would be expected if a professional staff only had been available.

Interestingly enough, reported attrition rates at other Responsive Parenting sites have been consistently lower than those at Shawnee Mission. For example, the LaGrange area program in suburban Chicago reported average attrition rates of 6%; the Menorah Medical Center in Kansas City, Missouri, reported 20%; and the May Institute program for parents of autistic children in Massachusetts reported an attrition rate of 0%. Possible reasons for this might be that the programs at these sites were initiated in recent years, after the program had been refined and developed to its present state. Also, the programs at LaGrange and the May Institute were primarily for parents of exceptional children and had largely professional staffs. Such parents may be especially motivated, particularly to work with staff members who have expertise in working with special children.

The Responsive Parenting Program has undergone a number of revisions that have incorporated changes suggested by feedback from program evaluations, parents, and staff. Among these have been the inclusion of an increasingly specific structure and instructions in the program director's and group leader's manuals, including suggestions for working with parents of secondary students and handicapped children, and the development of audio–visual tapes for training staff members. Other changes have included the elimination of formal tests and quizzes and an increased emphasis on using behavioral situations and behavioral rehearsals. Although the format of a large-group session followed by small-group sessions has remained in effect, the length of time devoted to large groups has been decreased and the time spent in small groups has increased. As previously mentioned, the number of weekly sessions has also been changed from 10 to 8, a move that seems to have contributed to a significant decrease in attrition without adversely affecting parent training.

Although there has been continuous modification of the program and training materials over the past several years, the project director and staff are satisfied that the program in its present form adequately meets the objectives set for Responsive Parenting. That is, using the materials and the training procedures developed, professionals have been able to implement the program in various settings and have been able to replicate the results obtained by its developers. The result has been a large number of parents provided with a basic knowledge of applied behavior analysis and some at least rudimentary skills in using systematic behavior change procedures.

Although the Responsive Parenting Program is basically the same at the various sites, a number of variations have been reported. For example, at the LaGrange area site, research design is not taught formally. Rather, the group leaders graph the parent data and use only AB designs in carrying out behavior change projects. They have also used videotaping of parents during behavioral rehearsals, in order to teach more effectively such procedures as social reinforcement, planned ignoring, and time out. The May Institute program has been modified extensively to include a great deal of information about autism and problems of special children. However, the basic information and activities included in the eight units presented in the Responsive Parenting Manual are provided at all sites.

It should be understood that no claim is made that these parents are skilled researchers, or that they will all necessarily use what they have been taught in their roles as parents. Nevertheless, the evidence provided by the home behavior change projects and the posttraining measures show that the parents have at least begun to understand behavior from the point of view of behavior analysis, and, according to self-reports and reports of others who have worked with graduates of the program (Kretsch, 1981; Pirnstill, 1981), they were able to apply that knowledge and those skills in other situations. Therefore, it would seem that Responsive Parenting is a promising program that provides at least a beginning step in meeting the need for training large numbers of parents to understand and use systematic behavioral procedures.

Acknowledgments

This program was supported in part by National Institute of Mental Health (NIMH) Training Grant MH 1453-03 to the University of Kansas, Bureau of Child Research, Lawrence, Kansas, and the Shawnee Mission Public Schools, Shawnee Mission, Kansas.

References

Azrin, H. H., Besalel, V. A., Hall, R. V., & Hall, M. C. (Eds.). *How to manage behavior series.* Lawrence, Kans.: H & H Enterprises, 1980.

Bureau of Child Research (Producer). *Responsive Parenting.* Lawrence: University of Kansas, 1978. (Film)

Bureau of Child Research (Producer). *Responsive Parenting: An overview; Responsive Parenting: Program director's responsibilities;* and *Responsive Parenting: Group leader's responsibilities.* Parsons, Kans.: Parsons State Hospital, 1981. (Audio–video training tapes)

Christophersen, E. D., Barnard, J. D., Ford, D., & Wolf, M. M. The family training program: Improving parent–child interactions patterns. In E. J. Mash, L. C. Handy, & L. A. Hamerlynck (Eds.), *Behavior modification approaches to parenting.* New York: Brunner/Mazel, 1976.

Hall, M. C. *Responsive Parenting Manual* (Rev. ed.). Shawnee Mission, Kans.: Responsive Management, 1981.

Hall, M. C., Grinstead, J., Collier, H., & Hall, R. V. Responsive Parenting: A preventive program which incorporates parents training parents. *Education and Treatment of Children,* 1980, *3,* 239–259.

Hall, R. V. *Behavior management series* (Part I, *The measurement of behavior;* Part II, *Basic principles;* Part III, *Applications in school and home*). Lawrence, Kans.: H & H Enterprises, 1977.

Hall, R. V., Axelrod, S., Tyler, L., Grief, E., Jones, F. C., & Robertson, R. Modification of behavior problems in the home with a parent as observer and experimenter. *Journal of Applied Behavior Analysis,* 1972, *5,* 53–64.

Hall, R. V., Christler, C., Cranston, S., & Tucker, B. Teachers and parents as researchers using multiple-baseline tactics. *Journal of Applied Behavior Analysis,* 1970, *4,* 247–255.

Hall, R. V., Copeland, R. E., & Clark, M. Management strategies for teachers and parents: Responsive teaching. In N. Haring & R. Schiefelbusch (Eds.), *Teaching special children.* New York: McGraw-Hill, 1976.

Hanf, C. *Modifying problem behaviors in mother–child interaction: Standardized laboratory situations.* Paper presented at the meeting of the Association of Behavioral Therapies, Olympia, Washington, 1968.

Hanf, C. *A two-stage program for modifying material controlling during mother–child (M-C) interaction.* Paper presented at the meeting of the Western Psychological Association, Vancouver, British Columbia, 1969.

Hanley, E. M. *Results of parent workshop program.* Unpublished manuscript, University of Vermont Special Education Program, 1972.

Hawkins, R. P. It's time we taught the young how to be good parents (and don't we wish we'd started a long time ago?). *Psychology Today,* 1972, *6,* 28–38.

Hawkins, R. P., Peterson, R. F., Schweid, E., & Bijou, S. W. Behavior therapy in the home: Amelioration or problem parent–child relations with the parent in a therapeutic role. *Journal of Experimental Child Psychology,* 1966, *4,* 99–107.

Herbert, E. W., & Baer, D. M. Training parents as behavior modifiers: Self-recording of contingent attention. *Journal of Applied Behavior Analysis,* 1972, *5,* 139–149.

Hirsch, I., & Walder, L. Training mothers in groups as reinforcement therapists for their own children. *Proceedings of the 77th Annual Convention of the American Psychological Association,* 1969, *4,* 561–562.

Howard, O. F. *Teaching a class of parents as reinforcement therapists to treat their own children.* Paper presented at the annual meeting of the Southeastern Psychological Association, Louisville, Kentucky, April 1970.

Kretsch, M. S. Training parents to teach their children to follow instructions. In M. C. Hall (Chair), *Five years of Responsive Parenting.* Symposium presented at the Seventh Annual Convention of the Association for Behavior Analysis, Milwaukee, May 1981.

Nordquist, V. M., & Wahler, R. G. Naturalistic treatment of an autistic child. *Journal of Applied Behavior Analysis,* 1973, *6,* 79–87.

O'Dell, S. Training parents in behavior modification: A review. *Psychological Bulletin*, 1974, *81*, 418–433.

O'Leary, K. D., & Kent, R. N. *A behavioral consultation program for parents and teachers of children with conduct problems*. Paper presented at the meeting of the American Psychological Association, New Orleans, March 1974.

O'Leary, K. D., O'Leary, S., & Becker, W. C. Modification of deviant sibling interaction pattern in the home. *Behaviour Research and Therapy*, 1967, *5*, 113–120.

Ora, J. P. *Instruction pamphlet for parents of oppositional children* (Regional Intervention Project for Preschoolers and Parents). Unpublished manuscript, George Peabody College, 1970.

Patterson, G. R., & Brodsky, G. A behavior modification programme for a child with multiple problem behaviors. *Journal of Child Psychology and Psychiatry and Allied Disciplines*, 1966, *7*, 277–295.

Patterson, G. R., Cobb, J. A., & Ray, R. S. A social engineering technology for retraining the families of aggressive boys. In H. E. Adams & I. P. Unikel (Eds.), *Georgia Symposium in Experimental Clinical Psychology* (Vol. 2). Oxford: Pergamon Press, 1970.

Patterson, G. R., Littman, R. A., & Hinsey, W. C. Parental effectiveness as reinforcers in the laboratory and its relation to child rearing practices and adjustment in the classroom. *Journal of Personality*, 1964, *32*, 180–199.

Patterson, G. R., McNeal, S., Hawkins, N., & Phelps, R. Reprogramming the social environment. *Journal of Child Psychology and Psychiatry and Allied Disciplines*, 1967, *8*, 181–195.

Peine, H. A. *Programming the home*. Paper presented at the meeting of the Rocky Mountain Psychological Association, Albuquerque, 1969.

Pirnstill, B. Teaching parents to toilet train their toddlers. In M. C. Hall (Chair), *Five years of Responsive Parenting*. Symposium presented at the Seventh Annual Convention of the Association for Behavior Analysis, Milwaukee, May 1981.

Pumroy, D. K. *A new approach to treating parent–child problems*. Paper presented at the annual meeting of the American Psychological Association, Chicago, 1965.

Wagner, J. I., & Ora, J. P. *Parental control of the very young severely oppositional child*. Paper presented at the annual meeting of the Southeastern Psychological Association, Louisville, Kentucky, April 1970.

Wahler, R. G. Oppositional children: A quest for parental reinforcement control. *Journal of Applied Behavior Analysis*, 1969, *2*, 159–170. (a)

Wahler, R. G. Setting generality: Some specific and general effects of child behavior therapy. *Journal of Applied Behavior Analysis*, 1969, *2*, 239–246. (b)

Wahler, R. G., Winkel, G. H., Peterson, R. F., & Morrison, D. C. Mothers as behavior therapists for their own children. *Behaviour Research and Therapy*, 1965, *3*, 113–124.

Walder, L., Cohen, S., Breiter, D., Daston, P., Hirsch, I., & Leibowitz, J. Teaching behavioral principles to parents of disturbed children. In B. Guerney, Jr. (Ed.), *Psychotherapeutic agents: New roles for nonprofessionals, parents, and teachers*. New York: Holt, Rinehart & Winston, 1967.

Walder, L., Cohen, S., & Daston, P. *Teaching parents and other principles of behavior control for modifying the behavior of children* (Progress report to the United States Office of Education). Washington, D.C.: U.S. Government Printing Office, 1967.

Walker, H. M. *Walker Problem Behavior Identification Checklist*. Los Angeles: Western Psychological Services, 1970.

Williams, C. D. The elimination of tantrum behavior by extinction procedures. *Journal of Abnormal and Social Psychology*, 1959, *59*, 269.

Wolf, M. M., Risley, T. R., & Mees, H. Application of operant conditioning procedures to the behavior problems of an autistic child. *Behaviour Research and Therapy*, 1964, *1*, 305–312.

Zeilberger, J., Samper, S. E., & Sloane, H. N., Jr. Modification of a child's problem behavior in the home with the mother as therapist. *Journal of Applied Behavior Analysis*, 1968, *1*, 47–53.

THE PORTAGE PROJECT
Teaching Parents to Teach Their Preschool Children in the Home

David E. Shearer
Utah State University

Craig R. Loftin
Portage Project

This chapter describes the Portage Project, provides insight into what are regarded as the major reasons for its success, and shares ways in which a behavioral parent training system can be evaluated, modified, and replicated.

The target population of early childhood education includes young children and their families. Providing an intervention program for preschool handicapped children and directly involving their parents in the educational process is an ever-increasing focus of attention. In the United States and in other countries, the young child, the parent, and the educational program are recognized as interdependent elements in the development of the society. To ignore parents, in their unique position as children's first and most natural educators, is to lessen the chances for a successful educational program.

PORTAGE PROJECT GOALS

The original goals of the Portage Project were these:

1. To develop an educational service for preschool handicapped children and their parents living in the rural areas of south central Wisconsin.
2. To develop a model that was practical, cost-efficient, and easily replicable.

3. To make a statement—a single declaration that parents can successfully teach their own children at home.

Originally funded in 1969, the Portage Project was an attempt to fill a void in services to families of handicapped children. Prior to the project, there were no educational services provided in rural Wisconsin to preschool handicapped children. Most community services were overburdened with existing workloads and were not anxious to take on additional responsibilities. In the initial activities of identification, screening, and provision of services, it never occurred to us that there should be a lower age limit where early intervention should begin. It was our firm belief that if early intervention does enhance a child's growth and development, then it should begin as soon as the handicap is diagnosed. We also believed that parent involvement was critical to program success. Today, well over a decade later, we maintain those beliefs more firmly than ever. Since its inception, the project has become known for many characteristics. It uses a home teacher as the change agent; it includes an ongoing assessment and evaluation process to assure appropriate curriculum planning; and it ensures that each child receives an individualized program. The Portage Model has a specific home teaching process. The parent and the home teacher record the behaviors each child learns, when the behavior was prescribed and accomplished, what developmental area it was in, and what skills the child is currently learning. The system is applicable for children from birth to the mental age of 6 and can be used with normal and handicapped children.

The basic premises of the Portage Model related to parents are these:

- Parents care about their children and want them to attain their maximum potential.
- Parents can, with instruction, modeling, and reinforcement, learn to be more effective teachers of their own children.
- The socioeconomic, educational, and intellectual levels of the parents do not determine their willingness to teach their children or the extent of gains their children will attain.

The Portage Project involves parents directly in their child's education, for several reasons:

1. Parents are the consumers. They pay, either directly or indirectly, for the programs and the services their children receive. Most parents want a voice in what and how their children are taught, and they want to participate in the teaching of their children (Fredricks, Baldwin, & Grove, 1974).
2. Knowledgeable parents can be strong advocates for program continuation and extension (Hayden, 1974; D. Shearer & Shearer, 1976). School boards, advisory councils, and state legislatures substantially change policy and laws as a direct result of parental advocacy.

3. Parents of handicapped children will have more responsibility for their children over a significantly longer period of time than parents of normal children will (M. Shearer & Shearer, 1972).

4. Parents know their children better than anyone else ever will. Thus, parents can serve as a vital resource in the selection of program objectives that will be most useful to the children in their own environment.

5. The problem of transferring learning from the classroom to the home can occur because of insufficient and ineffective communication between parents and teaching staff. Planned consistency between the classroom training and the educational experiences provided by the parents is vital. Without effective parent involvement, the best possible program for a child will have little effect (Lillie, 1974).

6. Studies have shown that parent training during the preschool years is of benefit not only for target children, but also for siblings (Gilmer, Miller, & Gray, 1968). This indicates that parents are able to generalize learned skills, thus making them better parent/teachers of all their children.

7. Training parents, who may already be naturally reinforcing, will provide them with the skills necessary to teach new behaviors effectively and to modify inappropriate behaviors that interfere with learning.

8. Parent involvement can greatly accelerate a child's rate of learning. A program without benefit of parental involvement cannot begin to accomplish what a program and parents can accomplish together. Fredricks, Baldwin, and Grove have demonstrated that a systematic program by the parent, in conjunction with the school, will almost double the rate of skill acquisition (Fredricks *et al.*, 1974).

THE PORTAGE MODEL

Administration and Target Population

The Portage Project operates administratively through a regional educational agency, the Cooperative Educational Service Agency (CESA) 12. This agency serves 23 school districts within its 3600-square-mile boundaries and provides a variety of services, including the Portage Project's early childhood program. Portage Project children range in chronological age from birth to 6 or older if there is not demonstrated readiness for a school program. All the children served have been diagnosed as handicapped in one or more developmental areas by professionals within each school's multidisciplinary team.

Assessment and Curriculum Planning

Each child is assessed to determine his or her present functioning level, which is used as the basis for further educational or curriculum planning. In the Portage Project, the Alpern–Boll Developmental Profile (Alpern & Boll, 1972) is administered as a parent questionnaire, and is combined with direct observation of the child's behavior whenever possible.

To facilitate planning for individual children, the project staff has devised the *Portage Guide to Early Education* (Bluma, Shearer, Frohman, & Hilliard, 1976). This curriculum guide, for use with children from birth through 6 years, consists of a manual of instructions; a checklist of sequenced behaviors, in five skill areas (cognition, language, self-help, motor, and socialization) and a section on infant stimulation; and a card file suggesting teaching activities for each of the 580 checklist behaviors.

The checklist, seen in Figure 5-1, pinpoints behaviors that the child already exhibits in each developmental area and indicates emerging skills (unlearned behaviors immediately following learned behaviors that the teacher and parent may target for learning). The user refers to the matching card in the card file, which suggests materials and methods for teaching that skill. This curriculum is simply a guide for the teacher. Many behaviors actually prescribed for children are not found in the checklist, but may lead to a long-term goal that is listed in the checklist. Thus, many checklist behaviors are long-term goals that must be divided into smaller behavioral segments. These may be chained together to achieve the long-term goal. The child determines the curriculum, not the checklist.

Writing and Implementing Curriculum Objectives

Following both formal and informal assessment, the home teacher suggests three or four emerging behaviors. Parents target a behavior, and the home teacher then writes the chosen goal, stated as a behavioral objective, and directions on an activity chart as represented in Figure 5-2. These prescriptions are written with the intention that the parent and child will succeed on the task within 1 week. As parents experience success and gain confidence in their ability to teach their children and record behavior, prescriptions are gradually increased to three or four per week. Weekly activities are presented from several areas of development. Parents may be working on reducing tantrums, buttoning, and counting all within the same week.

The most important point is for the home teacher to break tasks down and prescribe only those that can be achieved within 1 week. This provides parents with rapid reinforcement, for what the child learns is a direct result of parental teaching. The directions are clearly written, and recording is always uncomplicated.

cognitive

Age	Card	Behavior	Entry Behavior	Date Achieved	Comments
	82	Places objects behind, beside, next to		/ /	
	83	Matches equal sets to sample of 1 to 10 objects		/ /	
	84	Names or points to missing part of pictured object		/ /	
	85	Counts by rote 1 to 20		/ /	
	86	Names first, middle and last position		/ /	
5-6	87	Counts up to 20 items and tells how many		/ /	
	88	Names 10 numerals		/ /	
	89	Names left and right on self		/ /	
	90	Says letters of alphabet in order		/ /	
	91	Prints own first name		/ /	
	92	Names five letters of alphabet		/ /	
	93	Arranges objects in sequence of width and length		/ /	
	94	Names capital letters of alphabet		/ /	
	95	Puts numerals 1 to 10 in proper sequence		/ /	
	96	Names position of objects first, second, third		/ /	
	97	Names lower case letters of alphabet		/ /	
	98	Matches capital to lower case letters of alphabet		/ /	
	99	Points to named numerals 1 to 25		/ /	
	100	Copies diamond shape		/ /	
	101	Completes simple maze		/ /	
	102	Names days of week in order		/ /	
	103	Can add and subtract combinations to three		/ /	
	104	Tells month and day of birthday		/ /	
	105	Sight reads 10 printed words		/ /	
	106	Predicts what happens next		/ /	
	107	Points to half and whole objects		/ /	
	108	Counts by rote 1 to 100		/ /	

cognitive 58

AGE 3-4

TITLE: Copies series of connected V strokes VVVVVVVV

WHAT TO DO:

1. Draw a series of V strokes. Encourage the child to trace over the letter first with his finger and later with a crayon or pencil. Help by guiding his hand.
2. Have him draw with you making one line at a time.
3. Make a row of connected V strokes. Then have the child draw more rows as you give him verbal directions "up, down, up, down."
4. Have child make a row of V strokes on paper. When he finishes make it into a picture of mountains, grass, trees, etc. for him.

Figure 5-1

Portage Guide to Early Education checklist and activity card. (From *Portage Guide to Early Education*, revised edition, by S. Bluma, M. Shearer, A. Frohman, & J. Hilliard. Portage, Wisc.: Cooperative Educational Service Agency 12, 1976. Copyright 1976 by Cooperative Service Agency 12. Reprinted by permission.)

CREDIT: ____ yes ____ no

ACTIVITY CHART

Child's Name ______________________

Home Teacher's Name ______________________

Week of ______________________

WHAT TO TEACH:

STATE A TARGET BEHAVIOR

(WHO, WILL DO WHAT, WITH WHAT KIND OF HELP, HOW WELL)

WHAT TO RECORD:

SHOW THE SYMBOLS USED

TELL WHAT THEY MEAN

WRITE DOWN NUMBERS FOR RESPONSES

HOME TEACHER TAKES BASELINE

PARENT PRACTICES RECORDING DURING DEMONSTRATION

PARENT RECORDS DURING WEEK

HOME TEACHER TAKES POST-BASELINE

WRITE IN DAYS OF THE WEEK

DAYS

DIRECTIONS:

REMEMBER TO INCLUDE:

1. PLACE TO WORK IF IT IS IMPORTANT
2. MATERIALS AND HOW THEY WILL BE USED
3. HOW TO PRESENT THE MATERIALS AND GET THE CHILD TO RESPOND
4. HOW TO REINFORCE THE CHILD WHEN HE RESPONDS CORRECTLY AND HOW TO RECORD ON THE CHART.
5. WHAT TYPE OF AID TO USE AS A CORRECTION PROCEDURE AND HOW TO RECORD ON THE CHART
6. HOW MANY TIMES TO PRACTICE EACH DAY
7. ACTIVITY VARIATIONS

The Portage Project

Figure 5-2

Activity chart with instructions. (From *Portage Guide to Early Education,* revised edition, by S. Bluma, M. Shearer, A. Frohman, & J. Hilliard. Portage, Wisc.: Cooperative Educational Service Agency 12, 1976. Copyright 1976 by Cooperative Service Agency 12. Reprinted by permission.)

The Home Teaching Process (See Figure 5-3)

Step 1: Postbaseline Measurements

Before introducing activities for the coming week, the home teacher first takes postbaseline measurements on the previous week's activities to validate the accuracy of the parent's recording and to obtain feedback on the degree of success and readiness for the next sequential step. Based on these data, the home teacher alters the previous prescription or presents the new activities.

Step 2: Home Teacher Introduces New Activities and Models

The home teacher introduces the new activities to the parent and child and records baseline data—the frequency of correct responses—prior to instruction. These data are recorded on the activity chart. The home teacher then begins the teaching process—modeling teaching techniques for the parents, showing them what to do and how to do it.

Step 3: Parents Model for the Home Teacher

The parent takes over the instruction and works with the child, modeling for the home teacher. The home teacher offers suggestions and reinforcement, increasing the likelihood that the parent will successfully teach the child during the week.

Step 4: Review Activities and Recording Procedures

Before leaving, the home teacher reviews with the parent the activities to be conducted during the week, the teaching and reinforcement methods, and the recording procedures. This helps to ensure that the parent and home teacher agree, and it eliminates any possibility of misunderstanding. Throughout the visit, the home teacher stresses the importance of working with the child during the week, and the parent is encouraged to call the office if any question or problem arises. Teaching materials are primarily everyday items available in the home; however, materials are occasionally provided by the home teacher.

These four steps represent the Home Teaching Process, and the cycle is repeated at each home visit. Sometimes intermediate and/or additional steps are necessary to the parent teaching process. Parents differ, and it is as important to individualize the teaching process for them as it is for their children. Parents have successfully participated in the project who are themselves retarded (activity charts are not used; however, the parents still record utilizing adaptations in the charting system). Babysitters and other caretakers have

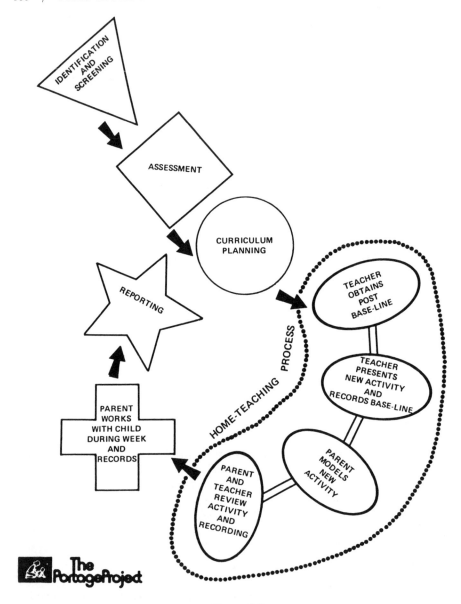

Figure 5-3

The Portage Model: The Home Teaching Process. (From *Portage Guide to Early Education,* revised edition, by S. Bluma, M. Shearer, A. Frohman, & J. Hilliard. Portage, Wisc.: Cooperative Educational Service Agency 12, 1976. Copyright 1976 by Cooperative Service Agency 12. Reprinted by permission.)

taught children, and the children's gains have been significant. Parents who, prior to project involvement, said they had given up trying to teach their children anything have, in fact, taught their children a great deal.

Data Collection and Accountability

Home teachers collect and turn in the activity charts at the end of each week. A weekly progress report lists prescribed behaviors from the previous week, states whether or not the child has attained the criteria for success, and records the prescriptions for the coming week. A behavior log, which details each activity and the data prescribed, is kept for each child. The log provides an ongoing record of every behavior prescribed, each success, and the duration of each prescription. The log also provides a percentage of success achieved by parent, child, and home teacher. The continual input of data allows supervisory personnel and home teachers to spot problems quickly, thus providing a continual feedback system for program monitoring and modification.

PROJECT EVALUATION

The Portage Project has engaged in many types of evaluation because of the types of questions we ask ourselves, and the questions others ask of us have changed as the program has grown and developed. Probably the first areas of interest were the abilities of parents to teach within the Portage Model and the effect these abilities had on the children's growth and development. To answer these questions, activity charts were analyzed, and before-and-after testing was done on the children in the project. It was found that the overall rate of daily recording by the 75 families in the project was 92%, and that an average of 128 prescriptions were written per child during the 8-month program. The children themselves were successful on 91% of the prescriptions. The average IQ of the children in the project was 75, as determined by the Cattell Infant Test (Cattell, 1940) and the Stanford–Binet Intelligence Scale (Terman & Merrill, 1960). The average child gained 13 months in mental age over 8 months.

Further, an experimental study was conducted involving randomly selected children attending local classroom programs for culturally and economically disadvantaged preschool children. The Stanford–Binet Intelligence Scale (Terman & Merrill, 1960), the Cattell Infant Scale (Cattell, 1940), and the Alpern–Boll Developmental Profile (Alpern & Boll, 1972) were given as pretests and post-tests to both groups. In addition, the Gesell Developmental Schedule (Gesell & Amatruda, 1947) was given to both groups as a posttest. Multiple analysis of covariance was used to control for IQ, practice effect, and age. The greater gains made by the Portage Project children in the areas of mental age, IQ, language, academic skills, and socialization skills were statistically significant, as compared to the group receiving classroom instruction (Peniston, 1972).

Using the children as their own controls, test results and behavioral gains were compared and measured. The mean gain in IQ scores on the Alpern–Boll Developmental Profile was 13.5 and was statistically significant beyond the .01 level. The mean gain in IQ scores on the Stanford–Binet Intelligence Scale was 18.3 and was statistically significant beyond the .01 level (M. Shearer & Shearer, 1972).

The Joint Dissemination and Review Panel of the United States Office of Education is responsible for the review of programs that have been developed through funding from the Department of Health, Education and Welfare, or, most recently, the Department of Education. This panel then selects exemplary models for validation and refers these models to individuals or agencies wishing to start programs of their own. In November 1975, the Joint Dissemination and Review Panel unanimously validated the Portage Project after an extensive review.

MAINTENANCE AND GENERALIZATION OF PARENTING SKILLS

In 1974, the Portage Project contracted with the Bureau of Education for the Handicapped (BEH), Research Projects Branch (Grant #G007500664) to conduct a study entitled "Acquisition and Generalization of Teaching and Child Management Behaviors in Parents of Preschool Handicapped Children: A Comparative Study" (see Boyd, 1978). This study attempted to answer two questions:

1. What effect had the Portage Project had upon the acquisition and generalization of child management and teaching behaviors of the parents served, not only in terms of the referred children across non-targeted behaviors, but also to nonreferred siblings?
2. Would a systematic program of strategies designed to increase parents' teaching and behavior management skills significantly improve the acquisition and generalization effects, in comparison with the Portage Project Model current at that time? If such strategies significantly improved these behaviors, the procedures were to be incorporated into the existing Portage Model.

To answer these questions, parent–child interactions in the areas of teaching and child management were analyzed using the antecedent–behavior–consequent (A-B-C) paradigm. Social learning theory simply states that most human behavior is determined by environmental forces. The environment, particularly a child's social environment, shapes and maintains most of the child's behavioral repertoire. When parent–child interactions are analyzed in the teaching and child management domains, it is assumed that the crucial elements controlling the child's behavior are the parental antecedent and consequent events (i.e., those parent behaviors that precede or follow the child's response). For example, the parent's behavior may serve as a significant model (antecedent event) for the child. If the child then imitates this behavior and is reinforced by the parent (consequent event), the probability that the behavior will be repeated is increased. This A-B-C paradigm has proven quite useful in terms of analyzing parent–child interactions and in implementing strategies either to decelerate maladaptive behavior or to accelerate adaptive behavior.

Effective parental antecedent and consequent behaviors were established through pilot study observations of parent–child interactions and a review of relevant research literature. The parental antecedent behaviors evaluated were commands and instructional aids, while the consequent behaviors included reinforcement of appropriate child behavior and correction and negation of incorrect or inappropriate child behavior.

The study was conducted in Portage, Wisconsin, using 48 families with preschool children who had been referred to the Portage Project for attention to their suspected exceptional educational needs as subjects. Forty of the families were subsequently enrolled for treatment, based on screening results that indicated a delay of at least 1 year between the children's chronological ages and functional ages. The families were randomly selected from the initial caseloads of seven home teachers who were participating in the research.

Two treatment groups were formed, one of which received Portage Model services only and the other of which received Portage Model plus Portage Parent Program services (to be defined later). Twenty families participated in each group. Four families within the Portage Model group and nine families in the Portage Parent Program group had at least one other child between 2 and 6 years of age who was observed for generalization of treatment effects. Eight additional families were selected for the nontreatment control group. These families were from among those whose children had been screened for services, but were not eligible because they did not exhibit developmental delays.

Treatment was conducted during 34 weeks for each of the families involved in each treatment group. The Portage Model group received weekly home visits that lasted 1½ hours. During these visits, families were provided with services following the procedures previously outlined for conducting the Portage Model. In this system, the parent serves as a mediator who carries out the instructional program prepared for the child by the home teacher. The responsibility for devising, writing, and evaluating the effectiveness of the instructional activities is primarily that of the home teacher.

The Portage Parent Program group received the services provided with the regular Portage Model, and were additionally exposed to a set of new strategies designed to enhance the acquisition and generalization of parental teaching and child management skills. This set of materials is called the "Portage Parent Program."

During the weekly home visit, the Portage Model of home teaching was followed; however, the teaching and management skills used by the home teacher were gradually and systematically transferred to the parent. The ultimate goal of intervention was to make the parent functionally independent of the home teacher. This was accomplished by emphasizing the parent–child interactions in terms of the A-B-C model. A Parental Behavior Inventory (see Boyd, Stauber, & Bluma, 1977) was used to rate the parent's baseline use of teaching and child management behaviors. Based on the baseline data, home teachers made data-based decisions to individualize a parent training strategy to meet the unique needs of each parent–child dyad. The *Portage Parent Program Instructor's Manual* was employed by the home teacher to develop intervention procedures, which typically were initiated by praising some aspect of the parent's interaction with the child and specifying a specific response that, if eliminated, modified, or acquired, would enhance the parent's skills. The techniques of modeling, prompting, recording behavior, and providing reinforcing or corrective feedback were widely practiced. As the parent mastered targeted skills, new objectives were established.

Each parent was provided with the *Portage Parent Program Parent Readings* (see Boyd *et al.*, 1977), which describe major topics and procedures in teaching and child management, in both the antecedent and consequent components of the A-B-C paradigm. These readings served as a point of departure for discussions between the parent and the home teacher.

In sum, the Portage Parent Program treatment thus utilized the Portage Model as a programmatic base, but sought to expand the use of basic behavioral principles to the parent as well as the child.

Data were collected on the type and frequency of parent–child interactions by trained observers, using a behavioral observation coding system. The behaviors recorded were coded during 10-second interval blocks, with the restriction that each behavior was coded only once during any 10-second interval. Observational data were collected approximately every 2 weeks, and each family was observed between 11 and 13 times. The data collected were analyzed, using a repeated-measures analysis-of-variance design, to determine whether parental antecedents, target children's behavior, and parental consequents changed differentially during the program year as a function of treatment.

The results of the study varied, showing positive effects of both treatment approaches as compared to no treatment, with limited differences between the changes brought about by either of the treatment strategies as compared with the other. In regard to parental antecedents, both treatment groups exhibited an increased percentage of effective instructional antecedents, while the control groups showed no change from baseline to postbaseline performance. Both treatment groups demonstrated significant increases over time on the percentage of appropriate child responses that were reinforced by the parents, while the control group exhibited a slight, nonsignificant increment regarding parental consequents. Treatment-group parents were also found to be more capable than control parents in the use of parental corrections given to incorrect child response, as well as in the percentage of effective corrections (i.e., corrections that resulted in appropriate child response). The children whose families participated in the treatment groups were found to engage in significantly fewer incorrect responses over time than were the children who were members of the nontreatment control group. There was no instance in which the control group outperformed the treatment groups. Generalization of child management and teaching behavior of the parents to nonreferred siblings could not be statistically analyzed, due to the small number of siblings (four in the Portage Model group, and nine in the Portage Parent Program group).

The treatment effects on the two treatment groups indicated the efficacy of both programs—the regular Portage Model and the Portage Parent Program. There was a significant increase in the absolute frequency of parental commands, instructional antecedents, and appropriate child responses during regular home visits, as opposed to the frequency of responses noted during task probe visits when the home teacher was not present. On the probe visits, the parents were asked either to select from the educational materials that the observer brought, or to use their own materials to teach their children something new. The parents were free to use the materials in any way they chose and were given no specific instructions by the observer. Nine visits were made to each family. Three baseline visits were made at ½- to 1-week intervals to assess initial skill level; three midyear visits were made at 6- to 9-week intervals during the school year; and three postbaseline visits were made at approximately 1-week intervals after the end of the school year.

Qualitative improvements were found in relations to several parent and child behaviors: percentage of effective commands, percentage of effective instructional antecedents, percentage of parental reinforcement of appropriate child responses, and percentage of parental corrections of incorrect child responses. The Portage Parent Program parents demonstrated a greater gain in the percentage of effective corrections and a reduction in the percentage of negative feedback following incorrect child response, both during treatment and follow-up.

Immediate treatment effects were evident from baseline to the first three observations. These improvements were generally maintained by both groups across the treatment phase. Generalization of treatment across behaviors from the Parental Behavior Inventory was found for both groups, with the exception of a decrease in both the frequency of all parental antecedents and in the percentage of instructional aid, and a corresponding decrease in the frequency and percentage of inappropriate child response for both treatment groups.

Postbaseline performance was maintained on the 10-week follow-up visit for all parent and child behaviors among both groups, with one exception.

There was a small decrement in the percentage of effective parental correction by the Portage Parent Program group.

The results of the study indicated that both treatment conditions produced superior results on certain parent and child measures, as compared to the control condition. This is attributed to the use of precision teaching and modeling by the home teacher in the Portage Model (Boyd et al., 1977).

The experience gained through this investigation taught us that each parent is truly unique, with differing abilities, skills and needs. We developed great respect for the skills that parents already have, and gained a greater repertoire of techniques that instructors can utilize in working with parents. Parent training is an interactive process in which everyone learns from the other; parent, child, and home teacher (Boyd et al., 1977).

REPLICATION OF THE PORTAGE MODEL

The development and implementation of the Portage Model had been a success. Studies indicated that the delivery system was effective and valid for providing services to handicapped preschoolers and producing positive change in their developmental status. The role of parents as the principal educators of their young children with special needs was established and realized. Despite the excitement and enthusiasm, however, the staff knew that the work had just begun. There were many questions yet to answer. The ensuing years provided the opportunities for the Portage Project to expand into new areas, and for the staff to examine the efficacy of the Portage Model when utilized in varied cultural contexts.

The remainder of this chapter reviews the efforts of the Portage Project in these areas. Wherever pertinent, program characteristics, practical issues, and research findings are discussed to describe any changes made in the project's methodology. Additionally, a systematic staff development system is presented to offer a means of ensuring well-trained and prepared change agents to work with parents. Particular attention is paid to the needs and interests of the parent training practitioners, program administrators, and students of parent training.

Once the effectiveness of the Portage Model had been established, the need to replicate the findings was apparent, if the approach was to have broader applications. In 1972, funding from BEH provided the opportunity to measure the effects of replication. From 1972 to 1974, nine replication sites were established across the country. The replications varied in the preschool populations they served, from children with diagnosed communicative disorders to multiply handicapped or developmentally delayed preschoolers. One replication was based at a Head Start program serving disadvantaged, but primarily normally developing, children. The administrative structures of the replication sites also varied. Public schools operated six of the sites while two were administered by community-based agencies and one by a Head Start program. To determine whether the service would be equally effective in urban as well as rural areas, replications were established in Milwaukee and Atlanta.

At each replication, the administrative and direct service staff was trained in Portage methodology, assessment, curriculum planning, precision teaching, use of the *Portage Guide to Early Education*, making of home visits, and working with parents. Each replication agreed to implement the Portage Model as described and to collaborate on data-gathering activities, and the Portage Project provided technical assistance throughout the program year. Two annual visits served to monitor program implementation, identify problem areas, and to provide training in identified areas of need.

At each of the nine original replication sites, the children were assessed to measure the program's impact on their development. A common measure was obtained across sites through before-and-after applications of the Alpern–Boll Developmental Profile. The results were clear: The gains made by the children at all of the sites were similar to those made by the children in the original Portage study (Weber, Jesien, Shearer, Bluma, Hilliard, Shearer, Schortinghuis, & Boyd, 1975). The developmental gains made by participating children ranged from 1.2 to 1.8 months for each month that they participated in the program.

With the knowledge that the Portage Model could be successfully replicated in both rural and urban locations and in varying administrative structures, Portage Project staff members began providing training and technical assistance to others interested in implementing the model. A recent evaluation was conducted at a public-school-funded replication in Seattle, Washington, during 1980–1981. At this site, 22 multiply handicapped children and their parents received Portage Model services over a 5.6-month period. Developmental gains ranged from 1.3 months to 3.1 months gain per month of participation (D. Shearer & Shearer, 1976).

Table 5-1 summarizes the results of evaluations conducted at four of the Portage replications. Repeatedly, the Portage Model has proved to be an effective means of teaching parents to teach their preschool children.

MODIFICATION
OF THE PORTAGE MODEL

Empirical support for the Portage Project and its Head Start experience with the Milwaukee replication led to funding for the project to provide training and technical assistance to Head Start programs in Federal Region V as a Home Start Training Center. At that time, 1975, the Portage Project assumed operational responsibility for Operation Success in Milwaukee.

This growing involvement with Head Start necessitated modifications to the Portage Model. There were significant differences between Head Start and

Table 5-1

Child Gains in Months on the Alpern–Boll Developmental Profile for Four Portage Project Replications

Replication site/population served	n	Months gained per month in program in five developmental areas				
		Physical	Self-help	Social	Cognitive	Communication
Clinton Early Learning Project, Clinton, Iowa (1973–1974) Multiply handicapped/developmentally disabled	35	1.7	1.8	1.5	2.3	1.4
Project PACE, Dubuque, Iowa (1973–1974) Multiply handicapped/developmentally disabled	30	1.3	1.5	1.3	2.0	1.3
Operation Success, Home-Based Head Start, Milwaukee, Wisconsin (1973–1974) Disadvantaged/normally developing	53	1.4	1.7	1.7	1.9	1.3
Education Service District 121, Seattle, Washington (1980–1981) Multiply handicapped/developmentally disabled	22	2.3	3.1	1.9	2.4	1.3

the programs for the handicapped with which the Portage Project had worked in the past. For example, families enrolled in the Head Start program participate for very different reasons than do parents whose children are enrolled in programs for the handicapped. Their needs and motivations are different. Because Head Start emphasizes the parents in their roles as educators of their children, as changing individuals, and as program policy makers, it became apparent that the parent focus of the Portage Model required elaboration.

Secondly, Head Start responds to the obvious needs not only of the children, but of the total families that comprise its service population. A truly effective program, producing lasting gains, must affect a child's total development. This "total child" approach includes modifying the child's environment by addressing both educational requirements and health, nutritional, and social service care. Previously, the Portage Model had dealt specifically only with educational aspects.

Finally, if gains being made by child and parent alike were to be maintained and generalized, a systematic approach was needed to plan for and provide ongoing opportunities to practice the use of acquired behaviors within the context of the normal daily routine.

In an attempt to respond to all these considerations, the Home Teaching Process of the Portage Model was modified. The modifications permitted each of these aspects to be addressed by relying on clear strengths of the Portage Model: specifically, precision teaching, individualization, learning in the natural environment where the generalized skills are utilized, and full family participation in the teaching–learning process. Figure 5-4 reflects this modified Home Teaching Process.

The Structured Activities section, the first segment of the home visit, is the original Home Teaching Process. It is the critical step in the process of both the child's and the parent's acquiring essential skills. As such, it continued to serve as the principal opportunity to assist parents in their efforts to teach developmental skills to their children. Two additional segments were added: Informal Activities, to address skill maintenance and generalization; and Parental and Family Activities, to expand the parental knowledge base and to develop strategies for identifying and satisfying family needs and concerns. Although these activities were informally incorporated into the original Portage Model, they were neither structured nor planned.

The Informal Activities segment of the home visit occupies the second 30-minute division of the 1½-hour visit. The home teacher preplans Informal Activities to promote the expansion of the skills that both the child and the parent have previously acquired.

Failure to provide experiences that will assist the maintenance and generalization of behavior has been identified as a frequently encountered problem when using behavioral checklists (Harkin, 1977; May & Schortinghuis, 1980). The Portage Project home teacher plans maintenance and generalization

THREE PARTS OF A HOME VISIT

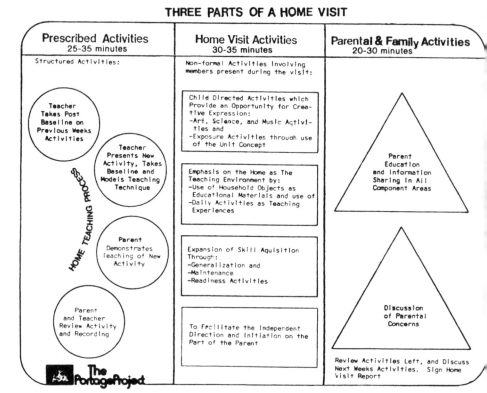

Figure 5-4
Modified Home Teaching Process. (From *Portage Guide to Early Education,* revised edition, by S. Bluma, M. Shearer, A. Frohman, & J. Hilliard. Portage, Wisc.: Cooperative Educational Service Agency 12, 1976. Copyright 1976 by Cooperative Service Agency 12. Reprinted by permission.)

opportunities for the child by reviewing the child's *Portage Guide to Early Education* checklist.

Skills that have been recently acquired are then targeted for maintenance or generalization. Activities are prepared that will set the occasion for expanding the child's use of the skill in the desired direction. While specific skills are pinpointed for change, the home teacher designs the activities to encourage the child's initiation, while limiting the adult's direction. Discriminations are strengthened by the consequences planned into the activity or by the nature of the materials provided. While the child is executing an activity, care is taken to reinforce the child's attempts to use skills in novel situations, with new materials, or in original combinations. Thus, a child who is not familiar with playground equipment, but has acquired such motor skills as hopping on one foot, jumping over obstacles, climbing, and so on, may be taken to a park where he or she can put these skills into use with the equipment. Subsequent visits to the park would provide opportunities for further expansion of the use of these and other newly acquired skills.

Maintenance and generalization of the skills acquired by the parent are, of course, as essential as the maintenance and generalization of those acquired by the child. Training the parent during the Structured Activities section in parenting and teaching skills prepares the parent for the transfer of those skills to parent–child interactions that occur spontaneously. Rather than assuming that this transfer actually is taking place, the home teacher takes a proactive position. The Informal Activities are planned to resemble normal, routine activities, and they emphasize the home as a teaching and learning environment. When the parent has demonstrated consistent success in using a skill in a structured setting, the home teacher models the use of that skill in the informal activities and reinforces the parent's generalized use of the skill. Under these conditions, the likelihood increases that the skills will be more readily transferred to other, similar situations. A frequently targeted child management skill is the use of procedures for correcting a child's error and noncompliance. Parents often respond to child error with punishing remarks that do little to keep the child from repeating the error. To assist a parent in acquiring skill in the use of correction procedures, the home teacher demonstrates positive ways of correcting the child's errors while working on structured tasks, thus reinforcing the parent's use of the technique. The long-range goal of this training is to enable parents to use the technique during general, daily interactions with their children. To aid a parent's generalization of this technique, informal activities are planned, such as cooking experiences, laundry tasks, and neighborhood walks. For the child, the activities provide opportunities to maintain and generalize developmental skills. For the parent, the home teacher reinforces the parent's spontaneous use of correction procedures, or demonstrates the use of the technique when the parent has missed an opportunity.

The final segment of the home visit, Parental and Family Activities, expands the parent's knowledge base in areas that directly or indirectly affect the child and family. Topics addressed include child development, child management, nutrition, health care of the young child, and many others. Topics are selected for discussion on the basis of the parent's expressed interests. The home teacher provides the parent with supportive literature whenever possible, to serve as the focus of the discussion and as a permanent resource. The home teacher and parents plan practical applications of the information. Subsequently, they attempt to include these applications in future home visits so that the knowledge acquired by the parent may be employed for the betterment of the home environment. Home safety, meal planning, and selecting toys for children are among many topics that are discussed and followed up.

This segment of the home visit also allows the parent to discuss concerns that affect the family. Frequently, parents share their frustrations and needs with the home teacher, with whom they have developed a strong rapport. Concerns may relate to the needs of the child or to other family members. While home teachers infrequently have the training or expertise to advise the family in all areas, they are in a unique position to assist. Rather than assuming the posture of an expert, the home teacher serves as a resource and advocate to the family. The approach employed is based on a modification of the precision teaching model (Lindsley, 1968), and the home teacher uses the Portage Project Family Action Plan (Figure 5-5) to guide the process.

The home teacher's role in assisting parents is limited to the following steps. When the parent expresses a need or concern, the home teacher encourages the parent to elaborate, thus obtaining a better understanding of the problem as the parent views it. Once the needs are clearly identified, the home teacher and parent list them in precise terms on the Family Action Plan log sheet in order of importance.

The need that has the highest priority is then transferred to the Family Action Plan work sheet. Together, the parent and home teacher list the resources currently available within the family that can be used to assist in resolving the problem. A sequence of steps then is generated that, when undertaken one by one, will gradually satisfy the need. The individual responsible for undertaking each step is also specified. Every attempt is made by the home teacher to have a family member accept each responsibility. A Community Resource Directory provided to each family during program enrollment identifies community agencies that could be of assistance.

For example, a parent may share with the home teacher her concern over her husband's alcohol abuse. Perhaps she has been physically abused and has no money with which to buy food for the children and pay for heat. Through discussion, the parent may indicate that she would like to do something about the alcohol problem eventually, but at the moment she is most concerned with the food and heat emergency. Having these problems addressed is her greatest concern. Together, the parent and home teacher list the resources available within the home that will be useful. These resources might include a telephone for calling assistance agencies, an older child who could seek gainful employment, and a sister living nearby who would be willing to care for the younger children, if necessary. Using the Resource Directory, agencies in the community would be identified that might be able to assist in meeting the urgent needs of the family, until a long-term solution is found.

Finally, the home teacher and the parent discuss their action plan and target the steps that will be accomplished during the week. The home teacher provides assistance as necessary to enable the parent to accomplish the steps independently. This may include role playing the steps with the parent or helping to formulate correspondence. When the home teacher returns for the next home visit, the previous week's plan is reviewed to identify outcomes and assist the parent, if necessary, in planning the course of action for the upcoming week.

FAMILY ACTION PLAN PART II
LOG SHEET

Family's Interests/Needs	Component Area	Priority	Date Initiated	Date Completed
Mrs. Abrams needs emergency assistance with food, fuel, rent.	Social Service	1	11/2	11/6
Mr. Abrams is looking for a job. He's skilled as a lathe operator.	Social Service	2		
Mr. and Mrs. Abrams are concerned with their son, John's, suspected drug use.	Mental Health	3		

The Portage Project

FAMILY ACTION PLAN PART III
PLAN OF ACTION

Component Area Social Services   Objective Family will obtain emergency assistance

Family Resources:

Date Started	Steps	Who	Outcomes	Date Completed
11/2	1. Review Head Start Resource Directory to determine a community resource agency providing immediate emergency food.	Mrs. Abrams	Agency: Catholic Charities	11/2
11/2	2. Call this agency and ask about service hours and qualifications for assistance.	Mrs. Abrams	Provided 2 days worth of groceries.	11/2
11/2	3. Call Dept. of Social Services and arrange interview for Food Stamp Program, also rent and fuel assistance.	Mrs. Abrams	Interview: Nov. 6 10:00 am	11/3

The Portage Project

Figure 5-5

Portage Project Family Action Plan log sheet and work sheet. (From *Portage Guide to Early Education*, revised edition, by S. Bluma, M. Shearer, A. Frohman, & J. Hilliard. Portage, Wisc.: Cooperative Educational Service Agency 12, 1976. Copyright 1976 by Cooperative Service Agency 12. Reprinted by permission.)

113

The Portage Project Family Action Plan permits the home teacher to support the parent when confronted with a concern, while encouraging the parent to look within the family for resources to address the concern. Independence of the family from external systems is the goal.

APPLICATION OF THE PORTAGE MODEL TO DIFFERING CULTURAL CONTEXTS

As the Portage Project developed relationships with agencies in the United States, requests for information began to arrive from other countries as well. The project has responded to requests from over 75 nations. To date, the *Portage Guide To Early Education* has been translated into eight languages and dialects: Spanish, French, Swedish, Japanese, Samoan, Papiamento, Jamaican vernacular, and Haitian Creole. Work is currently under way on other translations, including Chinese, Arabic, and Hebrew. In 1980, representatives of the Asian Federation on Mental Retardation nations voted to adopt the Portage Model for parent training. Each country will translate and adapt the Model to fit its individual needs.

Since 1975, the Portage Project has been actively assisting agencies and governments from around the world in replicating or adapting the Portage methodology in their own countries. Training and technical assistance has been provided to the Wessex Regional Health Authority and the Welsh National School of Medicine in the United Kingdom; the Fundacion de Asistencia para Ninos y Adultos con Retardo Mental in Ecuador; the Peace Corps of the United States serving various Latin American nations; the Centro de Rehabilitacion in the Dominican Republic; and numerous programs in Canada, the Pacific area, and Latin America. The programs developed by the Portage Project for use with these groups have primarily served a preschool-age handicapped population. Others, however, have served disadvantaged but normally developing children. All efforts are based on the parent training emphasis of the Portage Project.

Of the work that has been done in foreign nations, two programs exemplify the efforts involved: the adaptations of the Portage Model in the United Kingdom, and the "Validation of the Portage Model" Project in Peru.

Adaptation of the Portage Model in the United Kingdom

The decade of the 1970s in the United Kingdom was marked with a heightened awareness of the needs of the handicapped. The Department of Health and Social Security (DHSS) began to scrutinize the services that were available to this population, and it reviewed the effectiveness of various approaches to providing responsive quality programs. The availability and benefits of services were inconsistent at best. Early intervention and parent training in the home setting using the Portage Project offered one possible solution to the problems of transportation, shortage of adequate group facilities, and limitations of group parent training (Revill & Blunden, 1977). Further, the use of the Portage Model was seen as a possible remedy for the lack of coordination among services being delivered to families with handicapped children from health, education, and social services agencies (Smith, Kushlick, & Glossop, 1977).

In 1976, two groups in the United Kingdom—the Mental Handicap in Wales Applied Research Unit of South Glamorgan, and the Health Care Evaluation Research Team of Wessex—opted to implement and evaluate a Home Training Service based on the Portage Project. Portage Project trainers provided short, intensive training workshops and consultation to these groups, which set up their programs independently of each other. The service delivery system of each followed the Portage Model precisely, and the *Portage Guide to Early Education* served as the principal curriculum-planning instrument. Specific characteristics and evaluation of each program differed, and the two therefore warrant separate consideration.

Revill and Blunden (1977) reported on the Mental Handicap in Wales Applied Research Unit Portage Service. The service was delivered by two Home Advisors, who were trained nursery nurses. The program was offered to 19 families, all of which accepted the service. During the 6-month pilot phase, 5 of the original 19 withdrew from the program for domestic reasons. The target children ranged in age from 8 months to 4 years. Children were enrolled who scored 78 or less on two or more subtests of the Griffiths Mental Developmental Scale (Griffiths, 1970), who were receiving no more than five half days of nursery or play-school experience per week, and who were born on or after January 1, 1972.

The service was conducted under the auspices of the South Glamorgan Health Authority. Program activities were supervised by two senior clinical psychologists and supported through the collaboration of professionals from a number of agencies, who met with the home advisors periodically to assist in problem solving. The principal research question of the South Glamorgan program was whether preschool developmentally delayed children could be successfully taught new skills, using the Portage Model of service delivery.

A time-series design using the subjects as their own controls (Wolf, Risley, & Mees, 1964) was employed. Baseline was taken during the 2-month period prior to intervention. The results of the study indicated that the program had successfully increased the children's skill acquisition. Of the 306 skills targeted for acquisition, 270 (88.2%) were achieved, typically within 1 week after a skill was targeted. A mean of 9.5 skills listed in the Portage checklist was acquired per month during intervention, as compared with a mean of 3.7 skills per month during baseline. Of particular interest are the findings related to the importance of the activity chart to the rate of skill acquisition. An average of

87.65% of those targeted tasks for which activity charts were left for the parent's use was achieved, contrasted to the average of 11.5% for which no activity chart was presented.

Parental satisfaction with the service also was high. In a survey conducted with all participating families, 75% of the mothers considered that the program was very helpful; 93.7% expressed a desire to continue in the program; and 100% preferred receiving the service in their own home rather than at a local center. Thus, the Portage Project was successfully replicated in South Glamorgan and yielded similar results to the Wisconsin program.

The Wessex Portage Project, reported by Smith *et al.* (1977), was developed similarly to the South Glamorgan program. The Wessex program differed, however, in its focus. Evidence indicated that services were being provided to families with preschool handicapped children through uncoordinated and duplicative programs provided by health, social service, and education agencies. Families generally were dissatisfied, since the services were not helping them to solve the problems they were encountering with their young handicapped children. Thus, the Wessex group was concerned with administrative structure and interagency coordination. Implementing the Portage Project was viewed as a possible means of overcoming the problem. Improved multiagency collaboration and consistent, relevant assistance to parents of handicapped children were the goals.

It was determined that, if the program were to be considered successful, the services would have to be provided by personnel from agencies mandated to serve families with handicapped children; services from all relevant agencies would have to be provided in a coordinated fashion, with one home advisor serving as the contact for a family and provider of multidisciplinary services; personnel training in the system would have to be no longer than 1 week; managers from all agencies would have to be involved in all program-monitoring activities; and child gains would have to be identified, together with reports from parents regarding their satisfaction with the service.

Three full-time staff members were selected as home advisors to provide home-based Portage Services to families for no more than 20 hours per week, or one-half of their working hours. They were supervised by an educational psychologist who had not previously supervised teachers, and they were given technical assistance on an "as-needed" basis by a management team consisting of health, social services, and education professionals. The home advisors and supervisor were provided with an intensive 3-day training session by Portage Project staff members. Subsequently, the service delivery system was based directly on the Portage Project methodology and employed its materials. Home teaching services were provided to 13 families, each with a child who was diagnosed as handicapped. The 13 children ranged in age from 6 months to 4 years 6 months, and were provided services throughout a 6-month intervention period.

The Wessex report concluded that the program had met its objective of providing comprehensive, coordinated services to the families involved. The children enrolled gained an average of 37 new skills over a treatment period of 22 weeks. Measurement of parent satisfaction indicated that the program was considered to be very helpful. All families to whom the service was offered participated. Of the 236 home visits scheduled, only one was missed because the parent was not at home at the scheduled time. Every one of the participating parents reported that they would recommend the service to others and indicated that their confidence in dealing with their children had markedly increased as a result of the program. Smith *et al.* (1977) reported that "the parental responses to this home teaching project are much more favorable than, and qualitatively different to, the responses reported in other English studies of parents of developmentally retarded children who had received home visits from professionals such as health visitors, social workers, educational psychologists, and general practitioners" (p. 8).

Findings related to the organization and coordination of services were likewise favorable. The key interventionist for each family was the home advisor, and effective coordination of services was a reality. No conflicts arose regarding primary responsibility for a family, nor did any agency attempt to pass its responsibility for serving a family on to another group. The various agency program managers reported that they had never received such complete information regarding the work conducted with families prior to this program.

The Portage Model in these two projects in the United Kingdom successfully met the needs of the agencies providing services to families with handicapped children, as well as the needs of the families themselves. This was accomplished using resources that were already available, without the need for establishing others. The outcomes of these programs resulted in the expansion of the home training services into other communities, one of which has successfully replicated the findings of the Revill and Blunden study (1977) in Ceredigion by the Dyfed Health Authority (Revill & Blunden, 1978). In Wessex, the project has become part of the statutory services offered by the local agencies (Pugh, 1981), and a training manual has been developed to assist other agencies in establishing their own programs based on the Portage Project.

"Validation of the Portage Model" Project in Peru

In 1977, the Portage Project agreed to assist Peru's Ministry of Education with the development and implementation of a home-based, parent-focused early education program. The program would abet the government's attempts to provide cost-effective services to the nearly 1 million preschool-age children in that country living in conditions of extreme poverty. As conceived, the program focused on helping parents to promote the physical and psychosocial development of their children. It utilized existing community human resources and operated within the Ministry of Education.

To ensure that the program conformed to the basic tenets of Peru's educational law, members of the Ministry and of the Portage Project formed a program development group. This group developed a program methodology based on the Portage Project's precision teaching system, a curriculum appropriate for both the culture and the program methodology, and a systematic evaluation designed to measure the program's effects and to provide feedback for program modifications (Jesien, Llanos, Bustamante, Alcantara, Palma, Loftin, & Winkler, 1979). Each of these developments exemplify practical considerations for transferring a program methodology to multifarious contexts.

The curriculum designed was a modification of the Peruvian National Initial Education Curriculum, which reflects the social, cultural, and political objectives of the Educational Reform of 1973. The national curriculum consists of three developmental areas: biopsychomotor, which includes fine and gross motor skills, health, hygiene, and personal safety; intellectual, which includes cognitive and language development; and social–emotional, which includes social development and interpersonal relationships, as well as music and folklore appreciation (General Directorate of Initial Education, 1973).

To use this national curriculum with the developmental–prescriptive approach employed by the Portage Project, the objectives in each developmental area of the national curriculum were subdivided and operationalized to represent specific behavioral events. Objectives were evaluated and adopted on the basis of cultural appropriateness, feasibility of implementation given available teaching resources, and compatibility with the General Education Law. Objectives were then sequenced to generate a checklist, which served as an instrument for educational assessment and curriculum planning; it was used by the home teachers and parents to plan an individualized program for each child. The resulting Basic Initial Education Curriculum for Non-Formal Home-Based Programs consists of the developmental checklist, a series of activities suggesting teaching strategies for each skill included in the checklist, and an organizational document that describes the interrelationships of the skills.

The home teachers, who were primarily responsible for the application of the curriculum and the provision of direct services to families, were selected from the study communities by local educational staff and community officials. All of the home teachers were paraprofessionals with little previous experience in working with young children. Urban program teachers averaged a tenth-grade education; rural Andean teachers, a fifth-grade education. To prepare these home teachers to provide home-based services, a 4-week intensive training session was conducted, covering such topics as project methodology, child development, educational assessment, and planning and implementing home visits. Home teachers also met weekly with their supervisors, who monitored their performance and provided ongoing training (Loftin, 1979).

The program served 60 families living in urban squatters' ghettos surrounding the capital city of Lima, and 90 families living in remote rural communities located in the Cuzco region, high in the Peruvian Andes. The methodology for teaching parents during weekly home visits replicated that of the United States Portage Project.

The program operated for 1 year, except during a 2-month interruption caused by a national teachers' strike. All educational programs in the country were closed during this time. The implementation of the program was accompanied by an evaluation of its effects. An experimental–control group, pretest–posttest design was used. The McCarthy Scales of Children's Abilities (McCarthy, 1972) was used to measure developmental changes and general cognitive functioning; a Parent Questionnaire (Llanos & Alcantara, 1977) was developed to measure changes in parent knowledge and practices in regard to child rearing; and the Leiter International Scales of Performance (Leiter, 1969) was used in the rural communities to obtain a nonverbal measure of general cognitive functioning, necessitated by the predominance of Quechua, an unwritten indigenous dialect, as the primary language spoken in the homes. Change scores, generated by subtracting each subject's pretest scores from his or her posttest scores, were utilized to provide a measure of the subject's change over time, as well as independent observations for statistical analyses. Program effects were measured independently for the urban and rural programs.

The findings of the evaluation were generally supportive of the program. Analyses of the data indicated that the intervention had a significant impact on the perceptual–motor and general cognitive development of the children involved in the urban program, and on the verbal and general cognitive development of the children involved in the rural program.

While the differential gains of the experimental children over the control children were not large, generally falling within one-half of one standard deviation, this can be attributed to several factors: contamination of the sample due to kinship ties and geographical proximity of the experimental and control groups; insufficient curricular content related to quantitative and memory skills; and the 2-month interruption of services due to the national teachers' strike previously mentioned.

Measures of parent change varied considerably from the urban to the rural programs. In the urban programs, small but significant changes were found on the total Parent Questionnaire and on the child development and hygiene subtests. No significant changes were found with the rural samples. Thus, the treatment did not have a large impact on parents' knowledge or beliefs in respect to developmental progress and the needs of young children. Nevertheless, the differential gains of the experimental children, together with anecdotal records maintained by program staff members, suggest that the parents had improved as educators of their children.

The evaluation results were not as favorable as had been anticipated. However, the program was well received by the families and the communities, and was effectively installed into the administrative structure of the local, regional, and national educational system. In 1979, the Ministry of Education determined that the adapted Portage parent-focused home-based model was valid for use in Peru as a cost-effective alternative for providing urgently needed services to poverty families in rural and urban communities.

TRAINING PARENT TRAINERS

The major strength of the Portage Project lies in its emphasis on individualized parent training provided in the natural environment. The implication of providing the one-on-one parent training is clear in respect to the personnel resources required: If the home teacher is to plan for and provide adequate training, his or her caseload should be limited to between 10 and 15 families. The cost-effectiveness of providing such training for parents must be questioned if professionally trained home teachers are relied on exclusively. The availability of a sufficient number of such professionals to implement the system on a large scale also raises doubts about the feasibility of this system.

However, when paraprofessionals are considered for employment as home teachers, these issues become less troublesome. Paraprofessionals are recognized as a valuable resource in the field of education. Increasingly, their function is expanding to include planning, conducting, and evaluating educational experiences for diverse groups of learners. Since its inception, the Portage Project has recognized the value of paraprofessionals and has relied on these individuals to provide parent training services.

The term "paraprofessional" has become ambiguous as the role of paraprofessionals in the field has expanded. It is worthwhile to clarify, therefore, that paraprofessionals who have worked as home teachers using the Portage Model have varied considerably in their preparation for the position. Some have been in the process of working toward a baccalaureate degree in early education or special education; others have completed only five years of formal education and have lacked previous work experience.

The value of employing paraprofessionals as home teachers is, of course, relative to the degree of their effectiveness. The positive results of the various evaluations of Portage Project programs lend support to the use of paraprofessionals as change agents. Furthermore, Shortinghuis and Frohman (1974) indicated that paraprofessionals were as effective as their professional counterparts in teaching parents to teach specific behaviors to their children.

In the study, 21 handicapped children and their parents were served by paraprofessionals and 16 by professionals. The paraprofessionals involved in the study had all completed high school, but none had more than 1 year of college. All had previously worked with children in structured group situations. The professional home teachers had a minimum of a bachelor's degree in special education or a related area. Prior to working with the parents and children, all home teachers attended a 1-week preservice training session intended to provide an orientation to the project and its goals, educational assessment techniques, and precision teaching and behavior modification techniques.

Two measures were selected for study: child gains made on the communication and academic subtests of the Alpern–Boll Developmental Profile. The investigators found that there was no significant difference between the communication gains made by children who were served by paraprofessional home teachers and the gains made by those served by professional home teachers. However, a significant difference in favor of the paraprofessionals was found on the academic subtest. The study concluded that paraprofessionals can successfully provide quality parent training services when provided with an intensive training experience in a data-based precision teaching program.

Our work with paraprofessional and professional home teachers has indicated that certain conditions enhance the home teacher's effectiveness in training parents to teach their preschoolers. Access to a professional resource staff on an "as-needed" basis is essential, since the home teacher frequently encounters parents and children with a wide variety of needs. Often a home teacher lacks adequate educational preparation to assist with the diversity of these needs. The resource staff ensures that the home teacher's needs are met by assisting with family referrals or accompanying the home teacher on a home visit to provide technical assistance.

Another favorable condition for home teacher effectiveness is ongoing observation and supervision of performance. Due to the autonomous nature of the home teacher's position, it is difficult to view his or her performance objectively unless he or she is accompanied periodically on home visits. Routine supervision visits made by direct supervisors or peers can help the home teacher to identify techniques that are being successfully employed and, at the same time, to pinpoint problems.

Weekly staff meetings of all home teachers are also conducive to home teaching effectiveness. These staff meetings provide an opportunity to share ideas, resources, and problems. Discussing the problem with a peer frequently generates ideas for resolving it without further assistance. These meetings also allow for the program supervisor to provide ongoing training of the entire staff, based on the needs identified through the in-home observations of the home teachers.

To ensure that these conditions are met, a staff development model has been developed (Loftin, 1979). The steps in this model, represented in Figure 5-6, offer a system to ensure that each home teacher receives the individualized and group training experiences that will improve both planning and executing home visits, without interrupting services to the families served.

All home teachers receive a short, intensive preservice training session at the beginning of the program year and then begin their field experience. After

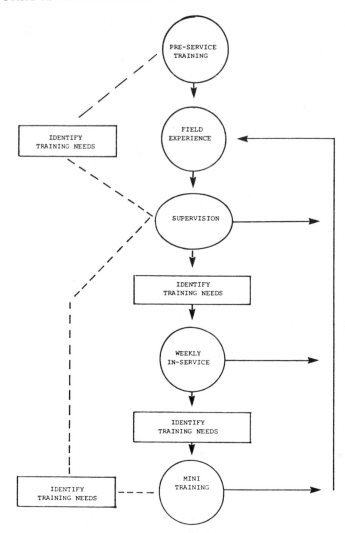

Figure 5-6

A model for staff development. (From *Initial Education Non-Formal Home-Based Program Training Manual* by C. R. Loftin. Portage, Wisc.: Cooperative Educational Service Agency 12, 1979. Copyright 1979 by Cooperative Service Agency 12. Reprinted by permission.)

1 month of service, each home teacher's performance is monitored by the home-based supervisor. The supervisor reviews the documentation generated by the home teacher during the month and accompanies the home teacher on a home visit. Following the visit, the supervisor records all observations and within 1 week meets for an individual conference with the home teacher. Together, they discuss the observations, establish two performance objectives for the home teacher to work on during the upcoming month, and formulate a plan for meeting the objectives.

The supervision process is repeated each month with each home teacher. Clearly, the supervisor observes but a small sampling of the home teacher's performance. Nevertheless, it is sufficient to identify trends, both for individual home teachers and for the entire staff. In this way, training can be tailored to meet the needs of each staff person on either an individual basis, in small groups, or with the entire group together.

Given the necessary support and training based on identified needs of each individual staff member, home teachers can provide good-quality parent training, regardless of their educational histories. Adequate supervision by a qualified professional and accessibility to professional resource services are essential.

FINAL COMMENTS

Home-based parent training is a rapidly expanding field. As more and more programs become interested in implementing a home-based service, it becomes important to identify those components that enhance the success of such programs. This places pressure on all programs, but particularly those viewing themselves as model programs, to be able to define their intervention strategies to evaluate specific components. This must be done at the original site, and it must be put to the test in the field. There are far too many programs in isolated cases or studies that can define their success in terms of child growth, yet are unable to define their intervention strategy clearly enough to allow others to replicate it. No longer does a program need to "sell" the home-based parent training concept; it is widely accepted as an effective, productive, and rewarding service. However, simply providing such a program is not the mysterious end-all in education. It simply implies that teaching is taking place in the home and that it is being done by the parent. It is time to take a critical look at what makes a successful home-based parent training program. Initiating a home-based parent training program does not ensure that parents will be active and effective, nor does it ensure that the children will benefit.

There are many reasons why the Portage Model has met with a high degree of success, both at the original site and at its replications:

1. It is community-based and uses community resources to provide the expertise lacking within the staff structure.

2. It is affordable, since in order to replicate the Portage Model, a program does not need a large resource staff.
3. The parents, who are already their children's natural reinforcing agents, are provided with the skills necessary to teach new behaviors effectively and to modify inappropriate behaviors that interfere with learning.
4. It follows a highly structured approach that is complex in design, yet simple in its implementation.
5. It follows a specific sequence that insures objective planning, a specific teaching process, and a built-in ongoing evaluation procedure.
6. It uses a curriculum that reflects the project's basic philosophy and practices.
7. It allows for individualized instruction because of the application of the precision teaching approach, and because the teaching takes place in the home.
8. It is easy to staff, since it has been demonstrated that paraprofessionals, with proper resources and supervision, can conduct the approach as effectively as professionals can.
9. It is cost-effective.

We have learned a great deal from the Portage experience and from our many fruitful and constructive relationships with other programs and parents. But, as educators, the greatest lesson we have learned as we have developed an early childhood education program is this: A program cannot work with children and parents and ignore the needs of the family. We have learned that unmet family needs not only inhibit a child's learning, but also must be addressed for the betterment of the entire family. As we enter the era of parent training, we need to be reminded of this lesson. It is easy to teach parents to teach their own children. The task at hand is to develop systems that will help families develop an enriching and stimulating environment that will ensure child growth and development—not in spite of the family dynamics, but because of them.

References

Alpern, G., & Boll, T. *Developmental Profile.* Indianapolis: Psychological Development Publications, 1972.

Bluma, S., Shearer, M., Frohman, A., & Hilliard, J. *Portage guide to early education* (Rev. ed.). Portage, Wisc.: Cooperative Educational Service Agency 12, 1976.

Boyd, R. *Final report—Acquisition and generalization of teaching and child management behaviors in parents of handicapped children: A comparative study.* Portage, Wisc.: Cooperative Educational Service Agency 12, 1978.

Boyd, R., Stauber, K., & Bluma, S. *Portage Parent Program.* Portage, Wisc.: Cooperative Educational Service Agency 12, 1977.

Cattell, P. *The measurement of intelligence in infants and young children.* New York: Psychological Corporation, 1940.

Fredricks, H. D., Baldwin, V., & Grove, D. A home-center based parent training model. In J. Grim (Ed.), *Training parents to teach: Four models.* Chapel Hill, N.C.: Technical Assistance Development Systems, 1974.

General Directorate of Initial Education. *El curricular básica de educación inicial.* Lima, Peru: The Ministry of Education, 1973.

Gesell, A. L., & Amatruda, C. S. *Developmental diagnosis* (2nd ed.). New York: Hoeber, 1947.

Gilmer, B., Miller, J. O., & Gray, S. W. The early training project for disadvantaged children: A report after five years. *Monographs of the Society for Research in Child Development,* 1968, *33* (Serial No. 120).

Griffiths, R. *The abilities of young children.* London: University of London Press, 1970.

Harkin, C. Educational assessment. In L. Cross & K. W. Goin (Eds.), *Identifying handicapped children.* New York: Walker & Company, 1977.

Hayden, A. H. A center-based parent training model. In J. Grim (Ed.), *Training parents to teach: Four models.* Chapel Hill, N.C.: Technical Assistance Development Systems, 1974.

Jesien, G., Llanos, M., Bustamante, G., Alcantara, M., Palma, S., Loftin, C., & Winkler, D. *Project "Validation of the Portage Model": Final report.* Portage, Wisc.: Cooperative Educational Service Agency 12, 1979.

Leiter, R. G. *The Leiter International Performance Scale.* Chicago: Stoelting, 1969.

Lillie, D. Dimensions in parent programs: An overview. In J. Grim (Ed.), *Training parents to teach: Four models.* Chapel Hill, N.C.: Technical Assistance Development Systems, 1974.

Lindsley, O. R. *Training parents and teachers to precisely manage children's behavior.* Paper presented at the C. S. Mott Foundation Children's Health Center, 1968.

Llanos, M., & Alcantara, M. *Cuestionario para padres.* Portage, Wisc.: Cooperative Educational Service Agency 12, 1977.

Loftin, C. R. *Initial education non-formal home-based program training manual.* Portage, Wisc.: Cooperative Educational Service Agency 12, 1979.

May, E., & Schortinghuis, N. *Ten problems frequently encountered when using behavioral checklists.* Wisconsin Department of Public Instruction Summer Memorandum, 1980.

McCarthy, D. *McCarthy Scales of Children's Abilities.* New York: Psychological Corporation, 1972.

Peniston, E. *An evaluation of the Portage Project.* Portage, Wisc.: Cooperative Educational Service Agency 12, 1972.

Pugh, G. *Parents as partners.* London: National Children's Bureau, 1981.

Revill, S., & Blunden, R. *Home training of pre-school children with developmental delay. Report of the development and evaluation of the Portage service in South Glamorgan.* Research report, University of Wales, Welsh National School of Medicine, 1977.

Revill, S., & Blunden, R. *Home training of pre-school children with developmental delay. Report of the development and evaluation of the replication of the Portage service in Ceredigian Health District, Dyfed.* Research report, University of Wales, Welsh National School of Medicine, 1978.

Schortinghuis, N., & Frohman, A. A comparison of paraprofessional and professional success with preschool children. *Journal of Learning Disabilities,* 1974, *17,* 245-247.

Shearer, D. *Staff training manual.* Portage, Wisc.: Cooperative Educational Service Agency 12, 1970.

Shearer, D., & Shearer, M. The Portage Project: A model for early childhood intervention. In T. Tjossem (Ed.), *Intervention strategies for high-risk infants and young children.* Baltimore: University Park Press, 1976.

Shearer, M., & Shearer, D. The Portage Project: A model for early childhood education. *Exceptional Children,* 1972, *36,* 172-178.

Smith, J., Kushlick, A., & Glossop, C. *The Wessex Portage Project: A home teaching service for families with a pre-school mentally handicapped child.* Research Report No. 125, University of Southampton, 1977.

Terman, L., & Merrill, M. *Stanford–Binet Intelligence Scale*. Boston: Houghton Mifflin, 1960.

Weber, S. J., Jesien, G. S., Shearer, D. E., Bluma, S. M., Hilliard, J. M., Shearer, M. S., Schortinghuis, N. E., & Boyd, R. D. *The Portage guide to home teaching*. Portage, Wisc.: Cooperative Educational Service Agency 12, 1975.

Wolf, M., Risley, T., & Mees, H. Application of operant conditioning to the behavior problems of an autistic child. *Behaviour Research and Therapy*, 1964, *1*, 305–312.

CONTINUING EDUCATION FOR PARENTS OF INFANTS AND TODDLERS

Edward R. Christophersen
University of Kansas Medical Center

Harriet H. Barrish
I. Jay Barrish
Shawnee Mission Medical Center
and private practice, Shawnee Mission, Kansas

Miki R. Christophersen
Shawnee Mission Medical Center

In the United States, pediatricians have long been responsible for maintaining the health and welfare of the children for whom they provide care. The pediatrician is expected to provide well-child care, as well as to manage routine acute illnesses (e.g., ear infections) and chronic diseases (e.g., asthma). Most of the time that a physician spends for training in pediatrics (cf. The Task Force on Pediatric Education, 1978) is in subspecialty clinics learning to manage sick newborns, cancer in children, upper respiratory infections, and the like. Relatively little of a pediatrician's formal training is in well-child care, yet one major study showed that approximately 50% of the pediatrician's office time is spent providing well-child care (Bergman, Dassel, & Wedgwood, 1966). Given that the average pediatrician sees 27 patients during each work day that is spent seeing patients, the average patient only spends 13 minutes with the doctor (Bergman *et al.*, 1966).

Reisinger and Bires (1980) found that very little time is spent providing anticipatory guidance to parents. The most time, 97 *seconds*, was spent with parents of children from birth to 5 months of age. Even in the second year of life (12–23 months), only 72 seconds of the visit was spent on anticipatory guidance. In the age range from 13 to 18 years, an average of 7 seconds was devoted to anticipatory guidance. The authors' definition of "anticipatory guidance" includes "feeding, sleeping, safety and accident prevention, growth, immunizations, development, behavior, future medical issues, and sex education" (p. 890).

Obviously, no pediatrician can provide comprehensive coverage of each of these topics during the minute and a half that is currently available. When consideration is also given to the fact that there are an estimated 50 million children in the United States under the age of 16 (cf. The Task Force on Pediatric Education, 1978), the need for someone to provide the anticipatory guidance that is now lacking in pediatric practice is immense.

The remainder of this chapter is devoted to a comprehensive discussion of a program that we developed for the express purpose of providing a forum for anticipatory guidance to parents of young children.

OVERVIEW

Within the limits imposed by a child's developmental status, parents must have two separate but related sets of skills. Some behavioral deficits or behavioral excesses can be changed if the parents possess the appropriate mastery skills. Other behavioral deficits or excesses are age-appropriate and usually cannot be changed; this fact necessitates that the parents either have or acquire appropriate coping skills.

In actual practice, mastery and coping skills are usually utilized conjointly. For example, if a parent is encountering problems at mealtime—such as the child's poking and stalling throughout the entire meal, then begging for snacks over the next 3 hours—the parents need to be taught several different but related skills. They are taught how to manage the actual mealtime situation by setting time limits and refraining from nagging or threatening the child, and then removing the child's plate after the time limit is reached. However, in order for any parent to implement these procedures effectively, he or she must be able to cope with the child's reaction to the newly imposed limits. This relatively simple mealtime example incorporates each of the major components of the Continuing Education Program:

1. The parent must know at what age a child can reasonably be expected to sit with the rest of the family for a meal.
2. The parent must know that limits need to be set and must be specifically taught how to set them.
3. The parent must know that the child initially is not going to like having such limits imposed and must be able to draw on several different

coping skills while waiting for the mealtime behavior problems to subside.

4. The parent must know that a child will not starve to death or be placed in a life-threatening position by virtue of having missed three or more meals in a row.

Each of these component sets of skills is discussed in detail below.

GROWTH AND DEVELOPMENT

Growth and development are introduced to parents of infants and toddlers through a presentation on norms, handouts on normative development and a summary review, group interaction between attending parents and group leader(s), and a question-and-answer period between attending parents and group leader(s). Most new parents have at some time or another been introduced to norms. Some have taken courses in child development; some have anxiously read books or articles on child development; some have heard about norms through friends or relatives; and others have been presented with charts by their child's physician. For most new parents, norms become a very key ingredient in preparing for parenting in a society that may offer little preparation for being a parent. In some instances norms can help signal that further evaluation of a child is advisable, but more commonly norms can easily become discriminative stimuli for parent anxiety, insecurity, guilt, anger, and/or depression. With this realization, it has been helpful to parents to make them more skilled consumers of information regarding their children's development.

Development is introduced as a process of growing, maturing, and learning, and norms are introduced as both a description of development and an estimate of when a behavior might be expected to appear. Information is provided on how norms are calculated and why they are important as a descriptive tool. It is also readily pointed out that many normative charts show what appears to be conflicting information, which often further confuses new parents. A normative range is introduced as being perhaps more realistic and helpful to the new parent.

Emphasis is further placed on the difference between using tables based on controlled studies and using a "parental reading" of children in the neighborhood. Perhaps one of the most frustrating circumstances new parents endure is the realization that most neighborhood children "did it first" or are "already doing it." Many new parents' anxiety level and confidence have been affected by well-meaning neighbors and grandparents or by the parents themselves in, for example, a circumstance in which "everybody's kid" is walking by 12 months and their child is not walking until 14, 15, or 16 months. Norms in this situation, when used intelligently and correctly, can help parents regain a certain perspective on the unique timetable of development for each child. In a situation in which the mother, for example, is very insecure in her new role, such information can be a critical variable in encouraging the continued nurturance the mother is to provide.

After a presentation on norms, handouts on normative development are provided, and the presenter provides an oral summary review. Any one of a number of current normative charts may be selected for presentation. Charts used by a sample of area physicians treating this age group may also be integrated. Of more particular concern is the inclusion of charts that present a normative range for developmental occurrences and those that include a variety of specific but typical behaviors parents will encounter. Some good examples might include "Some Selected Norms in Toddler Development" from *The Toddler Center* (O'Brien, Porterfield, Herbert Jackson, & Risley, 1979). At this time the leader emphasizes that early occurrence of a behavior does not necessarily signal the arrival of a genius, nor does delayed occurrence of a behavior necessarily signal retardation or an error on the part of the parent.

Following the leader's summary review of handouts, parent participants are asked to rearrange chairs into a circle in order to promote group interaction on the topic of norms and child behavior in general. Usually the presentation has prompted many head nods and reactions, suggesting an easy identification with the material presented and with some of the words of caution about norms. Shifting into a group circle facilitates the sharing of many of these identifying comments with other supportive parents. Usually this dialogue offers a natural transition into a question-and-answer period with the leader(s) as primary information giver(s).

In summary, an introduction to growth and development, primarily through norms, acquaints new parents with behaviors of the infant and toddler; perhaps even more importantly, it begins to shape the parents into observers of child behavior. As observers, parents can more skillfully pinpoint problem areas for intervention with behavior management skills. At the same time, they begin to realize that with each stage of development goes a repertoire of child behaviors that must be taken into account when talking about parental expectations for child behavior. Thus, with this kind of information, parents can more successfully identify positive normal developmental behaviors in their children and realize that other parents experience similar problematic behaviors with their children of similar chronological age. While many child behaviors are nonetheless frustrating for the parents, they soon realize that some of the very behaviors of concern are often signals that development is progressing on a normal course. Thus, parents are moved toward a body of information that, together with parent coping skills and applied behavior management skills, will set the stage for parents to cope more positively with child behaviors, to solve problems, and to engage in the parent behaviors necessary for effective parental interventions.

PARENT MASTERY SKILLS

The mastery skills module of the Continuing Education Program has as its rationale the assumption that parents need to have concrete, practical management protocols for commonly encountered behavior problems. These are provided in the form of written handouts that are limited to one or two typed pages. Each handout is composed of an outline detailing specifically what to do and when. The handouts draw heavily upon the existing literature on parent training. The actual handouts are provided elsewhere (Christophersen & Rapoff, 1979), as are the rationales for each handout (Christophersen, 1977).

The handouts presently include the following:

- Dressing Problems
    Teaching Dressing Skills
    Poking and Stalling
- Mealtime Problems
    Not Eating/Stalling
    Behavior Problems
- Bedtime Problems
    Crying at Bedtime
    Getting Out of Bed
- Behavior Problems in Public Places
- Using an Automobile Restraint Seat
- Using an Infant Restraint Seat
- Increasing Attention Span
- Using Time Out for Behavior Problems
- What to Do When Time Out Doesn't Work

Each of the couples attending the classes receives copies of the handouts at the start of the first class. The procedures for using time out are discussed and actually modeled for the parents. The time-out procedure is chosen because discipline is the only area about which virtually every parent is interested and concerned. Also, since several of the other handouts suggest the use of some variation of time out, the actual physical demonstration of the time-out procedures functions as a good starting point. Table 6-1 contains the time-out handout as it is distributed to parents.

After the time-out demonstration and the discussion of discipline, the focus is shifted to automobile safety for infants and children. A film, *Infants and Children in Car Crashes*, from the Insurance Institute for Highway Safety (1980), is shown, and two handouts on auto safety are discussed. As a homework assignment, the parents are asked to apply any of the handouts during the week and return with the questions for the next class on parent coping skills.

Table 6-1
Time-Out Handout Distributed to Parents

Using Time Out for Behavior Problems: Guidelines for Parents[a]

Time out involves placing your child on a chair for a short period of time following the occurrence of an unaceptable behavior. This procedure has been effective in reducing such problem behaviors as tantrums, hitting, biting, failure to follow directions, leaving the yard without permission, and others. Parents have found that time out works better than does spanking, yelling, or threatening their children. It is most appropriate for children from 18 months through 10 years.

A. *Preparations*:
  1. You should purchase a small portable kitchen timer.
  2. A place for time out should be selected. This could be a chair in the hallway, kitchen, or corner of a room. It needs to be a dull place (*not* your child's bedroom) where your child cannot view the television or play with toys. It should *not* be a dark, scary, or dangerous place. The aim is to remove your child to a place where not much is happening, *not* to make your child afraid.
  3. You should discuss with your spouse which behaviors will result in time out. Consistency is very important.

B. *Practicing*:
  1. Before using time out for discipline, you should practice using it with your child at a pleasant time.
  2. Tell your child there are two rules when in time out:
     Rule 1: The timer will start when the child is quiet. Ask your child what would happen if he or she talks or makes noises when in time out. Your child should say that the timer will be reset or something similar. If he or she does not say this, remind him or her of the rule.
     Rule 2: If the child gets off the chair before the timer rings, you will give *one* hard spank and replace him or her in the chair. Ask your child if he or she wants to get off the chair and get one hard spank to learn this rule. Children generally decline this offer.
  3. After explaining the rules and checking out your child's understanding of the rules, go through the steps under "C." Tell your child you are "pretending" this time.
  4. Mention to your child that you will be using this technique instead of spanking, yelling, or threatening. Most kids are pleased to learn this.

C. *Procedure*:
  Step 1: Following an inappropriate behavior, say to the child, "Oh, you . . . [describe what the child did]." For example, "You hit your sister. Go to time out, please." Say this calmly and only once. It is important not to lose your temper or begin nagging. If your child has problems getting to the chair quickly, guide him or her with as little effort as needed. This can range from leading the child part way by the hand to carrying the child to the chair. If you have to carry your child to the chair, be sure to hold him or her facing away from you so he or she doesn't confuse a hug with a trip to time out.
  Step 2: When your child is on the chair and quiet, set the timer for a specific

Table 6-1 (*Continued*)

number of minutes. The rule of thumb is 1 minute for each year of age up to 5 minutes. A 2-year-old would have 2 minutes; a 3-year-old, 3 minutes; and a 5-year-old, 5 minutes. For children 5 years and above, 5 minutes is the maximum amount of time. If your child makes noises, screams, or cries, reset the timer. Do this *each* time the child makes any noises. If your child gets off the chair before the time is up, give him or her *one* hard spank on the bottom, replace the child on the chair, and reset the timer. Do this *each* time the child gets off the chair. If these procedures are followed carefully, spanking will rarely be necessary after about 3 days.

Step 3: After your child has been quiet and seated for the required amount of time, the timer will ring. Go to the time-out chair and ask your child if he or she would like to get up. Do not speak from across the room. A nod of the head or a positive or neutral answer is required. Answering in an angry tone of voice or refusing to answer is not acceptable. If your child is still angry, he or she will probably get into trouble again in a short period of time. Should your child answer in an angry tone or refuse to answer, reset the timer. Your child may then answer appropriately, but once the timer is reset it must go to the full amount of time. You are the one who should decide when your child gets off the time-out chair, not your child.

Step 4: As soon as your child is off the time-out chair, you should ask if he or she wishes to repeat the behavior that led him or her there in the first place. For example, "Would you like to hit your sister again so I can put you in time out and then you will learn the rule?" Generally, children say no or shake their heads. You can then say, "I'm happy you don't want to hit your sister." If your child should take you up on this offer and repeat the unacceptable behavior, calmly place him or her in time out. Although this may sound as though you are daring your child to misbehave, it is better if he or she repeats the behavior in your presence. That way, your child will have several opportunities to learn that unacceptable behaviors result in time out.

Step 5: After your child finishes a time-out period, he or she should start with a "clean slate." It is not necessary to discuss, remind, or nag about what the child did wrong. Within 5 minutes after time out, look for and praise good behavior. It would be wise to take your child to a different part of the house and start him or her in a new activity. Remember, "catch 'em being good."

D. *Summary of the Rules*:
   1. *For Parents*:
      • Decide about behaviors you will use time out for ahead of time. Discuss these with your child.
      • Do not leave your child in time out and forget about him or her.
      • Do not nag, scold, or talk to your child when he or she is in time out. *All family members should follow this rule!*
      • Remain calm, particularly when your child is being testy.
   2. *For Children*:
      • Go immediately to time out when you are asked to. Do not argue.
      • Remain quiet and stay on the time-out chair until you are asked to get down. You will spend less time there that way.
      • The timer is not to be touched by any child in the house. If you do touch it, you will be placed in time out.

(*continued*)

Table 6-1 (*Continued*)

3. *Brothers and Sisters:*
   - If you tease, laugh at, or talk with your brother or sister while he or she is in time out, you will be placed on the chair and your brother or sister will get down.

Things to Check When Time Out Doesn't Work[b]

1. Be sure you are not warning your child one (or more) times before sending him or her to the time-out chair. Warnings only teach your child that he or she can misbehave at least once (or more) before you will use time out. Warnings only make things worse, not better.

2. All adults who are responsible for disciplining your child at home should be using the time-out chair. You should agree when and for what behaviors to send your child to time out. (You will want new sitters, visiting friends, and relatives to read and discuss the time-out guidelines.)

3. In order to maximize the effectiveness of time out, you must make the rest of the day ("time in") pleasant for your child. Remember to let your child know when he or she is well behaved ("Catch 'em being good") rather than taking good behavior for granted. Most children would prefer to have you put them in time out than ignore them completely.

4. Your child may say, "Going to the chair doesn't bother me," or "I like time out." Do not fall for this trick. Many children try to convince their parents that time out is fun and therefore not working. You should notice over time that the problem behaviors for which you use time out occur less often. (Time out is not supposed to be a miserable experience.)

5. When you first begin using time out, your child may act as if time out is a "game." He or she may put himself or herself in time out or ask to go to time out. If this happens, give your child what he or she wants—that is, put your child in time out and require that he or she sit quietly for the required amount of time. Your child will soon learn that time out is not a game. Your child may also laugh or giggle when being placed in time out or while in time out. Although this may aggravate you, it is important for you to completely ignore your child when he or she is in time out.

6. You may feel the need to punish your child for doing something inappropriate in the chair (e.g., cursing, spitting). However, it is very important to ignore your child when he or she behaves badly in time out. This will teach your child that such "attention-getting" strategies will *not* work. If your child curses when out of the chair (and it bothers you), be sure to put the child in time out.

7. Television, radio, or a nice view out the window can make time out more tolerable and prolong the length of time your child must stay in the chair by encouraging him or her to talk. Try to minimize such distractions.

8. You must use time out for major as well as minor behavior problems. Parents have a tendency to feel that time out is not enough of a punishment for big things and thereby discipline inconsistently. Consistency is most important for time out to work for big and small problems.

Table 6-1 (*Continued*)

---

9. Be certain that your child is aware of the rules that, if broken, result in time out. Frequently, parents will establish a new rule (e.g., "Don't touch the new stereo") without telling their children. When their children break the rule they do not understand why they are being put in time out.

10. Review the time-out guidelines to make certain you are following the recommendations. If your child is getting off the chair frequently, be sure to give one swat on the bottom and place your child back on the chair without talking.

11. When your child is in time out:
    - Do not look at him or her.
    - Do not talk to him or her.
    - Do not talk about him or her.
    - Do not act angry.
    - Do not stay in the room if possible.
    - Do remain calm.
    - Do follow the written guidelines.
    - Do find something to do (read magazine, watch television, listen to the stereo, phone someone or your therapist) when your child is crying and talking loudly in time out.

Note. From *Little People: Guidelines for Common Sense Child Rearing* (2nd ed.) by E. R. Christophersen. Lawrence, Kans.: H & H Enterprises, 1982. Copyright 1982 by Edward R. Christophersen. Reprinted by permission.

[a]Copyright 1977 by Edward R. Christophersen, Michael A. Rapoff, and Raoul Berman, Department of Pediatrics, University of Kansas Medical Center. Reprinted by permission.

[b]Copyright 1981 by Edward R. Christophersen, Jack W. Finney, Deborah Sosland Edelman, and Michael A. Rapoff, Department of Pediatrics, University of Kansas Medical Center. Reprinted by permission.

PARENT COPING SKILLS

The coping skills class of the Continuing Education Program has as its rationale the assumption that parents would profit from having better coping skills specific to predictable situations that often arise between the newborn period and 2 years of age. Thus, parents are taught not only how to respond to their children instructionally, but also how to manage their own emotional and behavioral responses better. The primary model utilized for coping skills training is a cognitive–behavioral model. This model emphasizes specific cognitive behavior that either assists or impedes the parents' ability to implement the specific applied behavioral management skills with their own children. It should be emphasized that in pinpointing cognitive deficits with parents, a situationally specific focus is emphasized, since in the short time allowed for each class it is unrealistic to be elegant in a cognitive sense. Finally, we assume that only by combining applied behavioral and cognitive–behavioral skills will the parents have sufficient skills to manage both their children and themselves.

The class on parent coping skills first presents a basic cognitive–behavioral framework pinpointing how appropriate and inappropriate behavioral and emotional responses are created by appropriate and inappropriate cognitive responses. Specific situations commonly experienced as being difficult coping situations are introduced, and a cognitive–behavioral analysis is undertaken.

Common situations covered with parents of newborns include severe colic that is unresponsive to medical intervention; crying in the middle of the night; feeding and nursing problems; mothers' acting overprotectively toward the newborn and excluding fathers from participating in child care; and parents' leaving their newborn with sitters. Common situations covered with parents of 1- to 2-year-olds include children's resisting being dressed, playing with feces, breaking something, playing with food, taking off clothes after being dressed, clinging to parents when guests are present, interrupting when parents are on the phone, refusing to have their hair washed, throwing public tantrums, and crying when they do not get their way.

Parents are solicited during this phase of the classes for specific problems with which they are having difficulty coping. As coping skills are identified for specific situations, applied behavioral management alternatives are also specified, so that the parent acquires some specific management responses to the situation. It is our assumption that, in many cases, applied behavioral management skills will be better implemented if the parents have better control over their own emotional and behavioral responses.

The primary emotional and behavioral responses pinpointed during the classes are anger, parental self-deprecation, low frustration tolerance, and anxiety. The creation of each of these inappropriate emotional and behavioral responses and their production are discussed generally and then discussed in relation to the specific situations. Emphasized throughout this class is a continuing focus on applying the data presented earlier on normative development to insure realistic expectation setting for both children and parents.

The leaders attempt, during question-and-answer sessions at the end of this and all classes following this class, to attend to both applied behavioral management issues and cognitive–behavioral coping skills issues.

HEALTH AND HOME SAFETY

The health and home safety class of the Continuing Education Program has as its rationale the knowledge, as previously discussed in this chapter, that pediatricians only spend 50% of their office time on well-child care and little time providing anticipatory guidance. It also has as its rationale the assumption that parents are fearful of illness in infants or toddlers, due to lack of experience with sick infants. Therefore, educating parents in the physical health of their infants has three distinct purposes. The first is to lessen the fear of an illness by giving anticipatory guidance until a child's physician or nurse is contacted by phone or observes the child. The second purpose is in the prevention of common health problems, and the third is reinforcement of what the family physician, nurse practitioner, or pediatrician tells parents about the physical care of their children during the first 2 years of life.

As dictated by the American Academy of Pediatrics, the frequency of checkups decreases with increasing age. Although the physician sees the child most often during the first 6 months, a parent's questions or concerns may not coincide with office hours. Parents often call upon relatives, friends, and neighbors first in order to learn about care for their children. Although the parents' intention is good (i.e., to avoid bothering the doctor), the information given may be inaccurate or may conflict with the doctor's recommendation. In the class discussion, communication with the physician is encouraged. Following are some suggestions for facilitating communication:

1. Write out questions on paper.
2. Call during office hours, except in an emergency.
3. Call for the benefit of the child, not the parent.
4. Have paper and pencil by phone in order to write down the orders given.
5. Observe unusual behavior or physical appearance and inform physician about same.
6. Listen to instructions and repeat them.

Parents are also informed of the fact that studies (Haynes, Taylor, & Sackett, 1979) indicate that only half of the orders given by physicians are correctly followed by parents.

The following list names, for the parents, those physical characteristics that must be individually evaluated by the physician:

1. Respiratory problems
2. Vomiting and diarrhea
3. Bowel problems
4. Excessive crying
5. Seizures
6. Temperature
7. Urinary problems
8. Decreased appetite
9. Color
10. Severe accident, poisoning, or acute illness—rush child to Emergency Room

Each characteristic is briefly discussed, and the parents are alerted to those characteristics that may constitute an emergency. Sometimes further teaching is necessitated: For example, in discussing respiratory problems, the normal rate per minute of respirations is given for different children's ages. Parents are then taught by demonstration how to count their children's respirations. Further education is given concerning what parents may do while waiting for the physician to return their phone call: For example, elevating the head of a child with nasal congestion may help relieve the condition.

It is also important for parents to understand that the medications prescribed by the physician may only help alleviate the symptoms; they may not necessarily cure the illness, but may make the child feel better while recuperating. Teaching parents about medications may be hoped to promote compliance with directions and proper administration of medications to children, although studies are being done to verify this fact. The following list gives suggestions for the proper administration of medication during the child's first 2 years.

1. Give no medication unless prescribed by physician.
2. Give the proper dosage. (Check label on medication carefully when removing the container from the shelf. Check label again for proper dosage when filling applicator and check again prior to administering to the child.)
3. Know exactly what medication you have (e.g., Tylenol® drops are a higher concentration per cc than syrup of Tylenol®).
4. Know the purpose and side effects of antibiotics.
5. Never call medication "candy."
6. Know how to administer medication.
7. Never rely on a babysitter to give medication unless absolutely necessary.
8. Discard medications after use or after 1 year.

Dental care for infants and toddlers is also included. Although parents may not have an appointment to see a child's dentist before the age of 3, prevention of dental decay may begin prior to then. The following list includes those items covered on dental care.

1. Dental caries are the most common nutritional disease in childhood.
2. Deciduous teeth are important for development of speech and provide location for permanent teeth.
3. Wash infant's teeth with washcloth during bath.
4. Avoid sweets, especially prior to bedtime, including milk or juices.
5. Never allow your baby to be put to bed with a bottle in his or her mouth.
6. Sucking the thumb or pacifier is normal at this age.
7. Fluoride is important for dental care.
8. If bruised or swollen dark areas on gum line are observed, let doctor or dentist evaluate.

Since we assume that most questions regarding whether to breast-feed or bottle-feed have been dealt with during prenatal classes or by physicians immediately before or after birth, little time is devoted to this subject. Parents are reminded of the "Basic Four" food groups to help them in selecting good diets after a child's physician has allowed solid food to be introduced. Feeding problems are dealt with, though; some of the common ones covered during class include underfeeding, overfeeding, spitting up, and preventing obesity. Parents are instructed that it is just as important for a child to be checked regularly regarding growth and development as it is for the child to be immunized. Weight and measurement charts are given to parents (similar to the ones used in pediatricians' offices) to allow parents to record their babies' growth themselves and perhaps to retain in their baby books.

The information covered in the classes, as previously discussed, is augmented by a discussion about accident prevention in the home and the automobile. A slide presentation and movies are used as teaching aids to demonstrate as many places as possible that accident prevention must be used. It is helpful to have one or more of the psychologists in attendance during this discussion for reference or questions by parents, because child discipline is closely related to accident prevention. For example, questions are typically asked about whether a parent should spank a toddler for running out in the street and whether to spank the hand of a 6-month-old infant for pulling an electric cord. Handouts are also given to the parents regarding dangerous plants and household products around the house.

This class has dealt specifically with the physical health and home safety of the infant or toddler. However, professionals from two distinct areas, namely nursing and psychology, attend every class period; the opportunity for questions relating to either profession is thus readily available at each of the four sessions, and the problem of parents' having to hold questions until another class is eliminated.

PROGRAM ORGANIZATION

We believe the following dimensions to be important to the success of the program.

1. Classes should be offered by a well-known hospital that has a firm commitment to public-information programs.
2. Access to the hospital (suburban location) and parking (free and close to the building) are necessities. Evening classes make attendance of both parents easier.
3. The hospital must have a large commitment to prenatal classes. These provide a mailing list for the class brochure.
4. One of the main sources of referrals should be the hospital staff doctors in pediatrics, family practice, and obstetrics/gynecology. Each of these groups should be approached prior to the first class and their feedback solicited.

5. The classes should *not* be identified with a mental health center, a psychiatry or psychology department, or the like. Most new parents believe, perhaps rightfully so, that mental health professionals deal with people who have "problems," not with normal infants and toddlers.

6. The faculty may be the most important part. In the present program, the faculty members have advanced degrees; they are well known in the community; they are willing to make a sizable commitment to the program; and they have young children of their own. Each of these factors may be important on its own.

   a. The faculty members need to be able to share "war stories" with the parents and be able to admit and talk about mistakes that they have made.

   b. A good sense of humor certainly helps.

   c. The individual practices of the faculty need to be stable, so that there is no conflict of interest (i.e., there is no temptation to refer parents to themselves for individual therapy).

   d. The faculty members need to have a wide variety of training, which allows them to discuss each of the identified areas of parenting.

7. Care may need to be exercised to insure that parents with problem children do not dominate the class discussions. This can be accomplished by referring families with moderate to severe problems to a mental health provider in the community. Such referrals may get a little touchy, but they may be essential to the success of the program.

8. No paid advertising (in the sense of radio ads, newspaper ads, etc.) should be necessary. Public-service announcements, physicians, and prior registrants should provide all of the referrals necessary.

9. The classes must focus on practical discussions of common problems that normal parents face. As such, there are no simple solutions that work with *everybody*. Somehow the faculty members have to convey the message that raising children is a very rewarding experience, but that some of the time the effort required, in terms of time, energy, and patience, is just plain unbelievable.

10. The present classes are offered on four consecutive Tuesday evenings during 8 months of the year, from 7:30 to 9:30 P.M. Local directors of continuing education programs are probably the best source of information on actual class scheduling.

PROGRAM EVALUATION

The Continuing Education Program is now in its second year of operation. During this time, over 150 families have attended the class, including several single mothers and, recently, six couples who are expecting children for the first time. The families have been predominately middle- and upper-middle-class, which is typical for the area that the hospital serves.

The major evaluation efforts have addressed the issue of consumer satisfaction. Generally, the respondents have indicated that the topics covered have been appropriate and that the amount of time devoted to each has been "just about right" on a 5-point Likert scale. Of the respondents who answered the question, "Will you be recommending this class to anyone else?", *all* indicated that they would. When asked for the "strengths" of the classes, the most frequently mentioned was the knowledge and presentation style of the instructors (three of us have PhDs in developmental and child psychology, and one has an RN with specialty training in pediatrics). The most frequently mentioned weakness of the classes was that they were not long enough. Numerous respondents stated that they would like the classes to last longer than the present 8 hours over four sessions—perhaps one or two additional sessions should simply allow more time for questions and answers and for sharing of experiences with the instructors (we, the instructors, are two married couples with a total of five young children).

The written materials that deal with mastery skills have all been previously evaluated, using a workshop format, with over 1000 pediatricians from across most of North America. They have been in daily use in the Pediatric Outpatient Clinic at the University of Kansas Medical Center and in numerous other pediatric groups. The handouts on child passenger safety and on bedtime problems have previously been subjected to an applied behavior analysis evaluation. In both cases, the provider met only once with each of the participants in the study to give them the appropriate handout and discuss briefly its important features. In the study using the child passenger safety handout, which had 1-year follow-up observation data, the parent's compliance with car seat usage was better than anything published in the literature to date (Christophersen & Gyulay, 1981). In the study using the bedtime problem handout, the results were less impressive; nevertheless, half of the participants were able to manage their toddler's bedtime problem effectively with only the provision of the handout and a brief conversation (Rapoff, Christophersen, & Rapoff, 1982). Obviously, using the continuing education format, which allows for repeated contacts as well as open group discussions and question-and-answer periods, the procedures would be expected to be even more effective.

SUGGESTIONS FOR FUTURE RESEARCH

Until such time as pediatrics is able to provide a feasible format of its own, within the context of routine well-child care, for providing the type of anticipatory guidance discussed herein, the Continuing Education Program's design will probably remain the format of choice. As it is presently being offered, the course is economical for the registrants ($25 for 8 hours of instruction vs. the current fee schedule in the Kansas City metropolitan area of \$15 to \$18 for a 15-minute well-child visit), and it is feasible for the instructors, since each instructor is responsible for only one evening per month and is able to net the same amount of money during that evening as he or she would have netted by seeing patients in his or her own office. The participating hospital is interested in continuing with the classes on a permanent basis, and we have been approached by several other hospitals in the area regarding the dissemination of the program to their clientele.

Research that attempts to evaluate the effectiveness of such prevention-type education programs can be categorized into at least two distinctly different types. The first type involves the parents' taking a written quiz before and after the course, over the terms and concepts that are specifically covered during the course. This type of evaluation, however, raises some serious and heretofore unanswerable questions regarding validity. That is, does the fact that parents can answer a written question after taking an educational offering give any indication of changes in their actual behavior with their children? In the absence of reliable observational data on parent–child interaction patterns before and after the class offering, the question of the validity of such paper-and-pencil evaluations cannot be answered.

The second form of evaluation would involve a prospective study with random assignment of parents to a "continuing education" group and a "no continuing education" group. Parent–child interaction data could be gathered at several points in time over a period of years in order to assess what changes might exist between the two groups. Obviously, a project of this size would be a major undertaking, but certainly one worthy of the effort involved.

CONCLUDING REMARKS

The need for the provision of anticipatory guidance for parents, to supplement the well-child care provided by pediatric health care providers, is well documented. Pediatricians have long acknowledged the need to provide anticipatory guidance to parents of infants and toddlers. However, even though parents frequently have questions about their children's development, many busy pediatricians simply find that they do not have the time to provide anticipatory guidance during the course of routine well-child care. The 11 to 13 minutes that pediatricians spend on a well-child visit is just not adequate. To ask the pediatrician to lengthen the amount of time devoted to well-child care may not be an efficient use of time; the similarity of the information that must be imparted to parents is probably more conducive to a group format. In the parenting classes described herein, parents are provided with most of the information that is usually included in discussions about anticipatory guidance. The format allows for group discussion, the sharing of experiences between the group leaders and the parents, and a question-and-answer period. The use of audio–visual aids (slides and a movie) is much better suited to the group format.

The type of information included under the general rubric of "anticipatory guidance" does not require that it be done by a pediatrician. In fact, the pediatric nurse and the developmental psychologist, because of their training, may be better suited for this endeavor. The format described herein has worked well from the perspective of the faculty (ourselves) and of the parents who have registered for the classes.

Acknowledgments

Preparation of this chapter was supported in part by a grant (HD 03144) from the National Institute of Child Health and Human Development to Edward R. Christophersen, Bureau of Child Research, University of Kansas.

References

Bergman, A. B., Dassel, S. W., & Wedgwood, R. J. Time–motion study of practicing pediatricians. *Pediatrics*, 1966, *38*(2), 254–263.

Christophersen, E. R. Children's behavior during automobile rides: Do car seats make a difference? *Pediatrics*, 1977, *60*, 69–74.

Christophersen, E. R. *Little people: Guidelines for common sense child rearing* (2nd ed.). Lawrence, Kans.: H & H Enterprises, 1982.

Christophersen, E. R., & Gyulay, J. E. Parental compliance with car seat usage: A Positive approach with long-term follow-up. *Journal of Pediatric Psychology*, 1981, *6*(3), 301–312.

Christophersen, E. R., & Rapoff, M. A. Behavioral problems in children. In G. M. Scipien, M. U. Barnard, M. A. Chard, J. Howe, & P. J. Phillips (Eds.), *Comprehensive pediatric nursing* (2nd ed.). New York: McGraw-Hill, 1979.

Haynes, R. B., Taylor, D. W., & Sackett, D. L. *Compliance in health care*. Baltimore: Johns Hopkins University Press, 1979.

Insurance Institute for Highway Safety (Producer). *Infants and children in car crashes*. Washington, D. C.: Producer, 1980. (Film)

O'Brien, M., Porterfield, J., Herbert Jackson, E., & Risley, T. R. *The toddler center*. Baltimore: Johns Hopkins University Press, 1979.

Rapoff, M. A., Christophersen, E. R., & Rapoff, K. E. The management of common childhood bedtime problems. *Journal of Pediatric Psychology*, 1982, *7*(2), 179–196.

Reisinger, K. S., & Bires, J. A. Anticipatory guidance in pediatric practice. *Pediatrics*, 1980, *66*(6), 889–892.

The Task Force on Pediatric Education. *The future of pediatric education*. Evanston, Ill.: Author, 1978.

THE TEACHING-FAMILY APPROACH TO TRAINING GROUP-HOME PARENTS
Training Procedures, Validation Research, and Outcome Findings

Curtis J. Braukmann
Kathryn Kirigin Ramp
Drenda M. Tigner
Montrose M. Wolf
University of Kansas

In the developmental research literature, two parenting variables have emerged repeatedly as being related to positive developmental outcomes for teenagers (see Conger, 1977). The first is "consistent guidance" by parents who provide appropriate reasons for their guidance actions. This broad variable encompasses much of what we have come to refer to as "social teaching" (Braukmann, Kirigin, & Wolf, 1980). The second variable often implicated in developmental research is the presence of an "attachment" relationship between parents and children. Slightly recast, this variable could be labeled "developing and main-taining a mutually reinforcing relationship"—a relationship in which the parent mediates important, positive reinforcers for the child, and the child mediates important, positive reinforcers for the parent (Braukmann *et al.*, 1980; Phillips, Phillips, Fixsen, & Wolf, 1974). The correlational literature has suggested that where such teaching and relationship variables are present at some strength, adolescents are more likely to achieve autonomy and self-confidence and to avoid delinquent behavior (Conger, 1977). These are developmental outcomes that are of importance to those of us involved in the Teaching-Family approach to group-home treatment for youths with behavior problems. We have em-phasized teaching and mutually reinforcing relationships in our efforts at creating both a family-style group-home treatment model for delinquent adolescents and a training program to prepare parent-like staff members to operate that treatment model.

We have come to view the two aforementioned parenting variables—teaching and the development of mutually reinforcing relationships—not only as individually important but also as mutually enhancing. In other words, we see that effective, positive teaching can increase the likelihood and strength of a mutually reinforcing relationship, and that such a relationship can increase the opportunities for and effectiveness of teaching. How can teaching enhance a mutually reinforcing relationship? We have found that teenagers value positive teaching behaviors (e.g., reasons, praise) and the adults who use them (Willner, Braukmann, Kirigin, Fixsen, Phillips, & Wolf, 1977). So by using positive teaching behaviors, parents may be directly making themselves more reinforcing, thereby making it easier for their children to like them. We can also see another way in which teaching can enhance relationships. Through effective teaching, parents can influence their children to behave in ways that are preferred by—that is, reinforcing to—the parents, making it easier for the parents to like their children.

Let us now look at the opposite direction of influence: How can a mutually reinforcing relationship enhance teaching? In a highly and mutually reinforcing relationship, the parent has a high reinforcing value. That is, the parent's behaviors can function as significant, differential reinforcers for the child's behavior. The more a parent is associated with significant reinforcement, the more the child is likely to spend time around the parent, to attend to the parent, to try to please the parent, and to imitate the parent (cf. Bandura, 1969; Staats, 1964). Spending time around, attending to, trying to please, and imitating the parent are all child behaviors that make it easier for the parent to teach the child.

An evolving appreciation for the importance of and interplay between teaching and relationship development has been at the heart of the development of the Teaching-Family model. The emphasis in the model on teaching and parent–child relationships is evident in the name, "Teaching-Family," and in the name given to the couples who operate Teaching-Family programs, "teaching-parents."

The Teaching-Family group-home treatment approach was originally developed at the Achievement Place for Boys group home in Lawrence, Kansas. It was designed for work with delinquent teenagers, but now has been adapted for use with autistic children (McClannahan, Krantz, McGee, & MacDuff, in press) and retarded adults (Sherman, Sheldon, Morris, Strouse, & Reese, in press). In a Teaching-Family model program for delinquents, teaching-parents live in a family-style group home in the community with an average of six young people who are between 12 and 17 years of age (Wolf, Phillips, & Fixsen, 1972). Prior to entering the group home, these young people have had repeated contact with the juvenile justice system and have been considered in jeopardy of being removed from the community. The average length of their treatment is 10 months.

The goal of the treatment approach is to provide not only youth-preferred but also effective treatment. Treatment effectiveness is thought to be fostered by the development of mutually rewarding relationships between the teaching-parents and the youths for at least two reasons. First, such relationships are thought to decrease the likelihood of delinquent behavior by increasing the positive reinforcement (e.g., the approval of the teaching-parent) that the youth would be putting at risk through delinquent behavior (Braukmann et al., 1980). Second, such relationships are thought to facilitate the teaching-parents' teaching (see earlier discussion of this point). Teaching by teaching-parents is central to the treatment program. Teaching-parents attempt to teach social, academic, vocational, and self-help skills that are more adaptive alternatives to delinquent behaviors. In their teaching, the teaching-parents use various teaching procedures and a flexible, individualized, token-economy motivational system, along with a self-government system where the youths are involved both in deciding what to teach and in the teaching itself.

The training of teaching-parents to use the Teaching-Family treatment approach and the teaching-parent role itself are the subjects we address next in this chapter. Then we give an account of some of our research, showing three things: Social teaching can change important behaviors of teenagers; we can teach the social teaching behaviors to teaching-parents; and youths like the teaching behaviors. We next present data suggesting that levels of social teaching and mutually reinforcing relationships in group-home programs are related both to youth satisfaction with the programs and to the effectiveness of the programs in controlling delinquent behavior. The latter findings can be seen as validating the Teaching-Family model's emphases on teaching and relationship development. Finally, we present data comparing Teaching-Family homes with comparison homes on measures of their teaching and relationship development and on measures of their effectiveness in controlling delinquency.

THE TEACHING-FAMILY TRAINING APPROACH

Teaching-parents learn the Teaching-Family approach through a year-long, pre- and in-service education sequence composed of skill-focused workshops, ongoing treatment consultation, and systematic performance feedback (Braukmann, Fixsen, Kirigin, Phillips, Phillips, & Wolf, 1975). Training programs based on this sequence are now ongoing at six regional training sites serving over 170 group homes in the United States (see Collins, Maloney, & Collins, 1981). Individuals involved in the training programs are often enrolled for academic credit in a master's program offered through a local university. The ongoing quality control of the training sites and of their member group homes is accomplished through a recently developed national organization, the National Teaching-Family Association. The association has established stringent criteria for the certification of training programs as well as teaching-parents, and monitors each training site and its affiliated group homes annually.

The year-long training sequence in effect at all Teaching-Family sites begins with a 1-week workshop. Prior to attending the workshop, each couple has been selected and hired by those who oversee their group-home program. For example, in the case of community-based programs, a local group-home board of directors will have recruited (often through newspaper advertisements), interviewed, and hired the couple. Selected couples are usually young, energetic people in their 20s and 30s. Often a couple has a child or children of its own. Usually, the husband, wife, or both have had experience in working with youths and have earned bachelor's or master's degrees in the behavioral or social sciences.

The first workshop provides the trainee couples with their first intensive exposure to the Teaching-Family approach. It provides instruction in the requisites for directing and administering a group-home treatment program, including procedures for teaching youths new skills; strategies for relationship building; techniques for motivating youths to learn and to change behavior; steps in developing a self-government system; techniques for working with parents and teachers; guidelines for adhering to ethical and legal criteria; skills for developing positive, professional relationships with community agencies; and skills in organizing and managing the overall program. The various workshop sections are presented by members of the training staff who have been selected for their expertise in the areas covered in their section. The training staff members are often current or former teaching-parents. To enhance their acquisition of many of these skills, trainees read and discuss written materials contained in *The Teaching-Family Handbook* (Phillips *et al.*, 1974) and in other sources, such as the comprehensive *Teaching-Parent Training Manuals* (Braukmann & Blase, 1979). The various workshop sections often include oral instructions and rationales concerning treatment activities and skills; videotaped examples of teaching-parents handling situations appropriately and perhaps, for contrast and discussion, inappropriately; and wherever possible, opportunities to rehearse skills in simulated situations. During skill rehearsals, trainees receive systematic, detailed feedback on their performance. The workshop sections are scheduled so that later sections build on the information and skills learned in earlier sections. Late in the workshop, each trainee couple visits a local Teaching-Family home to observe experienced teaching-parents handling both routine duties and simulated incidents. The trainees then handle similar situations in that home and receive feedback from both the teaching-parents and the youths. (The reader interested in more detail on the first workshop is referred to Willner, Braukmann, Kirigin, & Wolf, 1978, pp. 252–254.)

Following the first workshop, the couples return to their group homes and begin to implement the treatment program. The first 3 months or so constitute the first practicum and evaluation period. During this time trainees receive frequent telephone and periodic on-site consultation by experienced training staff members to provide the trainees with direction, advice, and feedback. At the end of this period, the program's consumers (e.g., the youths, their parents, the group-home board of directors, and personnel from the juvenile court, welfare department, and schools) complete rating scales asking them to indicate their level of satisfaction with the effectiveness and pleasantness of the teaching-parents and their program. In addition to this consumer evaluation, a professional evaluator makes an on-site evaluation of the program. The couple is given detailed feedback on the results of the consumer and professional evaluations, along with suggestions on how they might improve their performance in areas where they received a low rating.

Following this first evaluation, the trainees participate in a second practicum and evaluation period that extends until the end of the year-long training sequence. During this period, consultation continues, and a second evaluation is conducted covering any areas in which the couple received low ratings on the first evaluation. This second evaluation provides feedback to the trainees and the training staff on how well the trainees are correcting any problems. Early in the second practicum and evaluation period, the couple attends a second week-long workshop designed to extend and refine their teaching-parent skills. This advanced workshop provides a more advanced treatment of the various topics first introduced in the first workshop. Also, this workshop is designed to encourage individualized problem solving and the sharing of ideas and experiences by the trainees.

Approximately 12 months after the initial workshop, the first in a series of annual evaluations is conducted. The results of this evaluation are made known not only to the teaching-parents, but also to their board of directors and to the agencies involved in placing the youths in the program and in funding the program (e.g., the juvenile court and the welfare department). The results of this annual evaluation determine whether or not the couple will be certified as teaching-parents. Continued certification is contingent upon high evaluations on subsequent annual evaluations. The annual certification evaluations provide for the ongoing quality control of Teaching-Family model group homes (see Braukmann et al., 1975).

LIFE AS A TEACHING-PARENT

The lives of teaching-parents are full indeed. They daily teach youths interpersonal and self-care skills, assign and check their home maintenance tasks, supervise their meal preparations, counsel them about their problems, instigate and supervise their self-government systems, review their school performance for the day, tutor them during study hours, and engage in recreational activities with them. These activities can be rewarding. Effective teaching-parents can share in the successes of their youths and take pride in their growth. If they enjoy talking and joking with teenagers and helping them with the things that concern them, there are abundant opportunities for such behavior. Of course, the better the couple is at teaching the youths pleasant social skills and at developing positive relationships, the more pleasant the experience is likely to be.

Although there can be deep satisfactions associated with being a teaching-parent, the role is nevertheless an extremely difficult and taxing one. The job often produces fatigue and strain, diminishes private time with one's spouse and personal family, and curtails outside social activities. As one experienced teaching-parent said, "It is not like working at home; it is like living at work." Teaching-parents have full responsibility for their treatment program 7 days a week, 24 hours a day. And the days are filled with demanding professional activities. Teaching-parents must respond to more or less frequent and diverse problem situations, occurring not only at the group home but also in the natural family, at school, and elsewhere in the community. They must interact frequently with many community people, including the youths' parents, the home's board of directors, schoolteachers, and court and welfare agency personnel. The pace and challenges are such that neither teaching-parent can work outside the group home at a second job.

The teaching-parents do have some time during the week when they are not directly interacting with the youths. Usually, the majority of the youths go to school during the day and to their natural homes on the weekend. Also, teaching-parents usually have a half- or full-time assistant who handles some of the routine tasks, and this assistant occasionally can substitute while the teaching-parents take time off. Yet time away from the youths is not always time away from the job. While the youths are in school, teaching-parents need to engage in such activities as planning treatment, contacting agency personnel, scheduling treatment activities, keeping records, counseling parents, visiting teachers, arranging home repairs, planning the budget, planning the menu, and so forth. On those weekends when all the youths happen to be at their natural homes or when the assistant is covering for the teaching-parents, the teaching-parents are still fully responsible for their program, and usually need to be available in case any serious incidents arise.

Given the draining schedule, it is not surprising that for most couples the role is a temporary one. We have worked hard and successfully at securing more adequate salaries for teaching-parents and at obtaining assistants for them. These factors have helped increase the typical tenure to approximately 2 years. Even upon leaving their group homes, many teaching-parents do not leave the Teaching-Family field. A "career ladder" has developed for experienced, successful teaching-parents within the context of the National Teaching-Family Association. Such teaching-parents are finding that they have highly marketable skills as trainers, consultants, and evaluators of other teaching-parents. In fact, several former teaching-parents are now directing new regional training sites that we expect to become certified sponsor sites of the National Teaching-Family Association.

RESEARCH ON THE EFFECTS
AND TRAINING
OF SOCIAL TEACHING BEHAVIORS

In this section and throughout the remainder of this chapter, we describe a number of studies that concern teaching, or more precisely, social teaching (Braukmann et al., 1980). Although the exact definition and specific content of "social teaching" have varied slightly from study to study, the basic elements have remained the same. In each case, "social teaching" has consisted of four behavior classes directed toward the teaching of academic, social, or independent living skills. The first behavior class can be labeled "describing, demonstrating, or explaining what to do or how to do it." This behavior class includes giving specific descriptions, giving examples, and explicitly modeling desired behaviors. As part of their workshop training concerning how and what to teach, teaching-parents are encouraged to be behaviorally specific, to break down complex skills into components, and, wherever possible, to ask the teenagers to help select the behaviors to be taught.

The second component of social teaching is "providing reasons for doing something or for doing it in a certain way." Reasons are characteristic of what Baumrind (1968) has called "democratic, authoritative parenting," a style she contrasts with "authoritarian parenting." Research has shown that acceptance of parental authority has been better where reasons are given (Pikas, 1961), and that modeling of parents and association with parent-approved peers has been more likely where parents have used reasons to explain their demands and decisions (Elder, 1963). Through their training, teaching-parents are encouraged to give "rationales"—that is, reasons that specify the natural consequences of their teenagers' behaviors for the teenagers themselves as well as for others. Teaching-parents are also encouraged to base the rationales they provide on those natural consequences that they have found really matter to a teenager. To facilitate this process, teaching-parents are advised to have the teenager help generate reasons whenever that is feasible.

The third component is "supervising opportunities for practicing behaviors." Such practice is critical for the teaching of skills, because it allows the teaching-parent to help the youth refine and become comfortable with the skills. It also allows the teaching-parent to see whether his or her instructions have been understood. The final component is "providing positive feedback, including praise and token-economy consequences." Teaching-parents are taught that reinforcing appropriate behavior increases the likelihood that such behavior will be repeated. The use of positive feedback in teaching new skills not only increases the likelihood that the skills will be used, but also should help make the teaching interaction a pleasant experience. This is especially important where a youth is asked to participate in a considerable amount of teaching.

The first research studies we describe concern the effectiveness of the social teaching procedures in changing the behavior of youths in Teaching-Family group homes; we present two examples of this effectiveness. The first concerns the teaching of job interview skills to boys at the original Achievement Place group home (Braukmann, Maloney, Fixsen, Phillips, & Wolf, 1974). We attempted to teach the boys to engage in five classes of behavior: making use of appropriate social behaviors, presenting a neat and clean appearance, volunteering favorable information about themselves, maintaining an interested posture, and maintaining eye contact with the interviewer. We did several analyses, but describe only one here. Three boys were asked to participate in simulated interview sessions where measures were taken on each of the five behavior classes. Using a multiple-baseline design, we taught one boy between the fourth and fifth session, one between the sixth and seventh, and one between the eighth and ninth. The social teaching involved describing appropriate interview behaviors, giving reasons for using those behaviors, practicing the behaviors, and giving positive and corrective feedback on the use of the behaviors during the practice. In each case, the boy's performance on the behaviors improved immediately and considerably.

A second example of the effectiveness of the social teaching procedures was a study we conducted to examine the teaching of conversational skills (Minkin, Braukmann, Minkin, Timbers, Timbers, Fixsen, Phillips, & Wolf, 1976). We had identified two conversational behaviors that were reliably associated with ratings of good conversational skills. These behaviors were asking questions and providing positive feedback such as "I agree," or "Interesting," or "I see." These behaviors were taught to four girls from Achievement Place for Girls in Lawrence, Kansas. First, a baseline on each girl's use of the two behavior classes was obtained by asking the girls to engage in conversations with adults they had not met before. Then social teaching was introduced for each girl in multiple-baseline fashion, first on asking questions and then on positive feedback. For both behaviors of all four girls, teaching resulted in considerable, immediate increases. As an aside, we also found increases following teaching in ratings of the girls' conversational skills by 15 adults who viewed them in videotaped conversations. The girls' average rating on a 7-point scale, where 1 was "poor" and 7 was "excellent," was 2.9 pretraining and 4.3 posttraining. The average pretraining rating was below, and the average posttraining rating was between, average conversational ratings by the same judges of two other groups: 20 university females and 20 junior-high females who were the same age as the Achievement Place girls.

In the study described above, as in the case of the job interview study, we had evidence of the effectiveness of the teaching behaviors in changing teenagers' behavior. It needs to be noted that neither study examined the generalization of the trained behaviors across settings or over time. It also should be noted that in both studies the introduction of teaching involved monetary or token-economy contingencies. However, in one of the studies (Braukmann et al., 1974) and in another one not described here (Ford, Christophersen, Fixsen, Phillips, & Wolf, 1973), component analyses revealed that introducing the contingencies without the social teaching resulted in only small, if any, changes in behavior.

At the same time that we were doing studies to demonstrate the effectiveness of the teaching procedures, we were evaluating our effectiveness in training the social teaching procedures to individuals who were in training to become teaching-parents. In one study (Kirigin, Ayala, Braukmann, Brown, Minkin, Fixsen, Phillips, & Wolf, 1975), we compared the pretest and posttest performances of four couples who received instruction in the teaching procedures with the performances of two couples who did not receive such training. The training occurred in the first workshop described above. Training included a lecture describing what the teaching skills were, how they were to be used, and why they were important. Videotaped examples of correct and incorrect teaching were then provided, and trainee discussion was prompted. Then trainees practiced the skills in simulations and received detailed, positive, and corrective feedback. Thus, we used the teaching procedures—that is, description, reasons, practice, and feedback—to train the teaching procedures. The pretests and posttests involved simulations of typical situations that arise in group homes and that provide an opportunity for teaching. Examples of such situations included a report from a school, a poor performance on a home maintenance task, and an unpleasant comment by a youth. Before training, the trained couples were similar in skill level to the untrained couples. However, after training, the trained couples' average performance was twice that of the untrained couples. Thus, it appeared that we could indeed teach the teaching behaviors. However, the transfer of the acquired skills to the group home itself was not examined.

We next describe two additional studies that were quite similar to the one just described, in that they both concerned workshop teaching of teaching behaviors and used simulated situations to test trainees' skill acquisition. The first (P. D. Braukmann, Kirigin, Braukmann, Willner, & Wolf, 1977) focused on the rationale (reason) component of the social teaching procedures. Using a multiple baseline, we found that workshop training resulted in increased use of rationales by each of the 14 trainees. In this study, we also attempted to validate the importance of the rationale component of the teaching procedure. Five group-home girls rated some of the taped simulations of each of the 14 trainees. We found that when a rationale (as opposed to no reason or another type of reason) was used, the girls rated the taped interactions higher on dimensions of how well they liked the interaction, how effective it would have been in helping them change their behavior, and how good the explanation given was. Like the previous study, the rationale study showed that the teaching skills could be taught. In addition, the study indicated that rationales seemed to be viewed positively by group-home youths.

The third workshop training study looked at the effects of workshop training on both social teaching behaviors and other youth-preferred interaction behaviors (Willner *et al.*, 1977). In preliminary research, we found that youths in group homes liked interactions that contained teaching behaviors, as well as other positive behaviors and qualities such as joking, smiling, being enthusiastic, showing concern, and so forth. Since the other positive social behaviors were compatible with, and seemed to us to enhance, the social teaching behaviors, we taught them along with the teaching behaviors. The workshop training resulted in increases in the various trainees' use of the desired behaviors and brought such use into the range seen with experienced, successful teaching-parents. We attempted to validate the importance of the taught behaviors by asking group-home youths to rate randomly sequenced videotapes of pretraining and post-training test interactions and to indicate how much they liked the interactions. Rating increases matched the behavioral increases, validating the youths' preference for the teaching and other positive social behaviors. We were concerned about youth preference because we expected that if youths liked their teaching-parents' behavior, they would be more likely to spend time around them and imitate their behavior—important facilitators of treatment.

RESEARCH ON THE IMPORTANCE OF SOCIAL TEACHING AND RELATIONSHIP DEVELOPMENT

Our research to this point had shown us that teaching could change behavior and that we could teach people to use the teaching behaviors at least in workshop simulations. But we did not have data on the actual use and value of teaching in group homes. Was it being used? Was its use related to youth preference or satisfaction? These questions address the validity of the teaching procedures. Answers to these questions would tell us whether we should be focusing on teaching in training teaching-parents to work with delinquent youths. These are not easy questions to answer. We could not withhold training on the teaching procedures from some teaching-parents in order to introduce it later in an experimental fashion to see whether it helped. This would not be meeting our commitments to the teaching-parents, to the communities that contract with us, or to the youths in the programs. All these expect, and rightly so, that we will provide the best training we can.

Thus we have had to settle for correlational questions and answers. Is the amount of teaching we observe in group homes correlated with youth satisfaction with the program? Is it correlated with the program's effectiveness? To answer these questions preliminarily, we directly observed the teaching behavior of teaching-parents in 14 Teaching-Family group homes (Bedlington, Braukmann, Kirigin, & Wolf, 1979). Concurrently, we interviewed the youths in each home about their satisfaction with their program and their delinquent behavior. In the youth satisfaction interviews, we used the youth satisfaction scales that are used in the consumer evaluation process described in the earlier section on the training program. We found that there was considerable variation in the amount of teaching across homes, and as the amount of teaching increased, so did the satisfaction measures. The correlation was high and significant. The finding that teaching was related to youth satisfaction was compatible with the findings from the previous studies, where youth evaluative ratings of videotaped interactions of trainees increased after training in the teaching behaviors.

In order to see whether teaching also was related to program effectiveness in reducing delinquency, we used a self-report measure of delinquent behavior (Elliott & Voss, 1974). It would perhaps be useful here to say a word about self-report delinquency measures and their alternative, official police and court records. Those of us with a behavioral orientation would prefer to measure important behaviors through direct observation by independent observers using standardized observation formats. This simply is not feasible for the measurement of a person's delinquent behavior or drug use. Delinquency and drug-use measures derived from records kept by the police and juvenile court authorities can be useful, but they are limited. Records are limited because not all offenses are discovered, not all that are discovered are reported, and not all that are reported are recorded (Hindelang, Hirschi, & Weis, 1981). Further, agency policies that affect detection and recording can differ over time and over jurisdiction (Hawkins, Cassidy, Light, & Miller, 1977; LeFleur, 1975). In the self-report strategy, adolescents are asked directly about their illegal activities or use of drugs. The format used by delinquency researchers sometimes has been interviews and sometimes paper-and-pencil questionnaires (Kandel, 1978). Respondents are assured that their responses will remain confidential. Considerable research on a variety of self-report instruments has found them usually to yield impressive test–retest reliabilities and to be internally consistent (Hindelang et al., 1981). The validity of these various self-report instruments also has been examined, and "coefficients in the moderate to strong range" generally have been reported (Hindelang et al., 1981). These validity examinations have involved several techniques, such as comparing youths' self-reports with the reports and ratings of others concerning the youths' behavior (Elliott & Voss, 1974; Gold, 1970; Gould, 1969; Kandel, Kessler, & Margulies, 1978). Validity has most often been demonstrated by comparing self-reports with concurrent checks of official records (Elliot & Voss, 1974; Erickson & Empey, 1963; Farrington, 1973; Hirschi, 1969; Kulik, Stein, & Sarbin, 1968). Of course, the level of offending found in official records has been much lower than that found in self-reports. There are limitations to self-reports, just as there are to official measures. For example, unlike official records, self-report instruments can be dominated by nonserious offenses (Hindelang, Hirschi, & Weis, 1979).

In correlating each home's observed social teaching with the average self-reported delinquency of youths in that home, we found that where teaching was higher, delinquency was lower. The correlation was very high and negative. This relationship is probably due to the fact that amount of observed teaching was related both to the amount of alternative behaviors the youths were learning and to the moment-by-moment guidance and control of the teaching-parents. Thus, the data suggest that teaching is related to both youth satisfaction and delinquency. Because the data are correlational, we can make no causal statements, but the data are suggestive.

To this point, we have seen that social teaching can change behavior; that trainees can be taught to use it at least in simulations immediately following training; and that apparently the amount of it actually used is indicative of a program's effectiveness and its youths' satisfaction. Thus, teaching seems desirable and, under simulated conditions at least, increasable. An obvious further question is this: Does our training, as intended, result in more teaching behavior in the actual group-home setting than would otherwise occur? We have addressed that question using group comparison data, and it looks as though our training may indeed make a difference. But before we describe that research, we leave teaching for a while and return to the concept of reinforcing relationships.

As we make clear at the outset of this chapter, the Teaching-Family approach emphasizes the development of positive, mutually reinforcing relationships. Although such relationships do not lend themselves to the experimenter-controlled introduction and withdrawal necessary for single-subject designs, the role of such relationships could be examined using a correlational strategy. Is there less delinquency in homes with better, more positive relationships? We would expect that to be so, because the more a youth is in a reinforcing relationship with an adult who disapproves a delinquent behavior and who is somewhat likely to detect it, the more reinforcement loss the youth has to risk by being delinquent. Also, because better relationships mean that the teenagers are more likely to be around and to imitate, the teaching of the teaching-parents should be facilitated where there are good relationships.

Because we expected the relationship variable to affect delinquency by increasing the reinforcing value of the teaching-parent, we chose to try to measure the extent to which youths found their teaching-parents reinforcing. It is difficult to get natural observation measures of how much reinforcing value teaching-parents have for their youths; it is not as straightforward a problem as measuring teaching is. We selected two behaviors as indexes of teaching-parent reinforcing value, and while they were by no means unambiguous indexes, they did seem to make some sense. The measures were youths' proximity to teaching-parents and youths' talking to teaching-parents.

It seemed to us that the more that the social behaviors of a teaching-parent functioned as reinforcers for a youth, the more the youth would be likely to engage in behavior producing the reinforcing social behaviors of the teaching-parent. Being close to and talking to a teaching-parent are likely to produce the teaching-parent's social behaviors. To the extent that these social behaviors are reinforcers to the youth, they ought to maintain the youth's being close and talking. It therefore seemed that measures of youths' talking to and proximity to teaching-parents might be crude indexes of teaching-parents' reinforcing value. We did find, by the way, that the proximity measure was highly correlated with a self-report scale of youths' attachment to their teaching-parents (cf. Hirschi, 1969). If, indeed, talking and proximity are related to reinforcing value, then we would expect the measures to be correlated negatively with concurrent delinquent behavior.

We examined the correlation between the talk and proximity measures and self-reported delinquency over eight group homes (from Solnick, Braukmann, Bedlington, Kirigin, & Wolf, 1981). Proximity was defined as being within 3 feet of the teaching-parent. There were high negative and significant correlations between the average delinquency for a program and the amount of talk ($r = -.92$; $p < .01$) and proximity ($r = -.72$; $p < .05$) observed in a program. There were also negative correlations over individual youths, but those correlations were considerably lower ($r = -.28$ and $-.20$, respectively). We attempted to replicate this finding with another eight homes (Solnick, Braukmann, Kirigin Ramp, & Wolf, 1981). We again found high negative and significant correlations across homes and lower negative correlations over youths. To the extent that talk and proximity are indexes of relationship and reinforcing value, we have some evidence here that a mutually reinforcing relationship, like teaching, is negatively related to delinquency.

We would like to digress for a moment to discuss some data on social teaching and mutually reinforcing relationships in natural families of teenagers (P. D. Braukmann, Braukmann, Belden, Kirigin Ramp, & Wolf, 1981). A total of 29 youths were involved in the study. The study utilized a number of self-report measures: a delinquency-for-last-year measure, which was composed of drug-related and non-drug-related offenses; a drug-use questionnaire asking about the last year's use and about abuse at any time; and a repeatedly administered monthly drug use questionnaire asking about both use and abuse the previous month. We correlated the various self-report measures with directly observed teaching in the natural families of the youths. Consistently negative and usually significant correlations were found. The data suggested that teaching was making a difference in natural families as well as in group homes. We also directly observed negative interaction behaviors, which included negative feedback, derogatory remarks, statements of disagreement, and threats of aversive consequences. This measure was in almost every case significantly correlated positively with delinquency and drug use. We think that a high score on the negative behavior measure may reflect an absence of a teaching approach to behavior influence. It may also hinder relationship development. On the other hand, negative behaviors might also be a parental reaction to a child's delinquency or drug use. Thus negative behaviors may be both causes and effects of delinquency and drug use.

In the natural families, we also took measures of proximity and talking. The proximity measure was consistently negatively related to the self-report measures. Although none of the correlations was significant, the correlations were of comparable magnitude to those found over youths in the group-home studies by Solnick and his colleages (Solnick, Braukmann, Bedlington, Kirigin, & Wolf, 1981; Solnick, Braukmann, Belden, Kirigin Ramp, & Wolf, 1981). The talk measures in the natural families were unrelated to the self-report measures. We are not sure why this finding was discrepant with the group-home research.

RESEARCH COMPARING TEACHING-FAMILY AND COMPARISON PROGRAMS

We now return to the group-home context and to the question of whether our training increases the amount of teaching and of reinforcing relationships in our group homes. We have discussed earlier why it would be difficult to withdraw and introduce these variables in a single-subject experimental framework; we have had to settle for group comparisons. We collected observational data in 14 group homes for boys in Kansas (Bedlington, Braukmann, Kirigin Ramp, & Wolf, 1981). Seven of the homes were Teaching-Family homes, and the other seven were matched comparison group homes that implemented various kinds of treatments, generally based on group and individual counseling. The first data we discuss were collected during 1980 on the basis of one round of observations of all the homes. We were making such rounds every 3 months as part of a longitudinal study. We observed that Teaching-Family homes had more teaching, talking, and proximity, and that the differences were significant for all but proximity. A second round of observations was conducted early in 1981, in the same 14 homes. Again, the same differences were seen. These two rounds of data suggest that our training emphases on teaching and relationship development may be making a difference. If the training does produce higher levels of these variables, and if they are indeed functional variables, we would expect there to be less delinquency in the Teaching-Family homes. We turn to the delinquency comparison next.

We have gathered self-reported delinquency data concurrently with the two rounds of observational data just discussed (Kirigin Ramp, Braukmann, & Wolf, 1981). Thus far, we have preliminary data comparing the 3-month pretreatment and first 3-month during-treatment levels of delinquency of the Teaching-Family and comparison programs. We plan to add to our sample and to collect more during-treatment as well as posttreatment data in the months ahead. The self-report instrument we are using for the comparison contains frequency questions about 48 classes of delinquent acts and drug use. In the results thus far, the Teaching-Family youths reported more pretreatment delinquency than the comparison youths, but the differences were not significant. During treatment, however, the Teaching-Family youths reported significantly fewer acts than did the comparison youths. These are encouraging data. But self-reports are only one method of measuring delinquency. Would we see the same during-treatment differences if we used official record data?

While we have not yet collected official court and police data for our current samples, in the past we have compared Kansas Teaching-Family and comparison group homes on official measures (Kirigin, Braukmann, Atwater, & Wolf, 1982). In that study, we looked at the percentages of youths in the two samples involved in recorded offenses. Data were collected on both boys and girls for 1 year prior to group-home entry, for the during-program period, and for the 1-year postprogram period. For both boys and girls, there were no preprogram differences in percentages of youths with offenses. There were, however, during-treatment differences. Significantly fewer Teaching-Family boys and girls had offenses. There were also fewer Teaching-Family youths with offenses posttreatment, but these differences were not significant. In the same study, we looked at the official data in a different way: average number of offenses per year. We found that the Teaching-Family boys had reduced levels of offending during treatment and that the comparison boys had increased levels. The during-treatment differences were significant, but the posttreatment differences were not. The same pattern was evident for the girls. Again, the during-treatment differences were significant. We also found that the Teaching-Family programs were rated significantly higher by their consumers, including the youths in the programs, and that youth ratings correlated positively and inversely with reductions in delinquency during treatment.

Thus far in this section we have seen that Kansas Teaching-Family programs have apparently reduced during-treatment delinquency, whether measured by self-report or by official measures. There is more evidence that the Kansas homes are having such an effect. The data come from an independent evaluation by Richard Jones and his colleagues of Teaching-Family homes associated with three different training sites, including ours in Kansas. While Jones and his colleagues found that Teaching-Family homes were cheaper and more consumer-preferred than comparison homes, he found no overall differences in delinquency between the groups (Jones, Weinrott, & Howard, 1981). However, the independent evaluators gave us court record data that were analyzable by training site at a time when 80% of their total sample was in the study. We looked at the data from the homes associated with the Kansas site and again found that during-treatment offense levels for the Teaching-Family programs were considerably below those of the comparison sample.

It seems to be clear that Teaching-Family homes have more of a during-treatment impact on delinquency and drug use than do other group homes in Kansas. We also have more teaching and perhaps better relationships. We are pleased at such differences, because we attempt to teach teaching-parents to be teachers and to develop mutually rewarding relationships on the assumption that these strategies will help reduce delinquency. Indeed, as we have described in this chapter, we have found that teaching and relationship measures are inversely correlated with delinquency in our group homes and, for teaching, at least, in natural homes. Taken together, the data we have presented suggest that the Teaching-Family treatment approach and our training program have focused on important variables and have seemed to make a difference during treatment, at least in Kansas. We do not yet have a definitive answer about the effect of the model outside Kansas. The Jones *et al.* (1981) study does not fully answer the question for a number of reasons, including the fact of the newness of the two non-Kansas training sites at the time of the Jones *et al.* evaluation; indeed, one of those training programs was not fully implemented and was not supervised by an experienced Teaching-Family person during a considerable portion of the study. Those of us associated with the Teaching-Family approach to training group-home parents look forward to the opportunity of trying to improve our effectiveness further in Kansas as well as at other sites—particularly with regard to the posttreatment period. We are directing our current research efforts toward that end.

References

Bandura, A. *Principles of behavior modification.* New York: Holt, Rinehart & Winston, 1969.

Baumrind, D. Authoritarian versus authoritative control. *Adolescence,* 1968, *3,* 255–272.

Bedlington, M. M., Braukmann, C. J., Kirigin, K. A., & Wolf, M. M. Treatment interactions, delinquency, and youth satisfaction. In C. J. Braukmann (Chair), *Process and outcome research in group-home treatment of delinquents.* Symposium presented at the meeting of the Association for Advancement of Behavior Therapy, San Francisco, 1979.

Bedlington, M. M., Braukmann, C. J., Kirigin Ramp, K., & Wolf, M. M. *Process differences and outcome correlates in Teaching-Family and comparison programs.* Paper presented at the meeting of the American Psychological Association, Los Angeles, 1981.

Braukmann, C. J., & Blase, K. B. (Eds.). *Teaching-parent training manuals* (2 vols.). Lawrence: University of Kansas Printing Service, 1979.

Braukmann, C. J., Fixsen, D. L., Kirigin, K. A., Phillips, E. A., Phillips, E. L., & Wolf, M. M. Achievement Place: The training and certification of teaching-parents. In W. S. Wood (Ed.), *Issues in evaluating behavior modification.* Champaign, Ill.: Research Press, 1975.

Braukmann, C. J., Kirigin, K. A., & Wolf, M. M. Group home treatment research: Social learning and social control perspectives. In T. Hirschi & M. Gottfredson (Eds.), *Understanding crime: Current theory and research.* Beverly Hills, Calif.: Sage, 1980.

Braukmann, C. J., Maloney, D. M., Fixsen, D. L., Phillips, E. L., & Wolf, M. M. An analysis of a selection interview package for pre-delinquents at Achievement Place. *Criminal Justice and Behavior,* 1974, *1,* 30–42.

Braukmann, P. D., Braukmann, C. J., Belden, B. D., Kirigin Ramp, K., & Wolf, M. M. *Natural family interactions and their relationship to drug use and delinquency.* Paper presented at the meeting of the American Psychological Association, Los Angeles, 1981.

Braukmann, P. D., Kirigin, K. A., Braukmann, C. J., Willner, A. G., & Wolf, M. M. *The analysis and training of rationales for child care workers.* Paper presented at the meeting of the American Psychological Association, San Francisco, 1977.

Collins, S. R., Maloney, D. M., & Collins, L. B. (Eds.). *1981 directory of the National Teaching-Family Association.* Boys Town, Neb.: Youth Care Department, 1981.

Conger, J. J. *Adolescence and youth: Psychological development in a changing world.* New York: Harper & Row, 1977.

Elder, G. H., Jr. Parental power legitimation and its effect on the adolescent. *Sociometry,* 1963, *26,* 50–65.

Elliott, D. S., & Voss, H. L. *Delinquency and dropout.* Lexington, Mass.: D.C. Heath, 1974.

Erickson, M. L., & Empey, L. T. Court records, undetected delinquency, and decision making. *Journal of Criminal Law, Crimonology, and Police Science,* 1963, *54,* 456–469.

Farrington, D. Self-reports of deviant behavior: Predictive and stable? *Journal of Criminal Law, Criminology, and Police Science,* 1973, *64,* 99–110.

Ford, D., Christophersen, E., Fixsen, D. L., Phillips, E. L., & Wolf, M. M. *Parent–child interaction in a token economy.* Unpublished manuscript, University of Kansas, 1973.

Gold, M. Undetected delinquent behavior. *Journal of Research in Crime and Delinquency,* 1966, *13,* 127–143.

Gould, L. C. Who defines delinquency: A comparison of self-reported and officially reported indices of delinquency for three racial groups. *Social Problems,* 1969, *16,* 325–336.

Hawkins, J. D., Cassidy, C. H., Light, N. B., & Miller, C. A. Interpreting official records as indicators of recidivism in evaluating delinquency prevention programs. *Criminology,* 1977, *15,* 397–424.

Hindelang, M. J., Hirschi, T., & Weis, J. G. Correlates of delinquency: The illusion of discrepancy between self-report and official measures. *American Sociological Review,* 1979, *44,* 995–1014.

Hindelang, M. J., Hirschi, T., & Weis, J. G. *Measuring delinquency.* Beverly Hills, Calif.: Sage, 1981.

Hirschi, T. *Causes of delinquency.* Berkeley: University of California Press, 1969.

Jones, R. R., Weinrott, M. R., & Howard, J. R. *The national evaluation of the Teaching-Family model* (Final report to the National Institute of Mental Health Center for Studies in Crime and Delinquency). Eugene, Ore.: Evaluation Research Group, 1981.

Kandel, D. B. (Ed.). *Longitudinal research on drug use.* Washington, D.C.: Hemisphere, 1978.

Kandel, D. B., Kessler, R. C., & Margulies, R. Z. Antecedents of adolescent initiation into stages of drug use: A developmental analysis. In D. B. Kandel (Ed.), *Longitudinal research on drug use.* Washington, D.C.: Hemisphere, 1978.

Kirigin, K. A., Ayala, H. E., Braukmann, C. J., Brown, W. G., Fixsen, D. L., Phillips, E. L., & Wolf, M. M. Training teaching-parents: An evaluation of workshop training procedures. In E. Ramp & G. Semb (Eds.), *Behavior analysis: Areas of research and application.* Englewood Cliffs, N.J.: Prentice-Hall, 1975.

Kirigin, K. A., Braukmann, C. J., Atwater, J., & Wolf, M. M. An evaluation of Teaching-Family (Achievement Place) group homes for juvenile offenders. *Journal of Applied Behavior Analysis,* 1982, *15,* 1–16.

Kirigin Ramp, K., Braukmann, C. J., & Wolf, M. M. *Longitudinal outcome study of group homes: New methods and findings.* Paper presented at the meeting of the American Psychological Association, Los Angeles, 1981.

Kulik, J., Stein, K., & Sarbin, T. Disclosure of delinquent behavior under conditions of anonymity and non-anonymity. *Journal of Consulting and Clinical Psychology,* 1968, 375–382.

LeFleur, L. B. Biasing influences on drug arrest records: Implications for deviance research. *American Sociological Review,* 1975, *40,* 88–103.

McClannahan, L. E., Krantz, P. J., McGee, G. G., & MacDuff, G. S. Teaching-Family model for autistic children. In W. P. Christian, G. T. Hannah, & T. J. Glahn (Eds.), *Programming effective human services: Strategies for institutional change and client transition.* New York: Plenum Press, in press.

Minkin, N., Braukmann, C. J., Minkin, B. L., Timbers, G. D., Timbers, B. J., Fixsen, D. L., Phillips, E. L., & Wolf, M. M. The social validation and training of conversational skills. *Journal of Applied Behavior Analysis*, 1976, *9*, 299–331.

Phillips, E. L., Phillips, E. A., Fixsen, D. L., & Wolf, M. M. *The Teaching-Family handbook.* Lawrence: University of Kansas Printing Service, 1974.

Pikas, A. Children's attitudes toward rational versus inhibiting parental authority. *Journal of Abnormal and Social Psychology*, 1961, *62*, 315–321.

Sherman, J. A., Sheldon, J. B., Morris, K., Strouse, M., & Reese, R. M. A community-based residential program for mentally retarded adults: An adaptation of the teaching-family model. In S. C. Paine, T. Bellamy, & B. Wilcox (Eds.), *Human services that work: From innovation to standard practice.* Baltimore: Brooks, in press.

Solnick, J. V., Braukmann, C. J., Bedlington, M. M., Kirigin, K. A., & Wolf, M. M. Parent–youth interaction and delinquency in group homes. *Journal of Abnormal Child Psychology*, 1981, *9*, 107–119.

Solnick, J. V., Braukmann, C. J., Belden, B. D., Kirigin Ramp, K., & Wolf, M. M. *Group-home interactions and their relationship to drug use and delinquency.* Paper presented at the meeting of the American Psychological Association, Los Angeles, 1981.

Staats, A. *Human learning.* New York: Holt, Rinehart & Winston, 1964.

Willner, A. G., Braukmann, C. J., Kirigin, K. A., Fixsen, D. L., Phillips, E. L., & Wolf, M. M. The training and validation of youth-preferred social behaviors with child care personnel. *Journal of Applied Behavior Analysis*, 1977, *10*, 219–230.

Willner, A. G., Braukmann, C. J., Kirigin, K. A., & Wolf, M. M. Achievement Place: A community model for youths in trouble. In D. Marholin (Ed.), *Child behavior therapy.* New York: Gardner Press, 1978.

Wolf, M. M., Phillips, E. L., & Fixsen, D. L. The Teaching-Family: A new model for the treatment of deviant child behavior in the community. In S. W. Bijou & E. L. Ribes-Inesta (Eds.), *Behavior modification.* New York: Academic Press, 1972.

WINNING!
A Systematic, Empirical Approach to Parent Training

Richard F. Dangel
Richard A. Polster
The University of Texas at Arlington

WINNING! is a packaged parent training program designed to help parents solve complex child management problems; to promote child-rearing practices that facilitate healthy child development and rewarding parent–child interactions; to reach single- and two-parent families of 3- to 12-year-olds; and to reflect the concerns of diverse ethnic and socioeconomic populations. This chapter describes the methods used to select program content for WINNING!, as well as the training materials incorporating this content. It presents the conceptual base and an outline of the procedures employed to train parents who participate in WINNING!. Finally, the chapter summarizes several evaluation studies of WINNING!, and concludes with a discussion of issues germane to the development, evaluation, and dissemination of all large-scale parent training programs.

PROGRAM DESCRIPTION

Selecting Program Content

Despite the proliferation of programs, clear procedures for selecting parent training program content do not exist. Horowitz (1976) has cautioned against a focus on picking up socks and making beds, and behavioral programs in the schools have been accused of teaching children to be still, quiet, and docile (Winnet & Winkler, 1972). Nevertheless, program content often reflects only the theoretical biases or personal interests of the developer. To avoid such a narrow perspective, we used two criteria to select content for WINNING!: empirical support and social validity. Evaluating the empirical support for certain content was relatively easy. A thorough literature review produced substantial evidence attesting to the effectiveness of many procedures, largely derived from the laws of behavior, to solve complex parent–child problems (Barrett, 1969; Forehand, Wells, & Griest, 1980; Hawkins, Peterson, Schweid, & Bijou, 1966). Unfortunately, many parent concerns presented frequently in popular child care guides, newspaper advice columns, and television talk shows were neglected. Wolf (1978) argues that one important dimension of any program is its social validity. Socially valid programs have goals that society wants, treatment procedures that are acceptable to consumers, and important outcomes. We wanted to include socially valid content—the content that society wanted. And we wanted to teach parents acceptable parenting methods to use with their children.

Bushell's Project SCALE: School Client's Annual Local Evaluation (Bushell, 1978) provided a model for how we might accomplish these goals. In SCALE, groups of teachers and parents, enlisted through the PTA, constructed hundreds of statements descriptive of school environments. Thirty of these statements, generic to most schools, comprise a core questionnaire. The remaining questions form a pool from which to draw additional statements. Parents rate the importance of each item and how adequately they feel the school addresses the item. A quick tabulation of the results pinpoints major parent and school concerns—objectives for change.

Following Bushell's work, we (Dangel & Polster, 1982b) asked local PTA presidents to identify parents of 3- to 12-year-olds who had shown interest in their children's activities. We contacted 27 parents; nine made the time commitment necessary to serve as members of a Parents' Advisory Council (PAC). Table 8-1 shows demographic characteristics of the PAC members. Cumulatively, they represented 300 years of parenting experience and a diverse cross-section of society.

PAC meetings lasted 2 hours, twice per month. Meetings were recorded on audiotape; members received $10 per meeting to defray mileage and babysitting expenses. At the first meeting, we defined member responsibilities and established meeting guidelines. We asked PAC members, "What skills and knowledge do parents need to be good parents?" Throughout all discussions, we carefully avoided stating personal opinions and limited our input to questions, clarifying statements, and prompts for examples. Answering this simple question quickly consumed over a year's meetings!

The PAC identified nearly 300 topics, including everything from "ways to handle divorce" and "information about homosexuality" to "what to do about poor eating habits." Many of the topics were extremely broad or too personal, so we asked PAC members to help operationalize each topic and then to rank its importance. We constructed a lengthy questionnaire, including each topic as

Table 8-1
Parents' Advisory Council (PAC): Demographic Characteristics

Sex	*Children per family*
Two males	Range: one to five
Seven females	Mean: three
Ethnicity	*Sex of children*
Five whites	13 males
Four blacks	11 females
Age	*Age of children*
Range: 31 to 48 years	2 months to 27 years
Mean: 38 years	
Education	
Range: 10 to 16 years	
Mean: 14 years	

originally stated and two to four clarifying statements. For example, the original statement, "Take each child as he or she comes; share his or her terms," was operationalized to "Parents should not compare children" and "Parents should praise the good things that each child does, even though they may be different for each child." Using a 5-point scale, parents rated all statements on two dimensions: Does this statement say what you meant? and How clearly worded is this statement? Items below the mean were rewritten and rated again. Finally, parents rated all statements on a third dimension: How important is this statement? Items at or above the mean were retained. PAC members reduced the original list of nearly 300 topics to the 37 most important topics, shown in Table 8-2, and the 22 most common child management problems, shown in Table 8-3.

Parents, the experts, defined program content. Their values, experiences, and priorities expressed in this content reflected a broad, diverse, knowledgeable approach to parenting, consistent with at least a large segment of society.

Materials Development

Many PAC concerns addressed similar topics—for example, "Parents should help their children to understand that behavior has consequences" and "Parents should praise the good things their children do." We grouped related items from either list to form a single lesson. In addition, we categorized content as embodying either skills or information. Skill content specified observable behaviors, such as "Spend time talking with your child." Information content identified a body of knowledge, such as "Know the capabilities of children at different ages."

Table 8-2
Most Important Topics as Established by the PAC

Parents should know or do the following:

1. Know how to provide nutritious meals and teach their children healthy eating habits.
2. Teach their children to arrange their activities so that their time is used wisely.
3. Help their children to understand that behavior has consequences.
4. Teach their children that they are responsible for their own behavior.
5. Clarify their own values and be a constant model of those values to their children.
6. Spend time talking with their children.
7. Know their children's teachers.
8. Praise the good things their children do.
9. Encourage their children's physical activity.
10. Know the capabilities of children at different ages.
11. Praise their children for telling the truth.
12. Be cautious of overcriticizing their children.
13. Encourage their children's creative activities, such as drawing pictures or telling stories.
14. Provide children with toys that allow personal expression—for example, clay, finger paints, and building blocks.
15. Share their own interests with their children.
16. Allow their children to make some decisions.
17. Give their children chores.
18. Teach their children to respect the rights and privacy of others.
19. Teach their children to return what they borrow in good condition.
20. Discipline their children for destroying property.
21. Help their children to learn to solve their own problems.
22. Punish bad behavior immediately whenever it occurs.
23. Explain to children why they are being spanked.
24. Use spanking to show their disapproval and not to "get even."
25. Follow through when they say they are going to do something.
26. Use punishment that fits the child—for example, spanking for some, scolding for others.
27. Be aware that they are influenced by their children.
28. Be willing to bend the rules under special circumstances.
29. Teach their children to consider alternatives when their plans do not go as expected.
30. Encourage their children in academic activities.
31. Arrange activities with the elderly for their children.
32. Be supportive and understanding of their children's concerns about death and illness.
33. Teach their children good health habits, such as taking regular baths and brushing their teeth.
34. Arrange for time away from their children.
35. Explain a divorce in terms children can understand.
36. Encourage their children to look for the good in other people.
37. Become familiar with each of their children's likes and dislikes.

Table 8-3
Most Common Child Management Problems as Established by the PAC

1. Does not put away belongings.
2. Does not do household chores.
3. Does not do what parent asks.
4. Does not get along with brothers and sisters.
5. Has difficulty making friends.
6. Has poor health habits—for example, irregular bathing and brushing of teeth.
7. Whines, pouts, or nags.
8. Lies.
9. Steals.
10. Does not get ready for school on time.
11. Does not finish homework.
12. Makes unacceptable grades.
13. Gets in trouble in school.
14. Skips school.
15. Has temper tantrums—for example, yelling, kicking, holding breath.
16. Exhibits nervous habits, such as thumb sucking, nail biting, and so on.
17. Fights with other children.
18. Talks back to adults.
19. Has poor table manners.
20. Wets bed.
21. Exhibits hyperactivity.
22. Uses dirty words.

We developed two types of materials to deliver the content: 14 instructional booklets and 22 color videotape lessons. The instructional booklets cover information content; the videotape lessons cover skill content. Instructional booklets are approximately 1500 words long, illustrated, and written at about an eighth-grade level. Each booklet presents four or five main points, several practical examples, and concrete suggestions. Parents read, and keep for future reference, those booklets of interest to them. Table 8-4 lists the topics included in the instructional booklets.

Each videotape lesson is 14 to 25 minutes long and shows 35 to 50 brief scenes of parent–child interactions. We filmed several thousand scenes in homes, amusement parks, stores, restaurants, swimming pools, and supermarkets, using 300 volunteer "actor" families from various ethnic and socioeconomic backgrounds, and with children ranging in age from 2 to 14 years. When attempting to illustrate complex discriminations, the lesson uses both correct and incorrect examples. Narration focuses attention on specific behaviors. At times, it asks the viewer questions or provides prompts to participate. Lessons end with a summary of key points to remember and a weekly practice assignment.

Table 8-4
WINNING! Instructional Booklets

Lying	Parental Expectations
Stealing	Communication
No Friends	Creativity
Hyperactivity	Values
Negotiation and Contracting	Life Changes
Responsibility	Nutrition
Privacy	Sexual Curiosity

The first eight videotapes comprise the basic lessons; the second 14, advanced lessons. The basic lessons, shown in Table 8-5, each describe a specific skill and build on skills covered in previous lessons. Progress through the basic lessons is linear; parents must view all eight in order. The advanced lessons, shown in Table 8-6, each address a specific child management problem, show how to apply the skills covered in the basic lessons on the problem, and offer several alternative solutions. Parents choose only those advanced lessons that apply to their situations. They may view one, two, or even all 14. Viewing all basic lessons is prerequisite to viewing any of the advanced lessons; however, because the advanced lessons stand independently of one another, they may be viewed in any order.

While we have kept the videotape lessons entertaining, our main purpose has been to develop effective instructional tools, each with specific learning objectives. Never more than one point is introduced without multiple examples; most points are repeated several times with different examples.

Training Procedures

Conceptual Overview

Conceptually, WINNING! differs from other programs in that it employs a *deductive*, rather than an *inductive*, approach to training. In an inductive approach, parents select a particular child behavior problem, such as temper

Table 8-5
WINNING! Basic Lessons

1. Praise and Affection	5. Time Out
2. Rewards and Privileges	6. Removing Rewards and Privileges
3. Suggestive Praise	7. Physical Punishment
4. Ignoring	8. Compliance

Table 8-6
WINNING! Advanced Lessons

Temper Tantrums	Homework
Fighting	School Problems
Arguing and Backtalk	Mealtime
Chores	Bedtime
Annoying Habits	Good Behavior in Public Places
Bedwetting and Soiling	Allowances (Tokens)
Hygiene and Appearance	Home School Report Cards

tantrums, and learn several skills to correct the problem. For example, they may learn first to define and observe the problem, to collect baseline data, and then to apply a specific procedure, such as time out. Ongoing data collection indicates the effectiveness of the procedure. One assumption is that parents will learn from this experience to apply these same procedures to additional problems that they currently have, that may arise in the future, or that exist with other children in the family. The limited data available, however, suggest that generalization requires more than a single example (G. J. Allen, 1973; Stokes, Baer, & Jackson, 1974). Stokes and Baer (1977) recommend teaching several exemplars under different conditions.

In contrast, using a *deductive* approach, WINNING! teaches general skills, without focusing on application of these skills to any specific child problem behavior. For example, in Lesson One, "Praise and Attention," parents learn the general concept that praise can increase the good things their children do. They see parents praising children for everything from completing chores to studying, solving problems, and playing cooperatively. They see mothers and fathers praising, hugging, kissing, touching, and patting children of all ages. Lesson Five, "Time Out," shows parents using time out for problems ranging from fighting and lying to temper outbursts at the dinner table. The use of 40 scenes, all showing applications of the same skill, helps to prevent conclusions such as "That won't work with 7-year-olds," or "My problems are different from everyone else's." Most parents see at least several scenes resembling their situations, and after watching a lesson frequently remark, "My child does that same thing!" Showing a single specific skill used across diverse parents, children, behaviors, and settings is likely to facilitate generalization (Stokes & Baer, 1977).

If parents fail to generalize—that is, if they are unable to apply the skills from the basic lessons to their particular child behavior problems—WINNING!, as noted, offers 14 advanced lessons designed to facilitate generalization. For example, if a parent could not use several of the skills to stop a child's fighting, he or she would watch the advanced lesson, "Fighting." He or she would see 40 to 50 examples of parents applying skills from the basic lessons to the problem of fighting. The advanced lesson would also provide instructions related specifically to stopping fights.

WINNING! first employs a *deductive* training model, teaching general behavior change skills. Presumably, this method helps parents to generalize their new skills across problems, children, and settings. If more precise modeling or directions are needed, WINNING! employs a traditional *inductive* approach.

Training Model Characteristics

In addition to the training materials, WINNING! includes systematic, replicable training procedures. The procedures were originally packaged into a teacher training program, and were extensively field-tested by Hopkins and his colleagues (Dangel, Conard, & Hopkins, 1978; Hopkins & Conard, 1975) at the University of Kansas. More recent work has used the procedures to teach industrial workers the behaviors necessary to avoid dangerous exposures to potential carcinogens (Conard, Hopkins, Fitch, Smith, Anger, & Dangel, 1982). Application of the model with parents represents a systematic replication of this earlier work, and attests to the generalizability of the procedures (Sidman, 1960).

The training model has 11 major characteristics, listed in Table 8-7. These characteristics and the rationale for each are described below:

PROGRAM OBJECTIVES ARE IDENTIFIED BY CONSUMERS OR EMPIRICALLY DERIVED. Wolf (1978), in a seminal article on social validity, convincingly argues for enlisting society to determine the social appropriateness of treatment goals. Although widely accepted procedures for accomplishing this are only now being developed (Kazdin, 1977), the use of a PAC offers one approach. As the applied empirical literature on child management and related areas expands, there can be little excuse for not incorporating significant findings into programs. The Achievement Place research project (Phillips, Phillips, Fixsen, & Wolf, 1975) serves as a model for translating research results into usable programs, and then subjecting these programs to rigorous, comprehensive

Table 8-7
WINNING! Training Model Characteristics

1. Objectives identified by consumers or empirically derived.
2. Precisely defined objectives.
3. Objectives introduced by difficulty and prerequisite analyses.
4. Objectives taught in short units.
5. Quantitative criteria used to demonstrate mastery.
6. Cumulative criteria.
7. Modeling to show skills.
8. Opportunities to practice in the natural environment.
9. Closely monitored homework.
10. Immediate quantitative and qualitative feedback.
11. Self-paced, with remediation procedures.

analysis, evaluation, and redesign. Although several parenting programs are commercially available, few rely on science or society to determine program objectives.

PROGRAM OBJECTIVES ARE PRECISELY DEFINED. Considerable research in a variety of disciplines supports specifying learning objectives in behavioral terms (Bloom, 1956; Sundel & Sundel, 1975), and numerous procedural texts are available to assist in this process (Mager, 1962). Precisely defined objectives can facilitate learning rate and accuracy; when defined prior to program onset, they provide a standard against which behavior change can be compared, as well as criteria for assessing complementarity between program objectives and parent needs.

PROGRAM OBJECTIVES ARE INTRODUCED ACCORDING TO DIFFICULTY AND PREREQUISITE ANALYSES. Easy objectives precede difficult objectives. Complex tasks are divided into components; each is introduced until the entire skill is mastered. Programmed instruction research documents the utility of this approach (Markle, 1969). Procedures to conduct task analyses for mathematics curriculum (Resnick, Wang, & Kaplan, 1973), for pedestrian skills for the retarded (Page, Iwata, & Neef, 1976), and for complex managerial tasks (Feeney, 1976) have been explicated, along with countless examples of failures to program learning objectives sequentially by difficulty and prerequisites (e.g., in the public schools). Nevertheless, verification of the accuracy of even the most well-thought-out sequence of training tasks requires careful experimental evaluation.

As a case in point, an early version of Lesson One in WINNING! instructed parents to "Praise the good things your child does" and "Keep your praises descriptive." An unquestioned assumption was that parents had the prerequisite skill "to describe." While their praise rates increased as much as 800% following Lesson One, all too frequently praises consisted solely of repetitive phrases such as, "Well done, well done, well done, well done, and well done," indicating that we had made an incorrect assumption and an incomplete prerequisite analysis. Similarly, Lesson Four, "Ignoring," originally preceded Lesson Three, "Suggestive Praise" (differential reinforcement of other behavior). Pilot data on parent first-trial mastery of individual lessons suggested that "Ignoring" was more difficult than "Suggestive Praise," and that "Suggestive Praise" helped parents master "Ignoring." Consequently, "Ignoring" now follows "Suggestive Praise," and parents generally master "Ignoring" on the first try.

PROGRAM OBJECTIVES ARE TAUGHT IN SHORT UNITS. Several researchers (D. W. Allen, 1968; D. W. Allen & Ryan, 1969; Conard, Willans, Hatfield, & Hopkins, 1975) have successfully used short training units, usually only specifying one or two training objectives at each meeting. Short training units permit focusing on priority objectives, use training time expeditiously, and help maintain trainee interest. In WINNING!, parents concentrate on mastering one new skill at a time.

QUANTITATIVE CRITERIA ARE ESTABLISHED TO DEMONSTRATE MASTERY OF LESSON OBJECTIVES. Quantitative criteria reduce subjectivity in evaluations

(Pine & Boy, 1975), and because of their goal functions, may actually increase behavior change (Ritschl & Hall, 1980). The use of quantitative mastery criteria has strong support in both the teacher training (Saudergas, 1972; Vasquez & Hopkins, 1973) and parent training literature (Forehand, 1977). WINNING! employs quantitative mastery criteria, shown in Table 8-8, for all basic lessons.

MASTERY CRITERIA ARE CUMULATIVE ACROSS LESSONS. Thomas (1972) and Conard *et al.* (1975) concluded that previously mastered skills could be maintained throughout additional training if mastery criteria were cumulative. In WINNING!, for example, to demonstrate mastery of Lesson Two, "Rewards and Privileges," a parent not only must give two rewards and privileges in 10 minutes, but must also continue to give 10 descriptive praises in the same 10 minutes. In the basic lessons, mastery criteria are cumulative through Lesson Seven, "Physical Punishment."

LESSON SKILLS ARE MODELED. Bandura (1969) has demonstrated the effectiveness of modeling, which is widely used in training programs. However, trainers acting as models are often required to demonstrate skills repeatedly; allowing for differences across performances, this minimizes program exportability and generalizability. Videotape, which allows for editing out extraneous variables, insures identical demonstrations, and permits exporting of training materials, has proved to be a useful tool for training a wide variety of interactional skills (Mayadas & O'Brien, 1974). WINNING! relies heavily on the use of color videotapes to model complex parent–child interactions.

OPPORTUNITIES TO PRACTICE NEW SKILLS IN THE NATURAL ENVIRONMENT ARE PROVIDED. Many successful training programs use behavioral rehearsal or

Table 8-8
Basic Lesson Mastery Criteria

Basic lesson	Criteria
1. Praise and Attention	10 descriptive praises.
2. Rewards and Privileges	Same as Lesson One, plus two rewards and privileges.
3. Suggestive Praise	Same as Lesson Two, plus five suggestive praises.
4. Ignoring	Same as Lesson Three, plus no attention to inappropriate child behavior.
5. Time Out	Same as Lesson Four, plus one time out.
6. Removing Rewards and Privileges	Same as Lesson Five, plus two instances of removing rewards and privileges.
7. Physical Punishment	Same as Lesson Six, plus one physical punishment.
8. Compliance	Deliver two instructions; follow one with positive consequences, one with negative consequences.

role playing to teach new skills (Fawcett, Miller, & Braukmann, 1977; Matson, 1980). However, generalization studies suggest that problems of transfer to nontraining environments can occur (Koegel & Rincover, 1977). In programs where training occurs in the natural environment, transfer problems have been minimized (Walker & Buckley, 1972). In WINNING!, training takes place in the clinic and in the home.

PRACTICE HOMEWORK IS ASSIGNED AND MONITORED. Parent trainers frequently require parents to practice new behaviors between treatment sessions in the natural environment (Tams & Eyberg, 1976), to collect data, and to report on these practice attempts. While we recognize that clients often resist collecting data (Jahn & Lichstein, 1980) or report fabricated, exaggerated, or incorrect data (Foxx & Rubinoff, 1979; Lichtenstein & Danaher, 1976), and that empirically supported procedures for eliminating these problems do not exist, limited research supports the importance of homework assignments. In a pilot study we conducted (Dangel, Polster, & Sears, 1982), several parents, though able to demonstrate mastery of new skills in our presence, were not using the skills at other times. This failure to practice interfered with their acquisition of new, more complex skills, and resulted in continued problematic child behaviors. We found that specific homework assignments, which we now carefully collect every week, are necessary to increase parents' skill use between treatment sessions.

IMMEDIATE QUANTITATIVE FEEDBACK AND QUALITATIVE FEEDBACK ARE PROVIDED. Many parent training programs provide feedback to parents (Forehand, Cheney, & Yoder, 1974; Rose, 1969), often in the form of discussion or general comments. Feedback can be diffuse, disparaging, unrelated to skills being trained, or highly subjective, providing parents with little useful information. Quantitative feedback, corresponding to preestablished, objective mastery criteria, eliminates many of these problems (Peed, Roberts, & Forehand, 1977), and can change behavior (Van Houten, Nau, & Marini, 1980; Van Houten & Van Houten, 1977). Even qualitative feedback, when given according to carefully prescribed guidelines, can be quantified and objective. In WINNING!, parents receive quantitative feedback (a statement of the number of times they used each skill) and qualitative feedback (comments descriptive of their performance).

THE PROGRAM IS SELF-PACED AND INCLUDES SYSTEMATIC REMEDIATION PROCEDURES. Self-paced programs let participants who demonstrate mastery rapidly advance rapidly. Those requiring more practice, feedback, or instructions progress at a slower pace, yet continue to succeed. Systematic remediation procedures permit all participants to acquire the intended treatment gains. When the treatment program is not equally effective or is effective at different rates across participants, either behavior change agents must make a "best guess" about what to try next, or not all participants benefit from the treatment. Both of these outcomes are unacceptable; they quickly eliminate replicability, present evaluation difficulties, and raise ethical issues. Standardized procedures to accommodate individual differences in rate of skill acquisition can facilitate program evaluation, utility, replicability, and dissemination. Parents in WINNING! advance through lessons at their individual rates, only as they master skills from previous lessons.

Steps for Parents

WINNING! integrates the 11 characteristics described above into a systematic training program. Figure 8-1 illustrates the steps a parent completes when participating in the program.

Step 1: Parent Views Videotaped Lesson

Usually in groups of 15 or less, but sometimes individually, parents watch one of the videotapes. One basic lesson is shown each week, beginning with Lesson One, typically over 8 weeks. If a parent misses a meeting, he or she may watch the videotape lesson that he or she missed at the next meeting, after the scheduled lesson is shown. To encourage promptness, we always begin meetings on time. Other than social pleasantries and praise for reports of practice, the parenting specialist refrains from conversation with parents until after each videotape is shown. At the conclusion of the scheduled lesson, approximately 15 minutes are allotted for discussion. Because we have kept detailed recordings of meetings with hundreds of parents, we can now reliably predict which questions parents will ask after which lessons. The *Parenting Specialist Handbook* (Dangel & Polster, 1980) includes these questions with our standardized replies. The parenting specialist focuses conversation on content covered in the current or previously viewed lessons and on application of the content. Extraneous comments are gently and politely redirected or extinguished. By the third or fourth meeting, parents' comments relate directly to applications of lesson content.

Step 2: Parent Receives Written Materials

The parenting specialist distributes two types of written materials at the group meeting, a Mastery Criteria Sheet and a Practice Assignment Recording Form. The Mastery Criteria Sheet lists exactly what the parent must do to demonstrate mastery and includes suggestions on how to use the skill for that lesson. Figure 8-2 shows a Mastery Criteria Sheet for Lesson One. The parenting specialist asks parents to reread the sheet periodically through the week. The Practice Assignment Recording Form establishes a specific practice assignment for the week and provides a convenient recording form for parents' use. Figure 8-3 shows the Practice Assignment Recording Form for Lesson One. We suggest that parents fasten the form on the refrigerator door, so that it may serve as a

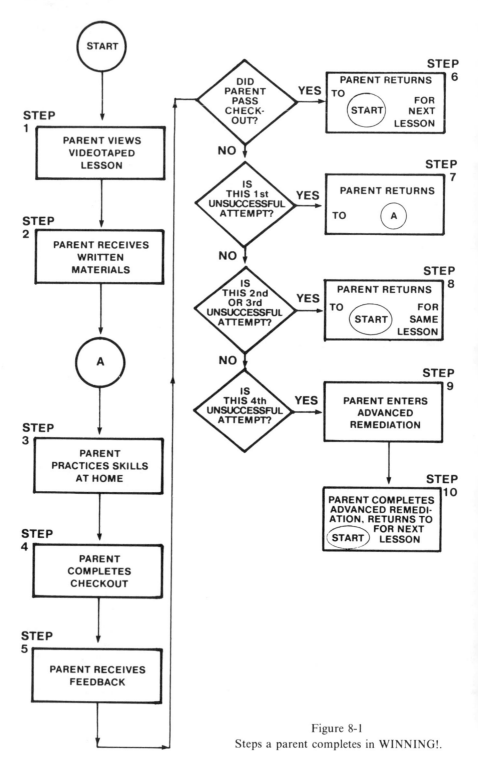

Figure 8-1
Steps a parent completes in WINNING!.

174

Criteria:

During the 10-minute Checkout, you must give:

10 descriptive praises.

Suggestions:

1. Keep your praises descriptive. For example, instead of saying, "Good boy," say "Good boy. You put all of your toys in the toy box."

2. Use hugs, kisses, and pats-on-the-head with your praises.

3. Praise **during** or **immediately after** good behavior.

4. Remember to praise the small good things your child does.

5. Don't pay attention to minor annoying behavior.

Figure 8-2
Mastery Criteria Sheet for Lesson One: Praise and Attention.

prompt to practice. After reading all material aloud, the parenting specialist answers any questions. This procedure accommodates parents with deficient reading skills, and helps to prevent misunderstandings about performance requirements.

Step 3: Parent Practices Skills at Home

Parents are given several days between meetings to practice the skills at home with their own children. During the group meetings, we repeatedly stress the importance of practice in skill acquisition.

Step 4: Parent Completes Checkout

After each lesson, the parenting specialist visits the parent at home at a scheduled appointment time to conduct a checkout. The checkout is the parent's

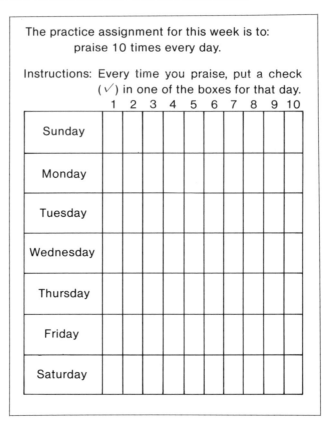

The practice assignment for this week is to:
praise 10 times every day.

Instructions: Every time you praise, put a check
(✓) in one of the boxes for that day.

	1	2	3	4	5	6	7	8	9	10
Sunday										
Monday										
Tuesday										
Wednesday										
Thursday										
Friday										
Saturday										

Figure 8-3
Practice Assignment Recording Form for Lesson One: Praise and Attention.

attempt to demonstrate mastery in the natural environment of the skills for a particular lesson. At the home visit, the parenting specialist collects the Practice Assignment Recording Form, and commends the parent if the form is complete. If it is not, the parent is reminded of the importance of practice, urged to complete the form *daily*, given a fresh form, and told that it will be collected at the next home visit. After reviewing the appropriate Mastery Criteria Sheet with the specialist, the parent attempts to demonstrate mastery of the required skills. All checkouts are conducted with the same child, selected by the parent. The parent and child can be involved in any activity during the checkout. Activities vary from checkout to checkout, and have included such tasks as getting ready for bed, cleaning the bathroom, watching television, and playing soccer. We advise parents to select different activities for each checkout to help increase generalization. Once the checkout begins, the specialist does not talk with either the parent or the child. Often at the first couple of checkouts, parents will ask, "How am I doing?," to which the specialist replies, "We have just a few minutes remaining in the checkout. Then we'll take a look. Keep going."

Step 5: Parent Receives Feedback

At the end of the checkout, the parent receives feedback recorded on a Checkout Sheet shown in Figure 8-4. The top portion of the Checkout Sheet includes identifying information and the number of times during each minute that the parent displayed each skill. For example, Figure 8-4 shows that Mr. Williams praised two times in the first minute, two times in the second, four times in the

Figure 8-4
Checkout Sheet for Lesson One: Praise and Attention.

Name: *Mr. Williams* Specialist: *D. Polster* Date: *2/14/78*

Activity: *Watching television* Time: *3:30* Attempt No: *1*

OBSERVATION

1	P P	6	P
2	P P	7	P
3	P P P P	8	
4	P	9	P P
5		10	P

RESULTS

Skills Being Observed		Criteria	Total Observed
P	Praise	10	*14*

COMMENTS   (Pass) Retake   New Criteria   Old Criteria

Wow! What a job you did sailing through this lesson. Your praises were very descriptive. And, you remembered to give them when little JoJo was behaving herself. I can tell you've been practicing - it shows! Keep it up! It's fine to use an occasional pat-on-the-head with your praises, too. Your daughter will love it. Nice job Mr. Williams.

third, and so on for a total of 14 praises during the 10-minute checkout, exceeding the required mastery criteria for Lesson One. The bottom portion of the Checkout Sheet indicates whether the parent demonstrated mastery. For example, the mastery criteria for Lesson Three, "Suggestive Praise," require the parent to give 10 descriptive praises, two rewards and privileges, and five suggestive praises. If the parent used two rewards and privileges and five suggestive praises, but only eight descriptive praises instead of the required 10, the parent would *not* have demonstrated mastery of Lesson Three.

The parenting specialist also writes at least seven comments, following closely specified guidelines explicated in the *Parenting Specialist Handbook* (Dangel & Polster, 1980). For example, one statement is made about passing the lesson, two statements about use of skills for the current lesson, two about the use of skills from previous lessons, one about the importance of practice, and zero to two suggestions for improvement. Similar guidelines exist for unsuccessful checkouts. The parenting specialist gives the original Checkout Sheet to the parent and retains a carbon copy for the parent's file. After allowing a few minutes for the parent to look over the completed Checkout Sheet, the specialist explains the results. We keep comments other than those on the sheet to a minimum.

Step 6: Parent returns to (START) for Next Lesson

If the parent passes the checkout, he or she views the next videotape lesson, and repeats Steps 1 through 6 until he or she finishes all eight basic lessons. If he or she does not pass the checkout, he or she goes to Step 7.

Step 7: Parent Returns to (A)

The parent continues to practice in the home for several days. The parenting specialist and parent then complete a second checkout. If the parent passes, he or she returns to (START) for the next lesson; if not, he or she goes to Step 8.

Step 8: Parent Returns to (START) for Same Lesson

The parent re-views the videotape lesson, on the assumption that the modeling component did not do its job the first time around. After reviewing the videotape lesson, the parent is allowed two additional checkout attempts. If he or she demonstrates mastery, he or she returns to (START) for the next lesson; if not, he or she goes to Step 9.

Step 9: Parent Enters Advanced Remediation

If after four attempts, the parent cannot pass the checkout, he or she enters Advanced Remediation. The sequence of events in Advanced Remediation is as follows:

1. Demonstrate skill, without child, for parent.
2. Parent imitates without child.
3. Repeat steps 1 and 2 for each skill.
4. Demonstrate skill, with child, for parent.
5. Parent imitates with child.
6. Repeat steps 4 and 5 for each skill.
7. Demonstrate mastery criteria.
8. Parent imitates; prompts given as necessary.
9. Parent completes checkout without prompts.

A parent entering Advanced Remediation is experiencing difficulty learning the material. He or she requires additional modeling, instructions, prompts, and praise. To keep this task pleasant, the parenting specialist provides considerable support and understanding to the parent. No parent has ever quit WINNING! while in Advanced Remediation, nor has any parent ever failed a checkout after completing Advanced Remediation.

Step 10: Parent Completes Advanced Remediation

The final event in Advanced Remediation requires the parent to pass the checkout without any assistance from the parenting specialist. The parent then returns to (START) for the next lesson.

Educational and Therapeutic Models

WINNING! can be employed as an educational model or as a therapeutic model. An educational model parallels the format for parent education classes routinely offered by mental health and social service agencies. When WINNING! is used as an educational model, parents attend a group meeting, view and discuss one of the videotape lessons, and go home. For many parents, this is sufficient to produce improvements in their children's behaviors, as shown in Figure 8-5. Parents also consistently report high levels of satisfaction with the program and are willing to recommend it to friends. Many agencies around the country now employ WINNING! exclusively as an educational model.

The therapeutic model may be necessary when families are unable to acquire new skills without more intensive intervention, are at risk of hurting their children, or are distressed. The therapeutic model uses all training procedures described earlier, including checkouts. In our research, we have been unable to identify any family characteristics, such as ethnicity, number of children, socioeconomic status, or child problem severity, that serve as reliable, strong predictors to assign a particular family correctly to one model over the other. Agency goals, resources and staff, and parent needs and preferences dictate which model is appropriate.

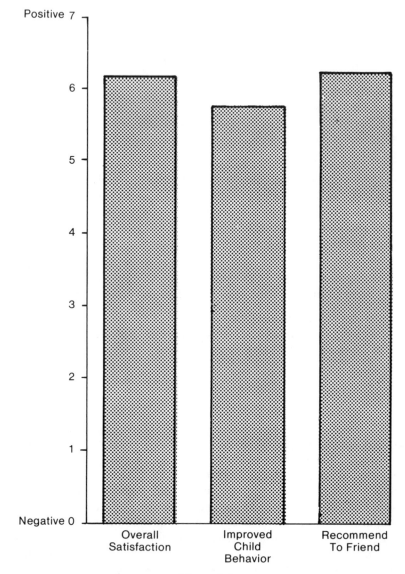

Figure 8-5
Parent satisfaction with WINNING! used as an educational model.

WINNING! has also been used in a wide variety of settings, shown in Table 8-9. Our successful work in residential care centers training houseparents has been especially encouraging. Houseparents report high levels of satisfaction with the skills, and observational data confirm maintenance of training gains.

PROGRAM EVALUATION

Since 1978, over 2000 families have participated in WINNING!. This section describes the various evaluation methods we have used, as well as the results obtained from some of our research.

Parent Recruitment

Many more parents could benefit from parent training than participate in it; often, those parents most in need of training are least likely to get it. We have used several methods to enlist a wide variety of parents in WINNING!. Three methods have been particularly successful.

Our initial attempts to obtain referrals from child protective service workers produced dismal results. We tried repeated written announcements, telephone calls, and presentations at weekly staff meetings, but received only four referrals in as many weeks. In a last-ditch effort, we invited 12 caseworkers as our guests for lunch at a popular Mexican cantina. All accepted. Over tacos and margaritas, we explained the program, answered questions, asked workers to identify families in their caseloads that could benefit from WINNING!, and distributed referral forms. We did everything possible to place all extra effort on us rather than on the social workers. Voilà! Follow-up phone calls 2 days later netted 27 referrals. We contacted families, completed all paperwork, and, when requested, supplied the social workers with written documentation of family participation.

Table 8-9
Settings Using WINNING!

Public libraries	Residential treatment facilities
Elementary schools	Public welfare offices
Mental health centers	Child protective service units
Private counseling offices	Inner-city housing projects
Children's hospitals	Day care centers
Universities	Group care homes
Preschool programs	Secondary schools

We also recruited families through the public schools. Figure 8-6 shows the half-page yellow flier distributed serendipitously on report card day to 12,000 elementary-school children. Clever teachers thoughtfully inserted the announcements in report card envelopes. Within 48 hours, 300 parents called the program office for more information. Several were neighborhood spokespersons representing entire blocks of families!

In Frazier Courts (Dangel & Polster, 1982a) a predominantly black, inner-city, government-subsidized housing project, we delivered 500 fliers door to door. Also printed on the fliers was, "Sign up any time Tuesday in Activity

Figure 8-6
Promotional flier used to enlist parents.

WINNING!

A Firm Approach To Child Management

Would you like to learn new ways to handle common child problems such as:

Arguing and Talking Back   Homework
Nagging and Crying   School Difficulties
Fighting   Hygiene
Not Doing What You Ask   Bedwetting
Temper Tantrums   Eating Habits
Chores   Bedtime

All you need to do is sign up for WINNING! You'll meet with other parents to watch short color movies which show ways to solve these problems.

The program is absolutely **FREE.**

For more information, call:

(817) 860-7915

Don't Wait! Call Today!
First come, First served

Center." Only one parent, a 72-year-old great-grandmother, parent to 35 children, attended, and she had no children living with her! In our second attempt, an influential black resident personally contacted several parents; more fliers were distributed; and we promised free toys to all parents who came to an informational meeting. Twenty parents attended.

Family Characteristics

A diverse cross-section of parents has participated in WINNING!. Except when research purposes dictate otherwise, the only screening criteria we use are that parents have at least one child between the ages of 3 and 12 years living at home. We have enlisted mothers, fathers, blacks, whites, Hispanics, single parents, parents with annual incomes ranging from under $3000 to over $50,000 and educational levels ranging from sixth grade to graduate education, foster parents, and child-abusive parents. Since our referrals come from an equally wide range of sources, we have worked with many agencies to accommodate their clients. For example, some families referred by child protective service agencies do not have children living at home; the children have been removed because of reported abuse. Usually, we arrange for the children to be returned home for several hours once or twice per week, so the parents can practice the skills they are learning in WINNING! and complete a checkout. In our work at Frazier Courts, we hold our meetings in the activity center, and parents drop in at times convenient for them. We believe that this flexibility has helped us to establish a strong referral network within the community and has provided us with an unusually large and diverse parent population. Nevertheless, about 60% of our parents are self-referred, white, middle-class, married mothers.

Children whose parents have participated in WINNING! range in age from 2 years 4 months to 13 years 4 months. Most have at least one behavior problem described by their parents as "serious." Many could belong to Bernal's "Brat Syndrome Club" (Bernal, Duryee, Pruett, & Burns, 1968). They fight, fail to do as their parents ask, and throw tantrums. Some also destroy property, lie, cry, steal, set fires, slash tires, and skip school. Classroom deportment problems and poor academic performance are common. A few are shy. Most have at least one sibling; some have as many as eight. A group of 30 parents, whose children had multiple physical and mental handicaps such as cerebral palsy and mental retardation, recently completed WINNING!.

Measurement Systems

We have used checklists, scales, inventories, role plays, in-home observations, and parent self-reports to evaluate the effects of WINNING! on parent and child behaviors. Originally we used the Parental Attitude Test (Cowen, Huser,

Beach, & Rappaport, 1970), which gauges parental attitudes and perceptions of child behavior with four measures: a school attitude measure, a home attitude measure, a behavior rating scale, and an adjective checklist scale. The school and home attitude measures consist of 4- and 7-item scales reflecting the parent's perceptions of the child's adjustment at school and home. The behavior rating scale consists of 25 items, each referring to a problem, and the adjective checklist scale consists of 34 adjectives, each describing a child behavior or personality characteristic. The test has been found to be a reasonably stable measure overtime (Cowen *et al.*, 1970), and Forehand, King, Peed, and Yoder (1975) demonstrated that parents of clinic children rated their children on the Parental Attitude Test as more maladjusted than did parents of nonclinic children.

While we obtained clear improvements on the Parental Attitude Test with many parents, we experienced the same difficulties with it as Radin and Glasser (1965) found with the Parent Attitude Research Instrument (Schaefer, Bell, & Bayley, 1958): Responses on the instrument varied widely for lower-class and middle-class parents. Many parents who participated in WINNING! could not read and were unfamiliar with labels such as "irritable," "boastful," or "sociable." Some parents complained about the length of the Parental Attitude Test, and (we suspect) completed it haphazardly. We have not yet found a convenient, reliable, useful pencil-and-paper test to measure parent attitudes and perceptions.

Checkouts, however, provide us with an excellent opportunity to evaluate parent skill acquisition. During the checkout, conducted in the natural environment with the parent and child, the parent displays mastery of new skills. Because we typically have different parenting specialists complete the checkouts on a particular parent from week to week, and because checkout criteria are cumulative, we have a form of test–retest reliability on the accuracy of our evaluations. Some basic lesson checkouts involve role playing. For example, to pass the checkout on Lesson Five, a parent must correctly use time out. If the child's behavior does not warrant time out, the parent and child role-play the situation. While role playing may not be as good a test as an actual performance, it does at least permit the parent to display his or her skill acquisition under simulated conditions. After some initial discomfort, parents routinely find checkouts helpful.

Our evaluation of WINNING! has relied most heavily on observational data collected in the home by highly trained, experimentally naive observers. A total of 35 undergraduate and graduate student observers completed approximately 60 hours of training in recording target behaviors from videotapes of parent–child interactions, as well as 15 to 20 hours of training in homes of families not participating in the research. Observers reached 80% interobserver reliability before starting actual data collection, and received weekly tests and booster training as needed to insure maintenance of accurate recording.

We have collected data on 11 categories of parent behavior and 8 categories of child behavior. The specific parent behaviors were praise, suggestive praise, rewards and privileges, removing rewards and privileges, directions, repeated directions, time out, attention, spanking, physical abuse, and parent–child interaction. The specific child behaviors were appropriate behavior, misbehavior, compliance, fighting, backtalking, household chores, temper tantrums, and whining. The operational definitions for these parent and child behaviors have been revised over the years, from study to study; we have also changed the conditions under which data are collected and the ways in which we analyze our data.

Early parent training research often required families to follow certain rules during data collection—for example, the television was to be kept off, telephone conversations were to be avoided, and the parent and child were to stay in the same room. While these rules may have facilitated data collection, they may also have functioned as significant, confounding independent variables. Because we have wanted our data collection to be as unobtrusive as possible, we have not imposed any rules on our families except that the parent and at least the target child be home during the observation. In some of our first studies, we collected data only during mealtime. Mealtime provided a somewhat standardized activity, which we hoped would reduce variability in the data across observations. We assumed that during mealtime parents and children would be in sight and hearing of each other and the observer; furthermore, mealtime has been identified as one situation where inappropriate child behavior is likely to occur (Ames, 1970; Breckenridge & Vincent, 1965)—thus, we hoped, providing frequent opportunities for parents to apply newly acquired skills. Recording of both parent and child behavior was done on an interval-occurrence basis. Each minute was divided into six 10-second intervals. Regardless of the number of times a target behavior occurred within a 10-second interval, it was recorded only once.

After collecting and analyzing about 250 hours of mealtime data, we decided for several reasons to collect data during other activities. First, contrary to our expectations, all data were highly variable, and inappropriate child behaviors only rarely occurred. Second, parents reported feeling particularly uncomfortable eating with observers present. Finally, we concluded that because mealtime was just one activity in family life, it did not adequately represent daily interactions.

In our studies since then, we have collected data at randomly selected periods during the day. We never observe the same family at the same time for two consecutive observations. Our only recording rule for parents is that they and their target child or children must be in the home or at an agreed-upon activity (e.g., a baseball game). If at any time during the observation, the parent or child is out of sight or hearing of the observer, observations are temporarily suspended; however, parents are not informed of this. We ask parents to do whatever activities they would ordinarily do. Because of this unstructured format, we have observed families under very natural conditions: sleeping, cooking, playing soccer, fighting, and watching television. While this allows us to capture a representative sample of parent–child interaction, it also introduces substantial variability in rates of behavior. Predictably, for example, a parent interacts significantly less, either positively or negatively, with his or her child when the child is frozen in front of the television or when the parent is talking on the telephone. Nevertheless, both events occur frequently. We have continued to use interval-occurrence data, most often 10-second but sometimes 5-second intervals. In our current work, we have divided each minute into a series of a 5-second interval followed by two 2.5-second intervals. During the 5-second interval, parent behavior is recorded. During the first 2.5-second interval, the behavior of the target child is recorded, and during the second 2.5-second interval, the behavior of a sibling is recorded. We also record to which child the parent's behavior was directed. This observation format allows us to measure generalization effects across children.

Interval data have been inadequate. Many of the behaviors of concern, for both parent and child, occur at extremely low rates. For example, a target child may throw a severe temper tantrum only once per day, and a parent may correctly use time out. Since an observer probably will not be present, both events go unrecorded. From the data, the deviant child looks well-behaved; the skillful parent looks as though he or she has not learned a new skill; and the parent training program looks ineffective—three incorrect observations.

We collect parent self-report data as one supplement to observational data. Each week parents complete a Practice Assignment Recording Form, which provides us with one index of their performance. Approximately 87% of the parents complete the form each week; however, they indicate informally that their recording may be inaccurate. In another study, we (Dangel, Polster, & Pike, 1982) instructed parents to call a 24-hour answering machine within 10 minutes of each episode of a preselected child problem behavior. Twelve mothers, all of whom reported severe, repetitive child behavior problems, participated. Despite frequent prompts and encouragement, only two parents complied with the instructions. Most of the other parents either quit the project or promised, but failed, to do better.

Finally, we use consumer satisfaction questionnaires completed by parents either shortly after they finish WINNING! or when they discontinue it. We typically ask questions such as these: "How well did you like the videotapes?", "How much do you use the skills on a day-to-day basis?", and "How much did your child's behavior improve?" Parents complete their consumer questionnaires anonymously.

Results

Though we have employed various methodologies across studies, the effects of WINNING! have been consistent. The data presented in this section summarize findings from four studies involving 62 families.

Figure 8-7 illustrates the percentage of parents showing changes in the desired direction in four categories of behavior. Positive consequences in-

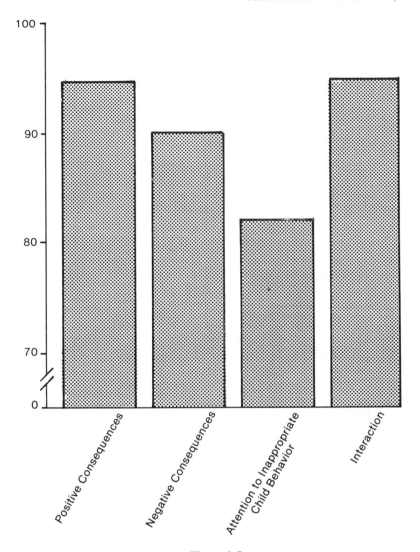

Figure 8-7
Percentage of parents showing changes in desired direction in positive consequences, negative consequences, attention to inappropriate child behavior, and interaction.

creased for 95% of all families; negative consequences increased for 89%; attention to inappropriate child behavior decreased for 82%; and interaction increased for 96% of all families.

Figure 8-8 shows the mean percentage of change from baseline for these same categories of behavior. Positive consequences increased by 153%, negative

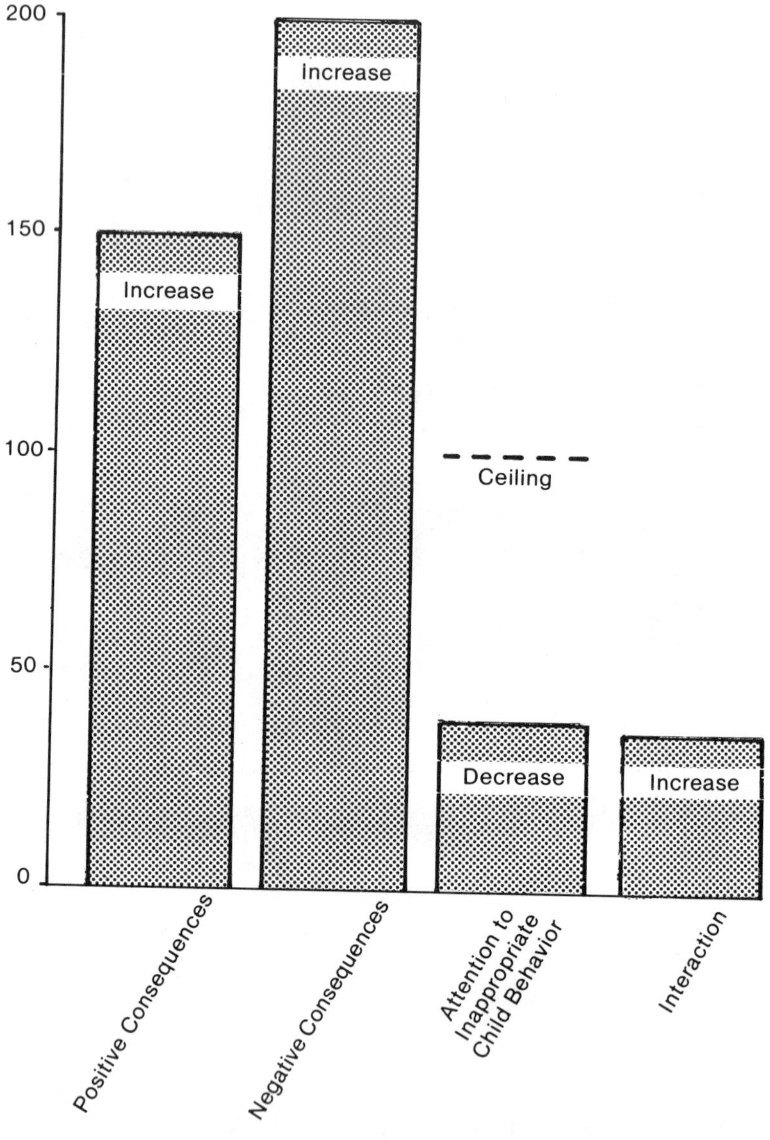

Figure 8-8
The mean percentage of change from baseline in positive consequences, negative consequences, attention to inappropriate child behaviors, and interaction.

consequences increased by 191%, attention to inappropriate behavior decreased by 44%, and interaction increased by 42%.

Figure 8-9 shows the percentage of children with decreased inappropriate behaviors and the mean percentage of decrease from baseline. Inappropriate behavior decreased for 86% of the children. The mean percentage of decrease was 44%.

Figures 8-10, 8-11, and 8-12 present sequential data. Figure 8-10 shows the percentage of appropriate child behaviors followed by positive consequences. Under baseline conditions, a mean of 2.5% of appropriate child behaviors were followed by positive consequences; under training conditions this rose to a mean of 9.3%, representing a 272% increase. Follow-up data, collected 3 weeks to 1 month later, indicate maintenance of change.

Figure 8-9

Percentage of children showing decreased inappropriate behaviors and mean percentage of decrease from baseline.

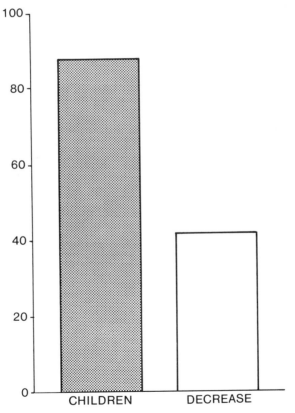

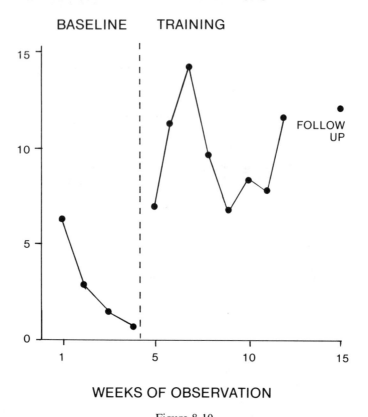

Figure 8-10

Percentage of appropriate child behaviors followed by positive consequences each week under baseline and training conditions.

Figure 8-11 shows the percentage of child misbehaviors (serious disruptions, fighting, noncompliance) followed by negative consequences. Under baseline conditions, a mean of 2.2% of child misbehaviors were followed by negative consequences; under training conditions this rose to a mean of 4.9%, representing a 122% increase. Follow-up data also indicate maintenance.

Figure 8-12 shows the percentage of inappropriate child behaviors (minor annoying behaviors) followed by parent attention. Under baseline conditions, 8.2% of inappropriate child behaviors were followed by parent attention; under training conditions, this fell to 3.1%, representing a 62% decrease. Again, changes were maintained 1 month later.

Figure 8-13 presents the results of a parent satisfaction questionnaire completed by all parents 1 week after final data collection or, for those parents who withdrew from WINNING! early, completed at that time. All question-naires were completed anonymously. On a 7-point Likert-type scale, with 1 representing a negative and 7 a positive evaluation, parents' ratings were as follows: "How well did you like the videotapes?," 6.4; "How much did the Practice Assignment Recording Form remind you to use the skills?," 5.5; "How comfortable were you with the checkouts?," 5.0; "How useful were the check-outs to help you learn the skills?," 6.0; "How much do you use the skills on a

Figure 8-11

Percentage of child misbehaviors followed by negative consequences each week under baseline and training conditions.

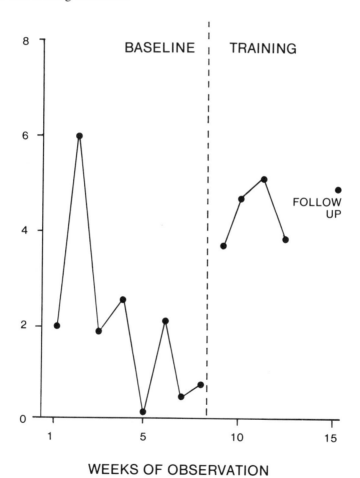

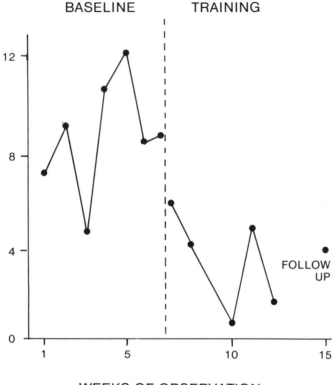

BASELINE   TRAINING

WEEKS OF OBSERVATION

Figure 8-12
Percentage of inappropriate child behaviors followed by parent attention each week under baseline and training conditions.

daily basis?," 5.2; "How much has your child's behavior improved?," 5.4; and "Would you recommend WINNING! to a friend?," 6.3.

Overall, these results indicate that WINNING! produces substantial desirable changes in parent and child behavior. These improvements occur across a diverse parent and child population: poor, wealthy, minority, nonminority, single-parent, two-parent, referred, and voluntary. All parents demonstrated mastery of all skills. Observational data show that parents used these skills at various times and activities during the day, that positive changes occurred in untrained behaviors (interaction), and that the effects appear to be maintained. Consumer satisfaction results indicate that parents enjoyed the program and found it effective in helping them with their children.

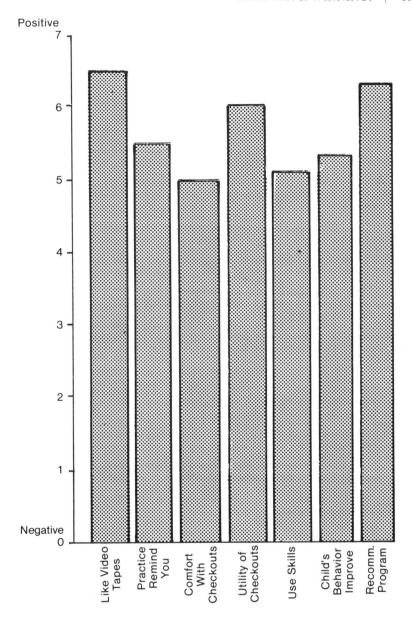

Figure 8-13
Parent satisfaction with several dimensions of WINNING!.

DISCUSSION

Dropout

Commonly, half or more of all parents who participate in parent training programs discontinue such programs before completing them (Chilman, 1975). This figure is astounding, especially considering that parents who enroll represent a sample biased toward participation. Discontinuance has been correlated with trainer variables (Lindsley, 1970), parent socioeconomic status (Chilman, 1975), spouse involvement (Sadler, Seyden, Howe, & Kaminsky, 1976), child age (Sadler *et al.*, 1976), and program dimensions (Cohen, 1970). Friedman (1979) recently suggested that there may be an inverse relationship between program response requirements and continued participation. As parents are asked to do more, such as collect data, practice skills, or complete homework assignments, they are more likely to withdraw from the program. If this is the case, then programs that include just those components most likely to produce behavior change may be the same programs least likely to retain participants! While research may eventually identify practical and manipulable variables capable of maintaining participation, such is not yet the case.

About 19% of the parents who begin WINNING! discontinue it between Lessons One and Four. After Lesson Four, only 1% discontinue it. These figures compare favorably with those from many other parenting programs. Comparison of observational data from parents who complete WINNING! and those who discontinue it indicates no significant differences during the time that both are in the program. In other words, no prediction can be made on the basis of observational data as to whether a particular parent will complete the program. Our examination of parent demographic characteristics, of whether parents were self- or agency-referred, and of child behavior problems also produced no reliable predictor of parent continuation.

Table 8-10 lists the reasons parents have given for not completing WINNING!. The clear diversity of reasons, the problems inherent in parent self-report data, and the limited sample size make interpretation of these data difficult. As more parent trainers collect data on why parents discontinue programs, perhaps appropriate interventions can then be developed.

Early discontinuance constrains the therapeutic impact of parent training and limits the generalizability of research findings. Many families who might benefit withdraw before new skills are learned. Researchers evaluate the effects of treatment only on those parents who, for unspecified reasons, complete the program. Nevertheless, critics often incorrectly entangle the issue of dropout with that of program effectiveness. While it can be argued that *one* measure of program success is how well the program keeps participants (if no one buys the service, the service shuts down), to say that a parenting program is ineffective solely because people discontinue it would be analogous to saying that a novel

Table 8-10
Reasons for Parent Early Withdrawal from WINNING!

Relocation	No longer interested
Too busy	Not what I expected
Child better	Did not like program
Illness	Did not like observer
Divorce	New job
Spouse died	Car broke down
Social worker said I could	Kids ran away
Child's pet missing	Already know stuff

is lousy because of a dull jacket cover. Since we are attempting to modify two separate response classes—attendance behaviors and parenting behaviors—two separate interventions, and two separate metrics, are required.

Cost-Effectiveness

Parent training requires equipment, staff expertise, and staff time. Each of these carries its own price tag. Many programs use inexpensive equipment already on hand, such as chalkboards or audiocassette players; no additional expenditures are necessary. Some packaged programs, such as Systematic Training for Effective Parenting (STEP) (Dinkmeyer & McKay, 1976), employ kits including audiotapes and display cards; others, such as Parent Effectiveness Training (PET) (PET, 1981), use books. STEP costs about $85 and PET about $12. WINNING! requires a videotape playback unit and monitor, the videotape lessons, and the *Parenting Specialist Handbook*. These items are expensive. Nevertheless, videotape is rapidly becoming a standard training medium, and the availability of excellent videotape programs (e.g., ASSET, 1981) justifies the acquisition of videotape equipment. We also encourage agencies to share (not to duplicate, which is illegal) materials and equipment, and distributors offer substantial discounts for multiple purchases. This allows, for example, each school within a district to own a set of materials. These methods reduce costs for any single agency, while still making innovative programs available.

With staff reductions commonplace, another important consideration is the amount of staff time required to implement a program. Individual therapy, where treatment goals closely parallel those of parent training programs, can take weeks, months, even years. In WINNING!, a parenting specialist spends approximately 85 hours to complete the basic lessons with a group of 10 parents. This includes 10 hours for group meetings, 50 hours for 100 checkouts, and 25 hours for travel time. These figures allow for parents who require more than a single attempt to demonstrate mastery on some lessons, and also for those unable to attend eight consecutive group meetings. Not included is time for record keeping and advanced remediation procedures. On the average, staff time equals about 8 to 10 hours per family to complete all Basic Lessons, or slightly over 1 hour per week. One hour per week per family is no more time than required by direct counseling. To use WINNING! as an educational model (without checkouts) requires considerably less time. A group of 35 parents can complete all basic lessons in eight weekly 1-hour meetings. The parenting specialist's time, including preparation and group meetings, is under 3 hours per week.

Parent training programs that rely heavily on clinical judgment or expertise often require costly doctoral-level counselors, social workers, or psychologists. The number of parents in need of services dwarfs the number of such qualified professionals. Consequently, programs that can be implemented by paraprofessionals or master's-level professionals can reach more people, cost less, and may have wide agency appeal. Of the 11 parenting specialists employed by our program, 9 were graduate students with clinical experience ranging from 0 to 15 years, working toward master's degrees in social work. We trained all parenting specialists in groups, according to systematic procedures described in a manual, *Training Parenting Specialists* (Dangel & Polster, 1979). The training closely resembles the procedures we use with parents, and requires about 20 hours to complete. We have not experimentally evaluated our parenting specialist training program. However, written Checkout Sheets, completed by parenting specialists on the job, provide a permanent retrievable performance measure. All Checkout Sheets complied with instructions in the *Parenting Specialist Handbook* at the 90% level or better. This suggests that trainees can learn to use WINNING! correctly with only 20 hours of training. Of course, completed Checkout Sheets reflect trainee competence in only one area; further evaluation, linked directly to changes in parent behavior, is necessary.

Physical Punishment

Originally, WINNING! did not include a lesson on physical punishment. Virtually no other popular programs do, and physical punishment of children is controversial (Gil, 1970). However, the PAC argued forcefully for the inclusion of such a lesson—generally on the grounds that PAC members had used physical punishment with their children, and had themselves as children been spanked, without adverse long-term effects. Surveys repeatedly find that most parents spank their children (Erlanger, 1974; Korsch, Christian, Gozzi, & Carlson, 1965; Sears, Maccoby, & Levin, 1957; Stark & McEvoy, 1970; Steinmetz & Straus, 1974; Straus, 1971). Anecdotally, finding an adult who was not spanked as a child is difficult. Contrary to frequently heard statements suggesting causal relationships between spanking and child abuse, between adults who were spanked as children and abusive parents, and between being spanked and psychological impairments, not a single study demonstrates any of these relationships. Data from carefully controlled studies on the long-term effects of spanking on children simply do not exist.

We subsequently added a lesson a physical punishment. The lesson falls late in the basic series, Lesson Seven, after parents have learned a variety of other powerful behavior change methods. The punishment lesson is divided into two parts. The first specifically states that physical punishment is not recommended, and describes several potential adverse side effects associated with the use of punishment, such as avoidance behavior, emotional responses, and diminished long-term effectiveness. The lesson also encourages parents to solve child management problems by using skills demonstrated in earlier lessons. The second part of the lesson prescribes guidelines for the correct use of physical punishment. We based these guidelines on reports in the empirical literature and on PAC recommendations. The lesson instructs parents to spank only for serious or dangerous behavior; to use brief, stern swats rather than lengthy, mild taps; to spank only with the hand, never with such objects as fly swatters, extension cords, belts, or wooden spoons; to spank only on the child's bottom or hands; and never to spank when angry or out of control. The lesson also shows an angry father contacting a social service agency to avoid hurting his children, and an out-of-control mother leaving the room.

Because parents spank their children, ethics dictate that professionals educate parents about the effects of punishment and caution against the incorrect use of punishment. In a survey of 28 professionals, we (Dangel, Polster, & Ross 1982) found that while 64% reported spanking their own children, 46% reported telling their clients not to spank, and only 42% gave instructions on how to spank. These same professionals viewed Lesson Seven, "Physical Punishment," and were able to answer with over 90% accuracy several procedural questions about spanking. Most found the lesson useful, easy to understand, helpful, and realistic. Many reported that they planned to discuss physical punishment with parents more than they had in the past.

Because physical punishment occurs so infrequently during in-home observations, we have not been able to evaluate the effects of Lesson Seven on parents' use of spanking. However, a pencil-and-paper test, completed by 98 parents from diverse ethnic and socioeconomic backgrounds who had viewed the videotape, indicated that they were able to answer several detailed questions about physical punishment correctly. These results show that the videotape lesson on physical punishment is an effective instructional tool to educate parents and professionals.

Program Dissemination

We have only recently begun dissemination of WINNING!. Over 40 agencies in 16 states now use the program. We are collecting data from these replication sites to determine the extent of program use and effectiveness. We have also prepared a completely packaged, self-instructional version of WINNING! designed for use in public libraries. Interested parents simply view, at their convenience, a videotape lesson; read the accompanying materials; and answer a brief quiz. Take-home Practice Assignment Recording Forms are included in the materials. We are collecting data on how many parents use WINNING! and which lessons are selected most often. The 8717 public libraries nationwide may provide an outstanding vehicle for wide-scale program dissemination.

Summary

WINNING! can teach child management skills to diverse parent populations. It is suitable for use as an educational or therapeutic model in schools, hospitals, libraries, mental health centers, social service agencies, day care centers, residential treatment facilities, and low-income housing projects. Continued evaluation is necessary to examine the generality of the program across training sites, trainers, and time.

Our current work focuses on the three areas. First, we are training parents who have completed WINNING! as parenting specialists for other groups of parents. We are also forming groups of WINNING! graduates as one possible strategy to facilitate maintenance of treatment gains. Second, we are examining generalization effects, specifically across child behavior problems. Prior to starting WINNING!, parents now identify at least three child behavior problems displayed by their children. Observational data are collected on how parents respond to these problems before and during treatment. Since the basic lessons in WINNING! do not focus on specific problems, we can evaluate whether parents learn to apply general skills to the specific problems they may be having. Finally, we are evaluating the 14 advanced lessons, both in terms of their effects on parent and child behaviors and their relative popularity.

Acknowledgments

The development and initial evaluation of WINNING! was supported in part by the Department of Health and Human Services, Office of Human Development, Administration for Children, Youth and Families, Grant No. 90-C-1776 and by the Graduate School of Social Work, The University of Texas at Arlington. We give our sincere thanks to Dr. Ray Rackley, a kind, thoughtful, encouraging grant manager; to the parents and children who have participated in WINNING!; and to our graduate students who assisted in the execution of the research reported here. Appreciation is extended to Martin Sundel for his helpful comments on an earlier version of this chapter. WINNING! is available from American Children's Foundation, P.O. Box 32, Arlington, Texas 76004-0032.

References

Allen, D. W. *Microteaching: A description.* Stanford, Calif.: Stanford University Press, 1968.

Allen, D. W., & Ryan, K. A. *Microteaching.* Reading, Mass: Addison-Wesley, 1969.

Allen, G. J., Case study: Implementation of behavior modification techniques in summer camp settings. *Behavior Therapy*, 1973, *4*, 570–575.

Ames, L. B. *Child care and development.* Philadelphia: Lippincott, 1970.

ASSET: A social skills program for adolescents. Champaign, Ill.: Research Press, 1981.

Bandura, A. *Principles of behavior modification.* New York: Holt, Rinehart & Winston, 1969.

Barrett, B. H. Behavior modification in the home: Parents adapt laboratory-developed tactics to bowel-train a 5½-year-old. *Psychotherapy: Theory, Research and Practice*, 1969, *6*, 172–176.

Bernal, M. E., Duryee, J., Pruett, H., & Burns, B. Behavior modification and the brat syndrome. *Journal of Consulting and Clinical Psychology*, 1968, *32*, 447–455.

Bloom, B. S. *Taxonomy of educational objectives.* New York: David McKay, 1956.

Breckenridge, M. E., & Vincent, E. L. *Child development: Physical growth through adolescence* (5th ed.). Philadelphia: W. B. Saunders, 1965.

Bushell, D. Personal communication, November 1978.

Chilman, C. S. Programs for disadvantaged parents: Some major trends and related research. In F. D. Horowitz (Ed.), *Review of child development research* (Vol. 4). Chicago: University of Chicago Press, 1975.

Cohen, H. C. *The PICA project: Programming interpersonal curricula for adolescents (Year 2: Project interim report).* Silver Springs, Md.: Institute for Behavioral Research, 1970. (ERIC Document Reproduction Service No. ED 044 717.)

Conard, R. J., Hopkins, B. L., Fitch, H. G., Smith, M. J., Anger, W. K., & Dangel, R. F. *A strategy to validate work practices: An application to the reinforced plastics industry.* Manuscript submitted for publication, 1982.

Conard, R. J., Willans, A., Hatfield, M., & Hopkins, B. L. *State of the art teacher training: Evaluation of a practical program.* Unpublished master's thesis, University of Kansas, 1975.

Cowen, E. L., Huser, J., Beach, D. R., & Rappaport, J. Parent perceptions of young children and their relation to indexes of adjustment. *Journal of Consulting and Clinical Psychology*, 1970, *34*, 97–103.

Dangel, R. F., Conard, R. J., & Hopkins, B. L. Follow-up on in service teacher training programs: Can the principal do it? *Journal of Educational Research,* 1978, *72*, 94–103.

Dangel, R. F., & Polster, R. A. *Training parenting specialists.* Arlington, Tex.: American Children's Foundation, 1979.

Dangel, R. F., & Polster, R. A. *Parenting specialist handbook.* Arlington, Tex.: American Children's Foundation, 1980

Dangel, R. F., & Polster, R. A. *Frazier Courts: Training high-risk parents in an inner-city housing project using a packaged, replicable parent training program.* Manuscript submitted for publication, 1982. (a)

Dangel, R. F., & Polster, R. A. *Programming social validity: Parents as partners in program development.* Manuscript submitted for publication, 1982. (b)

Dangel, R. F., Polster, R. A., & Pike, S. A. *The use of analogue experimental conditions to prompt inappropriate child behaviors and to assess a parent training program.* Manuscript submitted for publication, 1982.

Dangel, R. F., Polster, R. A., & Ross, G. *What parents and professionals think about physical punishment.* Manuscript submitted for publication, 1982.

Dangel, R. F., Polster, R. A., & Sears, M. J. *Packaged technology: A systematic, empirical approach to parent training.* Manuscript submitted for publication, 1982.

Dinkmeyer, D., & McKay, G. D. *Systematic Training for Effective Parenting (STEP).* Circle Pines, Minn.: American Guidance Service, 1976.

Erlanger, H. S. Social class differences in parents' use of physical punishment. In S. K. Steinmetz & M. A. Straus (Eds.), *Violence in the family.* New York: Dodd & Mead, 1974.

Fawcett, S. B., Miller, L. K., & Braukmann, C. J. An evaluation of a training package for community canvassing behaviors. *Journal of Applied Behavior Analysis*, 1977, *10*, 504.

Feeney, E. J. *BEST: Behavioral engineering systems training*. Ridgefield, Conn.: Feeney Associates, 1976.

Forehand, R. Child noncompliance to parental requests: Behavioral analysis and treatment. In M. Hersen, R. M. Eisler, & P. M. Miller (Eds.), *Progress in behavior modification* (Vol. 5). New York: Academic Press, 1977.

Forehand, R., Cheney, T., & Yoder, P. Parent behavior training: Effects on the noncompliance of a deaf child. *Journal of Behavior Therapy and Experimental Psychiatry*, 1974, *5*, 281–283.

Forehand, R. L., King, H. E., Peed, S., & Yoder, P. Mother–child interactions: Comparison of a noncompliant clinic group and a nonclinic group. *Behaviour Research and Therapy*, 1975, *13*, 79–84.

Forehand, R., Wells, K. C., & Griest, D. L. An examination of the social validity of a parent training program. *Behavior Therapy*, 1980, *11*, 488–502.

Foxx, R. M., & Rubinoff, A. Behavioral treatment of caffeinism: Reducing excessive coffee drinking. *Journal of Applied Behavior Analysis*, 1979, *12*, 335–344.

Friedman, B. *Analysis of participation in a training program for single parents*. Unpublished doctoral dissertation, University of Chicago, 1979.

Gil, D. G. *Violence against children: Physical child abuse in the United States*. Cambridge, Mass.: Harvard University Press, 1970.

Hawkins, R. P., Peterson, R. F., Schweid, E., & Bijou, S. W. Behavior therapy in the home: Amelioration of problem parent–child relations with the parent in a therapeutic role. *Journal of Experimental Child Psychology*, 1966, *4*, 99–107.

Hopkins, B. L., & Conard, R. J. Putting it all together: Super school. In N. Haring & R. L. Schiefelbusch (Eds.), *Teaching special children*. New York: McGraw-Hill, 1975.

Horowitz, F. D. Directions for parenting. In E. J. Mash, L. A. Hamerlynck, & L. C. Handy (Eds.), *Behavior modification and families*. New York: Brunner/Mazel, 1976.

Jahn, D. L., & Lichstein, K. L. The resistive client: A neglected phenomenon in behavior therapy. *Behavior Modification*, 1980, *4*, 303–320.

Kazdin, A. Assessing the clinical or applied importance of behavior change through social validation. *Behavior Modification*, 1977, *1*, 427–452.

Koegel, R. L., & Rincover, A. Research on the difference between generalization and maintenance in extra-therapy responding. *Journal of Applied Behavior Analysis*, 1977, *10*, 1–12.

Korsch, B., Christian, J., Gozzi, E., & Carlson, P. Infant care and punishment: A pilot study. *American Journal of Public Health*, 1965, *55*, 1880–1888.

Lichtenstein, E., & Danaher, B. G. Modification of smoking behavior: A critical analysis of theory, research and practice. In M. Hersen, R. M. Eisler, & P. M. Miller (Eds.), *Progress in behavior modification* (Vol. 3). New York: Academic Press, 1976.

Lindsley, O. R. Procedures in common described by a common language. In C. Neuringer & J. L. Michael (Eds.), *Behavior modification in clinical psychology*. New York: Appleton-Century-Crofts, 1970.

Mager, R. F. *Preparing instructional objectives*. Palo Alto: Fearon, 1962.

Markle, S. M. *Good frames and bad: A grammar of frame writing* (2nd ed.). New York: Wiley, 1969.

Matson, J. L. Preventing home accidents. *Behavior Modification*, 1980, *4*, 397–410.

Mayadas, N., & O'Brien, D. Use of videotape in the laboratory training of social work students. *TV in Psychiatry Newsletter*, May 1974, pp. 7–12.

Page, T. J., Iwata, B. A., & Neef, N. A. Teaching pedestrian skills to retarded persons: Generalization from the classroom to the natural environment. *Journal of Applied Behavior Analysis*, 1976, *9*, 433–444.

Peed, S., Roberts, M., & Forehand, R. Evaluation of the effectiveness of a standardized parent training program in altering the interaction of mothers and their noncompliant children. *Behavior Modification*, 1977, *1*, 323–350.

PET: Parent Effectiveness Training. Solana Beach, Calif.: Effectiveness Training Incorporated, 1981.

Phillips, E. L., Phillips, E. A., Fixsen, D. L., & Wolf, M. M. *The Teaching Family handbook.* Lawrence: University of Kansas Printing Service, 1975.

Pine, G. J., & Boy, A. V. Necessary conditions for evaluating teachers. *NASSP Bulletin,* 1975, *59,* 19–23.

Radin, N., & Glasser, P. H. The use of parental attitude questionnaires with culturally disadvantaged families. *Journal of Marriage and the Family,* 1965, *27,* 373–382.

Resnick, L. B., Wang, M. C., & Kaplan, J. C. Task analysis in curriculum design: A hierarchically sequenced introductory mathematics curriculum. *Journal of Applied Behavior Analysis,* 1973, *6,* 679–710.

Ritschl, E. R., & Hall, R. V. Improving MBO: An applied behavior analyst's point of view. *Journal of Organizational Behavior Management,* 1980, *2,* 269–277.

Rose, S. D. A behavioral approach to the group treatment of parents. *Social Work,* 1969, *14,* 21–29.

Sadler, O. W., Seyden, T., Howe, B., & Kaminsky, T. An evaluation of "Groups for Parents": A standardized format encompassing both behavior modification and humanistic methods. *Journal of Community Psychology,* 1976, *4,* 157–163.

Saudergas, R. A. *Setting criterion rates of teacher praise: The effects of videotape in a behavior analysis follow-through classroom.* Unpublished doctoral dissertation, University of Illinois, 1972.

Schaefer, E. S., Bell, R. Q., & Bayley, N. Development of a maternal behavior research instrument. *Journal of Genetic Psychology,* 1958, *95,* 83–104.

Sears, R. R., Maccoby, E. E., & Levin, H. *Patterns of child rearing.* Evanston, Ill.: Row & Peterson, 1957.

Sidman, M. *Tactics of scientific research.* New York: Basic Books, 1960.

Stark, R., & McEvoy, I. Middle class violence. *Psychology Today,* November 1970, pp. 52–65.

Steinmetz, S. K., & Straus, M. A. (Eds.). *Violence in the family.* New York: Dodd & Mead, 1974.

Stokes, T. F., & Baer, D. M. An implicit technology of generalization. *Journal of Applied Behavior Analysis,* 1977, *10,* 349–367.

Stokes, T. F., Baer, D. M., & Jackson, R. L. Programming the generalization of a greeting response in four retarded children. *Journal of Applied Behavior Analysis,* 1974, *7,* 599–610.

Straus, M. A. Some social antecedents of physical punishment: A linkage theory interpretation. *Journal of Marriage and the Family,* 1971, *33,* 658–663.

Sundel, M., & Sundel, S. S. *Behavior modification in the human services.* New York: Wiley, 1975.

Tams, V., & Eyberg, S. A group treatment program for parents. In E. J. Mash, L. C. Handy, & L. A. Hamerlynck (Eds.), *Behavior modification approaches to parenting.* New York: Brunner/Mazel, 1976.

Thomas, D. R. *Self-monitoring as a technique for modifying teaching behaviors.* Unpublished doctoral dissertation, University of Illinois, 1972.

Van Houten, R., Nau, P., & Marini, Z. An analysis of public posting in reducing speeding behavior on an urban highway. *Journal of Applied Behavior Analysis,* 1980, *13,* 383–395.

Van Houten, R., & Van Houten, J. The performance feedback system in the special education classroom: An analysis of public posting and peer comments. *Behavior Therapy,* 1977, *8,* 366–376.

Vasquez, G. F., & Hopkins, B. L. *Education para niños* (Vol. 1). Mexico City: Colegio "Walden Dos," 1973.

Walker, H. M., & Buckley, N. K. Programming generalization and maintenance of treatment effects across time and across settings. *Journal of Applied Behavior Analysis,* 1972, *5,* 209–224.

Winnet, R. A., & Winkler, R. C. Current behavior modification in the classroom: Be still, be quiet, be docile. *Journal of Applied Behavior Analysis,* 1972, *5,* 499–515.

Wolf, M. M. Social validity: The case for subjective measurement, or how applied behavior analysis is finding its heart. *Journal of Applied Behavior Analysis,* 1978, *11,* 203–214.

INDIVIDUALIZED BEHAVIORAL INTERVENTION FOR HOME AND SCHOOL

Elsie M. Pinkston
University of Chicago

Intervention and training techniques for behavioral parent training represent a highly developed technology in applied behavior analysis (Berkowitz & Graziano, 1972; Johnson & Katz, 1973; O'Dell, 1974). With this technology, researchers and practitioners can evaluate the effectiveness of behavioral interventions in modifying relationships between family members and between children and school personnel. Several techniques based on behavioral principles are employed by parents to alter their children's behaviors in positive directions; similar procedures are effectively used by teachers to improve school-related child behavior. Although these techniques are evaluated and usually found effective, several problems with the delivery system for parent training remain. Engaging parents and teachers in behavioral change efforts was the purpose of the present research. The effectiveness of an abbreviated approach to parent training is tested and presented here.

This chapter is devoted to a description of a brief training program designed to remediate child behavior problems through the alteration of parent- and teacher-supplied consequences following child behaviors. First, a description of the Parent Education Program is presented with results and illustrated by a case example. Then follows a description of a modified version designed from the same program for intervention with single-parent–child dyads in a systematic replication of the original results (Hersen & Barlow, 1976; Sidman,

1960), the Single-Parent Program. An evaluation of these programs and conclusions for their use in direct practice are offered in the discussion.

These parent training techniques were assembled in the Parent Education Program at the University of Chicago (Pinkston, Friedman, & Polster, 1981; Pinkston, Polster, Friedman, & Lynch, 1982) to remediate aggressive child behavior through the alteration of parent- and teacher-supplied consequences to child behavior. These children ranged from 5 through 12 years in age and were regarded by teachers, social workers, and parents as having serious problems. In the Parent Education Program, the population was restricted to families with two parents living at home and required both parents' agreement to participate. Because of the potential problems of discontinuance, the program was designed as a brief intervention; that is, only two parent training sessions were conducted in the clinic, with at least two additional sessions conducted in the home.

The systematic clinical replication (Hersen & Barlow, 1976; Sidman, 1960) of the Parent Education Program extended to single-parent families with similar problems was designed to determine the generality of the parent training technology (Cox, 1982; Cox, Rzepnicki, Shibano, & Pinkston, 1980; Friedman, 1979; Rzepnicki, Shibano, Pinkston, & Cox, 1982; Shibano, 1983; Shibano, Cox, Rzepnicki, & Pinkston, 1982). The development of the programs is presented in sequence.

PARENT EDUCATION PROGRAM

The Parent Education Program was formulated on a social reinforcement model with an emphasis on modeling and reinforcement of desired behaviors. The interpersonal breakdown in families was viewed as the result of infrequent reciprocal reinforcement between parents and children. Procedures were developed to teach family members to increase their rate of positive reinforcement for behaviors involving interpersonal relations, including (1) relations with parents, siblings, and peers; (2) household chores; (3) school functioning; (4) communication; and (5) general behavior.

Treatment procedures focused on establishing positive patterns of interpersonal interaction. Behavioral contingencies were modeled by the therapist and rehearsed with the parents, teachers, and children. Contracting, a technique for specifying contingencies for the exchange of positive reinforcers between two or more persons, was practiced and subsequently instituted in the home; it was then instituted in the school when desirable. Emphasis was placed on positive reinforcement for contracted behaviors (point cards for children on token systems). Overcorrection procedures and time out for severely deviant child behaviors were used in specific cases.

Subjects

The Parent Education Program was developed for parents of aggressive children between the ages of 5 and 12 years who were referred for treatment by a public school social worker or a community outreach social worker. Following intervention with a child at home, the teacher was contacted for an assessment of the child's school behavior. If the teacher consented, then a program was developed for the treatment of existing school-related problems. A total of 73 families were accepted in order of referral. Exclusions were made only if both parents were not available or if no aggression problem existed.

Basic Research Design

In this research, a multiple-baseline, across-subjects design (Baer, Wolf, & Risley, 1968) was used. This design is useful as a control when attempting direct replication of treatment effects on individuals and has been used successfully in a number of studies (e.g., see Corte, Wolf, & Locke, 1971; Hall, Christler, Cranston, & Tucker, 1970; Panyan, Boozer, & Morris, 1970). It provides the opportunity to test the effectiveness of treatment across subjects and also over time.

Settings

The structured assessment tools—an initial interview and a parent training interview—were conducted at the School of Social Service Administration at the University of Chicago. This setting was equipped with video equipment, comfortable chairs, and a coffee table to simulate a living room. Written consent was obtained for research participation and videotaping. Before filming began, children were given an opportunity to "do some tricks" in front of the camera and then to view themselves to help them adjust. Interviews with teachers were conducted in the schools, usually in a classroom.

Basic Data-Collection Techniques

Assessment and evaluation procedures included an initial behavioral questionnaire and a comparison between baseline and self-observation data (direct observation). Reliability checks were conducted by independent observers in the home and school to insure the reliability of parent-recorded data. A consumer questionnaire was administered to the parents by mail; 3- and 6-month follow-up interviews were conducted by telephone.

Definition of behavior was a characteristic of this behavior modification treatment research and an essential part of the applied behavioral analysis. It was important to define the behaviors of interest in clear, simple, and specific language, emphasizing their physical and topographical aspects. It was also important that the definition was written in such a way as to allow the least possible interpretation. The efficacy of the behavioral code was determined by the ability of the observers to obtain reliable agreement. Observer agreements of 80% or more were considered acceptably reliable, and operational definitions yielding such reliability figures were then used at length. Reliability was recorded frequently throughout the research, at least once during baseline and once during each experimental condition, or whenever there was an appreciable change in the behavior.

When the records of parents and teachers were compared with observer, agreements were scored for occurrence and nonoccurrence of the target behaviors within a given time sample. The procedure operated without qualifications when recording a free operant (a behavior that could be emitted at any time free from external constraint), such as aggression or acting-out behavior. However, when measuring a discriminated operant (a behavior, the rate of which was determined or altered by the presence or absence of some stimulus), such as compliance with an instruction, it was necessary for the observers to record the instruction and the compliance or noncompliance of the client. It was then possible to record the consequence to the child from the parent or teacher who gave the instruction.

This research method was appropriate for the recording of occurrence data such as the frequency, duration, and quality of communication between parents and children, teacher and children, and counselor and children. Time and place of behavior were also recorded.

Initial Contact by Therapist

Following referral by the social worker, the therapist telephoned the parents. During this conversation, the therapist conducted a brief problem exploration with a parent, usually the mother, to determine relevance of the program to family needs. Although the social worker had previously explained the Parent Education Program, he or she again stressed that the program was educational in nature and that the parent would need to visit the clinic for two sessions plus at least one home visit by the therapist (see Figure 9-1 for flow chart).

During the initial conversation (see Figure 9-2), the social worker explained that he or she would be mailing a questionnaire to the parents regarding their interactions with their child, and that as soon as the questionnaire was received, their first appointment would be scheduled.

Figure 9-1
Outline of the Parent Education Program.

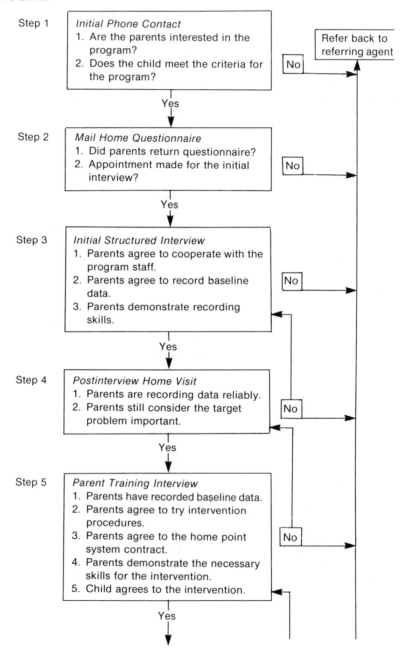

HOME PROGRAM

Step 1
Initial Phone Contact
1. Are the parents interested in the program?
2. Does the child meet the criteria for the program?

Refer back to referring agent

No

Yes

Step 2
Mail Home Questionnaire
1. Did parents return questionnaire?
2. Appointment made for the initial interview?

No

Yes

Step 3
Initial Structured Interview
1. Parents agree to cooperate with the program staff.
2. Parents agree to record baseline data.
3. Parents demonstrate recording skills.

No

Yes

Step 4
Postinterview Home Visit
1. Parents are recording data reliably.
2. Parents still consider the target problem important.

No

Yes

Step 5
Parent Training Interview
1. Parents have recorded baseline data.
2. Parents agree to try intervention procedures.
3. Parents agree to the home point system contract.
4. Parents demonstrate the necessary skills for the intervention.
5. Child agrees to the intervention.

No

Yes

Figure 9-1 (*continued*)

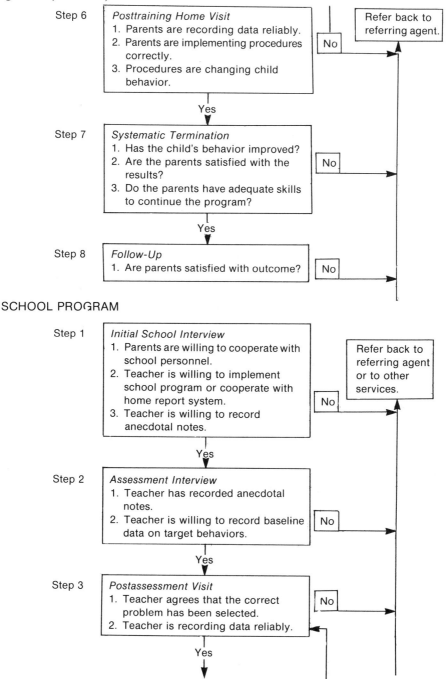

SCHOOL PROGRAM

(*continued*)

Figure 9-1 (*continued*)

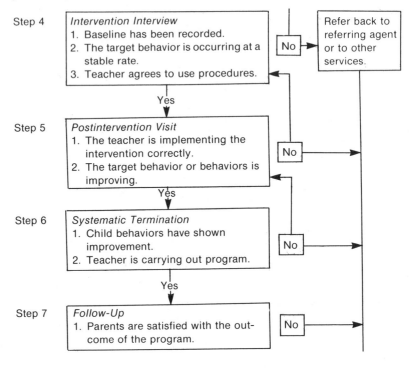

Home Questionnaire

The Home Questionnaire asked questions that examined the child's behaviors regarding (1) parent–child interaction; (2) interaction with siblings; (3) inter-action with peers; (4) household chores; (5) school functioning; and (6) general behavior. In addition, the parents were asked what they thought their child's strongest points were and what kind of consequences they provided for positive and negative behaviors. The questionnaire was designed to direct the parents to the kind of behaviors their children exhibited, rather than the kind of children they had—for example, "John does not answer me when I ask a question," rather than "John is a sullen boy." This was also the first response requirement from the parent. Help with the questionnaire was only provided if there was a language or an educational problem.

Initial Structured Interview

The goals for the first interview (see Figure 9-3) were these: (1) extension of the parents' knowledge regarding educational and behavioral approaches, and especially the present program's approach to family therapy; (2) definition of

Date: _____
Therapist: _____
Parent: _____

____ A. Identify yourself and affiliation.

____ B. Explain how family was referred.

____ C. Find out what parent already knows about program.

____ D. Briefly explain program.

    ____1. Parent Education Program is an educational approach to therapy. Skills for solving problems are taught in a positive and systematic way.

    ____2. Types of problems dealt with include school and parent–child interaction problems in the home.

    ____3. The training will be brief.

    ____4. Parent activity: Data collection and parental intervention between sessions is extremely important and requires client's interest, motivation, and cooperation. This includes a small time commitment each day to observe and record data on the problems chosen to work on with the child—but it actually shouldn't disrupt family routine too much.

    ____5. Cost for services. (This will vary, depending on the treatment setting.)

____ E. Behavior inventory: If parent expresses an interest in receiving our services, tell him or her that you would like to send him a behavior inventory to help determine some of the areas he or she might like to work on with his or her child. We will not ask for a strong commitment to participate until the program has been more fully explained in the first interview. (Make sure he or she knows this.)

____ F. Parental concerns: Ask what his or her concerns are regarding the child. Briefly, what sorts of problems are of concern at this time?

____ G. Benefits: If parents choose to participate, they may expect the following:

    ____1. Possible improvement of interaction between parent and child.

    ____2. Behavioral principles and skills to apply to *future* problems and with other children in the family.

    ____3. Principles and skills to help child develop in areas that may not to particularly problematic, but in which he would like to see an improvement.

____ H. Completion of behavior inventory: Tell parent that you will put the behavior inventory in the mail within the next day and that each parent should complete the inventory independently, and that the first appointment cannot take place unless the inventory is returned. When the inventory is returned, a call will be made to make an appointment for the first interview.

____ I. Find out convenient times and phone numbers to call.

____ J. If parent expresses lack of interest, request the reason.

_____

_____

_____

_____

Date behavior inventory mailed: _____

Planned date of second phone call: _____

Address: _____

Figure 9-2
Outline for initial therapist phone contact with the family.

I. Explain underlying rationale of Parent Education Program.

____A. Explain educational goals of the program.

____1. We will be teaching you skills so you can handle future problems.

____2. We will be training you how to modify problems in their early stages of development.

____3. We will help you become independent of us.

____B. Discuss different types of treatment and why an educational approach is most promising for their problem.

____C. Stress the convenience of a long training session rather than indefinite, short sessions. We will maintain phone contact but will be fading out of the treatment as soon as possible.

____1. Children learn how to get what they want from their parents, and parents learn from their children. Because parent–child relationships are reciprocal, we will be teaching you new ways to interact with each other that should make it easier for both of you to get what you want pleasurably.

____2. There are negotiable and nonnegotiable issues. We will be teaching you how to work out problems you may be having with each other through negotiation skills.

____3. If children do not comply with simple requests or follow directions, it is a problem of motivation, not learning. We will train you how to motivate your child to become more accomplished.

____4. This approach is directed toward accentuating the positive in a structured, nonpunitive manner.

II. Define responsibilities.

____A. Program staff

____1. Maintain phone contact when necessary.

____2. Be available to help when needed.

____3. Collect data in the school and attempt to ameliorate the problems the child is having in the school and at home.

____4. Teach parents how to collect data at home and teach them skills that will prepare them for future problem solving.

____B. Parents

____1. Collect data on child's behavior at home.

____2. Read *Parents Are Teachers* after training session.

____3. Carry out procedures we recommend or discuss alternatives if the procedures do not seem adequate. Honesty is extremely important if parents do not want to follow through with a procedure.

III. Parents read and sign contract.

IV. Explain data collection at home.

____A. Explain importance of data collection.

____B. Delineate and operationalize problems at home.

____C. Data-collection forms are organized.

____D. Explain the use of data-collection recording sheets and obtain final approval of behaviors that have been specified for observation.

V. Explain home observation.

____A. Reason for the observation.

____B. Explanation of how the observer will behave in the home.

____1. Observer will not talk or eat while collecting data.

____2. The reliability checker's visit is the time to add behaviors that the parents want to observe and collect data on.

____3. Training session will be scheduled after home observation.

Figure 9-3
Outline of initial interview with family.

the staff's responsibilities to them during the program; (3) specification and definition of target problems; and (4) instruction in data collection procedures for baseline assessment, including reliability procedures.

The therapist maintained quality control in the session, as in all contacts, by using a procedural checklist of goals for the session and recording videotapes of the two clinic sessions. At the beginning of the interview, the therapist explained the educational aspect of the program—that is, the parents would be taught skills that not only would help them with their current problems, but would also be useful in handling future problems. It was emphasized that they would be trained to discriminate and modify problems in the early stages of development, so that the parents would be independent of the social worker in a relatively short time. This was followed by a short discussion of different types of treatment and the reasons that the staff felt that an educational model, rather than a counseling or psychotherapy model, would be most useful to them. The therapist explained that two lengthy sessions (2 to 3 hours) followed by a home visit and phone contact would be most convenient and least expensive for them. It was noted that a behavioral child development approach involved changing their child's interaction with others at home and, if necessary in school.

During the session, the children were described as having inadequate skills for achieving their needs from their environment through appropriate means. Children were characterized as learning to get what they wanted from their parents in inappropriate ways. On the other hand, the parents had learned that the only way to get their children to decrease negative behavior was to provide punitive and aversive consequences. The program would, then, teach the parents ways to get their children to behave appropriately through more positive means with less emphasis on punitive consequences. The therapist was careful to use plain English devoid of behavioral or other jargon.

In the second part of the interview, the therapist defined his or her responsibilities, which included the following: (1) being available for consultation when needed; (2) maintaining phone contact when necessary; (3) teaching parents how to collect data at home; (4) teaching parents procedures for future problem solving; and (5) collecting data in the school and attempting to work out a program at school as well.

The parents' responsibilities were listed as these: (1) attending two clinic sessions; (2) recording data on parent and child behavior at home; (3) reading *Parents Are Teachers* (Becker, 1981) after the training session; (4) carrying out the recommended procedures or discussing alternatives when these procedures seem inadequate; and (5) reading and signing an agreement to participate in data recording.

Data-recording procedures for the home baseline were the main focus of the third part of the interview. The therapist discussed the necessity for establishing an ongoing record of parent–child interaction. The importance of this information with regard to evaluation of the treatment effectiveness was stressed. Using the Home Questionnaire, the social worker explored specific behaviors that the parents had listed as troublesome and those that they would like for their child to achieve or improve. The behaviors of the child were then defined. The description of the behavior as provided by the parent was written on the observation form, preserving as much of the parents' language as possible and refined to make it more observable. A time was determined for observations when the behaviors were thought most likely to occur, usually a 1- to 2-hour period. Typically, a positive and a negative behavior were selected for baselining, plus three or four chores that the parents would like for the child to perform. Instructions were provided regarding the use of data-collection forms (see Figure 9-4). It was explained that 5 days of baseline data would be necessary before the training interview could be scheduled. The parent-recorded data were to be telephoned to the project telephone recorder on a daily basis.

Postinterview Home Visit

Three days to 1 week following the interview, a home visit was conducted (see Figure 9-5). There were four goals for the postinterview home visit: (1) to collect independent data on parent and child target behaviors; (2) to determine whether or not, based on the observations and parent input, the correct behaviors were defined; (3) to compare an independent observer's data with parent-recorded data to determine reliability; and (4) to answer any questions the parents may have had regarding the data collection or the program. Audiotapes were collected at this time and before the initial interview.

The observer collected data with the parent for about 10 minutes and then checked the results to ascertain whether or not the parent understood the behavioral definitions and reliability procedures. Then the observer and parent did not talk during the remainder of the reliability recording.

Parent Training Interview

Included in the educational goals for the parent training interview (see Figure 9-6) were

1. Presentation of operant behavioral principles.
2. Examination of family communication issues.
3. Review of parents' and therapist's responsibilities.
4. Contracting rules.
5. Exploration of available reinforcers.
6. Techniques for child management.
7. Specification of target child behaviors for treatment.
8. Development of a home point system.

Direct instructions, modeling, rehearsal, and feedback were the techniques used for training the parents.

Observation times _____ Date: _____
                                   Observer: _____

Child's behaviors	Tally	Parent responses
Definition:		Physical affection _____ Warned _____ Physical punishment _____ Praised _____ Sent to room or isolated _____ Discussed _____ Left room or home _____ Denied privilege _____ Repeated request _____ Reprimanded _____ Ignored _____
Definition:		Physical affection _____ Warned _____ Physical punishment _____ Praised _____ Sent to room or isolated _____ Discussed _____ Left room or home _____ Denied privilege _____ Repeated request _____ Reprimanded _____ Ignored _____

Check in box if task was done.

Figure 9-4
Sample data-recording form for home observations.

213

Date: _____
Therapist: _____
Parent: _____

I. Reliability.
____A. Record parent–child interaction concurrently with parent.
____B. Compare parent's recording with observer or worker's recording.
____C. Evaluate the correctness of behavioral definitions.
II. Relevance of behavior.
____A. Ask the parents whether they still consider the target behavior important. If not, redefine behavior and set up recording procedures.
____B. Discuss possible future targets for intervention.
III. Assessment of treatment procedures (if this follows training session).
____A. Determine whether parents are able to use the procedures.
____B. If parents are not using procedures correctly, retrain:
____1. Model.
____2. Rehearse.
____3. Give feedback.
____C. If parents are using procedures correctly, give positive feedback.
____D. If procedures are not effective:
____1. Review problem.
____2. Redesign procedures.
____3. Model for parent.
____4. Rehearse parents.

Figure 9-5
Outline of home interview and reliability observations.

Figure 9-6
Outline of parent training interview.

Date: _____
Therapist: _____
Parent: _____

I. Present behavioral principles and examples.
____A. Reinforcement _____ Example _____
____B. Extinction _____ Example _____
____C. Punishment _____ Example _____
____D. Target behaviors _____ Example _____
II. Communication.
____A. Reciprocal—parents teach children and children teach parents.
____B. Directions and requests should be explicit; no "Please" or "Okay?" at the end of a direction if compliance is expected.
____C. Parents must present a united front to the children.
III. Responsibilities of worker.
____A. Train skills.
____B. Organize program at home.
____C. Only work on parent-specified behaviors.
IV. Responsibilities of parent.
____A. Record data.
____B. Practice skill as trained and advise or discuss alternatives.

Figure 9-6 (*continued*)

___C. Gain independence from program.
___D. Be specific and explicit in expectations.
___ E. Follow through on behavioral assignments.
V. Contracting rules.
___A. Sit down with child.
___B. Select one behavior and define it in observable terms.
___C. Describe all the important aspects of the behavior, such as the following:
___1. How often should it be done.
___2. When (the specific time) it should be done.
___3. Where it should be done.
___4. Who will demonstrate and teach the behavior to the child.
___D. Agree on a reward that will be given for performing the behavior.
___ E. Decide who will determine whether the behavior was completed according to the definition.
___ F. Write down all of the above information in a contract format similar to the contract written in the training session.
___G. Both parents and child should agree to and sign the contract.
VI. Time out and overcorrection.
___A. Specify behavior and procedure.
___B. Time out _____ Example _____
___C. Overcorrection _____ Example _____
VII. Decision on target behaviors at home.
___A. Initial information on questionnaire is used to determine target behaviors.
___B. Determine reasonable rewards, privileges, and bonuses.
VIII. Point system.
___A. Explain earning and spending of points.
___B. Specificity of expectations is facilitated.
___C. Bonus rewards are possible and helpful.
___D. Determine value of behaviors on point system form.
___ E. Contract point system with child.
IX. Modeling.
___A. Praise _____ Example _____
___B. Ignoring _____ Example _____
___C. Points _____ Example _____
___D. Punishment _____ Example _____
X. Review program.

A brief overview of operant principles included a discussion of reinforcement, extinction, and punishment, and their relationship to child behavior. Although the principles were mentioned, they were taught mainly by example, and jargon was avoided. For instance, when discussing reinforcement, the therapist most frequently introduced the example of how pleased the parents had probably been when their child began to learn such basic skills as walking and talking. The therapist reminded them how positive and encouraging they had been with their child in regard to those skills—praising the child and calling each other's attention to that marvelous new response. Parents usually agreed that, yes, they had been very encouraging. In the beginning of the training session, as many examples were pulled from the parents' experience as possible. This procedure avoided defensiveness on the part of the parents and provided evidence that the therapist recognized some of their previous achievement with their children.

Family communications issues were addressed in terms of their relationship to parent–child interaction. The therapist emphasized that it was important for the parents to present a united front—that is, for them to agree on the kind of behaviors that were appropriate for the child and on their goals for the child. Further, it was stressed that they must agree or negotiate on the consequences provided for both the appropriate and inappropriate behaviors of their child. The result of their disagreements would be that the child would receive different messages from each of them, resulting in a state of confusion and stress. Unfortunately, the child would also be able to play them off against each other; thus he or she not only would avoid negative consequences for inappropriate behavior, but would be puzzled regarding appropriate ways to obtain positive consequences. It was also noted that the interaction between children and their parents is a mutual learning process, with both parents and children shaping each other's behavior.

Before going on to the next stage of training, the mutual responsibilities of the parents and the therapist were reviewed (see Figure 9-3).

The parents were introduced to a set of contracting rules based on those of Homme, Csanyi, Gonzales, and Rechs (1969), which included the following steps:

1. Sit down with the child.
2. Select one behavior and define it in observable terms.
3. Describe all important aspects of the behavior (e.g., how often it should be done, when it should be completed, where it should be done, and who will demonstrate and teach the behavior to the child).
4. Agree on a reinforcer that will be given for performing the behavior.
5. Decide who will determine whether the behavior was completed according to the definition.
6. Write down all of the above information in a contract format.
7. Have all parties agree to the contract and sign it.

Using the Child Questionnaire and the Home Questionnaire as a basis for discussion, the therapist identified some possible child reinforcers with the parents and the child. Because the success of the program relied so heavily on reinforcement, it was important to identify several backup reinforcers that could be exchanged for points. The parents were encouraged to list reinforcers already existing in their environment, such as television, free time, trips, or movies. Whenever possible, the therapist suggested that the parent engage in a positive activity with the child as a consequence for appropriate behavior.

The major techniques discussed with the parents were differential attention, shaping, time out, and overcorrection. Although differential attention was an important component of the program, greater emphasis was placed on praise and the awarding of points. In previous studies, it was found that it was easier to get parents to punish than to praise or to drop negative verbalizations. Because many of the target behaviors included aggression and other violent behavior, ignoring was not emphasized, although the rule of thumb, "If you don't want to reinforce it or punish it, don't see it," served as a guideline for the parents. Again, the techniques were heavily supported with examples, usually drawn from the parents' own experience with their child. In the typical home point system, desired behaviors were assigned points in accordance with the parents' and child's priorities.

Even though the program was designed to decrease negative interaction between parents and children, two punishment procedures were introduced: time out and overcorrection. The therapist stressed the importance of defining specific serious behaviors, such as hurting another person, that should occur before these techniques were used. Because of their research base, these procedures were judged to be the most likely to be successful when combined with differential attention and shaping to provide a powerful treatment package.

Decisions regarding the selection of child target behaviors for treatment at home were based on the baseline data collected in regard to specified behaviors and chores. In most cases the most noxious behaviors, as determined by the parents, and those occurring at a high rate were selected. Occasionally a behavior was dropped because the parents no longer considered it a problem or because it occurred at a very low rate.

The parents and child negotiated the home point system with the assistance of the therapist. During this negotiation, the therapist served as both teacher and child advocate. The child was included in the selection of chores, and his or her agreement was obtained for the other target behaviors. The child was most enthusiastically involved in the assignment of points, asking and receiving more points for the items he or she did not like to do and fewer points to the items he or she considered easy. A rule of thumb, devised by the therapist, was that if a child was young small numbers of points were used for the point system, and that if a child was older and understood larger numbers, larger numbers were used. The parents were encouraged to offer larger numbers of points for those behaviors that were essential to them. Negotiation continued until all members of the family involved in the home point system agreed. Point systems were developed for siblings of the target child when it was desired by the parents or when it was requested by the siblings.

Data-recording forms, definitions of completed tasks, and charts were provided by the therapist. Data-recording procedures were again reviewed. Once the home point system was developed, the therapist reviewed and modeled the other contingency management procedures.

During the final segment of the parent training interview, the therapist modeled differential use of parent attention, administration of points, and time-out and/or overcorrection procedures for the parent with the children. After modeling each procedure, the parents were asked to rehearse the procedure and were given positive feedback on their performance. If they were not able to carry out the procedure, they were given positive feedback on some aspect of their performance and provided with additional instructions. If they still had difficulty with some aspect of the procedure, the therapist praised specific aspects of their performance and modeled the procedure again.

At the end of this session, an appointment was made for the posttraining home visit, and instructions for calling in the data were reviewed.

Posttraining Home Visit

During the posttraining home visit, the therapist (1) recorded independent data on the targeted behaviors; (2) made any necessary revisions in the home data collection procedure (i.e., defined and included new behaviors in which the parents considered change desirable); (3) assessed the parents' use of the home point system; (4) discussed with the child any difficulties he or she might be having with the point system; (5) assisted the parents in rehearsing praise, ignoring, point-awarding, contracting, and punishment procedures; and (6) reviewed the intervention procedures being used. In most cases, this was a one-time visit. However, if the data failed to reflect improvement in the parent–child interaction, additional sessions were scheduled.

Systematic Termination

Termination of the Parent Education Program occurred when the parents had revised the home point system under the supervision of the therapist, had achieved a stable treatment effect from 2 to 3 weeks, and had gradually removed the child from the home point system. The parents were provided data-collection material for the development of home point systems, should other problems occur; were asked to complete an evaluation form; and told that the staff would contact them in 3 months to see how they were doing. They were also told that they could call the staff in the future if their child had further problems and they felt they needed our assistance.

Follow-Up

At 3 and 6 months following termination, the parents were called and asked the following questions:

1. Are you presently recording data on any behaviors? If yes, describe the behaviors you are observing.

2. Are you using a point system? If so, for what behaviors?
3. Would you rate the point system's effectiveness as: High ____, Little Value ____, No Value ____, More of a Problem than a Help ____?
4. Have you been using any procedures you were taught by the staff of the Parent Education Program? If yes, what are they?
5. Have you communicated with your child's teacher recently? If yes, what was the topic of communication?

School Program

Initial School Interview

Following a successful intervention in the home, the therapist met with the parents and the educational staff to explore the possibility of an intervention in the school or between the school and home. The therapist emphasized the efforts the parents were extending to help their child with his or her difficulties, as well as their willingness to support school programs. Before this meeting, the therapist coached the parents as to the appropriate positive way to interact with the principal and the teacher. The intent of this meeting was to repair the relationship between parents and school personnel. The therapist's role here was one of mediator and family advocate.

Assessment Interview

Once agreement had been reached that it was possible for the family and school to work jointly on the child's school problems, the therapist then met individually with the teacher to assess the child's school problems. This assessment included an evaluation of the following:

1. Academic performance in such subjects as reading, math, social science, art, gym, and science.
2. Behavior problems, including crying, screaming, whispering, mumbling, echolalia, aggression toward peers or teachers, daydreaming, tardiness, attention-getting behaviors, or leaving seat without permission.
3. Definition of major problems, times at which they occurred, frequency, and consequences.
4. The child's behavioral strengths in the classroom.
5. Special remedial classes.
6. The teacher's willingness to participate—for example, to record data, to implement classroom procedures, to sign the home report card, and to meet occasionally with the therapist to discuss and evaluate progress.

The assessment produced three possible outcomes: a classroom intervention, a home report card intervention, or no intervention. If the teacher agreed to work with the therapist, the teacher and therapist defined one or two behavioral targets in objective, observable terms and devised a simple data-recording system, usually based on task completion and a frequency tally of targeted behaviors during specific time periods. Of key importance to the recording of classroom data was the simplicity of the data-recording technique; teachers are very busy, and if the data-recording requirements are too high, they will not be able to meet them. At the end of this session, the therapist made an appointment to conduct a classroom observation, in order to establish the reliability of the teacher's data recording and to assess the appropriateness and relevance of the target behaviors.

Postassessment Visit

During the postassessment visit, the therapist or an assistant observed the child concurrently with the teacher to assess the accuracy of the teacher's data recording. Following the observation, the two records were compared and reliability calculated as in the home program. The therapist, with the teacher, also assessed the social relevance of the target problem at this time. If it was decided that the wrong problem had been selected, a new behavior (or behaviors) was selected, and baseline recording was begun again.

Intervention Interview

During this interview, the therapist and the teacher reviewed the baseline behavioral data to determine the current level of child behavior and, whenever possible, the consequences for that behavior. Then an intervention was designed to alter that level of behavior in the desired direction. Two types of programs were designed as interventions—a home report card system and/or a classroom intervention. The programs were selected based on the available teacher time, the ability of the parents to cooperate with the school, and the necessity of social consequences in the classroom.

The home report card system was selected when the parents were willing to participate with the teacher in providing positive consequences at home for on-task and desired school behaviors. This intervention was accomplished through a daily report card listing specific behaviors to be achieved in designated periods. At the end of each period or at the end of the day, the teacher noted which behaviors the child had achieved. The child was given points by the parents for taking the report card home and was awarded reinforcers for points earned at school. In many cases, this system was incorporated into the existing home point system.

A classroom intervention was attempted when the teacher's behavior was an important consequence for the child's behavior and when the teacher had adequate time to carry out the intervention. The classroom intervention usually involved an alteration of teacher attention following the child's target behavior— ignoring undesirable behavior, redirecting the child, and providing positive consequences following desirable behaviors. The types of behaviors usually treated with these procedures were "attention-getting" behaviors, such as being out of seat and talking without permission.

Postintervention Visit

Approximately a week following the initial intervention, the therapist or an assistant visited the classroom to assess the effect of the intervention on child and teacher behavior and to assess the reliability of the teacher's data recording. The therapist also reviewed the teacher's data and provided positive feedback regarding his or her implementation of the program and her data recording. If the teacher was having difficulty with either, adjustments were made either by modeling the procedures or by revising them.

Systematic Termination

In most cases, further contacts were made by telephone, unless there were difficulties with the data or the intervention. The therapist made a weekly call for approximately 3 weeks, then monthly calls, and finally a 6-month call. If problems persisted, the therapist returned to the intervention stage of the program with the teacher or referred the teacher to the school social worker or the referring agent.

Follow-Up

At 3 and 6 months following termination, the teacher was asked to report the progress of the child, specifically to assess progress on the target behaviors and his or her use of the procedures. Referral was made back to the school staff if the problems persisted.

RESULTS

During the 4 years of this research, 73 families began the Parent Education Program, with 63 families completing all phases. Of those families completing the program, 52 were considered successful by the researcher; that is, the identified problem child in each case showed substantial behavioral improvement, and the parents reported that the program had been helpful and that their child had improved. It should be noted that all parents who completed the program reported improvement in their children's behavior, although this was not always supported by the data. The average total amount of time for completed interventions, including both home and school programs, was 23 hours; 20 hours were spent on the intervention and 3 hours on evaluation. Approximately 10 hours (not counting travel) were spent on home intervention.

School programs were developed for 46 children. Of these, 17 cases involved structured interventions with the teacher in the classroom, and 29 involved home report card systems. Of these interventions the home report card system was easier to use and required less therapist time. This can be attributed to the fact that while most teachers were willing to make a daily report card, few were willing, had the skills, or had the time to involve themselves in the program enough to alter their interaction in the classroom systematically. In two cases, the teachers were so negative about the children that transfers to other classes with different teachers were arranged.

Following is an example of an individual case involving a home intervention, a school intervention, and a failure to engage one of the teachers. This case is fairly typical in terms of the failure of the program to engage the father fully in the intervention, even though he was included in the training.

CASE STUDY

Harold was a 6-year-old kindergarten student. Both his parents and teachers regarded his behaviors as immature for his age. He was described as noncompliant, inappropriately affectionate, clinging, nagging, and whining. In school, he was diagnosed as deficient in reading and therefore spent part of his day in kindergarten and the other part in first grade; although it should be noted that most of the time he received specific tutelage until the last 6 weeks of school. Although he was behind academically and was occasionally aggressive to other children, his teachers seemed to be most upset about him because he was a pest. His parents regarded his noncompliance to their requests as his most serious problem.

Both parents were involved in the parent training sessions, although the program was primarily carried out by the mother. The mother was employed as a minor executive in a travel firm and was required to do some traveling as part of her employment. She was 36 years old, with a 1-year degree from a business college. She had no history of mental illness or therapy. The father was a graduate of a 2-year premedical junior-college program; he worked two jobs, as a full-time policeman and a part-time real estate agent. He was 47 years old.

The parents were referred to the Parent Education Program as a result of a school staff meeting on the child. Both parents agreed to participate in the program. One of Harold's two teachers, however, did not feel comfortable with an observer in her classroom; she agreed to record data herself, but would not agree to a reliability observer. The second teacher was fully cooperative, both in allowing observers in the classroom and in participating in the intervention program.

Initial Interview

Problems—Home

The problems identified in the home were these: (1) putting away toys and books after one request; (2) putting away clothes after one request; (3) going to bed after one request; (4) tantrums; (5) nagging and whining. The parent and child behaviors were defined as follows:

PARENTAL REQUEST. A complete parental request was defined as complete mention of the objects to be put away or the behaviors to be performed: for example,

> "Please put these books on the shelves in your room."
> "Harold, it is time for you to go to bed."
> "Put your clothes in your closet."

Parental requests were recorded in four categories: to get ready for school, to put toys away, to put away clothes, and to go to bed.

CHILD COMPLIANCE. Complying with parental request within 2 minutes of that request was defined as compliance to a request to get ready to go to school, to put toys away, to put away clothes, or to go to bed.

GETTING READY FOR SCHOOL. This involved moving in the direction of performing self-care tasks, such as putting on an article of clothing or brushing teeth.

PUTTING TOYS AWAY. Toys and books had to be put on the shelves in the subbasement specifically designated for those items.

PUTTING CLOTHES AWAY. Clothes had to be put into the clothes hamper, hung in the closet, or folded and put in the drawer that contained similar clothes.

GOING TO BED. Going to bed was defined as being fully in the bed, with the covers drawn up at least to chest height.

CHILD TANTRUM. A tantrum was defined as shouting, screaming, stomping feet, and crying, accompanying a refusal to comply or insistence upon the performance of a behavior either by Harold or his parents.

Recording Method

Data were recorded during the time before and after school that Harold and his mother were home together. This period averaged about 2 hours, with occasional breaks when she was out of town on business. She was asked to record a tally mark on a recording form for each request and to circle marks of requests complied with by Harold. Reliability checks were recorded by an independent observer four times during the study across both experimental conditions in the home.

Parent Training Interview

Following a week of baseline observation, the parents and Harold returned to the clinic for the parent training session. During that time, specific interventions were developed to increase the positive consequences for Harold's appropriate behaviors and to structure negative consequences for some of his behaviors.

Home Point System

A home point system was designed in which Harold was required to earn 5 points for access to his everyday privileges. These included watching television, playing outside, and eating dessert. All points earned beyond the 5 points could accumulate toward a bonus prize, such as a trip to the aquarium, a movie, or the purchase of a toy airplane model. Harold was given the choice of selecting from the bonus list; all items cost 15 bonus points. The schedule for earning points was as follows:

1. Putting clothes in closet or hamper   1 pt.
2. Going to bed
    a. Putting on pajamas   1 pt.
    b. Being in bed with covers at chest height   1 pt.
3. Taking a bath to get ready for school
    a. Turning on water   1 pt.
    b. Closing the drain   1 pt.
    c. Hanging up towels   1 pt.
4. Putting toys away
    a. Putting toys in appropriate drawer   1 pt.
    b. Putting toys on appropriate shelves in closet   1 pt.

Time Out

The parents were taught to use a 3-minute time out in a chair as a consequence for Harold's tantrums. Following each tantrum, the parents were instructed to place Harold on a chair and set a kitchen timer for 3 minutes. Once the timer rang, Harold was allowed to leave the chair, and the parents were asked to praise him as soon as possible when he engaged in an appropriate behavior of any kind.

Ignoring

The parents were asked to ignore Harold for a brief moment (a minute or so) following each instance of whining. As with time out, the parents were instructed to praise desirable behavior soon after they had ignored undesirable behavior.

Results—Home

Parental requests to get ready for school, to put away toys, and to go to bed are displayed in Figure 9-7. These data indicate a decrease in parental requests following the implementation of the home point system. These decreases were correlated with an increase in Harold's compliance with requests. On no occasion did Harold fail to earn the 5 points necessary for his daily privileges. His tantrum behavior also decreased following the use of a time-out procedure (see Figure 9-8). There was a relapse following a 1-week business trip of his mother in which he was left with his grandmother. Harold, however, had tantrums only twice during the last 20 days of the intervention. Although the baseline was inadequate for comparison, it is useful to note that whining occurred only once during the final 20 days of the study. Occurrence reliability estimates ranged from 93% to 100% across all behaviors and experimental conditions.

The lack of consistency in the administration may have resulted in the deterioration that occurred on all aspects of the program. Harold continued to earn his minimum points, but his mother was observed to use the point system in a punitive way by threatening not to give him the point if he did not comply. The inconsistent way in which the mother applied the program may indicate that after one request she did not allow adequate time for Harold to comply, or that she gave him the points after nagging him into compliance, rather than waiting for the point system to work. Reinstruction in the correct way to administer the point system produced improvement in the administration of the program; even though there was still occasional inconsistency. This inconsistency, however, was true of most parents in the program and is probably true of parents in the general population. Fortunately, positive effects are often achieved, despite some inconsistency in parenting skills.

Follow-Up

As with most parents in the program, the parent telephone follow-up revealed that at 3 months following termination the mother was no longer recording data on parent or child behaviors. She was, however, still using the point system as a reward for bedtime behaviors, bathtime activities, and putting away toys. She was also using time out and rated the home point system as having

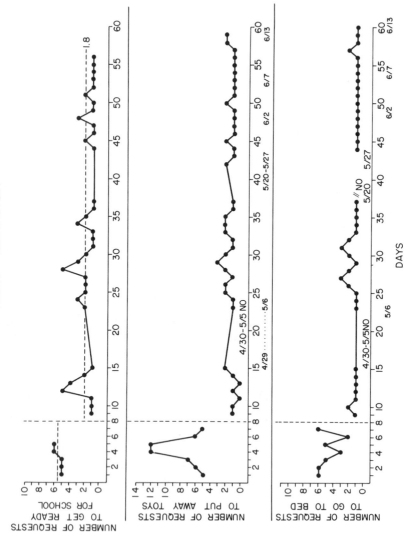

Figure 9-7

Number of parental requests to get ready for school, to put away toys, and to go to bed.

226

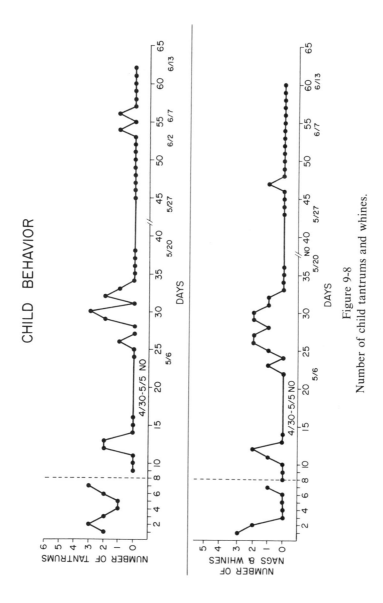

Figure 9-8

Number of child tantrums and whines.

227

been of medium value. She volunteered that she would engage in the program again if she had any major difficulty.

On the 6-month interview, the mother reported that she was neither recording data or using the home point system; though she rated the system as having been high in value. She also reported that she was still using rewards such as television programs and time out with Harold. Her husband had visited with the teachers recently and said that Harold's work was satisfactory at school. During the final 1-year interview, she reported that she was not recording data and that she had worked out a "breakfast program" which was timed and that while she was doing that she was teaching Harold how to tell time. She was also maintaining the point system for the original behaviors.

Problems—School

The major school problem identified by teachers was Harold's low rate of on-task behavior in class. Other problems, such as out-of-seat behavior and inappropriate affectionate demonstrations, were viewed as part of his inability to engage in on-task behavior. Therefore on-task behavior was selected as the primary behavioral target at school.

On-task behavior was defined as Harold's being seated at the desk with his face oriented toward his work, and being engaged in writing, drawing, or looking at work. Following 7 days of on-task baseline, the therapist developed a classroom token system in which the teacher was asked to present tokens and praise to Harold following on-task behavior at least three times during the half-day of class in kindergarten. The first-grade teacher, who was unwilling to allow direct observation in her classroom, recorded the frequency of problems and reported that Harold had improved after 2 weeks of observation and that they had no problems to work on.

Results—School

After the implementation of the token economy, Harold's on-task behavior increased from an average of 42% during baseline to an average of 67% following intervention. This, of course, produced a decrease in out-of-seat behavior. It did not produce a general decrease in undesirable affection.

His teachers informally reported more appropriate play with other children. This, however, could not be attributed to the program. Harold's improvement in school, again according to informal reports, included more interest in reading. There was no opportunity for follow-up, because the school term ended and Harold was assigned a new teacher the following year. According to the final interview with his mother, he did not experience difficulty in school the next year. This was supported by reports from the school social worker.

SINGLE-PARENT PROGRAM

The Single-Parent Program was a systematic clinical replication to evaluate the program generality of the Parent Education Program for the remediation of single-parent–child interaction problems and child behavior problems in school. Single parents were chosen as the primary subjects of this clinical research, because they represent the second largest group of families in the United States; they constitute no fewer than 17% of families (Wattenburg & Reinhardt, 1979). They were selected as a secondary population because they also suffer from special problems in terms of sparse resources of time, money, and social support. These minimal resources insure the likelihood that parenting may be more stressful for single parents. They are, however, established and continuing providers of child rearing in our culture (Blechman & Manning, 1976), and as such can benefit from parent training.

Revisions of the Parent Education Program for the Single-Parent Program included extensions of the parent training to four sessions and transfer of the training setting from clinic to home. These changes were implemented in order to decrease the stress of individual sessions by decreasing the time of each session; to increase practitioner contact and support; and to reduce the problem of generality across settings.

Characteristics of Single-Parent–Child Dyads

The single-parent families were referred for behavioral intervention by school and agency social workers. Referral social workers were provided a checklist including a description of the Single-Parent Program and the following criteria:

1. The family is headed by a parent who is currently not married.
2. The family must include at least one child who is between the ages of 5 to 10 years, with behavior problems at home and/or school.
3. The family is expected to be in the area for approximately 6 months.
4. The parent does not have a severe mental illness and has not been diagnosed as an alcoholic.

Setting

All sessions were conducted with each family at home or with school staff in the public school. The home and the school were also the settings in which behavioral changes were expected to occur.

A brief outline of the program is presented in Figure 9-9. This outline presents the program in its final form (Shibano, 1983), including three additional sessions to enhance the parent's use of the program over time. Essentially, the

Figure 9-9

Flow chart of the Single-Parent Program. (From *Development and Evaluation of a Program of Maximizing Maintenance of Treatment Effects with Single Parents* by M. Shibano. Copyright 1983 by M. Shibano. Reprinted by permission.)

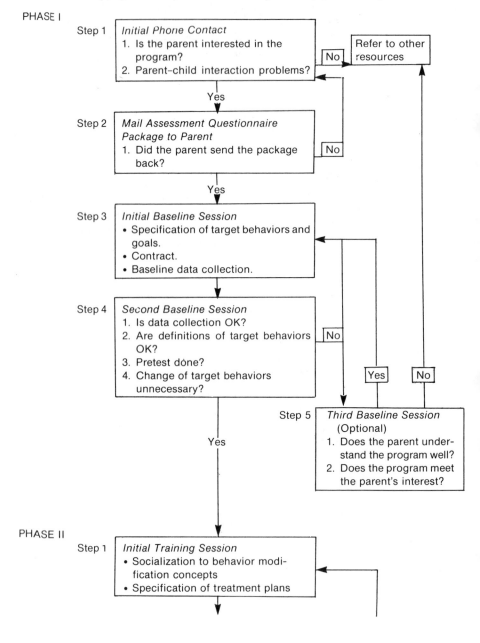

Figure 9-9 (*continued*)

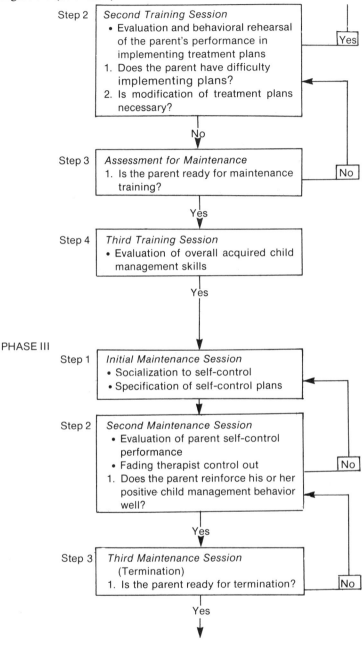

(*continued*)

Figure 9-9 (*continued*)

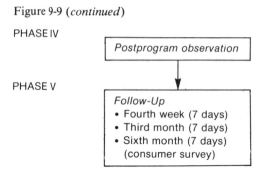

PHASE IV

PHASE V

content of parent training was the same as the Parent Education Program; therefore, the major difference was one of format. The therapist followed an outline for each step of the program similar to those presented in this chapter.

Initial Contacts by Staff

The initial contacts by staff consisted of a telephone call and a behavioral checklist and a family inventory (submitted by mail). As in the Parent Education Program, the initial phone contact was used to discuss the reason for referral, to describe the program, and to tell the parent that the inventory–checklist package would be mailed to them. When the package was returned to the program, the first appointment was scheduled.

Assessment Questionnaire Package

The assessment questionnaire package, as noted, was mailed to the parent to be completed and returned before the first interview; thus, some prompting was necessary at times to get the questionnaire returned. Included in the package were a family history, a behavioral inventory, and a behavioral checklist of potential problems. The goal of this assessment package was to guide the therapist in helping the parent to specify the problem areas of greatest concern and to assess many of the resources available to help with the intervention.

Initial Baseline Interview

The Single-Parent Program initial interview was revised from the Parent Education Program interview as a result of feedback from parents on the

Consumer Satisfaction Questionnaire (Friedman, 1979; Levitt, Friedman, Cox, & Pinkston, 1980), indicating that the parents thought the therapist was more interested in the data than in their problems. The format, therefore, was altered to begin with a discussion of child behavior problems in which the practitioner used the assessment questionnaire package to guide the discussion of the problems the family was experiencing. This was followed by the administration of parental attitude questionnaires to assess attitudes of the single parents toward their children and toward themselves. These questionnaires (Index of Self-Esteem and Parent Attitude Index) were developed to be administered over time to determine attitude changes during intervention (Hudson, 1981). In this program, they were used to determine whether or not there was an association between behavior change and reported changes in attitude.

The next step was a more complete description of the program, similar to that in the original Parent Education Program. That is, the emphasis was on the parent's educational focus and skill development as the method for changing child behavior.The benefits to the parent were described as improvement in child behavior, the ability to apply principles and skills to future problems, and the ability to use principles and skills to help the child develop desirable behaviors.

The explanation of participation was simplified to include the necessary time commitment, as well as observation and recording of parent and child behaviors. The parents were expected to make themselves available for four home training sessions, to observe and record data for 1 to 2 hours per day, and to be available for reliability observations during baseline and intervention conditions.

Following an analysis of the behavioral checklist and family inventory with the parent and a discussion of the characteristics of the program, the therapist and the parent specified and defined behavioral goals. In general, the behaviors selected were those that were of immediate concern to the parent, were aversive, provided obstacles to change of other problems, or were self-injurious. The parent was encouraged to define and talk about the problems in behavioral and objective terms. In addition to behaviors, the parent and the therapist selected some chores (usually 6 to 10) in the household that the child should perform.

The parent was then taught data-recording procedures; daily recording times were established; and procedures for phoning the data in to the answering service were explained. While recording procedures varied among parents, most parents were asked to tally the behaviors of their child and the responses or consequences they provided for the behaviors. In instances where child compliance was an issue, parents were asked to record their instructions or requests. Reliability procedures were explained to the parent, and usually an appointment was made for an observer visit before the next interview.

Second Baseline Interview

The second baseline interview was used to continue the assessment process. This entailed examination of any problems the parent may have had with problem definition or with the data-recording procedures. If the parent still did not regard the original problem definitions or goals as relevant, these were revised. If the data-recording system was too difficult, it was simplified or explained again. During this interview, a pretest for knowledge of basic behavioral principles was administered to the parent. A third baseline interview was scheduled only if major problems in defining goals or recording data occurred.

Initial Training Interviews

The purpose of the first training interview was essentially the same as in the Parent Education Program (see Figure 9-6). The parent was taught basic behavioral concepts; treatment plans were developed and specified; and the parent was taught through modeling, rehearsal, and feedback to use them. During the second training interview, the parent was asked to demonstrate once again his or her ability to use the procedures, and an assessment was made of his or her skills. The general procedures of positive reinforcement, ignoring, contracting, point systems, and time out were reviewed at this time.

If the parent improved his or her child management skills and the child improved behaviorally, maintenance training was therefore in order. A final training session was thus scheduled in which the therapist reviewed the improvement with the parent and scheduled the initial maintenance training interview. If the parent did not improve, he or she was asked to engage in additional training sessions if he or she was still interested in pursuing a solution to the problem.

Initial Maintenance Interview

The maintenance part of the program (Shibano, 1983) involved teaching the parent foundations for the concept of self-control and ways in which to set up a self-management program. The parent was taught to use self-evaluation and self-praise as ways of maintaining improved behavior, as well as to award himself or herself points for good child management behaviors and to trade those points for items he or she had placed on a payoff "menu."

Second Maintenance Interview

This interview was used to evaluate the effectiveness of the program in maintaining parental performance. It was also used to clean up any loose ends the parent may have had with the program or questions that may have been unanswered. Small revisions were still occasionally necessary.

Third Maintenance Interview

This interview was essentially the termination interview. First, the therapist and parent reviewed whether or not the agreed-upon criteria had been reached and whether or not the parent had learned to use the self-management procedures. If not, another maintenance session was scheduled. If the criteria had been reached, the therapist congratulated the parent and worked out the post-program observations and follow-up schedule.

Postprogram Observation and Follow-Up

The postprogram observation consisted of 7 days of additional observation following termination for assessment. This period resembled the baseline in terms of therapist control. The follow-up observation occurred 3 months following termination and involved a week of observation by the parent with a reliability check. The final follow-up was conducted 6 months following termination, with a reliability check and a week of observation. The consumer survey was administered at this time by a trained staff member who had not been involved with the client.

RESULTS

A total of 56 single parents were introduced to the Single-Parent Program; 37 of them completed the program. After the first year, in which 10 of 13 clients dropped out before intervention and only three completed the intervention successfully (Friedman, 1979), the program was revised with much better results. A survey of the first- and second-year clients (Levitt *et al.*, 1980) revealed that discontinuing clients could be discriminated from continuing clients by their belief that therapists were more interested in data recording than in their problems. All individuals with this belief were first-year clients. The second year of the program, 17 clients were treated successfully, with only three dropouts; this low rate of dropout was attributed to additional time spent in discussing the importance of the data to the treatment effort and talking to the parents regarding problem assessment. The therapists also attempted to increase their supportive statements to the clients. Seven of the clients were seen in group parent training, a procedure that apparently worked as well as individual treatment but was more difficult to organize. After the first year, most of the parents responded positively to the single-parent program (86% rated the program highly), although they were not as positive as were the two-parent families in the Parent Education Program, which was practically unanimously given high ratings even when the children did not improve greatly. Only five parents completed the maintenance program, and the follow-up is not completed yet. Of the 37 clients who completed the program, all showed improvement in their interactions with their children, and their children's behavior also improved. With one exception, follow-up observation showed continued parental use of praise at a higher rate than during baseline, and negative attention at a lower rate. It should be noted that there was some return to using negative attention, but not to the baseline level in 83% of the cases.

DISCUSSION

Clearly, both single and married parents can be taught to alter their behaviors as a way of altering their interactions with their children, and therefore altering their children's behaviors. These data indicate that this goal can be accomplished through a brief intervention with two-parent families, and with a slightly longer and more intensive involvement with single-parent families. In most cases, change can be accomplished following one or two training sessions, although others may require a longer intervention. These programs were designed to teach parents who could benefit quickly with a minimum of time investment on the part of parents, therapists, and in some cases teachers.

These procedures, based on reinforcement theory, can be taught with relative ease to parents to enable them to act as change agents for their children's inappropriate and appropriate behaviors. They provide a positive alternative to aversive control and can be modified to fit the specific problems presented by a variety of families. The most important aspect of this research, both from an economic and a humanitarian point of view, is that it provides a positive alternative to excluding children from normal interaction with their families. It can be used in community agencies and can provide clinical services to families of children with serious behavior problems. Essentially, the research is most valuable in situations in which contingency management is a major factor in the family dysfunction.

Perhaps the major advantage of behavioral parent training is the clinical use of data analysis to develop intervention alternatives. Decisions are then made through an informed assessment of parent and child progress. In altering this parent training model, more emphasis should be placed on educating the parents in the clinical value of data recording as part of the treatment, rather than as something the parents are doing for the therapist. The data are part of the parents' self-assessment and should be analyzed as a component of treatment in future research.

In addition, therapists should analyze their attention as a source of social reinforcement to parents and children. For single parents, social support by the therapist appears to be important and should be analyzed as a component of the intervention with the parents.

Brief evaluation tools (see Chapter 16 of this volume) for the practitioner could add greatly to the confidence of the therapist in the parent training procedure. Establishing parental skills and measuring them before trying to implement the procedures in the home would be an important improvement in achieving generality.

Acknowledgments

I would like to express my appreciation to Richard A. Polster, Benjamin S. Friedman, and Wendell Cox, the project directors of the Parent Education Program and the Single-Parent Program, for their assistance in carrying out this research. I am also grateful to the Illinois Department of Mental Health and Developmental Disabilities and the National Institutes of Mental Health for the funding that made the research possible.

References

Baer, D. M., Wolf, M. M., & Risley, T. R. Some current dimensions of applied behavior analysis. *Journal of Applied Behavior Analysis*, 1968, *1*, 91–97.

Becker, W. C. *Parents are teachers: A child management program*. Champaign, Ill.: Research Press, 1981.

Berkowitz, B. P., & Graziano, A. M. Training parents as behavior therapists: A review. *Behavior Research and Therapy*, 1972, *10*, 297–317.

Blechman, E. A., & Manning, M. A reward–cost analysis of the single-parent family. In E. J. Mash, L. S. Hamerlynck, & L. C. Handy (Eds.), *Behavior modification and families*. New York· Brunner/Mazel, 1976.

Corte, H. E., Wolf, M. M., & Locke, B. J. A comparison procedure of eliminating self-injurious behavior of retarded adolescents. *Journal of Applied Behavior Analysis*, 1971, *4*, 201–213.

Cox, W. H. *Behavioral group training of single-parent–child dyads*. Unpublished doctorai dissertation, University of Chicago, 1982.

Cox, W. H., Rzepnicki, T. L., Shibano, M., & Pinkston, E. M. *A cross validation study oj short-form scales in the evaluation of behavioral parent training*. Paper presented at the conference of the Association for Behavior Analysis, Dearborn, Michigan, 1980.

Friedman, B. S. *Analysis of participation in a training program for single parents*. Unpublished doctoral dissertation, University of Chicago, 1979.

Hall, R. V., Christler, C., Cranston, S. S., & Tucker, B. Teachers and parents as researchers using multiple-baseline designs. *Journal of Applied Behavior Analysis*, 1970, *3*, 247–255.

Hersen, M., & Barlow, D. H. *Single case experimental designs: Strategies for studying behavior change*. New York: Pergamon Press, 1976.

Homme, L. E., Csanyi, A., Gonzales, M., & Rechs, J. *How to use contingency contracting in the classroom*. Champaign, Ill.: Research Press, 1969.

Hudson, W. W. Development and use of indexes and scales. In R. M. Grinnel (Ed.), *Social work research and evaluation*. Itasca, Ill.: Peacock, 1981.

Johnson, C. A., & Katz, R. C. Using parents as change agents for their own children: A review. *Journal of Child Psychology and Psychiatry and Allied Disciplines*, 1973, *14*, 181–200.

Levitt, J. L., Friedman, B. S., Cox, W. H., & Pinkston, E. M. *Analysis of consumer evaluation across single-parent studies.* Paper presented at the conference of the Association for Behavior Analysis, Dearborn, Michigan, 1980.

O'Dell, S. Training parents in behavior modification: A review. *Psychological Bulletin*, 1974, *81*, 418–433.

Panyan, M., Boozer, H., & Morris, N. Feedback to attendants as a reinforcer for applying operant techniques. *Journal of Applied Behavior Analysis.* 1970, *3*, 1–4.

Pinkston, E. M., Friedman, B. S., & Polster, R. A. Parents as agents for behavior change. In S. P. Schinke (Eds.), *Behavioral methods in social welfare: Helping children, adults, and families in community settings.* New York: Aldine, 1981.

Pinkston, E. M., Polster, R. A., Friedman, B. S., & Lynch, M. A. Treatment of coercive family interactions. In E. M. Pinkston, J. L. Levitt, G. R. Green, N. L. Linsk, & T. L. Rzepnicki, *Effective social work practice: Advanced techniques for behavioral intervention with individuals, families, and institutional staff.* San Francisco: Jossey-Bass, 1982.

Rzepnicki, T. L., Shibano, M. Pinkston, E. M., & Cox, W. H. Treatment of stuttering through use of parental attention and structured programs for fluency. In E. M. Pinkston, J. L. Levitt, G. R. Green, N. L. Linsk, & T. L. Rzepnicki, *Effective social work practice: Advanced techniques for behavioral intervention with individuals, families, and institutional staff.* San Francisco: Jossey-Bass, 1982.

Shibano, M. *Development and evaluation of a program of maximizing maintenance of treatment effects with single parents.* Unpublished doctoral dissertation, University of Chicago, 1983.

Shibano, M., Cox, W. H., Rzepnicki, T. L., & Pinkston, E. M. A single-parent intervention to increase parenting skills over time. In E. M. Pinkston, J. L. Levitt, G. R. Green, N. L., Linsk, & T. L. Rzepnicki, *Effective social work practice: Advanced techniques for behavioral intervention with individuals, families, and institutional staff.* San Francisco: Jossey-Bass, 1982.

Sidman, M. *Tactics of scientific research: Evaluating experimental data in psychology.* New York: Basic Books, 1960.

Wattenburg, E., & Reinhardt, H. Female-headed families: Trends and implications. *Social Work*, 1979, *24*, 460–467.

COERCIVE INTERPERSONAL CONTINGENCIES AS A DETERMINANT OF CHILD MALTREATMENT
Implications for Treatment and Prevention

Robert L. Burgess
Rhonda A. Richardson
The Pennsylvania State University

Our objectives in this chapter are to describe what have come to be identified as major predictors of parents who mistreat their children, and to review recent efforts to build upon knowledge of those predictors in the development, implementation, and evaluation of treatment programs for dealing with abusive parents. As groundwork for our discussion, we need to establish a definition of "child abuse." Unfortunately, this is an especially difficult problem, in part because we are necessarily dealing with behavior that falls along a continuum of parent–child relationships (Burgess, 1979). In addition, four major types of parental maltreatment need to be considered. Perhaps the most commonly recognized and most frequently studied type is physical abuse. On a continuum of punitive intensity, such physically harmful acts range from pushing, slapping, or spanking to choking, punching, cutting, or burning a child. A second type is sexual abuse, which is the exploitation of a child for sexual gratification of an adult and includes exhibitionism, fondling of the genitals, incest, and rape. This form of parental maltreatment occurs most frequently between fathers and daughters, particularly within stepfamilies (Finkelhor, 1979).

Parental neglect represents the third major type of maltreatment, in that it involves the harming of a child through lack of care or supervision. It is a condition in which a caretaker responsible for the child either deliberately, or by extraordinary inattentiveness, permits the child to experience avoidable present suffering and/or fails to provide one or more of the ingredients generally deemed essential for developing a person's physical, intellectual, and emotional capacities (Polansky, Hally, & Polansky, 1975).

Along with discussing physical and sexual abuse and the neglect of children, it is essential that we include consideration of a fourth type of abuse—namely, emotional abuse. This last type provides a common thread linking the former three types of maltreatment. Emotional damage is frequently the underlying problem in many cases that first appear as other forms of abuse and neglect (Kinard, 1979). That is, there is growing recognition that emotional maltreatment is the central problem in child abuse, and that in most cases physical injuries are only of secondary concern (Garbarino, 1980b). Parental neglect and physical and sexual abuse of children merit concern in that they represent a threat to a child's emotional well-being.

Broadly speaking, the definition of "emotional maltreatment" should center on the parent's rejection of the child and the discouragement of the normal and naturally occurring behaviors that reflect the development of the child's competence. Two conditions should arouse special concern for the emotional well-being of a child (Garbarino & Garbarino, 1980). One is a child's seriously impaired competence in social relationships, including an inability to respond appropriately to adults, peers, and siblings, compounded by high frequencies of negative-affect behavior and low self-esteem. The second is evidence that a parent or guardian rejects a child by refusing to care for the child, by punishing normal prosocial behaviors, or by placing the child in a consistently negative light. In short, any parental behavior that threatens the development of a child's interpersonal skills, patience, ability to set reasonable personal goals, or self-esteem can be categorized as emotional maltreatment.

For our present purposes, each of these four types of parental maltreatment is subsumed under the heading of "child abuse" or "maltreatment" and is defined functionally as nonaccidental physical and psychological injury to a child under the age of 18, which occurs as a result of physical, sexual, or emotional actions of omission or commission perpetrated by a parent or caretaker and which threatens a child's developing competence (cf. Burgess, Garbarino, & Gilstrap, 1983).

We now turn our attention to identifying the major predictors of child abuse. This is followed by a review of recent research on treatment programs aimed at working with abusive parents. The chapter concludes with some thoughts about child abuse prevention programs targeted at parents.

PARENTAL FACTORS ASSOCIATED WITH ABUSE

Personal Characteristics

Early attempts to understand and explain the occurrence of abusive behavior within the family originated from within the medical profession. The parents were seen as the source of the problem, and research focused on identifying factors that distinguish abusive from nonabusive mothers and fathers. Thus, personal characteristics that place a parent at risk for child maltreatment include emotional disturbances (Elmer, 1967), difficulty in dealing with aggressive impulses (Wasserman, 1967), a rigid and domineering personality (B. Johnson & Morse, 1968), and low self-esteem (Spinetta & Rigler, 1972). Other factors linked to abusive parental behavior include alcoholism (Blumberg, 1974) and a history of having been abused or neglected as a child (Kempe, Silverman, Steele, Droegemueller, & Silver, 1962; Steele & Pollock, 1974).

Recently, attention has been directed away from such psychiatric profiles of abusive parents, and a more social-psychological approach has been used to determine personal characteristics of parents that are antecedents of child maltreatment. Results of such work suggest that a high level of life stress is associated with the incidence of abusive parental behavior (Conger, Burgess, & Barrett, 1979; Straus, 1980). The relationship may not be a direct one, however, since life crisis has its most significant impact on those parents with punitive history (i.e., those parents who themselves, as children, were subjected to maltreatment) (Conger *et al.*, 1979). Life change, physical and emotional health, and life experiences of a particular type are predisposing events that may turn the similar situations all parents face into an abusive encounter in one instance while not in another.

Another social-psychological situation in which abusive parents are disproportionately represented is finding oneself in the role of a stepparent (Burgess, Anderson, Schellenbach, & Conger, 1981; Finkelhor, 1979). In approximately 50% of the cases of documented child abuse collected by the American Humane Association, there were stepchildren in the home; in the majority of cases, the stepchild was the abused child. We should note that for the country as a whole, only 10–15% of families are stepfamilies. In short, then, a stepchild is 3.5 times as likely to be abused as is a child who lives with his or her biological parents (Burgess, 1980). Moreover, there is evidence that stepparents find it more difficult to develop deep affection for stepchildren than they do for their own biological offspring (Duberman, 1975).

This latter possibility leads to consideration of one other personal characteristic of parents associated with child abuse, which is essentially social-psychological in that it relates to the nature of the parent–child relationship. Lack of attachment to one's child may increase the probability of parental maltreatment (Klaus & Kennell, 1976). It is possible that the apparent lack of attachment to one's child is due to characteristics of the child that make that child unreinforcing and too difficult to handle, or to a mismatch of parent–child behavioral styles or temperaments. In any case, parental characteristics may also be involved, in that the parent may simply be unresponsive to the infant's needs or does not know how to manage a misbehaving youngster.

Deficient Parental Resources

Along with personal characteristics of parents, there is another set of variables— namely, deficient parental resources—that helps explain the occurrence of child maltreatment. Abusive parents often lack sufficient social and financial resources. Although child abuse is by no means restricted to lower-class families, low socioeconomic status and unemployment, perhaps because of the stress they place on parents, do result in a higher probability of child abuse (Garbarino, 1977; Gil, 1970; Light, 1973). There has also been some suggestion that adolescent parenthood increases the likelihood of child maltreatment (Straus, 1979). This association may, in fact, be explainable in terms of social class, since most teenage pregnancies occur among youths of lower socioeconomic status (Chilman, 1980). Indeed, recent evidence suggests that it is not age per se, but rather the socioeconomic status of a mother, that influences her interaction with her child (Philliber & Graham, 1981).

Other circumstances associated with child abuse also indicate a deficiency of parental resources. Single-parent households are heavily implicated in cases of abuse (Friedman, 1976; Gil, 1970; C. F. Johnson, 1974). Part of the reason for this may be the lower financial resources available to these families. In 1978, nearly half of all poor families were headed by women (U.S. Bureau of the Census, 1979). Over 70% of divorced women must work, and close to 85% must also care for children (Campbell, 1975); and they must do so without moral, economic, or psychological support from a husband or partner. Single parenthood is in itself a stressful experience, and the situation is aggravated further when financial and social resources are low. Data support the notion that the absence of a parent from the home may place considerable stress upon the remaining parent, and thus may increase the likelihood of aversive exchanges (Burgess et al., 1981). Single parenthood, particularly in families of lower socioeconomic status, contributes to an emphasis on the negative in parent–child interactions—a pattern that is associated with physical and emotional abuse as well as neglect (Kimball, Stewart, Conger, & Burgess, 1980).

Parental resources are also strained in families with a large number of children. Financial assets must be spread among more family members, increasing the likelihood of conflicts of interest over those goods. Such economic stress is particularly likely, given the fact that large family size is disproportionately found among parents who were under 18 when their first child was born (Chilman, 1980). The reader should recall that adolescent parenthood has already been described as occurring predominantly among youths of lower socioeconomic status.

In addition to financial assets, parental time and energy themselves, are limited resources, and it seems reasonable that their allocation per child may decrease as family size increases. In support of this are data showing that the larger the family, the less direct parental contact any one child receives (Burgess *et al.*, 1981). Furthermore, any attention a child does receive takes place in a more negative context (Burgess *et al.*, 1981). The more children there are in the home, the lower the frequency of positive contacts, including words and/ or actions expressing approval, support, or liking, between a child and a parent. At the same time, there is a slight increase in the frequency of negative behavior, such as physical or verbal indications of dislike, disapproval, or lack of support. Thus emotional and physical maltreatment of children is more likely in larger families. The reason for this great emphasis on the negative may be that greater numbers of children are associated with increasing parental frustrations in dealing with the complexities of individual personalities and needs (Kidwell, 1981). Furthermore, the day-to-day demands and pressures of family life become greater when there are more children to deal with, particularly in families where economic resources are limited. Thus, parents may find that they have less time and patience for displaying positive verbal behavior such as praise, approval, encouragement, or affection. What time they do spend attending to any one child must be used for disciplining him or her, a task that often involves punitive behaviors such as physical punishment and verbal threats. Clearly, parental resources, both financial and personal, are more deficient in families with more children—a fact that can explain the frequent association between large family size and the incidence of child abuse (Gil, 1970; Light, 1973).

Having one's children too closely spaced exacerbates the parental strain associated with large family membership. A narrow age spacing creates less breathing room in the family, leaving parents more stressed. It also means that there are more children placing affectional, disciplinary, and financial demands on the parents all at one time (Kidwell, 1981). Particularly for lower-class families, this increases the pressure of providing for many children, leaving the parents with even less time to devote to a given child on a one-to-one basis and fewer opportunities to engage in positive parenting. Support for the importance of child density as a risk factor for parents comes from research showing that with increased age spacing of children, parental influence become stronger and consists of less punitiveness, more reasonableness, and more supportiveness (Kidwell, 1981; Pfouts, 1980). Furthermore, children who are closer in age to their siblings experience fewer positive and more interactions with their mothers and fathers, a pattern most typical of abusive and neglectful families (Richardson, Burgess, & Burgess, in press).

The financial and personal resource deficits that place many parents at risk for child maltreatment become even more threatening when accompanied by a lack of social supports. Evidence suggests that abusive families tend to be socially isolated (Garbarino, 1977). The parents may be cut off from the neighborhood and community resources needed, for example, to help them cope with the stresses of single parenthood or limited parenting energy. In addition, lack of contact with people outside the family unit leads to more and intensified interactions with one's children, providing additional opportunities for conflicts of interest to arise, limiting tension-relieving outlets, and ultimately increasing the likelihood that violent behavior will erupt.

Parents who are socially isolated also receive less social monitoring of their behavior. This last suggestion points to the possibility that it is not simply a lack of social supports, but rather a lack of *proper* social supports, that places a parent at risk for abusive behavior. Burgess and Akers (1966) have argued that differential association and resultant social reinforcement can account for the development of deviant, antisocial behavior. With regard to child maltreatment, this would imply that a parent may develop abusive, unacceptable ways of dealing with his or her children merely because those people with whom he or she has contact reinforce such patterns of behavior. This reinforcement may not necessarily be in a direct verbal form, such as words of praise or encouragement for hitting one's child, but may consist of positive social actions such as respectful responses, smiling, or engaging in pleasant conversation while the parent neglects his or her youngster, disparages the child, or justifies the youngster's need of harsh treatment. The reason that such inappropriate reinforcement may occur could be that the members of the parent's social group—neighbors, for example—have developed norms prescribing such "deviant" forms of parental behavior. Given a large number of individuals living under similar conditions, they are likely to behave in similar ways (Burgess & Akers, 1966). Within such groups, many forms of social reinforcement may become contingent upon classes of behaviors that are outside the larger society's normative requirements. In the case of child abuse, the result would be neighborhoods in which less acceptable parenting behaviors are prevalent. Indeed, Garbarino and Crouter (1978) have documented the existence of "high-risk" neighborhoods where maltreatment of children is especially likely to occur. Thus, parents who lack social supports or whose social networks do not provide appropriate norms and social reinforcement for parenting behavior are more likely to abuse their children.

Many abusive parents exhibit a social skills deficiency that may, in fact, underlie many of the predictive factors we have discussed so far, including low socioeconomic status, difficulties in dealing with stress, and social isolation. Moreover, the lack of general social skills is especially likely to be manifested in the form of poor parenting skills (Burgess, 1979). Specifically, they may lack knowledge about normal child development and may be poor observers of their children's behavior (Patterson, 1979). This leads to unrealistic expectations for children's behavior and an inability to monitor appropriate and inappropriate actions. Inconsistent use of discipline may result (Patterson, 1976; Young, 1964). This general lack of parenting skills often results in higher rates of negative behavior and lower rates of positive behavior directed toward children in abusive and neglectful families (Burgess & Conger, 1978). It may also lead to an overall style of parent–child interaction referred to as a "cycle of coercion."

Interpersonal Contingencies and the Cycle of Coercion

One implication to be drawn from our discussion up to this point is that to predict and explain the occurrence of child abuse accurately, the maltreatment of children needs to be examined within a fairly broad social context (cf. Burgess, 1979). So far, we have considered a range of predictors, including such personal characteristics of the parent as emotional disturbance and the lack of parenting and social skills. We have also looked at parental characteristics that are clearly a product of a person's location within certain social structures of varying size or complexity. Thus, we have pointed out the importance of a person's place within the larger socioeconomic structure, reflected in the impact of poverty and underemployment. We have also suggested the importance of being isolated from proper social support networks such as friends and neighbors. Finally, we have considered the importance of family structure variables, such as being in a large family or being a single parent or stepparent.

However, not all variables are created equal, and it is necessary to consider how and why these predictors or parental risk factors presented so far result in child maltreatment in some cases, while in other instances effective parental functioning is maintained despite these predisposing factors. This requires an analysis of parent–child dynamics. As Burgess (1979, p. 168) has suggested, "abusive behavior patterns are more immediately traceable to contingency histories located within the family itself." Certain interpersonal contingencies or patterns of interaction increase the likelihood that abusive behavior will erupt. As first developed by Patterson and his associates, the most frequently invoked paradigm is one according to which the delivery of high-intensity aversive stimuli may result from an escalating cycle of coercive behaviors between individuals (Patterson & Reid, 1970; Patterson, 1976).

With respect to parent–child relations, the process works in the following way. Parental social actions, such as smiling, attending, or complying with a child's request, may function as positive reinforcers for a child. The child's aversive–oppositional actions are efficient ways of obtaining these. For example, a child emits a mand, such as shouting to his or her mother in a movie theater, "I want a candy bar." Noncompliance by the mother is punished; if she does not comply and buy the candy, the child will increase the amplitude of the manding behavior—he or she will yell louder. Further noncompliance will exacerbate the situation, such that the child may begin to scream and cry. The mother can stop her child's aversive actions by giving in to his or her command and buying the candy bar. Thus, termination of the tantrum serves as a negative reinforcer for the mother's compliance. At the same time, the child is positively reinforced for the aversive behavior, in that the mother complies. What results is a cycle of coercion whereby a parent's behavior is controlled by negative reinforcement and a child's is controlled by positive reinforcement.

Parents who lack knowledge of effective child management techniques may be particularly vulnerable to such a cycle. In addition, some parents may set the stage for aversive child behavior by placing unrealistic expectations on their children. For example, a 2-year-old boy might ask his mother to tie his shoes for him. The mother, on the other hand, might inappropriately respond by telling him to do it himself since she is busy feeding the baby. The toddler, unable to accomplish the task, will restate his request with more intensity. Thus proceeds the coercive process until the mother either stops what she is doing to tie her son's shoes or retaliates against his tantrum by striking out at him, forcing him to comply with *her* wishes as a way of terminating the maltreatment.

Most recently, Vasta (1982) has attempted to expand this social-interactional approach to explain why physical punishment sometimes erupts into abusive assault. Clearly, not all parents who are trapped in cycles of coercion with their children eventually commit physical child abuse. Some continually comply, while others may resort to ignoring the child completely (i.e., neglect) or to using verbal degradation as a means of retaliation (i.e., emotional abuse). To understand the occurrence of physical maltreatment as a response to the cycle of coercion, Vasta proposes a dual-component analysis. That is, he maintains that along with the instrumental component according to which a parent's behavior is controlled by negative reinforcment, there is also an impulsive component whereby parental aggression is reflexive in nature, occurring in response to excessive physiological arousal. Heightened arousal accounts for the escalation of the coercion cycle into physical abuse in two ways: It increases the intensity of the physical punishment administered by the parent, and it interferes with the rational, intellectual processes that would otherwise presumably thwart such an attack.

To understand the application of this principle, let us return to the example of the boy who wants his shoes tied. The mother's unrealistic expectations for her 2-year-old remain an important factor in increasing the probability of his aversive behavior. The subsequent whining and crying, while engendering a potentially functional response by the mother, also serve to increase her arousal. This condition is further heightened by the frustration and anger induced when the toddler's tantrum forces her to interrupt her present activity. By the time she approaches the child to administer physical punishment, the instrumental processes in operation (e.g., negative reinforcement) are accompanied by a very high level of autonomic arousal. Her initial slap produces only additional screaming by the child—inviting more punishment and, of course, heightening her arousal to the limit. As she continues to hit her son, the hitting actually increases rather than diminishes the frequency and intensity of his crying behavior. Since the arousal at this point is very extreme, the mother is probably unaware of the force she is using. Only when the boy ceases his tantrum and/or the mother becomes physically exhausted does the arousal subside and attack end.

Thus, according to this analysis, the personal characteristics and deficient parental resources presented earlier place parents at risk for child maltreatment, in that they increase the likelihood of conditions that can combine to ignite the cycle of abuse. Given the presence of certain parental characteristics, such as those outlined earlier, the commission of aversive behaviors by a child will begin a cycle of coercion that in turn may serve as a precipitant of abuse. Alternatively, there is the possibility that this coercion cycle may be important not as a precipitant but merely as a correlate of parental maltreatment. It may reflect an overall style of social behavior that is associated with poor parental functioning.

In line with the latter suggestion, Wahler (1980a) has demonstrated that multiple coercion traps are likely. A parent who finds that coercive interchanges are the most effective way to deal with his or her children may cease over time to find noncoercive exchanges reinforcing. That is, the same patterns of coercive interaction may be generalized to spouses, friends, and relatives. Indeed, within the social-interactional scheme, Gottman (1979) has extensively studied the nature of the husband–wife relationship. In particular, he has analyzed those characteristics of dyadic interaction that distinguish distressed and nondistressed couples. For example, in their actions toward each other, distressed spouses are considerably more negative than are nondistressed spouses (Gottman, 1979). The former spouses are also more likely than are the latter to reciprocate negative affect. This pattern of negative reciprocity is the coercion process we have been dealing with. Thus, the cycle of coercion frequently appears not only as a precipitant of child maltreatment, but as a general characteristic of other forms of family dysfunction.

When similar patterns of coercion develop between the parent and extrafamily members, the result is a multiply entrapped parent (Wahler, 1980b). This parent typically experiences generalized insularity, in that he or she finds little positive reinforcement value in most day-to-day contacts. Multiply entrapped parents have few positive social exchange options available to them within and outside their families. As a result, they tend to attribute negative qualities to themselves, to family members, and to extrafamily members. They also tend to be socially isolated, thereby being cut off from opportunities for outside monitoring of and feedback on their parenting behavior. Ironically, those parents who most need social supports to help them deal with stresses and to alter their aversive styles of interaction lack the social skills needed to obtain them. This cycle of coercion, as well as the resource deficits and personal characteristics discussed earlier, have implications for treatment and prevention strategies targeted at abusive parents. We turn now to a review of recent research on treatment programs and the application of knowledge of parental risk factors to preventive programs.

RECENT TREATMENT EFFORTS

Most studies of child abuse are largely descriptive in nature, focusing on characteristics of abusive parents and abused children. Even most articles dealing with intervention merely present descriptive outlines of treatment programs. Relatively few studies have empirically evaluated the effectiveness of treatment to reduce abusive parenting. A few recent efforts, however, show some promise of filling this void, and they are reviewed in this section.

All of the programs to be discussed are case studies, involving only one or two families. Although this may limit the generalizability of their findings, these studies nevertheless have merit in that they serve as models for empirically based treatment efforts. In addition, they suggest that the concept of coercive interpersonal contingencies is useful for treatment as well as for the explanation of child abuse. Finally, such efforts may have implications not only for decreasing the incidence of child abuse, but also, to the extent that the parental behaviors they seek to modify are exhibited by nonabusive parents, for increasing parental effectiveness in general.

Studies by Burgess and his colleagues (Burgess *et al.*, 1981) have revealed that there are certain patterns of interpersonal contingencies distinctive of abusive families. These families generally interact with each other less often than do individuals in nonabusive families; members are considerably less positive toward one another, while they are more negative and demanding; and they are more likely to reciprocate one another's negative behaviors than they are their positive responses. Information based on these interpersonal styles was used to design, implement, and evaluate a home-based parent training program for an abusive single-parent family consisting of a mother and four children ranging in age from 2 to 14 (Burgess *et al.*, 1981).

This family is an exemplar of those characteristics we have noted to be predictive of child abuse. The family was poor and lived in an isolated rural area with no telephone, no car, and few neighbors. Interpersonally, the mother displayed multiple behavioral deficits in diverse social skills essential to home and family management, such as obtaining medical and dental services for herself and her children, negotiating disputes with neighbors and the parents of her children's peers, budgeting for the household, and interacting with educational and service professionals of the community. The family as a whole exhibited low rates of interaction, and when members did relate to one another, they did so in a frequently aggressive manner, including fighting, teasing, lying, stealing, and destructiveness. The mother most often would ignore the escalation of these behaviors until they reached very high intensities, at which point she would interject an ambiguous negative command. The interaction would then escalate in aversiveness until her shouting was eventually followed by corporal punishment.

Given this pattern, a training program was designed to teach the mother to (1) specify undesirable child behavior correctly; (2) become a more accurate observer of her children's behavior; (3) issue precise-action directives to her children; and (4) apply appropriate contingencies of positive reinforcement for prosocial behavior and noncorporal punishment, such as "time out," for inappropriate behavior.

Observations and training took place in the home over a period of 9 months. Observations were taken in two ways: (1) continuous coding of behavioral flow with Datamyte 904 recorders, noting the type of interaction (verbal or physical), its quality or affective style, the referent, and, where appropriate, the type of action directive used or its outcome; and (2) a 10-second-interval time-sampling system. This latter system was used to provide data for immediate analysis of behaviors relevant for planning, implementing, and assessing intervention procedures. Further details are described in Burgess *et al.* (1981). A major focus of the training was noncompliant child behavior. The program involved teaching the mother about reinforcement and punishment contingencies, instructing her on how she was to respond to compliance and noncompliance, showing her how to behave, having her role-play, and then having her practice the behavior. Immediate feedback was given to her during the training phases.

Although the primary focus of the intervention was on behavioral parent training, the program also attended to the multiple environmental stresses that impinged on the family and exacerbated conflict within the family. These components of the program included (1) relationship establishment and the provision of support through positive social interaction and behavior feedback; (2) counseling in life management skills, such as advice in social and assertiveness skills necessary for effective resolution of interpersonal problems with neighbors, landlords, teachers, and social service workers; (3) referral to available community agencies for family support services; (4) advocacy by acting as a liaison to obtain health, financial, educational and legal services; and (5) the offering of such practical services as providing transportation or nutritional and financial management advice.

Nonetheless, the major dependent variable in the study was the observed patterns of interaction among family members. Thus, outcome data were systematically collected on the parent training component (Burgess *et al.*, 1981). In light of previous findings that higher rates of positive parental behavior are associated with nonabuse, the chief objective was to increase the frequency of positive interaction in the family. In general, the program was quite promising in that the mother increased her rate of verbal contacts with her children by

35%, thus suggesting that she had begun to take a more active role in managing their behavior. The most dramatic change was in her positive responses to her children, which increased over fivefold. Moreover, at the level of the entire family, there was a threefold increase of positive behaviors. Interestingly, there was even a temporary increase in the frequency of the children's positive behaviors toward one another.

In brief, there were significant increases in positive parent–child interaction during the intervention phases of this study, and these changes exhibited some durability through two follow-up phases. The degree of success of this program was perhaps most encouraging in light of the fact that this was an isolated rural family with extreme intellectual, interpersonal, and financial deficits. One regrettable failure of this program was the inability to reduce the rate of negative interaction in the family to any degree. Basically, the frequency of negative contacts remained unchanged throughout the study, although it is true that these negative contacts were included within a context of higher rates of positive interaction.

Information about the dynamics of parent–child interaction within abusive families, and in particular the cycle of coercion, formed the basis of another intensive behavioral parent training program developed by Wolfe and his associates (Wolfe, St. Lawrence, Graves, Brehony, Bradlyn, & Kelly, 1981). Working with a low-functioning abusive mother who displayed high rates of physical punishment and little ability to control the aversive behavior of her children, this team of professionals investigated the effectiveness of a direct training technique. The project began with home and laboratory observations, as well as discussion with the mother and caseworker to identify priorities for treatment intervention. Child compliance and family cooperation were selected for immediate attention. Structured activities were used to simulate these two problematic interactions and to provide in-clinic tasks that could serve as a basis for training. The child compliance task involved placing the mother and children in a room with 50 toys scattered on the floor and requiring the mother to direct her children to pick up all of the objects. Family cooperation was the goal of the second task, in which the mother was provided with crayons and coloring books and was asked to help the children color and draw pictures for a period of 10 minutes.

During these in-clinic mother–children interactions, several categories of parent behaviors were recorded for use as dependent measures. Hostile physical prompts were coded whenever the mother pushed or grabbed a child, or whenever she made a hand-raising motion toward a child but did not actually make physical contact with him or her. Hostile verbal prompts were scored as occurring when the mother threatened, labeled, or condemned a child. Both types of hostile parental prompts were targeted for reduction. In contrast, positive prompts were also scored and were targeted for increase. Positive physical prompts included hugging, patting, or touching a child when he or she was engaging in appropriate behavior, while positive verbal prompts were recorded when the parent specifically praised a child's behavior, thanked the child, or expressed other positive verbalizations toward the child. The total number of times that each of these behaviors occurred during a 10-minute fixed interval for every compliance and cooperative task was determined by an observer.

A total of 13 weekly 1-hour sessions were held. After obtaining baseline measures of the mother's behavior, training was introduced to decrease hostile parent behavior. A bug-in-the-ear device, whereby the therapist communicated with the mother through a microphone in the observation room to a miniature remote receiver worn in the mother's ear, was used to instruct the mother in strategies to deal with child noncompliance and noncooperation other than by hostile verbalizations or physical threats. Attention withdrawal and time-out procedures were encouraged. Following six sessions of this training, a similar approach was introduced to increase the parent's use of positive verbal and physical prompts. After observation demonstrated that hostile prompts had decreased and that other positive parental behaviors increased during the practice interactions, the use of the bug-in-the-ear device was terminated. Finally, throughout the 13 treatment weeks and at a 2-month follow-up, home probe visits were used to determine whether the parent would exhibit improved parenting behavior outside the clinic setting.

Overall, the results of this program were favorable. The direct parent training was successful in reducing hostile and increasing positive parental prompts. In addition, there was no physical evidence of abuse or excessive punishment during the 2-month follow-up period. Thus, one might conclude that through teaching new child management skills and terminating the cycle of coercion, the incidence of child maltreatment in this one family was significantly reduced. The use of behavioral parent training appears to be a promising approach.

Similar principles were applied in a more extensive treatment program by Conger, Lahey, and Smith (1981). Five different abusive families were treated, and although the program was individualized, the goals were the same in each case. Overall, the goal was to alter the pattern of parent–child interaction. In particular, this meant a reduction in the frequency of aversive parent–child interactions, an increase in the frequency of positive interactions, a reduction in the use of corporal punishment, and (given our earlier discussion, which shows these behaviors to be risk factors for parents) a consequent decrease in the risk of further abuse.

Reflecting an awareness of the interplay of multiple risk factors for parents, five treatment methods were used. These included (1) relationship formation, in which therapists attempted to establish friendly, warm, and supportive relationships with parents; (2) instruction in child rearing, where verbal instruction, modeling, and role-playing methods were used to instruct parents in child-rearing practices and appropriate expectations for child behavior and development; (3) stress management, including prompting and reinforcing assertive ways of handling environmental stressors (e.g., obtaining food stamps, obtaining appropriate employment); (4) couples therapy for those parents whose dysfunctional behavior extended into the marital relationship; and (5) relaxation training for parents who experienced anxiety or stress-related psychophysiological arousal (Conger et al., 1981). Clearly, these various techniques focus on the numerous factors presented earlier as contributing to and exacerbating the coercion cycle. That is, along with focusing on the instrumental component, the researchers gave attention to the impulsive component; their inclusion of relationship formation and couples therapy has implications for the problem of multiple entrapment.

To assess the effectiveness of these techniques in reducing the occurrence of dysfunctional parenting behavior, in-home observations were conducted on six separate occasions before treatment began, on three occasions during treatment, and on three occasions after termination of the treatment program. During these observation sessions, family members played games together (e.g., Tinkertoys, bean bag toss), and their interactions with one another were coded according to type of interaction (verbal or physical), the emotional affect of their behavior (neutral, positive, and negative), and certain content dimensions (commands and compliances). Results suggest that, overall, the abusive mothers in the social learning program appeared to decrease their use of aversive physical behavior, to increase their use of affectionate physical responses, to improve their child management skills in four out of five cases, and to reduce their degree of depression (Conger et al., 1981).

This treatment research is valuable in that it included use of a control group as a way of insuring that treatment gains were indeed due to the program itself. Although the project incorporated various approaches centering on the different risk factors for parents, it is unclear from the evaluative data which of these techniques was most responsible for the positive outcomes. Future efforts should be directed toward determining which elements of risk are most conducive to treatment and ultimately most worthy of investigators' attention in efforts to reduce the incidence of child maltreatment.

In reviewing this and other recent treatment efforts aimed at abusive parents, however, several issues arise. Despite the optimistic outlook portrayed by program reports, there are problems associated with current treatment attempts. One of these is the problem of measuring outcomes. Danish and Conter (1978) have pointed out that an intervention involves two sets of goals: distal (long-range) goals and proximal (short-term) goals. With regard to child abuse, the proximal goal of treatment efforts such as those we have reviewed is to alter patterns of parental behavior. Through observation and recording devices, the extent of attainment of such a goal is directly measurable. The distal goal of child abuse treatment programs, on the other hand, is to reduce the prevalence of child maltreatment. In this sense, measuring program success is extremely difficult. One faces, for instance, the recurring problem of defining and documenting child abuse. In addition, there is the issue of determining an appropriate time frame for assessing whether a parent has ceased being abusive. That is, at what point can one conclude that one has eliminated the potential for future abuse?

A second problem confronting recent treatment efforts is the difficulty in motivating parents to participate. In the programs reviewed above, this concern was less evident because participants were either court-ordered (Wolfe *et al.*, 1981) or paid for their attendance (Burgess *et al.*, 1981; Conger *et al.*, 1981). The problem remains, however, of how to reach those abusive parents who have not yet been brought before authorities. Clearly, what are needed are more attempts to market child abuse treatment services. Investigators and clinicians need to convince the public of the importance of functional parenting and to offer self-identification programs through the media so that parents can assess their child-rearing strengths and weaknesses. By placing more of the responsibility for identifying abusive parents in the hands of the parents themselves, those operating treatment programs would be respecting their rights to maintain control over their own lives. This might increase their trust in mental health programs and providers.

Building in this element of self-worth might also help to overcome a third issue: the lack of generalizability across situations and time. The programs reviewed above reveal that parents can be taught the functional child-rearing behaviors that our earlier review suggests are associated with nonabusive parenting. However, the skills that are acquired may not always carry over into other settings. Furthermore, progress may not be maintained once the intervention is terminated. Close examination of the data from the Wolfe *et al.* (1981) study, for example, reveals an increase in the number of hostile verbal behaviors and a decrease in positive verbal and physical behaviors over the 2-month follow-up period. Part of the reason may be that the correct treatment methods have not yet been found. However, client motivation may again be a key issue. Parents who have become convinced that it is the therapists rather than themselves who are responsible for changing and controlling their lives will not have the self-esteem or motivation to monitor their own behavior. Indeed, one approach to teaching parents and families conflict resolution skills designed to avoid conflict escalation (and hence physical and emotional abuse), which as demonstrated generalization and long-term effectiveness, carefully structures treatment in such a way that the participants see themselves as the change agents for one another (B. G. Guerney, 1977; B. G. Guerney, Vogelsong, & Coufal, 1981).

The problem of poor generalizability raises yet another problem facing current treatment efforts. This is the need to adopt a more holistic approach in dealing with abusive parents. Present knowledge of risk factors indicates that the source of the maltreatment problem is not confined to the family itself, but stems from the family's ecological setting as well. For example, multiple entrapment generally leads to insularity (Wahler, 1980b). The latter appears to be a key element in failure to maintain treatment gains (Wahler & Afton, 1980).

Parents need positive social contacts to reinforce their parenting abilities and general social skills. Indeed, in a recent review of successful treatment programs for child abuse and neglect, it was found that those clients receiving a service package that included lay services, such as participation in Parents Anonymous, were more likely to have their problems resolved (Cohn, 1979). Researchers have not yet made enough of an effort to build a community involvement component into their treatment programs. Another factor that has yet to receive systematic attention by child abuse interveners is the impulsive component discussed by Vasta (1982). Relaxation training such as that mentioned by Conger *et al.* (1981) and Frame and Lutzker (1981) should be investigated as a potentially valuable component of treatment services.

Finally, researchers and clinicians are still faced with the problem of the reincidence of abusive parental behavior even during treatment. In one study of 1724 parents, a full 30% were reported to have severely reabused or neglected their children *while they were in treatment* (Cohn, 1979). Even more discouraging is the fact that such reincidence is most likely among cases identified as "serious" at intake (Cohn, 1979). This would imply that those families who most need help are getting it least effectively. This and other issues raised suggest that although progress has been made, there is still much to accomplish in the area of helping abusive parents. Furthermore, a much more cost-effective strategy for reducing the incidence of child maltreatment would be to develop more programs aimed at prevention of the problem. In concluding this chapter, we now turn to a consideration of such strategies.

PREVENTION PROGRAMS

Over the past decade, the need for programs to prevent child abuse has been recognized. Several different strategies can be suggested, based on present knowledge of the risk factors for parents. Perinatal support programs to prepare individuals for parenting can provide education about infant development and parent–child relationships, and can supply information on community resources available to new parents and to infants and children. In addition, parent–child bonding may be enhanced by changing hospital childbirth practices to allow for family-centered childbirth and rooming-in (Garbarino, 1980a). Parent education programs to teach parents such things as financial management, social skills, methods of discipline, job training, and information about child development can reduce some of the stresses of parenthood and thereby can decrease the risk of child maltreatment. Public awareness campaigns to let parents know that being a parent is not easy and that it is all right to reach out for help, as well as to provide information about where to turn for help, may also play a role in preventing child abuse. Although very little direct research is available regarding the impact of such efforts, indicators such as increased reporting, additional state expenditures, and major interest in the theme of child abuse suggest that public awareness programs have been successful. Finally, in the past decade, many states have passed legislation requiring individuals whose work involves contact with children to report suspected cases of child abuse. At the federal level, the *Domestic Violence Prevention and Services Act* (H.R. 2977/S1843, 1980) provides funding for local programs and facilities aimed at reducing the prevalence of family violence.

Although isolated examples of each of these types of prevention projects exist, documentation of their effectiveness in reducing child abuse is scanty, and professionals continue to direct much of their time toward developing treatment programs to terminate ongoing abuse. The lack of attention to primary prevention probably stems from several sources. One is professionalism, or the belief that only "professionals" are truly capable of helping others (Broskowski & Baker, 1974). Treating problems, as opposed to preventing them, provides these professionals with opportunities to see themselves as making a significant impact on others and fulfills their needs to play that rescuer role (Danish, 1977). In addition to such professional barriers to the implementation of primary prevention programs are organizational barriers (Broskowski & Baker, 1974). Most service agencies depend on third-party reimbursement in order to maintain operations. Prevention activities become neglected because they leave people out of the reimbursement system. In addition, funding agencies typically do not provide support for preventive efforts. Particularly in the present era of funding cuts, accountability is essential in order for service organizations to maintain funding. Such accountability is difficult in the realm of prevention, since the acid test of such programming is the nonoccurrence of cases of psychopathology (Danish & D'Augelli, 1980).

Clearly, there is still a long way to go in setting the stage for successful implementation of programs to prevent child abuse. Professionals must first convince themselves of the value of the approach. They must then sell the idea to the people who hold the purse strings. Finally, the public must buy into the model so that the services will be utilized. One avenue of hope lies in programs giving children interpersonal skills, self-management, and coping skills in the classroom and through continuing education programs for adults in the public schools (B. G. Guerney, 1979; B. G. Guerney & Guerney, 1981).

Despite these issues, and in light of our review of parental risk factors, several thoughts come to mind regarding the prevention of child abuse. One is the importance of taking a developmental approach emphasizing changes across the life span. Danish and D'Augelli (1980) have argued that an inability to cope stems from three sources—a lack of knowledge, a lack of skills, or an inability to take risks. With regard to child maltreatment some of the problem may be due to lack of knowledge about parenting, child development, and so on. In giving people the knowledge they need to avoid dysfunctional parenting, however, those operating prevention programs must remain aware that the necessary knowledge base may differ according to the individual's phase in the life span. For example, an 18-year-old mother may need information about childbirth, infant care, and child safety, while a 40-year-old mother may lack knowledge about developmental concerns of her adolescent children and the importance of engaging in new activities after her children leave home. L. F. Guerney's (1978) parenting skills training manual integrates normatively appropriate age-related expectations with affectively oriented and behavior management skills for parents of young children; there is no reason why this could not be done for parents of children in other age groups.

The lack of skills is also evident as a risk factor for parents. In particular, what is known about the cycle of coercion and the problem of multiple entrapment suggests that the underlying deficit in many cases is a lack of general social competence. One way to prevent the development of abusive parental behavior and the insularity that exacerbates the problem and makes treatment difficult is to help people acquire a set of skills for interacting with other people effectively. The goal thus becomes not merely the prevention of child abuse, but the overall enhancement of a person's life skills and development. Such an approach is certainly cost-effective, in that it provides people with the resources to deal with a variety of life events across the life span (Danish & D'Augelli, 1980).

Wahler (1980a) has found that more severely troubled mothers appear to avoid interchanges with people outside their families. This avoidance behavior may be a direct function of manding approaches by the mothers' principal contact parties—extended family and helping agency representatives. An insular mother's pattern of extrafamily social contacts may have indirect effects on her child-rearing behavior. The nature of that pattern suggests that a shift from manding relationships to more friendly contacts might have beneficial effects on her child-rearing efforts (Wahler, 1980a). The present suggestion is that such a shift, if accomplished through developing the social competence of the mother, will also strengthen her repertoire of general life skills and will put her in a position to pass on positive social contacts to other troubled parents. Thus, if one could help these mothers (and fathers) to alter their community interactions in the direction of friendship relationships, that change might support more positive interactions between them and their children, as well as between them and their relatives, friends, and neighbors. Similarly, enhanced social skills could also have beneficial consequences in the workplace or, otherwise, improve the person's employability.

Optimizing positive neighborhood interactions is one way of facilitating this goal. The Community Helpers Project, designed by D'Augelli and his associates (D'Augelli, Vallance, Danish, Young, & Gardes, 1980), is an example of such a project. In this program, which was instituted in two rural communities in central Pennsylvania, persons who were "natural helpers" in the community were identified and recruited through the use of the media. The goal was to build upon and respect the native talent of these helpers, enhancing their natural helping function by giving them skills to use in dealing more effectively with common problems brought to them by friends, acquaintances, and family. In order to spread the impact of the training, a local network of trainers was developed. Thus, within the two communities, 32 trainers were trained by professional staff. These indigenous trainers then worked in pairs to offer the same program in basic helping skills to other local helpers, thereby increasing the number of social supports geometrically. This Community Helpers Project appears to be a valuable step in capitalizing upon the helping talents of natural caregivers and strengthening neighborhood-based support systems. Moreover, in this manner, researchers and clinicians can continue the movement in applied behavior analysis that began, as Bijou notes in his commentary in Chapter 1, with using the parent as the primary change agent for the child in the natural ecology of the family (i.e., the home rather than the clinic). Now, however, the parents' friends, neighbors, and relatives would be used as primary change agents for the *parents.*

References

Blumberg, M. L. Psychopathology of the abusing parent. *American Journal of Psychotherapy,* 1974, *28,* 21–29.

Broskowski, A., & Baker, F. Professional, organizational, and social barriers to primary prevention. *American Journal of Orthopsychiatry,* 1974, *44,* 707–719.

Burgess, R. L. Child abuse: A social interactional analysis. In B. B. Lahey & A. E. Kazdin (Eds.), *Advances in clinical child psychology* (Vol. 2). New York: Plenum Press, 1979.

Burgess, R. L. Family violence: Some implications from evolutionary biology. In T. Hirschi & M. Gottfredson (Eds.), *Theory and fact in contemporary criminology.* Beverly Hills, Calif.: Sage, 1980.

Burgess, R. L., & Akers, R. L. A differential association–reinforcement theory of criminal behavior. *Social Problems,* 1966, *14,* 128–147.

Burgess, R. L., Anderson, E. S., Schellenbach, C. J., & Conger, R. D. A social-interactional approach to the study of abusive families. In J. P. Vincent (Ed.), *Advances in family intervention, assessment, and theory: An annual compilation of research* (Vol. 2). Greenwich, Conn. JAI Press, 1981.

Burgess, R. L., & Conger, R. D. Family interaction in abusive, neglectful, and normal families. *Child Development,* 1978, *49,* 1163–1173.

Burgess, R. L., Garbarino, J., & Gilstrap, B. Violence to the family. In E. J. Callahan & K. McCluskey (Eds.), *Life span developmental psychology: Nonnormative life events.* New York: Academic Press, 1983.

Campbell, A. The American way of mating: Marriage si, children, only maybe. *Psychology Today,* May 1975, pp. 39–42.

Chilman, C. Social and psychological research concerning adolescent child bearing: 1970–1980. *Journal of Marriage and the Family,* 1980, *42,* 793–805.

Cohn, A. H. Essential elements of successful child abuse and neglect treatment. *Child Abuse and Neglect,* 1979, *3,* 491–496.

Conger, R. D., Burgess, R. L., & Barrett, C. Child abuse related to life change and perceptions of illness: Some preliminary findings. *The Family Coordinator,* 1979, *28,* 73–79.

Conger, R. D., Lahey, B. B., & Smith, S. S. *An intervention program for child abuse: Modifying maternal depression and behavior.* Paper presented at the Family Violence Research Conference, Durham, N.H., July 1981.

Danish, S. J. Human development and human services: A marriage proposal. In I. Iscoe, B. L. Bloom, & C. D. Spielberger (Eds.), *Community psychology in transition.* New York: Hemisphere Press, 1977.

Danish, S. J., & Conter, K. R. Intervention and evaluation: Two sides of the same community coin. In L. Goldman (Ed.), *Research methods for counselors.* New York: Wiley, 1978.

Danish, S. J., & D'Augelli, A. R. Promoting competence and enhancing development through life development intervention. In L. A. Bond & J. C. Rosen (Eds.), *Primary prevention in psychopathology* (Vol. 4). Hanover, N.H.: University Press of New England, 1980.

D'Augelli, A. R., Vallance, T. R., Danish, S. J., Young, C. E., & Gardes, J. L. *The community helpers project: A description of a prevention strategy for rural communities.* Unpublished manuscript, The Pennsylvania State University, 1980.

Duberman, L. *The reconstituted family: A study of remarried couples and their children.* Chicago: Nelson-Hall, 1975.

Elmer, E. *Children in jeopardy: A study of abused minors and their families.* Pittsburgh: University of Pittsburgh Press, 1967.

Finkelhor, D. *Sexually victimized children.* New York: Free Press, 1979.

Frame, R. E., & Lutzker, J. R. *Project 12-Ways: An overview of a program to treat and prevent child abuse and neglect.* Unpublished manuscript, Southern Illinois University at Carbondale, 1981.

Friedman, R. Child abuse: A review of the psychosocial research. In Herner Co. (Ed.), *Four perspectives on the status of child abuse and neglect research.* Washington, D.C.: National Center on Child Abuse and Neglect, 1976.

Garbarino, J. The human ecology of child maltreatment: A conceptual model for research. *Journal of Marriage and the Family,* 1977, *39,* 721–736.

Garbarino, J. Changing hospital childbirth practices: A developmental perspective on prevention of child maltreatment. *American Journal of Orthopsychiatry,* 1980, *50,* 588–597. (a)

Garbarino, J. Defining emotional maltreatment: The message is the meaning. *Journal of Psychiatric Treatment and Evaluation,* 1980, *2,* 105–110. (b)

Garbarino, J., & Crouter, A. Defining the community context of parent–child relations: The correlates of child maltreatment. *Child Development,* 1978, *49,* 604–616.

Garbarino, J., & Garbarino, A. C. *Emotional maltreatment of children.* Chicago: National Committee for Prevention of Child Abuse, 1980.

Gil, D. G. *Violence against children.* Cambridge, Mass.: Harvard University Press, 1970.

Gottman, J. M. *Marital interaction.* New York: Academic press, 1979.

Guerney, B. G., Jr. *Relationship enhancement: Skill training programs for therapy, problem prevention and enrichment.* San Francisco: Jossey-Bass, 1977.

Guerney, B. G., Jr. The great potential of an educational skill-training model in problem prevention. *Journal of Clinical Child Psychology,* 1979, *3,* 84–86.

Guerney, B. G., Jr., & Guerney, L. F. Family life education as intervention. *Family Relations,* 1981, *4,* 591–598.

Guerney, B. G., Jr., Vogelsong, E., & Coufal, J. *Relationship enhancement versus a traditional treatment: Follow-up and booster effects.* Manuscript submitted for publication, 1981.

Guerney, L. F. *Parenting: A skills training manual.* State College, Pa.: Institute for the Development of Emotional and Life Skills, 1978.

H. R. 2977/S1843, *Domestic Violence Prevention and Services Act.* Washington, D.C.: U.S. Government Printing Office, 1980.

Johnson, B., & Morse, H. A. Injured children and their parents. *Children,* 1968, *15,* 147–152.

Johnson, C. F. *Child abuse in the Southeast: Analysis of 1172 reported cases.* Athens, Ga.: Regional Institute of Social Welfare Research, 1974.

Kempe, C. H., Silverman, F. N., Steele, B. F., Droegemueller, N., & Silver, H. D. The battered-child syndrome. *Journal of the American Medical Association,* 1962, *181,* 17–24.

Kidwell, J. S. Number of siblings, sibling spacing, sex, and birth order: Their effects on perceived parent–adolescent relationships. *Journal of Marriage and the Family,* 1981, *43,* 395–332.

Kimball, W., Stewart, R. B., Conger, R. D., & Burgess, R. L. A comparison of family interaction in single versus two-parent abusive, neglectful, and control families. In T. Field, S. Goldberg, D. Stein, & A. Sostek (Eds.), *Interactions of high risk infants and children*. New York: Academic Press, 1980.

Kinard, E. The psychological consequences of abuse for the child. *Journal of Social Issues,* 1979, *35*, 82–100.

Klaus, M. H., & Kennell, J. H. *Maternal*–infant bonding. St. Louis: C. V. Mosby, 1976.

Light, R. J. Abused and neglected children in America: A study of alternative policies. *Harvard Educational Review*, 1973, *43*, 556–598.

Patterson, G. R. The aggressive child: Victim and architect of a coercive system. In E. J. Mash, L. A. Hamerlynck, & L. C. Handy (Eds.), *Behavior modification and families* (Vol. 1, *Theory and research*). New York: Brunner/Mazel, 1976.

Patterson, G. R. A performance theory for coercive family interaction. In R. Cairns (Ed.), *Social interaction: Methods, analysis, and evaluation*. Hillsdale, N.J.: Erlbaum, 1979.

Patterson, G. R., & Reid, J. B. Reciprocity and coercion: Two facets of social systems. In C. Neuringer & J. D. Michael (Eds.), *Behavior modification in clinical psychology*. New York: Appleton-Century-Crofts, 1970.

Pfouts, J. H. Birth order, age spacing, IQ differences, and family relations. *Journal of Marriage and the Family*, 1980, *42*, 517–531.

Philliber, S., & Graham, E. The impact of age of mother on mother–child interaction patterns. *Journal of Marriage and the Family*, 1981, *43*, 109–116.

Polansky, N. A., Hally, C., & Polansky, N. F. *Profile of neglect: A survey of the state of knowledge of child neglect*. Washington, D.C.: U.S. Department of Health, Education and Welfare, 1975.

Richardson, R. A., Burgess, J. M., & Burgess, R. L. Family density and the maltreatment of children: A social interactional analysis. *Analysis and Intervention in Developmental Disabilities,* 1983, in press.

Spinetta, J. J., & Rigler, D. The child-abusing parent: A psychological review. *Psychological Bulletin,* 1972, *77*, 296–304.

Steele, B. F., & Pollock, C. B. A psychiatric study of parents who abuse infants and small children. In R. E. Helfer & C. H. Kempe (Eds.), *The battered child*. Chicago: University of Chicago Press, 1974.

Straus, M. A. Family patterns and child abuse in a nationally representative American sample. *Child Abuse and Neglect*, 1979, *3*, 213–225.

Straus, M. A. Stress and physical child abuse. *Child Abuse and Neglect,* 1980, *4*, 75–88.

U.S. Bureau of the Census. *20 facts on women workers*. Washington, D.C.: Author, August 1979.

Vasta, R. *Physical child abuse: A dual-component analysis. Developmental Review*, 1982, *2*, 125–149.

Wahler, R. G. The insular mother: Her problems in parent–child treatment. *Journal of Applied Behavior Analysis,* 1980, *13*, 207–219. (a)

Wahler, R. G. The multiply entrapped parent: Obstacles to change in parent–child problems. In J. P. Vincent (Ed.), *Advances in family intervention, assessment and theory* (Vol. 1). Greenwich, Conn.: JAI Press, 1980. (b)

Wahler, R. G., & Afton, A. D. Attentional process in insular and noninsular mothers: Some differences in their summary reports about child problem behaviors. *Child Behavior Therapy*, 1980, *2*, 25–41.

Wasserman, S. The abused parent of the abused child. *Children,* 1967, *14*, 175–179.

Wolfe, D. A., St. Lawrence, J., Graves, K., Brehony, K., Bradlyn, D., & Kelly, J. A. *Intensive behavioral parent training for a child-abusive mother*. Unpublished manuscript, The University of Western Ontario, 1981.

Young, L. *Wednesday's children: A study of child neglect and abuse*. New York: McGraw-Hill, 1964.

PROJECT 12-WAYS
Treating Child Abuse and Neglect from an Ecobehavioral Perspective

John R. Lutzker
Southern Illinois University at Carbondale

HISTORY AND CONCEPTUALIZATION

The middle-class parents of a noncompliant 6-year-old boy have been working with apparent success with a third-year doctoral student behavior therapist in learning behavior management techniques. The "apparent" success comes from the perspective of the therapist, whose data show that after 8 weeks of parent training, the parents (who were self-referrals) have dramatically increased the frequency by which they deliver contingent praise and have mastered a simple time-out procedure. The therapist's in-home data are collected during twice-weekly observation sessions in structured activities in the living room. The parents are asked to minimize distractions by not having any guests in the house during the sessions, not accepting telephone calls, and having the television turned off. Praise is heaped on the therapist by a supervisor, who suggests that with a 3-month follow-up the data will probably be publishable. Is there something wrong here?

In another case, the state protective service agency has received an anonymous report from its hotline service that 5-year-old Robert has been abused by his 21-year-old mother and her 26-year-old paramour. The agency responds quickly with an investigation, discovering that the child has multiple bruises. Also, X-rays show two ribs that appear to be healing from fractures that occurred several months earlier. The mother, Jane, and her paramour, both of whom contend that Robert fell off a broken backyard swing, fit most of the demographic descriptors of child abusers. That is, Jane was unmarried when at age 16 she conceived and gave birth to Robert (Smith, Hanson, & Noble, 1973). At that time, she dropped out of high school. Her paramour, Stan, and she have lived together for 2 years, but this period has included several separations, two beatings of Jane by Stan, and drunkenness by Jane and Stan during their frequent arguments (Helfer, 1973). Jane has never worked and tries to "make ends meet" through her welfare payments. Stan is unemployed more often than not (Isaacs, 1981). Finally, Jane and Stan have few friends and engage in virtually no social or community activities. They surely could be labeled "insular" (Wahler, 1980). In this case, the protective service agency caseworker has formally charged Jane and Stan with child abuse, and has referred them to a research/treatment project at the university. The project's goal is to provide parent–child training for abusive parents. The undergirding philosophy of the university parent training project is that problems of child abuse and neglect result from parents' inability to manage their children's behavior successfully. The treatment offered to Jane and Stan is identical to the parent training provided the middle-class parents of the noncompliant 6-year-old. The training sessions also take place in the living room of the trailer in which Jane, Stan, and Robert live, and the same distraction restrictions are imposed on this family during treatment and observation sessions. Is something wrong here, too?

What is wrong in these two hypothetical case studies has been *partly* identified only recently in the behavioral literature. What is wrong is partly represented by what many of the critics of behavior analysis, behavior therapy, and behavior modification have been saying for years; that is, the focus of these approaches has been too narrow. For example, in the case of the hypothetical middle-class family, the description of the parent training situation could have been lifted out of any number of studies reported in the literature. But do we know about parent–child interactions in *any* setting outside of the living room, which, given the limitation on distractions, becomes in fact an analogue setting? Unfortunately, more often than not, the answer has very recently been "no" (Lutzker, McGimsey, McRae, & Campbell, 1983).

However, in 1974, Willems called for the measurement of child behavior from a molar or ecological perspective, rather than from the molecular level that had been examined previously. Rogers Warren and Warren (1977) collected and published a series of articles suggesting the need for an ecological or, more accurately, an ecobehavioral approach; and I (Lutzker, 1980) suggested that data and treatment both need to go beyond the home into the multiple settings in which children behave (e.g., classrooms, playgrounds, Sunday schools, relatives' homes, etc.). By "ecobehavioral," it is meant that human behavior must be examined within the context of the environments from which it comes. That is, in addition to observing an individual's behavior and the antecedent and consequential events that appear to affect it, investigators must look carefully at how the individual's behavior (and behavior change) affects others in the environment, and how many factors in the individual's life impinge upon his or her behavior. Also, Wahler and Fox (1981) have recently argued that much more emphasis should be placed on what they call "setting events" in assessing and treating complex family problems.

Recently, data have been presented on treatments stemming from this perspective. For example, Russo, Cataldo, and Cushing (1981) examined multiple factors in multiple settings in treating compliance in three deviant children, and Van Biervliet, Spangler, and Marshall (1981) looked at and rearranged the antecedent ecobehavioral events that affected mealtime language in retarded youths in a residential facility. Also, some innovative strategies for promoting the generalization of parent training techniques into community environments such as grocery stores and other settings were provided by Sanders and Glynn (1981).

Presented in this chapter is an *overview* of Project 12-Ways, an ecobehavioral approach to the treatment and prevention of child abuse and neglect. As soon becomes clear, Project 12-Ways is so large and multifaceted that a comprehensive description of the entire project would go far beyond the scope of a chapter. Thus, included here are (1) a brief history and conceptualization; (2) a review of the funding source, staffing pattern, referral process, and some demographic data on clients; (3) brief reviews of each treatment service; (4) a description of completed and ongoing research; (5) some ideas about "intangible" variables that operate in Project 12-Ways; and (6) some suggestions about future efforts.

In conceptualizing a treatment paradigm for the problem of child abuse and neglect, two issues seem paramount. First, planners must look at the existing demographic data on the environmental factors associated with the problem (e.g., unemployment, poor parenting practices, poor adult relationships, etc.); secondly, they must attack the problem of child abuse and neglect by following the suggestions of assessment and treatment from an ecobehavioral perspective. Thus, from these two basic tenets, Project 12-Ways was born. It seemed only logical that in looking at the factors that contribute to a problem as severe as child abuse and neglect, behavioral parent training alone, as presented in the hypothetical case of Jane, Stan, and Robert, would not be a durable functional approach. Surely, poor parenting practices alone do not lead to the severe beatings and gross neglect found in countless abuse and neglect cases.

Project 12-Ways can be considered "ecobehavioral" because it provides *in vivo* treatment (in homes, schools, foster homes, etc.) in many different areas: parent–child training, stress reduction, assertiveness training, self-control training, basic skills training for children, leisure time activity training, reciprocity marital counseling, alcohol treatment and referral, social support groups, job-finding training, money management training, unwed mother services, health maintenance and nutrition training, home safety training, and multiple-setting behavior management training (Lutzker, Frame, & Rice, 1982).

It should be noted that some ecobehavioral factors contributed to the creation of Project 12-Ways, too. It would be easy to suggest that the only factors were humanistic concern for treating this serious social problem and a desire to act on the conceptual issues articulated above. And, in fact, these were contributing factors; but at least three other more mundane elements also played a major role. Two of these others were related to the economics of education. That is, the Behavior Analysis and Therapy Program at Southern Illinois University at Carbondale (SIU-C) was in need of more external funding for its graduate students, and the training opportunities for its students that could be provided through a project such as this would be plentiful. In addition, the state protective service agency was looking for a qualified contractor with whom they could enter into a contract for the dissemination of the Title XX funds for which they were responsible. Thus, Project 12-Ways was created not only to explore an ecobehavioral approach to the treatment and prevention of child abuse and neglect, but also to provide a service for the state's protective service agency, and to provide funding and training to the students of the Behavior Analysis and Therapy Program at SIU-C.

FUNDING, STAFF, REFERRALS, AND CLIENTS

Funding

Project 12-Ways is funded by a Title XX Purchase of Service Contract with the Ilinois Department of Children and Family Services (DCFS), the Illinois Department of Public Aid, and the Rehabilitation Institute of SIU-C. Further, it is administered through the Governor's Donated Funds Initiative, wherein SIU-C contributes 25% of the funds. In fiscal year 1980 (July 1 to June 30), the level of funding was $531,205; in fiscal year 1981, the level of funding was $504,944; in fiscal year 1982, it was $481,827; in fiscal year, 1983, it was $542,338. Figure 11-1 shows the administrative and service structure of Project 12-Ways.

Staff

As can be seen in Figure 11-1, the project is a part of the Behavior Analysis and Therapy Program of the Rehabilitation Institute (in the College of Human Resources) at SIU-C. In fact, there is an inextricable interface between the program and the project. Under the supervision of the program coordinator is the program manager, who acts as the primary administrator (70%) and clinical supervisor (30%). The program manager holds a master's degree with emphasis in applied behavior analysis, and must have a minimum of 4 years of supervisory experience. The program manager supervises two rehabilitation counselor chiefs (a strange university bureaucratic title), who hold master's degrees with emphasis in applied behavior analysis. These master's-level specialists

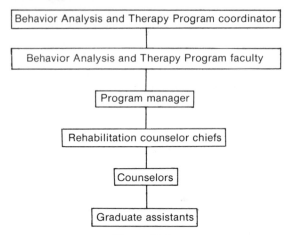

Figure 11-1
Project 12-Ways administrative structure.

supervise counselors (some of who hold master's degrees, others of whom are advanced students in the Behavior Analysis and Therapy Program). While the rehabilitation counselor chiefs provide some of the direct services to clients, the majority of the direct client services are provided by the counselors. Under the counselors' purview are first-year Behavior Analysis and Therapy Program graduate assistants, whose primary responsibilities involve data collection and "apprenticeships" with the counselors with whom they are assigned. Finally, a doctoral-level graduate assistant is involved in some case supervision and research. Thus, a sophisticated hierarchical system of supervision is used to provide service to the clients served by Project 12-Ways.

The Behavior Modification Program coordinator and the rest of the Behavior Analysis and Therapy Program faculty provide the professional training and staff development for the project. In addition to their apprenticeships with counselors, first-year graduate assistants receive academic training in the following courses: Basic Behavior Analysis (an overview course on principles, applications, and procedures); Behavioral Observation Methods (including *in vivo* applications); Scientific Methods (single-subject design in the first semester, group design in the second semester); Behavior Therapy (an overview of treatment and research strategies in adult clinical behavior therapy); and Legal and Ethical Issues in Behavior Analysis and Therapy. In addition, in the first semester, each student is assigned to a faculty adviser for an apprenticeship in the adviser's research program. Other program requirements include a practicum (often taken in the second semester of the first year); an internship (usually taken in summer and the second fall); and, for MA students, a thesis involving the manipulation of data, or, for MS students, a research paper that can be data-based or not (this option includes reviews, theoretical papers, and single-case experiments). Course electives in the program include Child Behavior (the focus of this course is on parent training), Sexual Behavior, Complex Behavior Analysis, Self-Control, Biofeedback, Behavior Modification with the Mentally Retarded, Behavioral Applications to Medical Problems, Community Behavior Analysis, and Staff Training and Development. Thus, graduate assistants and counselors who work for Project 12-Ways are exposed to an unusually rich background in behavior analysis and therapy.

Under development have been "packaged" training modules for Project 12-Ways staff, including, for example, stress reduction training and child-interaction skill training. These modules include readings and self-contained, self-managed video training tapes and quizzes. Clearly, relying solely on generalization by staff members from their Behavior Analysis and Therapy Program courses and applied experiences and from their project apprenticeships is not as "clean" a staff training model as would be desirable. Thus, validated protocols have been developed for stress reduction, interacting with children, interacting with other professionals (political/social skills), and training others to use time out. By "validated protocols," it is meant that the effect of the training module upon staff performance has been demonstrated to be functional. If the training packages based on these protocols, which are currently being formally assessed, prove functional, similar strategies will be applied to other project service components.

To deliver service, staff members use SIU-C fleet vehicles operated by the project, or staff members are reimbursed for their own auto expenses in making their visits to clients' homes and other service settings, attending meetings at local agencies, and making court appearances.

Referrals

The Illinois DCFS is the sole referral source for Project 12-Ways. Referrals are accepted from the five DCFS field offices included in the nine-county area currently served by the project. This nine-county area is in rural southern Illinois. The largest city in all of southern Illinois (27 counties) is Carbondale, with a population of approximately 27,000 (without the 22,000 SIU-C students). In fiscal year 1980, all 27 counties of southern Illinois were served by Project 12-Ways. Southern Illinois is a coal-mining, agricultural, and recreational area with above-average unemployment.

Self-referrals are possible in that an individual can request that DCFS refer him or her to Project 12-Ways; however, self-referrals comprise fewer than 10% of the clients served by the project.

When a referral is received, an investigation is made for verification of Title XX eligibility. Two criteria exist for eligibility for services by Project 12-

Ways. One is protective service status. This means that DCFS has determined, suspected, or judged a family to be at high risk for child abuse or neglect. Socioeconomic status (SES) plays no role in eligibility for protective service status. The other criterion *is* SES. Unwed mothers, who by their very status as such represent high risks for child abuse (Smith, Hanson, & Noble, 1974), qualify for the prevention component of Project 12-Ways if they fall at or below the state's criterion line for poverty status.

If verification for eligibility proves positive, the program manager determines the appropriateness of the case by reading the DCFS caseworker's referral report. Automatic exclusions include known drug addiction or psychosis. Also, referrals involving teenagers who are nearing 18 years of age, living at home, and referred because of conduct problems and "incorrigibility" are often rejected. However, 90% of DCFS referrals are accepted. Once a referral is accepted, it is assigned to a counselor (or occasionally to a rehabilitation counselor chief), who schedules an introductory meeting with the DCFS caseworker and the client(s). These meetings are held almost exclusively in the clients' homes. Project 12-Ways staff members then schedule future meetings for assessment, the development of treatment goals, and treatment itself. Frequently, adjunctive services are provided by DCFS homemakers, mental health agencies, public health nurses, and physicians. Direct and indirect behavioral assessment may take up to a month. When treatment goals are negotiated and formulated by the Project 12-Ways staff and the clients, they are then "signed off" by the project's primary counselor, the client(s), the DCFS caseworker, the supervisor (rehabilitation counselor chief), and the program manager and coordinator. That is, these parties sign a form agreeing to these specified treatment goals.

Clients

Most clients served by Project 12-Ways possess most of the descriptors of child abusers that have been reported by others (Isaacs, 1981). That is, they are poor and undereducated, are often single, and most often have more than one child in the home. Table 11-1 shows some demographic data on the clients served by Project 12-Ways in its first two fiscal years.

As can be seen in Table 11-1, the average family seen by Project 12-Ways would be a married couple with the wife listed as the head of the household, with three children. The primary client would be about 30 years old, and would have been reported for neglect. Accurate data on the SES of all Project 12-Ways clients have not been available for the first two fiscal years. However, most of our clients are either unemployed or underemployed, and most receive public aid. Since very few of the clients are self-referrals, and since the majority of them have protective service status, dropout rates are quite low.

Table 11-1

Available Demographic Data on Project 12-Ways Clients: Fiscal Years 1980 and 1981

	1980	1981
Total heads of household served	169[a]	156
Female heads of household served	129 (76%)	97 (62%)
Male heads of household served	23 (14%)	14 (9%)
Female and male heads of household served	17 (10%)	45 (29%)
Marital status		
Married	28%	37%
Divorced	21%	19%
Separated	9%	9%
Single[b]	34%	32%
Widowed	4%	3%
Status unknown	5%	0%
Average number of children per household	2.79	2.42
Range of children per household	1–6	1–6
Average age of primary clients	28.5 years	30.7 years
Range of age of primary clients	13–65 years	10–66 years
Referral for		
Abuse cases	15%	22%
Neglect cases	40%	53%
Prevention cases	45%	25%

[a]Data are unavailable on four families.

[b]This information may certainly be artifactual, in that some parents may list themselves as single, even though they were previously married.

One surprising outcome, however, has been the relatively high levels of compliance with treatment regimens. It is only speculation, but one of the beliefs about this high rate is that treatment may simply provide entertainment for clients. Most of these families have few friends and often are geographically isolated, with poor or no transportation available to them. Thus, when staff members visit their homes, listen to their problems, play with their children, drive them to an agency where they can recover lost medical services cards, and so on, they may be becoming their friends, or at least people who break up the tedium of their insularity. Also, counselors' coming to the homes (as opposed to expecting clients to show up for "clinic" visits) and dressing casually may affect compliance rates. Finally, counselors try to represent themselves to clients as professionals who might be able to help them become more independent and less involved with state agencies. That is, they try to stress that compliance with treatment regimens, among other things, might allow the agency to drop them from protective service status.

TREATMENT SERVICES

Table 11-2 shows the services that have been provided to families in the first two fiscal years, and the percentage of families each year that have received each service.

Parent–Child Training

Most families referred to Project 12-Ways have difficulties in parent–child relationships. In fiscal year 1980, 42% of the families who received services were provided with parent–child training. In fiscal year 1981, 66% of the families receiving the project's services were provided with this training. Thus, the parent–child training component represents the most commonly used treatment among the 15 services offered.

At the most formal level, the treatment provided in this area is a systematic replication of the parent training paradigm described by Peed, Roberts, and Forehand (1977). This training, in structured sessions, involves teaching parents to increase their use of alpha commands to their children (clear, understandable instructions with which the children can comply); to decrease their

Table 11-2

Percentage of Families Receiving Each Treatment Service in Fiscal Years 1980 and 1981

Service	1980	1981
Parent–child training	42%	66%
Stress reduction and assertiveness training	17%	16%
Self-control training	10%	21%
Basic skills training for children	21%	27%
Leisure time counseling	5%	21%
Marital counseling	—	7%
Alcoholism treatment or referral	3%	3%
Social support groups	5%	17%
Job-finding training	7%	13%
Money management training	6%	18%
Health maintenance and nutrition training	—	14%
Home safety training	—	14%
Multiple-setting behavior management training	11%	32%
Prevention services (unwed mothers)	16%	30%

Note. Since the majority of the families served received more than one type of service, these percentages do not total 100%.

use of beta commands (instructions that are vague and cannot be followed); to increase their use of contingent praise; and to make appropriate use of time out. This is a systematic replication, as opposed to a direct replication, in that some modifications in the Peed *et al.* (1977) model have been made. For example, in addition to observing parent–child interactions in the structured situations labeled by Peed *et al.* (1977) as the "Child's Game" and the "Parent's Game," generalization data are collected in unstructured settings inside and outside the home. Also, Peed *et al.* (1977) allowed their nonabusive parents a choice between learning time out or mild spanking for child noncompliance. No such choice is offered to Project 12-Ways clients; only time out is taught. This is because it was felt that abusive or potentially abusive parents should not be encouraged to use physical, corporal punishment on their children.

A major reason for choosing this model for parent training was the focus on antecedent control, as well as on consequences. That is, in addition to learning to praise appropriate behavior and to arrange a time-out consequence for noncompliance (consequences), the parent is taught to provide more salient discriminative stimuli (antecedents) in the form of clear, precise (alpha) commands. Also attractive about this model is the *a priori* specification of criteria for "movement" in training. That is, the mother (or, occasionally, the father) must meet a performance criterion in the Child's Game (wherein their level of alpha and beta commands and contingent reinforcers must change) before they move on to the next level of training, time out for noncompliance. Thus, the trainer has something more than intuition to work with in making "clinical" decisions in parent training.

The structured components of parent–child training in Project 12-Ways provide a special challenge with the families the project serves. Their homes and trailers are usually environments bordering on chaos. Often, Project 12-Ways graduate assistants must take other children away while the counselor, parent, and target child engage in the Child's Game or Parent's Game. This does, however, allow the graduate assistants some training time with the other children.

The age range of children who receive parent–child training under this format is 3–9 years. Older children find it boring; younger children do not have the prerequisite attention skills. By consulting specialists in child development and early childhood education, toys have been purchased and activities arranged that are appropriate to the ages of the children. Table 11-3 shows the kinds of activities used, according to age.

Many other modifications of the parent training model are necessitated by the idiosyncrasies of individual families, and are overlapped by other Project 12-Ways service components. For example, in addition to the formal training offered in sessions, counselors often ask (and teach) families to engage in more frequent, albeit brief, family activities. This has been loosely labeled "leisure time training"; however, it is also a part of parent-child training. Examples of this would include having a mother select and plan a different 15-minute

Table 11-3

Tasks and Age Ranges Used in Structured
Parent–Child Training

Task	Age range
Play-Doh	3–8
Jumbo wood beads	3–5
Large colored beads	4–7
Easy-grip pegs	3–7
Ring toss	4–9
Ball toss	3–9
Bean bag toss	3–8
Legos	4–9
Legos II	5–9
Tinkertoys	4–9
Plastic eggs	4–8
Hi-Ho Cherry Oh	5–9
Spin–Win	4–8
Cootie	5–9

activity to do with her child after school each day, or having an eight-member single-mother family that lives in public housing, with a room and table too small for family dining, to "set" a sheet as a surrogate table on the living room floor for a three-times-weekly family dining experience. It would seem only logical to consider these examples part of parent–child training; yet they are a far cry from the structured training done as a systematic replication of the Peed *et al.* (1977) model.

Also, counselors frequently arrange simple token economies for homework, housework chores, dry beds, and so on. Many programs focus on producing compliance at two of the most common problem times for families—getting off to school and bedtime.

Another idiosyncratic element is the use of didactic materials. Some parents ask for something to read, feeling that it helps, and are thus provided with a "guided tour" of *Parents Are Teachers* (Becker, 1979). Other parents neither ask for nor would be benefited by (because they would not or *could* not read) didactic materials. Thus, with respect to the use of reading materials, to be wed to one strategy or another would not be functional.

Two criteria determine whether or not the clients will be asked to participate in parent–child training. First, during the assessment phase through indirect or formal direct observations, the counselor may deem it a necessary component of treatment and thus may ask the parent to be allowed to articulate parent–child training as a treatment goal. Secondly, many parents simply request it. In addition to direct behavioral observations on parent–child inter-actions, counselors use a minimum of two indirect measures: the Walker Problem Behavior Identification Checklist (Walker, 1976) and the Becker Adjective Checklist (Becker, 1960).

In most cases, parental compliance with parent–child training has been quite high. There has been a concern that generalization outside of the struc-tured training sessions might be problematic, although the data seem contrary to this. However, in one case a mother was forthright enough to tell her counselor that she was only "performing" in structured sessions, and that she had no intention of "generalizing." Of course, only data can answer whether or not other parents are less forthright, but there is still a problem in the data collection itself. That is, observers might act as discriminative stimuli for parents and children to engage in "trained" behaviors, but those behaviors might not occur in the absence of the observers (Lutzker, 1980). Unfortunately, a service project as large and multifaceted as Project 12-Ways cannot afford the luxury of unobtrusive measures (e.g., hidden tape recorders) to procure "clean" measures of generalization.

An example of the ecobehavioral approach to parent training has been provided by Dachman, Halasz, Bickett, and Lutzker (1982). They examined the effects of an in-home ecobehavioral parent training program with a low-income single parent and her 7-year-old son. Generalization of training and main-tenance were also investigated.

A comprehensive assessment period lasted 10 weeks, during which in-formation was compiled from a variety of sources, including the DCFS case files; interviews with the caseworker, the parent, and the son's teacher; a series of casual observations at school; and informal and systematic observations at home. A variety of paper-and-pencil measures were also administered through-out training. The pretreatment and posttreatment measures included the Walker Problem Behavior Identification Checklist (Walker, 1976); the Becker Bipolar Adjective Checklist (Patterson & Fagot, 1967); and the Knowledge of Be-havioral Principles as Applied to Children examination (O'Dell, Tarler-Benlolo, & Flynn, 1979). The Therapy Attitude Inventory (Bernal, Klinnert, & Schultz, 1980) was issued as a posttraining client satisfaction scale.

A multiple-baseline, across-settings design was used. Treatment was staggered across three primary conditions, which included the training activity (play) and two generalization activities (schoolwork and unstructured). Training in descriptive praise consisted of modeling, role playing, giving corrective feedback, and having the client collect data and provide feedback on the counselor's use of descriptive praise. In addition to descriptive praise, the effects of training on untreated parent responses, such as nagging the child, were also measured.

The results indicated that training was effective in increasing the mother's frequency of descriptive praise in play, but generalization to the other activities (schoolwork and unstructured) did not occur. However, when training was introduced in the schoolwork and unstructured conditions, the use of descriptive praise by the mother during those activities increased significantly. Generalization then occurred across other parent responses in each activity. Criticisms decreased considerably, while physical positive affectionate interactions increased dramatically, though these behaviors were untreated. Maintenance probes conducted at 9 and 10 weeks following the end of training indicated that the effects were durable. A variation of the contingency management procedure reported by Jenson and Sloane (1979) was adapted to the home setting in response to the high frequency of tantrums displayed by the child. The procedure involved a "Grab Bag," which was a small paper bag with slips of paper representing activity, monetary, and edible reinforcers. These reinforcers were chosen by the parent and her child, and could be administered in the home. The second component of the procedure involved dot-to-dot drawings. Each picture was made from 60 to 130 dots. Interspersed among the regular dots were a number of larger dots. If 15 minutes elapsed and the child refrained from throwing tantrums, his parent issued a descriptive praise statement and allowed him to connect two dots. When the child reached a large dot, the parent praised him and gave him permission to reach into the grab bag for a special treat. The outline of each dot-to-dot drawing represented a bonus reinforcer, which included activities the parent and child could engage in in the community —for example, going to the park. These activities were scheduled and occurred as soon as possible after completing a drawing. In this component of treatment, a reversal design indicated a significant reduction in the frequency of tantrums over a 6-month period that was clearly attributable to the treatment program. Maintenance probes conducted 1 and 2 months after treatment suggest that the results were durable.

This single-case experiment exemplifies the ecobehavioral approach, and the ways in which each case on Project 12-Ways may receive variations of any given treatment service.

For very young children, less emphasis is placed on behavior management. The focus for them is on the other ecosystem factors that may contribute to their neglect or abuse situation. Parents of children from 2 to 3 years of age receive less structured training in reinforcement and time-out control of behavior. Parents of children older than 8 years of age are offered training in social reinforcement control and mutually negotiated token-reinforcement programs.

Stress Reduction Training

It has been noted that many parents involved in child abuse and neglect have difficulty in controlling stress and anxiety (Green, Gaines, & Sandgrund, 1974); thus, several parents served by Project 12-Ways receive treatment in stress reduction through deep muscle relaxation (Wolpe & Lazarus, 1966) and postural feedback (Schilling & Poppen, in press).

Sample work that has been done in this area on Project 12-Ways has been provided by Campbell, O'Brien, Bickett, and Lutzker (in press). In this case, a woman had been self-referred to Project 12-Ways after having repeated feelings of wanting to kill her 4-year-old daughter. After an intensive assessment process, three areas were chosen as high priority for treatment by Project 12-Ways counselors; parent–child training, marital counseling, and stress reduction. The stress reduction, done in the home (as are virtually all of the project's services), was an attempt to try to relieve the young mother of her severe migraine headaches. It is easy to understand how a rather unfortunate cycle of aversiveness could have developed, with the mother's poor relationship with her child and the mother's headaches. It was assumed that her headaches made it difficult to interact with her child in anything but a coercive manner. In turn, the coercive interactions between the mother and child produced more anxiety for the mother, which led to more headaches. Thus, an in-home stress reduction training program with a maintenance protocol was established with the mother, who recorded the frequency, duration, and intensity of her headaches. After 16 weeks of treatment and three follow-ups over a 16-week period of time, the mother's headaches were virtually eliminated (see Figure 11-2). Further, parent–child observational data and Marital Happiness Scale data indicated considerable improvements in those areas. In this case, it was clear that stress reduction played a major role in the ecobehavioral treatment package offered to this family. Service was terminated with the family after several formal follow-up measures showed maintained improvements in all treated areas. No subsequent incidences of abuse have ever been reported in this family.

In another case, an unwed mother was referred for neglect. One of her problems was frequent seizures. After several neurological and other medical workups, the interdisciplinary hospital team treating this young woman at a family practice center had concluded that her seizures did not appear to stem from any organic bases. Thus, they recommended that her Project 12-Ways counselor include stress reduction as one of the services that she was to receive. In this case, home portable biofeedback training was provided to teach the woman relaxation skills. The counselor helped this young mother identify antecedent events that seemed to precipitate the anxiety that brought on her seizures. She was then instructed to be sure to engage in her relaxation exercises whenever she could identify these antecedents, such as the onset of her menstrual period. After relaxation training, the woman's seizures were reduced from a rate of one or two per week to fewer than two every 3 months. In addition to working with this young woman on several aspects of infant care, she was also exposed to a modified Job Club approach to job finding (Azrin & Besalel, 1980). After three sessions, she procured a job as an aide at a local nursing home, had 12-Ways counselors help her find day care for her toddler,

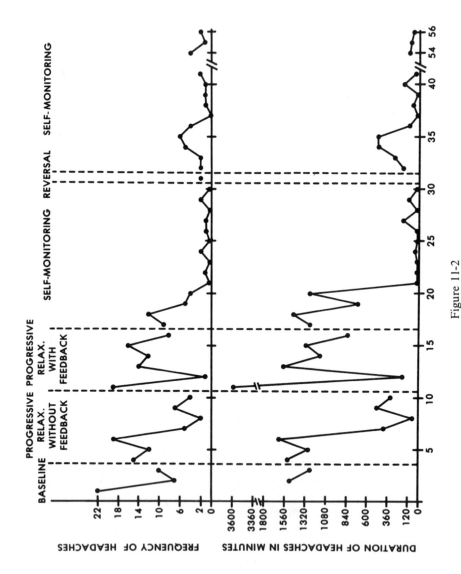

Figure 11-2

The frequency and duration of headaches of a highly stressed mother.

274

and was exposed to a money management program. An 18-month follow-up upon termination from Project 12-Ways determined the young woman's frequency of seizures to be once every 4 months; she was still employed and had not been reported for any incidents of abuse or neglect.

These cases provide good examples of how stress reduction is used as an adjunctive treatment to other services. It seems only logical that the outcome of stress reduction procedures would be facilitated by removing some of the environmental stressors that contribute to the anxiety's being produced in the client. Such seems the case with the mother with the migraine headaches, whose stress reduction treatment was embellished by parent–child training and marital counseling; or with the unwed mother, whose biofeedback stress reduction training was enhanced with child care training and job-finding training.

As Table 11-2 shows, only 17% of our clients received the stress reduction service in fiscal year 1980. For some clients, it is simply not functional or appropriate, and occasionally when it is recommended to a client, it will be rejected. As suggested earlier, stress reduction is not easy to accomplish in a small, unkempt home or trailer. Often, graduate assistants must occupy children, or even meet with a spouse or paramour in another room, while stress reduction is being conducted. However, it is clear that some of our clients find stress reduction to be reinforcing in and of itself, independent of any treatment goals. That is, they simply enjoy it, whether or not there are any specific outcome objectives to go along with the training. This phenomenon probably contributes to some clients' acceptance of our counselors in their homes week after week.

Assertiveness Training

Assertiveness training is offered to adult clients served by Project 12-Ways who have difficulty in expressing their feelings effectively. Both individual and group training formats have been used; the group format has been used exclusively with unwed mothers. Among the assertive behaviors that have been trained, when appropriate, has been teaching pregnant women to ask specific questions of their physicians and other medical personnel regarding their pregnancies. Also, clients have been taught to deal more assertively with their mates, children, paramours, and creditors. It has been clear that for many clients the ability to learn to act assertively without being aggressive has been an important element in their overall treatment strategies.

Self-Control Training

Special programs are designed to help parents control their tempers, lose weight, stop smoking, and so on. Not surprisingly, the most popular of these programs has been weight control. Cognitive strategies for temper control not only have been used with parents, but have also been applied with teenage clients. In one case, an aggressive 15-year-old delinquent was taught to reduce verbal and physical outbursts in his special education class in high school from an average of four per week to less than one per month. Self-control programs are virtually never attempted with clients until other problems in the ecosystem have been managed. This is because it is assumed that weight loss or smoking control programs, for example, could lead to added stress that would surely prove nonfunctional in trying to address problematic parent–child relationships and other difficulties. One disappointing outcome of these programs has been unwed mother clients' unwillingness to give up or reduce smoking.

Basic Skills Training

Many abused and neglected children lag behind their age-mates in developmental skills (Isaacs, 1981). A variety of skill training programs are delivered directly by Project 12-Ways counselors and graduate assistants. Some of these training packages include toilet training (Azrin & Foxx, 1974); shoe tying (Cooper & Etzel, 1969); bicycle riding (Lutzker, 1979); conversation skills (Jewett & Clark, 1979); and pleasant family shopping experiences (Greene, Clark, & Risley, 1977).

Project staff members have found these basic skill training programs especially useful in impressing upon clients some ability on the staff's part to produce productive behavior change. Also, since before-and-after indirect measures of parents' attitudes toward their children consistently show improvements, staff members have attributed this phenomenon not only to parent training, but also to the basic skills training when it has been utilized.

An example of basic skills training has been provided by Rosenfield, Sarber, Bueno, Greene, and Lutzker (in press). They trained two severely neglected children to bathe, to wash and comb their hair, and to dress in clean clothes on a daily basis. Services that were readily available from the state (homemaker services and allowances), but never previously distributed contingently or consistently, were used to maintain these hygiene skills with the two children in their home. Basic skills training programs have been used in both homes and schools.

Leisure Time Training

Family cohesiveness is enhanced by teaching families daily and weekly inexpensive and simple activities that help, among other things, to provide an environment that might be characterized as "enriched time in" (Solnick, Rincover, & Peterson, 1977). For example, a mother might be asked to post an activity board on the refrigerator at home. This board contains pocket envelopes for each day of the week, in which index cards are placed. The index cards that have been previously prepared by the parent and the counselor list simple, brief, inexpensive activities that the mother can choose to do in the late afternoon with her child(ren). A similar strategy of public posting of developmental activities was shown to be quite effective in increasing caretaker–infant stimulation activities in a day care facility for infants and toddlers (Kunz, Lutzker, Cuvo, Eddleman, Lutzker, Megson, & Gulley, 1982). Some of the activities include water play (in the sink), play with pots and pans, painting styrofoam balls, and so on. Again, as stated earlier, it is a bit difficult to discriminate this service component from parent–child training, because counselors frequently monitor these parent–child activities for generalization from parent–child training or give actual further training in alpha commands and contingent praise in these situations. Some clients' homes are so impoverished that finding even the most basic equipment (such as paper, scissors, or pencils) with which to conduct these activities has been difficult.

Marital Counseling

Marital conflict is a frequent problem for families involved in abuse and neglect (Isaacs, 1981). Couples who seek help in this area from Project 12-Ways are provided reciprocity counseling as described by Azrin, Naster, and Jones (1973), and contracting as described by Tearnan and Lutzker (1980). As shown in Table 11-2, only 7% of our clients received this service in fiscal year 1981. Of course, one reason for this comparatively low figure is the large proportion of single-parent families served by Project 12-Ways. Also, a frequent finding during assessment is that a wife or a single mother with a male paramour will express a desire to improve her relationship with her mate or partner, but that the spouse or paramour will refuse any involvement in any relationship therapy. In some cases, the male partner's refusal to participate in counseling, together with assertiveness training for the female partner (most frequently the primary client), has resulted in the woman's throwing the paramour or husband out of the house (and the relationship). In the few cases where couples have agreed to marital treatment, counselors have found it useful to combine reciprocity counseling, which focuses on communications and interactions, and the Tearnan and Lutzker (1980) contracting model, which focuses on some of the more mundane household routines from a *quid pro quo* contracting format.

Alcohol Treatment Referral

When alcoholism is a problem for a Project 12-Ways client, a referral is made, when possible, to agencies providing the community-based approach described by Hunt and Azrin (1973). When the referral is not possible, 12-Ways counselors provide a modified version of the community-based approach. Most often, the involvement by Project 12-Ways is to monitor drinking and to try to establish compliance programs for clients who are taking Antabuse as a part of the community-based treatment approach.

As any professional who has worked with low-SES rural families involved in child abuse and neglect knows, alcohol, especially beer, seems to be an ingrained aspect of that subculture that makes dealing with it professionally very difficult. In some cases, despite a desire to do more about problem drinking, the counselors must simply try to work around it. Curiously, several of our clients have been greatly benefited in their battle with drinking by becoming involved in fundamentalist religious groups. At least three of our problem-drinking clients have remained "off the wagon" for over a year after becoming involved with these groups. Truly, this involvement in religion may epitomize the ecobehavioral perspective.

Social Support Groups

Wahler (1980) has accurately described the insularity of many parents involved in child abuse and neglect. Thus, in communities where transportation and facilities make it feasible, social support groups have been organized for Project 12-Ways clients. These groups allow an opportunity for parents to have positive interactions with adults other than agency personnel or family members. The initial hope in conducting these groups was to try to have these insular clients learn to interact with one another and thus become less dependent upon agencies as their primary (and unpleasant) adult social contacts. Unfortunately, the large geographic area served by Project 12-Ways (over 4200 square miles) has made this difficult to accomplish for clients other than unwed mothers. With these young women, however, whom Project 12-Ways primarily serves in a one-county, two-community area, staff members have greatly facilitated their programs by conducting groups at local churches, women's centers, and high schools. This has worked quite well in that some of the young women have moved in together to share trailers, have acted as Lamaze coaches for each other during labor and childbirth, and have provided other reciprocal services such as babysitting and transportation.

Job-Finding Training

Unemployment is a serious problem for many families involved in abuse and neglect. Further, unemployment percentages are above the national average in southern Illinois. For clients interested in job finding, an individualized version of the Job Club (Azrin & Besalel, 1980) is used. This involves helping the client prepare a résumé, telephoning prospective empolyers for interviews, role-playing interviews, and, if necessary, accompanying the client to the interview. This component has also involved helping clients enroll in community college vocational training or general equivalency diploma programs. As can be seen in Table 11-2, only 13% of our clients participated in these efforts in fiscal year 1981. This figure is misleading, in part, in that several of our clients are already employed and thus do not need this service component. Other clients, however, express no interest in changing their current unemployment–welfare status. Thus, the job-finding service, which has a high success rate, is only offered to clients who express a strong desire to work.

Money Management Training

When clients served by Project 12-Ways have problems in money management, an individualized training protocol is used to teach them to live within their means, to handle creditors, and to shop economically. Since virtually nothing was available on this in the literature, particularly pertaining to living on welfare, Project 12-Ways was required to develop its own training program.

As with most of the project's services, the success of this component is dependent upon the client's motivation. Thus, this service is only offered to clients who express enthusiasm to try it. Among those eager clients, the interactions between the counselors and themselves have produced clear successes. Through such efforts, families have been taken out of debt and have even managed to produce some small savings.

Health Maintenance and Nutrition Training

Nutrition and hygiene deficiencies are frequently associated with child abuse and neglect (Tizard, 1975). Thus, individualized training has been provided in bathing, laundry, and other areas of self-hygiene (Rosenfield et al., in press). An example of the importance of this component was described by Sarber, Halasz, Messmer, Bickett, and Lutzker (in press). The 4-year-old daughter of a mildly retarded illiterate mother was removed from the home because the mother, who knew how to cook and serve meals, knew nothing about nutrition. The first phase of treatment involved teaching the mother the four basic food groups. This was accomplished by color-coding each major food group and teaching the mother to identify correctly pictures of foods belonging to each group. The mother's ability to plan several days of nutritious meals according to pictures prior to training was 0%. After training, her ability to plan three nutritious meals per day for her daughter was 100%. Follow-up data were collected at 8, 16, and 20 weeks. At the 20-week follow-up she was still planning nutritious meals 100% correctly, including demonstrating her shopping skills in different stores from the ones in which she was trained.

In addition to planning nutritious meals, it was necessary for the mother to be able to purchase the foods she had planned on her menu-planning board. Utilizing a multiple-baseline design across food groups, the mother was sequentially taught to transfer the information from her large meal-planning board at home to a "shopping list" that consisted of a small photo-album-like binder that she brought to the store. From average baseline percentages across groups from 25–60% correct items purchased, training produced 100% correct items across several sessions and a 12-week follow-up. Social validation data from caseworkers, nutritionists, and state agency homemakers provided testimony to the utility of the training. This training, along with some money management and parent training, allowed the child to be returned to the home after the original removal for neglect.

Home Safety Training

A sophisticated home safety checklist has been developed (Tertinger, Greene, & Lutzker, 1982) to assess and modify problems of safety in homes. These include (1) fire and electrical hazards, (2) suffocation by mechanical means, (3) suffocation by ingested objects, (4) guns, and (5) poisoning by solids and liquids. There are several reasons why home safety is an important component of an ecobehavioral approach to treating and preventing child abuse and neglect. Many clients' homes are physically dangerous. When a child approaches one of these dangers, such as an exposed electrical outlet, there is a tendency on the parent's part to intervene with inappropriate, abusive physical contact. This, in fact, was one of the reasons for one abuse referral to the project. Another reason that home safety is such a critical component is that the dangerous environments in which these families live place the children in those homes at high risk for injuries sufficient to produce lifelong handicaps, and handicapped children are at especially high risk for abuse. Also, the poor conditions in clients' homes are often major factors in the agency's classification of neglect. Thus, if families can be taught to improve the safety conditions in their homes, several agendas can be met: the risk of child abuse by the parents may be lessened; the risk of death or physical handicaps may be reduced; and the families may be able to have their neglect status reconsidered by the agency.

Several families have formally participated in the Home Accident Prevention Inventory (HAPI) program developed within Project 12-Ways. The purpose of the program was to reduce the number of potential hazards in the home that might endanger the lives of children from birth to 4 years of age. Data revealing the most common causes of childhood deaths in the home led to the inclusion of the five categories mentioned above that were found in the inventory. To identify dangerous situations in all five categories, 26 items were developed. These 26 items were sensitive to the many variations of hazards found in the home for all five categories.

The intervention package consisted of four components: education, modeling, practice, and feedback. Parents were educated by counselors about the potential dangers of the hazards included in the HAPI and were told how to child-proof their homes to make them safer. The process of child-proofing was modeled to the parents, in addition to practice sessions in which they demonstrated their competence in this task. Parents were also given feedback about the number and location of hazards found in their homes and were asked to make safety changes. These safety changes included tasks such as moving particular items to inaccessible locations or installing safety latches.

The results showed that the number of hazardous items was greatly reduced as a result of this intervention package. Regularly, two observers collected highly reliable data in the clients' homes. The data in Figure 11-3 are representative of the kind of results produced with the other families.

As can be seen in Figure 11-3, a multiple-baseline design was used across hazardous categories found during baseline data collection in the homes. In this case, three categories—fire/electrical hazards, poisons, and suffocation items—were determined to be problematic. Whenever treatment was introduced, there was a considerable reduction in the kinds and numbers of hazardous items found to be accessible to young children. Generalization occurred to the third hazard area, suffocation. In addition, as in the case illustrated here, several unannounced follow-up visits have shown the treatment effects to be durable over time. In fact, in one of the six families, treatment effects generalized in a very favorable manner to a new home (a trailer). Whereas Project 12-Ways is satisfied that this is a viable home safety intervention package, it should be recognized that this intervention, like the entire project effort, is quite invasive. Thus, current research efforts in the home safety component are focusing on "streamlining" the intervention package, so that it will be easier to teach to new counselors; so that it will be less invasive to clients (although social validation data from clients have indicated their satisfaction with this service); and so that it can be disseminated outside Project 12-Ways.

Multiple-Setting Behavior Management Training

Because clients' difficulties are not always limited to the home, Project 12-Ways counselors provide consultation pursuant to clients' interests and needs in settings outside of the home, such as day care centers, schools, foster homes, institutions, and so on. Schools in southern Illinois have been especially cooperative in allowing counselors and graduate assistants to consult with teachers, aides, and administrators, and to conduct in-class behavioral observations of Project 12-Ways clients. Teachers have been quite compliant with home–school token or daily report card systems for clients' academic and behavior problems. This is again reflective of the ecobehavioral approach. If a parent is receiving reports about problem behavior at school, the child may be

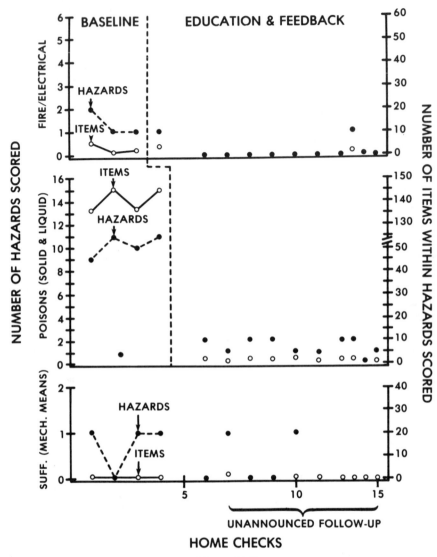

Figure 11-3

The number of hazards and items within a hazard category found in the home of a Project 12-Ways family.

at further risk at home unless a successful school intervention can be accomplished.

This multiple-setting behavior management component is often necessary. An example of home–school cooperation was described by Lutzker, Frame, and Greene (1980). They detailed the treatment of self-hygiene training of two grade-school children. Since the mother was physically handicapped and not cooperative in the plans for behavior management of bathing, toothbrushing, and other self-hygiene behaviors, the school teachers cooperated in school-based token-reinforcement program with the child.

Prevention Services for Unwed Mothers

Data indicate that young unwed mothers (Birrell & Birrell, 1968; Taylor, 1973) are especially at risk for child abuse and neglect. Christophersen (1979) reported a 30% recidivism rate of abuse in a control group of unwed mothers that he compared to the behavioral Family Training Program. Project 12-Ways counselors provide services to pregnant unwed women and carry these services throughout pregnancy, delivery, and the first few months of the new babies' lives. Services include preparation for childbirth, nutrition education, health care education, infant care and development, safety, family planning, and parent–child stimulation. A considerable number of didactic materials have been developed in this component of the project. This "software" has included testing materials on prenatal and postnatal development. Other Project 12-Ways services are also available to the unwed mothers. Most frequently, the other services they have sought have been training in stress reduction, money management, and job finding.

RESEARCH ON EFFECTIVENESS

How does one measure the outcomes and the effectiveness of a service as multi-faceted as Project 12-Ways? What are the dependent measures (variables) that might provide some answers to clinical and research questions? There are several answers to these questions, in that there are at least four levels of data collection and analysis on Project 12-Ways. The first level might be labeled simply "clinical." Clearly, the majority of the data collected on the project fit into this category. By "clinical," it is meant that the data are truly "unclean." There is no reliability; sometimes, there is no baseline; most often, there is no research design. Some of these data are collected by clients, some by staff members. Such data collection is anathema to good researchers, but it necessitated by the realities of clinical service. However, as good behaviorists, at least when it is realistic, staff members try to quantify data: "How many times did you praise your child this week?" "How many times did you lose your temper, and how many times did you successfully control your temper?" These are but a few examples of the kinds of events about which clients are asked to "take data." Sometimes they do; sometimes they do not. Sometimes they do, and an angry partner throws the data and the copy of *Parents Are Teachers* (Becker, 1979) in the fireplace. In any case, even without interobserver reliability, research designs, or baselines, these client-generated data can be useful adjuncts to more formal behavioral observations.

A second level of data collection involves single-case experiments. These are the cases where "clean" data are collected on a single individual or single family, using a simple single-subject research design. Examples of these cases have been provided, such as the Sarber *et al.* (in press) case on teaching nutritious meal planning and shopping skills to the retarded mother; the Dachman *et al.* (1982) case involving multiple measures in the parent training of a single mother; and the Campbell *et al.* (in press) case of parent training, stress reduction for headaches, and marital counseling. While these single-case experiments technically and empirically do not answer any questions about whether or not Project 12-Ways has any large-scale impact on child abuse and neglect in the region it serves, these studies do serve to demonstrate the impact of various treatment services on individual families involved in abuse and neglect. It may be hoped that as these single-case experiments appear in publications, they will be making contributions on how treatment can be effectively provided to these kinds of families. These single-case experiments also provide simple feedback as to the effectiveness of the intervention strategies employed.

The third level of data collection involves research. The research can use and has used both single-subject design (logic) with multiple subjects, or group designs. It has involved both applied behavior analysis (as in Tertinger *et al.*, 1982, in which intervention strategies for improving home safety in several families were examined) and behavioral assessment. In this latter case, for example, research was recently completed examining affection in Project 12-Ways families, compared to a group of low-SES families not involved in abuse or neglect. These data will contribute to a basic understanding of interaction patterns in families involved in abuse and neglect, and may aid in designing treatment strategies. The data can also be used to assess levels of affection in parent–child interactions and can thus be an assessment tool in helping to formulate treatment plans. It may be hoped that the data collected in these applied behavior analysis and behavioral assessment studies make contributions to the literature beyond the scope of the single-case experiments. That is, they should provide information on the behavioral characteristics of families involved in child abuse and neglect, and should also provide more sophisticated analyses of Project 12-Ways services. One major difference in this level of research is the issue of "external" validity across families within the project. That is, the applied behavior analysis research on the project allows us to determine whether treatment services are indeed replicable in the different homes and different families that the project serves.

The fourth level of data collection is program evaluation. Does Project 12-Ways have an impact on preventing the incidence of abuse and neglect among prevention clients (unwed mothers)? Do families that have been terminated from treatment for abuse or neglect refrain from abuse and neglect (recidivism)? Do families that the project treats repeat their abuse or neglect during treatment? How do the project's rates of prevention, repeated incidences of abuse and neglect during treatment, and recidivism rates compare to nationwide statistics and to untreated individuals in southern Illinois?

To date, Project 12-Ways is just short of being able to give formal answers to some of these research questions. However, staff members have analyzed some "primitive" data at this point, which can be shared here. For example, in an attempt to evaluate the prevention component of Project 12-Ways, all of the unwed mothers served by the project in fiscal year 1980 (July 1979 to June 1980) were evaluated. All of the women were considered "at risk" for child abuse and neglect at the time of referral. The treatment program consisted of numerous components, including prenatal and postnatal nutrition, physical care of the infant, infant stimulation, and general information about childbirth and the responsibilities of motherhood.

Data were gathered on the following variables: number of days in treatment, reason for termination, number of treatment goals, number of goals attained, number of goals partially attained, number of goals initially set but later deemed inappropriate, and number of goals not attained. Finally, a list of prevention clients served by Project 12-Ways was submitted to the Illinois State Central Registry to determine whether any of these clients had instances of child abuse and/or neglect since termination of treatment services. This represents a follow-up of at least 16 months.

Project 12-Ways prevention clients who *began* treatment during fiscal year 1980 spent an average of 167 days in treatment, ranging from 1 to 425. The mean number of goals specified was three, ranging from none to seven. (Some clients referred to Project 12-Ways terminated treatment before any goals could be established.) The average number of goals attained by prevention clients was 1.5 (ranging from none to five); the average number partially attained was .24 ranging from none to two). Very few goals were deemed inappropriate by Project 12-Ways staff ($\bar{x} = .19$, range none to four), and the mean number of goals not attained was .85 (range none to five).

Table 11-4 represents a breakdown of reasons for termination. For example, three clients, or 7% of the entire sample terminated "at the request of the client," while seven clients (14%) terminated as "successful" (i.e., all or most treatment goals were attained).

Data received from the Illinois State Central Registry indicated that one prevention client (2% of the total sample) had an indicative report of child abuse or neglect since termination of Project 12-Ways prevention services. The

Table 11-4

Project 12-Ways Prevention Clients: Reasons for Termination

Reason	Percentage
All or sufficient goals met	14
No reason specified	14
Failure to cooperate	12
No-shows	12
Client moved	9
Terminated by referring agency (DCFS)	7
Terminated at request of client	7
Services to area terminated	7
Other (child was placed, not Title XX eligible)	7
Gave up child	5
Inappropriate case	2
Client refused services	2
Client was never seen	2

Registry data also indicated that one other prevention client had abused or neglected her child during delivery of the services, but had not since termination of Project 12-Ways services. The Registry data also provided some additional information. Two other prevention clients had previously been *victims* of abuse or neglect (but were not perpetrators of abuse and/or neglect), with one of the clients being a victim in two separate incidents. Still another client had reported child abuse or neglect to the DCFS, but was *not* the perpetrator of the abuse or neglect.

This 2% rate of child abuse and neglect for prevention clients compares favorably with that reported by Egeland (1979). In that study, Egeland (1979) examined 275 pregnant women who were labeled as at high risk for child abuse or neglect. Of these, 60% were unwed at the time of delivery. At a 20-month follow-up, 26 of the 275 children had been abused, neglected or severely mistreated. This represents approximately 10% of the total sample, approximately five times the rate of child abuse or neglect found in the sample of Project 12-Ways prevention clients.

While these data are in fact promising, they are still only suggestive. Recently, however, data from a control group of prevention clients *not* served by Project 12-Ways were collected in order to compare their rates of abuse and neglect to rates from clients who received 12-Ways prevention services. This comparison eliminates any potential biasing factors (e.g., sampling error, measurement bias, etc.) and provides more conclusive evidence of the effectiveness and impact of these services.

Suggestive Trends

Until comparison data become available, detailed analyses of trends must wait; several other kinds of analyses are, nonetheless, possible. One such analysis is to look at reports of neglect within agency field offices served by Project 12-Ways as a function of amount of service provided. The unfortunate aspect of such an analysis is that it does not distinguish between *clients* served in any office by Project 12-Ways and those who were not; nonetheless, Figure 11-4 shows the mean frequency of indicative neglect per month as compared with the mean number of client service hours provided throughout the field offices of the protective service agency in the region. "Indicative neglect" means that the child protective service agency received a report of child neglect, investigated the neglect, and either substantiated the neglect or determined that there existed conditions of high risk for neglect.

A multiple-regression analysis was preformed to determine whether the number of client hours was related to the frequency of indicative neglect. In order to eliminate the possibility of certain biasing factors, three covariates were placed in the model. The model controlled for fluctuations in neglect across months (e.g., neglect is more likely in the summer than when school is in session), fluctuations across the number of reports called in (some field offices may be busier than others), and any overall differences among the field offices. Despite all of these attempts to "wash out" the effect statistically, the field office $\times$ client hours interaction term was still significant ($F = 2.37$, $df = 8,61$, $p < .027$). The correlation between the client hours variable and the neglect variable was negative ($r = -.282$) and significant ($p < .004$). This suggests an inverse relationship (i.e., that the more billable hours for which Project 12-Ways serves any one field office, the less indicative neglect is reported by that field office).

Another analysis was made that distinguished served from unserved offices in fiscal years 1979, 1980, and 1981. Since no offices were served in fiscal year 1979, some level of comparison can be made; but, again, it should be remembered that there is a gross confounding of clients. In order to evaluate the data, two data transformations were performed. To control for the frequency of reports, a proportion of neglect and abuse over the total number of reports for each month in each of the three fiscal years was obtained. This proportion more accurately controls for the nonlinear effects of the reports covariate. As in previous evaluations, overall differences among field offices and months of the year were also used as covariates (i.e., the contribution of these variables was portioned prior to any analysis) (cf. Lutzker *et al.*, 1982, for a more detailed description of this analysis). An analysis of covariance was done on the overall data set, with proportional abuse and proportional neglect scores as the dependent variables. There was a significant service effect ($F = 4.707$, $df = 1,303$, $p < .04$), indicating that less child abuse occurred in field offices when Project 12-Ways provided services than when services were not provided (mean served = .1060; mean not

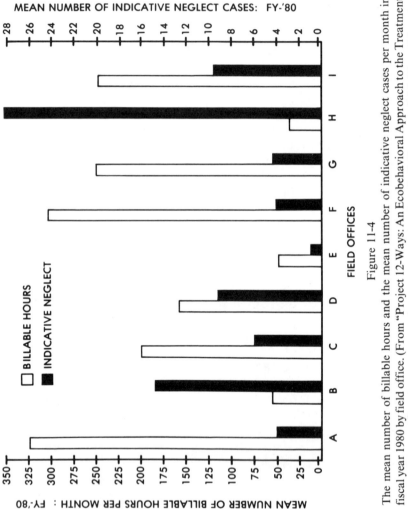

Figure 11-4

The mean number of billable hours and the mean number of indicative neglect cases per month in fiscal year 1980 by field office. (From "Project 12-Ways: An Ecobehavioral Approach to the Treatment and Prevention of Child Abuse and Neglect" by J. R. Lutzker, R. E. Frame, & J. M. Rice, *Education and Treatment of Children*, 1982, 5, 141–155. Reprinted by permission of the authors and *Education and Treatment of Children*.)

served = .1204). While there was no similar effect for neglect, there as a highly significant field office $\times$ service interaction ($F = 3.597$, $df = 8,303$, $p < .001$). Figure 11-5 illustrates this effect. All of the field offices except D and H had less child neglect when those field offices were served by Project 12-Ways than when they were not.

Analysis of the fiscal year 1981 data alone also supports the effectiveness of Project 12-Ways services. While there was no significant service effect with the abuse data ($F = .133$, $df = 1, 303$, $p = $ ns), there was a significant service effect for neglect ($F = 4.435$, $df = 1, 95$, $p < .04$).

All of these results are significant after partitioning out the efforts of reports, overall differences among field offices, and differences among months. Figures 11-4 and 11-5 display these effects.

In an attempt to examine the recidivism rates of child abuse and neglect among clients served by Project 12-Ways, 50 clients served by the project and terminated prior to January 1, 1981 were randomly selected. This list of clients was submitted to the Illinois State Central Registry to determine rates of indicated abuse and neglect during and after Project 12-Ways service delivery.

The Registry reported that four of these clients had an instance of indicated abuse or neglect following termination of Project 12-Ways services. This represents an 8% recidivism rate. There was a single instance of abuse or neglect during treatment (reincidence); this made the total recurrence rate 10% (see Figure 11-6).

These data compare favorably to the Illinois Region V recurrence rate, which for fiscal year 1981 was 21% (see Figure 11-7). This is over twice the rate seen by Project 12-Ways. It should be noted that this is still below other reported rates; thus, it appears that this state agency itself may have an unusually favorable impact on reducing repeated or recidivistic incidences of abuse and neglect.

Other descriptive data of interest include the average number of days in treatment ($\bar{x} = 115.4$), number of goals specified ($\bar{x} = 2.51$), number of goals attained ($\bar{x} = 1.0$), number of goals partially attained ($\bar{x} = .69$), and number of goals not attained ($\bar{x} = .612$). The correlation between recidivism and number of goals attained was $-.222$, suggesting an inverse relationship (i.e., the more goals attained, the lower the recidivism rate).

These recidivism data should be examined cautiously. The Project 12-Ways 10% recurrence rate suggests that these services are effective in relation to traditional casework. State Central Registry data on abuse and neglect have been collected continuously since the late 1970s. Subsequently, the probability of an increased recurrence rate is greater. Recently, a control group made up of clients *not* served by Project 12-Ways was developed to compare recidivism and repeat rates. The control group showed significantly ($p < .05$) more combined recidivism and repeat abuse and neglect than the Project 12-Ways group.

Cost-effectiveness data can often be as difficult to produce and understand as other kinds of program evaluation data can be. What staff members have

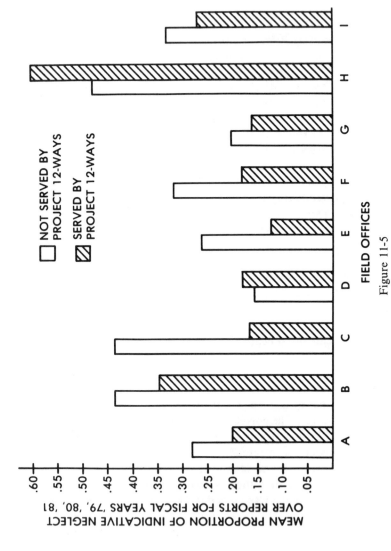

FIELD OFFICES

Figure 11-5

The proportion of indicative neglect for fiscal years 1979, 1980, and 1981 by field offices served and not served by Project 12-Ways.

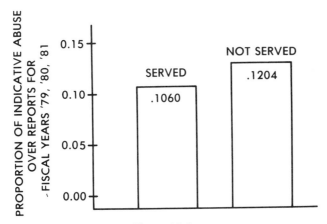

Figure 11-6

The proportion of indicative abuse over reports for fiscal years 1979, 1980, and 1981 by field offices in Illinois Region V.

been able to generate in this area is "gross" at best, but may be of some interest. In four fiscal years, Project 12-Ways has served over 350 families and delivered over 80,000 hours of service for a cost of approximately $2 million. This breaks down to $19.85 per hour in fiscal years 1981, $21.32 for fiscal year 1982, and $21.65 in fiscal year 1983. These unit cost figures are probably greatly lower than the costs per hour of providing services in mental health centers, but they can be misleading, because the figures do not take into account whatever it may cost the protective service agency and the public aid agency with whom Project 12-Ways holds its contract to interact with the project and facilitate its ability to provide service.

Summary

Any program evaluation data that are presented here are necessarily biased. Client assignment to Project 12-Ways, as described above, is hardly random. The agency personnel select and refer clients whom they feel are suitable for Project 12-Ways services, and the project accepts or reject clients on the basis of its own criteria. Thus, interpretation of program evaluation data *must* be conservative. On the other hand, as it turns out, the agency has taken to sending the project most of its most difficult cases. Thus, any successes that the project may have may be especially noteworthy.

A critical issue in the entire field of applied behavior analysis, and parent training in particular, is that of generalization and maintenance of treatment

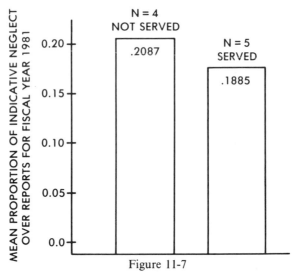

Figure 11-7

The mean proportion of indicative neglect over reports for fiscal year 1981 by field offices served and not served by Project 12-Ways.

effects. On one hand, Project 12-Ways staff members feel that the ecobehavioral model itself facilitates generalization and maintenance. This is because virtually all treatment services are offered in clients' homes; because the services attempt to remediate problems in the families' broad "ecosystems"; and because generalization measures (and programming) are often done in multiple settings. On the other hand, there is the notion that the 12-Ways approach is so invasive that even careful, gradual weaning of the family from project services might not be sufficient. That is to say, when the staff members have been so involved in rearranging so many events in a family's life and then terminate service, what cues remain in the family to maintain treatment gains? To a large extent, only long-term follow-up data on the gross measures of recidivism will answer any of the questions of maintenance. Almost paradoxically, however, only if a family engages in recidivism (abuse or neglect after treatment) can any other direct measures be collected. Part of the project's service contract is to try to produce behavior change, to terminate service, and ultimately to close the protective service case. Thus, long-term follow-up data collection is precluded by the very nature of the contract. Of course, as long as a case is kept "open," the staff can collect follow-up data and provide follow-up services. This has been the situation in many cases.

Social validation (Wolf, 1978) has been a relatively new concern in applied behavior analysis. It addresses these questions: Do clients feel benefited by treatment? Do experts agree on treatment goals, procedures, and outcomes? In individual research projects, such as the nutrition study (Sarber et al., in press), the home safety study (Tertinger *et al.*, 1982), and others, formal social validation at one or more levels has occurred. Project-wide, overall satisfaction evaluation by clients has not been accomplished for every case. This represents one of the future goals for Project 12-Ways.

INTANGIBLES OR "FUZZY ISSUES"

There are some aspects of Project 12-Ways that undoubtedly account for many of its successes; there are no data for these aspects and probably never will be, yet they need to be mentioned. For example, the project's relationship with the protective service agency (DCFS) at all levels (state, regional, and local field offices) is a positive one. With over 30 of the project's own staff members, the SIU-C administrative bureaucracy, the state agency's bureaucracy, and the very difficult legal and social problems of the clients, one might predict any number of conflicts at any number of levels. Such has not been the case. Any minor problems have been quickly resolved, and no major ones have ever occurred. It would be very comforting to be able to suggest many reasons why this relationship has worked out so well, but only a couple of speculations are possible. It seems that all parties concerned want to make Project 12-Ways work. Communication between the project and the agency has been excellent. The agency undoubtedly is pleased with the consistency of the project's effort. Despite being a university-based service, project staff members, like postal workers, have *delivered* service at all times of year under all kinds of conditions. Conversely, the project has been so pleased with the cooperation received at all levels from the state agency that there is always a willingness to compromise, to resolve issues that may come up, and to try to meet the agency's needs.

Another component that undoubtedly plays a major role in the success of Project 12-Ways is the fact that it functions within the Behavior Analysis and Therapy Program at SIU-C. A similar model would probably work only with similarly trained and supervised "behavioral" staff. Thus, it might not be as effective to try to replicate the model in a psychology department with one or two behavioral faculty members, whose students' time and interests might not allow for the intensive behavioral training and experience available in a program granting a degree in behavior analysis and therapy.

The issue of "behavioral" brings in another consideration. That is, our clients would probably not form good relationships with insight-oriented counselors. Many of our clients are not especially verbal, and most of them seem to appreciate the "action-oriented" model of behavior therapy. Some support for this speculation can be found in the recent work of Bernal and her colleagues (Bernal *et al.*, 1980), showing families' preference for behavior therapists over insight-oriented therapists.

It should be noted also that, despite the label "behavioral," our counselors have learned that a friendly relationship must be built with clients during the assessment phase, if the clients are going to comply with any treatment regimens. Also, although the project offers as many as 15 services, any individual service is seldom introduced simultaneously with another new service. Clients only seem to do well with one or two components at a time.

Finally, as suggested earlier, the in-home aspect of Project 12-Ways service is surely critical. Few of our clients, if any, would have the combination of motivation and transportation to show up for scheduled clinic visits. Also, again, in-home therapy presumably facilitates generalization.

FUTURE

Of foremost concern for the future of Project 12-Ways is continued funding. The project would like to believe that strong relationships within the state, consistent efforts, and reasonable successes would be sufficient to warrant continued funding, or at least to put the project near the front of the line at the "resources available" window. Of course, however, political and economic conditions will ultimately determine the project's fiscal future.

As suggested earlier, there is strong interest in conducting as sophisticated a level of program evaluation as possible. Of particular interest will be comparisons of recidivism or initial incidents of abuse and neglect between clients whose service from Project 12-Ways was terminated for 3 to 5 years prior to follow-up, and other clients in the region who also received state services, but not from Project 12-Ways.

Research has a way of snowballing, and that is an intentional design in Project 12-Ways. One home safety study has led to another; one infant stimulation study has led to another; the behavioral assessment study will undoubtedly lead to another.

Staff training and development are considered to be in need of continual improvement. As mentioned earlier, if some formal training modules have proven satisfactory, other ones will be implemented for other components.

Finally, if a model is truly ecobehavioral, it must adjust with the times. Perhaps we will need to increase our focus on job-finding training; perhaps we will discover the need to drop some service components and add others. But therein lies the challenge. I hope that this does not sound ingratiating, but it is truly our belief that whatever we have "given," we have gained more in return. Our clients have at once opened our eyes and taught us countless lessons. We hope to continue to learn enough from those lessons to be able to try to disseminate our new knowledge in a professional way.

Acknowledgments

A great number of people have contributed in one way or another to the completion of this chapter. The longer the list, the greater the likelihood of accidentally leaving someone out; however, risking an accidental omission is worth the opportunity to be sure that the following individuals' names are in print. Grateful appreciation is extended for the assistance of John Allen, Helen Auman, Sardari Bhasin, Alan Bickett, Gergory L. Coler, Kay Crist, Maria Halasz, Barbara Kohlenberg, Duane Lundervold, James McGimsey, Alice Rudolph, Gene Ruehmkorff, Rita Spiller, Dennis Stuckey, Richard Terry, Debbie Tertinger, Michael Tristano, Susan West, and George Williams. Special thanks are always in order for my "right-hand person," Sherry Siebel, and for some writing assistance from Randy Campbell, Ron Dachman, and Jim Rice (who also provides great help with data analysis). Finally, sincerest gratitude is extended to all individuals who have served as staff members on Project 12-Ways.

References

Azrin, N. H., & Besalel, V. B. *Job Club counselor's manual: A behavioral approach to vocational counseling.* Baltimore: University Park Press, 1980.

Azrin, N. H., & Foxx, R. M. *Toilet training in less than a day.* New York: Simon & Schuster, 1974.

Azrin, N. H., Naster, B. J., & Jones, R. Reciprocity counseling: A rapid learning-based procedure for marital counseling. *Behaviour Research and Therapy,* 1973, *11,* 365–382.

Becker, W. C. The relationship of factors in parental rating of self and each other to the behavior of kindergarten children as rated by mothers, fathers, and teachers. *Journal of Consulting Psychology,* 1960, *24,* 507–527.

Becker, W. C. *Parents are teachers.* Champaign, Ill: Research press, 1979.

Bernal, M. E., Klinnert, M. D., & Schultz, L. A. Outcome evaluation of behavioral parent training and client-centered parent counseling for children with conduct problems. *Journal of Applied Behavior Analysis,* 1980, *13,* 677–691.

Birrell, R. G., & Birrell, J. H. W. The maltreatment syndrome in children: A hospital survey. *Medical Journal of Australia,* 1968, *2,* 1023–1029.

Campbell, R. V., O'Brien, S., Bickett, A. D., & Lutzker, J. R. In-home parent training, treatment of migraine headaches, and marital counseling as an ecobehavioral approach to prevent child abuse. *Journal of Behavior Therapy and Experimental Psychiatry,* in press.

Christophersen, E. The family training program: Intensive home-based family-centered parent training. *Education and Treatment of Children,* 1979, *2,* 287–292.

Cooper, M. L., & Etzel, B. C. *The programming and development of pre-academic skills.* Paper presented at the meeting of the Society for Research in Child Development, Santa Monica, 1969.

Dachman, R. S., Halasz, M. M., Bickett, A. D., & Lutzker, J. R. *An ecobehavioral treatment package for the prevention of child abuse and neglect with a low-income single-parent family.* Manuscript submitted for publication, 1982.

Egeland, B. Preliminary results of a prospective study of the antecedents of child abuse. *Child Abuse and Neglect,* 1979, *3,* 269–278.

Green, A. H., Gaines, R. W., & Sandgrund, A. Child abuse: Pathological syndrome of family interaction. *American Journal of Psychiatry,* 1974, *131,* 882–886.

Greene, B. F., Clark, H. B., & Risley, T. R. *Shopping with children: Advice for parents.* San Rafael, Calif.: Academic Therapy Publications, 1977.

Helfer, R. E. The etiology of child abuse. *Pediatrics,* 1973, *51,* 777–779.

Hunt, G. M., & Azrin, N. H. A community-reinforcement approach to alcoholism. *Behaviour Research and Therapy,* 1973, *11,* 91–104.

Isaacs, C. A brief review of the characteristics of abuse-prone parents. *The Behavior Therapist*, 1981, *4*(5), 5–8.

Jenson, W. R., & Sloane, H. N. Chart moves and grab bags: A simple contingency management system. *Journal of Applied Behavior Analysis*, 1979, *12*, 334.

Jewett, J., & Clark, H. B. Teaching preschoolers to use appropriate dinnertime conversation: An analysis from school to home. *Behavior Therapy*, 1979, *10*, 589–605.

Kunz, G. R., Lutzker, J. R., Cuvo, A. J., Eddleman, J., Lutzker, S. Z., Megson, D., & Gulley, B. Managing care provider performance on health and developmental tasks in an infant care facility. *Journal of Applied Behavior Analysis*, 1982, *15*, 521–531.

Lutzker, J. R. *On the welfare of children.* Paper presented at the Fifth Annual Convention of the Association for Behavior Analysis, Dearborn, Michigan, June 1979.

Lutzker, J. R. Deviant family systems. In B. Lahey & A. Kazdin (Eds.)., *Advances in clinical child psychology* (Vol. 3). New York: Plenum Press, 1980.

Lutzker, J. R., Frame, R. E., & Greene, B. F. *An ecobehavioral approach to child abuse and neglect.* Paper presented at the Sixth Annual Convention of the Association for Behavior Analysis, Dearborn, Michigan, May 24–27, 1980.

Lutzker, J. R., Frame, R. E., & Rice, J. M. Project 12-Ways: an ecobehavioral approach to the treatment and prevention of child abuse and neglect. *Education and Treatment of Children*, 1982, *5*, 141–155.

Lutzker, J. R., McGimsey, J. F., McRae, S., & Campbell, R. V. Behavioral parent-training: There's so much more to do. *The Behavior Therapist*, 1983, *6*, 110–112.

O'Dell, S. L., Tarler-Benlolo, L., & Flynn, J. M. An instrument to measure knowledge of behavioral principles as applied to children. *Journal of Behavior Therapy and Experimental Psychiatry*, 1979, *10*, 29–34.

Patterson, G. R., & Fagot, B. I. Selective responsiveness to social reinforcers and deviant behavior in children. *The Psychological Record*, 1967, *17*, 369–378.

Peed, S., Roberts, M., & Forehand, R. Evaluation of the effectiveness of a standardized parent training program in altering the interaction of mothers and their noncompliant children. *Behavior Modification*, 1977, *1*, 323–350.

Rogers Warren, A., & Warren, S. F. (Eds.). *Ecological perspectives in behavior analysis.* Baltimore: University Park Press, 1977.

Rosenfield, M. D., Sarber, R. E., Bueno, G., Greene, B. F., & Lutzker, J. R. Maintaining accountability for an ecobehavioral treatment of one aspect of child neglect: Personal cleanliness. *Education and Treatment of Children*, in press.

Russo, D. C., Cataldo, M. F., & Cushing, P. J. Compliance training and behavioral covariation in the treatment of multiple behavior problems. *Journal of Applied Behavior Analysis*, 1981, *14*, 209–222.

Sanders, M. R., & Glynn, T. Training parents in behavioral self-management: An analysis of generalization and maintenance. *Journal of Applied Behavior Analysis*, 1981, *14*, 223–237.

Sarber, R., Halasz, M. M., Messmer, M. C., Bickett, A. C., & Lutzker, J. R. Preventing child abuse and neglect by training menu planning and grocery shopping skills to a mentally retarded mother. *Mental Retardation*, in press.

Schilling, D., & Poppen, R. Behavioral relaxation training assessment. *Journal of Behavior Therapy and Experimental Psychiatry*, in press.

Smith, S. M., Hanson, R., & Noble, S. Parents of battered babies: A controlled study. *British Medical Journal*, 1973, *4*, 388–391.

Smith, S. M., Hanson, R., & Noble, S. Social aspects of the battered baby syndrome. *British Journal of Psychiatry*, 1974, *125*, 568–582.

Solnick, J. V., Rincover, A., & Peterson, C. P. Some determinants of the reinforcing and punishing effects of time out. *Journal of Applied Behavior Analysis*, 1977, *10*, 415–424.

Taylor, C. The battered child. In D. Clifton & J. G. Wells (Eds.), *Deviancy and the family*. Philadelphia: F. A. Davis, 1973.

Tearnan, B., & Lutzker, J. R. A contracting "package" in the treatment of marital problems: A case study. *American Journal of Family Therapy,* 1980, *8,* 24–31.

Tertinger, D. A., Greene, B. F., & Lutzker, J. R. *The development, assessment, and implementation of a home safety program in homes of child abuse and neglect families.* Manuscript submitted for publication, 1982.

Tizard, J. Three dysfunctional environmental influences in development: Malnutrition, nonaccidental injury, and child minding. *Postgraduate Medical Journal,* 1975, *51,* 19–27.

Van Biervliet, A., Spangler, P. F., & Marshall, A. M. An ecobehavioral examination of a simple strategy for increasing mealtime language in residential facilities. *Journal of Applied Behavior Analysis,* 1981, *14,* 295–305.

Wahler, R. G. The insular mother: Her problems in parent–child treatment. *Journal of Applied Behavior Analysis,* 1980, *13,* 207–219.

Wahler, R. G., & Fox, J. J. Setting events in applied behavior analysis: Toward a conceptual and methodological expansion. *Journal of Applied Behavior Analysis,* 1981, *14,* 327–338.

Walker, H. M. *Walker Problem Behavior Identification Checklist.* Los Angeles: Western Psychological Services, 1976.

Willems, E. P. Behavioral technology and behavioral ecology. *Journal of Applied Behavior Analysis,* 1974, *7,* 151–166.

Wolf, M. M. Social validity: The case for subjective measurement or how applied behavior analysis is finding its heart. *Journal of Applied Behavior Analysis,* 1978, *11,* 203–214.

Wolpe, J., & Lazarus, A. A. *Behavior therapy techniques: A guide to the treatment of neuroses.* Oxford: Pergamon Press, 1966.

PARENT TRAINING FOR THE NONCOMPLIANT CHILD
Treatment Outcome, Generalization, and Adjunctive Therapy Procedures

Robert J. McMahon
University of British Columbia

Rex Forehand
University of Georgia

Noncompliance to parental instructions is consistently reported to be the most frequent problem among children who are referred to clinics for treatment of deviant behavior (Forehand, 1977). For example, Bernal, Klinnert, and Schultz (1980) reported that 35 of 36 parents who referred their children to the Family Intervention Project for treatment reported difficulties with this behavior, while Barkley (1981) has indicated that noncompliance is one of the primary problems of hyperactive children. Not only is noncompliance a common behavior problem, but severe manifestations of this and similar forms of conflict between parents and young children have serious ramifications for the development of adolescent and adult psychological problems (see Robins, 1979, for a review of this literature). Given the frequency with which noncompliance is found among clinic-referred children and the implications for later adjustment if noncompliance is left untreated, there is a need to develop treatment procedures for this behavior problem.

Recent reviews (Graziano, 1977; O'Dell, 1974; Wells & Forehand, 1981) have conclusively demonstrated the short-term efficacy of behavioral parent training for a wide variety of children's behavior problems. However, these authors have noted the scarcity of data on the generality of such treatment effects and have urged that future research be focused in this area. Generality is important for the success of a parent training approach from at least two perspectives (Forehand & Atkeson, 1977). From the viewpoint of treatment, generality results in a more optimal use of therapist time, since the therapist will no longer be required to treat recurrences of previously treated problems, problem behaviors in new settings, all of a child's problem behaviors, or the behavior problems of the child's siblings. From the viewpoint of prevention, generalization minimizes repeated professional intervention and should result in a diminution of future behavior problems of the child (and siblings). This would allow clinicians to move from a focus on tertiary prevention (i.e., the treatment of problem behaviors) to a focus on primary prevention (i.e., the enhancement of living conditions) (Caplan, 1964). An additional reason for assessing generality is that it allows therapists to monitor the potential occurrence of any "negative, second-order, or unintended" (Graziano, 1977, p. 281) side effects of parent training.

In a recent review, Forehand and Atkeson (1977) described four types of generality relevant to the effectiveness of parent training programs. These are (1) setting generality, which is the occurrence of treatment effects in settings other than the therapeutic one; (2) temporal generality, which is the maintenance of treatment effects following termination of treatment; (3) sibling generality, which is the effect of treatment on the behavior of the untreated siblings of the treated child; and (4) behavioral generality, which is the change in behaviors not specifically targeted for treatment. An additional facet of treatment outcome that may be considered to be relevant to generality is the concept of "social validity" (Kazdin, 1977; Wolf, 1978). This refers to the validation of treatment effects by demonstrating that therapeutic changes are "clinically or socially important for the client" (Kazdin, 1977, p. 429). Kazdin (1977) has proposed that this may be done by comparing the client's behavior before and after treatment to the behavior of nondeviant peers (social comparison) or by having the client evaluated by individuals who have contact with him or her to determine whether the client is perceived differently as a result of treatment (subjective evaluation). In addition, Wolf (1978) has suggested that therapists assess the social significance of the therapeutic goals, the acceptability of treatment procedures to the client, and the client's satisfaction with the outcome of treatment.

The purpose of this chapter is to describe a systematic program of research that has examined the treatment outcome and generalization of effects of a parent training program designed to modify child noncompliance. More recently, we have attempted to enhance the treatment outcome and generalization of our parent training program by developing and evaluating several adjunctive therapy procedures. These latter efforts have focused on the development of a written brochure for parents interested in improving their non-clinic-referred children's mealtime behavior, and on the addition of specific components to the treatment program. A brief description of the parent training program and of the various outcome measures employed in these investigations is presented first.

THE PARENT TRAINING PROGRAM

Program Description

A parenting program that has been specifically designed to treat child non-compliance was first developed by Hanf (Hanf, 1969; Hanf & Kling, 1973) and subsequently modified by Forehand and his colleagues (cf. Forehand & McMahon, 1981). This treatment program has served as the basic therapeutic intervention around which our explorations of treatment outcome and generalization and adjunctive therapy procedures have occurred. To date, over 100 mother–child pairs have participated in this ongoing project. The children, both male and female, were referred to the University of Georgia Psychology Clinic for treatment of noncompliance and other behavior problems. Severely retarded or autistic children were not included in this sample. Referral sources have included local pediatricians, school personnel, ministers, mental health workers, and the like. The children have ranged from 3 to 8 years of age. The socioeconomic status (SES) of the families has ranged from Class I (e.g., business executives) to Class V (e.g., welfare recipients) on the Myers and Bean (1968) scale. The majority of the families have been of a lower middle-class SES.

Unlike some other investigators, we have not made involvement of both parents in the treatment program mandatory. Consequently, much of our work has been completed with mothers only. Fathers have attended therapy sessions in only about one-third of our cases. Although our therapy program may be less effective because of this, we have chosen to provide services to as many parents and children as possible by not excluding families in which only one parent would participate.

The parent training program employs a controlled learning environment in which to teach the parent to change maladaptive patterns of interaction with the child. Sessions are conducted in a clinic setting with individual families rather than in groups. Treatment occurs in clinic playrooms equipped with one-way mirrors for observation, sound systems, and bug-in-the-ear (Farrall Instruments) devices by which the therapist can unobtrusively communicate with the parent. A table, chairs, and several age-appropriate toys are in each playroom. A number of discrete parenting skills are taught in a systematic manner. The skills are taught to the parent by way of didactic instruction, modeling, and role playing. The parent also practices the skills in the clinic with the child while receiving prompting and feedback from the therapist by means of the bug-in-the-ear device. Finally, the parent employs these newly acquired skills in the home setting.

The treatment program consists of two phases. During the differential-attention phase of treatment (Phase I), the parent learns to be a more effective reinforcing agent by increasing the frequency and range of social rewards and by reducing the frequency of competing verbal behavior. First, the parent is taught to attend to and describe the child's appropriate behavior. All commands, questions, and criticisms directed to the child are eliminated. The second segment of Phase I consists of training the parent in the use of verbal and physical rewards contingent upon compliance and other appropriate behaviors. The parent is taught to reward the child's ongoing appropriate behavior, to ignore minor inappropriate behavior, and to reward each instance of compliance. All of these skills are modeled by the therapist and cotherapist before the parent practices them with the child. Homework is assigned in the form of daily 10-minute practice sessions with the child using the skills taught in the clinic. The parent also is required to develop programs for use outside the clinic to increase at least two child behaviors using the new skills.

Phase II of the treatment program consists of training the parent to use appropriate commands and a time-out procedure to decrease noncompliant behavior exhibited by the child. The parent is taught to give direct, concise commands one at a time, and to allow the child sufficient time to comply.[1] If compliance is initiated, the parent is taught to reward or attend to the child within 5 seconds of the compliance initiation. If compliance is not initiated, the parent learns to implement a time-out procedure that involves placing the child in a time-out chair for 3 minutes (for complete details, see Forehand & McMahon, 1981). Following time out, the command that originally elicited noncompliance is repeated. Compliance is followed by contingent attention from the parent. This sequence is practiced by the parent with the cotherapist first and later with the child. When the parent is able to administer time out perfectly in the clinic, he or she is instructed to begin using the procedure for noncompliance at home.

During each treatment session in which a new skill is introduced (e.g., attends, rewards, time out), the parent is given a handout explaining the skill. Home data sheets are given to the parent after each session so that he or she can record home practice during Phase I and use of time out during Phase II.

Progression to each new skill in the treatment program is determined by the use of behavioral and temporal (number of sessions) criteria. The therapist uses observational data collected during each treatment session to determine whether the parent–child pair has attained the behavioral criteria necessary for movement to the next segment of treatment. The behavioral criteria insure that the parent has attained an acceptable degree of competence in a particular skill before being taught additional parenting techniques. In addition, these criteria allow for the individualization of the treatment program by allocating training time more efficiently, since they allow the therapist to concentrate his or her attention on the more serious parenting skill deficiencies. The treatment criteria have been delineated elsewhere (Forehand & McMahon, 1981) and are not reiterated here.

---

[1]These commands are referred to as "alpha commands." "Beta commands" are those to which the child has no opportunity to demonstrate compliance because of vagueness or parental interruption (e.g., "Act your age").

Outcome Measures

When parents accept treatment at our clinic, they also agree to participate in the ongoing process of data collection by which we can assess the effects of the parent training program. Multiple outcome measures are employed, since different categories of measures have been shown to have rather low intercorrelations (Atkeson & Forehand, 1978, 1981; Forehand, Griest, & Wells, 1979). Two primary types of measures have been employed in the studies examining the generalization and maintenance of our parenting program: direct observation and parent verbal report measures. These measures are collected immediately prior to treatment, immediately after treatment, and at the follow-up (where appropriate).

Direct Observation

Trained observers collect these data in the home (and/or school) setting, usually in blocks of four 40-minute observations conducted on different days. In the home, the parent is instructed to adhere as much as possible to the daily routine and to interact normally with the child. Similar instructions are in effect for the teacher in the school setting if observations occur there.

Undergraduate and graduate students serve as observers. Each observer spends at least 20 hours of training in the use of the coding system prior to beginning the observations. After the initial training sessions, biweekly 1-hour training sessions are held in order to maintain the accuracy of the observers. In addition, a second observer collects reliability data for approximately 25% of the observations. Interobserver agreements have been above 75% (Forehand & Peed, 1979), indicating that reliable data are being obtained.

In the coding system we have developed for use in the home setting (Forehand, Peed, Roberts, McMahon, Griest, & Humphreys, 1978), the following classes of parent behaviors are recorded: rewards, attends, questions, commands, warnings, and time out. Child behaviors that are recorded include appropriate behavior, inappropriate (deviant) behavior, compliance, and non-compliance. The behavioral coding system has been presented elsewhere (Forehand & McMahon, 1981). This coding system has also been adapted for use in the school setting.

Parent Verbal Report Measures

Two questionnaires have been employed either singly or in combination to assess parental perceptions of child behavior. Three scales from the Parent Attitudes Test (PAT) (Cowen, Huser, Beach, & Rappaport, 1970) have been employed. The Home Attitude Scale consists of seven items that reflect the parent's perception of the child's adjustment in the home. The Behavior Rating Scale consists of 23 items, each of which refers to a behavior problem, while the Adjective Checklist Scale consists of 34 adjectives, each describing a child behavior or personality characteristic. Cowen *et al.* (1970) have presented evidence demonstrating the reliability and validity of these scales. The second questionnaire is the Patterson and Fagot (1967) abridged version of the Becker Bipolar Adjective Checklist (Becker, 1960), which contains 47 bipolar adjective pairs anchoring the ends of 7-point Likert-type scales. The Becker is scored on the basis of the five factors derived by Patterson and Fagot (1967): "less relaxed," "less withdrawn and hostile," "more aggressive," "more intelligently efficient," and "more conduct problems."

In the later studies examining the role of parental personal adjustment in generalization, several widely used self-report measures have been employed. The Beck Depression Inventory (Beck, Rush, Shaw, & Emery, 1979) consists of 21 categories that are used to rate self-reported levels of depression. The inventory scores correlate significantly with clinicians' ratings of depression (Metcalfe & Goldman, 1965) and with objective behavioral measures of depression (Williams, Barlow, & Agras, 1972). The trait form of the Spielberger State–Trait Anxiety Inventory (Spielberger, Gorsuch, & Lushene, 1970) has been administered to obtain ratings of maternal anxiety, and the modified form of Locke's Marital Adjustment Test (Kimmel & VanderVeen, 1974) allows married parents to rate their marital satisfaction.

A Parent's Consumer Satisfaction Questionnaire (PCSQ) has been developed recently to measure parental satisfaction with treatment received in our parent training program (McMahon, Tiedemann, Forehand, & Griest, 1983). Several authors (e.g., Margolis, Sorenson, & Galano, 1977; Yates, 1978) have suggested that consumer satisfaction with a particular treatment strategy or an entire treatment approach is likely to be a factor in the ultimate effectiveness of the intervention. The PCSQ assesses parental satisfaction with the overall program, the teaching format, the specific parenting techniques taught, and the therapists. Items examining both the usefulness and difficulty of the teaching format and specific parenting techniques are included. In all of these areas, parents respond to items on a 7-point Likert-type scale. Parents also have the opportunity to reply to several open-ended questions concerning their reactions to the parenting program.

OUTCOME STUDIES
EXAMINING GENERALIZATION

Earlier outcome studies (Forehand & King, 1974, 1977) suggested the immediate effectiveness of the parent training program in improving parent–child interactions in a clinic setting. However, lack of proper experimental control and failure to assess parent and child behavior outside the clinic setting limited the conclusions regarding the efficacy of the program. Of primary importance, then, was the need to assess the generalization of these treatment effects across settings, time, behaviors, and siblings. In addition, it was important to determine whether these effects were socially valid and whether there were any side effects of the parent training program on other aspects of family functioning.

Generalization to the Home Setting

In order to evaluate the effectiveness of the treatment program in comparison to a no-treatment control group and to investigate the generality of treatment changes from the clinic to the home, Peed, Roberts, and Forehand (1977) undertook a study that compared six mother–child pairs who received treatment by way of the parent training program to six mother–child pairs who constituted a waiting-list control group. Each mother–child pair was randomly assigned to either the treatment or control group after the mother contacted our clinic expressing concern over her child's noncompliance. Each mother–child pair then underwent pretreatment sets of clinic and home observations. Following treatment or a waiting period of similar length, each mother–child pair again underwent the clinic and home observations (hereafter referred to as "posttreatment"). By assessing maternal and child behavior in both the clinic and home settings, the setting generality of the parenting program could be examined.

The results from the Peed et al. (1977) study indicated that in a free-play situation in the clinic setting, the mothers in the treatment group significantly decreased their frequency of questions and significantly increased their frequency of attends and rewards from pretreatment to posttreatment assessments. In a parental control situation in the clinic setting, the treatment group mothers decreased their use of beta commands and increased their use of contingent attention for child compliance from pretreatment to posttreatment. The children demonstrated a significant increase in compliance in the parental control situation. Thus, these data replicated earlier findings of improved mother and child behavior in the clinic setting. Of primary importance were the data concerning generalization of these treatment effects to the home setting. In the home observations, significant increases from the pretreatment to posttreatment assessments occurred for child compliance and for maternal rewards, attends, and contingent attention to compliance. Significant decreases occurred for maternal use of beta commands. For the control group, significant changes did not occur from the prewaiting to postwaiting period, providing support for the notion that the treatment program rather than the passage of time was responsible for the mother and child behavior changes in the treatment group.

The PAT and the Becker Bipolar Adjective Checklist were also administered to the mothers in each group at the pretreatment and posttreatment assessments. In general, mothers in both groups saw their children as better adjusted at posttreatment than at pretreatment, suggesting that the changes in perceptions of the mothers in the treatment group did not result from treatment per se. This finding suggests that a parent perception measure *alone* may not be an adequate criterion upon which to base judgments concerning the effectiveness of parent training programs, and again demonstrates the necessity of employing multiple outcome measures.

A recent investigation provided further support for generalization to the home setting by assessing the effects of SES on treatment outcome and generalization. We (Rogers, Forehand, Griest, Wells, & McMahon, 1981) divided 31 mother–child pairs who had completed the parent training program into low-, medium-, and high-SES groups according to the Myers and Bean (1968) index of social status. At posttreatment, the expected changes in parent and child behavior and parent perception of the child occurred for all three groups. There was no differential treatment effect across the three groups, indicating that the parent training program is equally effective across the range of SES.

Generalization to the School Setting

The Peed *et al.* (1977) study provided convincing data concerning the immediate effectiveness of the training program in changing parent and child behavior in both the clinic and home. However, the data were not provided concerning whether changes in child behaviors generalized from the clinic and home to the school setting. The effect of the treatment program on child behavior in the school as well as the home was of concern, because Johnson, Bolstad, and Lobitz (1976) had reported data suggesting that children may increase their deviant behavior in school when deviant home behavior is treated by parent training programs. In order to determine whether such a "behavioral contrast" effect existed, or whether setting generality (a decrease in deviant school behavior when noncompliance and other deviant behavior decreased in the home) occurred with our parent training program, two different investigations have been carried out.

In the first study, we (Forehand, Sturgis, McMahon, Aguar, Green, Wells, & Breiner, 1979) measured the total amount of deviant child behavior in the school (e.g., crying, demands for attention, tantrums, negativism) during observation sessions both before and after treatment for eight clinic-referred children. The standard home observational measures were also obtained for the clinic group. In addition, the classroom deviant behavior of eight randomly selected "normal" school children was measured before and after a time interval equivalent to the one that separated the treated children's pretreatment and posttreatment measures. Teacher responses to the treated and control children were also observed in order to determine whether changes in the school environment could account for the results obtained in the school setting. The results indicated that the expected changes in both parent and child behavior occurred in the home setting for the clinic group. In the school setting, three of the eight children treated for home noncompliance decreased their deviant school behavior, and five increased such behavior from pretreatment to posttreatment assessments. For the randomly selected control children, four increased and four decreased their deviant school behavior. Statistical analysis of the data revealed no systematic changes in school behavior. Teacher behavior was similar across both groups.

In a more recent study, which employed a larger sample of 16 subjects, Breiner and Forehand (1981) utilized a similar design. In addition, they assessed both compliance and general deviant behavior in both the school and home settings. The earlier study measured noncompliance in the home, but reported a general category of inappropriate child behavior in the school. As in the earlier investigation, while the expected changes occurred in both parent and child behavior in the home setting, there were no significant changes in the children's classroom behavior in either a positive or negative direction, nor did teacher behavior change from pretreatment to posttreatment observations. However, in contrast to the earlier study, which reported nonsignificant increases in deviant school behavior for some of the children, this study found a nonsignificant decrease in deviant school behavior and an increase in compliance for both treated and control subjects. Thus, the results of these two studies indicate that treatment-induced changes in child behavior in the home are not associated with significant behavior changes in the school (McMahon & Davies, 1980). Evidence for setting generality to the classroom was not generated by either study. However, these data also failed to support a behavioral contrast effect, since there were no systematic increases in deviant behavior in the classroom.

In both of the preceding studies, the treatment of behavior problems in the home was not associated with systematic changes in school behavior. However, in each study there were changes in all subjects' school behavior, although the direction and magnitude of change varied across children. Utilizing the clinic subjects from the Breiner and Forehand (1981) study, we (Forehand, Breiner, McMahon, & Davies, 1981) attempted to predict changes in child behavior in the school that occurred with the treatment of home problems. Two multiple-regression analyses employed pretreatment-to-posttreatment change scores in school compliance and oppositional school behavior as the criterion variables. The three variables used to predict change in school compliance were the pretreatment level of school compliance (since the degree of change that could occur in the criterion variable was limited by the initial level of occurrence of the behavior) and pretreatment-to-posttreatment change scores in home compliance and deviant home behavior. The three variables used to predict change in deviant school behavior were the pretreatment level of deviant school behavior and change scores from pretreatment to posttreatment in home compliance and deviant home behavior. The results indicated that changes in both compliance and deviant behavior in the school could be predicted by changes in deviant home behavior in combination with the pretreatment level of the criterion variable. This combination accounted for 55% of the variance in predicting changes in school compliance and 70% of the variance in predicting changes in deviant school behavior. Thus, this study provides some preliminary evidence that it may be possible to predict concomitant changes in school behavior for children who are clinic-referred for behavior problems in the home, on the basis of pretreatment-to-posttreatment changes in home behavior in combination with pretreatment levels of school behavior. It remains for future research to specify the relevant parameters affecting the magnitude and direction of such change. Such information can be of assistance in therapist decisions to monitor school behavior and/or to implement treatment in the school setting.

Temporal Generality (Maintenance)

At this point, our data indicated that the parenting program was immediately effective in changing parent and child behavior in both the clinic and home. However, the maintenance of these effects (i.e., temporal generality) was unknown. We have now conducted several studies that have examined the temporal generality of the parent training program (Baum & Forehand, 1981; Forehand, Rogers, McMahon, Wells, & Griest, 1981; Forehand, Sturgis, McMahon, Aguar, Green, Wells, & Breiner, 1979). In the first of these studies (Forehand, Sturgis, McMahon, Aguar, Green, Wells, & Breiner, 1979), the client sample consisted of 10 mother–child pairs, including the six mother–child pairs from the treatment group in the Peed et al. (1977) study. Data gathered in home observations both before and after treatment indicated that the subjects demonstrated pretreatment-to-posttreatment changes in the same parent and child behaviors as reported in the Peed et al. (1977) study. The temporal generality of the treatment program was assessed by means of single home observations gathered from the 10 mother–child pairs at 6 and 12 months following treatment. Observations in the home revealed that the changes in mother and child behaviors observed immediately after treatment were maintained. An exception was the maternal use of contingent attention, which did not differ from the pretreatment level at the 6- and 12-month follow-ups. Mothers continued to report, at both the 6- and 12-month follow-ups, the positive attitude changes concerning their children (as measured by the PAT) that were evident immediately following treatment.

The primary purpose of the 1981 study by Forehand, Rogers, McMahon, Wells, and Griest was to replicate and extend the results of the previous investigation by using a larger sample of mother–child pairs and by employing multiple observations in the home setting to assess temporal generality. Another purpose was to examine differences in mother–child pairs who would and would not participate in follow-up. All mother–child pairs who completed treatment at our clinic over a 2-year period were included in the sample ($n = 40$). However, at the time of the 8-month follow-up, four of the families had moved from the area. Eighteen of the remaining 36 families agreed to participate in the follow-up assessment, which included four home observations and the PAT. The observational measures of child behavior (compliance and deviant behavior) indicated that maintenance of treatment effects occurred at the 8-month follow-up. With respect to the observational measures of parent behavior, a reduced rate of beta commands was maintained. The frequency of attends plus rewards and contingent attention decreased significantly from posttreatment levels to follow-up; however, they still occurred significantly more frequently than at pretreatment. The parent perception measure indicated maintenance of positive attitude changes toward the children. Since comparisons of mother–child pairs who would and would not participate in follow-up generally failed to find differences between the two groups, this indicated that the positive results of this study were not an artifact due to participation at follow-up of only those clients who represented treatment successes.

Baum and Forehand (1981) examined the long-term maintenance of the parent training program by completing a follow-up assessment 1 to 4½ years after treatment for 34 mother–child pairs. The children ranged in age from 4.4 to 12.9 years at the time of follow-up. All parents completed the PAT and a modified version of the PCSQ. Furthermore, 20 of the parents and their children participated in two home observations. The results indicated that child compliance, deviant child behavior, and maternal perceptions of child adjustment changed significantly in the expected direction from pretreatment to posttreatment. Child compliance and maternal perceptions of child adjustment remained at the posttreatment levels at follow-up, while deviant child behavior was significantly lower at follow-up than at the posttreatment level. Maternal use of beta commands decreased from pretreatment to posttreatment, and the lower level was maintained at follow-up. Positive parent behaviors (attends plus rewards, contingent attention) improved from pretreatment to posttreatment. At follow-up, these behaviors occurred significantly more frequently than at pretreatment but significantly less frequently than at posttreatment. The PCSQ indicated that the parents were pleased with the treatment they had received. (These results are discussed below in the section on social validity.) There was no differential pattern of results on any of the outcome measures with respect to the length of follow-up. In addition, there were no differences between mothers who did or did not agree to participate in the home observations at follow-up on pretreatment and posttreatment measures or on the questionnaire measures at follow-up.

In summary, these investigations indicate that the parent training program possesses a high degree of temporal generality. Improvements in both child and parent behaviors and parental perceptions of the children generally have been maintained at follow-up assessments ranging from 6 months to 4½ years after treatment termination. The apparent exception to this pattern of maintenance has been the finding that, while such positive parent behaviors as attends plus rewards and contingent attention occur more frequently at follow-up than prior to treatment, they decrease from posttreatment levels. However, these decreases in positive reinforcement are programmed into the parent training program, since parents are told that the initial frequent use of reinforcement can be gradually decreased, but not eliminated, as the children's negative behaviors decrease.

Sibling Generality

We (Humphreys, Forehand, McMahon, & Roberts, 1978) also examined the generality of treatment effects from one sibling to another. During four to eight pretreatment home observations and four posttreatment home observations, the interactions of each mother and clinic-referred child and of the mother and a sibling of the clinic-referred child were observed. In all eight cases, both the clinic-referred child and the sibling were 3 to 8 years old, and the sibling was within 3 years of the clinic child's age. During treatment, the therapist did not discuss the application of the parenting techniques to the untreated sibling. If a mother initiated discussion of behavior problems in the untreated child, the therapist agreed that the procedures were general ones that were applicable to all children. No further elaboration of this point was made, and specific discussion of the sibling's behavior problems was deferred until after completion of the posttreatment observations.

The results indicated that from pretreatment to posttreatment, the mothers significantly increased their use of attention contingent on compliance, rewards, and attends, and decreased their use of beta commands toward the *untreated* children. In addition, the untreated children increased their compliance. These results suggest that mothers can generalize their skills for dealing with noncompliance to other children in the family without the aid of direct programming by the therapist, and that the untreated children respond by increasing their compliance to maternal commands.

Behavioral Generality

In their review of the different types of generality, Forehand and Atkeson (1977) concluded that behavioral generality (i.e., change in behaviors not specifically targeted for treatment) had the least support in the parent training literature. For example, large-scale studies by Patterson and his colleagues (Patterson, 1974; Patterson & Reid, 1973; Wiltz & Patterson, 1974) have all reported nonsignificant decreases in nontargeted deviant behaviors.

Of primary interest in examining behavioral generality in our parent training program was the relationship between a treated child behavior (noncompliance) and an untreated child behavior (other deviant behavior, including tantrums, aggression, crying, etc.). Wells, Forehand, and Griest (1980) treated 12 noncompliant clinic-referred children and their mothers. Observational data of child behavior were collected from these families as well as from a nonclinic comparison group of 12 mother–child pairs. Mothers in the nonclinic group were selected from community volunteers who responded to announcements requesting participants for a research project and whose children had no history of treatment for behavior problems. The clinic children significantly increased their compliance to both total and alpha commands from pretreatment to posttreatment, whereas the children in the nonclinic group did not change significantly on these measures. Further analysis indicated that the clinic and nonclinic groups differed significantly on both compliance measures at pretreatment but not at posttreatment. Most importantly, an examination of untreated deviant child behavior indicated that the clinic group decreased significantly from pretreatment on this measure and that the nonclinic group did not change. The clinic group was significantly more deviant than was the nonclinic group at pretreatment but not at posttreatment. These results provide evidence that generality from treated to untreated child behavior occurs with the parent training program, and suggest that the successful treatment of noncompliance is sufficient in many cases to reduce other deviant behaviors that are not treated.

Social Validity

The use of a normative comparison group has also been employed in an assessment of the social validity of the parenting program (Forehand, Wells, & Griest, 1980). Based on Kazdin (1977) and Wolf (1978), four social validation procedures were employed: social comparison, subjective evaluation, social acceptability of treatment, and consumer satisfaction. A total of 15 clinic-referred children and their mothers and 15 nonclinic children and their mothers served as subjects. Behavioral observations in the home setting were conducted at pretreatment and posttreatment and at a 2-month follow-up for the clinic group and at comparable times for the nonclinic group. Parental questionnaires regarding their own adjustment (Beck Depression Inventory) and the adjustment of their children (PAT) were also completed before and after the treatment period and at the 2-month follow-up. At 15 months after treatment, measures of consumer satisfaction and social acceptability of treatment were collected from mothers in the clinic group. Only mothers in the clinic-referred group completed the parenting program.

The social comparison method of assessing social validity indicated that children in the clinic (treatment) group were less compliant and more deviant prior to treatment, but not after treatment or at follow-up, than were children in the nonclinic group. Furthermore, children in the clinic group demonstrated an increase in compliance and a decrease in deviant behavior from pretreatment to posttreatment. Thus, this method of social validation suggests that treatment had the desired outcome. With respect to parent behaviors, mothers in the treatment group demonstrated a significant pretreatment-to-posttreatment improvement in positive attention (attends plus rewards, contingent attention) as well as in command behavior. At posttreatment and follow-up, mothers in the treatment group displayed more positive attention than did mothers in the nonclinic group, as well as similar levels of command behavior. There were also data to indicate that these behavioral improvements in both mother and child behavior were associated with improvements in self-reports of maternal depression. Depression ratings improved significantly from pretreatment to posttreatment for mothers in the treatment group, and did not differ significantly from those of the nonclinic group at posttreatment or follow-up.

With respect to the subjective evaluation procedure, mothers in the treatment group reported significant improvement in their children's adjustment from pretreatment to posttreatment; however, they still perceived their children as less well adjusted than nonclinic mothers perceived their children at posttreatment. At the follow-up assessment, the two groups of mothers did not differ in their perceptions of their children's adjustment. This suggests that changes in maternal perceptions of child adjustment to perceptions comparable to those held by mothers of non-clinic-referred children may follow rather than accompany changes in child behavior.

On the measures of social acceptability of treatment and consumer satisfaction collected 15 months after treatment termination, mothers in the treatment group indicated that they viewed the treatment procedures as appropriate for dealing with their children's behavior problems. Furthermore, they reported that they were satisfied with treatment; they viewed their children as improved; they felt confident in managing their children; they viewed the therapists as being very helpful; and they frequently used the skills taught in the program.

There have been two other investigations in which we have utilized consumer satisfaction indexes of social validity. In the long-term follow-up study discussed above, Baum and Forehand (1981) employed a modified version of the PCSQ to assess consumer satisfaction from 1 to $4\frac{1}{2}$ years after treatment termination. Mothers at all follow-up periods expressed a high level of satisfaction with the treatment program and with the therapists. They reported that they continued use of the parenting skills and that they found them useful and easy to implement. The mothers also reported that their children's behavior had improved at the end of the treatment program and at follow-up. There were no differences in satisfaction as a function of length of the follow-up period.

In a more thorough assessment of consumer satisfaction with our parent training program (McMahon et al., 1983), a total of 20 mothers who had completed the parent training program completed the PCSQ at posttreatment and at a 2-month follow-up. In addition to noting parental satisfaction with treatment outcome and with the therapists, comparisons of both perceived usefulness and difficulty among the various teaching methods and parenting skills were made. The temporal stability of these aspects of consumer satisfaction was measured by comparing results at treatment termination to those at the 2-month follow-up. Finally, we examined whether the inclusion of training in social learning principles into the basic parent training program differentially affected parental satisfaction. (This aspect of the investigation is discussed below in conjunction with the description of the adjunctive therapy procedures.)

Parents generally reported a high absolute level of satisfaction with the parent training program at both posttreatment and follow-up. The various teaching methods employed by the therapists were rated as quite useful and as relatively easy to follow. The more performance-oriented teaching methods in the clinic (e.g., therapist demonstration, practice with the child in the clinic) tended to be rated as more useful and sometimes as less difficult than the more didactic modes of instruction (e.g., lecture, written materials). With respect to relative satisfaction with the various parenting skills, rewards was generally the most useful and least difficult parenting skill, while ignoring was rated as one of the least useful and most difficult parenting skills. Alpha commands and time out tended to be seen as less difficult and more useful at the follow-up than at posttreatment.

The results also indicated that mothers generally maintained their high level of satisfaction with the various aspects of the parent training program. There were a few decrements in satisfaction by the 2-month follow-up. These included a slight decrease in satisfaction with the therapists, as well as declines in reported satisfaction with rewards (less useful), attends (more difficult), and the overall group of parenting skills (more difficult). It should be noted that the absolute level of satisfaction with these parenting skills remained quite high. Furthermore, most of the measures of satisfaction with the parent training program were maintained.

The overall results of these studies, in conjunction with the normative comparisons of Wells, Forehand, and Griest (1980) in their investigation of behavioral generality, strongly suggest that the parenting program is a socially valid one and that this social validity endures well after treatment termination.

Side Effects

In addition to our social validity research and the work in the areas of generalization previously delineated, we have also examined several side effects of our parent training program. As noted earlier, Forehand et al. (1980) found that maternal depression ratings improved significantly from pretreatment to posttreatment. Furthermore, while their scores differed significantly from those of mothers of nonclinic children at pretreatment, the two groups did not differ significantly at posttreatment and at a 2-month follow-up.

In another investigation, we (Forehand, Griest, Wells, & McMahon, 1982) presented evidence of a positive "side effect" of the parent training program with respect to marital satisfaction. In addition to significant improvements in parent and child behavior and in parental perceptions of the children, mothers with low levels of marital satisfaction prior to treatment improved significantly on this dimension after completing the parent training program. However, the gains were not maintained at a 2-month follow-up. Mothers with medium or high levels of marital satisfaction did not report any change in marital satisfaction. Thus, this positive side effect was temporary, and was limited to mothers with low levels of marital satisfaction.

ADJUNCTIVE THERAPY PROCEDURES

Once the basic treatment outcome and generality of the parenting program were established, our investigations shifted to the search for factors that might be involved in this process and ways in which we might enhance treatment outcome and generalization. Our attention has subsequently been focused on two rather different avenues of investigation: the development of a written brochure for parents interested in improving their non-clinic-referred children's mealtime behavior, and the addition of specific components to the basic treatment program. In this section, our work in each of these areas is described, and our findings to date summarized.

Written Instructions as Self-Help Materials

A variation of our parenting program that has been experimentally validated is the use of a written brochure to teach parents to improve their non-clinic-referred children's mealtime behavior (McMahon & Forehand, 1978). In recent years there has been a proliferation of self-administered behavior therapy programs for parents (see McMahon & Forehand, 1980, for a review). Their primary advantage is that they enable therapists to extend their services to a greater number of individuals with minimal increments in professional time. We have stressed the importance of empirically validating these self-help programs for parents (McMahon & Forehand, 1980, 1981). One area in which a self-administered therapeutic intervention seems appropriate is children's mealtime behavior. The importance of mealtime as an opportunity for a child to learn social, interactional, and cultural values has long been stressed (Dreyer & Dreyer, 1973). Surprisingly, there has been little research in modifying inappropriate mealtime behaviors in the normal child, although experts in child development have stated that the preschool child often engages in messy table behavior, leaving the table, and excessive demands for attention during meals (Ames, 1970; Breckenridge & Vincent, 1965).

Three preschool-aged children and their mothers participated in the project. All were from middle-class families. Observations were conducted in the home by independent observers during mealtime (supper for two families, lunch for one). A multiple-baseline design across subjects was employed to assess the effects of the treatment brochure. Prior to baseline observations, each mother specified the mealtime behaviors she wished to modify from the Mealtime Behavior Checklist, which includes a number of inappropriate mealtime behaviors. Following the final baseline observation, the experimenter delivered the brochure to the mother. The brochure described the procedures of rewards and time out by presenting a short rationale for each technique, along with step-by-step instructions for their implementation, and examples of their use at mealtime. There was no therapist–client contact other than an initial interview to describe the project and the delivery of the brochure to the mothers after baseline, and there was no feedback given to the mothers at any point in the study. After baseline, observations continued in the home during mealtime for 7–16 days. Approximately 6 weeks following the final observation, five additional follow-up observations were carried out to assess maintenance.

Results indicated that inappropriate mealtime behavior decreased substantially for each child following introduction of the treatment brochure. The amount of reduction in these behaviors ranged from 50% to 80%. Furthermore, the changes were maintained for all three children at the follow-up observations. Maternal behavior also changed in the direction dictated by the brochure. Following introduction of the brochure, all three mothers substantially increased both rewards to their children's appropriate mealtime behavior and suitable responses to inappropriate mealtime behavior compared to baseline levels of response. At the 6-week follow-up, successful handling of inappropriate mealtime behavior continued to improve or remained at a level comparable to that during the intervention phase. Rewards for appropriate mealtime behavior declined from intervention-phase levels at the follow-up; however, they still occurred more frequently than during the baseline. This uniform decline in the frequency of rewards was expected, since the mothers were instructed in the brochure to thin the schedule of reinforcement gradually. The degree of change manifested by these mothers was comparable to results obtained in the basic parent training program with clinic-referred children utilizing therapist instruction, modeling, and feedback (e.g., Peed *et al.*, 1977). Thus, this study indicates that written instructions alone can effectively prompt mothers to modify their children's inappropriate mealtime behavior in the home setting, and that these changes are maintained for at least 6 weeks. Written instructions for this particular problem behavior may be considered for use alone or in conjunction with the standard parent training program. In addition, this program for mealtime behavior can be viewed as an example of how written materials might be developed and evaluated for other common child behavior problems in the home (e.g., bedtime, bathtime, visitors in the home).

Additions to the Basic Parent Training Program

Three investigations have been concerned with enhancing treatment outcome and generalization by means of a constructive treatment strategy (Kazdin, 1980). In this approach, components are added to a treatment package to make it more effective. In one study, the use of maternal self-control procedures was examined as a means of promoting temporal generalization of the effects of the parenting program (Wells, Griest, & Forehand, 1980). In the second investigation, we (McMahon, Forehand, & Griest, 1981) examined the efficacy of incorporating formal training in social learning principles into the basic parenting program as a means of enhancing treatment outcome and generalization. In the most recent investigation of the addition of an adjunctive therapy to the basic parent training program, Griest, Forehand, Rogers, Breiner, Furey, and Williams (1982) assessed the efficacy of a multimodal family treatment approach (parent enhancement therapy) as a means of enhancing the generalization of the parent training program and improving the overall level of family functioning. Since the effectiveness and generality of the treatment program had been previously established, these studies were designed to focus on the *differential* effectiveness of incorporating additional treatment components into the parent training program.

Self-Control Training

The decision to incorporate a self-control strategy into the parenting program came about as a potential means of assisting parents in maintaining the use of their newly acquired parenting skills. It has been suggested that improvements in child behavior may not provide sufficient reinforcement to maintain good parenting behavior (Conway & Bucher, 1976). Similarly, after treatment, particular individuals (e.g., spouses, next-door neighbors, grandparents) may undermine continued change efforts by failing to reinforce or by punishing treatment-acquired parenting skills (Marholin, Siegel, & Phillips, 1976). Self-control procedures could conceivably circumvent these problems by providing a set of internally generated antecedent and consequent events necessary to control the parents' behavior, thereby reducing dependency on external reinforcement for the maintenance of treatment-acquired parenting skills.

Wells, Griest, and Forehand (1980) assigned 16 mothers and their clinic-referred noncompliant children either to parent training alone or to parent training plus self-control. All mother–child pairs participated in the parenting program. Mothers in the combination group also learned to self-monitor their use of their new parenting skills and to reinforce themselves for the use of these skills during a 2-month follow-up period. Each mother and the therapist composed an individualized self-control program immediately after the post-treatment assessment. A list of self-reinforcers was compiled, and the mother entered into a contract with the therapist in which she agreed to practice the parenting skills with ther child on a daily basis. Following each 15-minute "good parenting session," the mother administered one of these daily reinforcers to herself if she had provided positive attention to her child's appropriate behavior and provided the appropriate consequence for each occurrence of child noncompliance with time out. The mother was also encouraged to employ her treatment-acquired parenting skills as well as self-reinforcement strategies throughout the day.

Analyses of covariance using the pretreatment score as a covariate failed to find any differences between the two groups at posttreatment on observational measures of parent or child behavior. This finding was expected, since the self-control manipulation occurred *after* the posttreatment observations. Of primary interest were analyses of differences between the two groups at follow-up as a function of the self-control contract followed by half of the mothers. Children in the group receiving parent training plus self-control were significantly more compliant and less deviant than the children in the group receiving parent training alone. No differences were obtained between groups on the observational measures of parent behavior (rewards plus attends, beta commands, contingent attention). This finding was unexpected, particularly given the differences obtained in child behavior and the fact that the primary focus of the self-control contract was on the parental behaviors of rewards plus attends and time out. In addition, it should be noted that two mothers in the self-control group did not actively participate in the self-control program. Thus, while the results of this study provide some evidence that self-control procedures *might* be of benefit in the enhancement of temporal generality, the failure to find concomitant improvements in parent behaviors in this group and the failure of two of the mothers to participate actively in the self-control program suggest that this particular generalization enhancement strategy may be somewhat limited in its applicability. Future research is needed to determine which parents might benefit from such self-control training.

Training in Social Learning Principles

Another attempt to enhance the treatment outcome and generalization of our parenting program (McMahon, Forehand, & Griest, 1981) involved a second procedure that has been suggested as a potential means of enhancing generality —training parents in social learning principles, in addition to basic behavioral parenting skills. Reasons for training parents in social learning principles have included the hypotheses that parents need the theoretical framework supplied by such principles; that such training should allow subsequent performance of child management skills to accelerate more rapidly; and that generalization is more likely to occur (O'Dell, Flynn, & Benlolo, 1977). A number of parent training programs have incorporated such an approach into their treatment programs in varying degrees, while other programs have focused on training discrete behavioral skills.

Our study was designed to provide an analysis of the effectiveness of incorporating formal training in social learning principles into the parent training program as a means of enhancing treatment outcome and generalization. A total of 20 mother–child pairs who were referred for treatment of the child's behavior problems participated in the study. Each mother–child pair was assigned to one of two groups. The technique-alone (TA) parent training group received behavioral skill training via the program. Therapists did not include any reference to or explanations of social learning principles in their interactions with these parents.[2] The social learning (SL) parent training group also received training according to this format. In addition, mothers in this group were given specific didactic instruction and brief reading assignments in various social learning principles that were relevant to the parent training program, such as characteristics of positive and negative reinforcement, shaping, extinction, and punishment. Instruction in these principles was integrated into the program such that instruction preceded training of a particular technique, but relevant points were repeated throughout the program as the skills were being applied.

Multiple outcome measures were used to assess temporal and setting generality. As usual, home observational data were collected on both mother and child behavior, and the PAT was administered to assess maternal perceptions of child behavior. Additional parent verbal report measures included the Knowledge of Behavioral Principles as Applied to Children (KBPAC) test (O'Dell, Tarler-Benlolo, & Flynn, 1979), which was administered to assess parental verbal understanding of basic social learning principles, and the PCSQ, which was administered to assess the mothers' attitudes toward the particular treatment program they received. All but the PCSQ were collected prior to treatment, at the conclusion of treatment, and at a 2-month follow-up. The PCSQ was administered at the conclusion of treatment and at the follow-up.

Using the pretreatment score as the covariate, separate analyses of covariance were computed between groups on the posttreatment and follow-up scores for each dependent variable. At posttreatment and follow-up, mothers in the SL group demonstrated a superior knowledge of social learning principles as measured by the KBPAC, compared to mothers in the TA group. This indicated that the experimental manipulation (i.e., training SL mothers in social learning principles) was effectively carried out. The results of the parent perception measure suggested that mothers in the SL group generally viewed

---

[2]The TA parent training program, while very similar to the "basic" parent training program described in this chapter, was not identical to it. It should be noted that the basic parent training program is based on and utilizes social learning principles. However, parental exposure to formal instruction in these principles is limited.

their children in a more positive manner than did mothers in the TA group at both posttreatment and follow-up.

The results of the observational measures of parent behavior indicated that mothers in the SL group emitted higher percentages of contingent attention than did TA mothers at either posttreatment or follow-up, as well as a higher frequency of attends plus rewards at follow-up. There were no differences between the groups with respect to frequency of beta commands at either posttreatment or follow-up. The observational measures of child behavior indicated that children in the SL group were significantly more compliant to maternal commands than were children in the TA group at the follow-up. There were no differences in compliance at posttreatment, or in deviant behavior at either posttreatment or follow-up, between the two groups.

Mothers in both the SL and TA groups expressed a high level of overall satisfaction with their treatment program at both posttreatment and follow-up as measured by the PCSQ. Mothers in the SL group tended to be more satisfied with their program at posttreatment than did TA mothers. Both groups reported similar levels of satisfaction at the follow-up.

In a more extensive analysis of the consumer satisfaction data from the PCSQ (McMahon et al., 1983), mothers in both the SL and TA groups expressed high levels of satisfaction with their treatment program at both posttreatment and follow-up as measured by the PCSQ. However, mothers in the TA group found practice with the children in the clinic and therapist demonstration to be more difficult at both posttreatment and follow-up than did mothers in the SL group. At the follow-up, there were several additional differences between the two groups. One type of homework assignment, attends, and the overall group of parenting skills were judged significantly less useful at follow-up than at posttreatment for the TA group. The mothers in the SL group maintained their ratings on these measures. In addition, the SL group rated the overall group of parenting skills as significantly more useful than did the TA group at follow-up. These findings parallel and supplement the results of the first study described (McMahon, Forehand, & Griest, 1981), since many of the differences in parental satisfaction between mothers in the SL and TA groups became apparent only at the follow-up assessment. Thus, it appears that not only does the integration of formal training in social learning principles enhance treatment outcome, setting generality, and temporal generality with respect to behavioral and parent perception measures; it also results in higher levels of parental satisfaction and/or maintenance of satisfaction with the parent training program.

Parent Enhancement Therapy

The most recently developed adjunctive therapy is a multimodal treatment package designed to enhance general family functioning (Griest et al., 1982). There is evidence that various family-related issues, such as a parent's perception of a child's behavior, the parent's personal adjustment and marital satisfaction, and the parent's extrafamilial relationships, are associated with child behavior problems. Furthermore, these family-related issues may inhibit the effectiveness of behavioral parent training programs (see Griest & Forehand, 1982, for a review of these areas).

Several of our investigations have been concerned with the role of parental attitudes toward children and maternal personal adjustment. In one study with clinic-referred mother–child pairs (Griest, Wells, & Forehand, 1979), we found that maternal depression (as measured by the Beck Depression Inventory) was a more powerful predictor of maternal perception of child behavior than was child behavior per se. The more depressed mothers perceived their children as more maladjusted. In other studies, we have found that pretreatment levels of maternal depression (along with lower SES and higher rates of maternal commands) were also associated with an increased likelihood that mothers would fail to complete the parenting program (McMahon, Forehand, Griest, & Wells, 1981); if they did complete the program, the depressed mothers would be less likely to participate in follow-up assessments (Griest, Forehand, & Wells, 1981).

A more comprehensive assessment of the role of predictors of maternal perceptions of the child's adjustment was subsequently undertaken, utilizing both clinic-referred and non-clinic-referred mother–child pairs (Griest, Forehand, Wells, & McMahon, 1980). There were 20 mother–child pairs in each group. Measures included child and parent behavior recorded by home observers, mother-recorded rates of child behavior, maternal perceptions of child behavior (the PAT and the Becker Bipolar Adjective Checklist), and personal adjustment of the mothers. With respect to this latter dimension, the Beck Depression Inventory was used to rate levels of maternal depression; the modified form of Locke's Marital Adjustment Test allowed mothers to rate their marital satisfaction; and the trait form of the State–Trait Anxiety Inventory was administered to obtain ratings of maternal anxiety.

The results indicated that the clinic children were less compliant and were perceived by their mothers as significantly more maladjusted than were nonclinic children. The clinic mothers judged themselves to be significantly more depressed and anxious than did nonclinic mothers. In addition, parent perception of the child was found to be the best discriminator of clinic–nonclinic status.

Since the maternal perception measures of child behavior were the best discriminators between the groups, multiple-regression analyses were conducted separately with the clinic and nonclinic groups to examine whether child behavior or maternal adjustment best predicted parental perceptions of their children in each group. For the nonclinic group, maternal perceptions of child adjustment were best predicted by child behavior, whereas for the clinic group, maternal perceptions of child adjustment were best predicted by an interaction of child behavior and maternal personal adjustment (as measured by the State–

Trait Anxiety Inventory, trait form). Thus, clinic mothers appear to be less objective evaluators of their children's behavior, due to the influence of their own personal adjustment problems. This interaction of child behavior and maternal adjustment appears to be one critical factor that determines whether mothers will perceive their children as being in need of psychological services.

An attempt has been made to look more closely at this interaction of child behavior and maternal adjustment by examining differences in parent characteristics between two clinic-referred subgroups of children (Rickard, Forehand, Wells, Griest, & McMahon, 1981). Children in the deviant clinic group were significantly more noncompliant and deviant than was a nonclinic sample. On the other hand, children in the nondeviant clinic group, although referred for noncompliance and other behavior problems, did not differ from a nonclinic sample on either of these behaviors. Home observations by independent observers and parent questionnaires examining parental adjustment (the Beck Depression Inventory) and parental perceptions of child adjustment (the PAT) were completed. Results indicated that the mothers of the children in the nondeviant clinic group were significantly more depressed than were those in the remaining two groups. Since the children in the nondeviant clinic group were not more deviant or noncompliant than were those in the nonclinic group, it appears that the mother's personal adjustment (in this case, depression) rather than the children's behavior was a significant factor in the referral of these children for treatment. An additional finding was that mothers in the deviant clinic group issued more vague, interrupted (beta) commands than did mothers in the nondeviant clinic group, supporting the hypothesis that the deviant behavior of these children was associated with ineffective parenting skills.

Evidence from a recent study by Rickard, Forehand, Atkeson, and Lopez (1982) suggests that marital status and marital satisfaction also play a role in maternal interactions with clinic-referred children. Employing a sample of 41 mother–child pairs, these investigators found that low marital satisfaction was associated with increased maternal depression, whereas high marital satisfaction was associated with more positive parenting behavior (attends plus rewards) by the mothers, particularly in relation to the positive parenting behaviors emitted by the divorced mothers.

Wahler and his colleagues have presented data that link parents' interpersonal relationships outside the family to the occurrence of child behavior problems. Wahler and Afton (1980) identified two groups of parents: those with infrequent and aversive interactions outside the home, and those with frequent and positive interactions outside the home. The former group was termed "insular" and the latter "noninsular." Baseline observations in the home of these two groups indicated that children from insular families displayed more oppositional behavior than did those from noninsular families, suggesting that factors outside the home that affect the parents are related to the occurrence of child behavior problems in the home. Furthermore, Wahler (1980) has presented evidence that insular parents fail to maintain child behavior change at follow-up.

Thus, there appears to be strong evidence that factors such as parent perceptions of children, parental personal adjustment, parental marital status and satisfaction, and parental extrafamilial relations are associated with child behavior problems. The purpose of the Griest *et al.* (1982) investigation was to determine whether the inclusion into the basic parenting program of several additional treatment modules related to these broader family issues resulted in an enhancement of treatment outcome and generalization beyond the positive effects reported in some of our earlier investigations.

A total of 17 mothers and their clinic-referred noncompliant children were assigned either to parent training alone or to parent training plus parent enhancement therapy; 15 mothers and their nonclinic children served as a quasi-control group. All clinic-referred mother–child dyads were treated individually by way of the parent training program. In addition, mothers receiving parent training plus parent enhancement therapy also received treatment related to the following areas: parents' perception of the children's behavior, marital adjustment, parents' personal adjustment, and parents' extrafamilial relationships.[3] The emphasis of the additional treatment was that every parent plays a tripartite role that consists of being a parent, a spouse, and an individual, and that the three roles are integrally interrelated. Training consisted of didactic presentations, modeling, role playing, and homework assignments. Components of the parent enhancement therapy package were presented prior to, during, and after the standard parent training program. The sequence of treatment was as follows: perceptions and expectations of parents about their children's behavior, parents' moods and overall psychological adjustment, Phase I of the standard parent training program, spouse–partner communication, Phase II of the standard parent training program, spouse–partner problem solving, and parents' interactions outside the family.

The primary data in this project consisted of sets of four home observations conducted by independent observers prior to treatment, after treatment, and at a 2-month follow-up. A 3×3 analysis of variance, with groups and assessments serving as the factors, was performed on each of the mother and child behaviors. The results of the analyses of variance and subsequent simple effects tests indicated that parent training plus parent enhancement therapy was more effective than was parent training alone in changing deviant child behavior at posttreatment, as well as in maintaining the child compliance, deviant child behavior, parental rewards, and parental contingent attention at the follow-up. The two groups did not differ in effectiveness with regard to beta commands.

[3]The two clinic-referred groups were equated initially in each of the four areas addressed by the parent enhancement therapy. For example, the PAT was used to equate the two groups on parent perceptions of the child's behavior.

The control group did not change over the three assessment periods, suggesting that the behaviors measured were generally stable over the three assessment periods.

A second outcome measure for the two clinic-referred groups was a modified version of the PCSQ. For the group receiving both treatments, the parents' perception of the usefulness of the parent enhancement therapy was examined. For the group receiving parent training alone, the *potential* usefulness of the enhancement therapy was examined by asking parents to indicate whether such treatment would be helpful in future parent training. The consumer satisfaction measure was administered after treatment and at a 2-month follow-up. On a scale ranging from "extremely harmful" to "extremely helpful," the parent training plus parent enhancement therapy group rated the additional treatment as "helpful," while the parent training alone group rated the potential usefulness of the additional therapy as "slightly helpful" to "helpful."

The results of this study indicate that the effectiveness of parent training can be enhanced by combining this approach with a treatment package that focuses on parental perception of child behavior, parental personal and marital adjustment, and the parents' extrafamilial relationships. The parent enhancement therapy package was particularly effective in enhancing maintenance of treatment effects. This occurred with both child behaviors and positive parent behaviors. Furthermore, with respect to deviant child behavior, the parent enhancement therapy also facilitated treatment effects as well as maintenance of behavior. A parent consumer satisfaction measure indicated that parents perceived the additional treatment as helpful. It is important to note that the treated parent–child pairs in the present study were *not* selected because they demonstrated difficulties in one or more of the four areas targeted for treatment in the enhancement therapy. Therefore, the extent to which the present findings can be generalized to families with severe difficulties in one or more of the four areas is uncertain. The limited treatment delivered in the parent enhancement therapy package may not be sufficient with such families.

CONCLUSIONS

We have described a program of research that has examined the treatment outcome and generalization of the effects of a parent training program designed to modify child noncompliance. One group of studies was designed to assess the various types of generality of treatment effects. These studies indicated that setting (to the home), temporal, sibling, and behavioral generality occurred. The social validity of the parenting program was also demonstrated, since maternal and child behavior, as well as maternal personal adjustment (depression) and perceptions of child adjustment, were within normal limits immediately following treatment or at a 2-month follow-up. Some positive side effects, in terms of alleviating parental depression and increasing marital satisfaction, have also been noted.

More recent studies have replicated and extended these positive findings of generalization. Of particular interest are the findings that suggest that treatment gains endure up to 4½ years after treatment, that parents maintain their satisfaction with the parent training program well after treatment termination, and that the immediate effects of treatment are not differentially influenced by the family's SES. With regard to this last finding, a word of caution is necessary. Although treatment outcome was as effective for low-SES parents who completed treatment as for parents of middle and high SES, the low-SES parents were more likely to drop out of treatment. One area of future research might involve the development of methods for keeping low-SES parents in treatment.

Other limitations of the program's effectiveness were also demonstrated by these studies. There is no consistent evidence of setting generality to the school, but neither is there evidence of a behavioral contrast effect in the classroom. Preliminary evidence suggests that it may be possible to predict changes in school behavior on the basis of pretreatment levels of this behavior in conjunction with changes in home behavior. Until this predictability is better established, clinicians would do well to assess child behavior in the classroom when parent training is undertaken, so that a separate intervention may be developed in that setting if necessary. With respect to social validity, maternal perceptions of the child's adjustment after completion of the parenting program failed to reach levels comparable to the perceptions of nonclinic mothers until a 2-month follow-up. It may be that maternal perceptions of the child change more slowly than do maternal and child behavior or maternal adjustment. An alternative explanation is that our parent training program will need to develop treatment procedures that have a more immediate influence on modifying maternal perceptions of child behavior.

Another focus of our investigations has been the development and evaluation of several adjunctive therapy procedures to enhance treatment outcome and generalization. We have found that written instructions can be used in a self-administered fashion by mothers to improve their children's inappropriate mealtime behavior, and that these positive changes in both mother and child behavior are maintained. Future research may involve more extensive evaluation of this approach to parent training, using different types of brochures and extending the investigations to include clinic-referred as well as non-clinic-referred children and parents.

Most of our adjunctive therapy procedures have been developed as additions to the basic parent training program. These procedures have included a maternal self-control component, the integration of training in social learning principles, and a multimodal package to enhance family functioning. Self-control procedures appear to enhance positive child behaviors; however, more research is needed to determine which mothers are most likely to employ and to benefit from such an approach. Training mothers in social learning principles resulted in a greater enhancement of treatment outcome, as well as of temporal and setting generality. Of particular interest may be the finding that this component enhanced maternal perceptions of the children.

The incorporation of parent enhancement therapy into the basic parent training program also enhanced treatment outcome, setting generality, and temporal generality. This approach was a logical outgrowth of our research concerning the interactions among maternal perceptions of the children, maternal personal adjustment, maternal marital status and satisfaction, and parent and child behavior. This research indicated that the negative perceptions of the mothers of clinic-referred children are influenced by a combination of the children's behavior and the mothers' own level of personal adjustment. These mothers are more anxious and depressed than are mothers of non-clinic-referred children. Not only is this higher level of personal maladjustment associated with a more negative perception of their children, but lower levels of self-reported personal adjustment (e.g., depression) are also associated with failing to complete the parenting program or to participate in follow-up assessments at a later time. Marital satisfaction and status were also implicated in maternal interactions with clinic-referred children, since low marital satisfaction was associated with increased depression, and divorced mothers emitted fewer positive parenting behaviors than did mothers with high levels of marital satisfaction. A recent investigation has suggested that there are at least two identifiable subgroups of mothers of clinic-referred children: mothers with a deficit in parenting skills per se (and whose children are more deviant than are nonclinic children), and mothers who are experiencing personal adjustment problems but whose children are no more deviant than are nonclinic children.

These studies suggest a number of important steps that should be taken as a potential means of enhancing the treatment income and generalization of parent training programs. First, it is quite obvious that parental adjustment as well as parent perception of child adjustment, child behavior, and parent behavior must be assessed when these families are referred for professional assistance. Our assessment of maternal personal adjustment, although limited to self-report measures of depression, anxiety, and/or marital satisfaction, has indicated the importance of this aspect for at least some mothers. In some cases, treatment may need to focus on the parents' maladjustment rather than, or in addition to, the remediation of ineffective parenting skills. The parent enhancement therapy package is an initial attempt to deal with this issue. A focus of our future research will be to refine this adjunctive therapy and assess the relative contribution of each component to the enhancement of treatment outcome and generalization. An additional focus will be the application of these components to families who, in addition to reporting child behavior problems, are clinically distressed along one or more of these other dimensions. Finally, it is clear that adequate normative data for child behavior and for parent behavior, perceptions, and personal adjustment are necessary to determine whether treatment is required, and, if so, where that treatment should be focused (e.g., parental personal adjustment and/or parenting skills). This will allow us to individualize further the therapeutic programs we offer to families, and consequently to maximize the gains they can expect to achieve.

References

Ames, L. B. *Child care and development.* Philadelphia: Lippincott, 1970.

Atkeson, B. M., & Forehand, R. Parent behavioral training for problem children: An examination of studies using multiple outcome measures. *Journal of Abnormal Child Psychology*, 1978, *8*, 449–460.

Atkeson, B. M., & Forehand, R. Conduct disorders. In E. J. Mash & L. G. Terdal (Eds.), *Behavioral assessment of childhood disorders.* New York: Guilford Press, 1981.

Barkley, R. *Hyperactive children: A handbook for diagnosis and treatment.* New York: Guilford Press, 1981.

Baum, C. G., & Forehand, R. Long-term follow-up assessment of parent training by use of multiple-outcome measures. *Behavior Therapy*, 1981, *12*, 643–652.

Beck, A. T., Rush, A. J., Shaw, B. F., & Emery, G. *Cognitive therapy of depression.* New York: Guilford Press, 1979.

Becker, W. C. The relationship of factors in parental ratings of self and each other to the behavior of kindergarten children as rated by mothers, fathers, and teachers. *Journal of Consulting Psychology*, 1960, *24*, 507–527.

Bernal, M. E., Klinnert, M. D., & Schultz, L. A. Outcome evaluation of behavioral parent training and client-centered parent counseling for children with conduct problems. *Journal of Applied Behavior Analysis*, 1980, *13*, 677–691.

Breckenridge, M. E., & Vincent, E. L. *Child development: Physical growth through adolescence* (5th ed.). Philadelphia: W. B. Saunders, 1965.

Breiner, J. L., & Forehand, R. An assessment of the effects of parent training on clinic-referred children's school behavior. *Behavioral Assessment*, 1981, *3*, 31–42.

Caplan, G. *Principles of preventive psychiatry.* New York: Basic Books, 1964.

Conway, J. B., & Bucher, B. D. Transfer and maintenance of behavior change in children: A review and suggestions. In E. J. Mash, L. A. Hamerlynck, & L. C. Handy (Eds.), *Behavior modification and families.* New York: Brunner/Mazel, 1976.

Cowen, E. L., Huser, J., Beach, D. R., & Rappaport, J. Parental perceptions of young children and their relation to indexes of adjustment. *Journal of Consulting and Clinical Psychology*, 1970, *34*, 97–103.

Dreyer, C. A., & Dreyer, A. S. Family dinner time as a unique behavior habitat. *Family Process*, 1973, *12*, 291–301.

Forehand, R. Child noncompliance to parental requests: Behavioral analysis and treatment. In M. Hersen, R. M. Eisler, & P. M. Miller (Eds.), *Progress in behavior modification* (Vol. 5). New York: Academic Press, 1977.

Forehand, R., & Atkeson, B. M. Generality of treatment effects with parents as therapists: A review of assessment and implementation procedures. *Behavior Therapy*, 1977, *8*, 575–593.

Forehand, R., Breiner, J., McMahon, R. J., & Davies, G. Predictors of cross setting behavior change in the treatment of child problems. *Journal of Behavior Therapy and Experimental Psychiatry*, 1981, *12*, 311–313.

Forehand, R., Griest, D. L., & Wells, K. C. Parent behavioral training: An analysis of the relationship among multiple outcome measures. *Journal of Abnormal Child Psychology*, 1979, *7*, 229–242.

Forehand, R. Griest, D. L., Wells, K. C., & McMahon, R. J. Side effects of parent counseling on marital satisfaction. *Journal of Counseling Psychology*, 1982, *29*, 104–107.

Forehand, R., & King, H. E. Pre-school children's non-compliance: Effects of short-term therapy. *Journal of Community Psychology*, 1974, *2*, 42–44.

Forehand, R., & King, H. E. Noncompliant children: Effects of parent training on behavior and attitude change. *Behavior Modification*, 1977, *1*, 93–108.

Forehand, R., & McMahon, R. J. *Helping the noncompliant child: A clinician's guide to parent training.* New York: Guilford Press, 1981.

Forehand, R., & Peed, S. Training parents to modify noncompliant behavior of their children. In A. J. Finch, Jr. & P. C. Kendall (Eds.), *Treatment and research in child psychopathology.* New York: Spectrum, 1979.

Forehand, R., Peed, S., Roberts, M., McMahon, R., Griest, D., & Humphreys, L. *Coding manual for scoring mother–child interaction* (3rd ed.). Unpublished manuscript, University of Georgia, 1978.

Forehand, R., Rogers, T., McMahon, R. J., Wells, K. C., & Griest, D. L. Teaching parents to modify child behavior problems: An examination of some follow-up data. *Journal of Pediatric Psychology*, 1981, *6*, 313–322.

Forehand, R., Sturgis, E. T., McMahon, R. J., Aguar, D., Green, K., Wells, K., & Briener, J. Parent behavioral training to modify child noncompliance: Treatment generalization across time and from home to school. *Behavior Modification*, 1979, *3*, 3–25.

Forehand, R., Wells, K. C., & Griest, D. L., An examination of the social validity of a parent training program. *Behavior Therapy*, 1980, *11*, 488–502.

Graziano, A. M. Parents as behavior therapists. In M. Hersen, R. M. Eisler, & P. M. Miller (Eds.), *Progress in behavior modification* (Vol. 4). New York: Academic Press, 1977.

Griest, D. L., & Forehand, R. How can I get any parent training done with all these other problems going on?: The role of family variables in child behavior therapy. *Child and Family Behavior Therapy*, 1982, *4*, 73–80.

Griest, D. L., Forehand, R., Rogers, T., Breiner, J. L., Furey, W., & Williams, C. A. Effects of parent enhancement therapy on the treatment outcome and generalization of a parent training program. *Behaviour Research and Therapy*, 1982, *20*, 429–436.

Griest, D. L., Forehand, R., & Wells, K. C. Follow-up assessment of parent behavioral training: An analysis of who will participate. *Child Study Journal*, 1981, *11*, 221–229.

Griest, D. L., Forehand, R., Wells, K. C., & McMahon, R. J. An examination of differences between nonclinic and behavior problem clinic-referred children and their mothers. *Journal of Abnormal Psychology*, 1980, *89*, 497–500.

Griest, D. L., Wells, K. C., & Forehand, R. An examination of predictors of maternal perceptions of maladjustment in clinic-referred children. *Journal of Abnormal Psychology*, 1979, *88*, 277–281.

Hanf, C. *A two-stage program for modifying maternal controlling during mother–child (M–C) interaction.* Paper presented at the meeting of the Western Psychological Association, Vancouver, British Columbia, 1969.

Hanf, C., & Kling, J. *Facilitating parent–child interactions: A two-stage training model.* Unpublished manuscript, University of Oregon Medical School, 1973.

Humphreys, L., Forehand, R., McMahon, R., & Roberts, M. Parent behavioral training to modify child noncompliance: Effects on untreated siblings. *Journal of Behavior Therapy and Experimental Psychiatry*, 1978, *9*, 235–238.

Johnson, S. M., Bolstad, O. D., & Lobitz, G. K. Generalization and contrast phenomena in behavior modification with children. In E. J. Mash, L. A. Hamerlynck, & L. C. Handy (Eds.), *Behavior modification and families.* New York: Brunner/Mazel, 1976.

Kazdin, A. E. Assessing the clinical or applied importance of behavior change through social validation. *Behavior Modification*, 1977, *1*, 427–452.

Kazdin, A. E. *Research design in clinical psychology.* New York: Harper & Row, 1980.

Kimmel, D. C., & VanderVeen, F. Factors of marital adjustment in Locke's Marital Adjustment Test. *Journal of Marriage and the Family*, 1974, *36*, 57–63.

Margolis, R. B., Sorenson, J. L., & Galano, J. Consumer satisfaction in mental health delivery services. *Professional Psychology,* 1977, *8,* 11–16.

Marholin, D., Siegel, L. J., & Phillips, D. Treatment and transfer: A search for empirical procedures. In M. Hersen, R. M. Eisler, & P. M. Miller (Eds.), *Progress in behavior modification* (Vol. 3). New York: Academic Press, 1976.

McMahon, R. J., & Davies, G. R. A behavioral parent training program and its side effects on classroom behavior. *B.C. Journal of Special Education,* 1980, *4,* 165–174.

McMahon, R. J., & Forehand, R. Nonprescription behavior therapy: Effectiveness of a brochure in teaching mothers to correct their children's inappropriate mealtime behaviors. *Behavior Therapy,* 1978, *9,* 814–820.

McMahon, R. J., & Forehand, R. Self-help behavior therapies in parent training. In B. B. Lahey & A. E. Kazdin (Eds.), *Advances in clinical child psychology* (Vol. 3). New York: Plenum Press, 1980.

McMahon, R. J., & Forehand, R. Suggestions for evaluating self-administered materials in parent training. *Child Behavior Therapy,* 1981, *3,* 65–68.

McMahon, R. J., Forehand, R., & Griest, D. L. Effects of knowledge of social learning principles on enhancing treatment outcome and generalization in a parent training program. *Journal of Consulting and Clinical Psychology,* 1981, *49,* 526–532.

McMahon, R. J., Forehand, R., Griest, D. L., & Wells, K. C. Who drops out of treatment during parent behavioral training? *Behavioral Counseling Quarterly,* 1981, *1,* 79–85.

McMahon, R. J., Tiedemann, G. L., Forehand, R., & Griest, D. L. *Parental satisfaction with parent training to modify child noncompliance.* Manuscript submitted for publication, 1983.

Metcalfe, M., & Goldman, E. Validation of an inventory for measuring depression. *British Journal of Psychiatry,* 1965, *111,* 240–242.

Myers, J. K., & Bean, L. L. *A decade later: A follow-up of social class and mental illness.* New York: Wiley, 1968.

O'Dell, S. Training parents in behavior modification: A review. *Psychological Bulletin,* 1974, *81,* 418–433.

O'Dell, S. L., Flynn, J. M., & Benlolo, L. A. A comparison of parent training techniques in child behavior modification. *Journal of Behavior Therapy and Experimental Psychiatry,* 1977, *8,* 261–268.

O'Dell, S. L., Tarler-Benlolo, L. A., & Flynn, J. M. An instrument to measure knowledge of behavioral principles as applied to children. *Journal of Behavior Therapy and Experimental Psychiatry,* 1979, *10,* 29–34.

Patterson, G. R. Interventions for boys with conduct problems: Multiple settings, treatments, and criteria. *Journal of Consulting and Clinical Psychology,* 1974, *42,* 471–481.

Patterson, G. R., & Fagot, B. I. Selective responsiveness to social reinforcers and deviant behavior in children. *Psychological Record,* 1967, *17,* 369–378.

Patterson, G. R., & Reid, J. B. Intervention for families of aggressive boys: A replication study. *Behaviour Research and Therapy,* 1973, *11,* 383–394.

Peed, S., Roberts, M., & Forehand, R. Evaluation of the effectiveness of a standardized parent training program in altering the interaction of mothers and their noncompliant children. *Behavior Modification,* 1977, *1,* 323–350.

Rickard, K. M., Forehand, R., Atkeson, B. M., & Lopez, C. An examination of the relationship of marital satisfaction and divorce with parent–child interactions. *Journal of Clinical Child Psychology,* 1982, *11,* 61–65.

Rickard, K. M., Forehand, R., Wells, K. C., Griest, D. L., & McMahon, R. J. Factors in the referral of children for behavioral treatment: A comparison of mothers of clinic-referred deviant, clinic-referred non-deviant, and non-clinic children. *Behaviour Research and Therapy,* 1981, *19,* 201–205.

Robins, L. N. Follow-up studies. In H. C. Quay & J. S. Werry (Eds.), *Psychopathological disorders of childhood* (2nd ed.). New York: Wiley, 1979.

Rogers, T. R., Forehand, R., Griest, D. L., Wells, K. C., & McMahon, R. J. Socioeconomic status: Effects on parent and child behaviors and treatment outcome of parent training. *Journal of Clinical Child Psychology*, 1981, *10*, 98–101.

Spielberger, C. D., Gorsuch, R. L., & Lushene, R. E. *STAI Manual for the state–trait anxiety inventory.* Palo Alto: Consulting Psychologists Press, 1970.

Wahler, R. G. The insular mother: Her problems in parent–child treatment. *Journal of Applied Behavior Analysis*, 1980, *13*, 207–219.

Wahler, R. G., & Afton, A. D. Attentional processes in insular and noninsular mothers: Some differences in their summary reports about child problem behavior. *Child Behavior Therapy*, 1980, *2*, 25–42.

Wells, K. C., & Forehand, R. Child behavior problems in the home. In S. M. Turner, K. Calhoun, & H. E. Adams (Eds.), *Handbook of clinical behavior therapy.* New York: Wiley, 1981.

Wells, K. C., Forehand, R., & Griest, D. L. Generality of treatment effects from treated to untreated behaviors resulting from a parent training program. *Journal of Clinical Child Psychology*, 1980, *9*, 217–219.

Wells, K. C., Griest, D. L., & Forehand, R. The use of a self-control package to enhance temporal generality of a parent training program. *Behaviour Research and Therapy*, 1980, *18*, 347–358.

Williams, J. G., Barlow, D. H., & Agras, W. S. Behavioral measurement of severe depression. *Archives of General Psychiatry*, 1972, *27*, 330–333.

Wiltz, N. A., & Patterson, G. R. An evaluation of parent training procedures designed to alter inappropriate aggressive behavior of boys. *Behavior Therapy*, 1974, *5*, 215–221.

Wolf, M. M. Social validity: The case for subjective measurement or how applied behavior analysis is finding its heart. *Journal of Applied Behavior Analysis*, 1978, *11*, 203–214.

Yates, B. T. Improving the cost-effectiveness of obesity programs: Three basic strategies for reducing the cost per pound. *International Journal of Obesity*, 1978, *2*, 249–266.

CLINICAL CONSIDERATIONS IN TRAINING PARENTS OF CHILDREN WITH SPECIAL PROBLEMS

Michael F. Cataldo
John F. Kennedy Institute
and Johns Hopkins University School of Medicine

I N T R O D U C T I O N

To suggest that parenting can be reduced to simple stimulus–response terms is to deny the intense and complex relationship between parent and child. Yet much of this relationship is not well understood by scientists and clinicians. For parents who need professional help with their children, reliance on approaches having a sound empirical basis, such as operant psychology, is the most reasonable and effective strategy. Therefore, accepting the limitations of taking only one theoretical (albeit data-based) approach to parenting, this chapter addresses operant approaches to the parenting of children with special problems that often severely limit their activity and function, especially children with medical disorders or severe neurological damage resulting in mental and/or physical handicaps.

The chapter format provides a unique opportunity to approach this subject matter in a fashion usually not found in a professional journal. That is, the chapter format provides the opportunity to discuss clinical considerations for which investigators do not have research demonstration studies, but about which they are confident and which comprise an important aspect of a successful treatment approach. That operant approaches to clinical problems are based on considerable research is laudable. However, the fact is that much of what occurs in the clinic is not always patterned directly after a research study. Adaptations and extensions of research take place in the clinic, as do observations of phenomena that become the basis for further investigations. Nor does one need to wait for the research to be conducted in order to enjoy the clinical benefits of carefully considered observations. The clinical considerations raised in this chapter are based on the past 7 years of clinical services at the Kennedy Institute and 6 years of clinical services in the Behavioral Medicine Program at Johns Hopkins University School of Medicine. During that time, these two programs were responsible for approximately 400–600 patients per year. Thus, clinical considerations in this chapter are based on experiences with over 3000 cases.

The areas addressed in this chapter are not those of how to train parents in basic behavioral procedures. This is undoubtedly adequately covered elsewhere in this volume. Rather, the approach is to point out the most relevant clinical considerations often overlooked by behavior therapists new to the population of children with developmental disabilities or serious physical illness. Too often, the behavior therapist approaches complex clinical problems seeking only immediate consequences that can be manipulated in a behavior modification program. In many cases, a far better approach would be also to attempt a behavior analysis of the conditions maintaining the target behavior. While seeking causes for a particular problem is often associated with the medical and psychoanalytical model, determining the current contingencies and behavioral history of the presenting behavior problem can make the difference between success and failure of behavior therapy, particularly over long-term follow-up. Accordingly, basic behavior analysis considerations most often overlooked by new therapists are discussed, followed by considerations about behavioral treatment of behavior problems and medical problems of handicapped and physically ill children. To conclude, two general considerations about behavioral treatment approaches are addressed.

BASIC BEHAVIOR ANALYSIS

An operant approach is based on a three-term contingency analysis: (1) antecedent variables (e.g., setting events and discriminative stimuli); (2) an operational definition of the response or target behavior; and (3) the functional controlling consequences for either increasing or decreasing the response. Similar to Skinner's description of the speaker–listener relationship in his analysis of verbal behavior (Skinner, 1957), therapists must consider the functional participants in the parent training situation. In the latter case there are three, not two, participants: the child, the parent, and the therapist. A behavior analysis of the important, most often overlooked variables for all three is helpful in describing and constructing effective treatment.

The Child

Mental Handicaps

In the most simple analysis, the primary variables for the young child (up to 8-10 years of age) are the child's parents. Therefore, in conducting a preliminary behavior analysis of presenting problems and in designing a consequence system, the behaviors of the parents must be a major consideration. For the pre-adolescent and adolescent, the primary reinforcers tend to shift to the youths' peer group. For children with special problems, this analysis is also true but requires additional consideration. Again, in the simplest analysis, the retarded child has his or her parents as the primary reinforcers, but for a much longer time than with the normal child. This places additional burdens on the family to attend to a child who is physically an adolescent but whose behavioral preferences are those of a younger child.

Further, as the retarded child matures mentally into adolescence, two additional problems occur. First, the parents do not always recognize the shift in the child's interests, and the rebellion and desire for independence anticipated (although sometimes dreaded) in the normal child is seen as a behavior problem by the parents of the retarded individual. The solution to this first problem is to recognize the change and to try to arrange for the same maturing experiences that one would expect for the normal child. Of course, the matter is complicated by the fact that the retarded individual is often physically larger and thus more difficult to manage than is the normally developing child going through the same stage. Also, this problem requires contact with a well-organized group for retarded citizens so as to find peers of the same chronological age and level of development. A related problem is that the parents have often adjusted major portions of their life to accommodate the retarded child and have done so for such a long time that granting the child increased independence is even more difficult than for parents of a normal child. Parents of a retarded child are often unwilling to believe that their child may now have the intellectual ability necessary for greater independence.

This latter point is exemplified by a case at the Kennedy Institute of a mother and son. She was divorced and had arranged most of her work and social life to accommodate the boy; he was 19, physically large, strong, and entering maturational adolescence. The mother did not recognize the shift in her son's interests and continued to insist on a *status quo* routine at home. The resulting problems were arguments that sometimes escalated into foul language toward the mother and even an occasional shoving match between the two. While the referral to the Department of Behavioral Psychology was for cursing and aggression, and this was the mother's primary complaint, the solution was not solely a consequence (e.g., token or privilege) program to decrease these inappropriate behaviors. Such a program would fail or at best would result in a different problem. The solution was to implement a privilege program at home to decrease aggressive behavior *and* help the mother understand the change in her son; to arrange for him to get a part-time job at the Catholic school he attended; and to teach him to take public transportation. The latter necessitated the mother's following the two buses her son had to take between home and work until she was satisfied that he really could accomplish this task. That more than a consequence program was needed could be judged partially by the failure of many variations of a consequence program when instituted without the other considerations mentioned above.

The second problem related to mentally retarded adolescents is their emotional maturity. In addition to chronological age and mental capacities, the retarded, like everyone else, mature emotionally at different rates. Behavior problems of the adolescent are especially likely to result from emotional immaturity. Unfortunately, problems surrounding emotional immaturity are often compounded by an individual's size. What is emotionally immature but cute for a normal preadolescent is a major behavior problem for the retarded adolescent. Sexual exploration, overaffectionate behavior, and experimentation with inappropriate or forbidden words are all not only occasions for concern by parents but somewhat frightening, especially if the individual displaying them is a boy who is 6′ 3″ and weighs 220 pounds, or a fully developed girl who is capable of becoming pregnant. The solution again is not only a behavior modification program employing consequence control, but also the inclusion of the same type of "counseling" that a normal preadolescent or adolescent would receive from a teacher, parent, or other respected adult—which, from an operant analysis, represents instructional control.

Thus, for the retarded child or youth, the primary problem becomes one not only of providing a good behavior modification program, but also of insuring, as much as possible, that the naturally occurring reinforcers and opportunities to develop new behaviors are permitted, as they would be for a normal individual at the same level of mental and emotional maturation.

Physical Handicaps

A behavioral analysis of the physically handicapped child is, of course, much different. Our experience has been that the young physically handicapped child is provided with a good deal of adult attention and assistance. Relationships of these children with their environment produce few behavior problems, and the main therapeutic effort is that of physical habilitation. The primary problem occurs when the child approaches adolescence. At this time, primary reinforcers are to shift to the peer group, and explorations of independence and sexual awareness move into the foreground. However, because of the physical handicaps, these normal occurrences are hampered. The solution is less one of operant or behavior modification than it is of environmental design, as has recently begun to be reported in the applied behavioral literature. Especially important in environmental design is the arrangement of activities and opportunities for social interaction with peers, both handicapped and not. The goal is to establish a reinforcing context in the individual's social environment so that appropriate behavior can be reinforced and normal development can proceed. Our experience has been that such programs are notably lacking, and that this is one important area of research and clinical intervention that should be encouraged.

Illness

Concerning the physically ill child, a number of considerations arise. First are the behavior problems often noted with hospitalization and/or a prolonged illness, such as developmental regression, tantrums, and noncompliance. A simple behavioral analysis of these problems would suggest that high densities of parental attention, typical of those bestowed on an ill child, may also reinforce a response class of dependent behaviors prominent at an earlier stage of development; because the child is ill, parents are, in turn, likely to reinforce such dependent behaviors. For example, young children are sometimes noted to have feeding and toileting problems subsequent to a hospitalization, even though the admissions are not related to these problems. During hospitalization, parental attention and permissiveness may be similar to that at an earlier time in a child's life. A toileting problem in the hospital or soon after discharge may be attributed by the parents to the illness and may not be punished in the usual way, thus reestablishing earlier behavior patterns. Here, the solution is simply to reinstitute the same parenting rules relative to all behavior not connected with the illness as had existed before hospitalization.

More dramatic effects of hospitalization have been suggested (Cataldo, Jacobs, & Rogers, 1982) and relate primarily to the effects on the child of the hospital environment. While the primary means of intervention for these problems will rest with redesign of hospital activities and practices, the problems engendered for these reasons should quickly resolve after discharge.

Later in this chapter, the issue of employing operant procedures to treat physical disorders is discussed in greater detail. However, an important point to note here in a basic behavioral analysis is the importance of reinforcer selection. This is one of the aspects most frequently overlooked by therapists, particularly those moving from the graduate research setting to the clinic. The assumption is frequently made that the contingent application of what should be a reinforcing event is sufficient. Should the behavioral program succeed, there should be little reason for further concern. Should it fail, one does not know if the failure was due to reinforcer problems or some other factor. While this point may seem trivial, it is especially important when venturing into new treatment areas. For example, a previously reported study conducted at the Kennedy Institute (Cataldo, Russo, & Freeman, 1979) attempted to reduce the extremely high rate (300–400 per day) of myoclonic seizures of a 5-year-old girl hospitalized at Johns Hopkins. The plan was to make reinforcing events contingent upon low rates of clinical seizure activity. However, before beginning the procedure, events that were to be used as reinforcers were tested by making them contingent upon a known volitional behavior. In this case, a light discriminative for time out from the opportunity to obtain M & Ms was made contingent upon a high-rate behavior—turning around and talking to the therapist. Employing a reversal design over two sessions provided convincing data that the consequence procedure could be effective in modifying this volitional behavior. Only then was the time-out procedure applied (successfully) to reducing myoclonic jerking.

Similarly, reinforcers are tested on volitional behaviors prior to their use with our work at the Kennedy Institute and Johns Hopkins Unversity Hospital on electromyographic (EMG) biofeedback for neuromuscular disorders (Bird & Cataldo, 1978; Cataldo, Bird, & Cunningham, 1978). Especially with young children, some form of reinforcement, such as tokens or points, needs to be chained to biofeedback output. The instruction to perform according to the biological feedback information is not sufficient. An example of such a test of the reinforcer is presented in Figure 13-1. The patient described in the figure was a young boy referred for biofeedback treatment of a right-side intention tremor secondary to head trauma due to an automobile accident. The reinforcer under consideration (points traded for toys and privileges) was tested by making it contingent upon the patient's verbal behavior in repeating either "cat" or "dog" in rapid sequence. His verbal behavior was impaired by the head trauma, but was clearly under more volitional control than hand and arm movements were. Therefore, the boy was instructed that saying either "cat" or "dog" could earn points; that the therapists would not indicate which it was; and that the word that produced points would shift from time to time. The data demonstrated the reinforcement control of the points, which were subsequently used in biofeedback training to attempt to reduce the tremor.

Thus, for children with physical disorders, operant procedures are appropriate both to remediate problems resulting from the illness and to provide primary treatment. Most important to the clinician is that he or she follow the same precautions in implementing a behavioral procedure as would be used for a behavior problem of a child who is not physically ill or handicapped. The most overlooked precaution, in my experience, has been the proper selection and testing of reinforcers before treatment is initiated.

The Parent

The resources an adult calls upon as a parent are many: the experiences he or she had as a child in observing his or her own parents, experiences in raising younger siblings, books on parenting, advice from relatives and friends, experiences in raising another child, and the learning that takes place as the parent and child interact on a daily basis. Most of these are antecedent events that prepare the person for his or her role as a parent. None is usually adequate to prepare the parent for the problems presented by a handicapped or physically ill child.

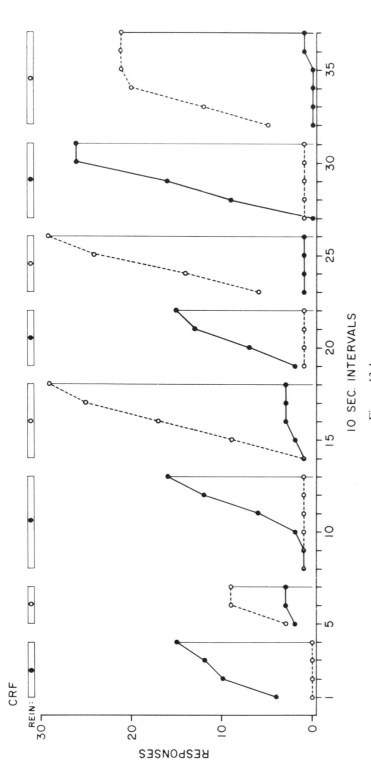

Figure 13-1

Verbal responses of "cat" (closed circles) and "dog" (open circles) were alternately followed by contingent points to test the reinforcing properties of the point-economy system for use in a biofeedback treatment program. The patient was a 13-year-old boy diagnosed as having status post closed head trauma with a right-side intention tremor and left-side hemiplegia. He had significant learning disabilities from the trauma and some speech impairment.

From the perspective of a treatment analysis, parents either have good parenting skills or do not, and the child who has special developmental or physical problems may benefit from an operant approach or may not. The child who cannot benefit from an operant approach is not the subject of this discussion. The child who can benefit either has a parent with good skills or does not, and the therapist's approach at this point differs. For the parent without parenting skills, or with poor skills, the approach is that typically seen with normal children demonstrating behavior problems—teaching parents operant-based approaches to successful parenting. However, many parents of children with special problems have good parenting skills but do not know how to apply them to a child with special problems. That this is the case should be no mystery. All the antecedent conditions for preparation of an adult to be a parent are usually conditions for raising a normal child. The handicapped or seriously ill child represents, in operant terms, a stimulus condition for which most parents are not adequately prepared. The solution, then, for the parent competent at raising a normal child, is for the professional to assist in determining which aspects of the special child's behavior are the results of the child's physical condition (mental handicap, physical handicap, or illness) and which aspects are not. The former are to be dealt with by extraordinary means (e.g., medical or behavior–medical treatment), and the latter should be dealt with as is any other inappropriate childhood behavior for which the competent parent already has a repertoire of successful techniques. While the professional may add to or refine the competent parent's repertoire, the primary assistance is one of assessing the child's behavior and interpreting this for the parent. Skills necessary for such assessment include not only behavior analysis but knowledge of normal child development, in the case of the retarded child, and knowledge of motor skills assessment and pediatric medicine, in the case of the physically handicapped or physically ill child. Since it is unlikely that the behavioral clinician will be well versed in all the areas he or she is likely to encounter in the clinical setting, the opportunity to have interdisciplinary case management is often of great benefit.

Thus, the most critical factor in a behavioral analysis of the parent with a handicapped or ill child is to assist the parent in applying his or her current parenting skills. This usually entails helping the parent to discriminate between behaviors that are directly related to the child's special problems and that cannot be treated by simple parental management procedures, from those that are the result of inappropriate parenting procedures and *can* be easily treated by appropriate parenting. In some cases, the professional may also need to assist the parents in understanding the benefits and life styles available to their child, especially as the child grows older.

The Therapist

While the problems encountered by therapists working with handicapped or ill children are diverse, those encountered most frequently are mentioned here.

First is the fact that the child with developmental delay or physical illness often presents with many behavior problems. The therapist's first problem often is one of categorizing and then assessing them all. Thereafter, the most important or pivotal behavior must be selected for treatment first. At the Kennedy Institute, staff members have found it helpful to use a checklist format for patient reports. This not only serves to reduce preparation time in completing patient reports, but provides a prompt to the therapist to check all likely behavior problems. An example of this checklist is provided in Figure 13-2. Other interview data sheets can be added for collecting information on the major behavior problems in terms of rate, topography, time of onset, trends, antecedents, consequences, and so on.

The second problem relates to the therapist's choice of treatment strategy. Where possible, my colleagues and I at the Kennedy Institute have used programs designed by other clinics. This saves the time it would take to develop our own and is likely to ensure success if the other clinic has done a conscientious job. To date, the most helpful have been those developed by Christophersen and his colleagues at the University of Kansas Medical Center.[1] For behavior problems that are not already part of an existing treatment package and that occur frequently, it is helpful to develop one's own packages. For more unique problems, a team input to the problem is the best strategy. With all cases in the Department of Behavioral Psychology at the Kennedy Institute, peer review of the treatment plan is conducted by the primary therapist presenting each case after the initial assessment, and then periodically during treatment. This helps to insure that ethical guidelines are followed (peer review of the proposed procedures makes them public and open to the scrutiny of one's colleagues) and provides the opportunity for the active department to provide input to difficult cases.

A problem that is encountered by therapists in parent training, and that is often overlooked by the new therapist, is that of the very few controlling variables the therapist has at his or her disposal in changing the behavior of parents. Unlike working directly with the child, the therapist can manipulate very few consequences relevant to the parents' behavior. The primary consequence, of course, is the provision of professional assistance. The withdrawal of this assistance is always the ultimate consequence. On occasion, parents will not want the help of the therapist, even though they are present for a therapy session. Pressure from the pediatrician, spouse, or social agency may force a parent to the behavior therapist. However, attempting to provide a behavioral program to an uncooperative parent wastes everyone's time, provides the wrong information to whoever is pressuring the parent to attend, and keeps the therapist from providing assistance to someone else in need. Therefore, it is a good idea to establish a set of rules to determine objectively whether parents are complying. A fixed number of missed appointments should result in termination of treatment. Similarly, parents' noncompliance with treatment procedures, such as collecting

[1]These treatment programs are available from Dr. Edward R. Christophersen, c/o Department of Pediatrics, University of Kansas Medical Center, Kansas City, Kansas 66103.

THE JOHN F. KENNEDY INSTITUTE

JFK NUMBER	
PATIENT'S NAME	
DOB	
ADM DATE	
DISCH DATE	
JHH NUMBER	

Date:

____Inpatient ____Outpatient

____ Evaluation & Recommendation

____ Evaluation, Recommendations &
Discharge Summary/Termination

P E D   H A B I L I T A T I O N   J F K I

Persons(s) present at evaluation: _____

Biographical: _____

Medical Information: _____

Medications: _____

Current Strengths: _____

BEHAVIOR PROBLEM CHECKLIST:

____ Noncompliant	____ Destructive	____ Toileting
____ Tantrums	____ Disruptive	____ Enuresis
____ Aggressive	____ Bedtime Problems	____ Encopresis
____ Verbally Abusive	____ Dressing Problems	____ Smears Feces
____ Pica	____ Feeding Problems	____ School Problems
____ Self-Injurious Behav.	____ Amt./Type of Food	____ Runs Away
____ Innap. Sexual Behav.	____ Not Self-Feeding	____ Inappropriate Play
____ Self-Stimulation	____ Vomiting	____ Activity: Hi___ Lo___
____ Steals	____ Disruptive	____ Language Problems

Other Problems: _____

Potential Reinforcers: _____

Problems Identified By: _____

Reason for Referral: _____

Problem: _____ Description: _____

Frequency: _____ Duration: _____

Onset: _____ Trend: _____

Setting: _____

Current Antecedents: _____

Current Consequences: _____

Additional Information: _____

Treatment Goals: _____

Direct Observation: _____

Suggested Measurement System: _____

Suggested Treatment: _____

*A Development of the Children's Rehabilitation Institute, Incorporated in Affiliation with
The Johns Hopkins University, through the School of Medicine, and The Johns Hopkins Hospital*

JFK 1-005 11/67

Figure 13-2

A sample of the patient report form used by the Department of Behavioral Psychology at the Kennedy Institute. The form serves to prompt therapists to cover all important problem areas during the intake interview. Because the relevant information can be noted directly on this form during the interview, therapist time is saved by not having to write a lengthy report afterwards; if it is written clearly, then typist time is saved, and the patient's problems can be quickly scanned for review and verbal report without referring to paragraphs of written text. Each important problem can be further reviewed with the parents one at a time, beginning at the bottom of this form and continued on subsequent forms by also noting frequency, duration, trends, and other characteristics essential to a behavior analysis.

home data or following intervention procedures, should be an occasion for terminating active treatment. Functionally, when the parent is noncompliant with procedures, treatment is not occurring, and it would be better to label the situation for what it really is. Some ethical concern arises when the parent does not comply with treatment plans but insists on scheduling repeated visits. Such requests for repeated contact should probably not be denied. At the very least, they represent continued opportunities to persuade the parent to employ the treatment procedure and to point out that the parent's own approach is not working. However, since the parent is not cooperating with the treatment plan, the visits should not be labeled as behavior therapy, but more accurately as sessions during which the therapist offers advice.

Related to a therapist's difficulty in judging that parents have functionally removed themselves from therapy (even though continuing to attend sessions) is the therapist's (particularly a new therapist's) insistence on attempting to design treatment programs for extremely difficult cases that require resources beyond those permitted by clinic time. Such cases are those for which there are few or no research demonstrations, but that should be theoretically remediable by behavioral methods. Graduate school trains students to believe that almost anything is possible. The behavioral student is most often convinced that operant approaches can solve almost any clinical problem. Graduate schools rarely prepare students for the practical constraints of the clinical setting, nor is the student usually prepared to admit that a case cannot be solved within these practical constraints. The problem is one of knowing these practical limitations, as well as knowing how to say no to someone in need of professional assistance. (One method clinicians use to say no is to refer the problem to someone else, such as a professional in another treating discipline.)

Thus, for the therapist, the primary problems are those of accurately identifying all the behavior problems of the child with developmental delay or illness, of selecting the best treatment approaches for those that can be treated, and of recognizing those problems that cannot be adequately addressed. For all these, physical prompts and peer review feedback are the best strategies.

BEHAVIORAL APPROACHES TO BEHAVIOR PROBLEMS

As noted above, children with special problems, such as developmental disabilities and chronic illness, often are referred for behavioral treatment because they have not just a few but many behavior problems. These problems require continued contact with the behavior therapist and often result in months, if not years, of active treatment programs. While such long-term assistance to parents is necessary, it is both expensive and time-consuming for all involved. Therefore, the design of a therapeutic intervention strategy for common behavior problems of children, which would reduce therapist and parent time, would be a significant contribution. For the past 5 years at the Kennedy Institute, my colleagues and I have been considering such an intervention strategy based upon assumptions about compliance as a generalized response class.

Currently, parent training about child management programs can be said to have two approaches to generalization of treatment. One is the program in which a target behavior problem is dealt with immediately and directly by providing parents with a specific behavioral procedure for the target or referring problem. Generalization of treatment procedures by the parents across problem behaviors rarely occurs. The consequence is that the parents then seek additional behavioral programs for each succeeding problem. A second type of program is one in which the target or referring problem is not dealt with immediately; rather, the parents are trained in behavioral principles. Later these principles are to be applied to specific presenting behavior problems. Because it is presumed that the parents are well versed in the principles, generalization of techniques to successive behavior problems is supposed to be enhanced.

Training compliance offers a third possibility. Parents can be taught to reinforce compliance using a standard, specific set of techniques. Since almost any behavior problem can be defined as a compliance problem, an immediate solution is provided for the target or referring problem. Generalization of effects to covarying behaviors can be expected to occur. Further, treatment techniques can be generalized to subsequent behavior problems, to the extent that these (as most behaviors) can be defined as failures to comply. Generalization is then inherent in the procedure, instead of a process that the parents must extrapolate from successive behavior programs or from being taught principles.

Our preliminary work on this notion has been conducted in the quasi-laboratory setting of the Kennedy Institute's inpatient unit. Here, children are admitted to the special pediatric inpatient service at the institute for residential stays that may last from 30 to 90 days. Medical and nonmedical problems are dealt with during this inpatient admission. This has provided us an opportunity to study these children's compliance behavior in detail. To date, we have not developed an extensive parent training program around this notion, nor have we collected extensive home data. However, we have trained parents in generalized compliance procedures via therapists' instructions during clinic visits and have obtained promising data on the children during their inpatient stays. Two in a series of these studies (as yet unpublished) have demonstrated that children's compliance with adults' requests to engage in certain behaviors increases as a function of reinforcing some, but not all, of those requests. That is, young retarded children who are asked to comply with five or six requests repeatedly during sessions conducted over a number of days will increase their compliance with all these requests as a function of direct reinforcement for compliance with only one or two of the targeted requests. These results suggest that, with these children, compliance to adult requests may belong to a response class. Bijou and Baer (1967) define a "response class" as "a group of responses which develop together. All grow strong or weak, even though the environment may be acting directly on only some of them" (p. 78). Should our preliminary findings hold true in that compliance may be trained as a generalized response class, then problem behaviors can be redefined as issues of compliance, and a great economy of treatment can be affected.

Indeed, other researchers have also noted that reinforcement of compliance to specific requests can result in increased compliance both to reinforced and to different nonreinforced requests (Bucher, 1973; Doleys, Wells, Hobbs, Roberts, & Cartelli, 1976). With very retarded individuals, additional training techniques, such as physical guidance and fading, may need to be used in combination with reinforcement of compliance. Further, generalization to nonreinforced requests does not always occur (Striefel & Wetherby, 1973). Nonetheless, reinforcement of compliance, when it does generalize across nonreinforced requests, may provide a considerable strategic improvement to current methods of parent training to reduce behavior problems.

The most intriguing aspect of compliance training and the modification of deviant behavior may lie in findings about the covariation of behavior. In a preliminary study of behavioral covariation, Sajwaj, Twardosz, and Burke (1972) applied behavioral procedures to selected problems of a 7-year-old while measuring other behaviors. The results indicated that "a response class may have member behaviors that covary directly and/or inversely. Some covariations may be socially desirable, others undesirable" (p. 163). Other investigators have shown that this observation about the covariation of behavior may be used to plan important therapeutic interventions. For example, using reinforcement procedures to improve minor behavior problems has been shown to decrease stuttering (Wahler, Sperling, Thomas, Teeter, & Luper, 1970), and reinforcement of academic behavior has resulted in decreased rates of disruptive behavior (Ayllon & Roberts, 1974). Similarly, procedures that increase compliance have been shown to result in a reduction in nocturnal enuresis (Nordquist, 1971), a decrease in hyperactive-type behavior, and an increase in some social behaviors (Zimmerman, Zimmerman, & Russell, 1969).

Such results as these suggest the possibility that deviant behaviors of developmentally disabled children or other children with many behavior problems may be modified by employing standard behavior change procedures (such as reinforcing compliance), which affect not only the target behavior but other behaviors that covary. This generalization of effects from target to other behaviors could also offer great economy of treatment, and could provide the additional advantage of avoiding some of the ethical difficulties facing behavior modification procedures. For example, if reinforcement of compliance could be shown to decrease aggressive and self-injurious behavior, the ethical problems of employing aversive techniques to suppress these undesirable behaviors could be avoided.

My colleagues and I have also recently begun to conduct pilot research on this covariation phenomenon. Again, using children admitted to the Kennedy

Institute, we have been able to demonstrate that reinforcement of compliance can be used as a treatment strategy not only to increase compliance but to decrease tantrums, aggression, and self-injurious behavior. In the first of these studies (Russo, Cataldo, & Cushing, 1981), three retarded children 3 to 6 years of age, with documented noncompliance and additional behavior problems, served as subjects. During all phases of the program, continuous measures of both compliance and the occurrence of other behaviors were made. Figure 13-3 shows the data from one of these children. As can be seen in the figure, a multiple baseline across three therapists was used to assess the effects of compliance training on compliance and on the two untreated corollary responses of hair pulling and thumb sucking. Each of these behaviors was mildly self-injurious, and the frequency was sufficient to warrant individual modification. As the figure indicates, baseline levels of compliance were low across all three therapists. With the beginning of treatment, compliance to each therapist's requests (a series of five standard requests) increased. In the Reinforced Compliance 1 condition, social praise and small bits of food were used as reinforcers. As compliance dropped in the later sessions of this condition, a second treatment (Reinforced Compliance 2) was instituted, in which the child received pennies for appropriate compliance. Her pennies could later be traded for a variety of backup reinforcers, such as a trip to a nearby store. For all three therapists, this produced immediate and stable increases in compliance.

Perhaps the most interesting aspect of these data is the behavior of the untreated corollary responses of thumb sucking and hair pulling over the course of compliance treatment. Visual inspection of the data shows correlated changes in behavior with respect to compliance, even though no specific contingencies were operative. Additionally, the protocol was designed such that corollary responses were not incompatible with compliance, and reinforcement of compliance could occur during instances of the nontreated corollary behaviors. That is, the child could be reinforced while sucking her thumb if she

---

Figure 13-3

Compliance and aberrant behavior of Patty, a girl aged 5 years 7 months who was referred to the Kennedy Institute for noncompliance, together with persistent hair pulling and thumb sucking. Psychological testing indicated an IQ of 60 on the Stanford–Binet; she had good language abilities and could follow several-step commands. Reinforcement of compliance with five standard requests resulted in increases in compliance and decreases in both aberrant behaviors relative to baseline. During the Reinforced Compliance 1 condition, as compliance decreased, a corresponding increase occurred in aberrant behaviors. Instituting a Reinforced Compliance 2 condition using tokens resulted in a sustained increase in compliance and decrease in aberrant behaviors. (From "Compliance Training and Behavioral Covariation in the Treatment of Multiple Behavior Problems" by D. C. Russo, M. F. Cataldo, & P. J. Cushing, *Journal of Applied Behavior Analysis*, 1981, *14*, 209–222. Copyright 1981 by The Society for the Experimental Analysis of Behavior, Inc. Reprinted by permission.)

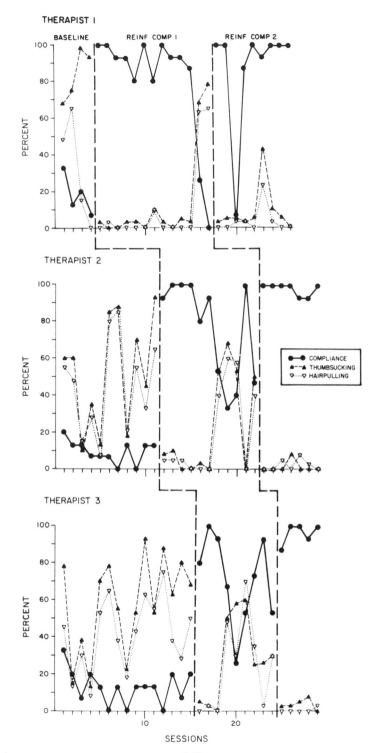

343

complied with the therapist's request to sit down. Data for the two other children showed similar effects.

One serious design question raised by these data is whether or not the increase in compliance and decrease in aberrant behaviors could be the result of the addition of pleasant events to the environment, rather than the presumed reinforcers' contingent relationship to compliance. This issue was addressed in a second study (Ward, Cataldo, Russo, Riordan, & Bennett, in preparation) in which a noncontingent control condition was added to the design. For some of the subjects, compliance increased and aberrant behaviors decreased during noncontingent reinforcement, but this effect was only temporary. All subjects demonstrated no long-term increase in compliance during noncontingent reinforcement, whereas during contingent reinforcement for compliance with adult requests, compliance was always high and aberrant behaviors decreased to near-zero levels.

An extension of this research has recently been completed, in which the effects of reinforcing an adult's requests to do certain behaviors were compared to the effects of reinforcing requests not to do certain behaviors (Neef, Shafer, Egel, Cataldo, & Parrish, 1983). The results of this study, presented in Figure 13-4, clearly indicated that compliance to "do" requests belonged to a different response class from compliance to "don't" requests. That is, when some members of a group of requests to do certain things were reinforced, all members in that presumed class increased in compliance; whereas there was no comparable increase in compliance to requests not to do certain behaviors. When the contingencies were reversed, compliance to "don't" requests increased and the compliance to "do" requests decreased. Only when reinforcement contingent upon some members of both presumed response classes occurred was compliance to all "do" and "don't" requests high.

Thus, it is becoming evident that an additional behavioral treatment strategy may be successful in resolving childhood behavior problems. This strategy, of characterizing behavior problems in terms of compliance and then increasing generalized compliance, may have considerable treatment economy in being able to address multiple behavior problems with one relatively simple procedure for parents.

BEHAVIORAL APPROACHES
TO MEDICAL PROBLEMS

Recently, interest in the application of behavioral principles to medical problems has increased. This is best characterized generally in terms of the growing area of behavioral medicine, and specifically with children in the growing area of behavioral pediatrics. With regard to behavioral pediatrics, three distinct areas can be delineated (Cataldo, 1982): (1) the remediation of routine behavior and developmental problems of children as identified through pediatric

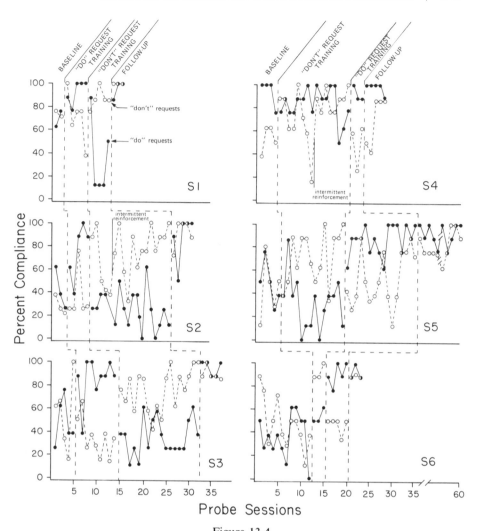

Figure 13-4

The percentage of compliance to "do" (closed circles) and "don't" (open circles) requests during probe sessions for subjects 1–6 across experimental conditions. Subjects were six children enrolled in a school for children with severe behavior disorders. Three were diagnosed as autistic and three as severely developmentally delayed. Data were collected in a room separate from their classroom, with only one child present at a time with the experimenter. Data displayed were collected during probe periods, when no reinforcement was programmed regardless of correct or incorrect responses. Only after periods when compliance with some examples of both "do" and "don't" requests was reinforced did compliance to all reinforced and nonreinforced types of requests increase. (Adapted from "The Class Specific Effects of Compliance Training with 'Do' and 'Don't' Requests" by N. A. Neef, M. S. Shafer, A. I. Egel, M. F. Cataldo, & J. M. Parrish, *Journal of Applied Behavior Analysis*, 1983, *16*, 81–99. Copyright 1983 by The Society for the Experimental Analysis of Behavior, Inc. Used by permission.)

clinic and office visits; (2) the identification and reduction of the iatrogenic behavioral effects of quality pediatric medicine; and (3) the modification of biological conditions to treat primary medical problems.

The first of these has come about primarily because the role of the practicing pediatrician has changed (Green, 1980). With a decline in infectious diseases from advances in public health and immunization, the pediatrician increasingly is asked to address problems in development, child rearing, and school performance. For many parents, the pediatrician represents an excellent first resource. Applications of the data base of operant and applied behavior analysis for use by the practicing pediatrician have been extensively discussed elsewhere (Christophersen, 1977; Christophersen & Rapoff, 1979). Increasing evidence exists that behavioral procedures may be provided to parents during pediatric clinic or private pediatrician office visits to treat behavior problems of noncompliance, tantrums, enuresis, encopresis, habit disorders, hyperactivity, and many problems related to developmentally disabled individuals (such as feeding, rumination, and mild self-injury).

The second example of the application of behavioral principles to pediatric medicine entails the iatrogenic behavioral effects of quality medical care. The magnitude of such behavior problems due to quality medical care is not trivial. A 1979 survey by the American Hospital Association of 6321 hospitals indicated that pediatric services provided over 55,000 beds (American Hospital Association, 1979). Based on an 80% census, this translates into over 16 million patient bed-days per year. Estimates on the incidence of these problems are variable, with early studies reporting the manifestation of problem behaviors to occur in 10–35% of hospitalized children (Cataldo et al., 1982). In addition to the considerations mentioned earlier with regard to analysis of the hospital environment from an operant approach, other intervention procedures have included the use of films and instructional materials and preparation of the child for hospitalization by parents and nurses, all of which can broadly be considered to be a desensitization approach. Also, in some hospitals the practice of allowing parents to spend considerable time with the child, including physically staying with the child during most of the hospital stay, has often proved to be beneficial.

Perhaps the most exciting area has been the application of behavioral principles to alter biological responses, including those diagnosed as medical problems. Behavioral research studies have demonstrated the modification of acute and chronic medically related problems of both normal and developmentally delayed pediatric populations (Cataldo & Bird, in press; Cataldo & Russo, 1979; Cataldo, Russo, Bird, & Varni, 1980; Russo & Varni, 1982). Both basic research and clinical research strongly suggest that behavioral procedures can now be added to the traditional armamentarium of medical and surgical procedures used in the direct treatment of medical disorders. The success of many of these procedures includes the use of direct intervention or at least follow-up by the parents.

For example, the extensive and very successful work on designing behavioral procedures for toilet-training young children is equally applicable when the children are of normal intelligence or mentally retarded. However, the procedures are difficult to apply with children who have afferent or efferent neuropathology of the bowel or urinary tract. Recent studies employing manometric equipment to provide discrimination of rectal distension and control of rectosphincteric activity report success in establishing continence in adult patients who were previously incontinent due to surgery or spinal injury, as well as in pediatric myelomeningocele patients (Cerulli, Nikoomanesh, & Schuster, 1979; Engel, Nikoomanesh, & Schuster, 1974; Wald, 1981; Whitehead, Parker, Masek, Cataldo, & Freeman, 1981). Follow-up studies on these initial procedures conducted at the Kennedy Institute clearly indicate the necessity for maintenance by parents of the gains obtained during clinic procedures.

Control of biological responses does not necessarily require biofeedback procedures, however. In an extension of the work that my colleagues and I at the Kennedy Institute have reported on biofeedback treatment of fecal incontinence secondary to myelomeningocele, preliminary results indicate that some patients can improve when positive consequences and prompting are provided for appropriate toileting. In another clinical demonstration (Russo, 1978), we have found that positive consequences for voiding completely on the first stream can be effective in remediating urinary retention and reflux in pediatric patients. Although initial training on this procedure took place while children were hospitalized with a suprapubic catheter, the procedure was successfully maintained by parents after removal of the catheter and discharge from the hospital.

A usual rule of thumb in designing and implementing these procedures is that the initial demonstration of the treatment procedure be conducted in the clinic setting, either while the child is an inpatient or during outpatient visits. This is exemplified in a recent study with a 7-year-old boy thought to have Gilles de la Tourette syndrome (Varni, Boyd, & Cataldo, 1978). Four discrete tics were reliably observed: facial grimaces, shoulder shrugging, rump protrusion, and the vocalization "huh." Data were obtained on these behaviors both during clinic visits and at home. Treatment in the clinic for facial grimaces was begun first and consisted of self-monitoring of tics, external reinforcement for increasing periods without tics occurring, and time out for tics. The results of clinic treatment are presented in Figure 13-5 and indicate that the procedures were effective in decreasing the occurrence of facial grimaces in the clinic to zero. Even though there was no intervention for the other tics, they also decreased in frequency concomitant with the facial tics. After a clear clinical improvement was noted in the clinic setting, a modified treatment procedure was provided to the parents for home use. The data on tics at home are presented in Figure 13-6. During the 4 weeks of baseline, facial grimaces averaged 93%, with a range of 74–100%, and the other behaviors were also variable but generally high. Starting with the third week of baseline, there was a

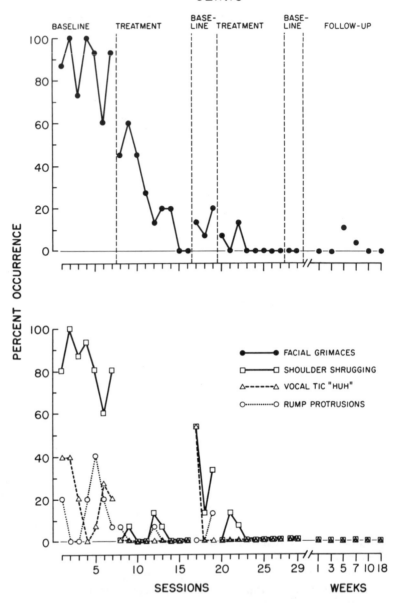

Figure 13-5

Percentage occurrence of tic behaviors across successive baseline and treatment reversals in the clinic. Treatment consisted of self-monitoring, external reinforcement (provided by the experimenter or parents), and time out. Only facial grimace tics were directly treated. (From "Self-Monitoring, External Reinforcement, and Time-Out Procedures in the Control of High-Rate Tic Behavior in a Hyperactive Child" by J. W. Varni, E. Boyd, & M. F. Cataldo, *Journal of Behavior Therapy and Experimental Psychiatry*, 1978, *9*, 353–358. Copyright 1978 by Pergamon Press, Ltd. Reprinted by permission.)

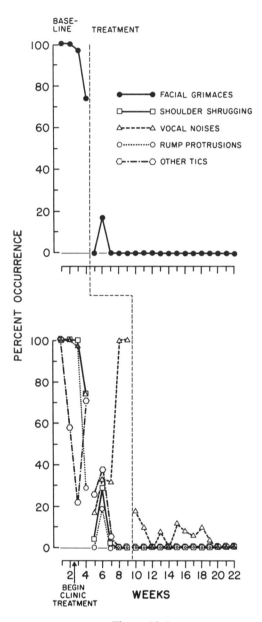

Figure 13-6

Percentage occurrence of the tic behaviors during baseline and treatment in the home. Facial grimaces were initially treated, then vocal noises. Shoulder shrugging, rump protrusions, and other tics were not directly treated. (From "Self-Monitoring, External Reinforcement, and Time-Out Procedures in the Control of High-Rate Tic Behavior in a Hyperactive Child" by J. W. Varni, E. Boyd, & M. F. Cataldo, *Journal of Behavior Therapy and Experimental Psychiatry*, 1978, *9*, 353–358. Copyright 1978 by Pergamon Press, Ltd. Reprinted by permission.)

slight downward trend in facial tics, shoulder shrugging, vocal noises, and rump protrusions (the other tic category was a chin-to-shoulder motion) in the home after the treatment was begun in the clinic (even though the mother was not told that the clinic treatment had begun). With the initiation of treatment procedures in the home, facial tics rapidly decreased to zero by the third week, with concomitant changes in other categories of tics. Further, an increase in vocal noises in the eighth and ninth weeks and the use of treatment procedures for all categories reduced all tics to zero except vocal noises, which eventually were eliminated by the 20th week.

GENERAL CONSIDERATIONS

Research versus Clinical Practice

There are two general considerations that are not necessarily specific to children with special problems, but that nonetheless are particularly important with this special population. The first of these has to do with the relationship between research and clinical service. Currently, discussion is taking place in the field of behavior therapy about the division of research and clinical practice (e.g., Wilson, 1981). One aspect of this argument is that research is often not particularly relevant or useful to problems of clinical practice. Another aspect has to do with the importance of clinicians' conducting research. One point of view is that the clinical environment is not suitable for the conduct of research and that the requirements necessary for high-quality investigations are too rigorous for the clinical setting. The primary contributors to this debate have tended to be individuals who conduct research but not clinical practice, or clinicians who do not do research, or individuals who do both but keep the two separate. At the Kennedy Institute and Johns Hopkins University Hospital, we have for a number of years conducted research separately from clinical practice, operated clinical services that have no research components, and combined research and clinical services in one comprehensive program. During this time the major distinctions between these areas have not been the collection of data, the use of reliability procedures, or the use of intervention designs to demonstrate causality, but rather the characterization of one's activities. That which separates clinical practice from research often involves the extent to which one is likely to try innovative techniques and the extent to which these techniques are justified to an audience of one's peers. Procedures attempted in clinical practice are usually bolder and more innovative than are those in formal research studies. The governing rule for the selection of procedures that can be attempted during clinical practice is usually that they must be in the best interest of the patient. In very severe cases, dramatic procedures can be warranted. Bold, innovative clinical procedures that are successful often first find their way into the professional literature in the form of a clinical report or case study. A number of case studies reporting a new technique often precede formal, controlled experimental research on the technique.

In a design of treatment procedures employing behavioral principles, the distinction between research and clinical practice need never be one involving the availability of data. Intervention techniques cannot be justifiably labeled as "behavioral treatment" unless behavioral data are obtained, the reliability of the data is determined, and a treatment design is planned that attempts to assess causality of improvements due to treatment. At the Kennedy Institute and Johns Hopkins University School of Medicine, behavioral treatment employed in this manner is the rule rather than the exception. Any clinical activities not conducted in this manner are considered professional advice, not an active treatment program. The main advantages of this approach are that clinical activities are more accountable and adhere to the same rules of evidence and objectivity as behavioral research; treatment procedures make direct contact with the research literature; and successful innovative treatment outcomes have all the necessary rigor for publication in professional journals. Further, a series of similar patients seen or techniques conducted over the course of clinical activities can also be reported in the research literature. At this juncture, formal clinical research and clinical activities conducted in a proper behavioral manner are one and the same. The objection often voiced about an approach to behavior therapy requiring data on patients is that it is too costly to be practical. Exactly the opposite is the case. It is much more costly, inefficient, and ineffective to attempt to conduct clinical interventions in the absence of data on the target behaviors. In addition, treatment interventions always require extra effort, and unless there is a clear indication that improvements are due to these treatment procedures, the effort should not be continued.

The second major objection raised about the routine collection of data during behavioral treatment is that objective, reliable data are very difficult to collect in the home setting. This is certainly true, and this methodological problem represents one of the major impediments to research and clinical advancement on parenting techniques. However, at the very least, parents can be required to obtain data on children's behavior in the home, and in some instances reliability on parents' data taking can be obtained with clinic personnel during parents' routine visits to pediatric clinics.

Symptom Substitution

Early in the development of behavior modification procedures for applied clinical problems, the question of symptom substitution arose. The usual answer was that behavior modification procedures were sufficient, that analytical techniques to determine the "cause" of the problem were unnecessary, and that symptom substitution did not occur. While this was and still is true in general, there are cases in which the therapist should exercise additional effort in attempting a behavior analysis of the current controlling and maintaining variables for behavior problems. Often the factors and remote contingencies that eventually maintain a behavior problem are not readily apparent, and will continue to result in behavior problems unless they are satisfactorily dealt with.

A collaborative case between the Departments of Behavioral Psychology and Psychiatry at Johns Hopkins will serve to illustrate this point. An adolescent retarded boy was referred to Hopkins because of extremely disruptive acting-out behavior at home. He refused to comply with his parents' requests and kept them awake at night by screaming; when his mother or father attempted to guide him manually to his bedroom, he would fall limp to the floor and remain there (he was larger than both his mother and his father), and on some occasions while lying on the floor he would urinate on himself. He was only moderately retarded, had an adequate verbal repertoire, and was otherwise well integrated into the school and community workshop activities. During the initial evaluation, it was clear that the parents' attention was contingent upon these aberrant behaviors. All attempts at establishing a parent-mediated program with this youth failed. Invariably, he would escalate and extend his repertoire of aberrant behaviors to circumvent any form of extinction, time out, or differential reinforcement of zero-rate procedures to the extent that he was finally admitted to the psychiatric unit at Hopkins on an emergency basis.

Further interviews with the parents revealed that they had been having marital difficulties over the past year and had decided to separate. It was at about this time the boy's tantrum-like behavior had developed. Based on this information, a more elaborate behavioral program was instituted, including a temporary suspension of the parents' plans to separate; increased activities with the parents, both singly and together, which were eventually made contingent upon appropriate cooperative behavior on the boy's part; increased involvement in community activities, so that the boy could establish relationships with other individuals; and counseling by the child psychiatrist to explain to this retarded individual his parents' problems and why they and the entire family might be happier if the parents separated. Over the course of a year this problem was satisfactorily resolved; the parents were able to effect a marital separation, and the boy maintained an increased contact with other community activities.

Another example of a child with a physical problem along the lines of a behavioral medicine consideration also provides a good example of the necessity for determining historical and underlying causes. This case involved the use of a behavioral analysis to determine the appropriate medical solution. An 11-year-old boy was referred to the Outpatient Pediatric Clinic at Johns Hopkins University Hospital for a rather difficult and long-standing case of encopresis.

There were no intestinal, bowel, or rectum problems, and the child was otherwise normal. The nature of his encopresis was typical to individuals who become extremely constipated and have overflow incontinence. During the initial interview, it was clear that there were appropriate contingencies for correct toileting and accidents, and that parents and child were highly motivated to solve this problem. It was difficult to see how any additional consequences or contingencies could improve the current circumstances.

Therefore, a more extensive history was taken. This revealed that the toileting problem began subsequent to a hospitalization 5 years earlier. During that time, a gastrointestinal (GI) disorder caused the child to have acute diarrhea for a few days. His soiling of the bed was remembered to be extremely embarrassing, and as the GI problem was resolved, he began to retain feces to avoid soiling the bed. As is usually the case, this resulted in constipation and unusually large and difficult bowel movements. The pain resulting from these bowel movements presented a second aversive consequence surrounding toileting, and the child further attempted to avoid having bowel movements; this resulted in even more difficult bowel movements when they did occur. Together, the pain and soiling of the overflow incontinence due to constipation made bowel movements extremely aversive events. In a typical behavior modification program, reinforcement is provided for appropriate toileting, and sometimes mild aversive consequences are provided for inappropriate toileting. However, in this case, what was needed was to reduce the aversive properties of bowel movements. In consultation with the pediatrician, a mild stool softener was provided. Over the course of the next 2 weeks, the child's bowel movements returned to normal and the encopresis problem was resolved—a problem that had existed for 5 years.

Not attending to "underlying" variables that maintain maladaptive behavior can result in serious consequences. This is particularly the case when the patient has selected a maladaptive behavior that is very dramatic and has medical aspects to it. In such situations, the individual has probably not selected that behavior at random, but rather has been shaped by the contingencies of the environment along a continuum of behaviors, each of which is more socially maladaptive and medically risky. Should the therapist use behavior modification procedures to eliminate this maladaptive behavior— without considering the previous history that has resulted in the current problem, without attempting to replace the behavior with a more appropriate one, *and* without attending to underlying *behavioral causes*—the individual is likely to select another maladaptive behavior to control his or her environment that is more dramatic and dangerous than the previous one. Such a selection would be consistent with this shaping history.

One example of this problem occurred at the Kennedy Institute when we first began our behavioral treatment program. An adolescent with a diagnosed seizure disorder was suspected of also faking seizures. The parents, the pediatric neurologist, and the behavioral treatment team all believed that she faked seizures in order to obtain adults' and peers' attention and to avoid or escape from certain situations, such as attendance at school. A behavior modification procedure was implemented for her seizure behavior at school. This was a step contingency, the goal of which was to eliminate her fake seizures at school. The consequence for these seizures had usually been that she would first be sent to the nurse's office and then eventually sent home for the day if the seizures continued. Contingencies were first placed on her for having six or fewer seizures at school. Soon the data indicated six or fewer seizures, at which point the contingency was shifted to five, then four, then three, with corresponding shifts in the data. When the contingency was placed on two or fewer seizures per day at school, the child attempted suicide by taking an overdose of her seizure medication. The significant key factor in this case was that the child had elected to fake seizures in order to control her social environment. For the epileptic, having seizures is a socially embarrassing event that often results in restrictions of a person's social sphere rather than the ability to manipulate it. That the child chose this behavior should have alerted the behavior therapists to look further. In retrospect, an analysis indicated that this child was overweight, had very few social skills, and otherwise was lacking in repertoires important to most adolescent girls. A more appropriate strategy would have been to employ contingencies to reduce the fake seizure behavior in conjunction with (and probably after) a program had been successfully initiated to teach her appropriate social skills and improve her physical appearance.

A more dramatic example is related by a colleague who was designing an intervention program for urinary incontinence on a geriatric ward. In this instance, a female geriatric patient had a history of enuresis, which was believed to be used as an operant to control staff behavior. A standard behavior modification procedure was implemented on the ward to reduce and then to eliminate this inappropriate urination. However, no compensatory procedures were employed to assist this woman in exercising more appropriate influence over her environment. Soon after inappropriate urination was successfully treated, the woman began to have episodes of tachycardia necessitating staff and medical attention. She was observed to induce this tachycardia by abnormal breathing on occasions when she attempted to control staff behavior in the geriatric environment. While these tachycardia episodes were extremely effective in obtaining staff attention because of her age, her heart was not capable of sustaining such erratic activity frequently, and during one of these episodes she had a major cardiovascular accident and died.

Therefore, it is particularly important that the behavioral clinician conduct as extensive a behavioral analysis as possible. The mere selection of consequences that could manipulate behavior does not ensure that behavior change will be maintained, or that it will not be replaced by another, possibly more severe, behavior problem.

SUMMARY

Since antiquity, assistance to parents in rearing their children has been provided by the extended family of grandparents, relatives, other siblings, and sometimes friends. As Western society has become more mobile, extended families have diminished as a parental resource. To this evolution have been added a cadre of social support systems, professionals on parenting, and a variety of scientific and quasi-scientific approaches. Medicine and psychology have also advanced in their ability to treat the special problems of mentally and physically handicapped and ill children, including involvement of parents in this treatment process. This chapter had provided information on clinical considerations in behavioral based treatment programs for children with such special problems. This information is based on a large clinical service for this population and focuses on the problems most frequently encountered by professionals when beginning to work in this area. Among these considerations are the following:

- The primary motivating factors for young children are their parents, whereas adolescents come increasingly under the stimulus control of their peers.
- This shift in primary social reinforcers, as well as emotional and other developmental changes, must be recognized by the parent and must result in appropriate changes in parenting.
- The goal for the parent and therapist alike is to ensure that the child can make contact with an environment that will differentially reinforce appropriate behavior and development.
- The clinician must also assist the parent in discriminating between behaviors that are the result of handicapping conditions or illness and those that are the result of inappropriate parenting.
- Only when a consequence has clearly been shown to change a known operant can it be ruled out as a cause of treatment failure.
- Therapists have few consequences to use to change parents' behavior; these must be identified and rules for their use clearly established, such as those for missed appointments and noncompliance with treatment plans.
- Children with handicaps and medical problems also often have many behavior problems as well, and these should be identified and prioritized for treatment.
- Peer review of all individual treatment plans should be conducted by clinic staff.
- Generalized compliance may represent a parsimonious approach to treating multiple behavior problems.
- Behavioral (operant) principles may be successfully used in treating

some medical disorders in conjunction with appropriate supervision by a physician; however, especially with new procedures, initial treatment should be carried out directly by the clinician before being given to parents for transfer to the home setting.

• Clinical services should include reliable data collection and treatment interventions to demonstrate causality for improvement as a standard, required practice.

• "Symptom substitution" does occur, and clinicians should conduct extensive behavioral analyses to avoid this problem.

Acknowledgments

Preparation of this chapter was supported in part by Grant 917 from the Maternal and Child Health Service, Department of Health and Human Services.

References

Ayllon, T., & Roberts, M. D. Eliminating discipline problems by strengthening academic performance. *Journal of Applied Behavior Analysis,* 1974, *7,* 71–76.

American Hospital Association. *Hospital statistics.* Chicago: Author, 1979.

Bijou, S. W., & Baer, D. M. Editors' comments for D. M. Baer and J. A. Sherman, "Reinforcement control of generalized imitation in young children." In S. W. Bijou & D. M. Baer (Eds.), *Child development: Readings in experimental analysis.* New York: Appleton-Century-Crofts, 1967.

Bird, B. L., & Cataldo, M. F. Experimental analysis of EMG feedback in treating dystonia. *Annals of Neurology,* 1978, *3,* 310–315.

Bucher, B. Some variables affecting children's compliance with instructions. *Journal of Experimental Child Psychology,* 1973, *15,* 10–21.

Cataldo, M. F. The scientific basis for a behavioral approach to pediatrics. *Pediatric Clinics of North America,* 1982, *29,* 415–423.

Cataldo, M. F., & Bird, B. L. Behavioral medicine in the treatment of children with physical handicaps. In T. J. Coates (Ed.), *Behavioral medicine: A practical handbook.* Champaign, Ill.: Research Press, in press.

Cataldo, M. F., Bird, B. L., & Cunningham, C. E. Experimental analysis of EMG feedback in treating cerebral palsy. *Journal of Behavioral Medicine,* 1978, *1,* 311–322.

Cataldo, M. F., Jacobs, H. E., & Rogers, M. C. Psychosocial factors in pediatric intensive care. In D. C. Russo & J. W. Varni (Eds.), *Behavioral pediatrics: Research and practice.* New York: Plenum Press, 1982.

Cataldo, M. F., & Russo, D. C. Developmentally disabled in the community: Behavioral/medical considerations. In L. A. Hamerlynck, P. O. Davidson, & F. W. Clark (Eds.), *History and future of behavior modification for the developmentally disabled: Programmatic and methodological issues.* New York: Brunner/Mazel, 1979.

Cataldo, M. F., Russo, D. C., Bird, B. L., & Varni, J. W. Assessment and management of chronic disorders. In J. Ferguson & C. B. Taylor (Eds.), *Advances in behavioral medicine.* Holliswood, N.Y.: Spectrum, 1980.

Cataldo, M. F., Russo, D. C., & Freeman, J. M. Behavioral analysis and treatment approach to myoclonic seizure control. *Journal of Autism and Developmental Disorders,* 1979, *9*(4), 413–427.

Cerulli, M. A., Nikoomanesh, P., & Schuster, M. M. Progress in biofeedback conditioning for fecal incontinence. *Gastroenterology*, 1979, *76*, 742–746.

Christophersen, E. R. *Little people: Guidelines for common-sense child rearing.* Lawrence, Kans.: H & H Enterprises, 1977.

Christophersen, E. R., & Rapoff, M. A. Behavioral pediatrics. In O. F. Pomerleau & J. P. Brady (Eds.), *Behavioral medicine: Theory and practice.* Baltimore: Williams & Wilkins, 1979.

Doleys, D. M., Wells, K. C., Hobbs, S. A., Roberts, M. W., & Cartelli, L. M. The effects of social punishment on noncompliance: A comparison with time out and positive practice. *Journal of Applied Behavior Analysis,* 1976, *9*, 471–482.

Engel, B. T., Nikoomanesh, P., & Schuster, M. M. Operant conditioning of rectrosphincteric responses in the treatment of fecal incontinence. *New England Journal of Medicine*, 1974, *290*, 646–649.

Green, M. The pediatric model of care. *The Behavior Therapist*, 1980, *3*, 7–8.

Neef, N. A., Shafer, M. S., Egel, A. I., Cataldo, M. F., & Parrish, J. M. The class specific effects of compliance training with "Do" and "Don't" requests. *Journal of Applied Behavior Analysis*, 1983, *16*, 81–99.

Nordquist, V. M. The modification of a child's enuresis: Some response–response relationships. *Journal of Applied Behavior Analysis*, 1971, *4*, 241–247.

Russo, D. C. *Behavior management approaches to genitourinary dysfunction in childhood.* Paper presented at the Vulnerable Child Conference, Johns Hopkins University School of Medicine, October 1978.

Russo, D. C., Cataldo, M. F., & Cushing, P. J. Compliance training and behavioral covariation in the treatment of multiple behavior problems. *Journal of Applied Behavior Analysis*, 1981, *14*, 209–222.

Russo, D. C., & Varni, J. W. (Eds.). *Behavioral pediatrics: Research and practice.* New York: Plenum Press, 1982.

Sajwaj, T., Twardosz, S., & Burke, M. Side effects of extinction procedures in a remedial pre-school. *Journal of Applied Behavior Analysis*, 1972, *5*, 163–175.

Skinner, B. F. *Verbal behavior.* New York: Appleton-Century-Crofts, 1957.

Striefel, S., & Wetherby, B. Instruction-following behavior of a retarded child and its controlling stimuli. *Journal of Applied Behavior Analysis,* 1973, *6*, 663–670.

Varni, J. W., Boyd, E., & Cataldo, M. F. Self-monitoring, external reinforcement, and time-out procedures in the control of high-rate tic behaviors in a hyperactive child. *Behavior Therapy and Experimental Psychiatry*, 1978, *9*, 353–358.

Wahler, R. G., Sperling, K. A., Thomas, M. R., Teeter, N. C., & Luper, H. L. The modification of childhood stuttering: Some response–response relationships. *Journal of Experimental Child Psychology*, 1970, *9*, 411–428.

Wald, A. Use of biofeedback in treatment of fecal incontinence in patients with meningomyelocele. *Pediatrics*, 1981, *68*, 45–49.

Ward, E. M., Cataldo, M. F., Russo, D. R., Riordan, M. M., & Bennett, D. *Child compliance and correlated problem behavior: Effects of contingent and noncontingent reinforcement procedures.* Manuscript in preparation.

Whitehead, W. E., Parker, L. H., Masek, B. J., Cataldo, M. F., & Freeman, J. M. Biofeedback treatment of fecal incontinence in patients with myelomeningocele. *Developmental Medicine and Child Neurology*, 1981, *23*, 313–322.

Wilson, G. T. Some thoughts about clinical research. *Behavioral Assessment*, 1981, *3*, 217–225.

Zimmerman, E. H., Zimmerman, J., & Russell, C. D. Differential effects of token reinforcement on instruction-following behavior in retarded students instructed as a group. *Journal of Applied Behavior Analysis*, 1969, *2*, 101–112.

COLLATERAL EFFECTS OF PARENT TRAINING ON FAMILIES WITH AUTISTIC CHILDREN

Robert L. Koegel
University of California at Santa Barbara

Laura Schreibman
Claremont McKenna College

Jean Johnson
Robert E. O'Neill
Glen Dunlap
University of California at Santa Barbara

INTRODUCTION

Behavioral treatment for autistic children has made considerable advances in the past 20 years, with parent training emerging as an integral component to promote increased breadth and maintenance of treatment gains. Also, it now seems probable that parent training approaches have influences beyond the direct changes in the children's behavior. That is, there seem to be several additional benefits to such an approach, including beneficial changes in the way parents of autistic children arrange their daily activities and family leisure time, as well as changes in parental attitudes toward the children and their treatment programs. In addition, from the therapists' point of view, there appear to be benefits relating to the scope of treatment delivery. Therefore, it is the thesis of this chapter that it is important to consider parent training with autistic children not only in terms of its direct effects upon the children's behaviors, but also in terms of the more widespread collateral effects that may result from this treatment delivery approach. Before considering these results, it is best to consider the behavioral characteristics of autistic children in the context of their family lives.

BEHAVIORAL CHARACTERISTICS OF AUTISTIC CHILDREN

Autistic children are generally characterized as exhibiting an extreme range of bizarre or deficient behaviors. One type of extreme behavior that is quite common is tantrumous behavior, which may be evidenced at the presentation of the slightest demand or request to the child. For instance, a parent might request that his or her autistic child use a fork to eat dinner. This might result in a severe tantrum. These tantrums may escalate into aggressive behavior in which the child tries to hit or bite another person. In some cases the child may exhibit self-injurious behavior, such as hitting his or her head on the corner of a table.

Many autistic children spend a great deal of their time engaged in repetitive, self-stimulatory behaviors, which seem to serve only to provide sensory input. These behaviors include rhythmic hand flapping, repetitive finger manipulations in front of the eyes, eye crossing, prolonged gazing, body rocking, and a wide variety of other behaviors. The children will typically prefer such activities to social companionship or appropriate play.

Autistic children typically display quite limited language abilities. Many of these children are nonverbal, meaning that they do not use words for communication. Other children may develop language, but it may be characterized by echolalic speech. "Echolalia" refers to speech that the child has heard previously and repeats back, either immediately or after a delay. Even when conversational speech becomes more elaborated, it is often characterized by word-order confusions, pronoun reversals, and immature grammar.

Finally, autistic children commonly show an extreme lack of social behavior, typically referred to as a failure to develop "social relatedness." Such symptoms are often reported to have been noticeable early in the child's life, as, for example, in the failure of an infant to show an "anticipatory response" to being picked up, or in the delay or absence of the development of a social smile. As young children, the reluctance to hold eye contact, preference for solitude, and failure to show an attachment to important people in their environment characterize the lack of social relatedness.

The types of behaviors described above can make some aspects of living with autistic children very demanding. The extreme lack of social relatedness and the apparent desire for solitary self-stimulatory activities often may make parents feel especially unneeded or unwanted. In addition, taking an autistic child out in public may risk a tantrum in the middle of a grocery store or a restaurant. Because the children can be destructive to property, it is often difficult to take them to friends' houses. It is usually difficult if not impossible to find sitters who are able and willing to sit with such children. Thus, it is common for parents of autistic children to relate that they feel "chained to their child" or "trapped in their house."

Because the severe behavioral extremes and deficits of autistic children have such dramatic effects on their parents and families, behavioral researchers have begun to focus outcome measures upon these people, as well as upon the autistic individuals themselves. The research to be presented in this chapter presents a comparison of different treatment approaches for autistic children, with an emphasis on some collateral effects that may result from parent training for families with autistic children.

PARENT TRAINING WITH AUTISTIC CHILDREN

Historical Development

Early work in behavior modification achieved a considerable degree of success in modifying deviant or problematic behaviors in laboratory and clinical settings. As reports of successful applications grew, it became increasingly desirable to introduce such techniques into more natural environments (Tharp & Wetzel, 1969), so that newly established behavioral controls and repertoires could be extended to a broader range of environments. Parent training began to be explored as a means of extending behavioral control to persons who have a natural relationship to the child and who have principal responsibility for further development and maintenance of learned behaviors. For instance, Wolf, Risley, and Mees (1964) gradually introduced the parents of an autistic child into his treatment program when it became desirable for the child to start returning home periodically on visits. In order to ensure the transfer and maintenance of those behaviors in his home, these investigators trained the parents to use the same behavioral treatment programs that were being successfully employed with the child in his residential setting.

The *importance* of parent training to the treatment of autistic children became clearly evident from a follow-up report of autistic children who had undergone 1 year of intensive behavioral treatment (Lovaas, Koegel, Simmons, & Long, 1973). These authors reported that children who were discharged to institutions or foster homes that did not employ behavior therapy programs lost most or all of their initial treatment gains, while children discharged to parents who had received training in behavior therapy maintained their treatment gains or continued to improve. These authors concluded that when contingencies were not in effect (i.e., for the institutionalized and foster-home children), the children's learned behaviors were effectively extinguished by their environment. However, when the parents were taught how to support their children's behavior through contingency management, the children remained motivated to perform those behaviors and learn new ones.

Parent Training Compared to Direct Clinic Treatment

The influence of parent training upon the maintenance of treatment gains suggested several implications regarding parents as primary treatment agents for their autistic children. Many of these questions have been systematically investigated by Koegel and Schreibman in a long-term study designed to compare the relative effectiveness of treatment delivery mechanisms for autistic children. The primary focus of the research has been to gather treatment outcome measures comparing *clinic treatment* of autistic children with *parent training*. The investigators were interested in extending the scope of treatment evaluation (which included traditional child measures, such as changes in appropriate and inappropriate behaviors and in social and academic functioning) to include the measurement of differential effects of the interventions for all family members, including parents and siblings (Koegel, Schreibman, Britten, Burke, & O'Neill, 1982; Schreibman, Koegel, & Britten, in press). Within this overall research program, individual investigations into generalization of treatment gains and special learning characteristics of autistic children (such as motivational difficulties and stimulus overselectivity) have also been conducted.

At the time of this writing, 49 parents have participated in various portions of the present research project. The families have been referred by school districts; by state regional centers for the developmentally disabled; by the National Society for Autistic Children; and by local pediatricians, psychologists, and psychiatrists. Every family with a child who has been reliably diagnosed as autistic has been included. The children have participated in this research through either the University of California at Santa Barbara or Claremont McKenna College.

The majority of the families have been in the middle to upper middle socioeconomic range. Most of the parents have been high-school or college graduates, while a small percentage have had less than a high-school education. The autistic children have ranged in age from 2 to 9 years, with a mean of 5 years. They have represented a broad range in terms of the severity of their handicaps. Social age scores on the Vineland Social Maturity Scale have ranged from .9 years to 5.8 years. The children have been mute or echolalic, have engaged in self-stimulatory behaviors, and have had minimal social and self-help skills.

In this study, families of autistic children were randomly assigned to one of the two groups. Children in the clinic treatment group attended the clinic for 1½–2 hours per day, 2 or 3 days per week for 1 year, or for a total of 225 hours of clinic treatment. The therapists were graduate and undergraduate students in speech pathology and psychology who had each completed two lecture and two laboratory classes in behavior modification and autism.

Children in the parent training group received treatment from their parents. The parents were trained using procedures designed to teach the general principles and procedures used in the behavior modification treatment of autistic children. The general-principles approach to parent training was based upon a previous study by Koegel, Glahn, and Nieminen (1978), which compared different approaches to parent training. This study demonstrated that parents who were provided a brief demonstration in how to teach a specific behavior were then able to teach their children that same behavior or skill, but were not able to teach other, previously undemonstrated tasks or skills. In contrast, when parent training concentrated on teaching general behavior modification principles and procedures, the parents were able to generalize their skills to teach new (previously undemonstrated) target behaviors to their children.

Parent Training Procedures

Our training program has six basic steps. The first step entails obtaining a premeasure on the parent's skills. The parent chooses a target behavior to work on with the child, and then is videotaped attempting to teach that behavior for 15 minutes. We score this tape for the parent's correct use of discriminative stimuli, instructions and questions, prompts, shaping and chaining, consequences, and discrete trials (for definitions and scoring procedures, see Koegel *et al.*, 1982). This provides us with a relatively precise estimate of how well the parent can teach the child, and allows us to compare the parent's performances prior to and after training.

STRUCTURED TRAINING SESSIONS. After the pretaping, the parent is given two training manuals to read. One manual is somewhat general, and presents basic behavior management principles and ways in which they can be applied to a variety of child behaviors (Baker, Brightman, Heifetz, & Murphy, 1976). The second manual deals primarily with autism and other severe handicaps, and the use of the behavioral approach with characteristics of such disorders (cf. Koegel & Schreibman, 1982). These manuals serve to give parents a general introduction to the treatment approach they will be trained.

Once parents have read the manuals, they are shown a 30-minute training videotape. This tape presents both good and bad examples of therapists using instructions, prompts, consequences, and shaping and chaining techniques. The important features of each of these trial components are presented and discussed. While showing the tape, the trainer also discusses how the procedures are applicable to situations other than those shown on the tape. This helps parents see how the principles generally apply to a variety of situations.

Following the viewing of the tape, each parent is given *in vivo* feedback while working with his or her own child on a specific target behavior. The parent conducts teaching trials, with the trainer periodically interrupting for a brief period to provide positive and/or corrective feedback on the parent's performance. *In vivo* feedback continues until each parent becomes relatively comfortable and proficient with the procedures. At this point, the parent and child are videotaped working on the same task as was used in the premeasure (which has not been worked on during training). If the parent then reaches criterion (80% correct overall use of the procedures), he or she is considered to be generalizing their skills to other tasks. If the parent fails to reach criterion, further training and tapings are done until he or she reaches the 80% criterion on the original task. Once this is accomplished, we present another task (not previously worked on) and again videotape and score the parent's performance. Such training and tapings continue until the parent reaches criterion on the first try with a new task he or she has not previously worked on. The use of these new tasks provides a further indication of how well the parent's skills are generalizing.

HOME TRAINING SESSIONS. Once a child's parents reach criterion in the clinic setting, the emphasis shifts to the home situation. During home visits, the trainer and parents discuss problems at home, focusing on how the parents can work with the child to correct them. These home sessions involve both discussion and *in vivo* feedback as each parent works with the child. At this point, the trainer begins to fade into more of a consultant role. Weekly phone calls and monthly home visits allow us to monitor the progress of parents and their children and to be available for support if a parent feels the need for a consultant.

As described, the training involves three general components. The premeasure (baseline) allows us to assess parents' initial need for training; the training (acquisition) component gives parents the basic knowledge and procedures they will be using; and the home visits (generalization) and follow-up procedures aid in teaching parents the use of the techniques in a generalized fashion.

Thus, children in both groups, clinic treatment and parent training, received treatments that were identical in procedure and curriculum. The only differences in the treatments were in (1) who provided the treatment (i.e., the parent for the parent training group, and the therapist for the clinic treatment group); and (2) how much professional time the treatment required (i.e., 225 hours for the clinic group compared to 25 to 50 hours for the parent training group).

Special Considerations in Training Parents of Autistic Children

Autism is often a very pervasive disorder; that is, it can involve a number of different symptoms in varying degrees of severity. This places a large burden on parents, in that they often have to deal with a great variety of problematic behaviors, including deficits (e.g., lack of speech, lack of play) and excesses (e.g., tantrums, self-stimulatory behavior). Autism is somewhat unique in this sense. Other populations of disordered children (such as noncompliant children, who are otherwise normal) often exhibit only one or two main symptoms, and training for parents of such children can be somewhat limited and aimed at specific target behaviors. In contrast, parents of autistic children need to be equipped with the skills to deal with the many different situations and behaviors they will encounter. These types of problems account for the emphasis on general behavior modification principles and procedures in the approach to parent training advocated by Koegel *et al.* (1978).

Relative Effectiveness of Treatments

Following 1 year of either treatment, children in both groups were videotaped in unstructured play interactions with their treatment providers, as well as with adults who were unfamiliar to the children. These sessions were analyzed for the percentage of 10-second intervals in which the children displayed appropriate behaviors. Appropriate behaviors included appropriate speech, social nonverbal behavior, and appropriate play. These data were compared to similar data collected prior to treatment, and both sets of data were compared to data gathered 3 months after the treatment had been discontinued (follow-up). The results describing the amount of appropriate behavior exhibited by children in both groups when observed with their treatment providers are presented in the solid lines in Figure 14-1. The ordinate describes the amount of change in appropriate behavior relative to the child's level at pretreatment (which is indicated as 0). The abscissa denotes measures taken at pretreatment, 1 year later at posttreatment, and 3 months after that at follow-up. As can be seen, the children in both groups evidenced significant gains at posttreatment and continued to improve at follow-up. These data indicate that the parents (who were treatment providers for children in the parent training group) were able to influence their children's behavior positively in unstructured interactions. Thus, the direct results of the comparison of parent training to clinic treatment suggested that parents were able to effect as much improvement in their children as could the clinicians in the clinic treatment group, for about 15% of the professional time involvement. In addition, both treatments showed durable gains following discontinuation of treatment. These findings lend considerable support to parent training as a treatment delivery mechanism for autistic children.

COLLATERAL EFFECTS
OF PARENT TRAINING

Additional data collected during the treatment comparisons allowed us to examine several possible collateral effects attributable to parent training—effects that were not evident with clinic treatment.

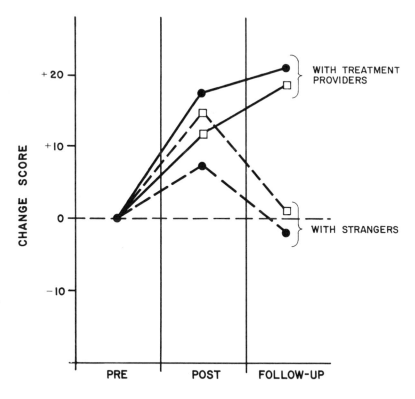

Figure 14-1

The change in amount of appropriate behaviors exhibited by the children of the clinic treatment and parent training groups from pretreatment to posttreatment, and 3 months later at follow-up. Solid lines depict the children's appropriate behavior with treatment providers; dotted lines depict appropriate behavior in interactions with unfamiliar adults.

Generalization

One of the first areas investigated concerned the generalization of the children's learned behaviors across settings and people. As can be seen in Figure 14-1, increases in appropriate child behavior were evidenced in an untreated environment when the children interacted with their treatment providers. Figure

14-1 also presents data representing the children's appropriate responding when they were interacting with unfamiliar adults. It had been hoped that the parent training would facilitate the generalization of learned behaviors across people, and the initial data at 1 year of treatment suggest that in fact this was the case. That is, the dotted lines in Figure 14-1 represent improvement or deterioration in the amount of appropriate behavior exhibited by the children in unstructured play interactions with adults who were unfamiliar to the children. For the clinic treatment group, very little improvement was evidenced with strangers at posttreatment. In contrast, the children in the parent training group evidenced considerable gains in appropriate interactions with unfamiliar adults at posttreatment, suggesting an initial generalization of treatment gains across novel persons. Follow-up data, however, reveal that generalization to strangers for both groups eventually fell to very low levels that reflect little change in appropriate behaviors from pretreatment.

These results have significant implications regarding the collateral benefits of parent training. The clinic treatment children evidenced clear differences in their behavior when they interacted with their treatment providers and when they interacted with unfamiliar adults. The data suggest the possibility that the operation of contingencies became highly discriminable to the clinic children and that they behaved accordingly. The parent training children, however, appeared to show initial generalization across strangers at posttreatment, suggesting that, for these children, the operation of contingencies was less discriminable. This initial generalization could be viewed as related to the operation of multiple therapists (i.e., both parents are trained to teach their child) as described by Stokes and Baer (1977). Relatedly, these initial results may be explained by the facilitory effects of training in multiple settings upon generalization (Handleman & Harris, 1980), since parents can teach concepts to their children in many natural settings.

Whatever the cause of the initial generalization across novel persons, the follow-up data confirm that eventually the children may disciminate the operation of contingencies and fail to generalize their appropriate behaviors, emphasizing the need for further study of the variables influencing generalization of treatment gains.

Influences on Family Activities

We have discussed the types of demands and limitations that autistic children can place upon their parents and families. Consistent reports by parents regarding the difficulties they encounter when their children accompany them to public places suggested an examination regarding the possibility that parent training might have facilitative effects upon the ability of parents to reduce the daily demands that their child can place upon them, and to facilitate the parents' ability to spend time alone or in family recreation. Preliminary data suggested that parent training has significant collateral benefits influencing the way in which families of autistic children arrange their daily activities.

Increased Teaching Time

One of the presumed benefits of a parent training approach for treating autistic children relates to the anticipated application by the parents of the training principles to the many natural activities in which they participate with their children. Thus, research has attempted to document the generalization of parents' skills to the home environment and its effects upon the child's behavior in that environment (Burke, 1982).

Information on parents' daily activities was collected by means of two 24-hour time–activity reports completed by the parents of both groups at post-treatment. The time–activity reports were then analyzed for the amount of time that the parents reported was spent in "teaching activities" with their children. "Teaching activities" included school-related work, educational games, exercises, housework, and work in self-help skills. The results showed that the parents in the clinic treatment group reported significantly less time engaged in teaching activities with their children than did parents who had undergone parent training. These results indicate that the trained parents reported using their teaching skills in many structured and unstructured interactions with their children at home.

Decreased Custodial Child Care

If trained parents were truly spending more time in teaching activities with their children than were parents in the clinic group, such teaching might be expected to have some effect upon the children's behavior. Thus, it might be expected that more time would be spent in teaching activities and less time in custodial-type child care activities. When the parents' daily activities were analyzed for the amount of time the parents spent in direct custodial-type care for their children, a dramatic result emerged. "Custodial activities" were defined as activities in which the parent was in direct contact with the child and engaged in what are typically considered self-help skills (e.g., bathing, toileting, dressing, feeding). The parents' time–activity reports indicated that trained parents reported a significantly smaller amount of time per sample engaged in these activities than did parents who did not receive parent training.

Thus, these results, in conjunction with the results regarding teaching activities, support the contention that trained parents generalize their skills to home environments and can achieve more freedom from custodial activities by promoting their children's own independent functioning.

Influences on Recreational and Leisure Activities

The ability of parents to promote greater independence and responding in their children does not directly address the common complaint by parents that they feel "trapped in their homes." Thus, we sought to analyze the possible effects of parent training on parents' leisure activities (Koegel *et al.*, 1982). Specifically, data were gathered on the amount of time that parents reported was spent in (1) visits from friends, (2) family outdoor recreation, or (3) quiet leisure time alone. The results indicated that prior to either form of treatment, parents of both groups indicated that they spent about the same amount of time in these activities. The treatments, however, clearly differed in their effect upon parents' leisure time. Figure 14-2 shows a clear dramatic facilitory influence of parent training on the leisure activities of parents in this group. In contrast, parents in the clinic treatment group actually reported a *decrease* in the amount of time they spent in leisure activities.

A summary of the results presented thus far illustrates that trained parents devote more time to teaching activities with their children, and at the same time devote less time to custodial child care responsibilities. In conjunction with these findings, there appear to be significant differential effects of the two treatments upon the parents' leisure activities. Still, however, the parents must take primary responsibility for the moment-to-moment supervision of their autistic child and may find it extremely difficult to spend time away from this child. Thus, preliminary data suggesting possible influences of parent training on the ability to obtain respite care are encouraging.

Respite Care

Subjective impressions of college students, who were naive with respect to autism and behavior modification, were sampled after viewing videotapes of the children taken before and after parent training (Schreibman, Koegel, Mills, & Burke, 1981). The children were shown in unstructured play interactions with their mothers. The college students were asked questions concerning their willingness, for example, to accept such children into their neighborhood, or to agree to babysit such children. The results indicated a clearly more positive attitude toward the children after their parents had been trained. That is, these respondents were more willing to agree to babysit the children when viewing parent–child interactions filmed after parent training was completed than they were when viewing tapes filmed prior to parent training. Thus, the preliminary results suggest a possible facilitory effect of parent training on the parents' ability to obtain respite care.

However, the data in Figure 14-1 suggest that, at follow-up, the parent training children were showing very poor generalization of appropriate behavior to strangers. And, in fact, some parents suggested anecdotally that this

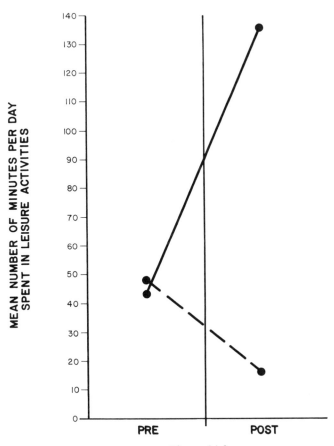

Figure 14-2

The amount of time devoted by families of autistic children to family leisure activities, measured at pretreatment and again at posttreatment. The solid line represents the parent training group, and the dotted line shows the clinic treatment group. (From "A Comparison of Parent Training to Direct Child Treatment" by R. L. Koegel, L. Schreibman, K. R. Britten, J. C. Burke, & R. E. O'Neill, in *Educating and Understanding Autistic Children*, edited by R. L. Koegel, A. Rincover, & A. L. Egel. San Diego: College-Hill Press, 1982. Copyright 1982 by College-Hill Press. Reprinted by permission.)

did happen. That is, they reported that no matter how nicely a child appeared to be interacting with his or her mother, the child quickly began to act as if he or she had never undergone treatment when left alone with a babysitter, and the sitter typically did not return. Thus, for now, the possible collateral facilitative effects of parent training upon the ability of parents to obtain respite care remain a subject for future research.

Summary

In summary, the data regarding the collateral effects of parent training upon the arrangement of the families' daily activities and leisure time suggest several additional benefits that are not evident with clinic treatment. Future research will help clarify the extent and/or limits of these collateral benefits, and should help to elucidate the relative efficacies of these two types of treatments.

SIDE EFFECTS FROM THE THERAPIST'S PERSPECTIVE

Direct Time Involvement

Figure 14-1 illustrates that trained parents can achieve as much behavioral improvement in their children as clinicians can. The two groups are similar regarding the durability of the treatment gains. However, the professional time involvement required for parent training (25–50 hours) to achieve comparable gains is about 15% of the time required for clinic treatment of each child (225 hours). The greater efficiency of parent training has clear implications for the cost of treating autistic children.

Since parent training takes less therapist time, the therapist can see a greater number of clients. The parent trainers in our research project typically see between two to four times as many clients in the period of 1 year as do therapists performing clinic treatment. Thus, parent training allows a less expensive treatment to become available to greater numbers of clients.

Availability of Service to Remote Areas

Since behavioral treatment for autistic children is still a relatively developing science, effective treatment services are often restricted to a very few large treatment centers located at universities or private schools. It is not uncommon for families to pack up their belongings and sell their houses in order to relocate in an area that can provide effective treatment services for their autistic child.

Parent training has several advantages with regard to families living in remote areas or in areas with few services. In the first place, if the parents can get to the training sessions without too much inconvenience, the parent training requires fewer visits per week. Also, it may be possible for parent trainers to travel to these areas for training sessions. In addition, the training is typically complete after a much shorter period of time. Traveling for parent training can be significantly reduced, compared to traveling for clinic treatment.

If, however, travel to the training center over a period of time is not practical (i.e., if the center is in a distant city or state), the advantages of parent training become even greater. The parent training lends itself to the possibility of intense training workshops for parents who must travel a great distance for training. At the University of California at Santa Barbara's Autism Research Center, we are currently developing and implementing such workshops for parents as well as professionals. Through such workshops, we hope to make it possible for more of the people who are in need of training to receive it. For example, parents and their autistic child attend a weekend or week-long workshop, and within that time achieve the same generalized parent training as when training is spread out across longer periods of time.

Parents as Professionals

Presently, the commitment of professional involvement to individual autistic children is both intensive and lengthy. The recruitment of an autistic child's parents into the child's teaching program allows the parents to serve new roles within the child's educational development that were previously filled by professionals. For instance, at present, professional involvement with autistic children may continue for several years. Professionals may be requested to aid with behavior problems as they emerge at school or in the community, or to do special programming for the children to expedite their learning of particularly difficult concepts. Thus, long after professional clinic involvement has been discontinued, the professionals may be called in as learning specialists for certain types of problems.

Such long-term demand on therapist time may be minimized to some extent by training the children's parents. That is, it seems that parent training can favorably influence parent–school interactions, such that parents whose suggestions may have been viewed as unrealistic or uninformed before training often find school districts to be more receptive after parent training. Provided that schools are aware of the training, the parent training program seems to alter the school personnel's perception of the parents' role in their child's education.

For example, after training, parents often assume a type of *consultant's* role in their child's education. If a teacher is having difficulty teaching a certain behavior or skill, he or she seems to be more apt to ask a trained parent how he or she might approach the situation. Parents may also be increasingly included or consulted regarding the child's curricular programming, thus being able to influence task selection and priorities in the child's curriculum.

After training, parents are also more likely to be employed as *continuity* agents or liaisons between home and school, maintaining reinforcement schedules and behavior programs such as time out and extinction for specific inappropriate or maladaptive behaviors. We have found such home–school feedback quite pertinent in certain programs.

For example, we have encountered children in our parent training program who had completed months or years of unsuccessful toilet training programs. For one child, as shown in Figure 14-3, baseline data collected from September of one year to March of the next indicate that toilet training implemented in one environment (at school) and then in two environments (school and clinic) was unsuccessful in increasing the child's percentage of toileting successes. However, upon the introduction of a toileting program that incorporated and was continuous across all of the child's natural environments (including home, school, and clinic), this child, with a 6-month baseline, became toilet-trained with remarkable ease and rapidity within the second block of 10 trials (Dunlap, Koegel, & Kern, 1981).

Parents have been recruited as continuity agents for other programs as well. In particular, current ongoing research is attempting to make an effective transfer of behavioral contingencies operating in the clinic to *all* of a child's natural environments. The procedure attempts to alleviate some of the problems in generalization across environments that we typically encounter in working with these children. Specifically, this program seeks to make the operation of contingencies virtually indiscriminable to the autistic student, such that it becomes extremely difficult for the child to know when contingencies are and are not in effect. The anticipated result is that the student will be unable to discriminate among environments and will thus be inclined to behave more appropriately for longer periods of time and across all environments (cf. Fowler & Baer, 1981). The success of such a program is illustrated in preliminary data in Figure 14-4.

The figure presents data taken in a work training center over a period of several weeks. This student exhibited frequent episodes of "autistic" self-stimulatory behaviors characterized by an extreme inattentiveness to environmental events (cf. Dunlap, Dyer, & Koegel, in press), which interfered with his learning and performance of the task at hand (cf. Koegel & Covert, 1972). Thus, the target behavior for this young man was defined as decreased frequency of autistic self-stimulatory activities, or, conversely, increased durations of continuous working without episodes of self-stimulation severe enough to interfere with his job.

This autistic adolescent had previously received extensive training in lengthening his periods of continuous working without engaging in self-stimulation within structured clinic sessions. During this intensive training in

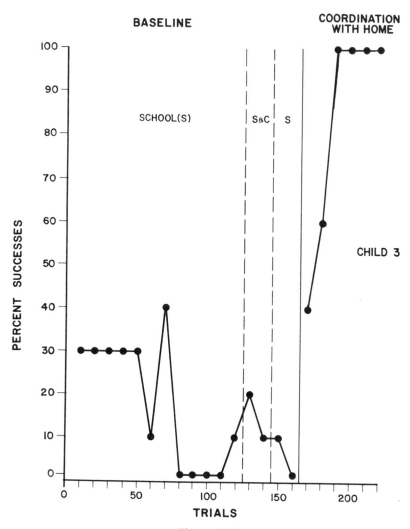

Figure 14-3

The percentage of toileting successes for one child when treatment was given first at school (S), then at school and at clinic (S & C), then at school alone again, and finally in all three environments, including the home. The ordinate depicts the percentage of successes, and the abscissa shows blocks of 10 trials.

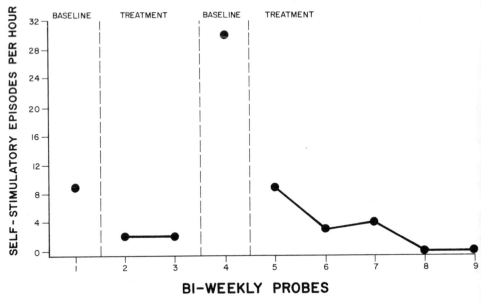

Figure 14-4

The number of self-stimulatory episodes per hour (ordinate), taken in biweekly probes (abscissa), for an adolescent boy. By the end of treatment, contingencies for self-stimulation were managed and implemented by the boy's parents at home.

the clinic, self-stimulatory activities that interfered with task performance were at first immediately punished, and then punished only after a small (gradually increasing) delay. Thus, if the young man began engaging in self-stimulation or nondirected gazing that interfered with his task, several minutes could elapse (after which the young man might return to his task) and consequences would still be forthcoming. The purpose of this procedure was to make it very difficult for the young man to discern when contingencies were in effect. Thus, if a small amount of self-stimulation occurred and was not immediately consequated, the young man would not be able to be certain whether he would eventually receive a consequence for the episode at a later time.

After delays between an episode of self-stimulation and its associated consequence had been gradually increased to about an hour, control over this adolescent's continuous working behavior was then transferred to his mother. This transfer process required the young man's mother to discuss with him the importance of working without engaging in self-stimulation. She explained that if she heard reports of him engaging in self-stimulation that caused him to work too slowly, then she would remove a favored activity from him that evening. A criterion level of self-stimulation was identified, after which the mother would be notified by the intervention team regarding her son's frequency of self-stimulation during his tasks that day.

Thus, the data in Figure 14-4 describe the student's number of self-stimulatory episodes per hour in his work training setting as contingencies were at first simply delayed within the setting, and then as control was transferred to the boy's home environment.

The data illustrate that the parent was able to exercise control over this student's working behavior simply by stating the contingency before he went to work and by implementing the contingency in the evening after work. Subsequent to this intervention and the implementation of the home–work feedback program (now monitored by the boy's natural supervisors at work and his parents at home), this adolescent works 15 hours per week (after attending daily classes at high school), maintaining his own responsibility for his work and productivity.

PARENTS' ATTITUDES
AND EXPECTATIONS

Before concluding our discussion of collateral effects, it is important to consider what effects parent training may have on the parents' perceptions of the treatment program and of their child as well. That is, clinic treatment and parent training are very different treatment mechanisms, and it is easy to see that one approach clearly requires more of the parents' thought and time. The question is, which do parents prefer, and why? Another question is also compelling. That is, do these two behavioral treatments affect parents' attitudes toward their autistic child? Does parent training have any particular effect upon the parents' expectations for their child's future? Do they differ from expectations of parents whose children receive clinic treatment?

These questions have been investigated by Klaila (1982). Parents of both groups were asked to complete questionnaires regarding their expectations for their children's short-term and long-term future. Parents' expectations regarding education, independent living ability, and work potentials were sampled using a Likert scale. The results showed that the parents' expectations for the child increased as a result of clinic treatment. In contrast, parents' expectations for children in the parent training group did not increase after a year. These data seemed surprising at first. Intuition suggested that the parents' ability to influence the children's behavior and teach new skills would increase their perception of the child's potential. However, the data may also suggest a different effect. Klaila discusses the finding as perhaps reflecting a change in parents' expectations, which become "more realistic" and more in concert with the child's current and future abilities. Whatever the cause of the differential parent expectations for the child, the finding suggests an important "side effect" of parent training that invites further research.

Klaila also compared the parents' satisfaction with the different treatment programs. That is, after 1 year of treatment, parents were asked if they were happy with their program, if they attributed changes in their child to the treatment the child received, and questions regarding how dedicated the parents felt the treatment program had been to their child's improvement. Anecdotally, it seemed as if both groups of parents felt quite satisfied in their respective training programs, and no apparent differences were noted. However, when an experimental analysis of the parents' attitudes was conducted under highly structured and controlled conditions, some apparent differences emerged. The results suggested that parents of children in the clinic were more satisfied in general, and attributed changes in their children over that year to the research/clinic program. Parents in the parent training group were less likely to attribute changes in their child to the parent training program, and also felt that the training indicated less dedication by professionals to their child's treatment.

These results, while somewhat disconcerting, are not surprising in retrospect. In the first place, a clinician who spends 225 hours with a child is likely to be viewed as more dedicated to the child's progress than is a clinician who spends only 25–50 hours with that family. Similarly, since in parent training the treatment provider is actually the parent, it probably makes the trainer's role regarding the child even less discriminable. Other factors, such as the parents' perceived increased responsibility for their child's improvement (or deterioration), may make parent training a more stressful treatment for parents. Finally, the clinic treatment provides incidental reinforcement by offering respite care to parents while their child is watched by someone else—a type of care that parent training does not provide. The variables influencing these parent attitudes require further thoughtful and empirical examination before conclusions can be drawn regarding parents' differential satisfaction with these treatment approaches.

For example, it seems that parents' attitudes toward the two types of treatments are different after the children have undergone both treatments than when the children have had one or the other treatment (but not both), as in the Klaila study. After parents have participated in both treatments and are asked which they prefer, the parents seem to favor the parent training (in contrast to Klaila's results). The parents report that they feel parent training is more helpful in dealing with their child on a daily basis. Thus, it seems clear that such variables as the degree of experience with the different treatments and perhaps the context in which questions are posed may influence the attitudes parents report. Clearly, further research is necessary before these variables are completely understood.

CONCLUSION

The development of effective treatments for autistic children has been remarkably successful in helping children who, 20 years ago, were generally considered untreatable, uneducable, and often even hopeless. One-to-one behavioral treatment in limited, highly structured environments laid the groundwork for more naturalistic treatment in unlimited, unstructured environments by persons who have a natural relationship (responsibility) to the children (cf. Tharp & Wetzel, 1969). The parent training approach to treatment provides several additional or collateral "side effects," which suggest that parent training may have more comprehensive advantages that do not appear evident or available with clinic treatment. However, despite equivalent (and in some cases, superior) treatment advances in the children, under some (as yet not fully understood) conditions the parent training approach seems to have a variety of influences on the extent of the parents' satisfaction with the program and their attitudes regarding their child's potential.

It is also possible that further collateral effects may become apparent as additional data are analyzed and understood. The delineation of the relationships between specific training techniques and associated collateral effects will undoubtedly facilitate the development of parent training programs that are more effective, both for the autistic children and for their families as a whole.

Acknowledgments

The research described in this chapter and the preparation of the manuscript were funded by USPHS Research Grant Nos. MH28210 and MH28231 from the National Institute of Mental Health and by Research Contract No. 300-82-0362 from the U.S. Department of Education—Special Education Program.

References

Baker, B. L., Brightman, A. J., Heifetz, L. J., & Murphy, D. M. *Behavior problems.* Champaign, Ill.: Research Press, 1976.

Burke, J. C. *Collateral effects of parent training on the daily interactions of families with autistic children.* Unpublished master's thesis, University of California at Santa Barbara, 1982.

Dunlap, G., Dyer, K. I., & Koegel, R. L. Autistic self-stimulation and intertrial interval duration. *American Journal of Mental Deficiency,* in press.

Dunlap, G., Koegel, R. L., & Kern, L. *Continuity of treatment: Toilet training in multiple community settings.* Unpublished manuscript, University of California at Santa Barbara, 1981.

Fowler, S., & Baer, D. M. "Do I have to be good all day?": The timing of delayed reinforcement as a factor in generalization. *Journal of Applied Behavior Analysis,* 1981, *14*, 13–24.

Handleman, J. S., & Harris, S. L. Generalization from school to home with autistic children. *Journal of Autism and Developmental Disorders,* 1980, *10*, 323–333.

Klaila, D. *Parental satisfaction with clinic treatment and parent training in the treatment of autistic children.* Unpublished master's thesis, Claremont Graduate School, 1982.

Koegel, R. L., & Covert, A. The relationship of self-stimulation to learning in autistic children. *Journal of Applied Behavior Analysis,* 1972, *5,* 381–387.

Koegel, R. L., Glahn, T. J., & Nieminen, G. S. Generalization of parent training results. *Journal of Applied Behavior Analysis,* 1978, *11,* 95–109.

Koegel, R. L., & Schreibman, L. *How to teach autistic and other severely handicapped children.* Lawrence, Kans.: H & H Enterprises, 1982.

Koegel, R. L., Schreibman, L., Britten, K. R., Burke, J. C., & O'Neill, R. E. A comparison of parent training to direct child treatment. In R. L. Koegel, A. Rincover, & A. L. Egel (Eds.), *Educating and understanding autistic children.* San Diego: College-Hill Press, 1982.

Lovaas, O. I., Koegel, R. L., Simmons, J. Q., & Long, J. S. Some generalization and follow-up measures on autistic children in behavior therapy. *Journal of Applied Behavior Analysis,* 1973, *6,* 131–166.

Schreibman, L., Koegel, R. L., & Britten, K. R. Parent intervention of autistic children: A preliminary report. In L. A. Hamerlynck (Ed.), *Proceedings of the XIII Banff International Conference on Behavior Sciences,* in press.

Schreibman, L., Koegel, R. L., Mills, J. I., & Burke, J. C. Social validation of behavior therapy with autistic children. *Behavior Therapy,* 1981, *12,* 610–624.

Stokes, T. F., & Baer, D. M. An implicit technology of generalization. *Journal of Applied Behavior Analysis,* 1977, *10,* 349–368.

Tharp, R. G., & Wetzel, R. J. *Behavior modification in the natural environment.* New York: Academic Press, 1969.

Wolf, M. M., Risley, T., & Mees, H. Application of operant conditioning procedures to the behaviour problems of an autistic child. *Behaviour Research and Therapy,* 1964, *1,* 305–312.

CHANGING THE OBSERVATIONAL CODING STYLES OF INSULAR AND NONINSULAR MOTHERS
A Step toward Maintenance of Parent Training Effects

Robert G. Wahler
University of Tennessee

Jean E. Dumas
University of Ottawa

Treatment strategies evolve, in part, from the conceptual model of deviance employed by the persons in charge of treatment. This is certainly true of parent training. This intervention strategy is based on a theoretical model that assumes that the problem child cannot be considered as an entity apart from the social system in which he or she interacts (Wahler, 1976). According to this model, when parents decide that some aspect of their child's behavior is deviant, this deviance is not so much a unique characteristic of the child as it is one of the social system within which he or she functions. Parent training has been most widely used in the treatment of deviant child behaviors in which the influence of the wider social context is often rather obvious—namely, oppositional–aggressive problems. These represent the most common behaviors classified as deviant by parents (Patterson, 1964; Rutter, 1976). They involve rule breaking or noncompliance with parental requests, and may take the form of both assertive activities, such as fighting or arguing, and more passive actions, such as ignoring rules and instructions.

Parent training has been and still is very successful in the treatment of oppositional–aggressive child behavior (e.g., Forehand, Sturgis, Aguar, Beggs, Green, McMahon, & Wells, 1979; O'Dell, 1974; Patterson & Fleischman, 1979; Strain, Steele, Ellis, & Timm, 1981; Wahler, 1975), especially when one considers that little in the form of treatment for such behavior was available before its development. However, there is mounting evidence indicating that parent training as practiced today can by no means be considered *the* answer to the problems of oppositional–aggressive children and their families. Some studies reflect a complete absence of therapeutic effects when these are evaluated with the help of objective behavioral measures (Ferber, Keeley, & Shembert, 1974; Johnson & Christensen, 1975), or the failure of such effects to be maintained in a follow-up phase (Forehand & Atkeson, 1977; Patterson, 1974; Wahler & Moore, 1975); others indicate that success or the lack of it is closely related to the socioemotional makeup of the family (Dumas & Wahler, 1981; Reisinger, Frangia, & Hoffman, 1976; Wahler, 1980). We believe that the problem raised by these treatment failures lies partly in the way in which investigators conceptualize the parental behaviors they attempt to modify through parent training. While the social learning approach they share assumes that child deviance is the result of an inadequate performance of child management skills on the part of the parents (Patterson, 1977), and that the parents therefore need to learn to improve their performance (i.e., need parent training), the nature of the training offered will depend on how a particular investigator conceptualizes this parental deficit.

TWO CONCEPTUALIZATIONS OF PARENTAL DEFICIT IN CHILD MANAGEMENT

The first conceptualization we describe is the traditional approach to parent training. It assumes that parents have a fairly sound knowledge of a child's developmental milestones but lack the necessary skills to implement it. In other words, the problem reflects a *behavioral* deficit: Parents whose children are oppositional or aggressive are essentially inept at "handling" them (i.e., at using positive and negative consequences to control their behavior). The purpose of training is primarily to equip parents with a set of management skills and to insure that they use these properly (Patterson, 1977). This approach makes three fundamental assumptions about child behavior: (1) Deviant behaviors are learned and sustained by the social attention children obtain from adults and peers. (2) A shift in social contingencies such that a child's desirable behaviors obtain these reinforcers will be therapeutic. (3) Behavior change will be maintained by a process of positive reinforcement. Since adults and children will both exchange reinforcers through their newly acquired behaviors, they will continue such behaviors, thus ensuring follow-up success. The training methods that reflect these assumptions (such as differential attention, time out, or contracting) are closely modeled upon a laboratory experiment that defines the parent as the experimenter (the independent variable) and the child as the subject (the dependent variable). Their primary focus is on the consequences of parental behavior, the *parent effects* upon the child.

The treatment failures mentioned above, together with the growing literature on child and social influences upon parents (Bell & Harper, 1977; Gewirtz & Boyd, 1976; Wahler & Fox, 1981), lead us to put forward another conceptualization of parental deficit. It assumes that parents have both an adequate knowledge of a child's developmental milestones and the skills required to implement it, but repeatedly fail to track the influence that their children's behavior and the behavior of other social agents has upon their own actions. In this case, the problem reflects an *attentional* rather than a skills deficit: Parents of deviant children commonly fail to monitor accurately the many environmental events that repeatedly "set them up" to act toward the children in ways likely to maintain their deviance. There are two classes of events of interest here—the immediate discriminative stimuli provided by the children, and, further removed in time, the many stimulus–response contingencies that involve the parents in interaction with the children or with other members of the environment. We refer to the former class as "stimulus events" and to the latter as "setting events" (Bijou, 1976; Bijou & Baer, 1961; Kantor, 1959; Wahler & Fox, 1981). Examples of stimulus events include child behaviors such as complaints, temper tantrums, or noncompliance; examples of setting events include a parent's history of interaction with a child, the quality of the parent's marital relationship, or the pattern of daily community contacts that the parent experiences. This approach makes three assumptions about child behavior that differ from those of traditional parent training:

1. A child's behavior is determined by a network of subsystems that form the components of other, more complex systems. At a first level is the covarying system of behaviors within the child's repertoire of responses. At the next level is the interacting behavior patterns of the child's primary groups (e.g., family, school). At the third level, the primary-group subsystems serve as components of the community system.
2. At each level, component elements are interdependent in the way they function. This can account for the interdependency of behaviors within the child and his or her primary groups.
3. Each level is affected by the dynamics of levels above and/or below it. This can account for the interdependency of behaviors within the child's social environment.

The emphasis of this conceptualization on the many influences that affect the parent–child relationship places the focus here on the *antecedents* of parental behavior—the *child* and *adult effects* upon the parent. As these have been found to influence parental behavior directed at the child (see below), even when they do not directly involve the child, we suggest that they ought to be taken into account in parent training. We present this new approach not as an alternative to, but as an expansion of, traditional parent training. This expanded view considers the parental behavior patterns that maintain child deviance to be only part of the therapeutic puzzle. The other part consists of both the stimulus and setting events that maintain these undesirable parental patterns. It is thus truly interactional, in that it considers adult and child behaviors as both independent and dependent, predictor and predicted values. It is also truly social, in that it goes beyond the limits of the discriminative stimuli provided by the child and analyzes the indirect influences that the wider social context exercises, through the parents, upon the child.

The new conceptualization we propose and the ways in which it might affect the theory and practice of parent training are discussed in detail below. Specifically, we argue that the effects of setting events require expansion of the traditional reinforcement model of parent training, and that their study ought to lead to some significant methodological developments in the area of child behavior disorders.

MOTHERING: ITS STIMULUS AND SETTING EVENTS

We open the discussion by presenting the evidence in support of the importance of stimulus and setting events to the mother–child relationship. We have so far been talking about parents and parent training. We will from now on talk almost exclusively about mothers and mother training, since mothers bear much of the responsibility for child rearing and for child therapy when the socialization process fails.

Mothering: A Challenging Job Description

While it has often been claimed that, during their first years of life, children require the almost continual presence and care of their mothers if they are to develop normally (e.g., Brazelton, 1969, 1974; Miller, 1968; Spock, 1976), we have argued elsewhere (Wahler & Dumas, 1981) that it may in fact be unreasonable to expect a single adult to do an adequate job of child rearing. Consider the level of vigilance required of the mother of a preschool child. When taking care of her 2- to 3-year-old, she is likely to have to monitor the youngster on an almost continual basis. Both laboratory (Forehand, King, Peed, & Yoder, 1975; Minton, Kagan, & Levine, 1971) and home (Patterson, 1976; Wahl, Johnson, Johansson, & Martin, 1974) observations of social interchanges in *normal* mother–child dyads indicate that mothers are apt to respond to child-provided stimuli by commanding or disapproving once every 3 to 4 minutes. Furthermore, the probability is one in four that the child will fail to obey a parental command (Johnson, Wahl, Martin, & Johansson, 1973). If these figures truly indicate that a solo caretaker spends much of her day warding off or responding to aversive child stimuli, one may well wonder how a normal mother finds the time to teach her child any prosocial behaviors and fulfill her homemaking responsibilities. In fact, looking at mother–child interactions in this light, we are not surprised to read that, in peacetime, the normal family is the most aversive of all human institutions (Straus, Gelles, & Steinmetz, 1980), or to find that normal mothers are five times more aversive when they interact with their own children as opposed to other preschoolers (Halverson & Waldrop, 1970).

The challenge of mothering is highlighted by the fact that social agents in general, and parents in particular, tend to respond to aversive child behavior in an aversive or inconsistent manner and more often than they respond to positive behavior. Johnson and his associates (Johnson et al., 1973; Wahl et al., 1974) found not only that level of child deviance was best predicted by level of parental aversiveness, but also that the more deviant children got a higher level of parental attention (both positive and negative) than their better-behaved counterparts. There is a considerable amount of evidence in support of this dual parental response tendency. Work by Delfini, Bernal, and Rosen (1976), Johnson and Lobitz (1974), Lobitz and Johnson (1975), Patterson (1976), Snyder (1977), and Wahler, Hughey, and Gordon (1981) has shown that a causal relationship exists between parental aversiveness (measured in terms of commands) and problematic child behavior; families of oppositional–aggressive children engage in aversive interactions that are more frequent, are more intense, and last longer, and in prosocial interactions that are less frequent, than those of families with nonproblem children. Comparable evidence can be found in studies that relied on indirect measures of parental aversiveness, such as parental perception of the child (Forehand et al., 1975; Green, Forehand, & McMahon, 1979; Lobitz & Johnson, 1975; Love & Kaswan, 1974; Patterson & Fleischman, 1979) or patterns of family communication (Alexander, 1973; Conger, 1976; Leighton, Stollak, & Ferguson, 1971; Love & Kaswan, 1974).

This picture is confirmed by the literature on parental inconsistency, whether one considers "intraagent inconsistency" (the extent to which the same person reacts differently over repetition of the same behaviors) or "interagent inconsistency" (the extent to which two or more persons react differently to the same behaviors). Observations of parent–child interaction in normal and deviant families have repeatedly shown that parents of aggressive children are more likely to reinforce deviant and punish prosocial behavior (Herbert & Baer, 1972; Lobitz & Johnson, 1975; Patterson, 1976; Snyder, 1977; Wahler et al., 1981); to show greater discrepancy between the verbal and nonverbal contents of their messages to the children (Bugental, Love, Kaswan, & April, 1971; Love & Kaswan, 1974); and/or to react in conflicting fashion to the same oppositional child actions (Love & Kaswan, 1974; Patterson, 1977). The importance of consistency in child management is also stressed by laboratory studies of the effects of different schedules of reinforcement and punishment on child behavior. These indicate that both types of inconsistency, when compared to consistent responding, lead to significantly more aggressive responses in young boys and increase the resistance of such responses to change under conditions of extinction and/or continuous, contingent punishment (Deur & Parke, 1970; Katz, 1971; Parke & Deur, 1972; Sawin & Parke, 1979).

Assuming that the tendency to respond to oppositional-aggressive child behavior with both increased aversiveness and inconsistency applies to most normal families, many of these families can be expected to drift into a habitual mode of coercive interchanges. As described by Patterson and Reid (1970) and Patterson (1976), "coercion" is a process in which one member of a dyad terminates the aversive behavior of the other by forcing a change. In turn, the coerced member changes his or her behavior to terminate the coercing behavior of the other. Both parties are thus negatively reinforced by the termination of behaviors they consider aversive, and are therefore more likely to act in a similar manner in other aversive interchanges. It follows that if maternal command or disapproval on the one hand and maternal ignoring of positive behavior on the other are aversive to the child, he or she can be expected to act aversively. Should this lead to a desired change in maternal behavior (e.g., the mother drops the command or gives increased attention), the child is likely to perform similar actions in comparable situations and, generally, to increase his or her use of coercive tactics. If this process is repeated often enough, the mother-child dyad will become engaged in aversive interactions that are more frequent and intense and last longer, and in prosocial interactions that are less frequent, than those of noncoercive dyads. We believe that such a coercive process is partly responsible for the development and maintenance of the oppositional-aggressive behaviors commonly seen by family therapists.

Mothering: The Importance of Setting Events

Our discussion until now has focused exclusively on the immediate discriminative stimuli provided to the mother by the child. We have noted that, with young children at least, many of these stimuli are aversive, and that should the mother respond to them aversively and/or by paying more attention to these stimuli than to prosocial behavior, a coercion process is likely to be initiated. However, because of our narrow focus on the immediate mother-child relationship, this bleak picture is overstated for most cases. Besides the stimulus events provided by her child, the caretaking mother obviously experiences several sources of social input, both from the child and from other social agents such as her spouse, relatives, and friends. Although the importance of these other sources of input is commonly acknowledged, little effort has been made to study the mother–child relationship in a truly social context or "setting." Attempts to evaluate the moderating influences that both child characteristics and social inputs have on this relationship have in fact only begun. The limited evidence available would seem to indicate that, while mothering is at the best of times a challenging task, it can be made easier or more difficult, depending upon the reinforcing functions served by the child and by the adults present in the mother's social system (Bates, 1980; Caplan, 1976; Cochran & Brassard, 1979). Specifically, the literature indicates that mothers who fail in their child-rearing task do receive more aversive and fewer positive social inputs than mothers who succeed do. The circumstances that make such input differences likely generally include one or more of the following: (1) The child is "difficult" to handle. (2) The nuclear family setting is a consistent source of aversive interchanges for the mother; her spouse or other children engage her repeatedly in coercive bouts, thus reducing the amount of positive inputs available to her. (3) The community setting is a consistent source of aversive interchanges for the mother; her relatives, neighbors, or helping agents also engage her repeatedly in coercive bouts, thus again reducing the amount of positive inputs available to her. We now consider the empirical evidence for a cumulative and deleterious effect of these circumstances.

Setting Events: The Child

The developing child is not without influence upon the environment. The initial arrival and, later, the mere presence of young children have been found to affect certain dimensions of parental behavior known to influence the mother–child relationship, such as maternal depression (Brown & Harris, 1978; Yalom, 1968) and marital disharmony (Lerner & Spanier, 1978; Russell, 1974). In addition, the newborn child rapidly learns to use crying and smiling as means of social control. While these responses are used by most infants, there are considerable individual differences among them (Brazelton, 1973; Carey, 1970), which directly affect their social environment. These differences appear to distinguish between infants and young children on a major dimension of "difficulty," involving irregularity, irritability, reactivity, and emotional lability (Bates, Freeland, & Lounsbury, 1979; Lamb, 1978a; Thomas, Chess, & Birch, 1968). For example, Frodi, Lamb, Leavitt, Donovan, Neff, and Sherry (1978) reported both self-report and psychophysiological data supporting the common-sense notion that a crying infant acts as an arousing and aversive stimulus. While such a stimulus generally increases the likelihood that an aggressive response will follow, in most cases the arousal remains limited, and the aversive situation is terminated by relieving the cause of the infant's discomfort. However, the situation is more complicated when one is dealing with a "difficult" infant, as these infants cry for longer periods and seem often inconsolable, despite their caretakers' repeated efforts (Thomas, Chess, & Birch, 1970). As a result and through a process of conditioning, the child may become an aversive stimulus whether it is crying or not (Lamb, 1978b); this in turn leads its mother to become less responsive and consistent in her caretaking behavior (Donovan, Leavitt, & Balling, 1978; Milliones, 1978; Sameroff, 1977). In this respect, one is not surprised to find that premature infants may run an increased risk of being negatively perceived by their parents, as their appearance is less attractive and their cry more aversive than that of full-term babies (Frodi et al., 1978), or that aversive patterns of infant activity are likely to elicit maternal anger during the first year of life (Butterfield, van Doornick, Dawson, & Alexander, 1979).

Setting Events: The Family

There is considerable evidence not only that separation and divorce are more common in referred than in nonreferred families, especially in the low socio-economic groups (Love & Kaswan, 1974), but also that intact families who seek help for child behavior problems commonly present high levels of marital discord. Specifically, there is a consistent negative relationship between measures of reported marital satisfaction (Johnson & Lobitz, 1974; Oltmanns, Broderick, & O'Leary, 1977) or measures of open marital conflict (Porter & O'Leary, 1980; Rutter, Yule, Quinton, Rowlands, Yule, & Berger, 1974) and observed child deviance, especially in boys. The role played by open conflict is emphasized in studies that observed couples (with or without children present) in laboratory situations which required interpersonal negotiations and/ or which were likely to lead to some degree of discord (Gottman, 1979; Leighton et al., 1971; Love & Kaswan, 1974; Weiss, 1978). These studies indicate that, compared to nondistressed couples, distressed dyads not only experience greater difficulties at communicating in a manner conducive to problem solving and perceive each other in a more negative light; they also engage in aversive interchanges at a higher rate and in positive ones at a lower rate, and they tend to reciprocate aversive behaviors more often. These characteristics of the distressed marital dyad are obviously strikingly similar to those of the coercive mother–child dyad described above.

Setting Events: The Community

While the existence of a relationship between a family's standing on socio-economic descriptors such as income, occupation, or education and child behavioral deviance has been known for a long time (Dumas, 1983), recent epidemiological studies have reported a relationship between a mother's pattern of social contacts and such deviance (Kellam, Ensminger, & Turner, 1977; Kolvin, Garside, Nicol, MacMillan, Wolstenholme, & Leitch, 1977; Lagerkvist, Lauritzen, Olin, & Tengvald, 1975). For our purposes, this second association is of greater importance than the first one, because it bears directly upon a mother's dynamic involvement with persons outside her nuclear family. This association has also been found in clinical samples. Much of the work in this area has been conducted by Wahler and his colleagues (e.g., Wahler, 1980; Wahler, Leske, & Rogers, 1979; Wahler et al., 1981). This work relies upon the concept of "insularity" (Wahler et al., 1979). "Insularity" may be defined as a specific pattern of social contacts within the community that is characterized by a high level of negatively perceived coercive interchanges with relatives and/or helping agency representatives and by a low level of positively perceived supportive interchanges with friends. Differences in maternal patterns of social contacts are associated with differences in deviant child behavior. Wahler et al. (1981) found that, while insular and noninsular mothers evidenced comparable rates of child opposition and maternal aversive and positive consequences when observed in their home environments, these coercive episodes lasted much longer for the insular dyads; moreover, the insular mothers were more likely to respond inconsistently (i.e., both negatively and positively) during these episodes. That these results reflect the existence of a covarying relationship between maternal community contacts and mother–child interactions at home, rather than the effect of a third, undetermined factor on both variables, is suggested by Wahler (1980). This study correlated, day by day, maternal self-reports of community contacts and observed aversive interactions between mothers and their children. On days marked by high proportions of maternal contacts with relatives and helping agents (high-coercion days), mothers were significantly more aversive with their children than on days in which their principal community contacts involved friends (low-coercion days). Thus, as is the case with distressed marital relationships, coercive community exchanges appear to impede a mother's ability to relate to her child in a noncoercive way. In other words, it impedes effective parenting.

To recognize that mothers can be helped or hindered in their child-rearing responsibilities by events other than the immediate discriminative stimuli provided by the children is to acknowledge the importance of setting events. Although the findings just reviewed are mostly correlational in nature and thus say little about the direction of effects, their logic would lead us to suspect that such events may play a causal role in a parent's ability to provide effective caretaking. The issue centers, we believe, on the proportion of aversive to positive social inputs received by the mother: Should she become party to a large number of aversive social inputs in proportion to a small number of positive inputs, she can be expected to become unable to manage her child(ren) in a prosocial and effective manner, and her child(ren) can be expected to learn to behave in oppositional–aggressive ways. In this perspective, marital disharmony and aversive social interactions, which we see as forms of interpersonal and social coercion, run hand in hand with mother–child coercion to produce an aversive environmental context for any mother and a deviance-facilitating context for any child.

MULTIPLE COERCION:
THE STUMBLING BLOCK
OF PARENT TRAINING

If it is true that the continual presence of several sources of aversive stimulation —which we refer to as "multiple coercion"—generally impede effective parenting, we would predict that multiply coerced mothers would fare poorly in most if not all parent training programs designed to teach effective parenting. More specifically, we would predict that such mothers may be able to improve their parenting skills in the course of therapy, but would in all likelihood be unable to maintain these treatment gains following intervention. While follow-up studies of parent training programs are rare, the evidence available to date would seem to support the contention that multiply coerced mothers fail to benefit as much from parent training as their less coerced counterparts do. In the first comprehensive follow-up investigation of a behavioral treatment program for families of oppositional–aggressive children, Patterson (1974) noted that his results [fitted] our general impression that the most difficult case to treat was the welfare mother living alone with her children who perceived herself unable to cope with the myriad of crises impinging upon her" (p. 479). The importance of aversive inputs at the interpersonal or social level for the mother has been reported in several other studies as well. Although long-term maintenance of treatment gains, as measured by both behavioral observations and parental reports (Forehand et al., 1979) or by parental reports alone (Johnson & Christensen, 1975), has been reported, Forehand et al. (1979) noted that in these two studies subjects were typically from two-parent families and of relatively favorable socioeconomic status, which was not the case in Patterson's (1974) sample. A similar statement can be made about other studies that have reported positive results (e.g., Alexander & Parsons, 1973; Christophersen, 1976; Martin, 1977).

Considering marital discord or single parenthood first, there are both descriptive and experimental data indicating that interpersonal conflict frequently undermines parent training (Kent & O'Leary, 1976; Patterson, Cobb, & Ray, 1973; Reisinger et al., 1976; Strain et al., 1981). For example, Reisinger et al. reported that mothers who experienced no marital difficulties, in contrast to mothers who did, were better able to attend to their children's desirable behavior (through the use of differential reinforcement) in the home setting following clinic intervention. Their counterparts demonstrated less generalization and found it necessary to seek further clinical help to alter their children's behavior. It should be noted that contrary results have been reported by Oltmanns et al. (1977); their significance is unclear, however, as the authors only used parental reports of child behavior change as their outcome measure. Their results might have differed had they also used a behavioral measure of outcome.

Turning to wider social influences, there is evidence that both socioeconomic and social-interactional variables can affect parent training outcome.

Wahler and his colleagues (Wahler, 1980; Wahler et al., 1979; Wahler & Moore, 1975) found nonmaintenance of treatment gains associated with "high-risk" families (i.e., families suffering from insularity, poverty, and lack of education, and living in high-crime neighborhoods). In a recent extension of this work, we (Dumas & Wahler, 1981) followed up for 1 year 49 mothers who had received training for oppositional child behavior. Comparison of these mothers on two background variables—an index of socioeconomic disadvantage (reflecting family income, maternal education, family composition, family size, source of referral, and area of residence) and insularity—indicated that both factors were significant predictors of parent training outcome. In terms of probabilities, noninsular mothers experiencing little or no disadvantage could be almost assured of long-term success, while their insular counterparts suffering from high levels of disadvantage were almost certain of failure; noninsular mothers scoring high on the index of socioeconomic disadvantage or insular mothers scoring low on it, for their part, only had approximately one chance in two of long-term success.

The limited amount of evidence available thus appears to support the contention that multiply coerced mothers tend to fare poorly in parent training programs. If our coercion view is correct, it seems reasonable to expect that people living under constant duress would find it difficult to deal constructively with any one aspect of this duress. That is, how could a multiply coerced mother be expected to arrange and maintain new (i.e., noncoercive) social contingencies for her oppositional child in the context of a generally coercive environment? While this expectation may be reasonable, it does not, however, explain why multiply coerced mothers should fare poorly in parent training. The explanation for this antitherapeutic expectation lies, we believe, in the fact that *multiple coercion has both behavioral and attentional consequences for the mother*. The behavioral consequences center on the dual increase in parental aversiveness and inconsistency already discussed, while the attentional consequences result from the fact that troubled mothers commonly fail to monitor accurately the many environmental events that repeatedly set them up to act toward their children in ways likely to maintain their deviance. Since it is the mother who must deal selectively with key aspects of her child's problematic and desirable behaviors, she must be able to attend carefully to what the child does and does not do. It then stands to reason that her continued success in using newly acquired parenting skills will depend on her continued attention to the details of her relationship with the child. This argument, which forms the basis for the hypothesis of attentional deficit that we propose, was experimentally supported by Wahler and Afton (1980). These authors monitored maternal verbal descriptions of their coercive interchanges with their children before and during parent training. Mothers whose incomes were below the poverty level and who were multiply coerced were compared with middle-income mothers whose coercion problems were restricted to their children. All mothers were encouraged to describe their day-to-day coercive interchanges with their targeted problem children. These summary reports were videotaped and coded by professional observers into two categories reflecting the following qualities of each report: global versus specific, and presence versus absence of blame orientation. Assignment of blame to the child and diffuse information quality were both considered signs of attentional deficit, first, because coercion is always a two-way exchange, and therefore assigning blame to only one party is an inaccurate reflection of the process; and, secondly, because one's capability to alter a coercive process depends on specific information about it. Results showed that both groups of mothers were equally diffuse and blame-oriented when they provided their descriptions of child problems prior to parent training. During parent training, both groups demonstrated their ability to modify the coercive problems successfully. However, only the singularly coerced, middle-income mothers altered their observational reports during the parent training phase. Their multiply coerced counterparts, despite their proven ability to change child relationship problems, continued to describe these interactions in global, blame-oriented fashion. As might be expected, according to the results of Wahler (1980), these mothers gradually returned to coercive interchanges with their children during a follow-up phase. The singularly coerced mothers, however, maintained their therapeutic gains during this phase. The remainder of this chapter describes the hypothesis of attentional deficit just outlined.

STIMULUS PROPERTIES OF THE OPPOSITIONAL-AGGRESSIVE CHILD: PROBLEMS IN MATERNAL ATTENDING

It is generally agreed that parent training is designed to eliminate a coercive process that appears to sustain a deviant child's problem behavior and to replace it by a new social process best described by principles of positive reinforcement. As we outlined earlier, parent training in its traditional form assumes that such a therapeutic change ought to be maintained by a self-sustaining cycle of positive interchanges within the mother–child dyad: The mother is positively reinforced by her child's newly developed prosocial behavior, and the child is likewise reinforced by his or her mother's approval. Consider, however, the complexities involved in this supposedly self-sustaining cycle.

Problems in Maternal Attending

Helping a troubled mother to attain such a cycle can be usefully conceptualized as a task in stimulus class construction. The entrapped mother must come to *discriminate* certain key child behaviors and respond to them as at least three distinct classes. First, there are those mildly coercive actions, such as complaints and demands, that usually appear as the immediate precursors of the child's more aggressive attacks. These actions are important cues, because if the mother can learn to suppress their occurrences, the likelihood of more aggressive, difficult-to-manage child actions will be reduced. The second class, noncompliance, is distinct from the first, because the mother's instructional behavior is part of its defining properties. Maternal instructions must be defined as clear-cut child-directed commands before noncompliance can be considered as a stimulus class for later action by the mother. Finally, the third class is comprised of those child behaviors that are both noncoercive and judged adaptive for the child's successful functioning within the family and larger community. Once these three groupings of child behaviors become functional stimulus classes for the mother, it then becomes possible for her to respond differentially to their appearance. According to the usual parent training format, the first two classes will become discriminative for maternal use of a time-out or extinction contingency. The latter class would set the occasion for social or material reinforcement.

The difficulties inherent in such stimulus class construction become apparent when the kinds of stimuli controlling a troubled mother's behavior prior to parent training are examined. In this regard, consider a complex response often encountered in clinic referrals for mother–child relationship problems— namely, maternal self-reports of depression. These reports are usually based on paper-and-pencil instruments, such as the Minnesota Multiphasic Personality Inventory (MMPI) or the Beck Depression Inventory (BDI; Beck, 1967). Taken together, studies that have measured maternal depression in normal and clinic samples indicate that depression (1) is more common among clinic than nonclinic mothers; (2) correlates positively with maternal ratings of child deviance and negative perception of the child; and (3) predicts parent training failure. Thus, for example, in a comparison of normal and clinic-referred mothers, Patterson (1976) found that the latter were far more likely to endorse MMPI items that described them as lonely, worthless, or unmotivated, as well as other descriptors summed under the rubric "depression." Comparable findings, based on the BDI, have been reported by Forehand and his associates (Forehand, Wells, & Griest, 1980; Griest, Forehand, Wells, & McMahon, 1980; Griest, Wells, & Forehand, 1979; Rickard, Forehand, Wells, Griest, & McMahon, 1980). This work further shows that, besides discriminating between clinic and nonclinic mothers, depression also appears to predict maternal perceptions of their children. Griest et al. (1979) found the BDI to be a significantly better predictor of maternal evaluations of child behaviors in a clinic population than were the actual child behaviors on which these evaluations were supposedly based. In fact, neither measures of child compliance and noncompliance nor measures of total deviant behavior (e.g., whines, yells, tantrums) were significantly correlated with maternal perceptions of the child. Griest et al. (1980) further demonstrated that the BDI scores did not covary with the evaluations of mothers who were managing their children adequately. Finally, Ricard et al.

(1980) confirmed these results in a comparison of three groups of mother–child dyads: one in which mothers reported no problems, one in which mothers reported problems confirmed by direct observation, and one in which mothers reported problems that were not apparent on direct observation. As predicted, the BDI index placed this third group of mothers apart from the other two. Since, behaviorally, children in this group were not different from their counterparts in the normal group, depression appeared to be the only predictor of these mothers' evaluations of their children.

While these studies do not shed light on the specific nature of pretraining stimulus classes for mothers of deviant children, they clearly support the contention that changes in the stimulus function of their children's behavior are a necessary part of parent training. In keeping with the Wahler and Afton (1980) study described above, Forehand et al. (1980) reported a reduction in depression among mothers who completed a program designed to increase child management skills; this reduction was accompanied by improvements in child behavior, parenting skills, and maternal perceptions of the children. Comparable findings can be found in Patterson and Fleischman (1979).

The importance of maternal attending is further supported by several clinical examples attesting to the fact that pretraining stimulus classes for troubled mothers are quite different from those three classes we outlined above as functional for parent training. Most mothers are apt to describe their children's problems in abstract fashion and/or as the "end products" of coercive interchanges. Thus, a child may be described as "impossible," "destructive," "never completing work," "demanding," "a stealer," "having temper outbursts," and "having a bad attitude." Without prompting by the clinician, it is unlikely that one would know about child-produced stimuli comprising a workable set of cues for parent training. In an attempt to illustrate this phenomenon, we recently helped initiate an empirical assessment of child-produced stimulus classes for troubled mothers. In this project, 15-minute videotape recordings are made of mother–child home interactions once a week. The mothers are then asked to observe these tapes, with the intent of detecting instances of problematic child behavior (as defined by the mother). When the mother detects problem behavior, she is to press a button and hold it down as long as the problem continues. (Button presses activate an event recorder.) This procedure continues for the entire videotape. Thus far in the project, six troubled mothers have completed such coding with two of their own home videotapes. In all six cases, the mother coding occurred during a pretraining phase. The 12 videotapes were also coded by a professional observer who followed the Wahler, House, and Stambaugh (1976) definitions of problematic child behavior. These definitions essentially required the observer to discriminate the following child behaviors as a single class: noncompliance with mother instructions; violation of mother-imposed rules; complaints and demands; physical complaints such as hitting, kicking, and throwing objects at people. On three occasions, a second professional observer also coded tapes as a reliability check on the first observer.

As Table 15-1 shows, the six mothers separated themselves into three who consistently coded their two tapes into a relatively small number of short units of problematic child behavior and three who proved to be high-rate, long-duration coders. Of greatest interest, however, are the percentages of agreement between the mothers and the professional observer. It is clear from this table that neither set of mothers was responding to the same class of problematic child stimuli as was the professional observer. While the high-rate mothers were in better agreement with the professional, it is obvious that most of their button-pressing responses were cued by videotape stimuli having little to do with aggressive or oppositional child actions—the presenting problems for all six mothers.

It is likely that all six of these mothers were in fact basing their button-pressing responses on child behavior as portrayed on the videotapes. During all tape viewings, a staff member observed both the tapes and the mothers; occasionally, when a mother was observed to press the button during occurrences of apparently innocuous child behavior, the staff member would stop the tape and ask the mother what cued her button pressing. Typically the mothers would cite the previously viewed child action, but then would *elaborate* on that action, as in the following examples:

1. "He was walking over to there. It's just like when last week I had to tan his hide for breaking the window."
2. "I think he was planning to go into that room. He's always wanting to go outside when the ice cream truck comes."
3. "She asked me for something to eat. When that happens, she usually wants me to treat her like a baby. She'll start to whine."

Table 15-1

A Summary of Mothers' and Professional Observers' Coding of Videotapes Depicting Mother–Child Home Interactions

Coder(s)	Mean number of problem units	Mean duration per unit (sec)	Mean unit agreement	Mean tape agreement
Low-rate mothers (3)[a]	2.1	1.9		
			.07	.18
Professional observer	14.0	9.0		
High-rate mothers (3)[a]	17.8	15.9		
			.33	.43
Professional observer	8.2	6.2		
Professional observer versus professional observer			.90	

[a]Since the six mothers produced a clearly bimodal distribution of unit scores, they were separated into three low-rate coders and three high-rate coders.

If this laboratory demonstration accurately reflects troubled mothers' attention to their problem children's behavior, one must conclude that their observational coding style is unique. A good many of their button-pressing responses were cued by child actions that other people would consider innocuous (e.g., asking for something to eat). Thus, the mothers do not necessarily view their children's aggressive–oppositional actions as a stimulus class distinct from the youngsters' other behaviors. Small wonder, then, that their inconsistent consequating, as seen in the previously discussed home observational studies (e.g., Patterson, 1976), is such a prominent feature of their child care behavior. Now, the question of interest with regard to parent training concerns the stability of these haphazard coding styles. It is clear from the parent training literature that mothers can be taught to code their children's problematic and desirable behaviors into the three stimulus classes outlined earlier. But not much is known about stimulus determinants of these pretraining maternal coding styles. Is it not possible that such maladaptive observational procedures will continue to govern a mother's child interchanges in nontraining situations or once training is completed? If so, the likelihood of treatment maintenance and generalization would be slim. As we have argued repeatedly in this chapter, the training failures already reported in the literature might well be due to problems with maternal attention. We turn now to speculations concerning the development of these problems.

Stimulus Control in Haphazard Attending

The coercion hypothesis described above (Patterson, 1976; Patterson & Reid, 1970) provides a reasonable explanation for the stability of problematic child behavior. This hypothesis is based on numerous sequential analyses of observed interchanges between troubled mothers and their aggressive–oppositional children, as well as for nontroubled mother–child dyads. Based on these findings, it would appear that problematic child behaviors are powerfully influenced by their stimulus–response antecedents. That is, the more obvious problem actions, such as temper outbursts, have been found to be preceded by predictable sequences of less obviously deviant mother–child interchanges. Once a mother–child exchange of aversives (e.g., child whine–mother command) begins, the *duration* of these coercive episodes is predictive of more seriously aggressive actions by both parties: The longer the episode, the more intense the terminal coercive action. Perhaps the most interesting facet of these findings concerns durational differences between deviant and normal mother–child dyads. In the latter dyads, coercive episodes are significantly shorter than the same episodes with troubled dyads are. For some reason, the nontroubled mothers are able to stop their children's aversive actions before the more intense coercive exchanges can materialize. In a functional sense, the troubled mothers' aversive behaviors seem to operate as discriminative and/or reinforcing stimuli for child aggression, while the same aversives delivered by nontroubled mothers served a punishing function. It is probable that these differing episodes are determined by their stimulus consequences: positive and/or negative reinforcement contingencies. However, causal factors in such coercive episodes have yet to be demonstrated.

Because of this, we suspect a more complex explanation, centering on a stimulus control phenomenon described as "superstition" (Skinner, 1953). In this type of stimulus control, an individual's behavior is governed by antecedent stimuli that are in fact only randomly discriminative for reinforcement. As shown repeatedly in animal studies, producing the phenomenon requires two operational steps: First, the chosen response is brought under discriminative stimulus control through application of contingent reinforcement. Once the response is under stable stimulus control, its reinforcement contingencies are shifted to an intermittent schedule that is gradually changed to a random presentation of reinforcers. If the schedule shifting is gradual enough, the animal will continue to respond to the "discriminative" stimulus as if it were still discriminative. This sort of adventitious environmental control is in fact quite stable (Morse & Skinner, 1957; Herrnstein, 1966).

In recent years, evidence has been presented to document occurrences of superstitious stimulus control in children. One of the first such studies by Koegel and Rincover (1977) was also a nice demonstration of across-setting generalization. These authors began their demonstration by establishing modeling stimuli as discriminative for imitative behavior in autistic children. This was accomplished by making food and social praise contingent upon the children's appropriate imitative responses. Then the schedule of these reinforcers was shifted to thinly intermittent deliveries. As a final step, the children were seen in a different environmental setting, and modeling stimuli were once again produced for them. However, the children's actions following the presentations of these stimuli were only randomly reinforced. Despite such adventitious consequences, the children demonstrated appropriate and dependable imitation. Fowler and Baer (1981) continued this line of stimulus control inquiry through their experimental analyses of superstition in normal preschoolers. As in Koegel and Rincover (1977), across-setting generalization was also involved. The children's sharing with one another was selected as the target behavior of interest. This response was brought under instructional control in a morning free-play setting of the preschool by use of a point system of reinforcement for observed increases in the children's sharing. Observers also monitored the same children's sharing in an afternoon free-play setting of the preschool. Results showed that the children shared more in the morning setting but did not change their rate of sharing in the afternoon setting. Then the authors delayed the point-reinforcement deliveries to the end of each preschool day—still making points contingent on sharing in the morning setting only. In effect, this operation now placed afternoon sharing under adventitious or chance-point consequences. Results were as expected from the superstition model: The children increased their sharing in the afternoon setting; the morning instructional stimuli became discriminative for sharing in both settings, even though the behavior in the afternoon setting was randomly reinforced. The superstitious instructional control proved stable, and experimental manipulations proved the delay factor to be causal in producing the phenomenon.

We believe that the above demonstrations illustrate principles by which individuals can become responsive to "faulty" stimulus classes. For example, in the above studies, children became responsive to classes of modeling or instructional stimuli in which some of the stimuli *were not* discriminative for reinforced responding. That is, while some of the stimuli (referring to imitation or sharing in a designated setting) were actually discriminative for reinforcement, other stimulus properties of the classes had no observable reinforcement functions. Yet the children behaved as if each class as a whole was discriminative for reinforced responding—certainly a good example of "faulty" stimulus control.

Consider now some of the previously cited data on troubled mothers' observational reports of problematic child behavior. With some of these mothers, their problem children's behaviors seem to function as components of a larger stimulus class comprised of other unknown stimuli. Thus, Griest *et al.* (1979) found that troubled mothers' observational reports about their children were best predicted by the mothers' scores on a depression inventory. Rickard *et al.* (1980) extended this line of inquiry to mothers who reported their children as having behavior problems, despite the fact that direct observations by a professional observer found no evidence of such problems. These mothers were also found to report a larger number of depressive experiences, compared to mothers with confirmed child behavior problems. Once again, it would appear that these "depressed" mothers were responsive to stimulus classes that included their children's behavior *as well as* a good many other *irrelevant* events—our definition of faulty stimulus control.

The findings above suggest that troubled mothers are likely to become influenced by superstitious stimulus contingencies. The process by which this might happen is alluded to in several observational studies of troubled and nontroubled mother–child dyads. In the course of becoming involved in a coercive episode, a troubled mother and her problem child will primarily exchange aversive behaviors, although occasionally they will exchange positive–aversive combinations as well (Taplin & Reid, 1977). Of greatest interest in this respect are findings that compared troubled and normal dyads. Patterson (1976) reported that troubled mothers were more likely than normals were to respond aversively to their children's positive behaviors, as well as more likely to respond positively to their children's aversive behaviors. A similar finding was reported by Sallows (1973). This pattern of greater inconsistency for the troubled dyads indicates that conditions prerequisite to the development of superstitious stimulus control are most likely to be found in the troubled dyads. One may recall from the findings of Koegel and Rincover (1977) and Fowler and Baer (1981) that superstitious control is established by shifting a contingent reinforcement schedule to noncontingent presentations of these same reinforcers. In this process, the discriminative stimuli may retain their discriminative function for the individual's responding, even though these responses are only randomly consequated. In the case of troubled mothers, the question of interest concerns stimulus control of their child-directed aversive behaviors and their subsequent observational reports about the children. Presumably, both of these maternal responses can come under superstitious stimulus control. The haphazard or inconsistent aversive responding by mothers observed by Patterson (1976) and Sallows (1973) suggests that these mothers were responding to negative and positive child behaviors as if both were discriminative for maternal aversive behaviors. If, in fact, it is true that troubled mothers may react to positive child behaviors as if they were negative, the previously reviewed findings concerning erroneous maternal observational reports make sense (Griest *et al.*, 1979).

The breadth of stimulus classes involved in a troubled mother's superstitious behavior is probably even greater than that depicted above. Thus far, our speculations have been confined to mothers whose coercion problems are restricted to interchanges with their children. It is not uncommon to find troubled mothers who are multiply entrapped with kinfolk, spouses, boyfriends, and helping agents, as well as their children. Imagine, then, the impact of such diverse and sometimes simultaneous aversive approaches to such a mother by adults and children. One would expect maternal inconsistencies greater than those outlined in the observational studies limited to mother–child dyads. More importantly, it is also conceivable that the mother's child-directed aversive behavior might come under the stimulus control of all people who engage her in coercive episodes. In other words, the stimulus class relevant to her child-directed aversive behavior could be represented by significant adults as well as by her troubled child. Thus, if the mother has an aversive interchange with her husband, the event may function as a stimulus component of the class supposedly represented by her child. Therefore, when such an interchange occurs, she may be more likely to react aversively to her child and to judge the child as deviant. This sort of superstitious relationship between environmental components was described in Wahler's (1980) correlational study of multiply coerced mothers. On days in which these mothers had aversive encounters with kinfolk and helping agents, they were more likely to experience coercive interchanges with their oppositional children. This finding would suggest that the mothers' reactions to their problem children were at least partly determined by the episodes with kinfolk and helping agents. These episodes may have functioned "superstitiously" as setting events for the mothers' coercive encounters with their children.

If the above speculations have some basis in fact, one could generate a predictive dimension by which to judge the effectiveness of parent training: The broader the stimulus class governing a mother's child-directed aversive behavior, the more chronic the child behavior problem. In our opinion, stimulus class breadth for a troubled mother can be assessed by evaluating her observational accuracy in categorizing her troubled child's problem behavior. This argument presumes that the parent trainer's research-documented classes of oppositional child behavior are indeed the appropriate targets of intervention. Our entire argument is based upon this assumption. Thus, the greater the extent to which a mother codes her child's problem behavior differently from the parent trainer, and the more stable this style, the more difficult will be the task of parent training. While this hypothesis remains untested, there are data from our own research group pointing to multiple coercion as a predictive factor in parent training outcomes. We (Dumas & Wahler, 1981) discovered that troubled mothers who reported the majority of their extrafamily contacts as aversive or nonfriendly in nature did not fare well in parent training. We do not yet know how these mothers code their children's problem behaviors, but we would expect that their coding styles differ from our own and also from the coding styles of mothers who do well in parent training. The findings of Wahler and Afton (1980) suggest that mother–parent trainer coding style differences may be more stable for the multiply coerced mothers.

In Table 15-2, we present a schematic outline of a superstitiously constructed stimulus class controlling one mother's coercive entrapment with her problem child. As the table shows, this mother is apt to respond aversively to her oppositional child under very broad stimulus conditions. She behaves as if aversive reactions are "called for" whenever her child hits, cries, or pouts. When the opportunity arises, she will do likewise when her problem child approaches her, when her boyfriend argues with her, when her mother criticizes her, when her welfare worker threatens her, or when her aunt is sarcastic in a conversation with her. If her aversive reactions to her child are controlled by this stimulus class, then a child deviance report ought to be expected from her—regardless of the child's behavior. This multiply coerced mother is unlikely to profit from parent training. Even if her child were to reduce pouting, hitting, and crying, this mother would continue to act as if these stimuli were present. She may perform well under the instructional fabric of parent training, but she cannot continue this adaptive performance when the training conditions have ended. As long as her boyfriend argues with her, her mother criticizes her, her child approaches her, her welfare worker threatens her, and her aunt acts sarcastically, this mother is apt to react aversively to her child and to judge him or her as deviant. We believe that the Table 15-2 schema is a realistic portrayal of the problem presented to clinicians who choose to work with these families. We think that the same superstition process operates with mothers who are coerced primarily by their children. However, the stimulus class affecting these mothers is surely more narrow and therefore more likely to be modified by parent training.

Table 15-2

A Schematic Illustration of Superstitious Stimulus Control in the Development of Coercive Mother–Child Relationships

Other people as stimuli	Maternal aversive behavior directed to child	Stimulus consequence	Mother summary report
Child hits (S1)	R	Reinforcement	
Child approaches (S2)	R	Random	
Child cries (S3)	R	Reinforcement	"My child
Child pouts (S4)	R	Reinforcement	is a
Boyfriend argues (S5)	R	Random	difficult
Mother criticizes (S6)	R	Random	problem."
Welfare worker threatens (S7)	R	Random	
Aunt is sarcastic (S8)	R	Random	

Note. This multiply coerced mother's child-directed aversive behavior (R) is depicted as controlled via a faulty stimulus class comprised of discriminative and nondiscriminative events. An important outcome of this process is the mother's erroneous summary report concerning her child's behavior.

THE MAND REVIEW PROCESS: A SUPPLEMENT TO PARENT TRAINING

Our superstition model of mother–child entrapment centers on stimulus class control of two maternal behaviors: the mother's aversive behavior directed toward her oppositional child (this behavior appears to maintain her child's aggressive and oppositional actions), and her summary report supposedly describing her child's undesirable actions. As we have argued, both of these maternal behaviors appear determined by a superstitiously constructed stimulus class; this class is partly comprised of problematic child behavior and partly comprised of stimuli having very little to do with this behavior. In mothers whose coercive entrapment is restricted to their children, we believe that the controlling maternal stimulus class is relatively narrow in breadth and restricted to child-produced stimuli. However, in multiply entrapped (e.g., insular) mothers, we think that the class is apt to be broad in scope and made up of adult-produced stimuli as well as those produced by the oppositional children.

There is little doubt in our minds that parent training is an efficient means of changing a troubled mother's aversive reactions to her oppositional child. We would go so far as to present parent training as *the* treatment of choice. In the case of mothers whose coercive entrapment is restricted to their oppositional children, we know that their summary reports about their children are modified by parent training. However, it is unlikely that these reports will change following parent training with multiply entrapped mothers (Wahler & Afton,

1980). These mothers, despite their success experiences in parent training, are still apt to code their children's behaviors negatively. If so, these latter mothers cannot be expected to perform well in all phases of parent training. The question of interest, then, centers on a means of changing these broad and inaccurate summary reports—a means of attenuating superstitious stimulus control of the reports and thereby increasing their discriminative power. If in fact these erroneous reports are controlled partly by stimulus events having little to do with problematic child behavior, what would happen if the mother were taught to discriminate the full range of child and adult stimuli that control her behavior? In essence, she would have to specify correctly the full range of child and adult behaviors correlated with her child deviance report. Were this to be accomplished, one would expect the child deviance report to become a "people" deviance report and her summary report to become an accurate representation of *all* coercive interchanges in her day-to-day life. We also believe that an increase in the accuracy of the summary report would be associated with more accurate attentional tracking by the mother. As an end product, she ought to profit more from the educational experience of parent training.

In Figure 15-1, we offer a summary report network associated with the mother described earlier in Table 15-2. This multiply coerced mother summarizes her entrapment in global terms reflecting the coercive process and her position in that entrapment ("I am a dishrag"). However, when she is asked to be specific in describing this entrapment, she points only to three of her child's coercive actions—despite the fact that she also admits to painful encounters with other people. Thus, as far as this mother is concerned, the descriptive process "I am easily pushed around" is a *child* deviance report. It does not include similar coercive actions by her boyfriend, her mother, her welfare worker, and her aunt. As the parent trainer listens to the mother's use of the report network, he or she has reason to suspect that these other coercive episodes will also influence the likelihood of the Figure 15-1 global reports. In essence, the parent trainer views the reports as superstitiously controlled by a wide variety of stimuli.

How does the parent trainer know which stimuli are in fact controlling a troubled mother's summary reports? Currently, this aspect of our clinical work is highly subjective. We do know that a multiply entrapped mother will describe day-to-day coercive encounters with a number of people. We also know that such a mother is quite selective when she is asked which of these encounters belong in her summary report network. Typically, the referred child will be represented, and possibly an adult as well. But, by and large, a *very small subset* of her recalled coercive episodes will be viewed as summarized by her chosen global descriptors. For two reasons, however, we would argue that all of the coercive episodes are functionally (via superstition) connected to her global descriptors. (In fact, even some noncoercive episodes, such as social approaches by the child, might be connected within the network.)

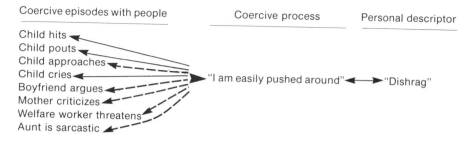

Figure 15-1

A summary report network used by a multiply entrapped mother. At the global report level, the mother uses metaphoric descriptors of her relationships with people. When she is then asked to specify people and episodes summarized at the global level, she points to three common episodes with her child (solid arrows). However, when recalling these episodes for the parent trainer, she also describes other episodes occurring in the same time frame. The parent trainer believes (dotted arrows) that these additional episodes also influence the mother's summary reports. The mother denies that these additional episodes are relevant to her summary reports.

The first reason for our argument centers on Wahler's (1980) correlational findings on multiply coerced mothers' aversive reactions to their problem children. These mothers were more likely to produce such reactions on days in which they reported coercive interchanges with adults than they were on days marked by positive exchanges with adults. Secondly, preliminary results in our tracking study of maternal attention indicate a relationship between a mother's coding of her child on videotape and her summary report network. Initially, when a troubled mother recalls her coercive encounters and her summary report network, only a few of the encounters or episodes are cited as belonging in the network. In addition, that mother's coding of her child's problem behavior (as depicted on videotape) is quite unlike that of a professional observer. Then, as the mother brings more coercive episodes into her summary report network (via the mand review process to be described below), her coding style when viewing the videotapes begins to match that of the professional observer. It is tempting to argue (but not to conclude) that this matchup in mother–observer coding of child behavior is constructed via changes in the mother's summary report network. As she uses that network to describe all coercive encounters in her day-to-day living, it may be that she becomes a more reliable observer in her assessment of each encounter. If this is indeed the case, the mother ought to function more effectively in parent training. Since accurate attending is a prerequisite skill for the mother's use of contingency management procedures, making her a reliable observer is bound to produce benefits in the overall training process.

We turn now to an outline of the mand review process. The core of this process is best represented by principles of operant concept learning (also called "abstraction"; see Skinner, 1953, pp. 134–136). According to these principles, it is possible to bring one response under the control of multiple stimulus events sharing a common property. Thus, if one wanted to teach a mother to use the response "oppositional" whenever her child produced a particular group of rule-violating behaviors, the teaching procedure would entail concept learning: The child's grouping of behaviors would be presented to the mother as separate stimuli randomly interspersed with other child-produced stimuli. When one of the rule-violating stimuli occurs and the mother responds "oppositional," she is reinforced by the teacher. The same response to non-rule-violating stimuli is ignored. Eventually, the stimulus class comprised of rule-violating child behaviors will exercise discriminative control of the mother's labeling response "oppositional."

We think that the above concept teaching is best accomplished within the context of a friendship relationship between mother and parent trainer. In examining the many descriptive accounts we have obtained from troubled mothers, a friendship relationship specifies that the other party *listens to* and *understands* what the mother says. Friends do not command, and they do not instruct; they typically listen, ask for clarification, and occasionally give opinions. One of the principal deficits in the lives of multiply coerced mothers is the absence of friendship relationships (Wahler, 1980). Compared to singularly coerced mothers, these mothers report few instances of adult contact in which the other party is primarily a listener. Rather, the other party (usually a relative, helping agent, or boyfriend) criticizes, demands, or otherwise instructs the mother to behave differently. Since parent training is an instructional process, we are concerned about the possibility that the parent trainer might become part of that coercion-maintaining stimulus class. Thus, we think it wise to initiate the mand review sessions by having the parent trainer function primarily as a listener.

In the process of listening to a troubled mother describe her coercion problems, the friendship-oriented parent trainer must also *understand* what the mother is talking about. "Understanding," in our frame of reference, is equivalent to a matchup in the observational coding styles of mother and parent trainer. But, as we demonstrated earlier, the parent trainer and the troubled mother are likely to have very different coding styles at the beginning of training. That is, the mother is apt to use global categories in which the specific referents summarized are not at all clear. If a matchup in coding styles is to occur, the parent trainer must respect the mother's use of these global summary reports and use these reports in talking with her. At first, the parent trainer will be groping in the dark with this style of communication. In this initial phase of the mand review process, the parent trainer is a "reflective" counselor (Rogers, 1951) who encourages the mother to describe her coercion problems and then reflects back to the mother what appear to be her principal categories. For example, if the mother is repetitive in her use of the term "bending over backwards," the parent trainer may choose to isolate this category in responding to the mother as follows: "It seems to me that this is what happens to you over and over again when you try to deal with your child."

After the parent trainer identifies the mother's key summary report categories and both parties are using these codes to discuss the mother's weekly coercion problems, the parent trainer must initiate the concept-teaching process. The mother's specific, concrete reports of coercive interchanges with people must now be integrated within her global summary report categories. The mand review discussions would at this point resemble a matching-to-sample learning process, in which global categories are compared to numerous specific categories. The quest for understanding between mother and parent trainer centers on summarizing specific reports of coercion within the mother-preferred global categories. Typically, the matching-to-sample process works in two directions. If the mother recalls a specific coercive episode (e.g., her spouse told her to shut up and she argued), the parent trainer will describe the mother's summary report network and ask whether the episode "fits" (e.g., "You've said that when people push you around, you get to feeling like a dishrag. Is this an example?"). Or, if the mother offers a global report concerning coercion (e.g., "Boy, I was really grouchy last week") the parent trainer will cite the mother's summary report network and ask for specifics (e.g., "Did somebody push you around? How?").

The bidirectional matching-to-sample illustrations above provide a good outline of the concept-teaching process. We cannot, however, provide clear rule descriptions of how the parent trainer responds to the mother's answers to the inquiries. In the initial sessions, the mother's answers are likely to be negative— the mother will not discriminate a matchup. If so, the parent trainer never attempts to "force" a fit. Rather, the topic is simply dropped for the moment, and the parent trainer will usually ask the mother to recall other problem episodes. Or the parent trainer may choose to review previous mother-specified matchups and then repeat the previous inquiry. We have found this aspect of the teaching process to vary widely across our group of parent trainers. While sheer repetition of the comparisons between global and specific reports is the rule of thumb, there is undoubtedly much more to the process. We know that some parent trainers are very good at this supplementary teaching and some are not—certainly an index of the "art versus technology" status of mand review.

One must keep in mind the goal of mand review: The mother's global categories reflecting coercion must come to summarize *all* of her coercive encounters. This being the case, the rate of progress in reaching such a goal ought to be a partial function of the actual number of coercive episodes in the mother's day-to-day life. Our findings support this conclusion. Mothers whose coercive entrapment is restricted to their children move rapidly through the mand review process, whereas multiply entrapped mothers progress at a much slower rate. It is also true that the latter tend to be more poorly educated than singularly coerced mothers (Dumas & Wahler, 1981), a factor likely to exercise a sizable impact on the teaching process. But it is also true that the concept-learning task is more complex for multiply coerced mothers. Consider, for example, a mother who describes her child as a singular source of distress, when in fact she is also coerced by her husband, mother, and neighbor. The sources and numbers of coercive encounters to be reorganized are vastly different than would be true of a mother whose principal problems center on her child.

Our current findings indicate that multiply coerced mothers maintain their parent training gains when the mand review process is added to their treatment program (Wahler & Dumas, 1981). With singularly entrapped mothers, the additional process appears unnecessary. We have yet to prove which aspects of mand review are instrumental in supporting the parent training outcomes. In addition to the concept-teaching process, other likely explanations are clearly in order. The experimental analyses crucial to such conclusions are now in progress. We turn now to a case study portraying the current state of our "art versus technology" process of parent training.

THE MAINTENANCE OF PARENT TRAINING OUTCOMES: A CASE STUDY IN MAND REVIEW

Mrs. Case was referred to our program by the Department of Human Services because of parental neglect. Her 10-year-old son, Jimmy, had been in repeated difficulties with neighbors, school officials, and the police because of stealing, physical assault, and marijuana use. The telling incident leading to this "forced" referral concerned Jimmy's knife assault on another child. Mrs. Case described Jimmy as "impossible to control" and a "carbon copy" of his father, who was serving a prison sentence for second-degree murder.

Mrs. Case (aged 30) was a clear-cut example of an insular, multiply entrapped mother (Wahler, 1980). She was single, lived with her mother, had only a grade-school education, and was relatively friendless. While she admitted that she would not have sought psychological help for Jimmy on her own initiative, she did express a strong interest in "doing something to keep him from turning out like his father." She described her interchanges with Jimmy as largely coercive. He would "act like a baby," "never do what I tell him," "demand all kinds of attention," and "pitch a fit when things don't go his way." In Mrs. Case's daily reports of extrafamily interactions, it was apparent that her average of three contacts per day was restricted to kinfolk, helping agents, and people in her work setting. Frequently, these contacts were described by her as coercive.

Assessment procedures for Mrs. Case and Jimmy were of two types. Home observations of mother–child interchanges were scheduled twice weekly, and these employed the Wahler, House, and Stambaugh (1976) standardized observation codes (SOC). Four of the codes reflected Jimmy's oppositional and aggressive behavior, and two were used to assess mother-aversive responses to Jimmy. Thus, SOC observations provided a direct picture of coercive interchanges between Jimmy and his mother. Mrs. Case also attended once-weekly mand review sessions as soon as the home observations began. These sessions were videotaped and later coded by observers using mand-oriented review codes (MORC; see Wahler & Afton, 1980). Based on these codes, it is possible to describe a mother's summary report network—her global categories and those specific reports summarized by the categories. For example, when a mother offers a global report such as "I was at the end of my rope," the parent trainer will usually ask for specifics if the mother's preferred global categories are already known. When she then provides the specific reports summarized by this statement, the MORC coder will list people and interchanges specified by the mother.

The total treatment program for the Case family has currently encompassed five phases: baseline and mand review; parent training and mand review; second home baseline and mand review; third home baseline only; fourth home baseline and mand review. The mand review sessions followed the strategy described in the previous section. Parent training was conducted in the home setting and comprised a time-out contingency for Jimmy's coercive actions, plus a schoolwork contract consequated by points.

Table 15-3 indicates mother and child coercive interchanges over the five phases of treatment. The reader may notice a sharp reduction in these interchanges during the parent training phase; in addition, it is evident that the reductions were maintained a full 10 weeks after parent training. The only

Table 15-3

Mean Percentage of Occurrences of Jimmy's Oppositional and Aggressive Behavior and Mrs. Case's Aversive Behavior Directed to Jimmy over Five Treatment Phases

Behavior	Baseline and mand review (4 weeks)	Parent training and mand review (8 weeks)	Second home baseline and mand review (10 weeks)	Third home baseline only (8 weeks)	Fourth home baseline and mand review (4 weeks)
Oppositional and aggressive child behavior	11.2 (5–22)	3.0 (0–10)	3.5 (0–8)	20.0 (4–60)	4.0 (0–15)
Aversive maternal behavior	8.0 (2–18)	1.5 (0–8)	0.8 (0–3)	10.0 (5–50)	2.0 (0–10)

Note. The range of observation scores is set in parentheses. The observations were based on the SOC observational format (Wahler, House, & Stambaugh, 1976).

"treatment" contact with the Case family in this phase centered on the once-weekly mand review sessions with Mrs. Case and the twice-weekly home observations. The likelihood that some currently unknown facets of the mand review sessions were responsible for maintenance is seen in the fourth and fifth phases. The 8-week termination of mand review in the fourth phase was clearly associated with a loss of the parent training improvements. Then, with a resumption of mand review sessions in the fifth phase, the improvements in mother–child interchanges are once again evident.

Unfortunately, while the results of this experimental manipulation do suggest a causal maintenance function of mand review, the same data depict a very unstable effect. If 22 weeks of mother participation in mand review can be "washed out" in 8 weeks, the likelihood of follow-up success is slim. The maintenance reversal could mean that mand review serves only a friendship support function—that it provides the opportunity for an insular mother to engage in one of her rarely reported friendship interchanges. Earlier correlational data by Wahler (1980) showed that insular mothers and their problem children engaged in fewer coercive bouts on days when the mothers' friendship contacts were proportionately higher than their kinfolk and helping agent contacts.

Another possible explanation for the weak maintenance seen in Table 15-3 presumes that the concept-teaching components of mand review are important in the maintenance of parent training gains. Furthermore, it would be assumed that the new summary report network resultant from this teaching requires constant practice and corrective feedback from other people—an unlikely set of conditions in the insular mother's natural environment. To explore these explanations further, it is now relevant to examine data taken from the mand review videotapes. By coding Mrs. Case's global and specific reports of coercion in each tape, it is possible to construct her summary report network at various points across sessions.

Figure 15-2 depicts Mrs. Case's summary report network as used by her in the first two sessions of mand review. In the inner circle, we see her often-used global description of how she tended to become engaged in coercive relationships. On the periphery of the outer circle are four people Mrs. Case reported as frequent sources of coercive contact. However, in describing how her global category was connected to these people, she summarized only two coercive episodes with two people. Thus, her personal formulation of the concept "patient–hard" was very narrowly relevant to her ex-husband and her son, Jimmy.

After another six sessions, Mrs. Case expanded the referents for her "patient–hard" global category (see Figure 15-3). She now connected three people and five coercive episodes as components of her summary report network.

Finally, after another 10 sessions, Mrs. Case's summary report network became quite complex (see Figure 15-4). All four people originally noted as her coercive partners were now represented in the "patient–hard" process through a

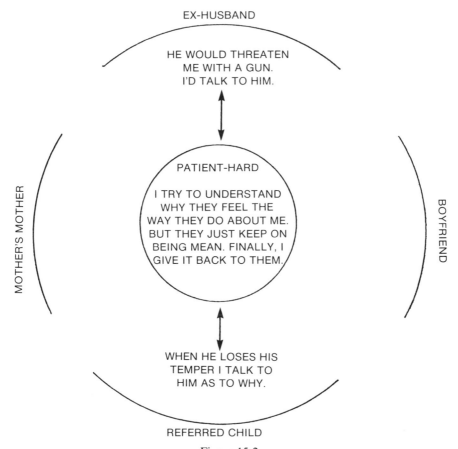

Figure 15-2

A multiply coerced mother's summary report network, taken from two initial mand review sessions. The center description is the mother's summary account of how she tended to get involved in coercive exchanges. On the periphery are four people the mother described as typical sources of coercion. However, she cited only two episodes with two of the people as connected to the "patient–hard" summary process.

total of 10 common episodes. It is of interest to note that, in one of these sessions, Mrs. Case announced: "Good Lord! I get into this mess with every one of them! It's the same thing every time."

Figure 15-5, by contrast, depicts the marked constriction in Mrs. Case's summary report network after the 2-month interruption of mand review sessions. While she continued to report four people as likely sources of coercion, only her ex-husband and Jimmy were designated as connected to her global process category. We find it intriguing to see that the Table 15-3 maintenance

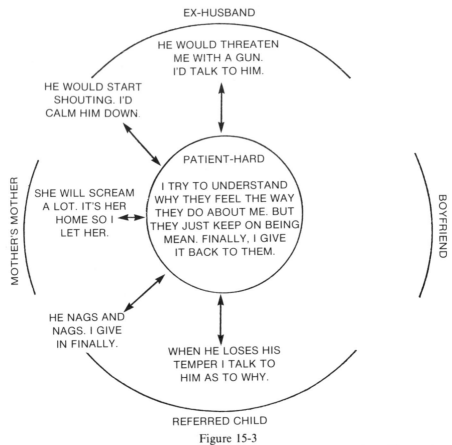

Figure 15-3

The Figure 15-2 summary report network after eight mand review sessions. The mother now described five coercive episodes involving three people as connected to her summary process, "patient–hard."

failure in parent training coincides roughly with this sparsely connected network. There is thus a suggestion here that Mrs. Case's more delimited summary report network may have adversely affected her interchanges with Jimmy.

The recovery of Mrs. Case's parent training gains as seen in the last phase of Table 15-3 was associated with a once-again-expanded summary report network (Figure 15-6). As she demonstrated in mand review sessions prior to the 8-week interruption, coercive episodes with all significant people in her life could be summarized by the "patient–hard" descriptive process. Thus, for the second time, reductions in coercive home interchanges between Mrs. Case and Jimmy were associated with the mother's expanded summary report network. We find these rough covariations encouraging enough to pursue further experimental analyses on the function of mand review as a behavior maintenance

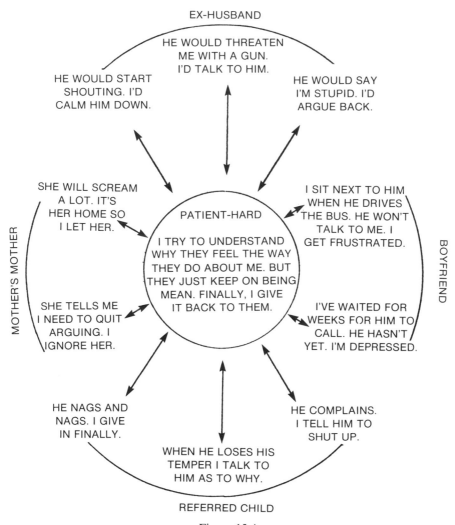

Figure 15-4

The summary report network of Figures 15-2 and 15-3 after 18 mand review sessions. The mother now described 10 coercive episodes involving four people as connected to her summary process, "patient–hard."

process for troubled mothers. However, even if we are able to document those components in mand review that are responsible for maintenance, it is also obvious that we do not yet have a treatment procedure leading to stable follow-up effects. Mrs. Case is only one of a number of multiply coerced, insular mothers who are now in an indefinitely prolonged mand review process. Much is yet to be understood concerning ways of effect stable therapeutic changes—those that will persist without continual contact with professional helpers.

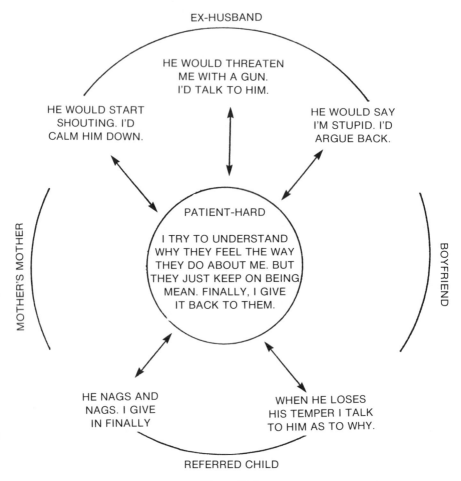

EX-HUSBAND

HE WOULD THREATEN
ME WITH A GUN.
I'D TALK TO HIM.

HE WOULD START
SHOUTING. I'D
CALM HIM DOWN.

HE WOULD SAY
I'M STUPID. I'D
ARGUE BACK.

MOTHER'S MOTHER

PATIENT-HARD

I TRY TO UNDERSTAND
WHY THEY FEEL THE WAY
THEY DO ABOUT ME. BUT
THEY JUST KEEP ON BEING
MEAN. FINALLY, I GIVE
IT BACK TO THEM.

BOYFRIEND

HE NAGS AND
NAGS. I GIVE
IN FINALLY

WHEN HE LOSES
HIS TEMPER I TALK
TO HIM AS TO WHY.

REFERRED CHILD

Figure 15-5

The summary report network of Figures 15-2–15-4, following a 2-month interruption of mand review sessions. The interruption occurred after 18 mand review sessions. The mother now described only five coercive episodes with two people as connected to her summary process, "patient–hard."

CONCLUSION

Maintenance of therapeutic outcome with multiply coerced mothers continues to be an elusive phenomenon. Certainly investigators' understanding of their entrapment has become clearer in the past few years. It does seem evident that the functioning of mothers under conditions of multiple coercive input is qualitatively different from that of singularly coerced mothers. The former

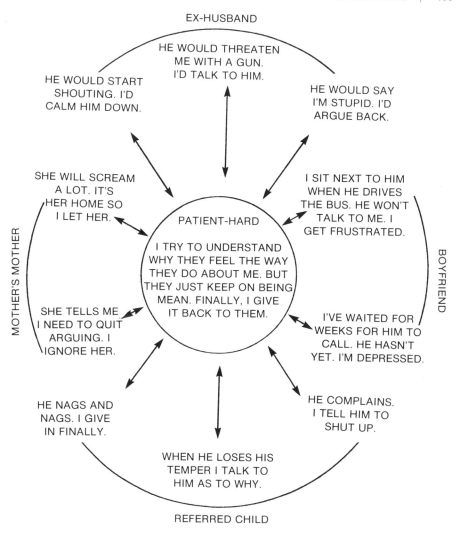

Figure 15-6

The summary report network of Figures 15-2–15-5, following a two-session resumption of the mand review process. The resumption occurred following the 2-month interruption described in Figure 15-5. Once again, the mother described 10 coercive episodes involving four people as connected to her summary process, "patient–hard."

appear to utilize observational coding strategies that foster a continuation of the entrapment. That is, when a multiply coerced mother responds to any one of her coercive partners, that response is influenced by *all* of her partners in coercion. The mother "believes" that she is attending to and responding to the coercive cues of the moment—for example, the nagging and demanding behavior of her problem child. In fact, however, her cue pattern is much broader than this; she is also influenced by previous coercive encounters with other significant people in her life. We think that this "superstitious" stimulus control is established under conditions of multiple coercive input. Such conditions appear to maximize a mother's inconsistency in responding to any one of these aversive episodes. Thus, as the mother vacillates unpredictably in her ways of dealing with her child, boyfriend, kinfolk, and other demanding people, her accuracy in attending to and summarizing these encounters will diminish. Then she becomes trapped. We have begun to develop a procedure aimed at improving the multiply coerced mother's attending. If this capability were to be maintained, it is likely that the mother could utilize her given interpersonal skills in almost any situation, including child management situations. The skills can be taught through parent training and other educational approaches to interpersonal behavior (e.g., assertion training). The missing link, in our opinion, centers on a means of maintaining the mother's attentional focus. In our next research strategy, we intend to incorporate the multiply coerced mother's friends into the mand review process. This strategy presumes that her friendship interchanges could become a vehicle for continued practice in the accurate use of her summary report network. If a friend can be a trained "sounding board" for discussion of the mother's day-to-day problems, it is less likely that the mother will return to her haphazard attentional style.

Acknowledgments

The research data reported in this chapter were generated by support from Grant No. R01-1068-58 from the National Institute of Mental Health, Crime and Delinquency Section.

References

Alexander, J. F. Defensive and supportive communications in normal and deviant families. *Journal of Consulting and Clinical Psychology*, 1973, *40*, 2, 223–231.

Alexander, J. F., & Parsons, B. V. Short-term behavioral interaction with delinquent families: Impact on family process and recidivism. *Journal of Abnormal Psychology*, 1973, *81*, 219–225.

Bates, J. E. The concept of difficult temperament. *Merrill–Palmer Quarterly*, 1980, *26*, 4, 299–319.

Bates, J. E., Freeland, C. A. B., & Lounsbury, M. L. Measurement of infant difficultness. *Child Development*, 1979, *50*, 794–803.

Beck, A. T. *Depression: Causes and treatment*. Philadelphia: University of Pennsylvania Press, 1967.

Bell, R. Q., & Harper, L. V. *Child effects on adults*. Hillsdale, N.J.: Erlbaum, 1977.

Bijou, S. W. *Child development III: Basic stage of early childhood.* Englewood Cliffs, N.J.: Prentice-Hall, 1976.

Bijou, S. W., & Baer, D. M. *Child development I: A systematic and empirical theory.* Englewood Cliffs, N.J.: Prentice-Hall, 1961.

Brazelton, T. B. *Infants and mothers: Differences in development.* New York: Delacorte Press, 1969.

Brazelton, T. B. *The neonatal behavioral assessment scale.* Philadelphia: Lippincott, 1973.

Brazelton, T. B. *Toddlers and parents.* New York: Delacorte Press, 1974.

Brown, G. W., & Harris, T. *Social origins of depression.* New York: Free Press, 1978.

Bugental, D. E., Love, L. R., Kaswan, J. W., & April, C. Verbal–nonverbal conflict in parental messages to normal and disturbed children. *Journal of Abnormal Psychology*, 1971, *77*, 6–10.

Butterfield, P., Van Doornick, W., Dawson, P., & Alexander, H. *Early identification of dysparenting.* Paper presented at the meeting of the Society for Research in Child Development, San Francisco, March 1979.

Caplan, G. *Support systems and community mental health.* New York: Behavioral Publications, 1976.

Carey, W. B. A simplified method of measuring infant temperament. *Journal of Pediatrics*, 1970, *77*, 188–194.

Christophersen, E. R. *Outcome of parent training in families of delinquent children.* Paper presented at the meeting of the Association for Advancement of Behavior Therapy, New York, 1976.

Cochran, M. M., & Brassard, J. A. Child development and personal social networks. *Child Development*, 1979, *50*, 601–616.

Conger, R. D. Social control and social learning models of delinquent behavior: A synthesis. *Criminology*, 1976, *14*(1), 17–40.

Delfini, L. F., Bernal, M. E., & Rosen, P. M. Comparison of deviant and normal boys in home settings. In E. J. Mash, L. A. Hamerlynck, & L. C. Handy (Eds.), *Behavior modification and families.* New York: Brunner/Mazel, 1976.

Deur, J. L., & Parke, R. D. Effects of inconsistent punishment on aggression in children. *Developmental Psychology*, 1970, *2*, 403–411.

Donovan, W. L., Leavitt, L. A., & Balling, J. D. Maternal physiological response to infant signals. *Psychophysiology*, 1978, *15*, 68–74.

Dumas, J. E. *Family correlates of antisocial behavior in children and adolescents.* Manuscript submitted for publication, 1983.

Dumas, J. E., & Wahler, R. G. *Predictors of treatment outcome in parent training: Mother insularity and socioeconomic disadvantage.* Manuscript submitted for publication, 1981.

Ferber, H., Keeley, S. M., & Shembert, K. M. Training parents in behavior modification: Outcome of problems encountered in a program after Patterson's work. *Behavior Therapy*, 1974, *5*, 415–419.

Forehand, R., & Atkeson, B. M. Generality of treatment effects with parents as therapists: A review of assessment and implementation procedures. *Behavior Therapy*, 1977, *8*, 575–593.

Forehand, R., King, H., Peed, S., & Yoder, P. Mother–child interactions: Comparison of a non-compliant clinic group and a non-clinic group. *Behaviour Research and Therapy*, 1975, *13*, 79–84.

Forehand, R., Sturgis, E., Aguar, D., Beggs, V., Green, K., McMahon, R., & Wells, K. Generality of treatment effects resulting from a parent training program to modify child noncompliance. *Behavior Modification*, 1979, *3*, 3–25.

Forehand, R., Wells, K. C., & Griest, D. L. An examination of the social validity of a parent training program. *Behavior Therapy*, 1980, *11*, 488–502.

Fowler, S. A., & Baer, D. M. "Do I have to be good all day?": The timing of delayed reinforcement as a factor in generalization. *Journal of Applied Behavior Analysis*, 1981, *14*, 13–24.

Frodi, A. M., Lamb, M. E., Leavitt, L. A., Donovan, W. L., Neff, C., & Sherry, D. Fathers' and mothers' responses to the faces and cries of normal and premature infants. *Developmental Psychology*, 1978, *14*, 5, 490–498.

Gewirtz, J. L., & Boyd, E. F. Experiments on mother–infant interaction underlying mutual attachment acquisition: The infant conditions the mother. In T. Alloway, P. Pilner, & L. Kranes

(Eds.), *Attachment behavior: Advances in the study of communication and affect* (Vol. 3). New York: Plenum Press, 1976.

Gottman, J. M. *Marital interaction: Experimental investigations.* New York: Academic Press, 1979.

Green, K. D., Forehand, R., & McMahon, R. J. Parental manipulation of compliance and noncompliance in normal and deviant children. *Behavior Modification,* 1979, *3,* 245–266.

Griest, D. L., Forehand, R., Wells, K. C., & McMahon, R. J. An examination of differences between nonclinic and behavior problem clinic-referred children and their mothers. *Journal of Abnormal Psychology,* 1980, *89*(3), 497–500.

Griest, D. L., Wells, K. C., & Forehand, R. An examination of predictors of maternal perceptions of maladjustment in clinic-referred children. *Journal of Abnormal Psychology,* 1979, *88,* 277–281.

Halverson, C. T., & Waldrop, M. F. Maternal behavior toward own and other preschool children: The problem of "ownness." *Child Development,* 1970, *41,* 839–845.

Herbert, E. W., & Baer, D. M. Training parents as behavior modifiers: Self-recording of contingent attention. *Journal of Applied Behavior Analysis,* 1972, *5,* 139–149.

Herrnstein, R. J. Superstition: A corollary of the principles of operant conditioning. In W. K. Honig (Ed.), *Operant behavior: Areas of research and application.* New York: Appleton-Century-Crofts, 1966.

Johnson, S. M., & Christensen, A. Multiple criteria follow-up of behavior modification with families. *Journal of Abnormal Child Psychology,* 1975, *3*(2), 135–154.

Johnson, S. M., & Lobitz, C. K. The personal and marital adjustment of parents as related to observed child deviance and parenting behavior. *Journal of Abnormal Child Psychology,* 1974, *2,* 193–207.

Johnson, S. M., Wahl, G., Martin, S., & Johansson, S. How deviant is the normal child?: A behavioral analysis of the preschool child and his family. In R. D. Rubin, J. P. Brady, & J. D. Henderson (Eds.), *Advances in behavior therapy* (Vol. 4). New York: Academic Press, 1973.

Kantor, J. R. *Interbehavioral psychology.* Granville, Ohio: Principia Press, 1959.

Katz, R. Interactions between the facilitative and inhibitory effects of a punishing stimulus in the control of children's hitting behavior. *Child Development,* 1971, *42,* 1433–1446.

Kellam, S. G., Ensminger, M. E., & Turner, R. J. Family structure and the mental health of children. *Archives of General Psychiatry,* 1977, *34,* 1012–1022.

Kent, R. N., & O'Leary, K. D. A controlled evaluation of behavior modification with conduct problem children. *Journal of Consulting and Clinical Psychology,* 1976, *44,* 586–596.

Koegel, R. L., & Rincover, A. Research on the difference between generalization and maintenance in extra-therapy responding. *Journal of Applied Behavior Analysis,* 1977, *10,* 1–12.

Kolvin, I., Garside, R. F., Nicol, A. R., MacMillan, A., Wolstenholme, F., & Leitch, I. M. Familial and sociological correlates of behavioural and sociometric deviance in 8-year-old children. In P. J. Graham (Ed.), *Epidemiological approaches in child psychiatry.* London: Academic Press, 1977.

Lagerkvist, B., Lauritzen, S., Olin, P., & Tengvald, K. Four-year-olds in a new suburb: The need for medical and social care. *Acta Paediatrica Scandinavica,* 1975, *64,* 413–420.

Lamb, M. E. Influence of the child on marital quality and family interaction during the prenatal, perinatal, and infancy periods. In R. M. Lerner & G. B. Spanier (Eds.), *Child influences on marital and family interaction: A life-span perspective.* New York: Academic Press, 1978. (a)

Lamb, M. E. Social interaction in infancy and the development of personality. In M. E. Lamb (Ed.), *Social and personality development.* New York: Holt, Rinehart & Winston, 1978. (b)

Leighton, L. A., Stollak, G. E., & Ferguson, L. Patterns of communication in normal and clinic families. *Journal of Consulting and Clinical Psychology,* 1971, *36,* 252–256.

Lerner, R. M., & Spanier, G. B. (Eds.). *Child influences on marital and family interaction: A life-span perspective.* New York: Academic Press, 1978.

Lobitz, W. C., & Johnson, S. M. Parental manipulation of the behavior of normal and deviant children. *Child Development,* 1975, *46,* 719–726.

Love, L. R., & Kaswan, J. W. *Troubled children: Their families, schools, and treatments.* New York: Wiley, 1974.

Martin, B. Brief family intervention: The effectiveness and the importance of including the father. *Journal of Consulting and Clinical Psychology,* 1977, *45,* 1002–1010.

Miller, M. *Sunday's child.* New York: Holt, Rinehart & Winston, 1968.

Milliones, J. Relationship between perceived child temperament and maternal behavior. *Child Development,* 1978, *49,* 1255–1257.

Minton, C., Kagan, J., & Levine, J. Maternal control and obedience in the 2-year-old. *Child Development,* 1971, *42,* 1873–1894.

Morse, W. H., & Skinner, B. F. A second type of superstition in the pigeon. *American Journal of Psychology,* 1957, *70,* 308–311.

O'Dell, S. Training parents in behavior modification: A review. *Psychological Bulletin,* 1974, *81,* 418–433.

Oltmanns, T. F., Broderick, J. E., & O'Leary, K. D. Marital adjustment and the efficacy of behavior therapy with children. *Journal of Consulting and Clinical Psychology,* 1977, *45,* 724–729.

Parke, R. D., & Deur, J. L. Schedule of punishment and inhibition of aggression in children. *Development Psychology,* 1972, *7,* 266–269.

Patterson, G. R. An empirical approach to the classification of disturbed children. *Journal of Clinical Psychology,* 1964, *20,* 326–337.

Patterson, G. R. Intervention for boys with conduct problems: Multiple settings, treatments and criteria. *Journal of Consulting and Clinical Psychology,* 1974, *42,* 471–481.

Patterson, G. R. The aggressive child: Victim and architect of a coercive system. In E. J. Mash, L. A. Hamerlynck, & L. C. Handy (Eds.), *Behavior modification and families* (Vol. 1, *Theory and research*). New York: Brunner/Mazel, 1976.

Patterson, G. R. Mothers: The unacknowledged victims. In J. H. Stevens & M. Matthews (Eds.), *Mother–child, father–child relations.* Washington, D.C.: N.A.E.Y.C., 1977.

Patterson, G. R., Cobb, J. A., & Ray, R. S. A social engineering technology for retraining the families of aggressive boys. In H. E. Adams & I. P. Unikel (Eds.), *Issues and trends in behavior therapy.* Springfield, Ill.: Charles C Thomas, 1973.

Patterson, G. R., & Fleischman, M. J. Maintenance of treatment effects: Some considerations concerning family systems and follow-up data. *Behavior Therapy,* 1979, *10,* 168–185.

Patterson, G. R., & Reid, J. B. Reciprocity and coercion: Two facets of social systems. In C. Neuringer & J. L. Michael (Eds.), *Behavior modification in clinical psychology.* New York: Appleton-Century-Crofts, 1970.

Porter, S., & O'Leary, K. D. Types of marital discord and child behavior problems. *Journal of Abnormal Child Psychology,* 1980, *8,* 287–295.

Reisinger, J. J., Frangia, G. W., & Hoffman, E. H. Toddler management training: Generalization and marital status. *Journal of Behavior Therapy and Experimental Psychiatry,* 1976, *7,* 335–340.

Rickard, K. M., Forehand, R., Wells, K. C., Griest, D. L., & McMahon, R. J. *An assessment of mothers of clinic-referred deviant, clinic-referred nondeviant, and nonclinic children.* Unpublished manuscript, University of Georgia, 1980.

Rogers, C. R. *Client-centered therapy.* Boston: Houghton Mifflin, 1951.

Russell, C. S. Transition to parenthood: Problems and gratifications. *Journal of Marriage and the Family,* 1974, *36,* 294–301.

Rutter, M. *Helping troubled children.* New York: Plenum Press, 1976.

Rutter, M., Yule, B., Quinton, D., Rowlands, O., Yule, W., & Berger, M. Attainment and adjustment in two geographical areas: III. Some factors accounting for area differences. *British Journal of Psychiatry,* 1974, *125,* 520–533.

Sallows, G. *Responsiveness between aggressive behavior in children and parent perception of child behavior.* Paper presented at the meeting of the Midwestern Psychological Association, Chicago, 1973.

Sameroff, A. J. Concepts of humanity in primary prevention. In G. Albee & J. M. Jaffe (Eds.), *Primary prevention of psychopathology* (Vol. 1). Hanover, N.H.: University Press of New England, 1977.

Sawin, D. B., & Parke, R. D. Inconsistent discipline of aggression in young boys. *Journal of Experimental Child Psychology*, 1979, *28*, 525–538.

Skinner, B. F. *Science and human behavior.* New York: Macmillan, 1953.

Snyder, J. J. A reinforcement analysis of intervention in problem and nonproblem children. *Journal of Abnormal Psychology*, 1977, *86*(5), 528–535.

Spock, B. J. *Baby and child care* (3rd ed.). New York: Pocket Books, 1976.

Strain, P. S., Steele, P., Ellis, T., & Timm, M. A. *Long-term effects of oppositional child treatment with mothers as therapists and therapist trainers.* Unpublished manuscript, University of Pittsburgh, 1981.

Straus, M. A., Gelles, R. J., & Steinmetz, S. K. *Behind closed doors: Violence in the American family.* Garden City, N.Y.: Anchor/Doubleday, 1980.

Taplin, P., & Reid, J. B. Changes in parent consequation as a function family intervention. *Journal of Consulting and Clinical Psychology*, 1977, *4*, 973–981.

Thomas, A., Chess, S., & Birch, H. G. *Temperament and behavior disorders in children.* New York: New York University Press, 1968.

Thomas, A., Chess, S., & Birch, H. G. The origin of personality. *Scientific American*, 1970, *223*(2), 102–109.

Wahl, G., Johnson, S. M., Johansson, S., & Martin, S. An operant analysis of child–family interaction. *Behavior Therapy*, 1974, *5*, 64–78.

Wahler, R. G. Some structural aspects of deviant child behavior. *Journal of Applied Behavior Analysis*, 1975, *8*, 27–42.

Wahler, R. G. Deviant child behavior within the family: Developmental speculations and behavior change strategies. In H. Leitenberg (Ed.), *Handbook of behavior modification and behavior therapy.* Englewood Cliffs, N.J.: Prentice-Hall, 1976.

Wahler, R. G. The insular mother: Her problems in parent–child treatment. *Journal of Applied Behavior Analysis*, 1980, *13*, 207–219.

Wahler, R. G., & Afton, A. D. Attentional processes in insular and noninsular mothers. *Child Behavior Therapy*, 1980, *2*(2), 25–41.

Wahler, R. G., & Dumas, J. E. *On the social ecology of troubled mothers: Discriminative and environmental restructuring.* Paper presented at the Banff International Conference on Behavior Modification, Banff, Alberta, Canada, March 1981.

Wahler, R. G., & Fox, J. J. Setting events in applied behavior analysis: Toward a conceptual and methodological expansion. *Journal of Applied Behavior Analysis*, 1981, *14*, 327–344.

Wahler, R. G., House, A. E., & Stambaugh, E. E. *Ecological assessment of child problem behavior: A clinical package for home, school and institutional settings.* New York: Pergamon Press, 1976.

Wahler, R. G., Hughey, J. B., & Gordon, J. S. Chronic patterns of mother–child coercion: Some differences between insular and noninsular families. *Analysis and Intervention in Developmental Disabilities*, 1981, *1*(2), 145–156.

Wahler, R. G., Leske, G., & Rogers, E. S. The insular family: A deviance support system for oppositional children. In L. A. Hamerlynck (Ed.), *Behavioral systems for the developmentally disabled* (Vol. 1, *School and family environments*). New York: Brunner/Mazel, 1979.

Wahler, R. G., & Moore, D. R. *School–home behavior change procedures in a "high-risk community."* Unpublished manuscript, 1975. (Available from Child Behavior Institute, 1720 Lake Avenue, Knoxville, Tennessee 37916.)

Weiss, R. L. The conceptualization of marriage from a behavioral perspective. In T. J. Paolino & B. S. McCrady (Eds.), *Marriage and marital therapy.* New York: Brunner/Mazel, 1978.

Yalom, I. D. Postpartum blues syndrome. *Archives of General Psychiatry*, 1968, *28*, 16–27.

BEHAVIORAL ASSESSMENT IN APPLIED PARENT TRAINING
Use of a Structured Observation System

Karen S. Budd
Pamela L. Fabry
University of Nebraska Medical Center

INTRODUCTION

The central thrust of behavioral parent training research since its inception some 20 years ago has been to develop effective interventions for modifying dysfunctional parent–child interactions. These interventions are aimed at teaching parents to rearrange the social contingencies they provide to child responses, and thereby to modify the children's deviant behavior. Although gaps still exist in the present understanding of how to design and implement effective treatments for some families (cf. O'Dell, 1982; Wahler, 1980), researchers over the past two decades have established an impressive record of success in altering deviant family interactions (see reviews of the research literature by Altman & Mira, 1982; Gordon & Davidson, 1981; Graziano, 1977; O'Dell, 1974). Demonstrations of how and when specific management techniques affect particular child behaviors, the delineation of procedures to teach these techniques to parents, and the discovery of variables that increase the generality of interventions form the base of a young but growing technology of behavioral parent training.

A technology of parent training is essentially a collection of practical "know-how," based on empirical research, that can be used by clinicians, counselors, and educators in parent training programs. To the extent that the technology

417

contains the necessary ingredients for conducting interventions, therapists in applied settings can extend the impact of parent training research far beyond the families that participate in experimental laboratory programs. However, if the parent training technology is missing essential ingredients, parent training in applied settings becomes more difficult. In these cases, therapists often are responsible for improvising procedures on the basis of their own experience or orientation.

A technology for training parents to rearrange their social contingencies consists of several dimensions. To date, research efforts contributing to the technology have focused primarily on three dimensions: (1) techniques of behavior management effective in remediating child behavior problems in the home; (2) methods of teaching parents to use these techniques; and, more recently, (3) procedures for enhancing the generalization and maintenance of training effects. These three dimensions represent the basic core knowledge essential for successful interventions, whether in an experimental or an applied parent training program. Findings on these topics have been disseminated to parent training practitioners through research reports in professional journals (e.g., *Behavior Modification, Behavior Therapy, Journal of Applied Behavior Analysis*) and books (Mash, Hamerlynck, & Handy, 1976; Mash, Handy, & Hamerlynck, 1976); guidebooks for therapists on what and how to train parents (e.g., Forehand & McMahon, 1981; Miller, 1975; Patterson, Reid, Jones, & Conger, 1975); and instructional materials for parents (e.g., Baker, Brightman, Heifetz, & Murphy, 1976; Becker, 1971; Christophersen, 1977; Patterson, 1975; Sloane, 1976).

In addition to the basic core knowledge outlined above, parent training technology needs to encompass other dimensions specific to its implementation in applied, as opposed to laboratory, programs. These other dimensions include (4) techniques for therapist assessment of parent and child behaviors for clinical evaluation purposes; (5) methods of tailoring interventions to particular families and referral problems; (6) strategies for training persons as therapists; and (7) organizational methods for establishing and implementing parent training programs in field settings. Unlike the three core knowledge dimensions, the latter four have received little systematic study by parent training researchers.

In part, research has been scanty in these areas because experimentation on an implementation technology is contingent on demonstration that a viable treatment technology exists—a demonstration that is just now beginning to gain recognition, due to the brief history of the field. However, it also is likely that parent training researchers in laboratory settings are naive to some of the conditions present in applied environments that call for systematic research. The types of families being seen, parents' motivation and cooperation in treatment, the amount of time available to therapists for individual families, and the nature of staff training all are factors that affect the way clinicians conduct parent training. Laboratory settings control for many of these factors, thereby making possible systematic data collection but also limiting the generalizability of the technology to applied settings.

Fleischman (1982) has elaborated on the discrepancy between laboratory and applied parent training in a recent description of an attempt to implement a behavioral intervention model developed by Patterson and his colleagues (Patterson *et al.*, 1975) within a community mental health agency. To evaluate the parent training provided by agency therapists, Fleischman collected extensive data on parent and child outcomes; thus, his research did not examine issues related to therapist assessment (the fourth dimension listed above). However, Fleischman reported several problems in implementing the treatment model, which he attributed to difficulties in training agency staff and in integrating the intervention model within the overall service system of the agency. These problems, which reflect the sixth and seventh dimensions listed above, were found to be specific to applied settings and thus were not anticipated from research in the laboratory. Fleischman's experience highlights the need to conduct research directly in applied clinical environments on procedures for implementing parent training programs.

The present chapter focuses on one dimension of the parent training technology that has not been well developed for applied use, despite the fact that the seeds of a technology in this area exist as a research tool. This dimension concerns methods of assessing parent and child behaviors for the purpose of clinical evaluation in parent training.

THE ROLE OF BEHAVIORAL ASSESSMENT IN APPLIED PARENT TRAINING

Assessment is functional for any therapeutic approach as a means of verifying that a problem exists, specifying its nature, identifying intervention goals, and evaluating outcome. However, assessment is especially integral to a behavioral approach, in that interventions are individually tailored according to pretreatment assessment and altered during the course of intervention on the basis of subsequent assessment (Haynes, 1978). As Willems (1974) suggested, the accuracy of the initial diagnostic observation process—by which the therapist views complicated behavioral interactions, selects certain responses for treatment, and predicts that they will be amenable to contingency control—often may distinguish successful from unsuccessful behavioral interventions. Yet the rules and procedures for diagnostic observations are not explicit, nor have they been subjected to study.

Many research-oriented parent training programs employ sophisticated direct observation systems (e.g., Reid, 1978; Wahler, House, & Stambaugh, 1976) in which several parent and child behaviors are measured in a naturalistic setting with few restrictions on parent–child interactions. These assessment methods are appropriate for experimental analysis, but they are not feasible for practitioners, due to the extensive time, training, and resources required. While the technology for direct observation of families exists as a research tool, it has yet to be simplified into practical systems applicable to professionals in clinical settings.

Without behavioral assessment procedures relevant to clinical settings, therapists must rely on indirect or informal measures, such as parent reports and clinical impressions, for diagnostic evaluation. These procedures increase the possibility that therapists will be inaccurate in identifying parent–child problems, in selecting procedures to remediate the problems, and in determining whether or not parents have acquired the skills taught to them. When objective data are not available, therapists can be misled by parents' verbal behavior into assuming that the parents are more or less competent in applying social contingencies than is actually the case. One illustration of this problem is discussed later in this chapter. Therapists who have little background in using behavioral assessment devices are particularly vulnerable in this regard, in that they are liable to view assessment as expendable to the intervention process and thus liable to rely heavily on parent report.

The present chapter provides a step toward the development of a behavioral assessment technology for use in applied parent training programs. The purposes of the chapter are (1) to discuss issues in the design of practical behavioral assessment devices; (2) to describe an observation system we have developed as a clinical assessment tool in behavioral parent training; and (3) to report on the usefulness of this observation system as evaluated by parent training therapists not involved in its initial development. The chapter is intended to convey functional information for parent training therapists and to exemplify issues in the progressive development of a clinical assessment instrument.

PRACTICAL METHODS OF BEHAVIORAL ASSESSMENT

In approaching the issue of behavioral assessment in applied settings, the most immediate question is how to design an assessment instrument that provides meaningful information yet is convenient to use. Large caseloads and limited resources allow therapists little opportunity for comprehensive examination of individual cases; yet the variety of parent and child problems referred for treatment requires that an instrument be sufficiently broad in scope to apply to diverse families. Because of the practical limitations on evaluation in applied settings, behavioral clinicians often rely on parent reports or paper-and-pencil measures to assess treatment outcome (Christophersen, Arnold, Hill, & Quilitch, 1972; Hall, Axelrod, Tyler, Grief, Jones, & Robertson, 1972; Rinn, Vernon, & Wise, 1975; Rose, 1974; Salzinger, Feldman, & Portnoy, 1970). These methods provide indirect indicators of the impact of parent training; however, they do not constitute a direct, objective assessment of the primary variables at issue in training—parent and child behaviors.

One approach to clinical assessment that has shown promise for parent training professionals is the use of structured assessment procedure (cf. Haynes, 1978). In this approach, structure is imposed on parent–child interactions by the use of specific cues (instructions, signals, materials, or assigned activities) that set the occasion for behaviors of interest to occur. Structure also is imposed on the recording system by selecting a limited number of pertinent behaviors and a systematic framework for recording the occurrence of the behaviors. Hughes and Haynes (1978) reviewed several structured assessment procedures for evaluating parent–child interactions in laboratory situations. Their review included both complex recording instruments designed primarily for research analyses and a few simpler recording formats of potential value in clinical work.

Hanf (1968) was among the first behaviorally oriented clinicians to propose and implement a structured assessment procedure for clinical evaluation in parent training. Her standardized assessment system, which has since been modified and used extensively in applied research by Forehand and his colleagues (e.g., Forehand & King, 1974, 1977; Forehand & McMahon, 1981; Peed, Roberts, & Forehand, 1977), exemplifies the structured assessment approach. In this system, parent and child behaviors are recorded in two structured contexts: a command situation (the "Parent's Game") in which the rules and activities are determined by the parent, and a free-play situation (the "Child's Game") in which the rules and nature of the interaction are determined by the child. These two structured situations were designed to be analogous to typical problematic situations reported by parents. The observation code (as described in Forehand & McMahon, 1981) entails recording seven parent responses (alpha and beta commands, warnings, questions, attends, rewards, and time out) and three child responses (inappropriate behavior, compliance, and noncompliance) in each 5- to 10-minute structured situation. Eyberg and Robinson also developed a clinical assessment system based on Hanf's structured approach (Robinson & Eyberg, 1981; Eyberg & Robinson, 1981). A total of 24 parent and child behaviors are coded during three 5-minute standard situations: the Parent's Game, the Child's Game, and cleanup, in which the parent is asked to have the child put away toys used during the two preceding activities. While both of these assessment systems structure the nature of parent–child activities, they entail fairly sophisticated recording procedures. In Forehand's system, each occurrence of defined behaviors is recorded in continuous 30-second intervals. In Eyberg and Robinson's system, the frequency of each behavior is tallied continuously across the structured situations. Conceivably, additional structure could be imposed on the recording procedures to simplify observer scoring for clinical assessment.

For applied parent training programs, a structured observation procedure offers several advantages over other assessment techniques. First, the structure promotes occurrences of parent–child interactions of clinical interest within a more efficient time frame than can be accomplished in naturalistic observation. Second, because specific parent and child responses can be anticipated from the structure, the therapist can obtain maximal information on behaviors and environmental variables found to be relevant in other cases. Third, a consistent structure allows the therapist to compare findings across families, thus making structured assessment a viable research tool for clinical investigations. Fourth, the recording procedure (or a simplified form of the procedure) could be used for self-recording by parents, either as a training exercise or as a means of obtaining supplemental data in additional settings.

It should be noted that a structured observation procedure also entails some disadvantages for clinical evaluation. For one, the structure imposed on parent and child behaviors could create a reactive effect on family members or could mask problems, especially with older children. Second, by focusing on preselected behaviors and environmental events, a structured observation procedure presumes some factors about the functional relationships of variables. A therapist runs the risk of overlooking variables pertinent to the parent–child interaction by concentrating only on behaviors identified within the recording system. Third, to the extent that the structure imposes an artificial environment, behavior in the structured setting may not reflect parent–child interactions in the natural environment.

Thus, a structured assessment instrument must be appropriate to the clients, problems, and context in which it is used. It does not take the place of perceptive clinical judgment on its use, and it needs to be supplemented by additional (even if informal) measures of generalization. However, given the practical restrictions on assessment in applied environments, structured assessment is a potentially viable method of obtaining systematic measures of parent and child behaviors in applied settings.

ILLUSTRATION OF A STRUCTURED OBSERVATION SYSTEM

Background, Purpose, and Development

To explore the usefulness of structured assessment in applied parent training, Budd and her colleagues designed a structured observation system and implemented it as one means of evaluation within a clinical parent training program

(Budd, Riner, & Brockman, in press). This observation system consists of five brief, structured activities, each oriented toward a specific set of child management techniques for dealing with common behavior problems. The initial evaluation of the structured observation system, summarized in more detail later in the chapter, indicated that the system was highly reliable, was applicable across diverse families and behavior problems, and reflected considerable increases in parents' correct performance of child management skills correlated with training. However, the observation instrument was not found to be sensitive to the assessment of children's behavior, in that the child measures showed little change, despite indications on other assessment devices of positive treatment effects. Also, it was not clear whether other therapists not involved in the development of the structured system would find it reliable and clinically useful.

To investigate the system's portability to other therapists, Fabry, who initially was naive to the system, trained herself and three other therapists in its use. After implementing the system for clinical evaluation with a few families in parent training, modifications in two of the five structured activities were made to increase the sensitivity of the system to child behavior change. The revised system was then implemented with additional families to test the usefulness of the changes. The ensuing description of the structured observation system incorporates these changes.

The focus of this structured observation system is the behavior of parents and their preschool or early-elementary-school children referred for assistance because of serious behavior problems. The system is applicable for families of children with normal development and children with mental or physical handicaps. It is most appropriate for use with children functioning at a cognitive level of between 2 and 5 years.

The observation system is designed to assess parents' use of a variety of child management techniques for implementing effective social contingencies. Five different standardized situations are defined, each oriented toward a specific set of child management skills: (1) giving and following through with instructions; (2) differential social attention; (3) use of a token system; (4) teaching new skills; and (5) use of time out. These skills were chosen on the basis of the designers' professional experience and a review of the parent training literature, which indicated that they are common ingredients of successful programs for parents.

To serve as a practical tool for clinical evaluation, limitations had to be imposed on the number of responses to be recorded in each structured situation. The present observation system emphasizes recording of parent responses entailed in the child management procedures, with limited recording of child responses. The focus on parent behaviors was selected in view of previous research establishing the functional value of specific child management techniques for modifying children's behavior, as well as the paucity of practical observation systems for measuring parents' use of these techniques. However, given the limited value of the child measures in the earlier version of the observation instrument, the revised system increases the attention given to child behaviors in two of the five structured activities, and thereby provides more detailed information on child performance.

Description of Structured Activities and Recording System[1]

The structured activities, which each last between 5 and 12 minutes, can be carried out either in the families' homes or in a simulated home environment within a clinic. Table 16-1 summarizes the instructions to parents regarding their role, the recording format, and the parent and child behaviors recorded during each structured activity.

The first activity, "Instruction Giving," assesses parents' skill in delivering and following through with instructions to their children. Prior to the observation, parents are asked to prepare six instructions they know their children can carry out. During observation sessions they are requested to deliver the instructions and have their children complete them, using whatever means they normally use to obtain compliance. Parents are given a written description of the structured activity, with sufficient information to indicate their role but without any direct suggestions on how to obtain child compliance.

During Instruction Giving, nine defined parent responses and four child responses are recorded during each instructional trial. In the initial version of the code, the child compliance categories referred only to the final completion of an instruction and provided no information on how quickly a child should initiate some movement toward compliance. In the present version, a measure of initiating compliance within 10 seconds is included, as is information on estimated trial duration (specifically, an observer judgment, at the outset of a trial, of whether an instruction should take less than or more than 30 seconds for the child to complete). Thus, the revised version provides two additional indicators of child performance.

If a child's behavior precludes the opportunity for a specific parent response to occur, the observer notes that the category is not applicable for that trial. For example, if a child complies quickly and independently with an instruction, the observer records that the physical assistance categories are not applicable. Responses occurring between trials on prespecified instructions are not recorded. Based on data obtained from the observations, calculations are made of the proportion of desired parent responses per opportunity to obtain a total correct performance score.

---

[1]The description of the structured observation system provided in this chapter is patterned closely after the account of the original system appearing in Budd, Riner, and Brockman (in press). A complete copy of the written instructions to parents, observation codes, and recording forms for each structured activity may be obtained upon request from Budd.

Table 16-1

Structured Observational Activities

Parent role	Recording format	Parent responses	Child responses
		Skill 1: Instruction Giving	
Prepare and deliver instructions for six motor tasks the child can do (e.g., "Turn off the light," "Put the books on the shelf")	Occurrence of responses during six instructional trials (maximum time: 7 minutes)	Get child's attention Clear instruction Wait 10 seconds Only one repeat No other verbal cues Physical help within 20 seconds Physical help later in trial Praise compliance Estimated length of instructional trial	Comply within 10 seconds Comply later independently Comply later with help Instructional trial duration
		Skill 2: Differential Attention	
Ask child to play independently and not interrupt parent while parent reads or works	Occurrence of responses at 7 audio tones sounded at 45-second intervals and between audio tones (time: 6 minutes)	At audiotape tones— Praise Ignore Request physical response Request verbal response Descriptor Disapproval Other attention Between tones— Ignore all inappropriate behavior Praise appropriate behavior (frequency)	At audiotape tones— Appropriate play Inappropriate play Deviant Between tones— Inappropriate play (frequency)

(continued)

425

Table 16-1 (*continued*)

Parent role	Recording format	Parent responses	Child responses

Skill 3: Use of a Token System

Parent role	Recording format	Parent responses	Child responses

Direct child in completing a task (e.g., making bed, setting table) with minimal help, and use a reward system	Occurrence of preparatory and completion steps, plus occurrence of other responses during 1-minute intervals (time: 6 minutes)	Preparatory—
		  Get tokens out
		  Explain token earning
		  Describe reward
		  State criterion
		Work session—
		  Give token contingently
		  Praise when giving token
		  Take token contingently
		  Give reason when taking token
		Completion—
		  Count tokens earned
		  Explain performance
		  Praise success or encourage
		    better performance next time
		  Criterion-based reward
			Appropriate work
			Deviant

Skill 4: Teaching New Skills

Parent role	Recording format	Parent responses	Child responses

Direct child in practicing two skills (e.g., use of spoon, motor imitation) the child has not mastered, using five practice trials for each skill	Occurrence of preparatory and completion steps, plus occurrence of other responses during five practice trials per skill (maximum time: 12 minutes)	Preparatory—
		  Remove distractions
		  Select appropriate materials
		Work session—
		  Get child's attention
		  Simple command
			Comply independently
			Comply with help

Model
Wait 5 seconds
Physical help within 10 seconds
Descriptive praise
Completion—
   End session with child
     compliance

None

Skill 5: Use of Time Out

Role play requiring child to sit on chair in corner for serious misbehavior—part of child can be played by adult trainer

Occurrence of responses (maximum time: 5 minutes)

Beginning—
  State misbehavior
  Use no other verbal cues when
    stating
  Guide to chair within 15 seconds
Middle—
  Set timer for 3 minutes
  Set timer within 15 seconds of
    guidance
  Return to chair if child leaves it
  Restate rule during return
  Use no other verbal cues during
    return
  Give no other attention during
    time out
Ending—
  Announce end of time out
  Time out lasts 2–4 minutes
  Parent ends time out, not child
  No comments re: misbehavior
    when ending
  Praise next appropriate response

None

The second activity "Differential Attention," evaluates parents' skill at praising appropriate child behavior and ignoring mild inappropriate responses. Parents are asked to occupy themselves with an activity such as reading, writing, or straightening up a room, and to instruct the children to play on their own and not interrupt them for the next several minutes. An audiotape recorder is activated to produce a short beep every 45 seconds. Parents are told that they can respond to their children at the tones if they choose, but are asked to minimize their attention at other times during the period. As for all structured activities, the instructions to parents are delivered through a written description of the activity, with an opportunity for the parents to ask questions before beginning the observation.

During Differential Attention, an observer records the type of child behavior occurring at the tones and the nature of the parent response during the first 10 seconds following each tone. Deviant child behaviors (e.g., leaving the room, serious aggression) occurring at the audiotape tone are noted by the observer, but the parental response to that behavior is not considered in evaluating parents' use of differential attention. Rather, an additional audiotape tone is played to obtain a total of seven opportunities. Calculations are made of the number of occasions on which parents praise appropriate behavior and ignore mildly inappropriate behavior to provide a total correct performance score.

Because the recording of responses only at the tones provides a restricted sample of behavior, and because the tones themselves may prompt parents to respond in a certain manner, the revised version of the Differential Attention code incorporates measures of parent and child responses between as well as at audiotape tones. In the revised code, the therapist identifies particular inappropriate child behaviors and records their frequency during the intervals between tones. At the end of each interval, the observer determines whether or not a parent ignored all instances of inappropriate behavior in that interval, and also denotes the frequency of parent praise during the interval. Thus, the revised version provides additional information about inappropriate child behavior and information about spontaneous parent attention.

The third structured activity, "Use of a Token System," examines parents' ability to set up and implement a reward system while the children complete a task. In the preliminary instructions, parents are specifically asked to use a reward system to encourage their children to work steadily and cooperate with them during the task. They are given a variety of forms of tokens (stars, chips, and a "happy face" stamp) and are asked to provide their children with one or more tokens during the work period to signify the children's performance toward a reward. They are requested to use the tokens as best they can to promote the children's performance. At the end of the work period, they are asked to decide whether the children have earned the reward, and to provide or withhold the reward accordingly.

Defined parent responses during Use of a Token System are organized into preparatory steps, behaviors during the work session, and completion steps. Preparatory and completion steps are scored as occurring or not occurring at appropriate times during the activity, whereas behaviors during the 5-minute work session are recorded upon their occurrence in 1-minute intervals. No child responses are directly recorded; however, definitions for appropriate work and deviant child behavior are included so that observers can determine for each minute of the work session whether a parent had the opportunity to deliver or withdraw tokens. Correct parent performance is considered to be a minimum of one token (accompanied by praise) given each minute in which a child is working appropriately. In addition, all deviant child behaviors are to be followed by withholding or withdrawing a token, accompanied by statement of the reason for token removal. An overall measure of correct parent performance is calculated by dividing the number of occurrences of correct parent behavior by the total number of opportunities.

The fourth activity, "Teaching New Skills," assesses parents' skill in conducting a practice session with their children on two tasks the children have not mastered. It is designed for children functioning at the 2-year level or below who need intensive help to learn new skills. Parents are given help in choosing appropriate teaching tasks and preparing verbal commands to deliver in each practice trial. As in Use of a Token System, defined parent responses for this activity are divided into preparatory actions, behaviors during the work session, and a completion step. The work session consists of 10 practice trials (five per task), during which a parent presents a command and provides help as needed to assist the child to complete the task. Child compliance (independent versus with help) is recorded for each trial. Correct parent performance is calculated by dividing total occurrences of correct responses over total opportunities.

The fifth structured activity, "Use of Time Out," evaluates parents' performance in placing their children on a chair in the corner for serious misbehavior. Unlike the other structured activities, in which the parents interact directly with their children, this activity typically involves the use of another adult (a trainer or student assistant) to play the role of a child. Parents are told to pretend that the adult is their child who has just done something highly disruptive or aggressive. They are asked to assume that their instructions to stop the behavior have not been successful, so as a disciplinary measure they are to have the "child" sit on a chair in the corner for a period of less than 5 minutes. The actor is given a script of behaviors to perform during the activity, in order to provide the parents with opportunities to use each step of the time-out sequence. A role-play format is used for this activity to avoid the problems of implementing time out with a child merely as a practice procedure; however, it can be applied directly within a parent–child interaction, contingent upon serious child misbehavior. A total of 14 appropriate parent responses are defined, and the occurrence or nonoccurrence of each response is recorded and later summarized over total possible responses to provide an overall correct performance measure.

ASSESSMENT OF THE STRUCTURED OBSERVATION SYSTEM AS A CLINICAL TOOL

The feasibility of the structured observation system was explored initially by using it as one means of evaluation with three small groups of parents who participated successively in a 10-week training program in child management (Budd *et al.*, in press). The participants were seven families (14 parents) of both normal and handicapped children, aged 3 to 8 years, who were referred to the Meyer Children's Rehabilitation Institute at the University of Nebraska Medical Center because of aggression, noncompliance, tantrums, and other disruptive behavior problems. Home observations were made of the families interacting in the structured activities on six to seven occasions across the 10-week period. Training in child management skills proceeded sequentially, and observations were scheduled before and after training of each skill, thus allowing for a multiple-baseline analysis of the effects of training on parent performance in the structured activities.

Two methodological aspects of the observation system were evaluated. Interobserver reliability was examined by comparing the independent observers' recordings during observations; and one index of validity was examined by comparing parent performance changes on the observational data to changes on two paper-and-pencil measures. These two measures were a Child Management Questionnaire, which assesses parents' knowledge of behavior management principles and their application, and a Parent–Child Behavior Inventory, which assesses parents' perceptions regarding the frequency of various appropriate and inappropriate child responses in the home.

Observations of families in the structured activities showed substantial changes in the levels of correct parent use of skills in each structured activity concurrent with clinic training. Mean levels of correct parent performance across all components of the structured activities were as follows: Instruction Giving, 55% before training and 86% after training; Differential Attention, 13% and 75%; Use of a Token System, 22% and 87%; Teaching New Skills, 42% and 88%; and Use of Time Out, 51% and 93%. All parents increased their levels of total correct performance on each trained skill, with similar changes for mothers and fathers.

The system also yielded high levels of interobserver reliability. After an observer training period estimated at 25–30 hours for all five structured activities, mean agreement levels of above 80% were achieved for 46 (or 79%) of the

58 response categories measured. Only two categories had mean reliabilities of less than 70%: complying with help in Instruction Giving (63%), and getting children's attention in Teaching New Skills (67%). Total agreement levels on all components for each structured activity ranged from 82–94%.

On the paper-and-pencil measures, parents showed statistically significant changes correlated with training. Scores on the Child Management Questionnaire increased from an average of 50% correct before training to 78% after training. These findings support the positive changes in parent performance observed during structured activities. Parents' ratings of their children on the Parent–Child Behavior Inventory also improved substantially and remained relatively stable at a follow-up conducted 6–12 months later. Thus, even though the child response measures in the structured situations showed minimal changes following training, parents perceived their children as significantly improved.

Overall, the initial evaluation provided an encouraging indication that the structured observation system is useful to evaluate parent training. The next question, which became the topic of the present research, was whether therapists who were not involved in the initial development of the system would also find it useful. Specifically, Budd and the other designers were interested in three aspects of its use by naive therapists: (1) acquisition of interobserver agreement; (2) outcome data on changes in parent and child behaviors with individual clinical cases; and (3) therapists' opinions regarding the advantages and disadvantages of the observation system.

An opportunity for evaluation arose when Fabry joined the staff of the Meyer Children's Rehabilitation Institute as coordinator of the parent training program. She had previous experience in parent training and behavioral assessment, but was unfamiliar with the structured observation system. After Fabry independently trained herself and three other therapists in the system, she obtained reliability data on the system using the naive therapists, proposed modifications in two of the five codes (as described earlier), and then implemented the revised system as an assessment tool in clinical parent training cases. The outcome of this evaluation is described below.

Acquisition of Reliable Recording

In addition to Fabry, the observer trainees were two graduate students in psychology who were currently obtaining experience in parent training, and another psychology staff member who was experienced in behavioral parent training. This last trainee joined the staff after the initial observer training was completed and thus received training on her own. Training materials consisted of the observation codes for each structured activity, recording forms, videotapes of families interacting in the activities, short-answer tests on the codes, and supplies (e.g., written instructions to parents, sample tokens, and audiotape with tones) required to carry out the observation sessions. To monitor the training process, a log was kept of training components and the time devoted to each component.

Training on each structured activity entailed the following steps: reading the observation code, discussing the definitions and recording rules, practicing recording from videotapes, taking a short-answer test on the code, practicing again with videotapes if needed, and practicing *in vivo*. Training proceeded across one activity at a time, until a criterion of 80% agreement was achieved between observers on individual behavior categories. Fabry trained herself in all five structured activities and trained the two students in four activities. (Due to time constraints, the students received no training in Teaching New Skills.) Training for the new staff member occurred after the observation system was revised and entailed only the modified Instruction Giving and Differential Attention codes.

After training was completed, interobserver agreement was assessed by having two therapists simultaneously observe families engaging in the structured activities, either in the clinic or in the families' homes. In some cases, observations were conducted as part of an initial evaluation of families referred for parent training; in other cases, the observations were part of a follow-up evaluation of families served previously. The observers' independent records were compared for agreement on each opportunity for occurrence of each behavior. To be scored as an agreement, both observers had to record the same judgment on whether the behavior occurred, did not occur, or was not applicable on each opportunity. A percentage of agreement was then calculated for each response category by computing the number of agreements divided by the number of agreements plus disagreements and multiplying the quotient by 100.

Table 16-2 summarizes the results of observer training and subsequent reliability checks by the naive therapists. Training for Fabry and the two graduate students on the original code for four structured activities required a total of 15.3 hours. Although observer training time was not monitored precisely in the initial evaluation by Budd and her colleagues, the overall training time for all five activities was estimated at 25–30 hours, which is considerably more than in the present project. The relative training time for specific activities is comparable between versions, with Instruction Giving requiring the greatest time and Use of Time Out the least. Training on the revised Instruction Giving and Differential Attention codes for the experienced therapist was shorter than for Fabry and the students, which may be related to greater familiarity with the code by the trainer, prior parent training experience by the trainee, or the fact that only one person received training.

As Table 16-2 shows, the naive therapists obtained high levels of interobserver agreement in all structured activities. The only mean levels below 77% for individual behaviors were in four cases where there were very few opportunities to score the responses across all reliability checks. For most behaviors, the mean interobserver agreement levels of the naive therapists were at

Table 16-2
Training Time and Reliability with Naive Therapists

Structured activity	Training Hours	Number of reliability checks	Range of mean reliability percentages across behaviors	Mean reliability across all components
Original code				
Instruction Giving	5.5	8	92–100	97
Differential Attention	5.0	14	77–100	97
Use of a Token System	3.5	2	50–100	96
Use of Time Out	1.3	4	67–100	96
Revised code				
Instruction Giving	4.5	6	90–100	95
Differential Attention	3.2	6	71–100	91

or above those obtained in the initial evaluation. Reliability on the new behaviors included in Instruction Giving and Differential Attention averaged 93–100% for individual responses. Thus, it appears that therapists naive to the structured observation system can train themselves within an efficient time frame to be reliable recorders of parent and child behaviors.

Use with Clinical Cases

A second issue regarding the applicability of the structured observation system for naive therapists concerns the validity of the instrument as a clinical tool. While the initial evaluation showed clear-cut changes in parent responses following training in the relevant skill areas, whether individual clinical cases would reflect similar changes in parent behavior concurrent with training was yet to be determined. In addition, the initial evaluation showed that the categories of child behavior reflected little change from pretreatment to post-treatment, while significant changes were seen in parent skills.

A related topic, which is discussed first, concerns the frequency with which therapists implement the structured observation system. Because the initial evaluation of the system used a multiple-baseline design, the designers conducted systematic observations of each family every 1 to 2 weeks across the training program. For clinical purposes, it may be infeasible or unnecessary to conduct observations this often for each structured activity. In applying the structured assessment system to clinical cases, Fabry conducted observations of structured activities when these were judged to be clinically useful.

Thus far, three parent training cases have been completed in which the structured observation system was implemented for clinical evaluation. The families involved were clinical cases referred for parent training because of child behavior problems (e.g., noncompliance, tantrums, excessive demands for attention, and destructive behavior) and scheduled for evaluation at the time this investigation was being conducted. The target child in each family was a boy who ranged in age from 2 years 10 months to 4 years 3 months and who was reported to be of normal intellectual development. The parents ranged in age from 27 to 43 years, had a minimum of a high-school education, and earned between $30,000 and $37,000 as a family. In all cases, both the mother and father participated in parent training. Interventions were individualized for each family, but focused on behavior management procedures such as praising, ignoring, use of physical guidance, and time out. The procedures were trained through readings, discussions, modeling, and practice in the clinic. For one family, several home visits were scheduled as well, after it became clear that the parents were not applying the procedures taught to them in clinic sessions. Training continued for 3, 5, and 13 sessions for individual families, with the most sessions provided to the family receiving training both in the clinic and home.

Scheduling of Structured Assessments

Typically, data were collected on parent and child behaviors in the structured activities twice per case—once before training and once at termination. Instruction Giving and Differential Attention were implemented with all families during the initial evaluation, as these situations have the most overall applicability to families who report difficulty managing their children's behavior. Based on the information gained in the initial evaluation, one or more other structured activities were selected for observation, depending on the nature of a child's problems and a judgment of the appropriate child management skills for remediating these problems. In some cases, observation of these structured activities was included in the initial evaluation; however, in other cases, assessment of performance in the additional structured activities was deferred until training was completed in more fundamental areas of child behavior management. Thus, it was found that assessments on additional structured activities could be conducted during the course of treatment, in accordance with the progress of intervention and decisions on skills to be trained.

With the family for which home visits eventually were scheduled, a midtraining assessment was also conducted, in order to assess the progress of intervention and to highlight areas in need of additional emphasis. After several clinic sessions with this family, recurrent inconsistencies were noted between the parents' verbal behavior, which indicated a thorough understanding of the procedures, and their interactions with their son, which showed little generalization of the procedures to spontaneous situations. Fabry was unsure whether this inconsistency represented only the need for one to two training sessions on facilitating generalization, or whether the parents had not yet acquired competence in using the skills. The midtraining assessment showed little improvement in parent or child behaviors in the structured activities, thus suggesting the latter interpretation. Based on the lack of change evident from the assessment, training was shifted to the home, where Fabry informally observed the family interacting in naturalistic situations and provided intensive *in vivo* coaching on the use of the behavior management skills. Thus, it was found that the structured assessment data were useful in planning changes in intervention, as well as in determining initial treatment goals and evaluating outcome.

Data on Parent and Child Behavior Changes

Measures of individual parents' performance in the structured activities before and after clinical parent training are presented in Figure 16-1. For Differential Attention, three behaviors are depicted to differentiate data obtained *at* audio-tape cues from the new measures (in the revised observation code) regarding behavior *between* audiotape cues. All six parents showed improvement in performance at audiotape cues following training, and some parents showed generalized use of these skills to the periods between cues as well. The other graphs in Figure 16-1 present total correct parent performance in other structured activities and indicate that all parents substantially increased their use of child management skills following training. The relative amounts of improvement shown by these parents in clinical training are comparable to the changes observed for parents in the initial study, except that gains in Differential Attention and Use of a Token System are slightly less dramatic for the later parents.

Figure 16-2 presents measures of child behavior during the two structured activities that were revised to provide additional information on child performance. Appropriate behavior at audiotape cues during Differential Attention increased from a mean of 70% before training to 92% after parent training. The amount of change was limited, due to relatively high pretraining levels for this response. Still, changes in appropriate behavior observed in these children were greater than in the earlier study, which reported average pretraining and posttraining levels across all children of 80% and 83%, respectively. The new measure—inappropriate behavior between cues—shows a large decrease following training for two parent–child pairs, a modest decrease for two other pairs, and no change or a slight increase for two additional pairs. These findings suggest that the usefulness of the measure of inappropriate behavior between cues is dependent on a child's engaging in frequent inappropriate responding during the pretraining assessment. For children who display problem behaviors in this activity at pretraining, the measure appears to provide a valuable indicator of change following training.

Three measures of child compliance in Instruction Giving are also presented in Figure 16-2. In four of the six parent–child pairs, the children eventually complied with all instructions even before parent training. A similar pattern was found in the initial study, thus indicating that eventual compliance is not a

PARENT BEHAVIOR

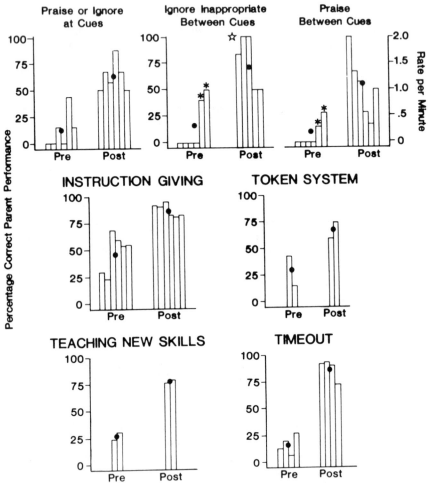

Figure 16-1

Levels of correct parent performance of child management skills before and after training during structured activities. Individual bars represent a single parent's data for one session, and solid dots indicate the mean performance across all parents. Bars for individual parents are arranged in a consistent order across pretraining and posttraining observations. Asterisks above some bars indicate that the bars contain data from a midtraining assessment for a mother and father whose pretraining assessment occurred before the observation system was revised to include these measures. The star in place of one bar denotes that no posttraining data were available for one parent on ignoring inappropriate behavior between cues, because no inappropriate behavior occurred during the observation.

CHILD BEHAVIOR

DIFFERENTIAL ATTENTION

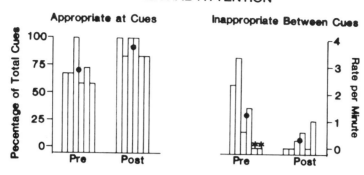

INSTRUCTION GIVING

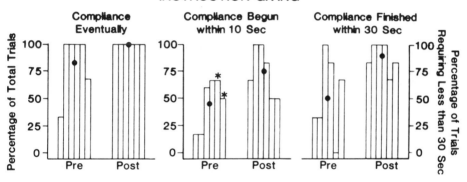

Figure 16-2

Levels of child behavior before and after training during structured activities. Individual bars represent a child's behavior with one parent for one session, and solid dots indicate the mean performance across all parent–child pairs. Bars for individual parent–child pairs are arranged in a consistent order across pretraining and posttraining observations and conform to the order in which the parents' data are presented in Figure 16-1. Asterisks above some bars indicate that the bars contain data from a midtraining assessment for two parent–child pairs whose pretraining assessment occurred before the observation system was revised to include these measures.

sensitive measure for most children. However, the new measures assessing whether compliance is initiated within 10 seconds and whether compliance is completed within 30 seconds (when appropriate to the task) showed more differential responding before and after training. These additional measures appear to enhance the sensitivity of the observation system to child behavior.

In summary, the pretraining and posttraining data from these three clinical parent training cases show improvements in parent skills similar to those found in the initial evaluation of the assessment instrument. These findings strongly support the usefulness of the structured observation system as a clinical assessment tool when training parents in effective social contingencies. Of course, without a controlled experimental design, the functional effects of training on parent and child behaviors cannot be verified; however, it is clear that the parents and their children performed better in structured activities after training than before. The new measures included in the revised version of the observation code increase the information available on child behavior and spontaneous parent attention without reducing the reliability of the recordings. The clear-cut differences in pretraining and posttraining performance on most measures suggest that, for many families, a single observation before training and another observation at termination are sufficient to provide the data needed for clinical evaluation. Additional assessments conducted periodically during the course of training can provide supplementary information about parents' acquisition and maintenance of behavior management skills.

Therapist Comments on Utility

After using the structured observation system with several families, Fabry and her fellow therapists found three of the five structured activities to be very helpful as clinical tools and found the two others to be moderately helpful. Instruction Giving, Differential Attention, and Use of Time Out were considered most useful, because they assess skills most often taught in behavioral parent training. The systematic framework allowed for careful examination of critical skills that often are examined only informally in clinical settings. The structured assessment device provided useful information in determining treatment needs, served as a baseline measure of parent and child behaviors, and provided a focus in writing evaluation and treatment reports. For the family whose progress in treatment was unclear, the assessment procedure provided an objective means of comparing pretraining and midtraining performance, thereby confirming the need for continued training in basic management skills. After the Instruction Giving and Differential Attention codes were modified to include additional measures of child behavior, they were judged to be valuable indicators of children's responsiveness to treatment as well.

In clinical experience, Use of a Token System and Teaching New Skills entailed some procedural problems that limited their usefulness. The work session in Use of a Token System often was too short to allow a child to complete the task specified by the parent, which in turn affected the parent's opportunities to deliver tokens. Also, the recording system provided limited information about parents' delivery of tokens and social attention during the activity. Teaching New Skills entails an invariant teaching procedure on each trial, such that it incorporates no provisions for shaping or fading procedures across trials. While the procedures assessed in Teaching New Skills are appropriate for initially teaching a child a new skill, they do not measure the parent's ability to alter the procedures as the child acquires increased skill on a task. Based on this experience, we presently are preparing a revised version of the Token System code. We also are considering a future revision of the Teaching New Skills code that would incorporate measurement of parents' skills in shaping and fading procedures (cf. Koegel, Glahn, & Nieminen, 1978).

An additional difficulty with Use of a Token System and Teaching New Skills is that they measure primarily parents' execution of skills, rather than parents' ability to plan, organize, solve problems, and progressively alter tasks and criteria. Thus, it is possible for parents to perform well in these structured activities, but not to be able to adapt the skills to unrelated tasks. To alleviate this drawback, a written test may be useful to supplement observation in the structured activities. The written test for each activity would assess specific issues in the design, revision, and analysis of child performance that cannot be evaluated efficiently by direct observation. We currently are preparing such a written test to supplement Use of a Token System.

Finally, the naive therapists who were trained to use the codes commented on some inconsistencies in the recording procedures. As the codes were developed and revised, gradual changes were made in the recording procedures to accommodate technical considerations. By the final revision, the recording forms were so familar to the initial developers of the system that they were unaware of any recording inefficiencies. Having therapists learn the observation system independently of the initial developers highlighted instances in which the recording format was less concise and systematic than it might have been. Although the naive therapists soon adjusted to these minor inconsistencies, they may increase observer training time or decrease the likelihood that naive clinicians would view the codes as useful. We currently are planning technical revisions in some of the recording forms to streamline data collection.

In summary, we found that the structured observation system had many positive attributes as a clinical assessment tool, but also had some procedural limitations. Therapist feedback has been very helpful in prompting revisions of the system and suggests that others will also find aspects of the system that need to be adjusted to meet their own clinical needs. Such changes often can be made while keeping the same structured framework for observation. We encourage other therapists to use the structured observation system, adapt it to their needs, and inform us of their opinions regarding its usefulness as an assessment tool. For it is just this sort of applied testing and feedback that will stimulate technological advances in behavioral assessment devices for parent training.

CONCLUSIONS

Clinical assessment of parent and child behavior is a critical dimension of a parent training technology for applied settings, and one that has received little systematic study. While research tools have been developed for evaluating parent–child interactions, these devices often require extensive observer training and resources for data collection and analysis. Even then, the instruments may be of limited use in applied settings, where therapists often train parents under different conditions than prevail in laboratory programs. A structured assessment format offers an efficient method of obtaining direct observational data on parent and child behaviors for clinical parent training. The objective data derived from structured observations provide an accurate base from which to identify treatment needs, monitor the effects of training, alter training as needed, and compare intervention outcomes across families.

Budd and her colleagues designed a structured observation system for use in behavioral parent training and implemented it as one means of evaluation within a clinical training program. Fabry and other naive therapists were then trained in its use and achieved reliable recording with only a few hours of training. When the observation system was used for clinical evaluation with individual families, it reflected considerable positive changes in both parent and child behaviors concurrent with training. Moreover, the system provided a means of clarifying the effects of parent training with a family whose progress in training was uncertain, due to conflicting information from indirect methods of assessment. Therapist comments indicated that three of the five structured activities within the observation system were particularly useful as clinical tools. Based on therapist experiences with the system, additional revisions are under way to enhance its applicability to clinical settings.

Thus far, the evaluation of the structured observation system has focused on its reliability, efficiency, and sensitivity as a clinical assessment instrument with a small number of families. Additional research plans on the system include the following:

1. Obtaining normative data on nonclinic families to assess whether the measures discriminate clinic from nonclinic families.
2. Implementing the structured observation system within a long-term follow-up evaluation of clinic families and assessing its appropriateness as a follow-up measurement tool.
3. Comparing pretreatment and posttreatment data on the structured observation system with data from unstructured home observations to examine its validity in reflecting parent–child interactions.
4. Obtaining data on more families and correlating structured observational data to other measures (e.g., parent reports, knowledge tests, and therapist impressions).

5. Assessing the types of children, parents, and problems for which the structured observation system is most appropriate as an assessment device.

Currently, research is under way on the first two of these topics.

Behavioral assessment is an essential ingredient of behavioral parent training. As treatment packages increasingly are being disseminated to therapists in applied settings, it is important that practical assessment devices also be developed and disseminated for applied use. The progressive development of the structured observation system, based on practice and evaluation in applied environments, exemplifies a useful research strategy for advancing a behavioral assessment technology in parent training.

Acknowledgments

We are very grateful to our staff colleague, Beth VonSeggern, and to Natalie Gendler and Gail Horras for serving as observers in this project. Their conscientious and cooperative involvement in learning the observation system was most helpful. Our sincere thanks goes to Stephen Greenspan of the Boys Town Center, who provided generous support and assistance to Budd throughout the preparation of the chapter. We also are appreciative of the Word Processing staff at the Boys Town Center, who prepared the written report. This project was supported in part by Project 405 from Maternal and Child Health Services to the Meyer Children's Rehabilitation Institute of the University of Nebraska Medical Center. Copies may be obtained from Budd at the Meyer Children's Rehabilitation Institute, University of Nebraska Medical Center, 42nd and Dewey Streets, Omaha, Nebraska 68105.

References

Altman, K., & Mira, M. Training parents of developmentally disabled children, In J. L. Matson & F. Andrasik (Eds.), *Treatment issues and innovations in mental retardation.* New York: Plenum Press, 1982.

Baker, B. L., Brightman, A. J., Heifetz, L. J., & Murphy, D. M. *Steps to independence: A skill training series for children with special needs.* Champaign, Ill.: Research Press, 1976.

Becker, W. C. *Parents are teachers.* Champaign, Ill.: Research Press, 1971.

Budd, K. S., Riner, L. S., & Brockman, M. P. A structured observation system for clinical evaluation of parent training. *Behavioral Assessment,* in press.

Christophersen, E. R. *Little people.* Lawrence, Kans.: H & H Enterprises, 1977.

Christophersen, E. R., Arnold, C. M., Hill, D. W., & Quilitch, H. R. The home point system: Token reinforcement procedures for application by parents of children with behavior problems. *Journal of Applied Behavior Analysis,* 1972, *5,* 485–497.

Eyberg, S. M., & Robinson, E. A. *Dyadic parent–child interaction coding system: A manual.* Unpublished manuscript, 1981. (Available from S. M. Eyberg, University of Oregon Health Sciences Center, Portland, Oregon 97207.)

Fleischman, M. J. Social learning interventions for aggressive children: From the laboratory to the real world. *The Behavior Therapist,* 1982, *5,* 55–58.

Forehand, R., & King, H. E. Pre-school children's noncompliance: Effects of short-term behavioral therapy. *Journal of Community Psychology,* 1974, *2,* 42–44.

Forehand, R., & King, H. E. Noncompliant children: Effects of parent training on behavior and attitude change. *Behavior Modification*, 1977, *1*, 93–108.

Forehand, R. L., & McMahon, R. J. *Helping the noncompliant child*. New York: Guilford Press, 1981.

Gordon, S. B., & Davidson, N. Behavioral parent training. In A. S. Gurman & D. P. Kniskern (Eds.), *Handbook of family therapy*. New York: Brunner/Mazel, 1981.

Graziano, A. M. Parents as behavior therapists. In M. Hersen, R. M. Eisler, & P. M. Miller (Eds.), *Progress in behavior modification* (Vol. 4). New York: Academic Press, 1977.

Hall, R. V., Axelrod, S., Tyler, L., Grief, E., Jones, F. C., & Robertson, R. Modification of behavior problems in the home with a parent as observer and experimenter. *Journal of Applied Behavior Analysis*, 1972, *5*, 53–64.

Hanf, C. *Modifying problem behaviors in mother–child interaction: Standardized laboratory situations*. Paper presented at the meeting of the Association of Behavior Therapies, Olympia, Washington, 1968.

Haynes, S. N. *Principles of behavioral assessment*. New York: Gardner Press, 1978.

Hughes, M. H., & Haynes, S. N. Structured laboratory observation in the behavioral assessment of parent–child interactions: A methodological critique. *Behavior Therapy*, 1978, *9*, 428–447.

Koegel, R. L., Glahn, T. J., & Nieminen, G. S. Generalization of parent training results. *Journal of Applied Behavior Analysis*, 1978, *11*, 95–109.

Mash, E. J., Hamerlynck, L. A., & Handy, L. C. (Eds.). *Behavior modification and families*. New York: Brunner/Mazel, 1976.

Mash, E. J., Handy, L. C., & Hamerlynck, L. A. (Eds.). *Behavior modification approaches to parenting*. New York: Brunner/Mazel, 1976.

Miller, W. H. *Systematic parent training*. Champaign, Ill.: Research Press, 1975.

O'Dell, S. Training parents in behavior modification: A review. *Psychological Bulletin*, 1974, *81*, 418–433.

O'Dell, S. L. Enhancing parental involvement in training: A discussion. *The Behavior Therapist*, 1982, *5*, 9–13.

Patterson, G. R. *Families* (Rev. ed.). Champaign, Ill.: Research Press, 1975.

Patterson, G. R., Reid, J. B., Jones, R. R., & Conger, R. E. *A social learning approach to family intervention* (Vol. 1, *Families with aggressive children*). Eugene, Ore.: Castalia, 1975.

Peed, S., Roberts, M., & Forehand, R. Evaluation of the effectiveness of a standardized parent training program in altering the interaction of mothers and their noncompliant children. *Behavior Modification*, 1977, *1*, 323–350.

Reid, J. B. (Ed.). *A social learning approach to family intervention* (Vol. 2, *Observation in home settings*). Eugene, Ore.: Castalia, 1978.

Rinn, R. C., Vernon, J. C., & Wise, M. J. Training parents of behaviorally disordered children in groups: A three-years' program evaluation. *Behavior Therapy*, 1975, *6*, 378–387.

Robinson, E. A., & Eyberg, S. M. The Dyadic Parent–Child Interaction Coding System: Standardization and validation. *Journal of Consulting and Clinical Psychology*, 1981, *49*, 245–250.

Rose, S. D. Training parents in groups as behavior modifiers of their mentally retarded children. *Journal of Behavior Therapy and Experimental Psychiatry*, 1974, *5*, 135–140.

Salzinger, K., Feldman, R. S., & Portnoy, S. Training parents of brain-injured children in the use of operant conditioning procedures. *Behavior Therapy*, 1970, *1*, 4–32.

Sloane, H. N. *Behavior guides*. Fountain Valley, Calif.: Telesis, 1976.

Wahler, R. G. The insular mother: Her problems in parent–child treatment. *Journal of Applied Behavior Analysis*, 1980, *13*, 207–219.

Wahler, R. G., House, A. E., & Stambaugh, E. E. *Ecological assessment of child problem behavior*. New York: Pergamon Press, 1976.

Willems, E. P. Behavioral technology and behavioral ecology. *Journal of Applied Behavior Analysis*, 1974, *7*, 151–165.

WHAT TO DO?
Matching Client Characteristics and Intervention Techniques through a Prescriptive Taxonomic Key

Lynne H. Embry
University of Kansas

Most parent training efforts have been directed toward finding effective techniques to improve parent–child interactions. As a result, a large pharmacopoeia of techniques for improving parent–child interactions in dysfunctional family relationships now exists. Unfortunately, as direct service providers, when therapists have attempted to apply these techniques to clients, they have discovered that these techniques sometimes do not work with some, or all, of the clients. The worst part of that discovery is that they usually do not know why those techniques did not work. The frustration from those failures often results in therapists' saying, "Well, parent training isn't effective. Parents just don't care about their kids. Parents are not reinforced by their children's improvement. Our strategies are not effective."

There are some actual reasons why those techniques do not work. However, the techniques are not faulty or ineffective, nor are parents unresponsive to their children. Therapists may not know all the reasons parent training sometimes fails, but that does not mean that these problems are unresolvable or incomprehensible. They can understand the reasons; they can analyze why they have failed; and they will eventually acquire enough information to match intervention techniques successfully to the appropriate population with which they are working.

Just as drug researchers have discovered organism-specific characteristics that systematically interact with the therapeutic effects of particular treatments and drugs, it is probable that family researchers will find that family-specific characteristics interact systematically with the therapeutic effects of behavioral training procedures. In that context, researchers and therapists will discover that in order to *pre*scribe effective interventions for families, they will probably need to *de*scribe more of those critical, interactive family characteristics that facilitate or inhibit successful therapeutic outcomes. Some researchers have already begun to work with the types of characteristics or variables that are likely to influence, either positively or negatively, the outcome of their treatment programs. The research conducted by Robert G. Wahler and his associates on family insularity is a perfect example. Some of the work conducted by Gerald Patterson and his colleagues is also going beyond "parent only"-focused parent training. Patterson's program now simultaneously teaches the adolescent in the family the same skills that the parents are taught. Both Wahler's and Patterson's work are good examples of approaches that are going beyond the parent–child dyad to discover more about those characteristics that determine appropriate interventions for specific families.

In this chapter, I first describe a program of research that my colleagues and I have conducted at the University of Kansas for the past 3 years to identify the impact of specific family characteristics on parent–child interactions and on treatment outcome. We learned a great deal more about the impact of specific family characteristics on parent–child interactions than we did about the impact of those characteristics on treatment outcome. Few differences emerged in treatment outcome, apparently because our treatment program was effective in remediating dysfunctional parent–child interactions for all types of families. However, there certainly were differences across families to begin with that were very prescriptive of the training techniques necessary to be successful. Those differences are the subject of the second section of this chapter. Third, I describe an empirical method that we have devised to organize all the information and data that we have collected on families' interactions and characteristics (and that I recommend that other therapists collect as well). This method permits one to test hypotheses about matching family characteristics and available intervention techniques. There are, of course, many intervention techniques available. The difficulty is predicting which techniques are going to work with whom and how. This method may offer such predictive capabilities. However, first, let me describe how we came to develop this organizational model and to collect the data on families on which the model's development is based.

THE PARENT PROGRAM

The Parent Program is a research and service program for families with young children (typically, children between the ages of 1 and 7 years). Nearly all teaching and training takes place in client families' homes; my colleagues and I do very little in-office or in-clinic training. Actually, parents have relatively few problems with their children in my office—there are interesting toys available, and staff members provide excellent child care. Thus, parent training in child management skills seems less necessary in the office or the clinic setting.

Subjects

The mean age of the children is approximately 3½ years. Most of the children the Parent Program works with are between 2 and 5 years of age. These children are either normal, gifted, or handicapped. About one-third of the children are handicapped—developmentally delayed, learning-disabled, language-delayed, or behaviorally disordered.

About one-third of the families have very serious problems; they have often been referred by Child Protective Services for child abuse. Another third of the families are fairly standard, clinic-referred families; these fairly intact families have noncompliant, aggressive children. These parents may have some other problems, such as depression, but they have fewer and less serious problems than the multiproblem families do. The final third represents those wonderful, healthy, competent parents who are a joy to work with. These families are participating because they want to become better parents. This diversity of families has been both enjoyable and educational. My colleagues and I have learned much about interventions with families that are easy to work with, and just as much about interventions with families that are very difficult to work with. Although the outcomes are similar, the strategies for achieving such similar outcomes are quite different.

Therapists

The individuals working with families in the Parent Program come from a variety of backgrounds, including child psychology, special and elementary education, social work, and behavior analysis. Although the majority of them have been working on graduate degrees, that seems an unnecessary requirement. Other skills are far more important. Parent trainers in this program must be extremely precise in recording family interactions, and must simultaneously be able to make quick and appropriate decisions when giving feedback within sometimes chaotic home observations. That is, they must be able to recognize dysfunctional or supportive child and parent behaviors quickly, and they must be able to prescribe immediately effective ways to reduce or encourage target behaviors. Additionally, their commitment in training must lie with teaching parents (adults) the skills to improve their children's behavior and the family relationship. A commitment to improving children's behavior is not enough—it teaches few skills to parents that they may integrate into their daily interactions to prevent or resolve future problems. Finally, parent trainers must be able to work flexible hours, including weekends and evenings. Trainers work with families in their homes at the times they report difficulties, and such problems occur infrequently from 9 A.M. to 5 P.M.

Of course, a whole host of other skills are important. These include the capability to communicate directly and positively, to break a task into smaller goals attainable by even the most deficient parent, to enjoy working with a diversity of people, to tolerate and find value in variations in life style dissimilar to one's own, to persevere when frustrated, and to set clear limits about what one will or will not do. None of these skills is directly related to a particular content area or number of years in school. Thus, the Parent Program emphasizes process skills within the context of parent education.

Training

Families typically participate in the Practical Parenting Class, a 10-week parent education and support group. Each family also receives individual home-based training through weekly homechecks. The Practical Parenting Class focuses on two training areas. The first is problem-specific training, in which parents are taught to formulate and implement behavior change programs to resolve such setting-specific problems as shopping behavior, toilet training, or mealtime hassles. The second area of training is the teaching of child management skills to parents to improve their children's compliance—basically, general compliance training.

In problem-specific training, parents are taught a very standard behavioral problem-solving strategy. Parents select the target behaviors to change; they learn to observe and record their children's behavior; and they design and implement treatment programs. As parents are learning these techniques in the Practical Parenting Class, they are carrying out those procedures in the home with staff supervision and support during homechecks. The general compliance training runs exactly parallel to the problem-specific training. Trainers are working on general compliance training with parents at home simultaneously with the work on problem-specific techniques and training. The parent-managed behavior change projects address problem-specific issues and skills; the general compliance training provides parents with the basic child management skills that can be applied in any setting or used at any time.

Problem-Specific Training

Parent-managed behavior change projects are developed in a step-by-step process in such a way that, as each step in the sequence is introduced in a class session (e.g., observing and recording behavior), the parents will use that information to develop their behavior change projects. For example, when methods of recording are described and practiced during the second week of class, parents must choose their own methods of recording and devise data sheets to measure their previously chosen and behaviorally defined target behavior(s). The home assignment for that week is to begin observing and recording the children's target behaviors on a daily basis for the rest of the course. Once the parents have collected the baseline data and completed reliability checks with staff members during the weekly home visits, they develop treatment programs to change their children's target behavior. These treatment programs are based on the behavior change techniques parents learn in the Practical Parenting Class. The techniques taught include descriptive positive feedback, use of stickers and "happy face" charts, shaping, time out, response-cost procedures, contracting, and so on.

Typically, parents select behavior problems to work on, such as bedtime battles, mealtime hassles, getting dressed quickly, room cleanup, and so forth. Self-care skills, such as toilet training, self-dressing, or shoe tying, are also frequently chosen target behaviors. Less often, academic or preacademic skills, such as letter labeling, writing, or learning numbers, or colors, are selected for problem-specific behavior change projects.

Parents are assisted both at home and in class by staff members in designing and carrying out these behavior change projects. Figure 17-1 displays a typical parent-managed behavior change project, in which the parent selected and defined the target behavior to modify (quiet independent play by her 4-year-old son); recorded the data for 30 minutes on a daily basis using a 5-minute interval-by-interval method of recording; graphed the data; and implemented a treatment program to increase quiet independent play by having the child self-record each 5 minutes, having the child earn a preferred snack later that afternoon, and using a door-shut time out for noisy play or interruptions.

General Compliance Training

In addition to the problem-specific training, each parent simultaneously receives general compliance training. During each weekly homecheck, staff members observe parents and children interacting in two other settings, an Instructional Training (IT) setting and a Routine Times (RT) setting.

In the first observational setting, IT, parents are required to ask their children to put away a series of easily nameable toys in one of four easily nameable containers. For very young or developmentally delayed children, the number of toys and the number of containers may be reduced, or the parent may simply hand the toy to the child and point to a container. This task requires an ambulatory child. This task is designed to assess child compliance in a short period of time (5–15 minutes). This IT task is extremely effective in indicating, in a very short period of time, whether children will be cooperative or compliant with parental instructions; what children will do when they are noncompliant; and what parents will do when their children are compliant or noncompliant.

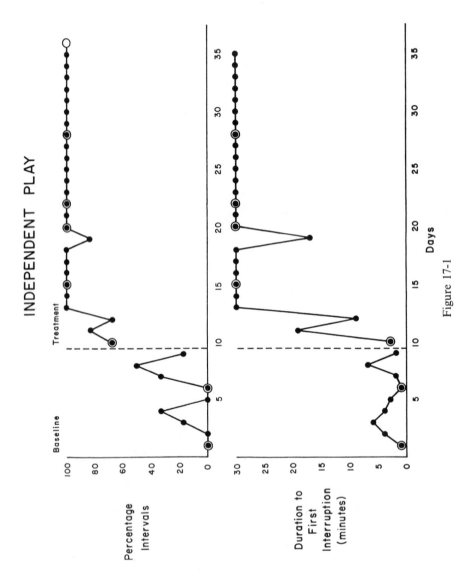

Figure 17-1

Parent-managed behavior change project to increase a 4-year-old boy's independent play.

The second observational setting, RT, is essentially a generalization setting. Staff members ask parents to choose times in which they are likely to have difficulties managing their child's behavior and in which they give at least three instructions to the child during the 16-minute observation period. Families do a variety of things during those times. Some families may teach their children; some families may engage in a specific routine, such as mealtime or bedtime; and other families may interact with their children in a variety of ways. Staff members collect data on the types of instructions parents give; on children's compliant, noncompliant, appropriate, and inappropriate behaviors; on the frequency and types of attention parents direct toward their children; and on the types of limit-setting techniques parents may use.

A 10-second interval method of recording is used in which only the first occurrence of a behavior is recorded. Additionally, reliability observations are conducted during approximately 60% of all home observations. The reliability observers are other parent therapists. Frequent reliability checks conducted during the weekly homechecks insure accurate recording of parent–child interactions and appropriate use of parent training procedures by therapists. Weekly review of reliability scores and family progress also insures the integrity and consistency of program implementation across program staff members.

Once baseline data have been collected, usually in three to five sessions, staff members begin teaching the parents during these homechecks. Once a parent has learned the basic child management skills in the Practical Parenting Class, training is begun at home in the use of those skills during the two observational settings. Thus, the home observations serve not only as evaluation settings for parent and child behavior changes, but also as training opportunities to teach parents the skills identified as helpful in successful child rearing. Those child management skills include differential attention, descriptive feedback, time out, physical guidance, and appropriate instruction giving.

Training is accomplished by interacting directly with the parents as they are interacting with their children during the home observations. The trainers provide verbal and graphic feedback to the parents and children. Additionally, parents are taught to self-record specific behaviors such as instructions or positive feedback with wrist counters. Trainers determine what skills parents need to learn from the ongoing evaluation system, which describes both successful and dysfunctional parent–child interaction patterns in the high-demand (IT) and more routine (RT) settings. Although feedback and training are directed primarily to the parents, children often actually participate in the graphic feedback phase. That is, the children are taught to read their own and their parents' graphs.

Examples of general compliance training with two different families may be found in Figures 17-2 and 17-3. The family depicted in Figure 17-2 was a low-stress, two-parent family. The target child was 3½ years of age, the youngest of three, and the only male child in the family. The mother enrolled in the Practical Parenting Class, reporting difficulties in controlling her son's noncom-

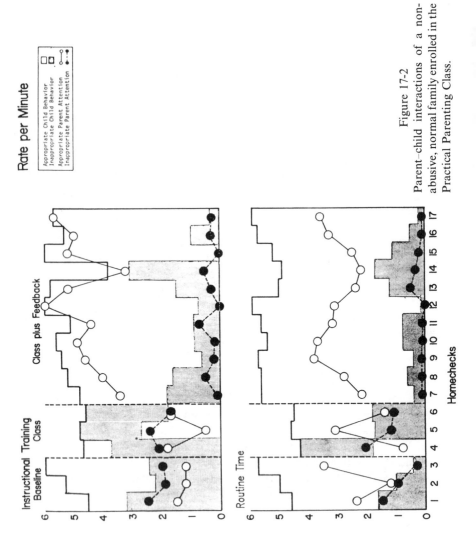

Figure 17-2
Parent-child interactions of a non-abusive, normal family enrolled in the Practical Parenting Class.

450

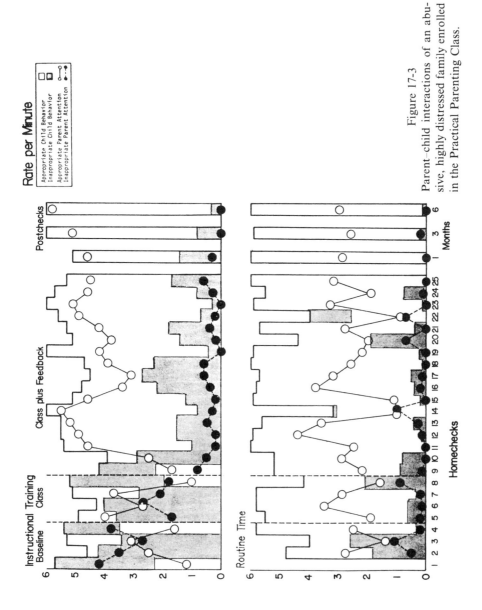

Figure 17-3
Parent–child interactions of an abusive, highly distressed family enrolled in the Practical Parenting Class.

451

pliance. This family was referred to the Parent Program by a friend, a parent who had previously completed training through the Practical Parenting Class. The top graph, which displays the child's compliance and noncompliance and parent attention to compliance and noncompliance in the IT setting, indicates that during baseline the child was indeed quite noncompliant, and his mother was very attentive to his noncompliance. However, during the much less demanding RT observation, the child's levels of appropriate and compliant behaviors were much higher, and his mother was also more responsive to his appropriate behavior. With home-based feedback, the mother's use of positive attention and planned ignoring improved, and the child's behavior improved a great deal in both settings. Follow-up data are not available for this family, because they moved to a distant community shortly after completing treatment.

The data presented in Figure 17-3 are from a severely stressed family with a 3-year-old, language-delayed, severely aggressive boy. The mother was a single parent who had recently separated from her alcoholic husband. The mother was also on antipsychotic medication and had been hospitalized for mental illness several times in the past year. The family was referred by Child Protective Services for abuse and neglect. Both the child's behavior and the parents' behavior were quite variable during baseline in both the IT and RT settings. This variability persisted for quite some time during training. However, following 9 months of training, the family's interactions were much improved, and these gains were maintained at 1, 3, and 6 months posttreatment. Obviously, this family took much longer to train, and the course of treatment was far more variable in comparison to that of the low-stress family presented in Figure 17-2. Nevertheless, despite these difficulties, the parent did acquire the target skills; she was able to improve her child's behavior substantially; and both the child and the parent maintained those improvements through the 6-month follow-up.

The differences between these two families during baseline and treatment were remarkable. The low-stress family had fewer skill deficits that took much less time to remediate, and the course of treatment was stable and of fairly short duration (approximately 5 months). The severely stressed family displayed much greater variability both during baseline and training, and it took many more training sessions to produce comparable behavioral improvements in the observed parent–child interactions (approximately 9 months). Clearly, family characteristics interacted with the types of interventions implemented, although the outcomes for both families were similarly favorable.

PROGRAM OF RESEARCH

The program of research that my colleagues and I carried out was designed to answer two major questions. First, we wanted to know whether a group parent training program produced changes in parent–child interactions in the home;

that is, could parents generalize the skills they had learned in behavioral child management course to daily interactions at home with their children? Second, we wanted to know what differences there were in family interaction patterns that were correlated with various stress factors affecting the family system, and whether treatment outcome varied in association with these factors and/or interaction patterns. Thus, as each parent–child dyad participated in the Practical Parenting Class in a similar manner, the stress factors impinging on each family were identified and later analyzed. The results of these two major research efforts are described below.

Study 1: Generalization of Group Parent Training

Three cohorts of families ($n = 9$, $n = 8$, $n = 9$) participated in the Practical Parenting Class and were observed interacting with their children during weekly homechecks in the two observation settings described previously, the IT and RT settings. Baseline data were collected during the first 4 weeks of the class, during which time the parents learned how to write behavioral definitions and record and graph their children's behavior for the parent-managed behavior change projects. Intervention techniques were not discussed, nor were suggestions on how to teach or manage children's behavior provided.

During the second condition, class only, parents learned about behavioral child management skills, including positive reinforcement, time out, response-cost procedures, and point systems. Additionally, they were assisted in developing and carrying out problem-specific treatment programs as part of their behavior change projects. This included direct feedback to the parents in the home during the behavior change projects to insure correct use of the behavior management techniques and treatment success. However, no feedback nor instruction was provided during the weekly generalization observations in the IT or RT settings.

A third condition, class plus feedback, was initiated when an individual parent–child dyad evidenced no, or limited and stable, generalization in the IT or RT settings. Direct home-based feedback was provided sequentially, first in one setting and then in the other setting. This resulted in a series of individual multiple baseline experimental designs within families across the two generalization settings.

The data presented in Figure 17-4 are the group mean scores for each weekly observation for a single cohort, Cohort B. These data are representative of the findings for the other two cohorts. Each bar represents the mean score for all families in Cohort B during a given week's home observation. The baseline data are from the 4 weeks of observations prior to the weekly class sessions on behavior management techniques. The class-only data are from the three weekly observations for each family in that condition, and the class-plus-feedback data are from the final five weekly observations for each family prior

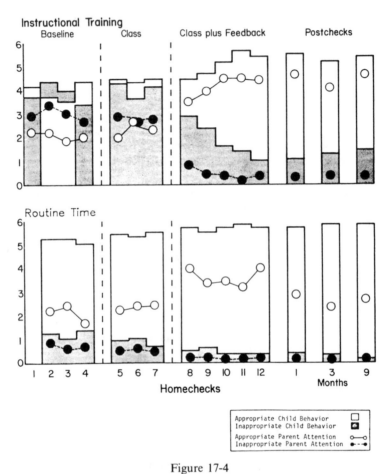

Figure 17-4

Cohort B: Analysis of the generalization from classroom to home of child management skills taught in the Practical Parenting Class and in the home.

to completion of training. The bars to the right are group means for all families during follow-up at 1, 3, and 6 months posttraining.

During baseline in the IT setting, the children were quite noncompliant, and their parents were more responsive to the noncompliance than they were to their children's compliant behavior. However, in the RT setting during baseline, the children were far more compliant, and their parents were more responsive to the compliance than to the noncompliance.

With the onset of the class-only condition, there was no evidence of generalization by either parents or children in the more difficult, problematic IT setting. In the RT setting, however, both parents and children showed some improvements—children's appropriate, compliant behavior increased slightly and their noncompliant behavior decreased slightly, and parental attention to appropriate, compliant behavior also increased slightly. Thus, there was some evidence of generalization to the setting in which there were few problems to begin with, and no generalization to the setting in which serious problems did exist.

The introduction of direct training in the home in the generalization settings, the class-plus-feedback condition, resulted in sizeable improvements in both parents' and children's behavior in the IT setting; additional moderate gains were made by both parents and children in the RT setting. The postcheck data indicated that the gains made during treatment were maintained 1, 3, and 6 months posttraining.

This study answered the question of whether parents can and do generalize from the classroom to the home. Parents were able to generalize the skills taught to affect improvements in their children's behavior in a less serious problem setting, but were unable to do so in a more serious problem setting. These findings suggest that group parent education programs attempting to teach problem-specific child management techniques may be quite successful at remediating mild interaction problems, but are unlikely to be successful at remediating moderate to severe problems. However, the addition of a direct training component (e.g., home-based feedback) is likely to remediate even seriously dysfunctional family interactions.

Study 2: Impact of Stress on Family Interactions

This research was directed toward analyzing the impact of differing family characteristics on parent–child interactions. The family characteristics chosen for analysis were defined as stress factors that had been identified by other researchers (e.g., Bronfenbrenner, 1976; Farber & Ryckman, 1965; Kempe & Kempe, 1978) as likely to have an adverse impact on family functioning. The characteristics selected for these analyses included the following: abusive parents; presence of a handicapped child in a family; presence of marital stress; parents with less than a high-school education; and multiproblem families in which two or more stress factors were identified. A number of other stress factors were identified but not included in these analyses, such as the presence of a chronically or critically ill immediate family member; legal contact by an immediate family member as a defendant or through arrest; hospitalization for psychiatric treatment; and others.

Objective criteria were used to decide whether a given stress factor existed within a family. The criteria were as follows:

Abusive parents: The family had an open case file with Child Protective Services.

Handicapped child: The child's handicap was identified by another agency or school program; the child lived at home; and the child was a target child for the home observation and parent training.

Marital stress: The parents (in two-parent families) had participated in marital counseling in the past year; they had been separated and lived apart because of marital problems in the past year; or an episode of physical abuse by a spouse had taken place in the past year.

No marital stress: The parents (in two-parent families) had not participated in marital counseling or been separated, and no episodes of domestic violence had taken place.

Less than high-school education: The participating parent had neither a high-school diploma nor a general equivalency diploma (GED).

High-school education or greater: The participating parent had a high-school diploma or a GED, or had gone to college.

Severe stress (the Multiproblem family): Two or more stress factors were identified.

Low stress: No stress factors were identified within a family.

For comparison purposes, three groups were formed. The low-stress group was composed of families for whom no stress factors were identified. These families were usually healthy, competent families. Families without evidence of marital stress formed the comparison group for the maritally stressed group, and families in which the mother had a high-school education or more formed the comparison group for families in which the mother was less well educated. The composition and size of the groups are given in Table 17-1.

The total number of parent–child dyads included in this research was 45. Some families fell into more than one group because of the presence of two or more stress factors; other families were included in only one group.

Every family in the study had a target child between 3 and 7 years of age and participated in the Practical Parenting Class. The data presented are from mother–child dyads only, although, in slightly more than half of the two-parent families, both mothers and fathers completed the training program.

Data on parent–child interactions were collected during the weekly home observations of the IT and RT settings. Again, the data presented in Figures 17-5 through 17-7 are the group mean scores for each weekly observation; that is,

Table 17-1
Composition and Size of Stressed and Comparison Groups in Study 2

Distressed families	n	Comparison groups	n
Abusive parents	7	Low stress	10
Handicapped child	9	Low stress	10
Marital stress	11	No marital stress	15
Less than high-school education	10	More than high-school education	20
Severe stress	10	Low stress	10

each bar represents the mean score for all families in that group during a given week's home observation. Data only from baseline and the final 6 weeks of training are presented because of the tremendous variation in length of time in treatment across families. The length of time in treatment varied from 3 to 9 months. Length of time in treatment also served as a dependent measure of treatment outcome, and the results are reported in the section that follows. Finally, only data from the IT setting observations have been presented. Differences in interaction patterns among groups were most distinctive in the IT setting, the setting in which the most serious problem behavior occurred.

Our findings were as follows:

1. Handicapped children were the most noncompliant during baseline, followed by children in maritally stressed families. Abused children, children with poorly educated mothers, and children in multiproblem families were all about equally noncompliant. Children in the low-stress families were the most compliant.
2. All groups of children exhibited fairly stable behavior patterns through baseline, except for children in maritally stressed families; these children became increasingly noncompliant.
3. All of the children's behavior improved considerably following parent training through home-based feedback.
4. During baseline, distressed parents were consistently more negative than positive in responding to their children's behavior.
5. Comparison parents were more positive than negative in response to their children's behavior. Parents in the low-stress group were the most consistently positive.
6. Parents of handicapped children exhibited both the highest rates of negative and positive attention.
7. All groups of parents exhibited fairly stable interaction patterns through baseline, except maritally stressed parents; these parents became increasingly negative, as did their children.
8. All parents learned to use positive feedback and limit-setting techniques

Mean Rate per Minute Scores of Positive and Negative Parent Attention
and Appropriate and Inappropriate Child Behavior

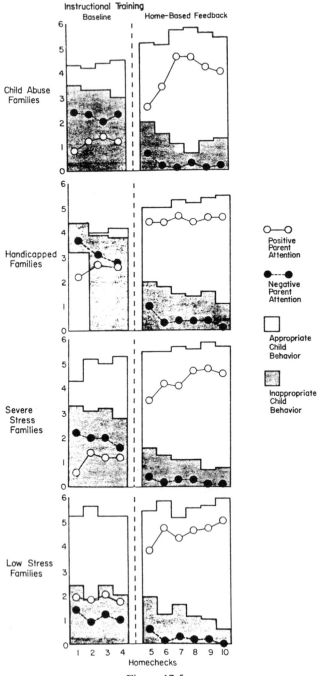

Figure 17-5

A comparison of the impact of specific family characteristics on parent–child interactions and treatment outcome.

Mean Rate per Minute Scores of
Positive and Negative Parent Attention
and
Appropriate and Inappropriate Child Behavior

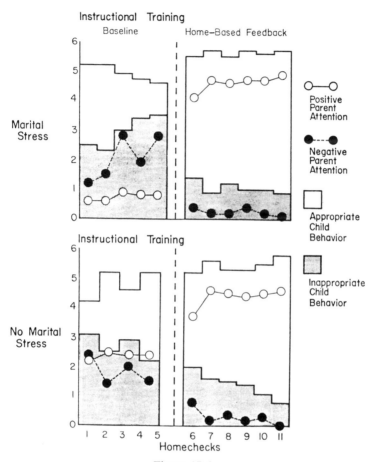

Figure 17-6

A comparison of the impact of marital stress or its absence on parent–child interactions and treatment outcome.

Mean Rate per Minute Scores of
Positive and Negative Parent Attention
and
Appropriate and Inappropriate Child Behavior

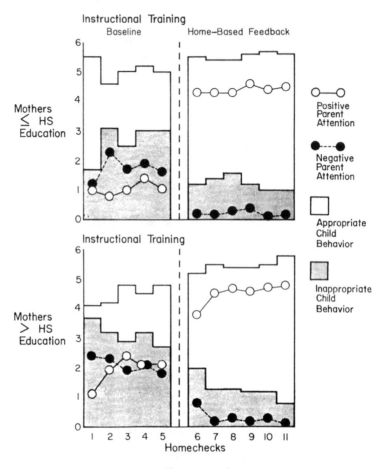

Figure 17-7

A comparison of the impact of mothers' education levels on parent–child interactions and treatment outcome.

effectively, increasing their children's positive, compliant behavior. All parents were far more positive than negative following training.

9. Length of time in treatment to achieve comparable levels of success varied across groups. As the level of stress increased (the number of identified stress factors increased), the number of weeks in training increased. Families in the severe-stress group took twice as long as families in the low-stress group to learn and reliably use the child management skills taught.

These data indicate that the existing types of parental skill deficits vary considerably across families experiencing differing types of stress. Parent training programs need to be prepared to teach different child management skills to different families. For example, parents of handicapped children needed only to learn to withhold attention for noncompliant behavior and to use other limit-setting procedures, because they were already very positive and responsive to their children's compliant behavior; however, abusive parents needed to learn not only to increase their positive attention to their children's compliant behavior, but also to decrease their negative attention to their children's noncompliant behavior. And, surprisingly, families experiencing marital stress may be at the greatest risk for interactional difficulties and in the greatest need for support and training. Once again, the importance of analyzing individual differences and designing family-specific interventions is emphasized. Careful assessment of families' interactional styles is crucial to efficient and effective interventions.

Our question about the impact of stress on treatment outcome was answered only in a limited way. Because our training program terminated only when a family exhibited criterion-level improvements over a 3-week period, there is little variation in final outcome. If this program had terminated training following a predetermined and limited time period, as many programs do, the results might have been clearer, but fewer families would have acquired the target skills. There are a number of ways to measure treatment outcome, however. The measures we used were length of time in treatment and dropout rate. Additionally, one could measure the strength of generalization and maintenance of behavior changes. Such measures have been completed but have not yet been analyzed.

Length of time in treatment did vary a great deal among groups—families with few or no problems learned the skills taught and effected positive behavior changes in their children most quickly (3 months), whereas the multiproblem families were the slowest to acquire the skills and improve their children's behavior (9 months). When training takes that long (as much as 9 months), the reinforcer of immediate child behavior change is available neither to parents nor therapists to encourage either parents' continued use of the newly learned behavior management techniques or therapists' continued training efforts.

Nevertheless, these parents did learn these skills and, on an individual basis, appear to be maintaining the behavior changes.

Dropout rates among groups did not differ. The overall dropout rate for all families participating in this research was 10%. In comparison to most other programs' dropout rates, which range from 30% to 90% (Szykula, 1979), this rate was considerably lower. Why this is the case is not clear. It may be the result of a combination of factors, including the use of structured home visits, group and individual treatment, training in both problem-specific techniques and general compliance training skills, or the extensive use of graphical feedback on various aspects of child and parental behavior changes. Even the highest-risk families, who were in treatment for many months, stayed in the program. It may be that just as each family's problems differ, the reasons families stay in or leave treatment differ.

In summary, Study 2 indicated that family-specific characteristics are associated with very different patterns of parent–child interactions, and that these characteristics interact systematically with the therapeutic effects of behavioral training procedures. In order for behavioral parent training to be more effective, not only must our analyses, or diagnostic assessments, of family skills and problems become more precise, but our training programs, our therapeutic interventions, must also be tailored to individual family needs.

The "shotgun" approach we are currently using is neither efficient nor (probably) effective with many families. Most families need additional training beyond classroom discussion and modeling, including direct training of general child management skills in the home. And families with more serious problems may need considerably longer training periods to learn to use child management skills consistently and to effect stable improvements in their children's behavior.

INTEGRATION: THE TAXONOMIC KEY OF FAMILY FUNCTIONING

I have already commented on the importance of obtaining more precise information on family relationships in order to prescribe better interventions for families. Naturally enough, that request also implies that I think it is important for behavioral researchers and therapists to increase the categories and amount of information that they acquire on families. Just collecting that information causes some organizational problems. What do therapists do with that much information? How can they use it in a helpful, therapeutic way? If they simply collect more data but have no way to integrate it into a comprehensible body of information capable of guiding therapeutic decision making, then it is a ridiculous waste of valuable time and effort. What I would like to suggest, in this next section, is a relatively simple, easily understood method of organizing and analyzing the mountains of information that therapists could (and probably should) acquire on family functioning.

But first, I discuss the hallmark of this approach, behavioral assessment. Then I describe the kind of assessment strategy that must be adopted by the field before therapists will be able to prescribe consistently successful intervention strategies.

The behavioral approach to assessment essentially provides descriptive information about the rate of particular behaviors, the topography of those behaviors, and the contingent relationships that exist between specific behaviors. In parent training, therapists look at the relationship between parents' interactions and children's behavior. Behavioral assessment does provide prescriptive information about dysfunctions in that relationship. For example, if a parent rarely responds to a child's appropriate social initiations (requests made in a regular tone of voice), and the parent quickly reacts to the child's inappropriate initiations (requests made by whining), then the therapist knows why the child whines a great deal and knows what behavior management techniques need to be taught to the parent.

Behavioral assessment does identify specific facilitative and dysfunctional relationships that are likely to enhance or remediate the target behaviors. Unfortunately, behavioral assessment only indicates what skills to teach. It does not indicate how to teach those skills; how the family is likely to respond to teaching efforts; how long it will take for the parent and child to learn new ways of interacting; or what can go wrong and what to do if something does go wrong. All these questions are left to an individual's therapeutic judgment.

Ecobehavioral Assessment of Family Relationships

Obviously, there are other factors in family environments that influence both the process and outcome of therapy. The measurement of those factors is popularly known as "ecobehavioral assessment." An ecobehavioral approach to assessment describes family relationships as the intersection of behavioral contingencies, characteristics of the physical setting, family history, and family perceptions or expectations about those relationships.

The ecobehavioral assessment of family functioning might be thought of as a set of concentric circles. The first circle is the one most often discussed, and it is certainly the most influential; this center circle is child-focused. Information important to acquire (which most behavioral therapists and researchers do acquire) includes the child's current behavioral skills and problems, the child's developmental level and progress, and the child's developmental history. The next circle represents the impact of the parent and the other immediate family members on the child, especially the other spouse. A therapist needs to know the health status of the marital relationship, how child-rearing responsibilities are assigned, and what the parents' own child-rearing experiences have been.

The outermost circle represents the family's relationship with the community. The kinds of community resources (e.g., friends, schools, health care) available to and used by parents appear to have a significant impact on parent–child interactions (Garbarino, 1976; Wahler, 1980). First the child, then the parent, then the parents' marital relationship, and then the family's community support network from these expanding circles of influence. All have an impact on family functioning—some quite directly and intensely, others in a more diffuse but encompassing manner.

The ecobehavioral approach examines relationships from a contextual perspective. Each context, or perspective, adds to an understanding of the family relationship. For example, if a behavioral therapist is confronted with a family in therapy and the identified problem is that the child will not help around the house, the therapist might first respond, "The child will not help around the house because the consequences are inadequate for maintaining the behavior." If the therapist takes a developmental perspective, other questions are asked: "How old is the child? What tasks is the child actually asked to do? Are those age-appropriate demands? Does the child have the prerequisite skills necessary to complete the task?" If the therapist takes an ecological perspective, sill other inquiries are made, and those inquiries relate to whether the physical environment is designed to support the completion of the tasks: "Is it possible for this child to do the tasks? Are the necessary materials available? Is someone available to monitor the completion of the task?" (In two-career families with older children, this problem may be a significant barrier to treatment success.)

The importance of taking an ecological perspective was confirmed for me when working with a particular family. The family had a visually handicapped 11-year-old who was supposed to wash the dinner dishes each evening. He did so, but very poorly. His parents were furious with him for continuing to do the job sloppily. On one of several home visits, while I was watching the boy wash dishes, it became quite clear why he did such a poor job—there was only one light in the kitchen, and it was directly behind the child's head while he washed dishes. The child's own shadow blocked him from being able to see whether the dishes were clean or dirty as he washed them. Because the child was visually handicapped, this physical characteristic of the setting was a major stumbling block to the successful completion of the dishwashing task.

The final perspective a therapist might also adopt is the examination of the family's, and especially the target parent's, social environment. If the only topic of discussion a parent has with a spouse or friends is the child's noncompliance, and the therapist attempts to reduce the child's noncompliance, the parent will lose the major basis of communication with the spouse or friends. If the basis of the friendship or marital relationship is complaints about the children, efforts to improve child compliance may well be met with great resistance.

Thus, an ecobehavioral analysis of family relationships provides valuable information not only about the behavioral contingencies circumscribing each family's interactions, but also about the impact of a variety of factors on each family's coping skills and informational needs, the development of individually tailored intervention plans, the commonalities of needs and effects across families, and a systematic evaluation of differing intervention strategies' effectiveness both within and across families.

The Concept: A Taxonomy of Family Functioning

Of course, an enormous amount of data on the parameters of family relationships will be accrued if an ecobehavioral approach to assessment is adopted. The task of organizing that data into a coherent form useful to the practitioner in direct contact with distressed families becomes a critical concern.

Currently, a service provider acquires information on certain characteristics of the family's interactions and history; examines these data for the presence of diagnostic cues; formulates a diagnosis of the family's skills and skill deficits; and implements an intervention that may remediate the family's difficulties and enhance the family's relationship. Basically, this classification approach is known as "clinical inference." It is likely to be very functional for a well-experienced practitioner. However, the direct service provider with immediate concerns, limited experience, and limited access to a skilled family therapist is likely to find this trial-and-error method an inefficient, lengthy, and possibly harmful learning process. Thus, a significant problem in the area of family research and therapy is the development of an objective method of duplicating this inferential technique.

I would like to recommend a method of information processing known as a "taxonomic key." This process involves taking the information acquired on a given family and evaluating it by asking a series of specially structured questions that relate family characteristics to diagnosis, prescription, and treatment outcome. This method is built upon the formation of an integrative framework that incorporates and organizes the information obtained through the ecobehavioral assessments of many families' relationships; evaluates through multiple outcome measures the effects of various intervention strategies employed with those families; and then provides prescriptive analyses for service providers working with individual families based on this body of data. This integrative framework is designed to handle a sample of one, although its initial formulation must be based on many cases. Thus, a direct service provider seeing relatively few families each year would have access to the same quality of clinical inference employed by the well-experienced practitioner. Indeed, if the inferences made by family therapists were examined, their inferences would be found to resemble this keying method in logical form.

The taxonomic key is a classification method that has been used in biology for three centuries. Taxonomic keys are used by biologists to determine the particular class that an individual specimen or case fits, although they are not a means of classifying a species (Sokol & Sneath, 1965). The keying method, essentially a diagnostic method, is a way of locating an individual within the framework of a preexisting, established taxonomic system. This method represents a type of reasoning by elimination, a method similar to a technique of diagnosis described by Wechsler (1958) as the "method of successive sieves." Such an approach is described earlier in this chapter, in the formation of a low-stress comparison group (see p. 456).

The use of formalized taxonomies is not without precedent in educational or therapeutic fields. Taxonomies have been developed to describe and analyze educational environments (Bloom, Englehart, Furst, Hill, & Krathwohl, 1956); to assist nurse practitioners in the examination and diagnosis of childhood diseases (Chinn & Leitch, 1974); and to help social workers identify and interact with apathetic, neglectful mothers in rural Appalachia (Polansky, DeSaix, & Sharlin, 1972).

To build a prescriptive key of family functioning, it is obvious that the keying method used in biology needs to be modified, since characteristics of family relationships vary tremendously. The usual taxonomic system is "monothetic"—that is, defining features are unique; a single characteristic or set of characteristics defines a group. Sokol and Sneath (1965) point out that in a monothetic system, all members of the group must have all characteristics in the set to be classified in that group. However, in a "polythetic" system, identification is based on the greatest number of shared features, such that no single feature is essential or sufficient to make an organism a member of the group. (An example of the use of a polythetic classification is described earlier in this chapter, in the criteria used for classifying a family as a "multiproblem family." See p. 456.)

A polythetic system of classification of family functioning may be built upon the information on a number of child, parent, and family characteristics gained through the ecobehavioral assessment. For such a taxonomy to function in a prescriptive manner, information on the effectiveness of various intervention strategies—measures of treatment outcome—will have to be correlated with those identified family characteristics. Initially, as individual families are evaluated and treated, the findings are incorporated into a rudimentary structure of the classification system in order to generate a more extensive and accurate keying system. As the taxonomy assumes a more prescriptive role, each additional family's ecobehavioral assessment and treatment outcome measures would provide validation of the key's prescriptive accuracy and capability. Quite quickly, then, such a classification system, a taxonomic key, would enable a service provider working with distressed families to identify target families by their specific characteristics and to prescribe proven interventions to enhance healthy family relationships and to remediate dysfunctional family relationships.

In summary, the ecobehavioral assessment of family relationships would not only provide information on planning family-specific interventions, but would also provide a sensitive monitoring technology to evaluate the impact of those interventions systematically. The development of a taxonomic key of family functioning would assist service providers in the identification of families at risk and in the prescription and implementation of successful intervention strategies.

An Example: A Preliminary Taxonomy of Family Functioning

I now describe a prototype of a taxonomic key devised by Dennis Embry and myself (Embry & Embry, 1981). The prototype itself may be found in Figure 17-8. The first component of this taxonomy is a risk assessment of the seriousness of a family's dysfunction. The risk assessment begins with the set of information obtained through the ecobehavioral assessment of the child's behavior and history, the innermost circle of those concentric circles of influence on the family relationship described earlier. The risk assessment then moves progressively through the other circles of influence by asking a series of structured questions about the data collected on parent–child interactions, marital interactions, and community interactions.

The first step in the risk assessment is based on an analysis of the family's observed interactional difficulties. Behavioral observations of parent–child interactions collected during the diagnostic phase (baseline) form the basis for the initial assignment of risk. The severity of risk is determined by the identification of particular interaction patterns that have been closely associated with various levels of severity of family problems (e.g., child abuse).

An examination of the data from a hypothetical family, Susan and Buddy Smith, may make the process of using a toxonomic key clearer. Buddy Smith is 4 years old, and his mother, Susan, has been divorced from Buddy's father for 2 years. Susan works full time, and Buddy spends part of his day at preschool and part of the day at a babysitter's. Susan found out about the program during a parent–teacher conference when she told the teacher of the battles she had with Buddy in getting him ready for school each morning and to bed each evening. During the initial interview and through the diagnostic assessment phase, much information on the family's interactions and history has been acquired. The therapist is ready to develop a treatment program for the Smiths.

Turning to the "Parent–Child Behavior" section of the risk assessment, the therapist examines the Smiths' home observation data and locates the Smiths on the table there. Step 1 is to examine the relationship between the child's level of appropriate behavior and the parent's responsiveness to that appropriate behavior. Buddy's mother does attend to approximately 60% of his appropriate behavior, but Buddy's behavior is only appropriate about 40% of the time. The Smiths are assigned a "risk factor" of 3.

Turning the page, the therapist goes on to Step 2, which evaluates the overall distribution of parental attention. Unfortunately, Buddy's mother is consistently more attentive to his negative, oppositional behavior than to his positive, cooperative behavior. In fact, of all the time she spends interacting with Buddy, 80% of her time is spent in nagging him, repeating commands,

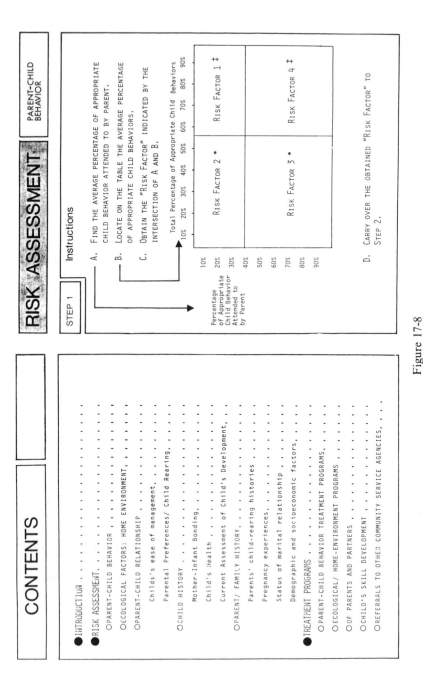

Figure 17-8

Taxonomic key of family functioning. These pages exemplify the construction of a taxonomic key of family functioning based on the ecobehavioral assessment of family relationships. ‡Partially supported by data from Embry and Herbert-Jackson (1977); also proposed for further investigation. *Proposed for further investigation.

RISK ASSESSMENT

INSTRUCTIONS

FOR EACH HISTORY PERIOD (E.G., PRENATAL), ENTER THE APPROPRIATE NUMBER OF POINTS FOR EACH PERIOD. WHEN ALL ENTRIES ARE MADE, ADD THE NUMBERS TOGETHER. USING THE SUM, ADJUST, AS INDICATED, THE PARENT-CHILD BEHAVIOR PROGNOSIS.

(Entries)

● PRENATAL

If severe medical complications (See Appendix to the manual for definitions), add 5 points. . . . . . ____

● POSTNATAL

○ If mother and child were separated for 48 hours after birth, add 10 points. . . . . . ____

○ If the child(as an infant) was hospitalized after the mother was discharged, add 2 pts. for each day . . . . . ____

○ For each day that the child (as an infant) was not visited by the mother, add 1 point . . . . . ____

TOTAL HAZARD POINTS . . . . ____

PARENT-CHILD BEHAVIOR PROGNOSIS ADJUSTMENT

IF THE SUM IS EQUAL TO OR GREATER THAN 30 POINTS, THEN MOVE THE PROGNOSIS UP ONE DEGREE IN SEVERITY.

IF THE SUM IS BETWEEN 15 AND 29 POINTS, THEN MOVE THE PROGNOSIS UP 1/2 DEGREE IN SEVERITY.

IF THE SUM IS LESS THAN 15 POINTS, MAKE NO ADJUSTMENT IN THE LEVEL OF PROGNOSIS SEVERITY.

(continued)

| STEP 2 | Instructions |

A. LOCATE RATIO OF PARENT ATTENTION TO APPROPRIATE AND INAPPROPRIATE CHILD BEHAVIOR.

B. LOCATE OBTAINED "RISK FACTOR" ON THE TABLE.

C. OBTAIN RECOMMENDED THERAPEUTIC PROTOCOL AND CORRELATED FAMILY FUNCTION PROGNOSIS

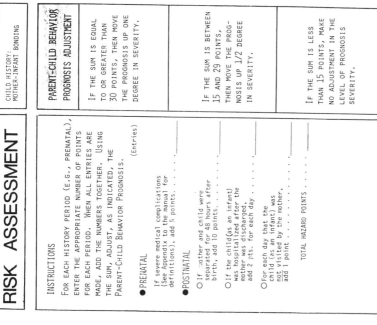

RISK FACTOR

	1	2	3	4
90% app/ 10% inapp	Behavior Treatment Program:* (i) 1 B (ii) 1 C — Prognosis: SERIOUS	Behavior Treatment Program:* (i) 1 B, if ecology assessment has score of 80 or more. (ii) 1 C — Prognosis: MODERATE	Behavior Treatment Program:* (i) 1 C (ii) 1 D — Prognosis: MILD	Behavior Treatment Program:‡ (Not indicated unless score on Parent Attitude Survey is greater than 25, then 1 C) Prognosis: GOOD
80% app/ 20% inapp				
70% app/ 30% inapp				
60% app/ 40% inapp				
50% app/ 50% inapp				
40% app/ 60% inapp	Behavior Treatment Program:‡ (i) 1 A (ii) 1 B (iii) 1 C — Prognosis: CRITICAL	Behavior Treatment Program:* (i) 1 B (ii) 1 C — Prognosis: SERIOUS	Treatment‡ (i) 1 C (ii) 1 D — Prognosis: MODERATE	Treatment‡ (i) 1 C — Prognosis: MILD
30% app/ 70% inapp				
20% app/ 80% inapp				
10% app/ 90% inapp				

D. CONSULT APPROPRIATE BEHAVIOR-TREATMENT PROGRAM, SEE RISK ASSESSMENT: ECOLOGY.

Figure 17-8 (*continued*)

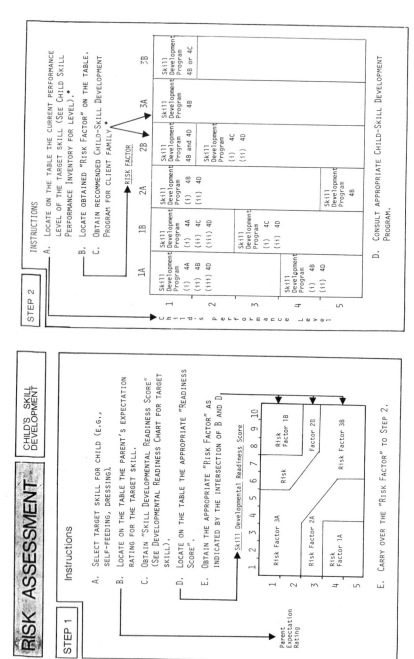

RISK ASSESSMENT | CHILD'S SKILL DEVELOPMENT

STEP 1

Instructions

A. SELECT TARGET SKILL FOR CHILD (E.G., SELF-FEEDING, DRESSING).

B. LOCATE ON THE TABLE THE PARENT'S EXPECTATION RATING FOR THE TARGET SKILL.

C. OBTAIN "SKILL DEVELOPMENTAL READINESS SCORE" (SEE DEVELOPMENTAL READINESS CHART FOR TARGET SKILL).

D. LOCATE ON THE TABLE THE APPROPRIATE "READINESS SCORE".

E. OBTAIN THE APPROPRIATE "RISK FACTOR" AS INDICATED BY THE INTERSECTION OF B AND D

E. CARRY OVER THE "RISK FACTOR" TO STEP 2.

Skill Developmental Readiness Score

	1	2	3	4	5	6	7	8	9	10
1	Risk Factor 3A						Risk Factor 1B			
2						Risk				
3	Risk Factor 2A						Factor 2B			
4	Risk Factor 1A						Risk Factor 3B			
5										

Parent Expectation Rating

STEP 2

INSTRUCTIONS

A. LOCATE ON THE TABLE THE CURRENT PERFORMANCE LEVEL OF THE TARGET SKILL (SEE CHILD SKILL PERFORMANCE INVENTORY FOR LEVEL).*

B. LOCATE OBTAINED "RISK FACTOR" ON THE TABLE.

C. OBTAIN RECOMMENDED CHILD-SKILL DEVELOPMENT PROGRAM FOR CLIENT FAMILY*

RISK FACTOR

	1A	1B	2A	2B	3A	3B
Child's performance Level 1	Skill Development Program (i) 4A (ii) 4B (iii) 4D	Skill Development Program (i) 4A (ii) 4C (iii) 4D	Skill Development Program (i) 4B (ii) 4D	Skill Development Program (i) 4B and 4D	Skill Development Program 4B	Skill Development Program 4B or 4C
2						
3		Skill Development Program (i) 4C (ii) 4D		Skill Development Program (i) 4C (ii) 4D		
4	Skill Development Program (i) 4B (ii) 4D		Skill Development Program 4B			
5						

D. CONSULT APPROPRIATE CHILD-SKILL DEVELOPMENT PROGRAM.

470

CODE | DESCRIPTION

1A IMMEDIATE, INTENSIVE, INDIVIDUAL THERAPY
Designed to provide crisis intervention, emphasizing non-physical alternatives to managing the disruptive behavior of a handicapped child.

1B INDIVIDUAL THERAPY
Designed to teach positive child-management skills, maximizing the growth and development of supportive family environments for a handicapped child.

1C PRACTICAL PARENTING CLASS
Designed to teach positive child-management skills in a supportive social environment, which reduces the social isolation of parents of children and maximizes the maintenance of newly acquired parenting skills.

1D SETTING-SPECIFIC TREATMENT PROGRAMS
Designed to remediate dysfunctional parent-child interactions occurring in specific contexts (e.g., mealtime, bedtime, and going shopping).

1E PARENT-CHILD RESPONSIVITY TRAINING
Designed to increase the child's social responsiveness, thereby strengthening the reciprocal parent-child relationship.

2 ECOLOGICAL/ HOME-ENVIRONMENT PROGRAMS
Designed to rearrange (where appropriate and possible) the physical characteristics of the child's environment, which will optimize parent-child interactions and the child's development.

3 OF PARENTS AND PARTNERS
Designed to train a father and mother in mutual-support techniques that facilitate their roles as partners in the parenting of a child.

4A CHILD'S SKILL DEVELOPMENT
Designed to teach skills to children, which reduce the risk for family dysfunction. The emphasis of the program is on manipulation of the child's home-educational environment to maximize incidental learning.

4B CHILD DEVELOPMENT
Designed to improve a parent's understanding of both normal and special children's development, causes and treatments of particular handicapping conditions, and appropriate skill-level assessment of a child's capabilities.

5 REFERRAL SERVICES
Designed to connect parents with other services in the community relevant to the health, welfare, and development of their child.

arguing with him, and reprimanding him. Although Susan does respond to much of Buddy's appropriate behavior (60% in Step 1), this only accounts for about 20% of her total interaction time with Buddy. This results in a prognosis of moderate difficulty in Column 3.

Prescription of family-specific interventions also begins at this point, although final decisions about a comprehensive treatment program must be determined by interpreting the information obtained on other aspects of family functioning. In this case, treatments 1C and 1D are recommended. (See the "Treatment" section of Figure 17-8 for a listing of possible intervention components.)

The second section of the risk assessment, "Child History: Mother–Infant Bonding," is based on the finding that children with problematic pre-, peri-, and postnatal histories are at greater risk for child abuse, developmental delays, and later emotional and behavioral problems. All risk factors that are known to be related to compromised development are noted, and the service provider simply checks those that exist in the target family's history. The risk factors are each assigned "hazard" points as a function of the strength of the correlation with later developmental problems. Those hazard points are totaled and entered into the overall risk assessment.

Buddy's early history indicates that Susan's prenatal history was without incident, but that within 2 days after birth, Buddy developed hyperbilirubinemia and had to remain in the hospital for phototherapy 4 days after his mother's discharge. Susan visited him each day and, in fact, continued to nurse Buddy as well. Because of the 4-day hospitalization, 8 "hazard" points are assigned in this section. However, 8 points are not enough to change the treatment prognosis at this point.

As the service provider moves through the taxonomy, additional critical analyses and intervention prescriptions are built into a comprehensive treatment plan for this specific family. This plan is based on the past data and experience gained by others from working with a great diversity of families, some of whom may have been similar to the target family. Thus, the ecobehavioral assessment of the family may be readily translated into the prescription of a family-specific ecobehavioral treatment program of proven effectiveness.

As yet, such a taxonomy of family functioning exists only on paper. Future work in the area of behavioral family therapy must begin to expand the analysis of family relationships, so that efforts such as these will strengthen both therapists' understanding of family development and therapists' skill in intervening with families.

CONCLUSION

Through the use of information-processing methods, such as the taxonomic key, it seems likely that family researchers will begin to discover the crucial family-specific characteristics that systematically interact with the therapeutic effects of particular behavioral interventions, just as drug researchers have identified organism-specific characteristics that systematically interact with the therapeutic effects of particular treatments and drugs. But until researchers begin to achieve some understanding of those critical variables, parent training will continue to be limited to the "shotgun" approach in which therapists give a family everything they have and hope that something works. Unfortunately, the shotgun approach may be neither consistently effective nor very efficient. Just as there are site-specific drugs that are more effective than wide-spectrum drugs, it seems likely that family-specific interventions that pinpoint target relationships for enhancement or remediation will considerably improve the effectiveness and efficiency of family therapy. It is my contention that the adoption of an ecobehavioral approach to family assessment and intervention will supply the information needed to attain that goal. And the development of a taxonomic key of family functioning will make that information available to clinicians and researchers committed to establishing and supporting happier, healthier family relationships.

References

Bloom, B. S., Englehart, M. D., Furst, E. M., Hill, W. H., & Krathwohl, D. R. *Taxonomy of educational objectives.* New York: David McKay, 1956.

Bronfenbrenner, U. Who cares for America's children? In V. Vaughn & T. B. Brazleton (Eds.), *The family: Can it be saved?* Chicago: Yearbook Medical Publishers, 1976.

Chinn, P. L., & Leitch, C. J. *Child health maintenance: A guide to clinical assessment.* St Louis: C. V. Mosby, 1974.

Embry, L. H., & Embry, D. D. *Ecobehavioral assessment and intervention for distressed families with young children.* Unpublished manuscript, 1981.

Embry, L. H., & Herbert-Jackson, E. *Group training for parents: Mechanics of effectiveness.* Paper presented at the 11th annual meeting of the Association for Advancement of Behavior Therapy, Atlanta, 1977.

Farber, B., & Ryckman, D. B. Effects of severely mentally retarded children in family relations. *Mental Retardation Abstracts*, 1965, *2*, 1–17.

Garbarino, J. A preliminary study of some ecological correlates of child abuse: The impact of socio-economic stress on mothers. *Child Development*, 1976, *47*, 178–185.

Kempe, R. S., & Kempe, C. H. *Child abuse.* Cambridge, Mass.: Harvard University Press, 1978.

Polansky, N. A., DeSaix, C., & Sharlin, S. A. *Child neglect: Understanding and reaching the parent.* New York: Child Welfare League of America, 1972.

Sokol, R., & Sneath, P. *Principles of numerical taxonomy.* San Francisco: W. H. Freeman, 1965.

Szykula, S. *Dropouts: The Achilles heel of mental health service delivery systems.* Paper presented at the 13th annual meeting of the Association for Advancement of Behavior Therapy, San Francisco, December 1979. (Available from S. Szykula, Primary Children's Hospital, Psychology Training Program, 363 12th Avenue, Salt Lake City, Utah 84103.)

Wahler, R. G. The insular mother: Her problems in parent–child treatment. *Journal of Applied Behavior Analysis*, 1980, *13*, 207–219.

Wechsler, D. *The measurement and appraisal of adult intelligence* (4th ed.). Baltimore: Williams & Wilkins, 1958.

III

ISSUES AND DIRECTIONS

CONSUMER ISSUES IN PARENT TRAINING

Martha E. Bernal

University of Denver

INTRODUCTION

Some background of my parent training work and research is provided as an introduction to the topic of consumer issues in parent training. The history of this work with conduct-problem children dates from 1965, with the introduction into my life of an 8-year-old boy whose outrageously abusive behavior led to the coinage of the term "the brat syndrome" (Bernal, Duryee, Pruett, & Burns, 1968). It might amuse the reader to learn how that term came to be, and also might provide some insight into the social context of behavior modification during the field's early development. The term evolved at the University of California at Los Angeles (UCLA) Neuropsychiatric Institute, the home of their Department of Psychiatry, during an era when psychoanalysis was the prevailing ideology; the social class organization of mental health professionals ranked psychiatrists at the top and the rest of us as second- or third-class citizens. This class structure was associated with different academic degrees and invoked the rule that only physicians could treat patients. This rule meant that psychiatrists, but not psychologists or social workers, were allowed to conduct psychotherapy. Experimental behavioral approaches were barely evolving at that time, and there was uncertainty about whether to classify them as treatment or heresy. I hasten to add that that era dates up to about the late 1960s, and that the UCLA psychiatric setting, along with that of many other university medical centers, has changed with respect to social structure and professional ideologies.

Such a psychosocial environment provided strong incentives for reciprocal aversive exchanges among its medical and nonmedical mental health professionals. When, in a department colloquium, my young graduate-student colleagues and I introduced to that setting the parent training procedures we had developed for the reduction of conduct problems in children, with objective data that demonstrated their efficacy, there was an aversive reaction character-ized by a description of our work as a regression to pre-Phillipe Pinel days, when mental patients were flogged. In response, my coauthors and I coined "the brat syndrome," a term designed to provoke the establishment to further aversive reactions because of its presumption of medical legitimacy. Then, in a recognizable passive–aggressive attempt to add insult to injury, we wedded this "brat syndrome" term to "behavior modification" in defiance of the psychiatric establishment's low regard for us and our behavioral treatment approaches. Fortunately for all of us, there was a waning of the intensity and frequency of coercive reciprocity as the mental health profession and its professionals matured.

What was learned about the scientific aspects, not the sociopolitical antics, of this early work? The critical data were that the parents of children with conduct problems could be trained to deal directly and effectively with their own children's behaviors; that very elementary but powerful social learning principles were the theoretical base of this training; and that very few hours of client contact time were required in which to achieve successful and beneficial parent and child behavior changes.

These early findings converged with those of other investigators, such as Hawkins, Peterson, Schweid, and Bijou (1966), Patterson (1966), Wahler, Winkel, Peterson, and Morrison (1965), and Williams (1959). As more referrals came in, particularly from pediatricians, however, it became apparent that the parent training procedures were not useful for every family. The characteristics of the parents who successfully improved their children's behaviors were as follows: They were in the middle or upper socioeconomic class; the mothers either stayed at home or had sufficient time and resources to care for the children; and the parents were loving, though floundering. The children were between 2½ and 8 years of age; demonstrated similar patterns of problem behavior in a broad range of settings; and were socially responsive to the parents, who were in control of the children's reinforcers, even though they might not realize it.

The parents who failed to benefit from parent training, or who dropped out before they received help, tended to be in the low socioeconomic bracket or were actually receiving some form of welfare assistance. Often the mothers were single, their time and resources were divided among several children, and they had no social support system. The children were highly noncompliant and showed many problem behaviors across settings, but were indifferent to the mothers' social reinforcers and spent much unsupervised time away from home.

While the foregoing may suggest that at that early time we knew a great deal about the kinds of families for which parent training was effective, that information was based on only six families who stayed in treatment. Further-more, most of the six families were private-practice referrals and did not represent the ordinary family seeking help at a neighborhood health center or a community mental health center. Thus, the representativeness of the sample was a problem, since it was clearly biased. Gerald Patterson addressed this problem in his presidential address to the Association for Advancement of Behavior Therapy in 1972, when he called for the treatment of continuously referred cases so as to reduce the bias in selected samples being treated by parent trainers.

Many other equally important issues remained to be addressed by parent trainers interested in learning about the effectiveness of what was then a set of experimental treatment procedures. A central issue was whether the behavioral parent training procedures accounted for the beneficial change found in families who were successful in helping their children. At least two alternative explanations were possible: The children would have improved in any case as they grew older; or perhaps the nonspecific effects of treatment, rather than the specific behavioral parent training components, had brought about improvement. The former explanation had some considerable support, since it had been reported widely that two out of three behaviorally disordered children improved significantly over a follow-up period of 2 to 5 years (Eysenck, 1966; Levitt, 1971; Rachman, 1971). Nevertheless, it was possible that such improvement did not take place over the shorter intervals involved in parent training. The nonspecific effects of treatment, which included those possible benefits derived from contact with a therapist and expectations that improvement will occur, had been known to be powerful factors in behavior change (Frank, 1961; Shapiro, 1971).

This primitive state of the art of parent training was the incentive that led to a major outcome study (Bernal, Klinnert, & Schultz, 1980), which sought to answer the question, "What is the most plausible explanation for child behavior change in parent training—the specific behavioral treatment components, the nonspecific effects of being in treatment, or the maturation of the child?" In 1972, when the study was initiated, these questions were virtually unaddressed in the literature. Subsequent studies of parent training for treatment of children's conduct problems that have incorporated waiting-list control groups have suggested that, when untreated, these children do not improve in periods of 4 to 8 weeks, relative to treated children (Karoly & Rosenthal, 1977; Peed, Roberts, & Forehand, 1977; Tavormina, 1975; Wiltz & Patterson, 1974). Research incorporating a control group in order to address the nonspecific effects question has suggested that the specific behavioral ingredients indeed might be the active therapeutic components in parent training; however, several problems plague this research, including failure to control therapist attention (Walter & Gilmore, 1973) and failure to provide empirical verification that the comparison treatment was delivered as described (Alexander & Parsons, 1973; Christophersen, Barnard, Barnard, Gleeson, & Sykes, 1981; Tavormina, 1975).

Our study was funded by the National Institute of Mental Health and was conducted at the University of Denver with the able assistance of many graduate and undergraduate students. The subjects of the study were the families of 36 5- to 12-year-old children with conduct problems, who had in common their parents' complaints that they frequently engaged in fighting, teasing, tantrums, destructiveness, talking back, arguing, and noncompliance.

Two serious problems plagued and jeopardized the project during its early years: recruitment of families, and dropout from data collection at posttreatment evaluation. Parents said, "Thank you for your help, but we cannot take part in your evaluation," and left. Our solution to the recruitment problem was to reach out widely to parents via frequent public-service television and radio announcements. Unfortunately, we began using the public media in the midst of a presidential election campaign, and could not get enough public-service announcement time. After the election, this method brought in the most parents, but it was also very consuming of staff time for screening families via telephone and intake appointments. Our solution to the dropout problem was to use an incentive system to keep parents involved through the posttreatment evaluation. Families paid from $1 to $15 per treatment session on a sliding scale based on family income, and we paid them from $50 to $100 for completing both treatment and the evaluation. Once this solution was instituted, our dropout rate from both treatment and posttreatment evaluation dropped to only 12%. Incidentally, the total amount we paid to all the families for the evaluation equaled the total amount they paid for treatment.

The design of the study was as follows. The families were screened and assigned in equal numbers to three groups: a group receiving behavioral parent training, a group receiving client-centered parent counseling, or an 8-week waiting-list control group. Families were assigned to the behavioral and client-centered groups at random until therapist loads were full; then families were assigned randomly to all three groups, including the waiting-list control. This method was used to maintain community referrals, but resulted in a departure from random assignment for the control group. All groups underwent a 5-week baseline period; then treatment groups were provided 10 1-hour training sessions over 8 weeks of time. The waiting period for the control group was equivalent to the period of treatment time for the other two groups. An independent check on the use of the two types of treatment models was conducted by coding therapist verbalizations from treatment videotapes. Variables that distinguished a behavioral approach from a client-centered one were coded independently by two unbiased observers. These variables focused on two process codes, instruction and reflection, and two content codes, behavioral and relationship/feeling, that were assumed to differentiate the verbalizations of the behavioral and the client-centered therapist respectively. Analysis of the observers' data corroborated the delivery of two different treatment models. Conduct of the entire course of the two therapies by project staff members assured that the two groups were equal in terms of therapist contact time, expectations communicated to parents regarding treatment, and length of the treatment.

The three major measures by which data were collected during baseline and posttreatment assessment were these:

1. The Tailored Checklist, which was obtained twice per week from the parents via telephone. It required that the parents report on the

occurrence of the five child behavior problems identified by the parents at intake as being of most concern to them.

2. "Overall deviance," a modified rate-per-minute measure of observed child deviance, which was based on twice-per-week 30-minute recordings by trained observers in the families' homes. This overall deviance measure combined occurrences of three behavioral categories: "annoying" (talking back, interrupting, yelling, arguing, bossing, teasing, threatening, lying, whining, crying, sulking, begging, noise making, grabbing or taking objects without permission, cheating, disrespectful hand or facial gestures, and intruding without permission or invitation), "deviant" (profanity, derogatory terms, destroying or attempting to damage objects, and physical attacks on or attempts to attack other persons), and "noncompliant."

3. The Becker Summary Score, a paper-and-pencil global perception of deviance measure, which was obtained from each parent at the end of each assessment period. The Summary Score combines Factors I, III, and V from the Becker Adjective Checklist.

Results for each measure were as follows:

1. The behavioral group was significantly lower in parent-reported child problems on the Tailored Checklist at posttreatment than the client-centered and waiting-list groups.

2. The difference on the overall deviance observation measure between the behavioral and control groups, and the client-centered group approached but did not reach significance ($p < .08$).

3. The behavioral and control groups did not differ on the overall deviance measure.

4. Both mothers and fathers of the behavioral group had significantly more favorable perceptions of their children on the Becker Summary Score at posttreatment than did either the client-centered or control parents.

These results, then, indicated superiority of the behavioral group on measures of parent reports and parent perceptions of child deviance, but not on the more objective home observation measure. Children who waited for 8 weeks improved as much in observed child deviance as did children whose parents received parent training.

In the discussion of these results, it was pointed out that, because of the randomization problem, the results for the control group were suggestive but not definitive. It also was suggested that there might be an artifact in the parental report and parental perception data involving a possible interaction between the parents' reports of occurrence of deviant child behaviors and the behavioral treatment, which emphasized changing of the same behaviors being monitored by the parents. That is, the parents in the parent training group may have reported improvement in child behavior as a result of their belief or expectation that the monitored behaviors were changing because they were working on them in treatment. This effect could extend as well to more global parent perceptions of child deviance.

Several considerations were raised in the evaluation of these results. First, my colleagues and I wanted to generalize the results to a population of parents of children with conduct problems (i.e., according to our criteria for "conduct problems") who seek professional help, are offered treatment, and accept it. The sample we drew, then, would represent this population, since the dropout rate was very low. A higher dropout rate would have produced a sample that was biased in some unknown manner. However, because families with poor prognosis for treatment may have stayed in treatment and evaluation in order to be paid, the sample may have contained many families who might otherwise have done poorly and dropped out. The sample of this study, then, may have been different from those of other published studies, because, in the general population from which our sample was drawn, there is a sizeable proportion of families who do not benefit from parent training. The 12% dropout rate of this study may be compared to 34%, the lowest reported in the related literature (Weinrott, Bauske, & Patterson, 1979), in support of the contention that our sample may have been less biased than that of other studies.

Two other considerations in evaluating these results were the use of graduate-student therapists and of time-limited therapy. Other studies using therapists of comparable experience for a roughly equivalent period of treatment had improvement rates for observed child deviance that ranged from 29% (Eyberg & Johnson, 1974) to 60% (Ferber, Keeley, & Schenberg, 1974), and the 41% improvement rate for the parent training group in our study was within this range.

Given all these considerations, the most parsimonious conclusion that could be made about the results of our study was that there was serious question about the effectiveness of either specific behavioral ingredients of parent training or nonspecific effects of being in treatment when families were not carefully selected into parent training. This statement could be particularly true as a result of our using less experienced therapists and time-limited therapy.

The implications of these findings brought us back to the need to understand what kinds of families benefit best from parent training, a topic that had surfaced very early in our work. Except for anecdotal reports about characteristics of families that do well or poorly, there is no empirical research on this topic. If parent trainers knew more about family characteristics differentiating successful from unsuccessful families, they could advise parents about their suitability for parent training, and could offer them alternative interventions that might be more effective. However, since more than suggestive information is not available, a different way to approach the problem of selection into parent training is to help parents become sophisticated consumers of parent training services.

The education of parents regarding parent training can help reduce the confusion that the public must have about the identity and functions of mental health professionals. When parents seek help for a physically ill child, they are likely to go to a clinic, hospital, or doctor's office to see a physician or nurse, and it is possible that they have some understanding of the training of these persons, their skills, the kinds of diagnoses they make, and the treatments they prescribe. When parents have a child with psychological problems, they may go to any of several types of agencies where some professional or paraprofessional of variously defined training may offer any of many approaches to treatment of the problem. Since the medical model is a useful referent for parents seeking help, and since there is room for public confusion about mental health professionals as opposed to physical health professionals, it would be helpful for parent trainers to educate parents about themselves. They should identify who they are; what training and degrees they have; what services they offer; the conceptual, theoretical, or philosophical rationale or framework for these services; and where they and their services may be found.

The remainder of this chapter is devoted to a discussion of the kinds of questions parents might ask and the kind of information I recommend that parent trainers who adhere to a framework of social learning theory have available in order to deal with parents' questions. Such discussion is attempted without at the same time trying to compare behavioral parent training with other types of parent training or with other mental health services, and without drawing conclusions about the superiority of behavioral parent training to other services. The information to be presented is based primarily upon my own experience as a parent trainer, and secondarily on the available literature. The professional parent trainer will find a recent review by Gordon and Davidson (1981) to be an excellent source of more detailed information that bears directly on many of the questions that follow.

QUESTIONS ABOUT PARENT TRAINING

What Is Parent Training?

Parent training may be offered by many types of professionals in many types of settings, but it is not just one kind of service. Rather, the term covers a spectrum of at least six approaches, each of which is based on a particular theoretical orientation. These approaches include the psychoanalytically oriented approach; rational–emotive therapy; transactional analysis; client-centered therapy; the Adlerian or Systematic Training for Effective Parenting (STEP) approach; and the social learning or behavioral approach. The child-rearing skills that these approaches teach are intended to be applied across a wide range of situations with a wide range of child-rearing problems. The philosophy on which each of these approaches is based influences its content and methodology.

What Is Behavioral Parent Training?

The behavioral parent training approach is based upon a philosophy that social beings mold each other's behaviors and that lawful, scientifically derived learning principles guide this molding. Understanding of these social learning principles and their applications to children permits parents to teach their children to behave in more socially desirable and positive ways, as well as to decrease negative or disturbing child behaviors. These child-rearing skills thus enable parents to shape and promote warm, loving, and mutually gratifying relationships.

The skills are taught to parents in a stepwise, systematic fashion (e.g., Miller, 1975), using a variety of methods, such as role playing and videotape demonstrations. Basic to this approach is the assumption that parents can have greater impact on their children than a therapist can, because the parents can teach the children on a day-to-day basis in many different kinds of situations. Another basic assumption is that parents may inadvertently teach inappropriate behaviors to their children as well as appropriate ones, and can learn to emphasize the teaching of appropriate child behavior patterns.

Much of the theoretical framework of social learning has been derived in the psychological laboratory. The approach emphasizes the collection of scientific data in naturalistic settings such as homes, schools, playgrounds, and even supermarkets, to assist in the testing of social learning hypotheses (e.g., Patterson, 1976) and to evaluate the effectiveness of the training of parents. The most common reason for collecting data on parents and children is the concern with assessing the effectiveness of intervention, and in this respect the behavioral parent training approach is unique among all other parent training approaches. That is, it is the one approach that makes claim to systematic evaluation of its services. This evaluation in turn permits the refinement of parent training technologies to improve their efficiency. In the remainder of this chapter, I use the term "parent training" to refer to the behavioral approach.

Where Are Parent Training Services Offered?

As has been mentioned earlier, many different agencies and institutions offer parent training services. This training is offered either in a group or individual format, or in a class designed to impart general child-rearing skills. The seriousness of a child's problem determines what format a parent should seek. If there are persons other than the parents who have complaints about a child, such as teachers, neighbors, or family members, then chances are that the problem is more serious than if the parents are complaining that the child is just a little more active or mischievous than other children. It is often difficult for a parent to assess degree of seriousness, of course, but if there is any doubt in the parent's mind as to whether services should be sought, that doubt should be resolved by talking with a professional. If the child's problem seems serious, individual or group treatment is best because of the time the parent will need from the parent trainer. Child guidance clinics, mental health centers, schools, and hospitals may have parent training services that are designed to deal with the more serious problems.

On the other hand, if a child's problem is not of serious concern, and the parent is seeking better general child-rearing skills, behavioral parent education classes sometimes are found either at the previously mentioned places or in other types of places, such as Planned Parenthood chapters; adult education programs; parent groups; or child development, psychology, and education departments of universities. Since the parent trainer should be screening families for their appropriateness for either parent training or parent education classes, an initial contact may suffice to clarify the severity of the problem and the appropriateness of the service. Parent education classes are not included in the discussion that follows.

For What Kinds of Child Problems Is Parent Training Useful?

Parent trainers work with children who show either an excess of certain behaviors (i.e., more of them than is developmentally or socially appropriate), or a deficit of desirable or appropriate behaviors. Examples of the types of excessive child behaviors with which parent trainers have worked include antisocial acts, immaturity, conduct problems, weight problems, oppositional behaviors, seizures, self-injurious or other injurious behaviors, school phobia and other fears, bedwetting, and encopresis. Examples of the types of child behavioral deficits with which parent trainers have worked include academic problems, toileting problems, and social isolation. Developmentally delayed and handicapped children can gain from parent training designed to teach speech, locomotion, toileting, self-help, and other skills. A more recent application of parent training technology has focused on parents with difficulties in controlling their aggressiveness toward their children (e.g., Denicola & Sandler, 1980; Wolfe & Sandler, 1981).

How Can Parent Training Be Helpful to a Child Who Has a Behavior Problem but Also Has Harmful Internal Feelings Such as Low Self-Esteem?

It is good professional practice to conduct an assessment to determine which of a child's behaviors, cognitions, and feelings are problematic to the parents and other persons, as well as to the child. Sometimes a child shows a clear-cut behavior problem that can be easily described and treated, but at other times the child may suffer from a whole set of difficulties. Thus, a child may be physically assaultive toward other children, and it may be relatively easy to intervene in this problem. On the other hand, the child may also experience low self-esteem that results from ostracism by other children because of the assaultive behaviors. It is not unusual to find combinations of problems in children, in which their maladaptive behaviors have an effect on their social relations, and their social relations in turn affect their feelings about themselves. In a circular fashion, these feelings produce negative self-labels, frustration, hurt, and anger, which then may lead to further aggression, and so on. For the parent trainer, the issue is where to focus the earliest intervention for maximum effect on all problems, not what is the most important problem. Since behavioral treatment technology is most effective with overt behaviors, it is often these behaviors that receive treatment first. The rationale for selecting the overt behavior for initial treatment is that, for example, if the child stops being assaultive, there is a chance that other children will become more accepting and that more positive social experiences will bolster self-esteem. Data from the assessment of social experiences and self-esteem should assist in determining whether intervention to improve social skills with peers will be necessary after the aggressive behavior has been treated. If social skills training is initiated and is effective, then self-esteem may improve, and so on. Behavioral techniques for changing children's cognitions and increasing self-control and feelings have been developed (e.g., Kendall & Zupan, 1981). These techniques can be useful in helping children change their self-statements and develop more personally satisfying ways of thinking about themselves.

What Are the Characteristics of a Helpful and Effective Parent Trainer?

Since parent trainers come in many professional forms and settings, and since there is no one course of study that is standard for qualification of the parent trainer, it is best to keep two things in mind: the general characteristics of the parent trainer as a therapist, and his or her specific experience and credentials. Generally, certain kinds of similarities between the client and the therapist can facilitate the client–therapist relationship. Similar educational, socioeconomic, cultural, and linguistic backgrounds promote communication between people, and communication is an essential feature of treatment. Aside from these similarities, therapists who communicate empathy, genuineness, nonjudgmental attitudes, and a sincere interest in helping their clients are more likely to be effective as therapists (Truax & Carkhuff, 1967). The therapist's credentials and experience are certainly relevant, but somewhat more difficult to evaluate in relation to parent trainer effectiveness. Parent trainers can describe their own education and experience in the field, and the more of such education and experience they have, the better their services are likely to be. But one should not expect a one-to-one relationship between education and experience related to quality of service. While higher success rates have been reported with more experienced parent trainers (Patterson & Fleischman, 1979), the results of a systematic study by Kent and O'Leary (1977) of the use of BA plus PhD teams versus PhD therapists working alone raises questions about the use of degrees alone as an index of parent trainer effectiveness. Although these investigators assessed the effectiveness of *teacher* trainers working with teachers on children's classroom behaviors, their well-executed study revealed no differences in therapist effectiveness due to having a BA-level person conduct two-thirds of the treatment. In fact, the teachers expressed a preference for working with the teams of BA and PhD therapists. In the field of child psychotherapy, length of experience and the profession of therapists have been found to be unrelated to outcome (Lessing & Shilling, 1966). Sometimes the parent trainer can describe someone who is well known in the field as his or her mentor. Parents should feel free to discuss such credentials, and the parent trainer should provide them.

What Kinds of Parents Do Not Benefit from Parent Training Services?

There are some personal and demographic characteristics of parents that have the potential for reducing the effectiveness of parent training, even if the parent does not drop out before the end of treatment. Among these characteristics are marital problems (Cole & Morrow, 1976; Johnson & Lobitz, 1974; Margolin & Christensen, 1981; Oltmanns, Broderick, & O'Leary, 1977; Wahler, 1980b); depression (McMahon, Forehand, Griest, & Wells, 1981); social isolation (Wahler, 1980); single parenthood (Sloop, 1974; Strain, Young, & Horowitz, 1981); low socioeconomic status (Blechman, Budd, Christophersen, Szykula, Wahler, & Embry, 1981); child-rearing philosophies that conflict with parent training philosophy (Bernal & Klinnert, 1981; Sloop, 1974); a severely negative, critical view of the child (Bernal & Klinnert, 1981; Cole & Morrow, 1976); and inability or unwillingness to devote sufficient time to carrying out parent training programs (Bernal & Klinnert, 1981).

Parent training procedures demand a great deal of the parents' time and effort; it is not possible simply to drop off a child at the therapist's door and come back to pick the child up after the therapist has solved the problem. They also require changes in the parenting skills of the adults in the household, and these changes include a cooperative effort to behave in more positive ways toward the child. For this reason, any factors that prevent a parent from investing the necessary amount of time and energy, or that prevent adults from working together, will prognosticate less effective treatment outcome or even dropout from treatment. Furthermore, factors that prevent a parent from cooperating with the parent trainer in carrying out programs also will predict lesser effectiveness.

I am not recommending that parents bearing any of the above characteristics should avoid parent training. Some investigators have developed, and continue to refine and evaluate, means for working more effectively with problem parents—for example, parents who have marital conflict (Margolin & Christensen, 1981; Patterson, Weiss, & Hops, 1976) and depressed parents (Griest, Forehand, Rogers, Rickard, McMahon, & Wells, 1980). The parent trainer needs to identify these prognosticators of poor outcome in discussion with such parents and to identify means for dealing with them in therapy.

My personal view of behavioral parent training is that it is best suited for white middle- and upper-class families, since it was developed for service to these families. Issues arise relevant to the match or mismatch between parent training (as well as parent trainers) and diverse populations, such as low-income and culturally or ethnically different families. The parent trainer who attempts to work with low-income families soon learns that the required appointments, homework, and monitoring of parent and child behavior are not family priorities when economic pressures and uncertainties disrupt schedules, plans, and availability of resources on a daily basis. These families may have needs for which a parent training approach may be inappropriate. Wahler (1980b) has discussed some important considerations for all parent trainers attempting to deliver family interventions to low-income, socially isolated parents.

The cultural or ethnic background of a family is an issue because some features of parent training—its behavioral prescriptions and the parent training materials, for example—may conflict with cultural traditions valued by some groups. A cultural mismatch between a parent trainer and a family may lead to formidable impasses in the parent training process, even when the parent trainer's attitudes and sensitivities are positive and refined. In general, the less acculturated and the more linguistically different the family is in relation to the white culture, the greater the need is for a cultural and linguistic match between the family and the parent trainer, in order to facilitate the adaptation of parent training procedures to the culture in the appropriate language.

These convictions stem from my experience as a parent trainer working with low- and middle-income black and Hispanic families and as a consultant to a group of investigators who were developing and assessing parent training materials for use with low-income black and Hispanic families. In my role as consultant, I carefully examined one of the most popular behavioral parent training manuals for its applicability to these families. Because the book was written according to the language and life style of the white middle-class family, I saw it as inappropriate for minority and low-income populations. I recommended that the group throw out the book and write its own manual, emphasizing language, examples, and procedures that were consonant with the life and cultural experiences of the intended consumer population.

What Happens in Parent Training?

Appointments

It is common for parent training to be conducted in a time-limited, weekly-appointment format. The meetings may be from 1 to 3 hours long and may take place over 6 to 12 weeks, though much more time may be needed. It is possible that parents will be seen individually by the parent trainer, in groups of parents who have children with similar problems, or in some combination of individual and group meetings. It often is required that children be included in the treatment, and that children join parents at meetings. Since the object of parent training is to teach parents skills that will be useful in such settings as playgrounds and supermarkets in which the children's problems occur, some meetings may take place in these settings.

The attendance of both parents in two-parent families is frequently requested. This requirement is based on the rationale that if one spouse cannot or will not attend, there is likely to be some discontinuity in the child management program when the absent spouse has to handle problems, and there may be a lack of coordination between parents about how to handle problems according to the parent trainer's instructions. Very little research has been conducted on the issue of the need for both parents to participate in parent training. Brockway and Williams (1976) presented single-family case data that suggested that the father's cooperation was needed in carrying out programs. However, Martin (1977) assessed the importance of including fathers when working with child problems in family intervention and found that therapy was equally effective when fathers were included and when they were not included. It is likely that there are no clear-cut answers to this issue, since much depends upon such factors as the marital relationship, the father's attitudes about participation in child rearing and willingness to identify problems in the child's behavior, and so on. Nevertheless, there is some evidence that it is possible to teach the mother skills for establishment of new behaviors in the child, such as dressing skills, and then have the mother teach the father these same skills successfully (Adubato, Adams, & Budd, 1981). Clearly, however, participation of both spouses at the same time is a time-saving measure.

Evaluation

Since parent trainers are committed to objective assessment of their services, it can be expected that one indicator of a good-quality service is that some type of evaluation will be conducted. The extent of evaluation may range from a brief paper-and-pencil form that assesses parental satisfaction with treatment, to parental recording of daily child behavior, to a very extensive and demanding regimen requiring a high level of cooperation from the whole family. The extensiveness of the evaluation depends upon the agency or group providing the service. In general, private practitioners and public mental health agencies and hospitals have fewer funds and less time for evaluation, while research groups of parent trainers located in universities or community research centers usually have funds for more extensive evaluation.

To determine what benefits, if any, that parents and children have obtained, several kinds of measures are used, and data on these measures may be obtained in several different ways. Measures also may be taken on both parents and children, as well as on their interactions. The kinds of measures for assessment of parent and child change include collection of data on actual ongoing behaviors; parental reports of desirable and undesirable child behaviors; paper-and-pencil checklists or rating scales that measure a parent's perception of the degree of a child's deviance; and other paper-and-pencil measures of marital satisfaction, personal adjustment, and satisfaction with the treatment and the therapist. Child and parent behaviors may be observed by trained human observers on one or more occasions, or audiotaped or videotaped and then scored by observers. Parents and children may be asked to collect data and bring them to meetings, or to report via telephone or in person on some regular basis on the occurrence of some set of behaviors of interest. Paper-and-pencil measures usually are obtained once before and again after the end of treatment. Any or all of these measures may be taken in whatever settings are of interest, depending upon where a parent needs to teach a child a new skill: parks, school playgrounds and classrooms, homes, stores, and so on. The measures also may include other important social agents who may influence the child, such as teachers, playmates, siblings, and other family members.

All persons who are to participate in evaluation should be fully informed about all expectations regarding participation, including ground rules for what to do during observations, length and frequency of appointments for data collection, and rules governing who needs to be present for what length of time. The cooperation of all participants should be obtained on a voluntary basis prior to the beginning of the evaluation. If the parent is discouraged by extensive evaluation demands that may characterize the services provided by a research group, it would be very important to clarify what advantages are to be gained, such as cost of the service, special expertise, and so forth. Referral to another agency that makes fewer assessment demands is appropriate when a parent requests it.

Incentive Systems

Two types of parent behaviors need to occur in order for parent training to have any chance of success: Parents must attend meetings regularly, and they must carry out instructions and programs with their children. When the more extreme type of failure to cooperate occurs and a parent drops out of treatment, much time and effort has been lost, and the child in need of help has not received it. Therefore, parent trainers make a point of reducing dropout from treatment whenever possible.

To achieve these goals, the parent trainer relies upon some of the same learning principles and techniques that a parent will learn to use in teaching a child. The parent trainer arranges for certain rewarding consequences to follow contingent upon the desirable parent behavior. Since parents need to learn to use these various techniques for changing child behaviors, it is a useful teaching method to have the parents themselves experience an incentive system.

The most commonly used form of incentive system for attendance and assignment completion involves the collection of an initial deposit, or some larger sum that pays for the entire training program, and then the refund of all or part of this deposit or sum to the parent contingent upon attendance and completion of assignments. Eyberg and Johnson (1974) systematically evaluated the impact of such an incentive system with a group of 17 families of children with behavior problems. They found significantly greater attendance and assignment completion for parents on the incentive system than for parents who were not put on the incentive system. Peine and Munro (1973) found similar effects in their earlier study of a similar incentive system. Fleischman (1979) used and evaluated the effects of a "parenting salary" of $1 per day on compliance with treatment assignments and attrition. The salary had a dramatic effect in reducing dropout in low-income single-parent families, and greater benefits for two-parent and middle-income families in treatment compliance.

An example of an incentive system for obtaining parent participation in a fairly demanding evaluation of treatment effectiveness has been presented earlier (Bernal et al., 1980). That system was highly successful, since the dropout rate prior to its being instituted was 74% in one year and as high as 91% in the next year of operation (Bernal, 1975). Szykula (Szykula, 1981; Szykula, Fleischman, & Shilton, 1982) has described a total service-delivery approach called "The Comprehensive Referral Pursuit and Maintenance Approach," which seeks to involve families and referral source agents actively in the referral and treatment process from a very early point of contact with the families. This approach significantly reduced the overall dropout rate of single-parent families and families on welfare, two groups that have high dropout rates, as well as for all families in general seen over a 1½-year period. The most comprehensive discussion of incentive procedures for use with parents in both individual and group parent training has been provided by Bates (1977), and it is highly recommended.

It might interest both parents and parent trainers that at least one type of behavior, excuse giving, has been found to be predictive of dropout (Bernal & Kreutzer, 1976; Bernal, North, & Kreutzer, 1974). An "excuse" was defined as a reason given for not receiving the therapist's intake phone call, not making the next appointment; not accepting therapy; or not agreeing to times, dates, or other conditions of an offered appointment, whether or not the reason could be judged to be legitimate. For parents taking part in a pretraining assessment, there was a moderate and significant relationship between excuse giving and dropout from the assessment (Bernal et al., 1974). Excuse giving identified 82% of the dropouts from a mental health center that had a base dropout rate of 53% (Bernal & Kreutzer, 1976). Thus, although 18% of the excuse givers did not drop out of treatment, it was possible to identify the majority of the dropouts by excuse giving. There seems to be some advantage to both parents and parent trainers to monitor excuse giving as a warning signal of impending dropout. When that warning occurs, discussion between a parent and a trainer to determine sources of reasons for dropout may be helpful in facilitating modifications in parent training services that are sensitive to family needs.

Parent Training Technology

In a broad sense, parent training technology may be organized according to a continuum of the degree to which a therapist assumes responsibility for providing the solution to a family's problem. Emphasis may be placed upon the parent trainer as teacher of skills to parents at one end of the continuum, and as facilitator of family-initiated solutions at the other end. This conceptualization is adapted from Blechman (1980), who describes a continuum of behavioral family interventions ranging from those that are imposed by the expert therapist to interventions that emphasize the encouragement by the therapist of effective client problem solving. While Blechman (1981) differentiates between parent training and other behavioral family interventions, my view is that all behavioral family interventions rely upon some degree of training of parents that is based upon the application of social learning principles, and therefore may be referred to as "parent training" in a broad sense.

Three specific parent training technologies may be defined along this continuum of therapist as instructor–facilitator. The contingency management approach involves a hierarchy of instructors, wherein the parent trainer determines the solution to a family's problem and teaches the parents new parenting skills; the parents then use these skills to teach the child new skills. This is a unidirectional model of parent training that is commonly applied to teach young children more appropriate behaviors (Bernal & Klinnert, 1981).

A second parent training model that falls between the ends of the continuum of therapist direction described above is contingency contracting (e.g., Alexander & Parsons, 1973; Weathers & Liberman, 1975). In this model, the parent trainer teaches a set of social contracting skills to the parents and the identified problem child, and the child is an active participant in the contract. The contract is a written agreement between parents and child that spells out consequences for given desirable and undesirable behaviors, as well as methods for monitoring compliance with the contract.

Family negotiation, the third model of parent training, lies at the facilitator end of the continuum, in that the parent trainer imparts a set of skills to the family unit that ultimately will allow complete family control of the intervention (e.g., Blechman, Olson, Schornagel, Halsdorf, & Turner, 1976; Kifer, Lewis, Green, & Phillips, 1974). The skills are negotiation and problem-solving strategies for dealing with interpersonal family problems. This approach is the least standard of the three models, and has received less evaluative attention than have the other two models.

All three models rely upon the law of effect, which states that a consequence that follows a behavior may have the effect of increasing or decreasing the future likelihood of occurrence of the behavior. In contingency management, child behavior change is brought about by controlling the nature and timing of the parent-produced consequences that follow child behavior. In contingency contracting, child behavior change is brought about by the agreement of parents and children to rules governing consequences for their behaviors. In the family negotiation model, contracts among family members are developed and negotiated that set rules for the management of certain interpersonal consequences for family member behaviors.

The fact that parent trainers rely on learning principles as the tools for behavior change means that parents may encounter a new conceptual and language system. When the parent trainer judges that it is necessary, appropriate reading and didactic instruction are recommended to introduce the parents to this system. Furthermore, since the central task of parent training is to change parent behaviors in order to change child behaviors, the parents will need to learn to talk very specifically about behaviors, treatment goals, and interactions among people. It is common in parent training to analyze ongoing chains of social interaction in order to understand how behaviors are established and maintained. Therefore, parents also will need to keep records of parent and child behaviors at the time they occur, and such commonly encountered assignments are an important part of treatment. Videotape or audiotape recordings of family interactions in *in vivo* settings may be used to facilitate such behavioral analysis.

How these teaching tools are communicated to parents may differ widely, but any or all of the following may be used: games, lectures, role playing, and modeling or demonstration, either live or with film or videotape. Sometimes parents and children may be asked to view videotapes of their interactions in order to improve their performance of new skills. A device called a "bug-in-the-ear" may be used. It is a wireless radio receiver for trainer-transmitted instruction by radio.

Very few empirical data are available on the topic of the relative effectiveness of different instructional methods in parent training, and results are inconclusive or contradictory (e.g., Flanagan, Adams, & Forehand, 1979; Nay, 1975; O'Dell, Mahoney, Horton, & Turner, 1979). There is some suggestion that, in comparison to behavioral rehearsal, written materials, and lecture, modeling is particularly effective (Gordon & Davidson, 1981).

Is It Necessary for Parents to Understand Social Learning Principles in Order to Be Successful?

The role played by knowledge of learning principles in increasing the effectiveness of parent training has not been widely investigated. Consequently, there is little information on how necessary it is that parents study and understand social learning principles in order to be able to apply them successfully. There are several published accounts of successful parent training where parents were merely told what to do, without any discussion of the principle underlying the instruction (e.g., Bernal et al., 1968).

Two studies have been reported in which some superior effects of teaching social learning principles were noted. Glogower and Sloop (1976) and McMahon, Forehand, and Griest (1981) evaluated the possible advantages of teaching social learning principles to parents. Neither group of investigators found any advantage of teaching these principles in terms of success in implementing behavior change programs. However, Glogower and Sloop found that parents who had learned the principles were better able to generalize their knowledge across situations. McMahon et al. found that social learning knowledge produced greater parent satisfaction with treatment, and that these parents perceived their children as better adjusted. On follow-up, Glogower and Sloop reported that the group instructed in learning principles successfully implemented more home programs for different child behaviors and were more successful in handling management problems. McMahon et al. found in their follow-up that their instructed parents were more rewarding toward their children and that their children were more compliant. Thus, there appears to be some advantage of teaching social learning principles, particularly at follow-up.

On the other hand, some parents may need only a minimal theoretical background in social learning principles for effective skill acquisition. O'Dell, Flynn, and Benlolo (1977) found no advantage of training in social learning principles on any measures. They reported that the parents had enjoyed the performance of skills and feedback they received about their performance, rather than the didactic discussion of principles.

The ultimate value of instruction in learning principles probably depends on a parent's level of curiosity, interest, and cooperation, as well as on the parent trainer's judgment about what amount of instruction will best prepare a particular parent with particular characteristics to be more effective. Although level of education is one of these relevant characteristics, parent training manuals are available for different reading levels (Bernal & North, 1978).

What Manuals Are Available to Help Parents
Help Their Own Children?

A recent survey (Bernal & North, 1978) of parent training manuals provides information on 26 commercially available behavioral parent training manuals, 20 of which were written for parents and six for professionals. Some of the manuals are applicable when parents are seeking general information about child rearing, while others are intended for use as background reading material for parents seeking professional guidance for specific child problems, such as toilet training. In the 1978 survey, these manuals are organized and presented in a table that provides various useful pieces of information, such as price, availability in foreign languages, characteristics of children for whom they were intended, and reading level required.

A review of the research literature dealing with these manuals, plus communication with the authors themselves, permitted evaluation of each manual in terms of available proof that it actually taught parents how to rear children or how to handle specific problems. Only 5 of the 26 manuals had been evaluated in a manner that provided relatively convincing conclusions regarding their effectiveness. The available evidence pointed to the greater usefulness of a manual that provided instruction for dealing with the more circumscribed child problems (i.e., problems that are very specific and whose occurrence is confined to a given time and place), as opposed to more diffuse, multiple problems occurring across settings.

Parents and parent trainers attempting to choose among parent training manuals should be aware of the dearth of evaluation efforts among authors of these manuals, and ought to seek information about such evaluation. Parent consumers also need to be aware that, as a general rule, obtaining such a manual and reading it will not be very useful in dealing with children whose problems are of serious concern. Scientific support for this warning has been provided by Christensen, Johnson, and Phillips (1980), who demonstrated the superior effects of individual or group parent training for parents of conduct-problem children over the effects of a procedure involving minimal therapist contact and self-instruction via reading. Parents of children already in trouble would do best to seek professional assistance, though they may be asked to read a manual as a supplement to treatment. Similarly, professionals seeking to learn parent training skills should keep in mind that parent training requires a broad set of skills and the ability to make sensitive clinical judgments, which can only be acquired through extensive supervised clinical experience that teaches the application of theory.

What Are the Relative Merits of Group versus Individual Parent Training?

Some parents prefer individual meetings, while others work best in conjunction with others; personal preference is an important consideration. I have worked with parents in both types of formats, and found that there are advantages and disadvantages to both. As a general rule, the individual meetings allow a parent trainer and a family to get to know each other better, and there are more opportunities to influence the parents to change, as well as for the parents to develop greater trust and confidence in the parent trainer. The parent trainer can give more individual attention to, and thus can tailor treatment more directly to, the family. All of these factors should result in a higher probability of success than a group training format should.

On the other hand, group training also has its distinct advantages, particularly since the presence of other parents who are also trying to change may facilitate parent change. The social group processes that function in group treatment may help parents who are less able to examine their own behaviors and the impact of these behaviors on their families. As an example, it seems possible that a parent who attempts to enforce rules and standards that are inflexible or unreasonable, or who is insensitive to developmentally appropriate needs and desires, would be more likely to realize his or her inflexibility or insensitivity in a group setting where more flexible and sensitive attitudes and rules are modeled by other parents, than in a one-to-one confrontation with a therapist (Cole & Morrow, 1976). Similarly, if a parent experiences discomfort in attending in a positive manner to a child, discussion of the problem with a parent group wherein some other parent experiences similar discomfort may reduce the threat implied by the problem and thus facilitate the emergence of warmer exchanges with the child. Furthermore, the demonstration by other parents of warm parent–child interactions may provide useful models.

Single parents are a group that may actually need the support of a parent group, but care should be taken when mixing single- and two-parent families to avoid the impact of a detrimental social polarization between coupled and single parents. Sometimes the individual parent trainer can determine that some parents would benefit from a group format, and will arrange for it. At other times, the group parent trainer may spend extra time with individual parents to facilitate progress. Much of the decision as to which format is offered to a parent depends upon economic considerations, and the group format is generally regarded as less expensive to the parent as well as to the agency, although Mira (1970) reported that it was more costly in terms of therapist time to work with parents in groups than individually. However, Mira's sample had a high proportion of parents with physically handicapped children, and individual parent training may have been more efficient with that group. Kovitz (1976) compared group and individual methods for parent training and found equivalent improvement for both groups. While the meager literature on the effects of group parent training is afflicted with the problem of measurement that is less elegant and methodologically clean than that of individual parent training outcome studies, because of the cost of more adequate evaluation, there is no evidence to suggest that group parent training is less effective than individual training.

How Cost-Effective Is Parent Training?

Parent training technologies are insufficiently advanced to permit statements about cost-effectiveness. Such statements would require that a program of parent training have fixed expendable operating costs so that such costs could be assessed, and perhaps compared to costs of other mental health services. The current availability of parent training services in a wide range of settings conducted by many types of professionals and paraprofessionals precludes the derivation of a cost estimate, since these different settings and service providers have different costs. Only when parent training procedures become sufficiently standardized in terms of technology, parent trainer salaries, and settings in which they are provided as a standard service will it be possible to begin to make cost estimates (Bijou, 1981).

How Effective Is Parent Training?

When a child's problems have changed in a desired direction as a result of the training of the parent, it is possible to claim that this form of intervention is effective. The claim that parent training as a general treatment approach is effective is one that is somewhat difficult to make, because of the many kinds of child problems, parent training programs and training methods used; the heterogeneity of parents and children involved; and the many types of outcome measures employed in different studies.

In general, the research literature indicates that parent training is effective in the treatment of a very wide variety of children's problems, particularly when the problems can be specifically defined and are relatively discrete. Child problems that are more complex and difficult to identify or specify are less responsive to parent training. An example of a discrete specific problem is a temper tantrum, which can be defined as some combination of kicking, throwing, hitting, and screaming that occurs when the child is thwarted. One can see it, describe it in words (specify it), and observe whether or not it occurs by matching the child's behavior to its behavioral specification. However, when there are multiple problems, or when a child's problems are attributed to internal causes such as negative attitudes, intervention is more difficult—in part because of the need for multiple interventions, and also because one must be able to see the behavior when it occurs in order to carry out an intervention procedure. To some extent, the skill of the parent trainer in helping a parent define a problem determines whether intervention is successful. However, child problems are also easier to treat if the consequences that maintain them can be identified, if the parents can control those consequences, if the desirable behaviors required are appropriate to the child's developmental level, if the behaviors occur frequently enough for there to be an opportunity to intervene, and if the behaviors occur at a time and place where a parent can be present to intervene. Stealing and fire setting are examples of behaviors that are difficult to treat for some of these reasons.

Are There Side Effects of Parent Training on Child Behavior?

There are two main types of side effects of parent training on child behavior; these are called "behavioral generality" and "setting generality." "Behavioral generality" refers to a change in some untreated child behavior that occurs when another child behavior is the focus of treatment. In "setting generality," the behavior that is treated in one setting also changes in another setting where it was not treated. Of course, similar types of generality or side effects also may occur for parent behavior (e.g., Koegel, Glahn, & Nieminen, 1978).

Behavioral generality has not received much attention in the literature. It is evaluated by focusing parent training on one child behavior, and simultaneously monitoring any changes in other designated child behaviors. A change in any of these other untreated behaviors would suggest that behavioral generality has occurred. Wahler (1975) has suggested that some child behaviors are organized in clusters that may permit intervention on one member of the cluster to generalize to other untreated members. This possibility has received empirical support in studies of children who present with several deviant behaviors. Untreated behaviors such as bedwetting (Nordquist, 1971), stuttering (Wahler, Sperling, Thomas, Teeter, & Luper, 1970), and crying, aggression, and self-injury (Forehand, Sturgis, McMahon, Aguar, Green, Wells, & Breiner, 1979) showed beneficial changes correlated with positive changes in treated behaviors.

Evaluation of setting generality typically involves training the parent to deal with a given behavior in the clinic, and then assessing changes in the same behavior in another setting, such as the home or school. Although there are some data on setting generality, there is no conclusive verification that it occurs in parent training. Several investigators have reported setting generality from clinic to home (Forehand et al., 1979; Humphreys, Forehand, Green, McMahon, & Roberts, 1977; Reisinger & Ora, 1977), while others have reported no setting generality (e.g., Embry, Kelly, Jackson, & Baer, 1979).

In general, although there is some evidence for both behavioral and setting generality of parent training effects, such effects are best assured by careful programming by the parent trainer. This programming may involve specific instructions to parents about dealing with untreated behaviors, and planning for ways to facilitate the generalization of treated behaviors across settings. Techniques include parent recordings of parent and child behaviors, practice of parenting skills in different settings, and frequent telephone contacts to monitor progress in these settings. Some programs for effecting child behavior change in the school setting by training parents to provide consequences for school behaviors when children arrive home have been very effective in producing beneficial effects across settings (e.g., Budd, Leibowitz, Riner, Mindell, & Goldfarb, 1981). The parent would do well to inquire in what ways the parent trainer plans to enhance the likelihood of behavioral and setting generality.

Other side effects of parent training that do not fit these types of generality have been discussed in the literature, the common perception of such side effects being in terms of some negative outcome. Although such negative outcomes have been reported—for example, Johnson, Bolstad, and Lobitz (1976) reported increases in school behavior problems associated with positive effects of parent training in the home setting—it is possible to intervene successfully when such problems develop. A requirement for such intervention is some foresight in planning careful monitoring of a child's treated and untreated behaviors in several settings.

Will Parent Training to Help the Problem Child Also Help the Parent to Deal More Effectively with Other Children in the Family?

"Sibling generality," the transfer of treatment effects from the identified problem child to other siblings, develops for at least two reasons: The parent has learned better ways of managing children in general, and the problem child is no longer engaging in problem behaviors that incite siblings and parents to react in a negative fashion. While there has been no attempt to separate these two different reasons in research on sibling generality, there are some meager research data demonstrating that such a positive radiating effect on siblings can be produced (Humphreys *et al.*, 1977; Lavigueur, 1976; Lavigueur, Peterson, Sheese, & Peterson, 1973). If the parent desires help with the behaviors of other children in the family, the best way to assure sibling generality is to incorporate them into the parent training program.

How Durable Are the Effects of Parent Training?

Gordon and Davidson (1981) indicate that the effects of parent training are maintained best over time when the behaviors on which treatment focuses are highly discrete and easily defined, and when problems of observation of outcome are minimized. They also point out that another factor enhancing maintenance is that some child behaviors show persistence of change, independent of parental behavior change. That is, the treated child behavior persists in its desirable form without any assistance from parents, probably due to its maintenance by nonparental social agents in the child's life, such as peers. Examples of the types of child problems for which parent training has the best effects and is best maintained over time are oppositional and tantrum behaviors in young children (e.g., Forehand & King, 1977). However, data on the maintenance of parent training effects over time are relatively scarce, and most of the available research is concentrated on certain types of child problems, such as noncompliance. Much work remains to be done to identify the characteristics of parents and children who benefit best from parent training technologies, and to adapt and develop technologies for a broad range of families and child problems. The field of parent training shows a strong future trend in this direction.

In conclusion, it is appropriate in a chapter addressing the issues that should be raised by parents about parent training to point out that the training of people for parenting should be an integral part of everyone's education. To my knowledge, Hawkins (1972, 1974) was the first to suggest this idea of universal parenthood training for young people in high schools; the idea has been echoed by many, although such training is still not conducted routinely in the schools, except perhaps in a few progressive settings. Beyond a doubt, parents are the primary determiners of children's behaviors and psychological adjustment, and are in the best position to teach children and arrange their lives in order to minimize the development of child problems and to promote mental health. Consumers of parent training services should be insisting that those services be provided to all potential parents as a standard part of their education for life.

References

Adubato, S. A., Adams, M. K., & Budd, K. S. Teaching a parent to train a spouse in child management techniques. *Journal of Applied Behavior Analysis*, 1981, *14*, 193–205.

Alexander, J. F., & Parsons, B. V. Short term behavioral intervention with delinquent families. *Journal of Abnormal Psychology*, 1973, *81*, 219–225.

Bates, D. The search for reinforcers to train and maintain effective parent behaviors. *Rehabilitation Literature*, 1977, *38*, 291–295.

Bernal, M. E. *Comparison of behavioral and nondirective parent counseling.* Paper presented at the meeting of the Association for Advancement of Behavior Therapy, San Francisco, 1975.

Bernal, M. E., Duryee, J., Pruett, H., & Burns, B. Behavior modification and the brat syndrome. *Journal of Consulting and Clinical Psychology*, 1968, *32*, 447–455.

Bernal, M. E., & Klinnert, M. D. *Further insights on the results of a parent training outcome study.* Paper presented at the XIII Banff International Conference on Behavioral Sciences, Banff, Canada, March 1981.

Bernal, M. E., Klinnert, M. D., & Schultz, L. A. Outcome evaluation of behavioral parent training and client-centered parent counseling for children with conduct problems. *Journal of Applied Behavior Analysis*, 1980, *13*, 677–691.

Bernal, M. E., & Kreutzer, S. L. Relationship between excuses and dropout at a mental health center. *Journal of Consulting and Clinical Psychology*, 1976, *44*, 494.

Bernal, M. E., & North, J. A. Survey of parent training manuals. *Journal of Applied Behavior Analysis*, 1978, *11*, 533–544.

Bernal, M. E., North, J. A., & Kreutzer, S. L. Cross-validation of excuses and cooperation as possible measures for identification of clinic dropouts and continuers. *American Journal of Community Psychology*, 1974, *2*, 151–163.

Blechman, E. A. Family problem-solving training. *American Journal of Family Therapy*, 1980, *8*, 3–22.

Blechman, E. A. Toward comprehensive behavioral family intervention: An algorithm for matching families and interventions. *Behavior Modification*, 1981, *5*, 221–236.

Blechman, E. A., Budd, K. S., Christophersen, E. R., Szykula, S., Wahler, R., & Embry, L. H. Engagement in behavioral family therapy: A multi-site investigation. *Behavior Therapy*, 1981, *12*, 461–472.

Blechman, E. A., Olson, D. H. L., Schornagel, C. Y., Halsdorf, M. J., & Turner, A. J. The family contract game: Technique and case study. *Journal of Consulting and Clinical Psychology*, 1976, *44*, 449–455.

Bijou, S. *Parent training: Actualizing the critical conditions of early child development.* Keynote address delivered at the National Conference on Parent Training, Dallas, September 1981.

Brockway, B. S., & Williams, W. W. Training in child management: A prevention-oriented model. In E. J. Mash, L. A. Hamerlynck, & L. C. Handy (Eds.), *Behavior modification approaches to parenting.* New York: Brunner/Mazel, 1976.

Budd, K. S., Leibowitz, M., Riner, L. S., Mindell, C., & Goldfarb, A. L. Home-based treatment of severe disruptive behaviors. *Behavior Modification*, 1981, *5*, 273–298.

Christensen, A., Johnson, S. M., & Phillips, S. Cost-effectiveness in behavioral family therapy. *Behavior Therapy*, 1980, *11*, 208–226.

Christophersen, E. R., Barnard, J. D., Barnard, S. R., Gleeson, S., & Sykes, B. Home-based treatment of behavior disordered and developmentally delayed children. In M. J. Begab, H. C. Haywood, & H. T. Garber (Eds.), *Psychosocial influences in retarded performance* (Vol. 2, *Strategies for improving competence*). Baltimore: University Park Press, 1981.

Cole, C., & Morrow, W. R. Refractory parent behaviors in behavior modification training groups. *Psychotherapy: Theory, Research and Practice*, 1976, *13*, 162–169.

Denicola, J., & Sandler, J. Training abusive parents in child management and self-control skills. *Behavioral Therapy*, 1980, *11*, 263–270.

Embry, L. H., Kelly, M. L., Jackson, E., & Baer, D. M. *Group parent training: An analysis of generalization from classroom to home.* Research brief, Kansas Research Institute, 1979.

Eyberg, S. M., & Johnson, S. M. Multiple assessment of behavior modification with families: Effects of contingency contracting and order of treated problems. *Journal of Consulting and Clinical Psychology*, 1974, *42*, 594–606.

Eysenck, H. J. *The effects of psychotherapy.* New York: International Science Press, 1966.

Ferber, H., Keeley, S., & Schenberg, K. Training parents in behavior modification: Outcome of problems encountered in a program after Patterson's work. *Behavior Therapy*, 1974, *5*, 415–419.

Flanagan, S., Adams, H. E., & Forehand, R. A comparison of four instructional techniques for teaching parents to use timeout. *Behavior Therapy*, 1979, *10*, 94–102.

Fleischman, M. J. Using parenting salaries to control attrition and cooperation in therapy. *Behavior Therapy*, 1979, *10*, 111–116.

Forehand, R., & King, H. E. Noncompliant children: Effects of parent training on behavior and attitude change. *Behavior Modification*, 1977, *1*, 93–108.

Forehand, R., Sturgis, E. T., McMahon, R. J., Aguar, D., Green, K., Wells, K. C., & Breiner, J. Parent behavioral training to modify child noncompliance. *Behavior Modification*, 1979, *3*, 3–26.

Frank, J. D. *Persuasion and healing.* Baltimore: Johns Hopkins University Press, 1961.

Glogower, F., & Sloop, E. W. Two strategies of group training of parents as effective behavior modifiers. *Behavior Therapy*, 1976, *7*, 177–184.

Gordon, S. B., & Davidson, N. Behavioral parent training. In A. S. Gurman & D. P. Kniskern (Eds.), *Handbook of family therapy.* New York: Brunner/Mazel, 1981.

Griest, D. L., Forehand, R., Rogers, T., Rickard, K., McMahon, R., & Wells, K. C. *The role of parental depression in parent behavioral training.* Paper presented at the meeting of the Association for Advancement of Behavior Therapy, New York, 1980.

Hawkins, H. P. It's time we taught the young how to be good parents, and don't you wish we'd started a long time ago? *Psychology Today*, 1972, *11*, 28–38.

Hawkins, R. P. Universal parenthood training: A proposal for preventive mental health. In R. Ulrich, T. Stachnik, & J. Mabrey (Eds.), *Control of human behavior* (Vol. 3, *Behavior modification in education*). Glenview, Ill.: Scott, Foresman, 1974.

Hawkins, R. P., Peterson, R. F., Schweid, E., & Bijou, S. W. Behavior therapy in the home: Amelioration of problem parent–child relations with the parent in a therapeutic role. *Journal of Experimental Child Psychology*, 1966, *4*, 99–107.

Humphreys, L., Forehand, R., Green, K., McMahon, R., & Roberts, M. *Generality of treatment effects resulting from a parent training program to modify child noncompliance.* Paper presented at the meeting of the Association for Advancement of Behavior Therapy, Atlanta, December 1977.

Johnson, S. M., Bolstad, O. D., & Lobitz, G. Generalization and contrast phenomena in behavior modification with children. In E. J. Mash, L. A. Hamerlynck, & L. C. Handy (Eds.), *Behavior modification and families.* New York: Brunner/Mazel, 1976.

Johnson, S. M., & Lobitz, G. K. The personal and marital adjustment of parents as related to observed child deviance and parenting behaviors. *Journal of Abnormal Child Psychology*, 1974, *2*, 192–207.

Karoly, P., & Rosenthal, M. Training parents in behavior modification: Effects on perception of family interaction and deviant child behavior. *Behavior Therapy*, 1977, *8*, 406–410.

Kendall, P. C., & Zupan, B. A. Individual versus group application of cognitive–behavioral self-control procedures with children. *Behavior Therapy*, 1981, *12*, 344–359.

Kent, R. N., & O'Leary, K. D. Treatment of conduct problem children: B.A. and/or Ph.D. therapists. *Behavior Therapy*, 1977, *8*, 653–658.

Kifer, R. E., Lewis, M. A., Green, D. R., & Phillips, E. L. Training predelinquent youths and their parents to negotiate conflict situations. *Journal of Applied Behavior Analysis*, 1974, *7*, 357–364.

Koegel, R. C., Glahn, T. J., & Nieminen, G. S. Generalization of parent training results. *Journal of Applied Behavior Analysis*, 1978, *11*, 95–109.

Kovitz, K. E. Comparing group and individual methods for training parents in child management techniques. In E. J. Mash, L. A. Hamerlynck, & L. C. Handy (Eds.), *Behavior modification approaches to parenting*. New York: Brunner/Mazel, 1976.

Lavigueur, H. The use of siblings as an adjunct to the behavioral treatment of children in the home with parents as therapists. *Behavior Therapy*, 1976, *7*, 602–613.

Lavigueur, H., Peterson, R. F., Sheese, J. G., & Peterson, L. W. Behavioral treatment in the home: Effects on an untreated sibling and long-term follow-up. *Behavior Therapy*, 1973, *4*, 431–441.

Lessing, E. E., & Shilling, F. H. Relationship between treatment selection variables and treatment outcome in a child guidance clinic. *Journal of the American Academy of Child Psychiatry*, 1966, *5*, 313–348.

Levitt, E. E. Research on psychotherapy with children. In A. E. Bergin & S. L. Garfield (Eds.), *Handbook of psychotherapy and behavior change*. New York: Wiley, 1971.

Margolin, G., & Christensen, A. *Treatment of multiproblem families: Specific and general effects of marital and family therapy*. Paper presented at the XIII Banff International Conference on Behavioral Sciences, Banff, Canada, March 1981.

Martin, B. Brief family intervention: The effectiveness and the importance of including father. *Journal of Consulting and Clinical Psychology*, 1977, *45*, 1002–1010.

McMahon, R. J., Forehand, R., & Griest, D. L. Effects of knowledge of social learning principles on enhancing treatment outcome and generalization in a parent training program. *Journal of Consulting and Clinical Psychology*, 1981, *49*, 526–532.

McMahon, R. J., Forehand, R., Griest, D. L., & Wells, K. C. Who drops out of treatment during parent behavioral training? *Behavioral Counseling Quarterly*, 1981, *1*, 79–85.

Miller, W. H. *Systematic parent training*. Champaign, Ill.: Research Press, 1975.

Mira, M. Results of a behavior modification training program for parents and teachers. *Behaviour Research and Therapy*, 1970, *8*, 309–311.

Nay, W. R. A systematic comparison of instructional techniques for parents. *Behavior Therapy*, 1975, *6*, 14–21.

Nordquist, V. M. The modification of a child's enuresis: Some response–response relationships. *Journal of Applied Behavior Analysis*, 1971, *4*, 241–247.

O'Dell, S., Flynn, J., & Benlolo, L. A comparison of parent training techniques in child behavior modification. *Journal of Behavior Therapy and Experimental Psychiatry*, 1977, *8*, 261–268.

O'Dell, S. L., Mahoney, N. D., Horton, W. G., & Turner, P. E. Media-assisted parent training: Alternative models. *Behavior Therapy*, 1979, *10*, 103–110.

Oltmanns, T. F., Broderick, J. E., & O'Leary, K. D. Marital adjustment and the efficacy of behavior therapy with children. *Journal of Consulting and Clinical Psychology*, 1977, *45*, 724–729.

Patterson, G. R. A behavior modification program for a child with multiple problem behaviors. *Journal of Child Psychology and Psychiatry and Allied Disciplines*, 1966, *7*, 277–295.

Patterson, G. R. The aggressive child: Victim and architect of a coercive system. In E. J. Mash, L. A. Hamerlynck, & L. C. Handy (Eds.), *Behavior modification and families*. New York: Brunner/Mazel, 1976.

Patterson, G. R., & Fleischman, M. J. Maintenance of treatment effects: Some considerations concerning family systems and follow-up data. *Behavior Therapy*, 1979, *10*, 168–185.

Patterson, G. R., Weiss, R. L., & Hops, H. Training of marital skills: Some problems and concepts. In H. Leitenberg (Ed.), *Handbook of behavior modification and behavior therapy*. Englewood Cliffs, N.J.: Prentice-Hall, 1976.

Peed, S., Roberts, M., & Forehand, R. Evaluation of the effectiveness of a standardized parent training program in altering the interaction of mothers and their noncompliant children. *Behavior Modification*, 1977, *1*, 323–350.

Peine, H. A., & Munro, B. C. *Behavioral management of parent training programs.* Paper presented at the annual convention of the Rocky Mountain Psychological Association, Las Vegas, 1973.

Rachman, S. *The effects of psychotherapy.* Oxford: Pergamon Press, 1971.

Reisinger, J. J., & Ora, J. P. Parent–child clinic and home interaction during toddler management training. *Behavior Therapy*, 1977, *8*, 771–786.

Shapiro, A. K. Placebo effects in medicine, psychotherapy, and psychoanalysis. In A. E. Bergin & S. L. Garfield (Eds.), *Handbook of psychotherapy and behavior change.* New York: Wiley, 1971.

Sloop, E. W. *Problems with parents as behavior modifiers: How to fail and how to succeed.* Paper presented at the meeting of the Southeastern Psychological Association, Hollywood Beach, Florida, May 1974.

Strain, P. S., Young C. C., & Horowitz, J. An examination of child and family demographic variables related to treatment outcomes during oppositional child training. *Behavior Modification*, 1981, *5*, 15–26.

Szykula, S. A. *An effective method of reducing child and family therapy dropouts: The comprehensive referral pursuit and maintenance approach.* Unpublished manuscript, 1981.

Szykula, S. A., Fleischman, M. J., & Shilton, P. E. Implementing a family therapy program in a community: Relevant issues on one promising program for families in conflict. *Behavioral Counseling Quarterly*, 1982, *2*, 67–78.

Tavormina, J. B. Relative effectiveness of behavioral and reflective group counseling with parents of mentally retarded children. *Journal of Consulting and Clinical Psychology*, 1975, *43*, 23–31.

Truax, C. B., & Carkhuff, R. R. *Toward effective counseling and psychotherapy: Training and practice.* Chicago: Aldine, 1967.

Wahler, R. G. Some structural aspects of deviant child behavior. *Journal of Applied Behavior Analysis*, 1975, *8*, 27–42.

Wahler, R. G. The insular mother: Her problems in parent-child treatment. *Journal of Applied Behavior Analysis*, 1980, *13*, 207–219.(a)

Wahler, R. G. The multiply entrapped parent: Obstacles to change in parent–child problems. In J. P. Vincent (Ed.), *Advances in family intervention, assessment, and theory* (Vol. 1). Greenwich, Conn.: JAI Press, 1980.(b)

Wahler, R. G., Sperling, K., Thomas, M., Teeter, N., & Luper, H. The modification of childhood stuttering: Some response–response relationships. *Journal of Experimental Child Psychology*, 1970, *9*, 411–428.

Wahler, R. G., Winkel, G. H., Peterson, R. F., & Morrison, D. C. Mothers as behavior therapists for their own children. *Behaviour Research and Therapy*, 1965, *3*, 113–124.

Walter, H. I., & Gilmore, S. K. Placebo versus social learning effects in parent training procedures designed to alter the behavior of aggressive boys. *Behavior Therapy*, 1973, *4*, 361–377.

Weathers, L., & Liberman, R. P. Contingency contracting with families of delinquent adolescents. *Behavior Therapy*, 1975, *6*, 356–366.

Weinrott, M. R., Bauske, B. W., & Patterson, G. R. Systematic replication of a social learning approach to parent training. In P. O. Sjoden & S. Bates (Eds.), *Trends in behavior therapy.* New York: Academic Press, 1979.

Williams, C. D. The elimination of tantrum behavior by extinction procedures. A case report. *Journal of Abnormal and Social Psychology*, 1959, *59*, 269.

Wiltz, N. A., & Patterson, G. R. An evaluation of parent training procedures designed to alter inappropriate aggressive behavior of boys. *Behavior Therapy*, 1974, *5*, 215–221.

Wolfe, D. A., & Sandler, J. Training abusive parents in effective child management. *Behavior Modification*, 1981, *5*, 320–335.

TRAINING PARENT TRAINERS AND ETHICISTS IN NONLINEAR ANALYSIS OF BEHAVIOR

Israel Goldiamond

University of Chicago

Behavior professionals and ethicists may be said to engage in parallel training patterns. The professional presumes to instruct parents in how they should train their children, and the ethicist presumes to instruct professionals in how they should train client/parents. It should be noted that professionals, and specifically their training procedures, are once again in the middle: They are the subjects whose object is changed parenting behavior; *their* change is the object of ethical procedures. This is so for two reasons. The first is that ethicists often function as formulators of morality (from the Latin, *mor*, "custom"; a translation of the Greek, *ethos*, "community customs, standards"). The second is that professionals are agents of the community or social system. Often, as in medicine, they are granted a state monopoly to engage in their services. The presumable reason for such license is that the services that have been delegated to them (in this case, changing parenting behavior so as to produce potentially contributing members of the community) are of putative interest to the social system. Indeed, ethical breaches often consist of violations of, or failures to meet, this implicit social–professional contract. Failures are often masked by stratagems whereby reports of numbers "seen" are substituted for (implicitly socially contracted) outcomes attained. Yet another stratagem involves offering explanations in lieu of outcomes. One is then reminded of a rumored cheer at University of Chicago football games, when that school was still in the Big Ten. "Score that point," the cheer went, "or explain the reason why."

Such stratagems may, in time, cease being accepted by the social system (it is worth noting that the University of Chicago subsequently dropped football).

For these and other reasons (e.g., the unresolved problems and their effects, the ethical issues raised), it may be worthwhile to examine the procedures used for analysis and change. These procedures may, at times, underlie violations of the social contract or failures to score its goals. And it may turn out on inspection that parallel analytical procedures are used by ethicists when they serve parallel training functions. Accordingly, it may be worthwhile for ethicists and practitioners (and clients as well) to examine not only the procedures used by professionals when they serve as socially authorized training agents, but also the procedures used by ethicists and other social commentators when they, like practitioners, serve as parallel social training agents.

The purpose of this discussion is to consider ways of analysis and change as they relate to the social endeavors of behavior professionals regarding clients, and as they relate to the social endeavors of ethicists regarding behavior professionals. Practical and ethical problems are considered within this context. Attention is focused on differences between linear and nonlinear analyses of behavior, and between topical and systemic approaches. It may be noted that, for the behavior professional, the social contract may be strained by application of a linear analysis where a nonlinear analysis is applicable; and that, for the ethicist, the social contract may be strained by similar misapplication, or by application of a simple nonlinear analysis where a more complex one is applicable.

LINEAR AND NONLINEAR BEHAVIOR ANALYSIS

The terms "linear" and "nonlinear" have a variety of usages, both within mathematics and among the various disciplines that employ them. They are used here in the context of the causality of a specified pattern of behavior; or, stated otherwise, in the context of the variables of which the referent behavior (RB)—that is, the specified behavior pattern at issue—is a function. Stated heuristically, the term "linear" is applied to those cases where the RB is considered to be a function of variables (which may include history) that a particular explanatory system assigns to the RB as its exclusive domain. Examples are the reinforcement history of a particular RB, its conditioning history, its maintaining variables, and so forth. The values of these variables in a given functional relation to the RB determine the value of the RB at any time. The term "nonlinear" is applied to those cases where, although the RB may be functionally related to the variables noted, the values in its exclusive domain enter into, but do not determine at any time, the values of the RB. To obtain its values, one must also consider similar, but exclusive, domains of alternative behaviors (ABs)—that is, behaviors other than the RB that are then functional. Stated otherwise, *no matter how extensive one's knowledge of the behavior at issue and of its linear determinants, one cannot make adequate predictions about the behavior in such cases.*

For example, in decision theory, as applied to signal detection research, the likelihood of reporting the presentation (RB) of a stimulus (signal, S) cannot be determined solely by variables in the exclusive domain of the RB—for example, signal–noise ratio, *a priori* probability, and payoffs (positive reinforcement when a signal presentation occasions the RB, and punishment when a noise presentation occasions the RB), among others. The RB can be determined *only* by *also* considering variables in the exclusive domain of ABs—in this case, reporting that the signal was not presented (Egan, 1975). For practical purposes, this challenges the validity of psychophysical curves (and other perceptual data) that are based on relating the probability of reporting stimulus seen (or some other RB) to stimulus intensity or to other stimulus attributes (Tanner, 1955). Needless to say, subliminal data based on such curves, and mental tests based on similar relations, are also challenged. Just as linear analysis is not confined to the linear respondent and linear operant examples noted in passing, nonlinear analysis is not confined to the decision theory example noted in passing. Each of the sets is far more extensive.

The crux of the distinction between linear and nonlinear behavior analysis is not whether one can diagram the RB and its determinants by a straight or curved line of the stimulus–response (S → R) type, or the operant occasion-behavior–consequence (S · R → S) type, or by a model requiring multiple lines of a decision theory type. Rather, the distinction lies in the causality, the determinants, and the domains, of which the RB is, respectively, the effect, the resultant, and the range. The issue is whether or not the RB can be understood (or predicted, etc.) solely by, or as a resultant of, variables assigned exclusively to it at any time by an explanatory system, regardless of whether one (unlinear) or more lines (branching, converging linear) or feedback loops (feedback linear) are used in the diagram. If it can be so understood or determined, the analysis or determination of the RB will be considered linear. Given a linearly depicted RB, whose type of linearity accords with the requirements of an explanatory system, if—no matter how adequate the explanatory system has historically been in explaining RB—it cannot be explained on its own, but its explanation requires simultaneous attention to the determinants of one or more ABs, the analysis or determination of the RB will be considered nonlinear. A theoretical implication is that when a unilinear operant analysis, say, of the RB does not provide adequate explanation of the RB, the answer is not necessarily to reject operant analysis in such cases in favor of, say, a cognitive analysis (cf. Skinner, 1980, pp. 89–90). One might first try a nonlinear operant analysis, in which neither the RB nor the ABs can be explained by sole reference to the operant unilinearity of either, but in reference to the combined contingencies the operants represent (Goldiamond, 1975a). It should also be noted that a linear analysis of the RB is often explanatory. Occasionally, a given linear analysis is not explanatory, but a different linear analysis is. The issue is, then, not the rejection of linear analyses, but rather understanding the differences among linear analyses and between these and nonlinear analyses.

Example 1: A Case of Bulimia

The difference may be exemplified by a case of persistent binge–vomit behavior (bulimia). The client was a young married woman, aged 21, with a child 18 months old, whose presenting complaint was the twice-daily occurrence of binge–vomit episodes.[1]

History

Within a year after graduation from high school, the client and her husband, who was of a different faith, were married. Her parents disowned her, and the couple moved away from her neighborhood into the home of his parents, who received her warmly. He found a job as an appliance salesman in a discount outlet that was open from noon to late evening, to attract couples after work. When she became pregnant, they found an apartment of their own—a "railroad" flat (all rooms in a row) in which the only sunlit room was the large kitchen. Her social life was completely disrupted, and she was alone from 11:00 A.M. until 8:00 P.M. Occasionally, they went out with his crowd; he often stayed out with the "boys." When their son was born, these conditions were not changed. Her parents reaccepted her. They spent every Sunday afternoon at her parents' house, where the family ate Sunday dinner and then watched television.

According to the client's records, at about 2:00–3:00 P.M. most weekday afternoons, she sat at her kitchen table, watching her child play with toys on the floor, and ate (1) a 1-lb box of Oreo cookies, (2) a package of ladyfingers, (3) a 1-lb angel food cake, (4) a dozen doughnuts, and (5) a quart of milk. She then went to the bathroom and "undid" (her term) in the toilet. The process took over an hour, and was substantially repeated at about 6:00 P.M. At 8:00 P.M., she and her husband had a regular supper together. On Sundays, she partook similarly of her mother's cakes, and "undid" there. The pattern had been going on since the couple's latest move; they discussed it regularly. There had been occasional binge–vomit episodes when they had lived with her husband's parents. She had told her husband, before marriage, that she had resorted to occasional binge–vomit patterns all during high school, he pooh-poohed it, along with her other apprehensions (e.g., about her family's attitude). As can be gathered, he did well as a small-appliance salesman; she was quiet and soft-spoken. She was 5'3" tall, of normal weight for her height and build.

---

[1]All cases, unless stated otherwise, were treated at the University of Chicago. In the bulimia case cited, patient sessions were conducted in the presence of a graduate class in behavior analysis for nutrition students, conducted as one of the degree requirements of the university's Committee on Human Nutrition and Nutritional Biology, in which I hold an appointment.

Sessions were conducted weekly in the presence of four graduate students in the nutrition program. Treatment rationale is presented in Table 19-1. The behavior at issue—that is, the referent behavior (RB)—is considered in this case to be the disturbing behavior (DB) of binge–vomiting; DB is a subset of RB, and properties attributed to RB apply to DB.

Intervention

Intervention was mainly nonlinear, as is evident in Table 19-1. The program was carried through in about 15 weeks, with the spouse called in from the waiting room for slightly under half of these. Minor linear rearrangements were made in the kitchen once the social agenda had been set. These consisted of pushing the kitchen table to the wall, so that when the client was seated for snacks, she would have to turn her head to watch the child. Another table was to be used for writing and telephoning, and was to be placed so that the refrigerator was not in the line of sight of the table. Nonlinear intervention was directed toward three major areas.

The first nonlinear area was for the client to reestablish a social life of her own, in which she could actively participate without neglecting her child. To the extent that this circle included mothers in similar situations, the problems would be simplified. In a large city, many people find themselves in similar situations. The problem is to find them and bring them together—and to make the necessary time available for searches and meetings. Part of the intervention was directed toward these ends: Her husband was required to release time for her by taking care of the child during the search, and thereafter while she was with her friends. This involved training her husband in the nonlinear program. (With other bulimics, the parents have been so trained.) Unfortunately, there were few social resources in their vicinity set up for such purposes. The client herself located the Y mentioned as among possible resources (her Intervention 1 in Table 19-1). It had a program precisely directed toward this population—the swimming pool had a swimming crib attached, so that mothers could leave their children to wade and swim while they swam in an adult pool. In addition to swimming, she registered for two classes: psychology and hypnosis.

The second major area consisted of reestablishing relations with her parents in an area that was central to their life (and without which she was restive)—namely, the church of her parents and grandparents. Her present relations with her parents, centered as they were on dinner and then watching television all afternoon, were dull and restrained, with little chance to do anything but eat, and with few pleasant comments to make other than on the excellence of her mother's cooking and polite trivia. By going to Mass in the mornings and returning to her parents' house briefly thereafter, she would make them delighted, and she and her husband could then spend the rest of an enjoyable Sunday elsewhere. This change was the last one instituted. It involved resolving in practice religious differences (and similarities) between the wife and the husband in this area, as opposed to the theoretical discussions prior to marriage. The Sunday binge–vomit pattern was the last to go; this target change was the last to be instituted.

The third area was central to the other two. It involved producing the first two outcomes in a manner consistent with attention to the child and attention to the relations of the husband and wife with each other. The latter would involve, for the husband, an increase in his circle of friends through her friends (and for both, an increase in friendships developed as a couple); a chance to be with his child; a more alert wife with more things to talk about when he returned from work; and, most important, the cessation of the threat to her health. During the last two sessions, she was very much on her own with her husband. Furthermore, she asked if there were any point in continuing to come. She felt she could handle the problem.

Comments

Linear programs were directed toward eating and were minimal. The client's vomiting was simply considered to be a natural effect of bingeing, with bingeing analyzed as a procedure that occupied her and enlivened an otherwise dull day. The binge–vomit pattern also produced concern from her husband who, then, together with her, sought professional attention. No control procedures were directed toward vomiting, but records were kept of both eating and vomiting.

The various nonlinear programs (nonlinear with respect to the presenting symptoms) were not only suggested, but carried out, with weekly monitoring of records that, although kept by the wife, also reported her husband's involvement. This was then ascertained in his presence. With regard to eating, the paradigm was not classically that of differential reinforcement; this procedure would involve, for the same situations (stimulus controls), withholding of reinforcement upon eating and reinforcing behaviors other than eating. It was the social context that was changed: New conditions were established under which new behaviors, not otherwise available, supplied those important reinforcers hitherto contingent only on bulimic patterns; numerous other reinforcers were now also available. One can speculate that the premarital bulimia was also accompanied by the same critical reinforcers, given the social isolation of a shy girl in a high school whose classmates valued other patterns. It should be noted that the client can still vomit, she can still overeat—these have, so to speak, not been "eliminated." Their absence is explained nonlinearly (i.e., by alternative contingencies). There are simply better ways for the client to spend her life, and, apparently, she can now assert such agendas for herself.

Much of the intervention concerned her husband and involved changes in his behavior as well as changes in hers, with regard both to him and to other features of her environment. It may also be noted that explicit attention was directed toward the benefits *for him* that were contingent on changes in his and her behaviors. Her husband may be considered, for the purposes of elucidating

Table 19-1

A Case of Bulimia: Treatment Rationale

Occasion	Alternative behaviors	Costs	Benefits
	Disturbing behavior (DB)		
Client alone with child at home, in kitchen while husband at work; housework done; 2:00–3:00 P.M.	1. Eating excessively, vomiting	Medical risks and "psychological risk," worry over interpretation; food and money wasted	Whiles away her time; occupies her while watching child, and after housework is done
6:00 P.M.	2. Same pattern	Same costs	Child having slept, bathed, and now playing, foregoing benefits are potent; leaves her time to prepare supper thereafter
Sunday, client at her parents' house in afternoon	3. Eating mother's cakes, ice cream, and cookies to excess	Same costs, plus risk of discovery of pattern	Mother expresses delight that her daughter enjoys her cooking; whiles away boring afternoon
	Target behavior (TB)		
Afternoons	1. Find other young mothers with similar problems; new circle of friends	Usual risks attached to forming friends; arrange for friends and husbands to meet husband; keep him informed; thank him for release of time	Enjoyable time occupies her while child is cared for; housework done (other mothers have same problem)

Evenings	2a. Arrange with new friends to go shopping for meals, in early evening; start other activities	Same, plus scheduling problems and breakdowns	Child is cared for; client does things with friends; leaves her time to prepare supper
	2b. Go out with own circle of friends twice a week	See above	Friendships, social circle
Sundays	3. Arrive Sunday morning, go to Mass with parents; leave after luncheon snack	Stress and indicate importance of marriage; stress and plan afternoon	Mother and father express joy over lost daughter found; avoids boring afternoon; afternoon with husband and son

Note. Bulimic nonlinear intervention: Daily event logs kept by client, turned in weekly, food eating and vomiting to be recorded. Re: Targets—

1. Discuss and check on social resources for groups of young mothers: neighborhood churches—no resources, community colleges—no groups, women's groups—none in neighborhood, local Y—regular classes for mothers during afternoons, swimming periods, with supervised children "cribs" (shallow pools) in same room as pool. Register in courses there.

2. Find friends from Resource 1, make arrangements for shopping, swapping child care. Discuss ways to have husband take over child care two evenings a week, while group goes out.

3. Discuss with husband change in Sunday pattern.
   Intervention with spouse:

1. Program and rationale discussed; consent obtained.

2. Come home early two afternoons a week. (Spouse's initial reaction: "Good, then we'll go out together." Therapist's answer: "You go out with the boys, don't you? Let her go out with the girls.")

3. Spouse to get up early to allow his wife to attend Mass. (Had no objections to wife's religion, feared possible use by parents to get her back completely. Agreed that they would not try to break up their marriage, which could be strengthened by having Sunday afternoons to themselves.) To read paper at her parents' house while waiting; babysit.

4. To move to better house as job prospers.

511

parent training procedures, where disturbing behaviors of a child are the presenting problem, as functioning *in loco parentis*. In other cases of bulimia, wherever it has been possible to involve parents, their behaviors have been made part of the program. Interventions are directed toward changes in their behaviors, in the child's behaviors, and, often, in the behaviors of other significant members of the environment.

In one case, this consisted of the elimination of the father's requirement that all of his children attend the excellent local college on whose board he served as a prominent businessman alumnus (and where the tuitions he paid were reduced). The mother, who had hitherto engaged in volunteer work, obtained independent full-time employment for herself. The young woman broke with her boyfriend, who had insisted she spend all her waking time with him; during the academic year, she dropped from ingesting 50,000 calories weekly to 8500, and from vomiting up to 22 times in a week to no vomiting (Goldiamond, 1979). At every weekly session, I conducted parent training (with another significant other, when possible), while the young woman was seen by Carol Collins, a doctoral student at the Behavior Analysis Research Laboratory. The separate periods were followed by a joint period at each session. Neither vomiting, nor its control as a habit, nor its control by other linear means was the subject of intervention. Intervention was directed mainly toward nonlinear changes of the social context in which, prior to change, bingeing was an impressive operant (among other things, the vomiting that ensued got her out of attending the next class with her boyfriend).

For a young college student of similar age, intervention was entirely nonlinear and also involved parent training, but to a lesser extent. She is currently a graduate student at an Eastern university, and, when she finds herself bingeing, attends to the social contingencies, which involve relations with boyfriends.

Intervention may consist of parent training alone. In a case of this type, the daughter was 21 and was classified as schizophrenic as well as the Prader–Willi syndrome (stature under 5 feet, gross obesity, small hands and feet, and continual ingestion of food up to 16,000 calories in one day). She was "seen" separately, mainly to allow discussion to go on with her parents. In the initial interview, in response to the question, "If we were successful, what would be your outcome?" (Goldiamond, 1974), one of the parents replied, "Helene would be dressed during the day." The response was, "What would the outcome be for *you*? What your daughter gets is up to *her*." Her mother, it turned out, could get advanced training and an advanced degree, while her father could do other work at home; both outcomes were blocked by the inordinate drain of time and energy demanded by their daughter's egregious behaviors. Changes in her behavior were contingent on changes in their behavior; her responses selectively reinforced their parenting behaviors. The interlocking patterns, where the behaviors of one are the stimuli of the other (and the reverse) (Skinner, 1957), were monitored by the parents and myself from their records and were discussed during weekly programing sessions. Their outcomes were attained within 5 years; 5 years thereafter (and at present), their daughter weighs 135 pounds, and recently appeared to speak to parents of other such children in conjunction with a talk by her mother on her procedures. (Her parents and I are preparing a monograph.) The program contained both linear and nonlinear procedures.

Example 2: A Case of Gilles de la Tourette Syndrome

A program in which the contingencies supplied by significant others entered into the maintenance of a disturbing pattern, and probably into its establishment, but in which neither the parents nor others could be seen for training, is exemplified by an early program applied to a case of Gilles de la Tourette syndrome, with whom I worked in conjunction with Dr. Sheldon Glass, then a psychiatric resident.[2] This was the second admission of a young woman whose first admission had been 2 years earlier, with outcome unresolved at the age of 17. On the flight back home after her first hospitalization, she met a young man who was now her fiancé. She returned for hospitalization, reporting concern that she might "spoil the [wedding] ceremony" by erupting into the full-blown syndrome. This consisted of a sharp jerking of her head over her left shoulder; simultaneously, she would pull clenched fists to her collar bones without quite striking them, rapidly shaking her fists back and forth with a traverse of about an inch from her collar bones; she would grimace, with her mouth pulled to the left, and utter an audible prolonged "f—f—f—f" merging into "uck," equally audible. She would then relax completely. Two types of intervention were planned and introduced within the first few days of her 3-week stay. One involved linear operant shaping and fading procedures. The other involved a nonlinear analysis dealing jointly with an operant DB, an operant AB, and an operant target behavior (TB). The case exemplifies both types of analysis.

History

Grace was born a "blue baby," with mitral anomalies, but it was decided to postpone heart surgery until she was 11. Her father's family was German Swiss, and her mother's Mexican. Both sides of the family were devoutly Catholic. She attended the neighborhood parochial schools, and the Sisters were instructed to treat her as a normal child. She participated in all games during recess, with her mother coming to the schoolyard to approve and watch for any emergency. She was hospitalized in the local Catholic hospital on schedule; the surgical outcome was considered successful, but she and her parents were instructed that she was

---

[2]The case was the first one assigned to me upon my promotion to Professor of Behavior Analysis, Department of Psychiatry, Johns Hopkins University, in 1967. Dr. Sheldon Glass is now at Glass Mental Health, Inc., Baltimore, Md.

not to exert herself. (At 19, her terminal finger phalanges were slightly enlarged and bulbous; her nails and lips were bluish.) These instructions were ignored, as they had been up to then, in the interests of her having a "normal" childhood. It was during the hospitalization that her occasional and periodic tremors, which had consisted of a slight tic of the mouth and arms, became the full-fledged Gilles de la Tourette syndrome as described. She returned to her class in school, where the tic was accepted as an affliction beyond her control; she reported to me and to Glass that she had gained some notoriety among certain classmates as "the goil with the doity mouth." Her grades at the parochial high school were average, as were her school activities.

As noted, it was on her flight back home after her first hospitalization for the Gilles de la Tourette syndrome that she met the young man who was to become her fiancé. She reported having received medical advice not to pursue college full-time and, if she married, not to bear children. Nevertheless, she was now in college, and was determined to have a full family life, including children. She was alert, bright, and attractive, with, she reported, her father's fair skin and hair and her mother's dark eyes. She was seen by both programer/therapists twice a week, for sessions of over 1 hour; Glass visited her almost daily for part of an hour. The intervention program was planned during the joint sessions, with the daily visits used for practice in accord with the program. During one of the joint sessions, she asked, "Does my problem have anything to do with a death wish?" "Why, Grace, what makes you say that?" Glass asked interestedly, because the question accorded with one of the psychoanalytic interpretations of the syndrome. "Well," Grace answered, "every time I use the word 'death,' in a statement like, 'This will be the death of me,' all the doctors look at each other significantly, nod, and make a note in their notebooks."

Linear Intervention

Linear intervention was of two types, shaping and fading. Shaping initially involved breaking the syndrome pattern into three independent elements: (1) almost beating her chest with clenched fists; (2) turning her head; and (3) uttering the fricative followed by "uck." It was first ascertained that she could produce the entire syndrome upon instruction by either programer. She was then instructed several times to produce the terminal expletive alone (0, 0, 3), which she did each time, then the head turn–expletive sequence as a unit (0, 2, 3), then the entire sequence (1, 2, 3). The sequence was then made chest beat, head turn, no expletive (1, 2, 0); then chest beat without sequelae (1, 0, 0). Each of these was preceded by instructions, for example, "Grace, tic—arms, then head alone," followed by compliance and then an enthusiastic "Good," or "Terrific." Unit 1 (the chest beat) was then made the RB. It was to be shaped from its original form to a TB of a simple tremor confined to a small tightening of the muscles of her arms and hand, upon the instruction, "Tic!" A book was held against her chest, and she was to bring her fists almost to the book, then almost to two books held against her chest. The books were then withdrawn, and she was instructed to produce the arm tic almost that far on instruction. She was then successively to reduce her traverse, as though more books were added, until the TB alone resulted. Instructions were then given for various elements along the RB → TB progression, and for the independent emission of tic components 1, 2, or 3. Practice sessions between program meetings consisted of repetitive drilling in each of sequences 1, 2, 3; 1, 2, 0; and 1, 0, 0, then of RB → TB, with the RB = TB distance gradually increased.

Fading involved transfer of control over any of the foregoing units, in the following steps:

1. Grace was instructed to tic upon the programer command, "Tic."
2. Grace was instructed to tic upon completion of the programer command, "Tic, 1-2-3-4-5."
3. Upon the programer instruction, "Tic," Grace was to count from 1 to 5 silently, then tic.
4. Upon the programer's raising of a pointed finger, Grace was to say "Tic" silently, then count silently, then tic.
5. She was ad lib to say "Tic" silently, then count silently, then tic.
6. She was to say "Tic" silently, then tic.
7. She was to limit the spasm to the TB (simple tremor described) when it occurred.

The shaping progression took place in two sessions with both programers, and the fading progression in two similar sessions; overlap between sessions made the total three sessions. The effort was for Grace to demonstrate to the programers and herself that she could, upon command, engage in each of the program steps. No effort was made to ensure that each program step on its own controlled the required response; the time was simply insufficient. Glass engaged in repeated drilling in the steps during his regular daily visits.

Nonlinear Analysis

From discussions with Grace during the sessions, and from other information on group characteristics, inferences were made by the programers and confirmed or revised by Grace to the following effect: The Swiss side of Grace's family tended toward subdued emotional behaviors; its members spoke quietly. These were patterns that Grace considered worthy of emulation. The Mexican side was outgoing and emotional behaviors were vigorous; its members spoke loudly and gesticulated visibly. When they visited and became "too loud," the syndrome appeared, and everyone quieted down. Grace then withdrew. The syndrome appeared, as well, on other occasions when Grace was "under stress" —that is, for her (stress might be defined differently for others), the situation or context was to be escaped, avoided, or changed. With regard to the escape situation produced by the "loudness" of the Mexican side of the family, there was a discussion of the fondness for children and concern for others that often accompany the "loud" patterns; Grace reflected upon this with a perplexed

"Really?," then nodded assent. In the past, she had simply asked her relatives to be quiet; this had not worked, so she had stopped. It was suggested that, upon occasions requiring escape, she might resume asking her relatives to quiet down or to change other patterns and was also to cite her physical condition as an explanation. Grace again wondered whether this would work, was asked to consider her relatives' evident concern for others, and then nodded in agreement. Table 19-2 may clarify the analysis.

Comments

In contrast to the outcome of her previous hospitalization for the syndrome, Grace departed free of tics. She was presented before the staff at Grand Rounds, where she glared at them and spoke without distress. Electromyography revealed continual recurrence of muscle spasms, but she was able to confine the spasms to spasms, without "making a production" of them. The extent to which the analysis used for Grace holds for other cases of Tourette syndrome remains to be seen, but I have noticed the use to which children put the spasms. Conceivably, these need not be escalated. Conceivably, drugs can be effective in blocking the muscle spasm and therefore its sequelae, or can also thereby change reactions by the audience in other ways. However, carefully designed behavior analysis programs may, in the case of the muscle spasm, restrict it to a spasm without its disturbing sequelae, and may also be directed toward audience reactions—all without the possible complications that can attend use of drugs.

The intervention described took place during 3 weeks of hospitalization. Three joint sessions were devoted to the shaping and fading program described, with the effort made to produce the patterns noted, rather than to maintain them or establish them under the control of occasions in Grace's day-to-day environment; the daily practice sessions were directed toward maintenance on occasions instigated by Grace's commands or by the muscle spasms themselves. Two joint sessions were devoted to discussing and formulating the nonlinear analysis described. Because of time limitations and the impracticality of having her family come with Grace (her case was turned over to me after her arrival), all that could be done was to present and discuss the analysis. It is presented here simply to illustrate the analysis, as well as the possible implications of a combined linear and nonlinear analysis in the treatment of a syndrome often handled chemically at present. It may also have implications for medical understanding of the establishment and maintenance of a syndrome to which many organic theories are presently directed. Organicity is involved, but this may be restricted to the variables entering into a spasm.

Subsequent to discharge, Grace's marriage took place as scheduled, with no untoward incidents. She has since been separated from her husband; she now works as an administrative assistant. In contrast to the preceding cases, where behavior analysis was continued beyond the original intervention period, she has not been involved in any behavior analysis programs since her participation

Table 19-2

A Case of Gilles de la Tourette Syndrome: Treatment Rationale

Occasion	Alternative behaviors	Costs	Benefits
Family gatherings; presence of other "noisy" people	**Disturbing behavior (DB)** Full tic; beating of chest, turning head, expletive fricative followed by "uck!"	Uncontrollable tic whenever there is a slight muscular spasm; may occur at wedding and may upset wedding plans; may prevent or destroy marriage	Shuts up "noisy" Mexican relatives; they become quiet, and atmosphere sedate; gets them and others to behave quietly around her, not to intrude into her privacy; sympathetic concern and consideration from others
	Available alternative behavior (AAB) Ask family to be quiet	Hates to keep nagging them	They continue on their way, or resume immediately, if they stop
	Target behavior (TB) Firmly tell relatives that such noise makes her sick, will cause tic; thank them for doing so, and join in conversation; express appreciation of their heritage	Mention tic (less costly than doing it) and sickness; capitalize on it	Mexican relatives, though "noisy," will be kind and understanding, delighted at her joining their conversation and being part of family; will respect her wishes

Note. Intervention: Resident to keep records at hospital. Resident to train client in programed diminution of tic to a simple occasional small spasm. Instructions for posthospitalization: Control tic at inception so that only spasm occurs.

517

in the program described, 15 years ago. She has been under the care of local physicians. The Tourette syndrome is reported as occasional, but in much milder form and with less frequent occurrence than ever before. The routine and accepted medicines in such cases have been prescribed.

In the foregoing case, the parents were not seen as part of the program. Grace had flown down without parental escort, and I was not in a position then to request that they join her, nor would such a request have been reasonable in the absence of prior arrangements. However, at present, where a child is involved or where the nature of the problem implies parental involvement, admission into any of the programs at the Behavior Analysis Research Laboratory is made contingent upon such involvement. Such involvement is routine in our fluency program. The child is trained in a new pattern of speech, using explicit linear programing procedures. The program and its linear and nonlinear rationales are gone over with the accompanying parent, who is trained to serve as a programer and program monitor at home. There is in-session monitoring of parental monitoring of the child. Suggestions are made to the parent and child on changing home contingencies to those conducive to maintenance of the pattern at home. Following discharge, logs are mailed on a regular basis, and are returned with analysis and recommended changes to the parents and children involved.

TOPICAL AND SYSTEMIC ANALYSIS

In the case of bulimia that is described in Example 1, the binge–vomit pattern is described as a symptom. As I have noted earlier (Goldiamond, 1965a), the term "symptom" accords as well with behaviorist formulations as it does with formulations in the routine and accepted practice of medicine. In the medical care, an illustration may be provided by a patient who sees a dermatologist for an itching skin rash. The professional may diagnose the problem as, say, numular eczema, and prescribe a cortisone ointment; the rash is gone within 2 days. On the other hand, the professional may ask, "Does your skin flush when you get up in the morning?" Upon further investigation, the patient is referred to a cardiologist, whose treatment is addressed toward the cardiovascular system rather than toward the presenting skin problem; analogously, the dermatologist's own treatment may be directed toward an allergy, allergens, and the immune system, rather than toward the presenting skin problem. In the latter two cases, the presenting complaint is defined as "symptom" (or "sign")— intervention is directed elsewhere. Such interventions are generally "systemic," as opposed to the area-localized "topical" treatments, exemplified by the cortisone ointment (Goldiamond, 1979; Guimaraes, 1979). Whereas "area," "localization," and "system" are anatomical or anatomical–functional in medicine, such terms are generally metaphorical in psychology. In behavior analysis, "topical" treatment would generally refer to interventions defined by the presenting problems and addressed toward those "areas," and "systemic" treatment would generally refer to interventions initiated by the presenting problems but addressed toward different behavior–contingency "systems." Both types of analysis and intervention are presented in the preceding section, and have been noted earlier (Goldiamond, 1965a). Nevertheless, psychoanalytic writers keep equating behaviorally oriented procedures with linear topical treatments—for example, "In *behavior therapy* . . . target symptoms define procedures" (Davanloo, 1978, p. 75; emphasis in original). The equation may hold for linear analysis, but does not define nonlinear analysis (which includes both topical and systemic procedures, and hence is equated with neither). With regard to such critics of behaviorism, one wonders, along with the refrain from "Where have all the flowers gone?," "When will they ever learn? When will they ever learn?" To the extent that behaviorally oriented practitioners continually restrict their analyses to localized topical interventions, the refrain may apply to them, as well. As I note in the next section, when the discussion is extended to ethicists, the refrain may also apply.

Two points are worthy of note. The first is that in *both* topical and systemic intervention, as defined medically, intervention may be addressed to the variables of which the presenting complaint is a "function." In the topical case cited, for example, the cortisone does not remove the skin (although some topical interventions in other cases might have been so addressed). It was addressed toward the vascular edema relations of which the rash was a function. In the systemic case, treatment is directed toward the cardiovascular or immune systems of which the rash is a function. Accordingly, differentiation between the two types of treatment is not purely on the basis of "function" (as the term is used in algebraic set theory). In a parallel discussion in the preceding section, it is noted that in linear analysis, intervention could be directed toward the referent behavior itself (e.g., shaping, analogous to gradual replacement of anomalous skin), or to variables *of which the DB is a function* (e.g., change in stimulus control or in maintaining consequences, among others). The differences are considered shortly.

Second, it is important to emphasize that, regardless of differences in analysis, application, and implication, both topical and systemic analyses are useful and legitimate forms of analysis and intervention in behaviorist approaches, even as they are in medicine. The issue is simply their appropriate use. It is inappropriate and wasteful to apply systemic analysis when topical analysis is appropriate (e.g., as in the case of the stutterer who, after 5 years of psychoanalysis, informed me that "I—I—I s—s—still s—s—stutter b—b—but now I un—n—nderstand why"). It is also inappropriate and wasteful to apply topical analysis when systemic analysis is appropriate (e.g., as in the case of the bulimic who, after several sessions of habit control elsewhere, informed me that "I feel much better," but still had binge–vomit episodes twice a day).

As noted, although linear analysis is, almost by definition, topical (i.e., a linear analysis is restricted to the specific "area" or domain of the RB), nonlinear analysis may be either topical or systemic. Accordingly, it may be convenient to consider, first, the common nonlinear analysis that topical and systemic interventions share, and then, the differences between their analytic systems.

Common Nonlinear Analysis

In both topical and systemic nonlinear analysis, changes in the RB are attributable to changes in the relations between (1) the linear determinants of the RB, on the one hand, and (2) the linear determinants of the available alternative behaviors (AABs), on the other hand. In the economic format to be employed in the present discussion, the linear determinants of the various behaviors are mainly their respective consequences. Stated otherwise, the nonlinear determinant of the RB is the relationship between its consequences and those of the various other relevant behaviors. This relation may be defined as "the resolution of the payoff matrix."

It should be noted that among the determinants of the RB, the AABs, and the TB are not only the consequences but also the occasions (S^D) when behavior is consequential. The occasions have been omitted from the discussion for two reasons. The first is to avoid the awkwardness that might arise from continual coupling of "when S^D" or "upon specified occasions" with any behavior discussed, and from the necessity for distinguishing an occasion–behavior relation (which is the object of the reinforcement) from the relation between the various payoffs of the different occasion–behavior relations. Omission of the occasion simplifies the presentation. The second reason is that the critical difference between linear and nonlinear analyses in the economic models to be presented lies in their systematically different treatment of the consequential (or payoff) determinants, rather than of others. Although these others may then not be necessary for comparative purposes, they nevertheless do remain determinants and must be considered in any analysis. The paradigm presented in Table 19-3 may help clarify the terms. The particular economic format to be used is that of the cost–benefit analysis (cf. Mishan, 1976) noted in Tables 19-1 and 19-2, with an added column, namely, development costs–benefits.

Although the format is economic, the analysis and procedures for change are those of consequential behavior analysis. The costs and benefits are neither predefined negative nor positive monetary values, nor their equivalents in shock, food pellets, tokens, or hypothesized survival values. Rather, they refer to demonstrable decremental and incremental effects upon behavior (cf. Goldiamond, 1975a), which derive from contingency histories under specified conditions, as exemplified by Morse and Kelleher (1970), who programed the maintenance of behavior "by electric shocks presented under fixed-interval schedules" (p. 183). Electric shocks made contingent on behavior would intuitively be entered as economic costs of that behavior. As arranged by Morse and Kelleher, they are benefits in terms of the present discussion. The decision rules, strategies, or decision criteria whereby the economic matrix is resolved (to be discussed shortly) are to be understood in the context of "rule-governed behavior" (Skinner, 1966), or "instructional–abstractional control of behavior" (Goldiamond, 1966). The terms refer to a history of complex behavior–environment relations. The economic format is used because it provides a convenient framework for examining complex behavior contingencies in nonlinear relation.

Three types of consequential costs are mentioned. The "punitive costs" (1a in Table 19-3) refer to delivery of social or other aversive stimuli contingent on behavior, or to such contingent elimination of reinforcing stimuli (as in conventional time out). Although punishment may be defined by its attentuative effects (Azrin & Holz, 1966), and the RB is not attenuated, the punitive costs are, nevertheless, punitive. Their attentuative effect is being overridden by the augmentative effects of the reinforcers that are contingent on the same behavior. There is ample laboratory evidence for such linear overriding (e.g., Holz & Azrin, 1961). The "losses" (1b in Table 19-3) refer to the opportunities for behavior or other outcomes lost while one is engaging in the behavior or thereafter. For example, as long as a child is verbally abusing someone indoors, that child cannot be playing outdoors. "Preemptive costs" (1c in Table 19-3) refer to later consequences. For example, if a student learns how to pass examinations through cheating, the cheating may replace learning of the subject matter; learning of skills based on that subject matter may thereby be preempted.

Consequential costs are differentiated from development costs in Table 19-3. In economics, the latter are often entered into the consequential costs and hence need not be considered separately. In economic analysis, where an enterprise is not yet established, a cost is assigned to its construction. The cost may be borne by a loan whose amortized repayments become part of the operating or consequential costs of delivering the services for which it was ostensibly constructed. (Double-entry bookkeeping may change the profit–loss picture, but not the analysis.) In behavior analysis, where a behavior pattern or its stimulus relations are not established, the efforts for such establishment cannot be amortized—that is, they cannot be attached to the target behaviors as consequences along with the consequential reinforcers. Accordingly, a separate column is attached in Table 19-3. It should be noted that the TB (and $S^D \cdot RB$ relations) and AABs (and their S^D relations) may be well established. Little or no development cost may then be required. However, the topical and systemic TB or $S^D \cdot TB$ relations may not be well established. Considerable time and effort may then be required to establish them. (In a case noted above, the effort required for the parents was 5 years of daily programing to establish the appropriate TB for a child whose RB had been patterns diagnosed as irreversibly retrogressive schizophrenia. The progress of their daughter's behaviors and event–behavior relations, augmented by the explicit statement of the progres-

Table 19-3

Paradigm for Development of Cost–Benefit Analysis and Intervention

Development costs–benefits	Occasions	Alternative behaviors	Consequential	
			Costs	Benefits
A. Analysis (topical and systemic)				
1. RB (or S_x^D · RB) well established	1. S_x^D	1. Referent behavior (RB), symptom or sign, disturbing behavior (DB), with DB $\subseteq$ RB	1− a. Punitive b. Loss c. Preemptive	1+
2. AAB (or S_x^D · AAB)	2. S_x^D	2. Available alternative behaviors (AAB$_{2,\ldots,n}$), (RB$_{2,\ldots,n}$)	2− $(\ldots n)-$	2+ $(\ldots n)+$
B. Intervention (topical)				
T3. TB (or S_x^D · TB) to be established or transferred	T3. S_x^D	T3. Target behavior (TB), outcome, objective	3− $|3| < |1|$	3+ $3 \geq 1$ $\mathrm{Ben}_{TB} \supseteq \mathrm{Ben}_{DB} \supseteq RB$
C. Intervention (systemic)				
S3. TB (or S_x^D · TB) to be established or transferred $|(3-)| > |(1-)|$, $(3+) > (1+)$	S3. S_x^D	S3. Target behavior (TB), outcome, objective	3− $|3| < |1|$	3+ $3 \geq 1$ $\mathrm{Ben}_{TB} \supseteq \mathrm{Ben}_{DB} \supseteq RB$

Note. A. Analysis: Resolution of (consequential) payoff matrix, in accord with decision rule, favors RB. *B. and C. Intervention:* Resolution of payoff matrix, in accord with decision rule, favors TB. *Consequential and development costs–benefits:* Costs to be considered include not only payoff costs, but response efforts and development costs to establish, transfer, and maintain DB, AABs, TB, and program. Similarly, benefits to be considered include payoff benefits, and also response and developmental benefits.

sions in the various records kept, were among the variables that maintained and differentially reinforced the parents' training patterns.)

A more adequate discussion of development costs would require a chapter in itself, and would lead far afield of the present discussion. However, several points (among many) are briefly noted here. The foremost of these is that the significance of the area is almost precisely matched, but inversely, by the number of systematic studies directed to it. Kipling's "six honest serving-men"[3] may serve here: *What* are the costs (e.g., what is the client expected to do)? *Why* undertake them (e.g., outcome, alternatives, payoffs)? *When* are they borne (e.g., how often, over how long a period)? *How* are they arranged (e.g., see below)? *Where* are they to be assumed (e.g., locales for acquisition and application)? And *who* is to bear them (e.g., parents, child)? The answers may suggest the conditions under which clients postpone entry into or drop out of program participation in a well-articulated program that would, if maintained, produce the target outcomes; they may suggest correctives.

A related point about development costs concerns their interaction with the payoff matrix. Although *intervention* in behavior analysis requires separation of development costs from payoff costs, *prognosis* for program success (as well as client participation) requires integration of development costs and payoff costs, as in economics. Put most simply, the assumption is made that if the RB and the TB produce the same benefits, and the TB is far less costly than the RB, the payoff matrix will be resolved in favor of the TB instead of the RB. However, if the net development costs of the TB exceed the payoff costs of the RB (more technically, if they exceed the difference between the RB and TB costs), the program "ain't worth the effort." It may then not be undertaken; or may not be completed if undertaken; or may not be transferred to the everyday environment, if completed. It is at such points, in conjunction with Kipling's Who, that coercive procedures for participation are often suggested or resorted to. "After all, it's to their advantage that they be involved." It should be noted that development costs can be attenuated by providing the reinforcement at each step, and can even be totally transformed into development benefits by appropriate attention.

One final point: Kipling's How may not be that formidable. In most cases with adults, it is not necessary to shape, successively approximate, and so on. The pattern may be present, but under different stimulus control. An example is a depressive patient who considered herself to be antisocial—she had never invited guests for meals or other occasions. She attributed this social lack to her mother, who had been an isolate and had never done so, either. It turned out that the patient had been a very successful producer of religious talk shows on local television, and had produced programs considered to be very exciting. It

---

[3]"I keep six honest serving-men / They taught me all I knew; / Their names are What and Why and When / And How and Where and Who."—Rudyard Kipling, *Just So Stories*. From *Rudyard Kipling's Verse: Definitive Edition* (Garden City, N.Y.: Doubleday, Doran, 1944).

was suggested that she treat her dinner guests like television guests—select them for an interesting evening, arrange their seating, and so forth. "I never thought of that!" she said. The various procedures may be reduced to three general ones:

1. "Do as I say" (i.e., instruction, with "frame" completion reinforced).
2. "Do as I do" (i.e., a transfer program, with each successful unit reinforced; the transfer may be imitative transfer, also known as "modeling"), "do as you do" (transfer from one's own repertoire that is under different stimulus control—e.g., the talk show host), "do as you did" (historical transfer from one's own past repertoires), "do as others do" (observation, then imitative transfer).
3. "Do as I arrange" (i.e., routine and accepted fading, shaping, contingency management).

The last—the surest, but often the most time-consuming—is the one most required where new patterns are to be established, as is often *assumed* to be the case with children. I emphasize "assumed," since the pattern may, in some cases at least, exist partially or *in toto* elsewhere in their repertoires. In all events, all programs require arrangement. The question is; how are they to be applied?

The payoff matrix whose resolution governs behavior (or, more properly, a given occasion–behavior relation) is, for the RB and ABs, the set of RB costs (1−), RB benefits (1+), AAB costs (2−), AAB benefits (2+). Where there are other available alternatives (2, 3, . . . , n) the costs of these (. . . , $n-$), as well as benefits (. . . , $n+$), must also be entered into the matrix. The simplest case is for two classes of behavior (occasion–behavior relations), and the discussion is restricted to these.

Various decision rules, strategies, or decision criteria (Birdsall, 1955; Luce & Raiffa, 1957) may be applied. A "net-gain" rule would involve matrix resolution toward the behavior pattern whose benefit–cost difference is greater than the benefit–cost difference of any other behavior pattern; a "minimax" might be described in terms of the behavior patterns whose losses (negative differences between benefits and costs) best serve not to exceed certain values; in a "maximin," the profits (positive benefit–cost differences) would not fall below certain values. Other rules may be applied (von Neumann & Morgenstern, 1944). Where the probability of a given pattern of behavior accords with such a rule, the "choice" of that behavior (i.e., its probability in relation to that of others) is said to be "rationalized," and it is then described as a "rational choice." It is the assumption of this discussion that where the probability of a disturbing pattern of behavior (e.g., bulimia, depression, schizophrenia) can so be described, and interventions so directed can be effective—that is, where desirable changes in probabilities are produced in accord with the model—then the disturbing pattern (in that case) can be treated as though it were a rational choice.

No implication should be drawn that the use of such a model requires the behaver to behave this way *on purpose*, to accord with Lewis Carroll's ditty,

"Speak roughly with your little boy, / And beat him when he sneezes. / He only does it to annoy, / Because he knows it teases." As has been known for some time (Hefferline, 1962; Hefferline, Keenan, & Hartford, 1959), the probability of behavior can be changed independently of the behaver's tacting (Skinner, 1957, p. 81ff.) the behavior, or tacting the consequence as a consequence, or the contingent relation of one on the other (see also Goldiamond, 1965b). Decision theory, cost–benefit analysis, and related consequential economic theories may be used descriptively, as the typical scientific model is applied. They may also be used normatively—that is, to indicate how one should behave. This may involve thinking of and planning a course of action, and behaving accordingly. However, if the entries in the payoff matrix are changed—say, by an economic depression or by a laboratory investigator—the investor may change plans and investments in the former case, and the pigeon may change comparative behavior probabilities in the latter case. The pigeon's shifts might accord with a strategy which, when it occurs in humans, demonstrates knowledge of calculus. The issue is, then, not the one the theoreticians of cognitive "behavior" modification would like to state as the issue—namely, "Do we think, then act; act, then think; act and think independently; or do all three, as permitted by cognitive theory? Or do we allow only act then think, and act and think independently, as (allegedly) restricted by the radical behaviorists?" The existence of any of these is not at issue. What is at issue is their *causality*. As the payoffs (consequences) change, and as the contingent relations of payoffs to behaviors change, then *both* thinking and behavior will change, although not necessarily at the same rate, nor in any particular ordering relation to each other. They have different histories of, and types of, contingent relations to the consequences of behavior (Goldiamond, 1979, pp. 387–388).

Implications

In linear analysis, the referent DBs (disturbing patterns of occasion–behavior relations) are often considered to be functions of their currently maintaining variables or of their historically establishing and maintaining variables. They are often considered to be maladaptive, or pathological, or outcomes of deficient histories. Intervention is defined by these DBs or the variables that maintain them—*they* constitute the problem.

In the nonlinear analysis depicted in Table 19-3, however, the referent DBs are considered as functions of the decision rules as they are applied to the entries in the payoff matrix (*a priori* probabilities and similar variables may also enter into this, but are excluded from the present discussion, since they do not affect the general analysis). They are analyzed *as if* they were rational choices. Stated otherwise, the DB is reinforced behavior and is explained in matrix terms as occurring, despite the high costs entailed, because if we compare these costs and benefits to the costs and benefits of the AABs, the DB turns out to be the pattern of (rational) choice. It is the most economic way of producing the critical reinforcer (a consequence "which is preferred in all choice situations," given certain regnant conditions and procedures—e.g., deprivation; see Goldiamond, 1976a, p. 23). Neither the DBs nor their choice constitutes the problem. Rather, it is the resolution of the matrix through an RB that is costly, or that jeopardizes the individual, that constitutes the problem. Intervention is directed toward other resolutions of the matrix.

The Basic Rule for Matrix Resolution

The rationale for intervention, given nonlinear analyses of the type indicated, is to find and program a TB that produces, at the very least, reinforcers of the same stimulus (or behavior) class whose delivery maintains the DB (in Table 19-3, the entry $Ben_{TB} \supseteq Ben_{DB}$ in the Benefits column for the TB row indicates, in set terminology, that the classes of reinforcers maintaining the TB [Ben_{TB}] include the classes of reinforcers maintaining the DB [Ben_{DB}]; stated otherwise, the TB produces the same maintaining consequences as the DB, and possibly even more [$\supseteq$]), and at less cost than the DB (in Table 19-3, $3+ \geq 1+$, and $|3| \leq |1|$). Development costs and benefits must also be considered. Given the same critical reinforcer for both patterns, with one pattern (DB) heavily punished and costly otherwise while the other (TB) is not, the TB will not only be the theoretical pattern of choice; it will also be the empirical pattern of choice (Herman & Azrin, 1964; Holz, Azrin, & Ayllon, 1963). Stated otherwise, the rule for intervention is to ascertain the critical reinforcer whose delivery governs the DB and, rather than necessarily withholding it upon occurrence of the DB, making its delivery *also* contingent on a TB that is less costly to the individual and that is of greater benefit to the individual and to the referent social system (in parent–child training, the parents). The client is not deprived of a choice; rather, the client's range of choices is extended.

In both topical and systemic intervention, a new (to the matrix) pattern of behavior (TB) has been added, but the *maintaining* consequence (the reinforcer) includes that for the DB matrix entry. Hence, the significant consequential element that enters into the definition of an operant contingency is the same (with others added). Although the costs differ, and although this will affect the relative probabilities of TB and DB, the definition of the contingency is not altered (see Goldiamond, 1975a).

Topical Intervention

In topical nonlinear intervention, the S^D for the TB, $S_x^D = S_x^D$, the S^D for the DB. The maintaining consequence for both is also the same. Since the contingency events that bracket the TB and the DB are the same, the TB and the DB may be considered to be in the same response class. They are in the same general "area" of behavior (occasion–behavior relation); intervention is then defined as topical. An example of such intervention can be found in the case of a person whose presenting complaint was smoking. Among his various patterns was one in which he escaped a monotonous task every hour on the hour by putting down the ledgers, relaxing in his chair, and smoking a cigarette. After discussion, he was instructed to put down the ledgers every hour on the hour and take an explicit 10-minute break; he was to tell his secretary that this was necessary to ensure accuracy (which was probably true). The two were to have a cup of tea, or he was to exercise briefly, or something of the sort. The cigarettes dropped out of the daily routine.[4] The DB and TB occasion, 50 minutes of ledger work, was the same. The DB and TB reinforcer, 10 minutes of no ledger work, was also the same, as was the escape contingency. However, the DB and TB escape behaviors differed. It is as though a pigeon resets the timer (whose time down, when the key is green, produces shock) by striking the key with its wing (TB), rather than with its beak (DB). The two responses are functional equivalents in a topical substitution.

The outcome may also be changed by changing the S^D component of the occasion–behavior relation, rather than the behavior component. In this case, since behavior and consequence are identical to those of the original components of the contingency, an equivalent S^D has been programed, and the intervention is topical.

Systemic Intervention

Systemic intervention is nonlinear by definition. In such an intervention, the S^D for the TB, $S_x^D \neq S_{x'}^D$, the S^D for the DB. The maintaining consequences for both overlap, in accord with the basic rule for matrix intervention. However, the other events, which together with the consequences bracket the TB and the DB, are not the same for the TB and the DB. Occasions and behaviors differ; consequences alone overlap. Hence the TB is in a different class or area from the DB, and the intervention is systemic. An example of such intervention can be found in the case of bulimia (Table 19-1). The clients' parents' joy (S') at having her in their home in the afternoon (S_x^D) was not contingent on her eating their food with gusto (then vomiting, DB). Rather, her parents' joy (S') at seeing her at church in the morning ($S_{x'}^D$) was contingent on her rejoining (TB) their (and her own) religious communion. Similarly, her social community at her home was extended from her husband alone to him *and* her peers and friends. In both situations, the target outcome (critical consequence) was a community considerably enlarged from the originally restricted one of her DB.

---

[4]From research performed in collaboration with Dr. Margaret Nellis, now at Johns Hopkins University School of Medicine, Division of Behavioral Sciences, Baltimore, Md.

This is a far cry from the intervention centered on the binge–vomit episodes, which too many psychoanalytic writers would seek to equate with the behavior therapies. In the process of obtaining such enlarged community, the client adopted the assertive patterns necessary to ascertain available resources, to keep her husband in line in sharing child care, and to part from her parents after lunch, among others. There were record keeping and contingency analyses, as well as changes in stimulus control. The point being made is that the routine and accepted practices of behavior analysis are used in systemic as well as in topical intervention, just as the routine and accepted practice of medicine is used in systemic as well as in topical intervention.

A Rule of Thumb

A quick rule that seems to distinguish between nonlinear topical and systemic interventions may be derived from the comparison in Table 19-4.

For each row, there are two entries that are similar to each other, and one that differs from the other two. In the topical row, equality is found under both the S^D and Benefits columns ($Ben_{TB} \supseteq Ben_{DB}$ implies $Ben_{TB} = Ben_{DB}$, or equality plus extra benefits for Ben_{TB}); nonequality is found under Costs. In the systemic row, inequality is found under both S^D and Costs; equality is found under Benefits. If we examine the *odd* entry in each row, it pertains to Costs in the topical row and Benefits in the systemic row. Using the odd entry as a rule of thumb, one might say that in topical intervention, intervention is focused upon a TB (or S^D) that will *reduce* the costs of the DB, while maintaining the benefits of the DB. In systemic intervention, intervention is focused upon different behaviors and contexts that will, nevertheless, maintain the benefits of the DB. This emphasized difference between topical and systemic interventions, it should be noted, is only a rule of thumb. Both require attention to the benefits and to the programing of the context–behavior relations that maintain these benefits.

In many of the linear interventions, which are, by definition, topical, therapeutic attention is devoted to reducing the costs of the DB. These interventions may use either constructional procedures or eliminative-pathological procedures (Goldiamond, 1974). On the other hand, systemic interventions, as presently applied, are constructional.

The foregoing presentation is admittedly incomplete in several ways. The theoretical discussion has focused on changes in the matrix produced by changed behaviors of the referent client. The important roles of the referent significant others, or the referent social system, were empirically reflected in the bulimic intervention (where the husband was enlisted), but this is not systematically reflected in the theoretical discussion. Changes in the determining matrix cannot always be made the sole responsibility of the client (even when aided by a resourceful practitioner). Others must then be recruited into the task. The

Table 19-4

Rule of Thumb for Distinguishing between Topical and Systemic Interventions

Intervention	S^D	Costs	Benefits
Topical	$S_{TB}^D = S_{DB}^D$	$Cost_{TB} < Cost_{DB}$	$Ben_{TB} \supseteq Ben_{DB}$
Systemic	$S_{TB}^D \neq S_{DB}^D$	$Cost_{TB} < Cost_{DB}$	$Ben_{TB} \supseteq Ben_{DB}$

cost–benefit analysis of development must then be extended to them as well, as part of a program. Furthermore, such roles function within social policy (i.e., under certain social policies), the costs to family members are less prohibitive than under others. For example, our laws of relative responsibility often function to make family costs prohibitive: Relatives of a dependent are often simply considered responsible for appropriate caretaking as a moral obligation; they may not be offered the financial and other social aid offered to nonrelated caretakers, or may even lose such aid when they undertake responsibility (e.g., a paid caretaker for a quadriplegic lost her salary when she married him!). This may affect care—and caring (B. Goldiamond, 1982; Moroney, 1980).

Still other areas that require consideration are procedures that simply alter the values of the matrix entries, without establishing new TBs. This often enters implicitly when a system seeks to increase the penalites for a DB (as has occurred in certain jurisdictions with respect to drug abuse), or seeks to reduce the benefits of a DB. Certainly, AABs may be made more potent through change in matrix entries; their range can also be broadened.

Finally, among the other areas that merit elaboration are unresolved ambiguities in the present discussion. It may at times be difficult to distinguish between complex nonlinear topical interventions and simple nonlinear systemic interventions. This difficulty extends as well to medicine, where the distinctions between symptoms, signs, and nonsymptomatic interventions can become blurred. The field then adopts arbitrary classifications, and proceeds with interventions whose procedures are clearly defined.

Nevertheless, the present discussion is intended to focus attention on a method of analysis that has proven highly fruitful in other social disciplines, and much of which remains to be explored in those disciplines as well as in behavior analysis. Linear consequential behavior analysis derives from experimental investigations in which the AABs are effectively excluded from consideration: The pigeon pecks the key for food, or engages in AABs and starves. Such cases can be considered as nonlinear investigations in which the matrix entries in the benefits column are 0 for all AABs. Such experimental isolation of variables is often necessary for scientific purposes. However, it should be distinguished from the more general case in application, where there are matrix entries for AABs that must enter into the consideration of the RB. Problems are raised when conclusions from the limiting case are extended to the general case. Investigators might start focusing on the general case of which the limiting cases are legitimate subsets.

IMPLICATIONS FOR ETHICISTS

The *Harvard Medical School Health Letter* recently inaugurated its seventh year of publication by reprinting what it considered to be "perhaps [the most] important" and "germane" of its articles—namely, its "guidelines for evaluating new medical information" ("Evaluating Medical Information," 1981, p. 6).

Of the four points, the opening and closing points (peer review over unreviewed reports; wariness regarding claims for unusual remedies for incurable diseases) are general. The second and third points are specific. They concern, respectively the effectiveness of treatment in its safety. The concluding statements in each of these paragraphs are these: in regard to effectiveness, "[*A*]*sk yourself if the treatment in question was compared either to other treatments or to 'doing nothing'*"; in regard to safety, "When you encounter information about 'safety,' *ask yourself—'safe compared to what?'*" (Emphases in original.) Both risks (probable health costs) and benefits (health) are to be considered, and for each, treatments are to be compared with one another. This produces a social intervention matrix of the type in Table 19-5.

Development costs and benefits have been added to the system implied in the *Harvard Medical School Health Letter*. Although they may enter into an individual's choice of treatment, the costs of enrolling in a treatment can be separated from the health risks (and benefits) *produced* by the treatment. Where "a social system" is substituted for "an individual," ethicists are obviously dealing with a comparison of different therapies that are addressed to similar presenting problems—the equivalent ($x = x$) occasions of Table 19-5.

The analysis may also be addressed to different problems, when competing allocations of funds are considered: For example, will scarce funds be allocated to a well-baby clinic providing limited care (to many), or to a dialysis clinic

Table 19-5
Social Intervention Matrix

Development costs–benefits	Type of (health) problem		Costs (health risks)	Benefits (health)
A±	X	Intervention A	A−	A+
B±	X	Intervention B	B−	B+
n±	X	Intervention n	n−	n+

providing intensive care (to few)? Ethicists thus enter into the realm of conflicting social decision rules and policies and conflicting ethical decisions.

The format need not be restricted to payoff entries that are monetary. What is salient about the use of monetary entries is not that they are quantifiable, but that their quantifiability permits the formulation of behavior–environment relations (economics) that can be validated and that permit control. It should be noted that reinforcing and aversive consequences, which have been the entries in the present discussion, also enter into formulations of behavior–environment relations (behavior analysis) that can be validated and that permit control. While comparative values on a magnitude dimension generally cannot be as readily assigned in behavior analysis as they are in economic analysis, relative positions or ranges on a magnitude dimension can be assigned.

The format is one of high generality. Problems arise when it is ignored, or when the limiting case is made the general one. Such a limiting case is found, as previously noted, when the ABs to the RB (and their contingencies) are annulled. Yet another limiting case is found when ABs (choices) are presented, but analysis is restricted to only one of the consequential columns (e.g., costs), thereby ensuring that the opposite effects (benefits or reinforcers, in the same example), which are also necessary for the analysis, are annulled. The discussion is restricted to the generality of rules drawn from these two types of limited cases, although others could be considered as well (e.g., omitting development and maintenance costs and benefits). The discussion is focused on two areas— namely, ethical analysis of professional behavior, and recommendations for social behavior (implementation). Space precludes extended discussion of these and related issues. Accordingly, discussion centers around one or two examples, case studies, or issues under each heading.

Professional Behavior—Linear Analysis

A case that I have discussed in some detail exemplifies such analysis and the tragic outcome of its effects.

> A colleague at a different university showed us a deeply moving film. The heroine was an institutionalized primary-grade girl. She was a head banger, so a padded football helmet was put on her head. Because she could take it off, her hands were tied down in her crib. She kept tossing her neck and tore out her hair at every opportunity. She accordingly had a perpetually bruised face on a hairless head, with a neck almost as thick as that of a horse. She was nonverbal.
>
> My colleague and his staff carefully planned a program for her, using all kinds of reinforcers. She was remanded to their program, but persisted in her typical behavior. In desperation, the ultimate weapon was unwrapped. When she tossed her head, my colleague yelled "Don't!," simultaneously delivering a sharp slap to her cheek. She subsided for a brief period, tossed again, and the punishment was delivered. My colleague reports that less than a dozen slaps were ever

delivered and that the word "Don't!" yelled even from across the room was effective. Its use was shortly down to once a week, and was discontinued in a few weeks. In the meantime, the football helmet was removed and the girl began to eat at the table. She slept in a regular bed. Her hair grew out, and she turned out to be a very pretty little blond girl with delicate features and a delicate neck. In less than a year, she started to move toward joining a group of older girls whose behavior, it was hoped, she would model. She smiled often.

The initial institution and her parents discovered that she had been slapped. They immediately withdrew her from the custody of my colleague's staff. The last part of the film shows her back at the institution. She is strapped down in her crib. Her hands are tied to a side. She is wearing a football helmet. Her hair is torn out, her face is a mass of bruises, and her neck is almost as thick as that of a horse. (Goldiamond, 1974, pp. 62–63)

As noted above, she was removed from the program. The argument raised was an ethical one: Given a child who is under treatment for an ailment whose symptoms include head banging, to punish her for displaying signs of her ailment is morally repugnant.

The analysis of institutional behavior was a linear one: occasion, head bang; RB, "Don't!" or slap; outcome, attenuation (or punishment) of behavior (stated symbolically, S^D - RB → S^a). A more detailed analysis of institutional behavior is presented in Table 19-6. The disapproved and approved linear analyses are each enclosed in a three-term rectangle. As is evident, such analyses are only part of the larger story in the table. Interestingly, in the restricted analysis that underlay removal of the child, *costs* were the only consequences considered for the referent institution; for the original institution, *benefits* were the only consequences considered. For the referent institution, benefits produced by participating in the program, which were made possible by removing the restraints, were ignored. For the original institution, costs produced by the restraints—namely, the physical force necessary to hold down the child when restraining her head and hands and observed lack of progress produced by concomitant restraints on behavior—were ignored.

The point is not being made that the original institution is representative. Chemical sedation is often substituted for physical restraints; other programs may use neither type of restraints. Rather, the case is being made that too often an outcry is raised over the use of some procedure considered to be punitive and repugnant, in line with the reasoning underlying the moral repugnance expressed by the child's parents and the institution. No attention is then paid to the constructional program that is thereby made possible.

The implicit social contract between the social system and the professional system involves the costs and benefits to each system of helping the child. Presumably, it is beneficial to the social system to have appropriately functioning children, and, for this outcome, it will undergo the costs of professional treatment and social support by the professionals. In return for such benefits to them, professionals are to invest time and skill, at cost to them. In the development cost–benefit analysis of Table 19-6, the ABs are those that the psychological staff directs toward the child; the development costs are those for these behaviors; the consequences are the professional behaviors that are outcomes of the alternative treatments. These outcomes, of course, derive from the effects on child behavior that the treatments produce. This feedback model— → (1). preparatory behavior (developmental) → (2) alternative treatments → (3) (continued or new child behavior) → (4) continued or new professional behaviors, opportunities (consequences) → (1) preparatory . . . —is only one of many development cost–benefit analyses that can be made. These analyses are considered in greater detail shortly.

One other analysis is considered in this section. Where the *child's* ABs are the subject, and the consequences include social effects, a different table ensues. In such a table, a linear analysis would consider only the head banging and self-mutilation. In a systemic analysis, these would be the RBs or the DBs.

For these DBs, the consequential costs are as follows: organic costs, such as lacerations, potential blindness, and brain damage; punitive costs, such as aggressive responses from others; losses, such as avoidance by other children, restrictions by parents, and preemption of social development and speech. In contrast, for the TBs, the costs are those related to participating in the program.

For these DBs, the maintaining benefits derive from a complex history of interactions with significant others, which include (but are not limited to) coerced, intense, and special concern of the significant others. For the TB, the maintaining benefits of the TBs include the benefits of the RBs, but in a different manner. The staff is required ("coerced") by the nature of the program (establishing self-grooming, dressing, social eating, etc.) to attend intensely to the fine grain of the child's behavior in a program specially tailored to her changing behavior. (For an early step-by-step account of fine-grain procedures that were used to establish imitative patterns for children "who apparently showed no imitation whatever," and that culminated in vocalization of specific vowel and consonant sounds minimally necessary for speech, see the sensitive report by Baer, Peterson, & Sherman, 1967.)

The difference between the intense concern produced by the RBs and that produced by the TBs is that, in the first case, the concern is produced because distraught parents and staff "don't know what to do," but in the second case, concern is produced as a requirement of an articulated fine-grain program previously designed by professionals. Reinforcers in addition to these were also made contingent on the TBs. Space precludes further analysis.

To treat such a program as though it is a topical program, and one confined to punitive treatment at that, neither does the program nor the child justice, nor is it intellectually or morally justified. Returning to Table 19-6, the previously noted concentration on institutional *costs* in one case (the referent institution) and *benefits* in the other (the original institution) suggests a selectivity that requires no comment.

The issues still abound. I was very recently appointed to a state task force to examine the use of "aversives" (costs) by an institution for developmentally disabled children. The task force was not charged to relate these institutional

Table 19-6

Alternative Institutional Behaviors Regarding a Head-Banging Girl: Feedback Effects on Staff

Development costs–benefits	Occasions	Alternative behaviors	Consequential	
			Costs	Benefits
Referent institution				
Patterns available in repertoire	$S^{D}1_a$: Preparatory head toss	RB1$_a$: "Don't!"	Continual monitoring; use of aversives	Physical restraints removed; allows TB programing to proceed
Costs Detailed advance preparation of programs; scrapping and new programs when program failures	$S^{D}1_b$: Head banging Varied	RB1$_b$: Slap TB: Constructional step-by-step programs; self-grooming, dressing, mealtime, academics, games, social, verbal, etc.	Continual monitoring, assessment, reinforcement	"Job satisfaction": observation of accomplishment, staff learning new skills, analysis, publication, institutional
Reinforcers Decreasing time for new programs as skills improve				
Original institution				
1. Equipment available commercially 2. Strong attendants available	$S^{D}1_a$: Bruised head $S^{D}1_b$: Torn hair, facial lacerations	RB1$_a$: Football helmet emplaced RB1$_b$: Hands tied down, other restraints	1. Periodic monitoring to ensure restraints in place; physical force to tie down child; behavior stasis and observation of lack of progress	1a: Escapes head banging, protects child 1b: Avoids self-removal of helmet, self-mutilation
Staff training in patience, pleasant demeanor, attitudes	Mealtimes, occasional visiting periods	RB2: Greeting child warmly, explaining restraints, possible goals, aspirations; attempts to "reach" child	2. Emotional drain on staff, hardening or burnout and turnover	Possible future reaching of the child; difficulty "of treating such cases" rationalizes outcomes to date; "humane" approach approved

behaviors to any constructional programs applied by the institution, nor was it charged to compare the overall effects with those of other institutions (as the parents of the children strongly urged). Subsequently, I was asked to participate in writing guidelines for the use of aversive procedures. This task was declined. If the reasons have not been made evident thus far, they are made more explicit in the ensuing discussion.

Analysis of Alternatives Restricted to One Consequential Column and Implementation

In a linear analysis, there is omission of the effects on the RB of consequences attached to ABs. A different type of omission can occur when both the RB and its ABs are specified. In this type of omission, there is no matrix containing both behavior-attenuating and behavior-augmenting consequences. Instead, the alternative behaviors are simply compared on the basis of one type of consequence only. An example of this type of omission is the normative rule designated as "the *least* restrictive *alternative*." The rule states that, given a variety of available institutional procedures, one should choose the least restrictive of these. It assumes that the procedures can simply be located as values on one least–most dimension—namely, $least = r_1, r_2, \ldots, r_n = most$. If the procedures are multidimensional with regard to restrictions, it is implied that such a dimension can be derived, and that this one dimension governs behavior.

This rule has been swallowed whole by many behavior professionals. It has been translated to "the least aversive alternative," and hierarchies of aversiveness have been explicitly stated, in line with the least–most dimension described. If some self- or other-destructive behavior occurs, the least aversive alternative that *attenuates* the RB (to criterion) is to be used, and a more aversive one is justified only if a less aversive alternative does not work. In this case, although alternative costs are involved in the choice of professional behavior, the alternative benefits are not considered. To the extent that these differ markedly, the omission becomes critical. For example, in the case of the head-banging child, the "Don't!"-slap consequence apparently attenuated the RB rate (to 0). The slap was provided in the context of a program in which the ABs to the RB could be shaped to the TB.

As noted earlier, the general case is the nonlinear one, in which the matrix involves at least two consequences for each alternative behavior, as exemplified by the set $AB_1: x_1, y_1; AB_2: x_2, y_2; AB_3: x_3, y_3; \ldots ; AB_n: x_n, y_n$, where x and y are costs and benefits. The least restrictive alternative is a limiting case, in which benefits do not even enter into consideration, as exemplified by the set $AB_1: x_1, \emptyset; AB_2: x_2, \emptyset; AB_3: x_3, \emptyset; \ldots ; AB_n: x_n, \emptyset$, where $\emptyset$ is the empty set. Another limiting case involves annulment of benefits and costs for AABs to the RB, as exemplified by the set $RB_1: x_1, y_1; AB_2: 0, 0; AB_3: 0, 0; \ldots ; AB_n:$

0, 0, where 0 represents acknowledged entries whose value is 0. Under the latter conditions, which generally are *explicitly* instituted in the operant laboratory, the most parsimonious analysis of the RB may be linear. However, such analysis for the general case is unwarranted, unless the conditions that justify linear analysis have been demonstrated to exist. The conditions that might justify the limiting case of a least aversive (or restrictive) alternative have typically not been demonstrated to exist. Stated otherwise, until the omitted column of benefits (or reinforcers) is ascertained, neither normative analysis nor descriptive analysis nor implementation is justified.

It might be argued that the situations to which the least restrictive alternative is applied as a rule are those in which the benefits are identical, as exemplified by the set AB_1: x_1, y_1; AB_2: x_2, y_1; AB_3: x_3, y_1; . . . ; AB_n: x_n, y_1, where $y_1 = y_1$ represents the same benefits. This valid type of nonlinear treatment is described as "cost-effectiveness analysis." Since the benefits are the same for each alternative behavior, the decision rule may simply be matrix resolution in favor of the least costly alternative. Where the benefits as well as the costs of the alternatives differ, formal use of a cost–benefit model is required. Such a case is exemplified by a situation in which the least restrictive alternative (leaving children free to their own devices) produces fewer benefits than does a more restrictive alternative (requiring children to go to school). Given a variety of alternative methods of treatment, with a variety of restrictions as well as therapeutic benefits, the rule of the least restrictive consequence no longer applies.

Historically, the ethical use of this rule may derive from alternative methods of treatment (or "correction," in the case of prisons), each of which was equally ineffective (or, more properly, was effective to the same small degree), but which differed in their restrictions, as exemplified by the set AB_1: x_1, 0; AB_2: x_2, 0; AB_3: x_3, 0; . . . ; AB_n: x_n, 0. The formal use of the cost-effectiveness model may then have been justified. However, procedures change over time, new technologies are developed, and assumptions that were related to such procedures and that were applicable at one time are not necessarily applicable at another. Formally, cost-effectiveness models are limiting cases of more general cost–benefit models, just as linear analyses are limiting cases of more general nonlinear models. In behavior analysis, the justified use of the limiting case model derives from the explicit emplacement of the appropriate limits. In economic analysis, the appropriate limits are explicitly demonstrated or explicitly justified otherwise. In neither case are the nullified variables (whose annulment justifies the formal use of a limited model) simply not acknowledged. In all cases, whether for the purpose of inclusion of all elements in an analysis, or for the purpose of exclusion by annulment, specification of at least two consequential columns is minimally necessary.

The establishment of guidelines for intervention that are restricted to the use of punishment and aversives, and to the conditions and safeguards under which they are to be deployed, is accordingly questionable. The therapeutic outcomes that are produced, the program steps, and their development costs and benefits must also be considered. These conclusions may be derived not only from the format presented, but also from a sociolegal analysis. The social system has a vested interest in guarding against abuse of those whom it assigns to professionals. Such abuse is not restricted to those implied in the "cruel and unusual punishments inflicted" clause of the Constitution (Eighth Amendment), nor to those that "abuse the privileges of citizens of the United States . . . [or] deny to any person within its jurisdiction the equal protection of the law" (Fourteenth Amendment), nor that deprive any person "of life, liberty, or property without due process of law" (Fifth and Fourteenth Amendments). Abuse also derives from depriving a person of the opportunities to develop new repertoires and patterns of behavior that, continuing in the same vein, increase the likelihood of "life, liberty, and the pursuit of happiness." Guides that specify aversives or their conditions should specify equally meticulously the repertoires to be constructed, their means of construction, and their conditions—and the interactions between the two classes.

Social Oversight Restricted to One Model Rather than Alternative Models

Various social efforts have been directed, and are being proposed, for social oversight and monitoring restricted to behaviorally oriented interventions. Such restriction poses various problems, which have been discussed in greater detail elsewhere (Goldiamond, 1975b, 1976b) and are accordingly simply noted here. The discussion focuses on the linear analysis implied by these social efforts, and proposes a nonlinear analysis, in accord with the theme of the present discussion.

A recurrent issue found in these restricted social efforts is the confusion of nomenclature and analysis, on the one hand, with intervention procedures, on the other.

> Consider, for example, a case of increased privileges made contingent on progress. This occurs in every psychiatric institution. How different is this in principle from a graded-tier system or a token economy? In a token economy, progressive increase in tokens earned progressively purchases more privileges. It is not easy to distinguish among applications of such principles in a penal institution by prison officials, in a mental hospital by a humanist psychiatrist, in a token economy by an operant behaviorist, or in advancement through the grades of school by an educator. Yet, in all these systems consequences are applied when behavior changes. . . .
>
> Is the issue whether the therapist believes that the change is due to consequences he provides, or whether he believes that the changes have occurred some other way and he merely increases freedom as a consequence? Stated otherwise, does he believe that the behaviors change because of anticipated or actual consequences, or that the consequences were presented because the behaviors changed?

The operations are identical in both cases, and legal examination also should be. . . .

Difficult questions are raised when a procedure with application to two or more orientations is regulated when employed in one orientation or profession but not in another. If procedures presently associated with routine psychiatric practice are operationally identical to the regulated procedures of behavior modification, the question arises whether the psychiatrist also must apply for prior clearance. Indeed, as behavior modification expands and moves away from the model of the animal laboratory, an increasing number of procedures in the more classical approaches will be subsumed by its concepts. Similarly, if a given procedure, considered to be a behavior modification procedure, is identical to a procedure also considered to be a standard humanist procedure, and if legal regulation is required in the first case but not in the second, grounds for legal action exist. Arguably, equal protection of the right to practice psychotherapy is denied. (Goldiamond, 1975b, pp. 111–112)

The foregoing quotation is from a comment on a proposal for social oversight restricted to applied behavior analysis (Friedman, 1975). It has also been suggested that professional oversight be restricted to self-help manuals whose orientation is behavioral (Rosen, 1976); again, there is overlap between certain assertiveness training procedures ("behavioral") and Dale Carnegie procedures ("nonbehavioral"). The foregoing should not be interpreted to suggest that there are no differences between the various procedures. Genuine differences are to be found, but these are not in the areas that are cited to justify restriction of social oversight to behaviorally oriented procedures. The differences are (1) in the degree of explicitness and nonambiguity of assumptions and of formal and empirical operations; and, accordingly, (2) in their amenity to scientific analysis, correction, and advance, using the routine and accepted procedures of science. It is questionable whether a rule that subjects to social oversight the most explicitly stated alternatives is to the social interest. One is reminded of the drunk on all fours whom a policeman observed circling around a lighted lamp post on a dark street. He had lost his keys elsewhere on the street. "Where else can I search, officer?" he explained indignantly. "It's the only place that's lighted!"

The overlap described between procedures classified as "behavioral" and those derived from different orientations makes it difficult to differentiate procedures by means other than the names assigned to them or the orientations from which they derive. This overlap extends as well into the various behavior schools, and makes it difficult for nonpsychologists to distinguish between these (e.g., Friedman subsumes systematic desensitization under "applied behavior analysis"). This poses another problem frequently found in the works of social critics. Public (and literary) assignment of $S \rightarrow R$ causality to operant formulations is almost legendary. However, the clear separation of the two is currently being subjected to professional questioning (Locurto, Terrace, &

Gibbon, 1981). Yet another example is the overlap between the "imitative transfer" of radical behaviorism (e.g., Baer *et al.*, 1967) and the "psychological modeling" of social learning theory (Bandura & Walters, 1963). In contrast to imitative transfer, which necessarily incorporates reinforcement of successive imitations, modeling, which is related to observational learning, does not. When reinforcement becomes incorporated into modeling procedures for "participant modeling," overlap with imitative transfer increases. Accordingly, it becomes difficult to distinguish procedurally among the various schools that consider themselves "behavioral," and between these schools and those that consider themselves by designations other than "behavioral." Investigators are apparently left with differences in the names of these procedures and in the orientations from which they are derived. Such differences are not grounds for differential social attention. The other difference mentioned, explicitness, could provide a basis for differential social attention; however, as noted, the normative rule for such attention as presently oriented ("muzzle 'em, they're explicit!") raises questions as to its social desirability.

A distinction should be made among a specific procedure as applied in a given circumstance, the general procedure that it exemplifies, and the integrated body of practice (or school or model) from which it is drawn. A *specific* time-out procedure can be used injudiciously or judiciously, depending on the conditions of its use and on its analysis in a cost–benefit matrix of the type applied to the "Don't!"-slap procedure in Table 19-6. The *general* procedure which time out exemplifies might be described as "punishment" by means of withdrawal of positive reinforcers or of the opportunity to obtain such reinforcers (Ferster, 1958). Proscription of this treatment, *sui generis*, would involve proscription of all the various societal and interpersonal control mechanisms directed toward the attenuation of some undesirable pattern of behavior through removing socially desirable commodities or the opportunity to obtain them when the behavior occurs (e.g., through fines and incarceration) (cf. Reese, 1978). The singular attention to the administration of loss of liberty or property described by "due process of law" might also require peer or other review of a teacher who keeps a child from recess, a psychiatrist who isolates a patient after an obnoxious outburst, and so on. The theoretical justification for the actions may differ in these cases, but the general procedures do not. The *school* from which time out is drawn, *when it is designated as time out*, is applied behavior analysis; however, as is noted shortly, time out can have other designations when it is applied as a procedure derived from other schools.

On what basis might one model be socially selected over another? In one form, the question might be stated as the basis on which a social system approves of one type of intervention over another. As noted earlier, there are three parties that enter here—the social system that sanctions the professional change agent, the professional change agent, and the individual whose improved functioning (by means of the professional) is of benefit to the social system.

Social evaluation of the professional system accordingly depends in part on the adequacy with which the professionals improve individual functioning (or produce other results). The matrix described in Table 19-5 is appropriate here.

Professional behaviors are the alternative behavior patterns that are to be evaluated or selected. In terms of the present discussion, instead of health intervention A, B, . . . n, these might be an intervention that is behaviorist in orientation, yet another available intervention, and so on, as well as no particular intervention. One basis for evaluation might be the differential effects upon the patient's presenting problem (described as type of health problem x), as rationalized through matrix resolution of the beneficial and deleterious consequences, for the patient, of each type of intervention. These are integrated with the development costs and benefits necessary for the intervention to occur.

A variation on Table 19-5, which has not been presented, would consider the same alternative interventions in terms of their effects on the referent social *system*, which would thereby encourage or discourage professional behavior. What strains are imposed on a system by the intervention, and to what extent have the funds provided preempted solutions elsewhere?

The development costs of an intervention system include the costs of emplacing it. A referent social system may lumber along with what it recognizes as a less effective intervention system, simply because the development costs of replacing it outweigh the gains produced for the system. Hence, the difficulty that new systems encounter in getting established does not necessarily reflect prejudices that are difficult to overcome, but may derive from the rationality of the system. Indeed, the prejudices that exist may simply represent the emotional–ratiocinative accompaniments of the contingencies governing the stay-put behaviors. The observation that new theories do not replace the old because of their virtues, but because the old scientists die, may reflect similar rationality.

Comparative effects of alternative professional interventions upon other professional behaviors (through changes or continuation of patient behavior) have been presented in Table 19-6, which concerns the child who banged her head. It was the truncation of this table that provided the basis for ethical rejection of the behavior procedures used. The professional RB occasioned by the S^D (the patient's DB) need not be the slap presented in that table. The RB occasioned by the S^D may be an analysis of the contingencies of the various behaviors, for immediate use in a constructional systemic or topical intervention, in accord with Table 19-3. Stated otherwise, there may be no need for intervention directed toward a patient's DB. On the other hand, immediate chemical relief while the TB is being established may often be a necessary adjunct (and may eliminate the necessity for aversive consequences); it may also be used in conjunction with such a program.

A social analysis of delivery systems for human services in a particular (or general) case would consider at least six possible tables and their interactions. These are derived from the tripartite social–professional–professional analysis, in the following manner:

1. The various alternative patterns of the referent social system, as they are rationalized by the (developmental and consequential) costs that attenuate them and benefits that maintain them, supplied by (a) professionals, and (as a separate table) (b) patients or clients.
2. The various alternative behaviors of the professionals, as rationalized by matrix entries supplied by (a) the social system, and (b) patients or clients.
3. The various alternative behaviors of the clients, as rationalized by matrix entries supplied by (a) the social system, and (b) the professionals.

Intervention would involve either change of the values of the matrix entries to rationalize the choice of an available alternative rather than the referent behavior, or establishment of a new target behavior with matrix entries that rationalize choice of that pattern (or both types of change, among others).

The referent social system for a professional might include the agency that provides, as consequences of professional behavior, such benefits as social recognition and authority, professional advancement, income, facilities, and so on. These may be attached not only to those professional behaviors that involve patient change, but to professional recognition through publication, professional committees, and the like. The development costs of these behaviors (e.g., being kept from other activities) also have to be considered, as do other referent social systems, such as professional societies.

The referent social system for a child or other dependent might be the parents. In a marital program, this might be a spouse. Generally, the referent social system may be defined by the power relations involved (Goldiamond, 1975a). Other tables would be necessitated by parent–parent–child combinations. It is difficult to work with children and not be sensitized to the fact that proposed TBs for a child are often (openly or subtly) opposed by one or more parents because of the costs or losses such change would then produce for *them*. Any ethical analysis that concentrates only on one table, let alone a truncation of that table, to the exclusion of the interacting tables may be as inadequate as is intervention that is restricted in this manner.

The use of economic models and behavior analysis models should not be taken to imply that ethical rules or behaviors are economic in nature or follow laboratory prescriptions. The models described are simply efforts to specify and define formally, in unambiguous terms, the assumptions, designatory terms, and relations that researchers and therapists use when they establish and justify normative and descriptive rules for their behaviors.

An example of conflicting outcomes of application of the same formal rule to economic and ethical analysis is supplied by the rule of the least restrictive alternative. Ethically, therapists would certainly consider locking a child in a back ward (with "the key thrown away") under heavy sedation to be a far *more* restrictive alternative than allowing the potentially violent child free movement with peers, without sedation, would be. However, the continual supervision required for the latter, and its absence in the former, may make the back ward the *less* costly alternative (in dollars). That the same formal rule of a cost-effectiveness or cost–benefit model is being applied in both the economic and ethical analyses, with opposite results, should not be interpreted to challenge the usefulness of the analysis. The formal models call for analysis of the benefits, as well as the costs (without which either is incomplete), and the fact that they collide with each other indicates precisely why social institutions may often behave in a blatantly unethical manner.[5] That institutions often value economic costs above other human costs, and do so on a rational basis, suggests minimally that they share with others adherence to a common rational system. The task then becomes one of transferring that rationality to an ethically oriented matrix. Such transfer procedures are part of a behavioral repertoire. If ethical analysis is needed, so, too, is a behavior analysis that may provide better means of implementation than presently exist—providing that both areas use the same format, among other requirements. If ethical and legal implementations are wanting—to the extent that such implementations have tended to concentrate on the consequential costs of professional and institutional behaviors, to the exclusion of the consequential benefits or reinforcers that these behaviors may also produce—applied behavior analysts have been wanting to the extent that *they* have tended to concentrate on the consequential benefits they have produced, to the exclusion of the consequential (and developmental) costs of their behaviors.

The foregoing discussion should not be interpreted to imply that substitution of formal analysis for experimental analysis, nor to challenge as meaningless or outdated the data and relations of the experimental analysis of behavior.

With regard to formal–empirical relations, a particular formal system can describe a variety of possible empirical relations, some of which are valid and some of which are invalid. Accordingly, formal analysis can never substitute for familiarity with empirical procedures and their effects (cf. Skinner, 1980, p. 185). In the social sciences, especially, different languages are often employed to describe empirical procedures, and different formats often describe the relations between them. The differences can obscure the fact that the rule-governed behaviors represented by the procedures and relations often share common rules. An example is found in the governance of (1) detection of (2) signal

---

[5]Where the potentially violent child is allowed free movement, continual supervision may derive from the necessity to protect other children or the child. It may then be argued that it is the safety of others that is at issue, rather than economic–ethical conflict. However, the cost issue is raised because it enters as a determinant, no matter how slight. Another issue that can be raised is that monies saved by locking up the child can be used to provide considerable care to numerous others. As can be gathered, the issues are often not simple. The argument made here is simply that costs alone, rather than costs and benefits, are often made the issue.

versus noise alone by (3) a payoff matrix; in the governance of (1) decision under (2) different states of the environment through (3) systematic relation to payoffs; and in the control of (1) discrimination of (2) discriminative stimuli by (3) differential reinforcement. The parallel formats may be described by common rules of consequential contingency analysis. This general commonality may suggest a variety of specific commonalities in the disparate sets of procedures (e.g., signal detection theory and discriminative behavior), which may or may not be supported by experimental analysis. Where such commonalities *are* supported empirically, the special procedures developed by one field in the solution of (what it considers to be) its isolated problems may be transferred to the other field and may thus enrich its analytic, experimental, and applied repertoires (cf. Goldiamond, 1964, 1968; McCarthy & Davison, 1981).

Proclamation of the inadequacy and limitation of radical behaviorism is not a new phenomenon. It has been with behaviorists since the inception of the field, along with statements of its demise. At an earlier period, such objections came from those outside the field; they are now being joined by those with training in the field. If one considers the increasing infusion of behaviorism into psychological training, the change in the backgrounds of the critics is not surprising. Indeed, such change attests the contributions made by the field to date and those it is likely to make. I hope that the present chapter will be viewed in this light. The present discussion is a digression from a larger work in progress, which seeks to explore the field in the context of the consequential analysis of alternative contingencies. The fact that many of the established operant relations derive from the limiting case, in which alternative contingencies are annulled, does not nullify these established relations. The fact that many of the established "properties" of certain chemical elements derive from the limiting pure-element case, in which its various compounds are excluded, does not nullify these established properties, nor the various related rules of chemistry. When alternative contingencies are added, the outcome will vary with the new matrix, and when different elements are joined, the outcome will vary with the new compound. Certainly the fact that humanity lives in a world of few pure elements and thousands of complex molecules in no way suggests that the periodic table or its relational rules should be dumped. Chemists certainly have to study complex molecules—but in doing so must rely on their atomic bases.

The following article, reprinted in its entirety, appeared in the *Chicago Tribune* ("Teacher Places Boy in Box for Chatting," 1976); with the brief subsequent commentary, it brings together some of the major points of the present discussion. I admit to a feeling of queasiness when I began reading the article. "Uh, oh," I said, "here goes another blast at behavior modification because of some untrained person!" The last paragraph provided some relief from this burden, although the effects of the procedure on the parents and child were not changed by relating to procedure to a different therapeutic school.

TEACHER PLACES BOY
IN BOX FOR CHATTING

LIMA, Ohio [UPI]—Mr. and Mrs. Robert Seigler have been threatened with truancy charges because they removed their 11-year-old son, Ben, from school after his teacher confined him to a cardboard box to write a discipline agreement.

Ben earned his teacher's displeasure for talking to a girl in class. He was called a nonperson.

Mrs. Seigler says her 6th grade son's treatment at Bath Middle School was dehumanizing.

School officials called the treatment reality therapy, and a spokesman for the Bath Township school system referred to the box, a container for an appliance, as a social adjustment center.

Time out is frequently employed in a linear approach to attenuate undesirable behavior. While it may be as quick, efficient, and humane as its proponents claim, its use can occasionally be uningenious. The following incident arose from an in-service class I taught to the staff of a psychiatric hospital for children (cf. Goldiamond, 1970).

One day, the staff members on a particular ward informed the instructor of their resolution of a disturbing problem. Wake-up time was 8:00 A.M., but one child regularly woke at 7:00 A.M. and awakened the other children in the ward. The staff tried reasoning, threats, bribes, and withholding of privileges, to no avail. They decided on time out, and a special isolation room was equipped with aluminum sides. "We know you're going to disapprove," they informed me, "and say it's aversive. But we're going to do it anyway." During the following days, each time the child was dragged to jail, he kicked and screamed (describing the staff in Tourette terms) and awakened the whole school. The staff then requested instruction.

It was suggested that the critical reinforcer was undistracted counselor involvement with the child without competition from others. The counselor was to arrive at 6:30 and do paperwork at his desk in the ward. When the child awoke, the counselor was to smile, come to his side, and whisper: "Psst. If you tiptoe to the bookcase and get a book, I will read it to you. But let's be quiet about it, because if the others wake up, I won't be able to, because I'll have to take care of all of them." The child was quiet, as suggested; the others awoke at 8:00. The date after, the child awoke at 7:30, and at other times thereafter. He was always quiet, and the ward slept. "How long do we have to go on like this?" the staff asked. It turned out that there was a sale of do-it-yourself and pop-up books. These were bought, and the child was told that he could play with these on his own, or ask the counselor to read to him. Other such articles were bought. In effect, the parent-relieving properties of toys had been rediscovered.

Readers are invited to draw their own matrices for the various behaviors involved.

Acknowledgments

This chapter was written with support from a grant from the State of Illinois, Department of Mental Health and Developmental Disabilities, entitled "Staff Training in Topical–Systemic Diagnosis and Treatment." The views expressed are my own. I wish to express my appreciation to Dr. Paul Andronis, Dr. Jefferey Grip, and Terrence (Joe) Layng for critical comments.

References

Azrin, N.H., & Holz, W. C. Punishment. In G. Honig (Ed.), *Operant behavior: Areas of research and application.* New York: Appleton-Century-Crofts, 1966.

Baer, D. M., Peterson, R. F., & Sherman, J. A. The development of imitation by reinforcing behavioral similarity to a model. *Journal of the Experimental Analysis of Behavior,* 1967, *10,* 405–416.

Bandura, A., & Walters, R. H. *Social learning and personality development.* New York: Holt, Rinehart & Winston, 1963.

Birdsall, T. G. The theory of signal detectability. In H. Quastler (Ed.), *Information theory in psychology.* Glencoe, Ill.: Free Press, 1955.

Davanloo, H. (Ed.). *Basic principles and techniques in short-term dynamic psychotherapy.* New York: Spectrum, 1978.

Egan, J. P. *Signal detection theory and ROC analysis.* New York: Academic Press, 1975.

Evaluating medical information. *Harvard Medical School Health Letter,* November 1981, p. 6.

Ferster, C. B. Control of behavior in chimpanzees and pigeons by time out from positive reinforcement. *Psychological Monographs,* 1958, *72* (Whole No. 461).

Friedman, P. Legal regulation of applied behavior analysis in mental institutions and prisons. *Arizona Law Review,* 1975, *17,* 39–104.

Goldiamond, B. Families of the disabled: Sometimes insiders in rehabilitation, always outsiders in policy planning. In M. G. Eisenberg (Ed.), *Disabled people as second class citizens.* New York: Springer, 1982.

Goldiamond, I. Response bias in perceptual communication. In *Disorders of communication* (Vol. 42, Research Publications, A.R.N.M.D.). Association for Research in Nervous and Mental Disease, 1964.

Goldiamond, I. Self-control procedures in personal behavior problems. *Psychological Reports,* 1965, *17,* 851–868. (Monograph Supplement 3-V17) (a)

Goldiamond, I. Stuttering and fluency as manipulatable operant response classes. In L. Krasner & L. P. Ullmann (Eds.), *Research in behavior modification.* New York: Holt, Rinehart & Winston, 1965. (b)

Goldiamond, I. Perception, language, and conceptualization rules. In B. Kleinmuntz (Ed.), *Problem solving: Research, method, and theory.* New York: Wiley, 1966.

Goldiamond, I. Moral behavior: A functional analysis. *Psychology Today,* September 1968, pp. 31–34, 69–70.

Goldiamond, I. A new social imperative. In M. Wertheimer (Ed.), *Confrontation: Psychology and the problems of today.* Glenview, Ill.: Scott, Foresman, 1970.

Goldiamond, I. Toward a constructional approach to social problems: Ethical and constitutional issues raised by applied behavior analysis. *Behaviorism,* 1974, *2,* 1–84.

Goldiamond, I. Alternative sets as a framework for behavioral formulations and research. *Behaviorism,* 1975, *3,* 49–85. (a)

Goldiamond, I. Singling out behavior modification for legal regulation: Some effects on patient care, psychotherapy, and research in general. *Arizona Law Review,* 1975, *17,* 105–126. (b)

Goldiamond, I. Protection of human subjects and patients: A social contingency analysis of distinctions between research and practice, and its implications. *Behaviorism,* 1976, *4,* 1–41. (a)

Goldiamond, I. Singling out self-administered behavior therapies for professional overview. *American Psychologist,* 1976, *31,* 142–147. (b)

Goldiamond, I. Behavioral approaches and liaison psychiatry. *Psychiatric Clinics of North America,* 1979, *2* (2), 379–401.

Guimaraes, A. *Topical and systemic analysis and treatment of conversion disorders: A radical behaviorist analysis.* Unpublished doctoral dissertation, University of Chicago, 1979.

Hefferline, R. F. Learning theory and clinical psychology—an eventual symbiosis? In A. J. Bachrach (Ed.), *Experimental foundations of clinical psychology.* New York: Basic Books, 1962.

Hefferline, R. F., Keenan, B., & Hartford, R. A. Escape and avoidance in human subjects without their observation of the response. *Science,* 1959, *130,* 1338–1339.

Herman, R. L., & Azrin, N. H. Punishment by noise in an alternative response situation. *Journal of the Experimental Analysis of Behavior,* 1964, *7,* 185–188.

Holz, W. C., & Azrin, N. H. Discriminative properties of punishment. *Journal of the Experimental Analysis of Behavior,* 1961, *4,* 225–232.

Holz, W. C., Azrin, N. H., & Ayllon, T. Elimination of behavior of mental patients by response-produced extinction. *Journal of the Experimental Analysis of Behavior,* 1963, *6,* 407–412.

Locurto, C. M., Terrace, H. S., & Gibbon, J. (Eds.), *Autoshaping and conditioning theory.* New York: Academic Press, 1981.

Luce, R. D., & Raiffa, H. *Games and decisions.* New York: Wiley, 1957.

McCarthy, D., & Davison, M. Toward a behavioral theory of bias in signal detection. *Perception and Psychophysics,* 1981, *29,* 371–382.

Mishan, E. J. *Cost–benefit analysis.* New York: Praeger, 1976.

Moroney, R. M. *Families, social services, and social policy: The issue of shared responsibility* (U.S. Department of Health and Human Services Publication No. ADM 80-846). Washington, D.C.: U.S. Government Printing Office, 1980.

Morse, W. H., & Kelleher, R. T. Schedules as fundamental determinants of behavior. In W. N. Schoenfeld (Ed.), *The theory of reinforcement schedules.* New York: Appleton-Century-Crofts, 1970.

Reese, E. P. *Human behavior: Analysis and application* (2nd ed.). Dubuque, Iowa: William C. Brown, 1978.

Rosen, G. M. The development and use of nonprescription behavior therapies. *American Psychologist,* 1976, *31,* 139–141.

Skinner, B. F. *Verbal behavior.* New York: Appleton-Century-Crofts, 1957.

Skinner, B. F. An operant analysis of problem solving. In B. Kleinmuntz (Ed.), *Problem solving: Research, method, and theory.* New York: Wiley, 1966.

Skinner, B. F. *Notebooks, B. F. Skinner* (R. Epstein, Ed.). Englewood Cliffs, N.J.: Prentice-Hall, 1980.

Tanner, W. P., Jr. On the design of psychophysical experiments. In H. Quastler, (Ed.), *Information theory in psychology.* Glencoe, Ill.: Free Press, 1955.

Teacher places boy in box for chatting. *Chicago Tribune,* October 22, 1976, Section 1, p. 10.

von Neumann, J., & Morgenstern, O. *Theory of games and economic behavior.* Princeton, N.J.: Princeton University Press, 1944.

FUTURE DIRECTIONS?
Or, Is It Useful to Ask, "Where Did We Go Wrong?" before We Go?

Donald M. Baer
University of Kansas

Bijou and his colleagues opened the field of behavior-analytic parent training in the early 1960s, and published the first scientific account of that kind of intervention into familial behavior problems in 1966 (Hawkins, Peterson, Schweid, & Bijou, 1966). Their report described teaching a parent to do some crucial behavioral analyses of the parent–child dyad, thereby remediating a class of troublesome problems for the family. The important characteristics of that study, especially for Bijou and his colleagues, went much further than its emphasis on absent and misapplied reinforcement contingencies as the essence of the problem. They also included objective definition of the parent and child behaviors thought to be at issue; direct and demonstrably reliable observation of those behaviors; and an experimental design showing cause-and-effect relationships between the intervention and the subsequent desirable behavior changes. Clearly, the team meant not only to solve a problem for a family that had asked their university clinic for help, but also to make a contribution to a better behavioral science in the process. (What, after all, is a university clinic for?) Clearly, they succeeded. A decade and a half later, in opening this volume describing the current state of the field thus initiated, Bijou has again recommended doing parent training only in ways that would be good behavioral science and make better behavioral science. Any further recommendations for future directions of the field can only suggest tactics for that strategy.

A previous tactic for promoting a better behavioral science was to scorn, rhetorically, "the medical model." One early function of that scorn was to reinforce abstinence from invoking physiological explanations of what might well be essentially behavioral processes. Another early function was to reinforce what then were quite worrisome leaps into almost unprecedented behavioral analyses of real problems of real people—who, above all, were not to be hurt, and certainly not in the name of some fledgling approach called behavior analysis. Those functions were useful, especially in conjunction with confirming data well measured in good designs. But the early days of this field are over, and that scorn is no longer needed or helpful. Now, we will do better to note that there is no such thing as *the* medical model; there are many medical models. Some of those models, in fact, can be quite useful to a behavioral discipline looking for future directions that will create better behavioral science. One of them is the history of our knowledge of tuberculosis, as described by Thomas (1979, pp. 16–17, 140).

Tuberculosis, Thomas wryly notes, was once considered a very complex disease. In its extreme form, it involved five different organ systems of its host. Even more complex than its manifestations, no doubt, were its correlates—for, not knowing its cause, the science of the day could only note its epidemiological patterns. The incidence of tuberculosis could surely be shown to relate—slightly—to variables such as age, sex, social class, ethnicity, housing conditions, nutrition, geography, and, probably (if only the epidemiologists of the day used psychometric instruments), personality attributes. Scientists of the time no doubt warned their students and their public, gravely, that the problem of tuberculosis had no simple answers (much as politicians of today characterize social problems like recessions). Thomas's discussion of this stage in our knowledge of tuberculosis is wry, because it is now known to be quite a simple disease. It is caused by a bacillus; thus, control of the bacillus yields corresponding control of the disease, and bacillus control is relatively simple these days—antibiotics.

Then why do those epidemiological relationships exist? Probably because they represent—indirectly—the conditions under which exposure to the tuberculosis bacillus is maximized or minimized, or the conditions under which resistance to it is maximized or minimized, or both. They represent not its analysis, but epiphenomena of the process that is its analysis.

Familial strife similarly may be considered a very complex behavioral problem, if we choose to study it that way. Some did, for quite some decades; they found that it too relates—slightly—to variables such as age, sex, social class, ethnicity, housing conditions, nutrition, geography, and, magnificently, personality attributes. But, since 1966, the explosive growth of behavior-analytic parent training, mainly because it was done as good science striving for better science, has rendered familial strife a simpler problem. Its bacillus is the reinforcement contingency. The problem is unapplied and misapplied reinforcement contingencies; its solution is correctly and abundantly applied reinforcement contingencies. Those contingencies are wielded by everyone in the family for (or against) the behaviors of everyone else in the family, and the training of parents in their use is demonstrably a workable entry point into all of that. The data making that simplicity clear are apparent in this volume and in its references.

Then why do its epidemiological relationships exist? Probably because they represent—indirectly—conditions under which the relevant contingencies are maximized or minimized, or the conditions that result from the relevant contingencies' being maximized or minimized. These conditions again represent not the analysis of familial dysfunction, but epiphenomena of the processes that are the analysis.

Thus, the medical model implicit in Thomas's analysis of the history of tuberculosis offers some profound lessons for the future directions of behavior-analytic parent training:

- Problems always appear complex before they are correctly analyzed.
- To approach a correct analysis, it is reasonable to examine the epidemiology of the problem.
- Epidemiological studies of the problem will show what, if anything, is related to it, but will not ordinarily show the nature of the relationship.
- Even so, at their best (or most fortunate), epidemiological relationships may indicate where to look for the correct analysis; so to speak, they mark a place where the bacillus may be operating, and so indicate a place where research has a better probability of analytic results than random, curiosity-guided, or sociologically trendy research.
- And nevertheless, at their worst (or least fortunate), epidemiological relationships may mark a connection to the bacillus so tenuous that research there has virtually no probability of uncovering analytic results and so, *from that point of view*, is a waste of time, resources, and effort.
- But, as in any behavioral endeavor where responses encounter short-term reinforcement, even for good reasons, those responses are likely to be controlled by those reinforcers, rather than by long-term reinforcers associated with even better reasons; the discovery of relationships to marker variables becomes an end in itself, always publishable, rather than a means to the better but much more difficult end of continuing to dig where the marker variables indicate that further (and probably quite different) research *might* yield a truly analytic answer.

Behavior-analytic parent training, as exemplified in these pages, did not in fact come about through close attention to its marker variables. It occurred instead because a few researchers, totally ignoring the wealth of marker-variable research available, took up a different model of behavior; obedient to the premises of that model, they asked repeatedly whether the model, superbly effective in the Skinner box, also had generality in the real-life arenas of human behavior—for example, in the case of familial strife. Indeed, the psychological study of familial strife just prior to then looked as if it represented only the final, most dangerous lesson of the tuberculosis model—the functional autonomy of marker-variable research for its own sake, rather than as a guide to different research with a higher probability of proving analytic. When marker-variable relationships become professional reinforcers rather than discriminative stimuli for different research, analysis becomes, if anything, less probable than it was before in the audience attentive to those marker variables. Marker-variable discovery then becomes the goal of research; by functioning as the goal, it obscures rather than stimulates the search for what it marks and why it marks it. It is no wonder, then, that the term "marker variable" has lately taken on an additional and probably more unusual meaning: a calibrating variable for the comparison of results from different studies, rather than a signaling variable for indicating where intensive research might uncover a solution to the original problem.

There is an occasional irony, then, in one current direction of parent training research: the sudden inclusion of marker variables *after* the essential analysis of the problem is clear! Studies of parent training recently have included psychometric measures of personality; assumptions about locus of control; perceptions of marital happiness; determinations of ethnicity, socio-economic status, and locale; and the like. In some of these cases, there seems to have been no better reason for including those variables than somehow to relate parent training better to the rest of social science by resembling it more. Perhaps this will create some affection for behavior-analytic parent training researchers among the rest of social scientists. Nevertheless, it is choosing to resemble the majority in one of their least useful, least rational, least questioned, and most ritualistic superstitions. Worse, yet, this is the superstition that most resembles a quagmire of quicksand. Anger joins irony when it becomes clear that some parent training researchers have not *chosen* to resemble the rest of social science in this way, but rather have had the act forced on them by their funding agencies; the agencies, too, seem to have forgotten the original, potentially useful function of the marker variables, and are caught up in the autonomous business of pursuing them as an end in itself. (The funding agencies will of course point out that such requirements emanate from their reviewers—our peers—and not from the agencies per se. But any spectators can point out that the agencies choose their reviewers, and choose them very carefully.)

If the analysis of familial dysfunction is in hand—if it is a matter of unapplied and misapplied reinforcement (and punishment and extinction) contingencies—then we need no epidemiological correlations to mark where to look for the analysis. We need, instead, to see what barriers there may be to the application of the analysis, and what its generality is when it is applied as widely as seems needful. And, indeed, enough experience has been gained with these questions to show that training parents in contingency management is not easy, and that its difficulty may vary with the kind of case to which it is applied. Because of that, a quite reasonable and thoughtful argument for a possible role of the marker variables arises: Can some marker variables be found that predict the relative difficulty of accomplishing parent training across various cases, and the relative effectiveness of it when it is accomplished? And if they are found, will their nature suggest to us how to look further to understand why we have differential difficulty and differential effectiveness? The second of these two questions is the essential one, of course. Relationships that satisfy the first question but do nothing for the second are useless for anything except publishing in fields that treasure the markers for their own sake. That suggests a third question: Can we avoid the behavioral trap implicit in the publishability of otherwise useless marker-variable relationships, and so remain useful?

Again, recourse to the medical model represented by tuberculosis may offer a model answer: Tuberculosis became a simple disease with the discovery that it is caused by a bacillus that lodges in lung tissue and causes effects that eventually disrupt four other organ systems. Its analysis was complete with the further discovery that two particular antibiotics are best in destroying the bacillus; but the application of that analysis remains incomplete, because it turns out that the delivery of those antibiotics to the bacillus is particularly difficult in lung tissue. Treatment often requires months of high dosages of these antibiotics. What remains, then, for medical researchers is an essentially technological problem of a sort familiar to us as well: the refinement of delivery systems. Perhaps the marker variables that relate to the length of saturation with antibiotics necessary to a cure in each case will illuminate how to look for a better delivery system; perhaps not. Medical researchers are attentive to those relationships; however, they also are attentive to research into delivery systems per se—research that need not wait for markers, but can proceed on the basic of the logic and facts of how antibiotics enter and are transported in physiological systems.

Then, while it is not unreasonable that we look for the markers of when our delivery systems work better or worse, it is also clearly possible to look at delivery systems as such, not waiting for or wanting marker-variables relationships, for we know enough about delivery systems in general to be able to question them immediately about this problem. Parent training is teaching; it is behavior modification. So we must already know enough about the processes involved to experiment with them directly, rather than waiting for an epidemiological relationship to suggest a better-than-random point for entry into the question. We are already far beyond random entry points. We know that it will be a matter of the most effective reinforcers, a thorough program dealing with all relevant stimulus controls, maintenance, and generalization. Those are labels for classes of processes, not solutions, but they are specific enough labels to set us to work in ways quite likely to yield solutions. Consider them a highly recommended set of future directions.

Furthermore, the prediction of when a delivery system will work better or worse is not a useful thing to have, if the delivery system itself is far from perfect and is soon to be replaced by a more effective one. The work reported in this volume is at once testimony to the fact that current parent training programs are indeed far from perfect, and that they are being improved steadily and intensively. In the early 1970s, behavior-analytic parent training programs looked strikingly similar; they taught parents to attend positively to desirable behavior, to ignore undesirable behavior as perfectly as possible, and to use time-out procedures, and they did these things in a very small variety of ways. But the parent training programs reported here are more specialized.

They differ in significant details so that they may deal with a variety of children. Cataldo (Chapter 13) describes the procedural variations suitable to handicapped and ill children; McMahon and Forehand (Chapter 12) adapt their procedures to noncompliant children; and Lutzker (Chapter 11) reports a program appropriate to abusive and neglectful parents. The programs seen here also differ in ways that allow them to deal better with a variety of parents. Thus, Dangel and Polster (Chapter 8) have developed branching techniques useful in working across cultural groups; and Wahler and Dumas (Chapter 15) have gone far toward finding the variant of parent training needed for societally and socially insular parents (significantly for this argument, they are not satisfied, and see themselves as still in transition). Finally, a sudden variety of delivery systems per se, largely independent of the parent training program to be conveyed within them, are apparent here. Braukmann, Kirigin Ramp, Tigner, and Wolf (Chapter 7) tell us how to train teaching-parents for halfway houses; Hall (Chapter 4) shows how programs may be delivered through schools, hospitals, and mental health centers; Pinkston (Chapter 9) integrates school and home delivery in very low-SES communities; Budd and Fabry (Chapter 16) have found ways to operate from outpatient clinics in medical settings; and Shearer and Loftin (Chapter 5) have well-tested means for delivering parent training directly to homes. These variations are only a sample of the diversity that the field is just now producing.

This diversity says that the prior programs were too homogeneous to suit every situation effectively enough to make obvious and worthwhile gains; we knew that was so, because we were using well-measured clinical research approaches. The diversification apparent in these reports (and in the rest of the field) is not at the level of fundamental approach, but at the level of detail. No one has abandoned the analysis; it is still a matter of unapplied and misapplied contingencies that need to be replaced by abundant, well applied ones. The issue is how to deliver that analysis; and development of the details necessary to accomplish that in various cases is clearly a matter for careful research. (Some members of this volume's audience no doubt find that research quite repetitive, as they already have in most of the other problem areas that we deal with better and better; to stay interesting to this audience, we should never try to finish a problem.)

The diversification of parent training delivery systems clearly is a response to diverse cases, and the diversity of those cases could be indexed by marker variables: by gross diagnostic categories (epilepsy, retardation, emotional disturbance, delinquency); by ethnicity or socioeconomic status or social insularity; and by locale (home, school, halfway house, hospital clinic). But those categories are so gross and so clear that the variables that mark them are virtually automatic; and the marking is for communication after the fact, rather than for guiding the detailed differential development that these cases have needed and are receiving now, apparently quite efficiently.

Thus, another much recommended future direction is to continue this diversification—not for its own sake, but only in response to less than useful current effectiveness, as measured by direct observation of the behavior of everyone involved (and also as measured by the social-validity questionnaires that they fill out for us—see below). The field has never assumed before, and need not assume now, that the next kind of child, the next kind of parent, and the next kind of locale should require a different kind of program than has proved useful in previous experience. Indeed, the field has usually assumed that the next case will probably work well in the *same* program—after all, so many "next" cases already have. In this case, diversification should follow only upon proof of a need for it. Since some experience in just that form has in fact been encountered, then certainly we should develop diversifications in response to it. However, we should pursue each of those developments as far as its optimization seems to require before developing yet other diversifications; we have only just started on them, and can hardly tell how effective we may be able to make them in another few years of intensive work. Closer to their optimum efficiency, they may very well cover a wider generality of cases than at their inception; if so, that wider generality may then be seen to cancel what earlier had seemed to be a good argument for creating another diversification for what only seemed to be another kind of case. Thus, a recommendation for diversification is instantly tempered by a recommendation to do the current diversifications very well before taking on any more. Since those diversifications are at the level of detail, not at the level of their fundamental analysis of the common problem, this research will be exquisitely technological research, and as such will be hard to justify to a very large segment of the scientific community—even our own scientific community (cf. Michael, 1980, and his references). Nevertheless, we should do it, as well as we can and as thoroughly as it needs to be done. To follow that recommendation may require that we seek funding from different sources than have thought us exciting in the past (since they may well find us derivative and repetitious if we follow this recommendation in the future—they like analyses, but not solutions); or may require that we find ways to do that research with very much less funding than we have been accustomed to using; or both. Both are feasible, in fact, as some very recent experience in the field demonstrates (and as some predictable near-future experience of all social research fields may well require!).

The technological refinement of our current adventures in diversification will not only limit the amount of future diversification needed, and perhaps reduce the amount that we currently think is useful; it can also finally realize some of the comparative research that other social scientists and funding agencies have wanted for so long. "Comparative research," in this context, means a comparison of the effectiveness of an entity called "behavior-analytic parent training" with some other entities called, for example, "psychoanalytic parent training," "Gestalt therapy," "nondirective counseling," "rational–emotive therapy," and so forth. The actual possibility of that kind of comparative research may in fact be a very long time off; behavior-analytic parent training presumably will continue to measure its effectiveness in behavioral terms, and some of those other approaches (to which many would like to compare it) are likely to continue assessing their effectiveness in nonbehavioral terms. The comparison of one side's apples to the other's oranges is not likely to be any more fruitful this time than it has been in any previous instance of incommensurable outcomes. However, between any approaches that share a common outcome, comparison is possible. But while it is always possible, it is fruitful only when something close to one side's optimum efficiency is compared to something close to the other side's optimum efficiency. Comparisons at earlier points than that are pointless, in that they compare an arbitrary degree of effectiveness of one approach with an equally arbitrary degree of effectiveness of the other approach. That much compounding of arbitrariness is not only abritrary, but frivolous and whimsical. Thus, to the extent that behavior-analytic parent training has not yet been pushed toward its optimum efficiency, and to the extent that its diversifications (admirable as their purposes are) have not yet advanced toward their optimum efficiencies, then comparison with other approaches or among themselves is useless (and, being expensive, worse than useless). Later, when parent training procedures either have approached a point of diminishing increments in additional effectiveness through additional components or variations, or else have become socially entrenched as standard practices (at optimum efficiency or otherwise), comparison will be useful and reasonably meaningful. Clearly, we are far from either outcome just now. Then a much-recommended immediate-future direction for the field is, while systematically perfecting and refining, systematically refraining from making comparisons just yet.

If we follow only these recommendations, we will have less to do with many of our nonbehavioral colleagues not engaged in parent training, at least temporarily. Abstinence from pursuing epidemiological relationships and from comparing our immature children to their immature children, and intensive pursuit of technological refinement, may insulate us from the neighbors (cf. Wahler & Dumas, Chapter 15). To whatever extent our behavior has been maintained in the past by their attention, it will now be at risk. What will take over their function in our behavior? The necessary answer seems to be that we must. We had better meet often for sharply differential reinforcement by all of us of all of our newest efforts; from now on, if we do not do that ourselves, no one else will. We had better be sure that at least some journals remain interested in technological refinement (and we had better not create yet another new journal for that purpose, for a variety of reasons). We can help to assure some of that refinement by being willing to participate in all aspects of our journals— as authors, cogently rational rebutters of misunderstanding reviewers, reviewers, and editors—whenever we can. We had better keep submitting our work to the neighbors' journals, symposia, poster sessions, paper sessions, and so on, as well as to our own, repetitive as that may seem. We had better keep stating the central importance of parent training to our science and to our society, self-evident as that may seem. And we had better keep clarifying the rationale underlying our current behavior, for ourselves and for the neighbors—neighbors understand their commendably busy neighbors better than their apparently snobbish ones. All of this is very important, because we do not want to become "insular," as Wahler and Dumas (Chapter 15) describe the term; and however intelligently insular we do become in service to the logic of these recommendations, we ought not to stay that way very long.

A good way to manage that may well be to increase our present levels of attention to what we now call "social validity" (Kazdin, 1977; Wolf, 1978). We are almost accustomed now to assessing the acceptability of our interventions to all those involved, by asking them in a variety of simple ways. What they say about our interventions does not, of course, constitute the data that contribute to an analysis; what they say is simply an index of whether the analysis realized in the intervention will ever prosper, or even survive, in social application. What they say is not to be believed as true of the intervention, but as true of them as participants in the intervention. Parent training clearly is one of the interventions most needful of valid social-validity assessments. Then a much-recommended future direction is to learn what social psychology and sociology already know about the valid assessment of as insubstantial (but as important) a behavior as social validity, and to use it. Validity of social validity means that when those involved in an intervention say in our questionnaire that they like the intervention, they will not then vote against it in the next election, denounce it to the media, or sue; instead, they will continue to testify in all ways that it is nice and does good things, in their opinion. Finding that out will take a long time and hard work; meanwhile, we can at least perfect our questionnaires. Those questionnaires might be viewed as a very special kind of epidemiological relationship, or marker; what they mark is verbal good will or ill will that might well become social action. If that is a reasonable use of the concept of "marker variable," then social validity estimates may be the one exception to the otherwise problematic nature of marker variables in this field. In that case, they need especially careful construction and use.

What is socially valid is not necessarily intrinsically valid; it may represent only a momentary quirk for our culture. Indeed, neither the experimental analysis of behavior nor its application has supposed that there are any intrinsically good or bad behaviors. Instead, they have supposed that all behaviors simply obey the laws of nature, and thus serve whatever environmental and organismic functions there may be. It is not that serving those functions is healthy or good; it is simply that serving them is inevitable, given sufficient encounter with them. Thus, there is no fundamental concept of "pathological behaviors." There are behaviors that lead an organism to injury or death, but even these can be imbued with the social function of self-sacrifice, heroism, duty, and the like, and so become desirable and admirable—even to their hosts. Yet we like to say that we are studying the process of solving problems— behavioral problems. If there is no fundamental concept of "pathological be-havior," is there any fundamental concept of a "behavior problem"?

Apparently, when we say that some behavior is undesirable and propose to modify it, we are typically saying only that we and/or our society do not like the behavior (or its predictable consequences). In that case, for what problem is parent training the solution? So far, it is simply the problem constituted by the fact that we, the parent training interveners, do not like the nature of some of the familial contingencies that we see. At first, we were merely responsive to the fact that certain parents did not like the kinds of interactions they and their children consistently created, and asked us for help; we agreed with the parents' estimate that help was appropriate, saw what contingencies they were misusing or failing to use, and taught them better ones for creating an interaction that they (and we) would like. Parent training was then the rather small solution to that essentially personal problem of them and us.

But Bijou and his colleagues correctly made parent training a matter of good science as well as of personal problem solving, and that meant, among other things, that it seemed to need a larger context. Applied behavior analysis, apparently without any serious analysis of the underlying issue, made it a social problem rather than an occasional personal one. As a result, we currently see large *programs* of parent training. Some of those programs personalize their interventions, to solve the problems that specific parents see as their particular problems and that the interveners agree are problems. But some (most?) of those programs are not individualized; they solve problems that the interveners see as uniform problems across (and despite) much of the variety of parents and children who come to them. Some of the parents (and children) may agree with the interveners' definition of their problem, and some may not; but most may stay in the program because they know that they have *some* problem and that these interveners enjoy at least some social definition as the correct clinical resource for their case. On what rationale are we teaching parents to run the contingencies that *we* like, if in fact they are not exactly the contingencies that would realize the outcome that the parents would like, or if in fact the parents do not really know yet what they would like?

Currently, a good deal of parent training programming is aimed at child-abusing parents and at parents of delinquent children. The strength of our common dislike for child abuse and for delinquency masks the question of what rationale we have for training these parents to interact differently with their children. And yet, a little perspective shows us that not very long ago, child abuse was almost universal and unquestioned in many societies, and that there are subcultures in which delinquency is a virtue.

Similarly, a good deal of current parent training programming seems predicated on the assumption that aversive contingencies between parents and children are a problem, and that their replacement with positive contingencies is a large part of the solution to that problem. But there is nothing intrinsically problematic about aversive contingencies: Many of our most useful skills, like walking or driving a car, are skills that get us to positive reinforcers, but that were learned and are maintained under severe, consistent punishment for almost any small errors. Yet we do not consider that our interactions with the surface of our planet or with our automobiles are problems in need of intervention, despite the pervasively aversive nature of the contingencies surrounding them.

We might solve this problem by returning to parent training as an essentially small solution to the particular personal problems that particular families present to us, and that we agree personally might well be changed through better family contingencies. Or we might continue purveying parent training on a programmatic, societal scale and ignore any further inquiry into why we do this, other than the fact that it is there to be done and that we and the parents like doing it (so far). Or we might ask whether there is a larger context within which parent training is the only logical thing to do on as wide a scale as we can learn to do it. Blechman (Chapter 3) suggests that a context called "competence" might have just that function, and ought to be pursued as such. The Christophersens and the Barrishes (Chapter 6) propose normal development as an alternative context: Should parent training teach contingencies so that normality will be shaped and managed where it does not appear "spontaneously"? Burgess and Richardson (Chapter 10) move from a thorough analysis of child-abusing families to a concept of family function within a social network; and Koegel, Schreibman, Johnson, O'Neill, and Dunlap (Chapter 14) reinforce with data the notion that familial contingencies exist within a larger system of behavior than the trained contingencies and their target behaviors: Do network and system constitute the larger context?

An excellent future direction is to continue asking these kinds of questions, and to reinforce such questioners for asking, even while we think through their suggestions as critically as we can. Surely, there is no better way to choose a future direction than to know where you are at the moment, and to speculate about all the places that you could and could not be.

References

Hawkins, R. P., Peterson, R. F., Schweid, E., & Bijou, S. W. Behavior therapy in the home: Amelioration of problem parent–child relations with the parent in a therapeutic role. *Journal of Experimental Child Psychology*, 1966, *4*, 99–107.

Kazdin, A. E. Assessing the clinical or applied importance of behavior change through social validation. *Behavior Modification*, 1977, *1*, 427–452.

Michael, J. Flight from behavior analysis. *The Behavior Analyst*, 1980, *3*(2), 1–22.

Thomas, L. *The medusa and the snail.* New York: Bantam, 1980.

Wolf, M. M. Social validity: The case for subjective measurement, or how applied behavior analysis is finding its heart. *Journal of Applied Behavior Analysis*, 1978, *11*, 203–214.

AUTHOR INDEX

559

SUBJECT INDEX

569